DATE DUE			
			PRINTED IN U.S.A.

SOMETHING ABOUT THE AUTHOR

ISSN 0276-816X

SOMETHING ABOUT THE AUTHOR

Facts and Pictures about Authors
and Illustrators of Books for Young People

EDITED BY
ANNE COMMIRE

VOLUME 46

GALE RESEARCH COMPANY
BOOK TOWER
DETROIT, MICHIGAN
48226

Editor: Anne Commire

Associate Editors: Agnes Garrett, Helga P. McCue

Assistant Editors: Dianne H. Anderson, Elisa Ann Ferraro, Eunice L. Petrini, Linda Shedd

Sketchwriters: Marguerite Feitlowitz, Rachel Koenig

Researchers: Kathleen Betsko, Catherine Ruello

Editorial Assistant: Lisa Bryon

Permissions Assistant: Susan Pfanner

In cooperation with the Young People's Literature staff

Editor: Joyce Nakamura

Assistant Editor: Heidi Ellerman

Research Coordinator: Cynthia J. Walker

External Production Supervisor: Mary Beth Trimper

External Production Assistants: Linda Davis, Amanda Wheatley

Internal Senior Production Assistant: Sandy Rock

Layout Artist: Elizabeth Lewis Patryjak

Art Director: Arthur Chartow

Special acknowledgment is due to the members of the *Contemporary Authors* staff
who assisted in the preparation of this volume.

Publisher: Frederick G. Ruffner

Editorial Director: Dedria Bryfonski

Associate Editorial Director: Ellen Crowley

Director, Literature Division: Christine Nasso

Senior Editor, Something about the Author: Adele Sarkissian

Contents

Introduction 9   Acknowledgments 15
Illustrations Index 233   Author Index 251

A

Abolafia, Yossi
  Brief Entry.................................21

Adamson, Gareth 1925-1982 21

Akaba, Suekichi 1910- 22

Asimov, Janet
  see Jeppson, J(anet) O(pal)................121

Atkinson, Allen
  Brief Entry.................................24

Augelli, John P(at) 1921- 24

Ayres, Patricia Miller 1923-1985
  Obituary Notice 25

B

Baron, Virginia Olsen 1931- 25

Bauer, Caroline Feller 1935-
  Brief Entry.................................26

Bentley, Roy 1947- 26

Berry, Joy Wilt
  Brief Entry.................................27

Bettmann, Otto Ludwig 1903- 27

Blair, Anne Denton 1914- 27

Blumenthal, Shirley 1943- 29

Boorman, Linda (Kay) 1940- 29

Bourdon, David 1934- 29

Bragg, Michael 1948- 30

Bridges, Laurie
  see Bruck, Lorraine 31

Bruck, Lorraine 1921-
  Brief Entry.................................31

Burke, David 1927- 32

Burt, Jesse Clifton 1921-1976.................32

Burton, Marilee Robin 1950- 33

Byars, Betsy (Cromer) 1928- 34

C

Cabral, O. M.
  see Cabral, Olga 47

Cabral, Olga 1909- 47

Cauley, Lorinda Bryan 1951- 49

Chamberlain, Margaret 1954- 50

Chambers, John W. 1933-
  Brief Entry.................................52

Christopher, Milbourne 1914(?)-1984.........52

Ciardi, John (Anthony) 1916-1986
  Obituary Notice 53

Clark, Mary Higgins 53

Corlett, William 1938- 54

Cox, William R(obert) 55

Craig, Helen 1934-
  Brief Entry.................................56

D

Dank, Gloria Rand 1955-
  Brief Entry.................................56

Davies, Sumiko 1942- 56

Davis, Gibbs 1953- 58

Delessert, Etienne 1941- 60

Denzel, Justin F(rancis) 1917- 69

DeWeese, Gene
  see DeWeese, Thomas Eugene 71

DeWeese, Jean
  see DeWeese, Thomas Eugene 71

DeWeese, Thomas Eugene 1934- 71

Duane, Diane (Elizabeth) 1952-
  Brief Entry.................................74

Dunrea, Olivier 1953-
  Brief Entry.................................74

E

Eastman, P(hilip) D(ey) 1909-1986
Obituary Notice 74

Eisner, Vivienne
see Margolis, Vivienne .152

F

Farquharson, Alexander 1944- 74

Francis, Dee
see Haas, Dorothy F. 80

Funai, Mamoru (Rolland) 1932-
Brief Entry. 76

G

Gee, Maurice (Gough) 1931- 76

Glass, Andrew
Brief Entry. 77

Goble, Warwick (?)-1943 77

H

Haas, Dorothy F. 80

Haller, Dorcas Woodbury 1946- 82

Hampson, Frank 1918(?)-1985
Obituary Notice 82

Hansen, Joyce 1942- 83

Hare, Norma Q(uarles) 1924- 84

Heath, Charles D(ickinson) 1941- 85

Heller, Linda 1944- .85

Hockaby, Stephen
see Mitchell, Gladys (Maude Winifred). 158

Howker, Janni
Brief Entry. 87

Hughes, Sara
see Saunders, Susan 195

Hurd, Thacher 1949- 87

Hyman, Trina Schart 1939- 90

Hyndman, Jane Andrews 1912-1978. 112

J

Jeppson, J(anet) O(pal) 1926-
Brief Entry. 121

Johnson, Charlotte Buel 1918-1982 121

Johnson

Johnson, Maud Battle 1918(?)-1985
Obituary Notice 122

Joyce, William 1959(?)-
Brief Entry. 122

K

Krauze, Andrzej 1947-
Brief Entry. 122

L

Langone, John (Michael) 1929- 122

Lehn, Cornelia 1920- 123

Leigh, Tom 1947- 124

Lester, Helen 1936- 125

Lewis, Alice C. 1936- 126

Lindgren, Barbro 1937-
Brief Entry. 127

Lurie, Alison 1926- 127

Lustig, Loretta 1944- 134

M

Macaulay, David (Alexander) 1946- 138

MacMaster, Eve (Ruth) B(owers) 1942- 151

Margolis, Vivienne 1922- 152

Marks, Hannah K.
see Trivelpiece, Laurel 206

May, Robert Stephen 1929- 153

May, Robin
see May, Robert Stephen 153

McInerney, Judith Whitelock 1945-
Brief Entry. 154

McLenighan, Valjean 1947- 154

McManus, Patrick (Francis) 1933- 156

Meyer, Kathleen Allan 1918-
Brief Entry. 158

Miller, Frances A. 1937-
Brief Entry. 158

Mitchell, Gladys (Maude Winifred)
1901-1983. 158

Mitchell, Joyce Slayton 1933- 159

Moore, Jack (William) 1941- 160

Morgan, Geoffrey 1916- 161

Morton, Miriam 1918(?)-1985
    Obituary Notice 161

Myra, Harold L(awrence) 1939- 161

N

Nash, (Frederic) Ogden 1902-1971 162

Newman, Gerald 1939- 177

O

Oriolo, Joe
    see Oriolo, Joseph .177

Oriolo, Joseph 1913-1985
    Obituary Notice 177

P

Pace, Mildred Mastin 1907- 177

Pinkwater, Daniel Manus 1941- 178

Pitman, (Isaac) James 1901-1985
    Obituary Notice 191

Pollock, Bruce 1945- 191

Price, Jonathan (Reeve) 1941- 191

R

Reeve, Joel
    see Cox, William R(obert) 55

Reid, Alastair 1926- 192

Reiner, William B(uck) 1910-1976 194

Rieu, E(mile) V(ictor) 1887-1972 194

S

Saunders, Susan 1945- 195

Scott, Bill 1920(?)-1985
    Obituary Notice 196

Seidler, Tor 1952-
    Brief Entry. 196

Shreve, Susan Richards 1939- 197

Skipper, G. C. 1939- 201

Small, David 1945-
    Brief Entry. 202

Smith, Joan 1933-
    Brief Entry. 202

Smith, Philip Warren 1936- 202

Springstubb, Tricia 1950- 204

Stratton, Thomas [Joint pseudonym]
    see DeWeese, Thomas Eugene 71

Sumiko
    see Davies, Sumiko 56

T

Tether, (Cynthia) Graham 1950- 205

Thomas, Victoria [Joint pseudonym]
    see DeWeese, Thomas Eugene 71

Torrie, Malcolm
    see Mitchell, Gladys (Maude Winifred). 158

Trivelpiece, Laurel 1926-
    Brief Entry. 206

W

Warren, Betsy
    see Warren, Elizabeth Avery. 207

Warren, Cathy
    Brief Entry. 207

Warren, Elizabeth Avery 1916- 207

Warren, Robert Penn 1905- 208

Watts, Franklin (Mowry) 1904-1978. 218

Wild, Jocelyn 1941- 219

Wild, Robin (Evans) 1936- 223

Wilson, Christopher B. 1910(?)-1985
    Obituary Notice 223

Wilson, Maurice (Charles John) 1914- 223

Wisler, G(ary) Clifton 1950-
    Brief Entry. 224

Worth, Richard
    Brief Entry. 225

Wyndham, Lee
    see Hyndman, Jane Andrews 112

Z

Zerman, Melvyn Bernard 1930- 225

Zwinger, Ann 1925- 226

Introduction

As the only ongoing reference series that deals with the lives and works of authors and illustrators of children's books, *Something about the Author (SATA)* is a unique source of information. The *SATA* series includes not only well-known authors and illustrators whose books are most widely read, but also those less prominent people whose works are just coming to be recognized. *SATA* is often the only readily available information source for less well-known writers or artists. You'll find *SATA* informative and entertaining whether you are:

—a student in junior high school (or perhaps one to two grades higher or lower) who needs information for a book report or some other assignment for an English class;

—a children's librarian who is searching for the answer to yet another question from a young reader or collecting background material to use for a story hour;

—an English teacher who is drawing up an assignment for your students or gathering information for a book talk;

—a student in a college of education or library science who is studying children's literature and reference sources in the field;

—a parent who is looking for a new way to interest your child in reading something more than the school curriculum prescribes;

—an adult who enjoys children's literature for its own sake, knowing that a good children's book has no age limits.

Scope

In *SATA* you will find detailed information about authors and illustrators who span the full time range of children's literature, from early figures like John Newbery and L. Frank Baum to contemporary figures like Judy Blume and Richard Peck. Authors in the series represent primarily English-speaking countries, particularly the United States, Canada, and the United Kingdom. Also included, however, are authors from around the world whose works are available in English translation, for example: from France, Jean and Laurent De Brunhoff; from Italy, Emanuele Luzzati; from the Netherlands, Jaap ter Haar; from Germany, James Krüss; from Norway, Babbis Friis-Baastad; from Japan, Toshiko Kanzawa; from the Soviet Union, Kornei Chukovsky; from Switzerland, Alois Carigiet, to name only a few. Also appearing in *SATA* are Newbery medalists from Hendrik Van Loon (1922) to Patricia MacLachlan (1986). The writings represented in *SATA* include those created intentionally for children and young adults as well as those written for a general audience and known to interest younger readers. These writings cover the spectrum from picture books, humor, folk and fairy tales, animal stories, mystery and adventure, science fiction and fantasy, historical fiction, poetry and nonsense verse, to drama, biography, and nonfiction.

Information Features

In *SATA* you will find full-length entries that are being presented in the series for the first time. This volume, for example, marks the first full-length appearance of Otto Ludwig Bettmann, Mary Higgins Clark, Etienne Delessert, Warwick Goble, Alison Lurie, Loretta Lustig, David Macaulay, Susan Richards Shreve, and Robert Penn Warren, among others. Since Volume 25, each *SATA* volume also includes newly revised and updated biographies for a selection of early *SATA* listees who remain of interest to today's readers and who have been active enough to require extensive revision of their earlier entries. The entry for a given biographee may be revised as often as there is substantial new information to provide. In Volume 46 you'll find revised entries for Betsy Byars, Trina Schart Hyman, Jane Andrews Hyndman, Ogden Nash, and Daniel Manus Pinkwater.

Brief Entries, first introduced in Volume 27, are another regular feature of *SATA*. Brief Entries present essentially the same types of information found in a full entry but do so in a capsule form and without illustration. These entries are intended to give you useful and timely information while the more time-consuming process of compiling a full-length biography is in progress. In this volume you'll find Brief Entries for Yossi Abolafia, Caroline Feller Bauer, John W. Chambers, Gloria Rand Dank, Janni Howker, William Joyce, Barbro Lindgren, Tor Seidler, and Laurel Trivelpiece, among others.

Obituaries have been included in *SATA* since Volume 20. An Obituary is intended not only as a death notice but also as a concise view of a person's life and work. Obituaries may appear for persons who have entries in earlier *SATA* volumes, as well as for people who have not yet appeared in the series. In this volume Obituaries mark the recent deaths of Patricia Miller Ayres, John Ciardi, Frank Hampson, James Pitman, and others.

Each *SATA* volume provides a cumulative index in two parts: first, the Illustrations Index, arranged by the name of the illustrator, gives the number of the volume and page where the illustrator's work appears in the current volume as well as all preceding volumes in the series; second, the Author Index gives the number of the volume in which a person's biographical sketch, Brief Entry, or Obituary appears in the current volume as well as all preceding volumes in the series. These indexes also include references to authors and illustrators who appear in *Yesterday's Authors of Books for Children*. Beginning with Volume 36, the *SATA* Author Index provides cross-references to authors who are included in *Children's Literature Review*.

You will also find cross-references to authors who are included in the *Something about the Author Autobiography Series,* starting with Volume 42. This companion series to *SATA* is described in detail below.

Illustrations

While the textual information in *SATA* is its primary reason for existing, photographs and illustrations not only enliven the text but are an integral part of the information that *SATA* provides. Illustrations and text are wedded in such a special way in children's literature that artists and their works naturally occupy a prominent place among *SATA*'s listees. The illustrators that you'll find in the series include such past masters of children's book illustration as Randolph Caldecott, Kate Greenaway, Walter Crane, Arthur Rackham, and Ernest L. Shepard, as well as such noted contemporary artists as Maurice Sendak, Edward Gorey, Tomie de Paola, and Margot Zemach. There are Caldecott medalists from Dorothy Lathrop (the first recipient in 1938) to Chris Van Allsburg (the latest winner in 1986); cartoonists like Charles Schulz, ("Peanuts"), Walt Kelly ("Pogo"), Hank Ketcham ("Dennis the Menace"), and Georges Rémi ("Tintin"); photographers like Jill Krementz, Tana Hoban, Bruce McMillan, and Bruce Curtis; and filmmakers like Walt Disney, Alfred Hitchcock, and Steven Spielberg.

In more than a dozen years of recording the metamorphosis of children's literature from the printed page to other media, *SATA* has become something of a repository of photographs that are unique in themselves and exist nowhere else as a group, particularly many of the classics of motion picture and stage history and photographs that have been specially loaned to us from private collections.

What a *SATA* Entry Provides

Whether you're already familiar with the *SATA* series or just getting acquainted, you will want to be aware of the kind of information that an entry provides. In every *SATA* entry the editors attempt to give as complete a picture of the person's life and work as possible. In some cases that full range of information may simply be unavailable, or a biographee may choose not to reveal complete personal details. The information that the editors attempt to provide in every entry is arranged in the following categories:

1. The "head" of the entry gives

       —the most complete form of the name,
       —any part of the name not commonly used, included in parentheses,
       —birth and death dates, if known; a (?) indicates a discrepancy in published sources,

—pseudonyms or name variants under which the person has had books published or is publicly known, in parentheses in the second line.

2. "Personal" section gives

   —date and place of birth and death,
   —parents' names and occupations,
   —name of spouse, date of marriage, and names of children,
   —educational institutions attended, degrees received, and dates,
   —religious and political affiliations,
   —agent's name and address,
   —home and/or office address.

3. "Career" section gives

   —name of employer, position, and dates for each career post,
   —military service,
   —memberships,
   —awards and honors.

4. "Writings" section gives

   —title, first publisher and date of publication, and illustration information for each book written; revised editions and other significant editions for books with particularly long publishing histories; genre, when known.

5. "Adaptations" section gives

   —title, major performers, producer, and date of all known reworkings of an author's material in another medium, like movies, filmstrips, television, recordings, plays, etc.

6. "Sidelights" section gives

   —commentary on the life or work of the biographee either directly from the person (and often written specifically for the *SATA* entry), or gathered from biographies, diaries, letters, interviews, or other published sources.

7. "For More Information See" section gives

   —books, feature articles, films, plays, and reviews in which the biographee's life or work has been treated.

How a *SATA* Entry Is Compiled

A *SATA* entry progresses through a series of steps. If the biographee is living, the *SATA* editors try to secure information directly from him or her through a questionnaire. From the information that the biographee supplies, the editors prepare an entry, filling in any essential missing details with research. The author or illustrator is then sent a copy of the entry to check for accuracy and completeness.

If the biographee is deceased or cannot be reached by questionnaire, the *SATA* editors examine a wide variety of published sources to gather information for an entry. Biographical sources are searched with the aid of Gale's *Biography and Genealogy Master Index*. Bibliographic sources like the *National Union Catalog*, the *Cumulative Book Index*, *American Book Publishing Record*, and the *British Museum Catalogue* are consulted, as are book reviews, feature articles, published interviews, and material sometimes obtained from the biographee's family, publishers, agent, or other associates.

For each entry presented in *SATA*, the editors also attempt to locate a photograph of the biographee as well as representative illustrations from his or her books. After surveying the available books which the biographee has written and/or illustrated, and then making a selection of appropriate photographs and illustrations, the editors request permission of the current copyright holders to reprint the material. In the case of older books for which the copyright may have passed through several hands, even locating the current copyright holder is often a long and involved process.

We invite you to examine the entire *SATA* series, starting with this volume. Described below are some of the people in Volume 46 that you may find particularly interesting.

Highlights of This Volume

BETSY BYARS......Newbery Medal-winning author from North Carolina who has been writing books for young people ever since her own children began to read. As the young wife of a graduate student and the mother of three small children, Byars found herself with hours of empty time that she filled by writing articles for magazines. As her children grew, however, she developed an interest in writing books for them. Her children, she remembers, "not only read my books and gave me their frank opinions," but they also offered "a refresher course in childhood." Byars' compassion for young people and her sense of humor and insight have won her a steady audience of readers in this country and abroad. Her books have won several awards, including the prestigious Newbery Medal, "an enormous pat on the back," that gave Byars the impetus to experiment with her craft. Subsequently, she has also written, produced, and directed an operetta for mentally retarded students, written and illustrated a picture book for young children, and has had several of her stories dramatized and presented on television.

TRINA SCHART HYMAN......children's book illustrator and artist who decided on an illustrating career when she was four years old. She grew up loving fairy tales, fairies, and drawing, but hated school until she entered art school. Her first illustrating job was for the Swedish children's book, *Toffe och den lilla bilen,* commissioned by Astrid Lindgren. Since then, Hyman has retold various classics, authored several books, and won the Caldecott Medal for her illustrations in *Saint George and the Dragon.* Although she has always longed to be an artist like Rembrandt or Goya, she considers herself primarily a book illustrator. "Books and illustrations are part of me," she claims. "They're not just what I do; they're what I *am.*"

ALISON LURIE......Pulitzer Prize-winning novelist who remembers making up stories and poems to amuse herself and her family while she grew up in Westchester, New York. Writing was another favorite pastime once she discovered that "with a pencil and paper I could revise the world." By the time she was a student at Radcliffe College, she had sold her first poems and a short story. Her first novel was not published until years later. Marriage, three sons, and numerous rejection slips did not deter her from pursuing her "writing habit." In subsequent years, Lurie has earned a solid international reputation as a sensitive and observant writer. Since 1969, she has also taught a children's literature course at Cornell University. Her writing for children includes such titles as *Fabulous Beasts, The Heavenly Zoo: Legends and Tales of the Stars, Clever Gretchen and Other Forgotten Folktales,* and the "Classics of Children's Literature" series, which she co-edited with Justin G. Schiller.

DAVID MACAULAY......author, illustrator, artist, and designer who spent his childhood in England until he was eleven. Those early years were "full of play," and he was encouraged by his parents to let his imagination soar. His childhood ended abruptly, however, when he moved with his family to the United States, where he had to adjust to a much faster pace. During this period, he began to draw seriously, copying "every photograph ever taken of the Beatles." He studied architecture in college, which later helped him to develop the discipline he needed to create books. Most of his books are concerned with architectural subjects, which require extensive research in many parts of the world. For his book *Pyramid,* for instance, he climbed to the top of the Great Pyramid in Egypt. In his work, Macaulay strives for economy, believing that "the more you do with less, the better the drawings because it leaves more room for the imagination."

OGDEN NASH......master of whimsical poetry and light verse. Growing up in New York and Georgia, he was educated at home by his mother until the age of fifteen when he entered prep school in Rhode Island. He later moved to New York and began his writing career in the advertising business, writing serious poetry in the evenings, until he began "to poke a little fun at myself." The result of this humorous writing was his first book of light verse. Nash, who gained fame for his mangled verse and unconventional rhymes, preferred to call himself a "worsifier." Children and adults find delight in his unique style in such books as *Parents Keep Out: Elderly Poems for Youngerly Readers* and *Custard, the Dragon.*

DANIEL MANUS PINKWATER......grew up in Chicago reading good books, "mainly adventure stories." This author and illustrator of children's books studied sculpture in college, a discipline that later helped him become a writer, "...because when you carve wood or stone, the moment comes when you've got to actually go *into* the piece of material and start knocking hunks off of it." In his books for young people he tries to portray courageous people—"people prevailing"—because he wants his readers to feel enlightened and encouraged. Pinkwater has the highest regard for his young audience and believes that only through art can young people make sense of the world around them.

ROBERT PENN WARREN......first poet laureate of the United States[1986]. While Warren's early years in Southern Kentucky have had a profound influence on his novels, his years as an undergraduate student at Vanderbilt University have greatly influenced his poetry. "Writing poetry was almost epidemic, even an all-Southern center on the football team did some credible lyrics." Warren's literary development continued while he was a Rhodes Scholar at Oxford University in England. "I saw practically nothing of England," he recalls; "I was always in France." There he was strongly influenced by American writers living on the Left Bank in Paris, such as Ernest Hemingway and F. Scott Fitzgerald. During his own long and distinguished writing career Warren has made significant contributions to fiction, poetry, drama, biography, and literary criticism. The only writer to be awarded the Pulitzer Prize in both poetry and fiction, he has also adapted a collection of the Greek myths for children.

These are only a few of the authors and illustrators that you'll find in this volume. We hope you find all the entries in *SATA* both interesting and useful.

Something about the Author Autobiography Series

You can complement the information in *SATA* with the *Something about the Author Autobiography Series (SAAS)*, which provides autobiographical essays written by important current authors and illustrators of books for children and young adults. In every volume of *SAAS* you will find about twenty specially commissioned autobiographies, each accompanied by a selection of personal photographs supplied by the authors. The wide range of contemporary writers and artists who describe their lives and interests in the *Autobiography Series* includes Joan Aiken, Betsy Byars, Leonard Everett Fisher, Milton Meltzer, Maia Wojciechowska, and Jane Yolen, among others. Though the information presented in the autobiographies is as varied and unique as the authors, you can learn about the people and events that influenced these writers' early lives, how they began their careers, what problems they faced in becoming established in their professions, what prompted them to write or illustrate particular books, what they now find most challenging or rewarding in their lives, and what advice they may have for young people interested in following in their footsteps, among many other subjects.

Autobiographies included in the *SATA Autobiography Series* can be located through both the *SATA* cumulative index and the *SAAS* cumulative index, which lists not only the authors' names but also the subjects mentioned in their essays, such as titles of works and geographical and personal names.

The *SATA Autobiography Series* gives you the opportunity to view "close up" some of the fascinating people who are included in the *SATA* parent series. The combined *SATA* series makes available to you an unequaled range of comprehensive and in-depth information about the authors and illustrators of young people's literature.

Please write and tell us if we can make *SATA* even more helpful to you.

Acknowledgments

Grateful acknowledgment is made to the following publishers, authors, and artists
for their kind permission to reproduce copyrighted material.

ADDISON-WESLEY PUBLISHING CO., INC. Illustration by Trina Schart Hyman from *Self-Portrait: Trina Schart Hyman* by Trina Schart Hyman. Copyright © 1981 by Trina Schart Hyman. Reprinted by permission of Addison-Wesley Publishing Co., Inc.

AGATHON PRESS, INC. Sidelight excerpts from an article "Betsy Byars: An Interview" by Elizabeth Segel, November 4, 1982 in *Children's Literature in Education,* Volume 13. Copyright © 1982 by *Children's Literature in Education.* Reprinted by permission of Agathon Press, Inc.

CAROLRHODA BOOKS, INC. Illustration by Jim Lamarche from *My Minnie Is a Jewel* by Tricia Springstubb. Copyright © 1980 by Carolrhoda Books, Inc. Reprinted by permission of Carolrhoda Books, Inc.

COWARD, McCANN & GEOGHEGAN, INC. Illustration by Trina Schart Hyman from *Why Don't You Get a Horse, Sam Adams?* by Jean Fritz. Text copyright © 1974 by Jean Fritz. Illustrations copyright © 1974 by Trina Schart Hyman. Reprinted by permission of Coward, McCann & Geoghegan, Inc.

CREATIVE EDUCATION. Illustration from *La Belle et la Bête* [*The Beauty and the Beast*] by Marie Catherine D'Aulnoy. Reprinted by permission of Creative Education.

THOMAS Y. CROWELL, INC. Illustration by Margot Tomes from "Molly Whuppie" in *Clever Gretchen and Other Forgotten Folktales,* retold by Alison Lurie. Text copyright © 1980 by Alison Lurie. Illustrations copyright © 1980 by Margot Tomes./ Illustration by Loretta Lustig from *Where Does the Garbage Go?* by Paul Showers. Text copyright © 1974 by Paul Showers. Illustrations copyright © 1974 by Loretta Lustig./ Illustration by Loretta Lustig from *Spaces, Shapes, and Sizes* by Jane Jonas Srivastava. Text copyright © 1980 by Jane Jonas Srivastava. Illustrations copyright © 1980 by Loretta Lustig./ Illustration by John Caldwell from *Beyond a Reasonable Doubt: Inside the American Jury System* by Melvyn Bernard Zerman. Text copyright © 1981 by Melvyn Bernard Zerman. Illustrations copyright © 1981 by John Caldwell. All reprinted by permission of Thomas Y. Crowell, Inc.

DELACORTE PRESS. Illustration by Ruth Sanderson from *The Animal, the Vegetable, and John D. Jones* by Betsy Byars. Text copyright © 1982 by Betsy Byars. Illustrations copyright © 1982 by Dell Publishing Co., Inc. Reprinted by permission of Delacorte Press.

JEAN-PIERRE DeLARGE. Illustration by Etienne Delessert from *Conte numéro 1 pour enfants de moins de trois ans* [*Story Number One for Children under Three Years of Age*] by Eugéne Ionesco. Copyright © 1969 by Editions Universitaires. Reprinted by permission of Jean-Pierre Delarge.

DODD, MEAD & CO. Illustration by Manus Pinkwater from *Blue Moose* by Manus Pinkwater. Copyright © 1975 by Manus Pinkwater. Reprinted by permission of Dodd, Mead & Co.

DOUBLEDAY PUBLISHING CO. Frontispiece illustration by Ronald Fritz from *The Adventures of a Two-Minute Werewolf* by Gene DeWeese. Text copyright © 1983 by Gene DeWeese. Illustrations copyright © 1983 by Doubleday Publishing Co./ Sidelight excerpts from an article "What Happened Next to Maggie?" by Lee Wyndham, November, 1953 in *Young Wings./* Sidelight excerpts from "We All Work Together" by Lee Wyndham, October, 1952 in *Young Wings.* Copyright 1952 by Doubleday & Co., Inc./ Illustration by Etienne Delessert from "The Cat That Walked by Himself" in *Just So Stories* by Rudyard Kipling. Illustrations copyright © 1972 by Etienne Delessert./ Jacket illustration by Stephan Marchesi from *Major Corby and the Unidentified Flapping Object* by Gene DeWeese. Copyright © 1979 by Gene DeWeese. All reprinted by permission of Doubleday Publishing Co.

E. P. DUTTON, INC. Illustration by Trina Schart Hyman from *How Does It Feel to Be Old?* by Norma Farber. Text copyright © 1979 by Norma Farber. Illustrations copyright © 1979 by Trina Schart Hyman./ Illustration by Daniel Pinkwater from *I Was a Second Grade Werewolf* by Daniel Pinkwater. Copyright © 1983 by Daniel Pinkwater./ Illustration by E. H. Shepard

15

from "Pirate Passes" in _The Flattered Flying Fish and Other Poems_ by E. V. Rieu. Copyright ©
1962 by E. V. Rieu. All reprinted by permission of E. P. Dutton, Inc.

EDITIONS GALLIMARD. Illustration by Etienne Delessert from _La souris et les poisons_ by
Anne van der Essen. Copyright © 1975 by Editions Gallimard. Reprinted by permission of
Editions Gallimard.

M. EVANS & CO. Illustration by Wendy Watson from _The Cruise of the Aardvark_ by Ogden
Nash. Text copyright © 1967 by Ogden Nash. Illustrations copyright © 1967 by Wendy
Watson./ Illustration by Hilary Knight from _The Animal Garden_ by Ogden Nash. Text
copyright © 1965 by Ogden Nash. Illustrations copyright © 1965 by Hilary Knight. Both
reprinted by permission of M. Evans & Co.

FAITH AND LIFE PRESS. Illustration by Keith R. Neely from _Peace Be with You_ by
Cornelia Lehn. Copyright © 1980 by Faith and Life Press. Reprinted by permission of Faith and
Life Press.

FARRAR, STRAUS & GIROUX, INC. Illustrations by Monika Beisner from _Fabulous
Beasts_ by Alison Lurie. Text copyright © 1981 by Alison Lurie. Illustrations copyright © 1981 by
Monika Beisner. Copyright © 1981 by Jonathan Cape Ltd. Both reprinted by permission of
Farrar, Straus & Giroux, Inc.

GARRARD PUBLISHING CO. Illustration by William Hutchinson from _Sampson: Yankee
Stallion_ by Justin F. Denzel. Copyright © 1980 by Justin F. Denzel./ Illustration by Gordon
Laite from "The Christmas Season in Scandinavia" in _Holidays in Scandinavia_ by Lee
Wyndham. Copyright © 1975 by Lee Wyndham. Both reprinted by permission of Garrard
Publishing Co.

GLOUCESTER PRESS. Illustration by Maurice Wilson from _Eskimos_ by Jill Hughes.
Copyright © 1977 by The Archon Press Ltd. Reprinted by permission of Gloucester Press.

HARPER & ROW, PUBLISHERS, INC. Illustration by Marilee Robin Burton from _Aaron
Awoke: An Alphabet Story_ by Marilee Robin Burton. Copyright © 1982 by Marilee Robin
Burton./ Jacket illustration by Ruth Sanderson from _The Two-Thousand-Pound Goldfish_ by
Betsy Byars. Text copyright © 1982 by Betsy Byars. Jacket art copyright © 1982 by Ruth
Sanderson. Jacket copyright © 1982 by Harper & Row, Publishers, Inc./ Illustration by Linda
Heller from "The Princess in the Tower" in _Elijah's Violin and Other Jewish Fairy Tales_,
selected and retold by Howard Schwartz. Text copyright © 1983 by Howard Schwartz.
Illustrations copyright © 1983 by Linda Heller./ Illustration by Thacher Hurd from _Mama
Don't Allow_ by Thacher Hurd. Copyright © 1984 by Thacher Hurd./ Illustration by Nancy
Ekholm Burkert from _The Scroobious Pip_ by Edward Lear. Completed by Ogden Nash.
Original unfinished text copyright 1953 by John Murray Publishers Ltd. Text as completed by
Ogden Nash copyright © 1968 by Harper & Row, Publishers, Inc. Introduction and illustrations
copyright © 1968 by Nancy Ekholm Burkert./ Photograph by Herman H. Zwinger from _A
Desert Country Near the Sea: A Natural History of the Cape Region of Baja, California_ by Ann
Zwinger. Copyright © 1983 by Ann H. Zwinger. All reprinted by permission of Harper & Row,
Publishers, Inc.

HOLIDAY HOUSE, INC. Illustration by Trina Schart Hyman from _The Water of Life_,
retold by Barbara Rogasky. Text copyright © 1986 by Barbara Rogasky. Illustrations copyright
© 1986 by Trina Schart Hyman./ Illustration by Trina Schart Hyman from _A Christmas Carol_
by Charles Dickens. Illustrations copyright © 1983 by Trina Schart Hyman./ Illustration by
Trina Schart Hyman from _Little Red Riding Hood_, retold by Trina Schart Hyman. Copyright ©
1983 by Trina Schart Hyman./ Illustration by Trina Schart Hyman from _A Child's Christmas in
Wales_ by Dylan Thomas. Text copyright 1954 by New Directions. Illustrations copyright ©
1985 by Trina Schart Hyman./ Illustration by Trina Schart Hyman from _Witch Poems_, edited
by Daisy Wallace. Text copyright © 1976 by Holiday House, Inc. Illustrations copyright © 1976
by Trina Schart Hyman./ Illustration by Trina Schart Hyman from "Dame Hickory" by Walter
De La Mare in _Fairy Poems_, edited by Daisy Wallace. Text copyright © 1980 by Holiday House,
Inc. Illustrations copyright © 1980 by Trina Schart Hyman. All reprinted by permission of
Holiday House, Inc.

HOLT, RINEHART & WINSTON GENERAL BOOK. Illustration by Margaret
Chamberlain from _The Tale of Fearsome Fritz_ by Jeanne Willis. Text copyright © 1982 by Jean
Willis. Illustrations copyright © 1982 by Margaret Chamberlain. Reprinted by permission of
Holt, Rinehart & Winston General Book.

THE HORN BOOK, INC. Sidelight excerpts from _Illustrators of Children's Books: 1967-
1976_, compiled by Lee Kingman and others. Copyright © 1978 by The Horn Book, Inc./

Sidelight excerpts from "Caldecott Medal Acceptance Speech" by Trina Schart Hyman, July/August, 1985 in *Horn Book*. Both reprinted by permission of The Horn Book, Inc.

HOUGHTON MIFFLIN CO. Illustration by Linda Shute from *The Other Emily* by Gibbs Davis. Text copyright © 1984 by Kathryn Kirby Gibbs Davis. Illustrations copyright © 1984 by Linda McElhiney Shute./ Jacket illustration by Martha Perske from *The Gift-Giver* by Joyce Hansen. Copyright © 1980 by Joyce Hansen./ Frontispiece illustration by Trina Schart Hyman from *Star Mother's Youngest Child* by Louise Moeri./ Illustration by Trina Schart Hyman from *The Mechanical Doll* by Pamela Stearns. Text copyright © 1979 by Pamela Stearns. Illustrations copyright © 1979 by Trina Schart Hyman./ Illustration by Lynn Munsinger from *The Wizard, the Fairy and the Magic Chicken* by Helen Lester. Text copyright © 1983 by Helen Lester. Illustrations copyright © 1983 by Lynn Munsinger./ Illustration by David Macaulay from *Castle* by David Macaulay. Copyright © 1977 by David Macaulay./ Illustration by David Macaulay from *BAAA* by David Macaulay. Copyright © 1985 by David Macaulay./ Illustration by David Macaulay from *City: A Story of Roman Planning and Construction* by David Macaulay. Copyright © 1974 by David Macaulay./ Illustration by David Macaulay from *Mill* by David Macaulay. Copyright © 1983 by David Macaulay./ Illustrations by David Macaulay from *Cathedral: The Story of Its Construction* by David Macaulay. Copyright © 1973 by David Macaulay./ Illustrations by David Macaulay from *Unbuilding* by David Macaulay./ Illustration by Lucinda McQueen from *Skunk and Possum* by Graham Tether. Text copyright © 1979 by Graham Tether. Illustrations copyright © 1979 by Lucinda Emily McQueen. All reprinted by permission of Houghton Mifflin Co.

ALFRED A. KNOPF, INC. Jacket illustration by Trina Schart Hyman from *The Nightmares of Geranium Street* by Susan Shreve. Copyright © 1977 by Susan Shreve./ Illustration by Diane de Groat from *The Flunking of Joshua T. Bates* by Susan Shreve. Text copyright © 1984 by Susan Shreve. Illustrations copyright © 1984 by Diane de Groat. Both reprinted by permission of Alfred A. Knopf, Inc.

J. B. LIPPINCOTT CO. Illustration by Wendy Watson from *The Cruise of the Aardvark* by Ogden Nash. Text copyright © 1967 by Ogden Nash. Illustrations copyright © 1967 by Wendy Watson./ Illustration by Hilary Knight from *The Animal Garden* by Ogden Nash. Text copyright © 1965 by Ogden Nash. Illustrations copyright © 1965 by Hilary Knight./ Illustrations by Jocelyn Wild from *The Bears' Counting Book* by Robin and Jocelyn Wild. Copyright © 1978 by Robin Wild and Jocelyn Wild. All reprinted by permission of J. B. Lippincott Co.

LITTLE, BROWN & CO. Illustration by Alexander Farquharson from *Conqueror and Hero: The Search for Alexander* by Stephen Krensky. Copyright © 1981 by Stephen Krensky./ Illustration by Trina Schart Hyman from *Saint George and the Dragon*, adapted by Margaret Hodges. Text copyright © 1984 by Margaret Hodges. Illustrations copyright © 1984 by Trina Schart Hyman./ Illustration by Trina Schart Hyman from *King Stork* by Howard Pyle. Illustrations copyright © 1973 by Trina Schart Hyman./ Illustration by Trina Schart Hyman from *Joy to the World: Christmas Legends* by Ruth Sawyer. Copyright © 1961, 1962, 1963, 1964, 1966 by Ruth Sawyer Durand./ Detail of a double-page spread by Trina Schart Hyman from *Snow White* by the Brothers Grimm. Translated by Paul Heins. Translation copyright © 1974 by Paul Heins. Illustrations copyright © 1974 by Trina Schart Hyman./ Illustration by Quentin Blake from "The Big Tent under the Roof" in *Custard and Company* by Ogden Nash. Selection and illustrations copyright © 1980 by Quentin Blake./ Illustration by Quentin Blake from "The Panda" in *Custard and Company* by Ogden Nash. Selection and illustrations copyright © 1980 by Quentin Blake./ Illustration by Linell Nash from *The Christmas That Almost Wasn't* by Ogden Nash. Copyright © 1957 by Ogden Nash./ Illustrations by Maurice Sendak from "Go Ahead, It Will Do You Good or Her Eyes Are Bigger Than His Stomach" in *You Can't Get There from Here* by Ogden Nash. Copyright 1953, 1954, © 1956 by The Curtis Publishing Co. Copyright 1953, 1954, © 1955, 1956, 1957 by Ogden Nash./ Illustration by John Alcorn from "The Paid Attendance" in *Everyone But Thee and Me* by Ogden Nash. Copyright © 1957, 1958, 1959, 1960, 1961, 1962 by Ogden Nash./ Illustration by Daniel Pinkwater from *Ducks!* by Daniel Pinkwater. Copyright © 1984 by Daniel Pinkwater./ Illustration by Ben Shahn from *Ounce Dice Trice* by Alastair Reid. Text copyright © 1958 by Alastair Reid and Ben Shahn. All reprinted by permission of Little, Brown & Co.

LOTHROP, LEE & SHEPARD BOOKS. Illustration by Michael Bragg from *The Writing on the Wall* by Leon Garfield. Text copyright © 1983 by Leon Garfield. Illustrations copyright © 1983 by Michael Bragg./ Illustration by Roy Doty from *Kid Camping from Aaaaiiii! to Zip* by Patrick F. McManus. Copyright © 1979 by Patrick F. McManus./ Illustration by Carolyn Bentley from *Quick and Easy Holiday Costumes* by Vivienne Eisner. Copyright © 1977 by Vivienne Eisner. All reprinted by permission of Lothrop, Lee & Shepard Books.

MACMILLAN, INC. Illustration by Warwick Goble from *The Water Babies* by Charles Kingsley./ Illustration by Warwick Goble from *Green Willow, and Other Japanese Fairy Tales* by Grace James./ Illustration by Trina Schart Hyman from *Caddie Woodlawn* by Carol Ryrie Brink. Copyright 1935, renewed copyright © 1963, 1973 by Carol Ryrie Brink. Copyright © 1973 by Macmillan Publishing Co., Inc./ Jacket illustration by Daniel Pinkwater from *Slaves of Spiegel: A Magic Moscow Story* by Daniel Pinkwater. Copyright © 1982 by Daniel Pinkwater./ Illustration by Daniel Pinkwater from *The Magic Moscow* by Daniel Pinkwater. Copyright © 1980 by Daniel Pinkwater./ Illustration by Tomie de Paola from *The Wuggie Norple Story* by Daniel Pinkwater. Text copyright © 1980 by Daniel Pinkwater. Illustrations copyright © 1980 by Tomie de Paola. All reprinted by permission of Macmillan, Inc.

McGRAW-HILL, INC. Illustration by Wesley Dennis from *Old Bones, the Wonder Horse* by Mildred Mastin Pace. Copyright © 1955 by Mildred Mastin Pace. Reprinted by permission of McGraw-Hill, Inc.

WILLIAM MORROW & CO., INC. Illustration by Suekichi Akaba from *The Crane Wife,* retold by Sumiko Yagawa. Translation from the Japanese by Katherine Paterson. Copyright © 1979 by Sumiko Yagawa. Illustrations copyright © 1979. English translation copyright © 1981./ Illustration by Loretta Lustig from *Get Rich Mitch* by Marjorie Weinman Sharmat. Text copyright © 1985 by Marjorie Weinman Sharmat. Illustrations copyright © 1985 by Loretta Lustig. Both reprinted by permission of William Morrow & Co., Inc.

OXFORD UNIVERSITY PRESS. Illustration by Etienne Delessert from *The Endless Party* by Etienne Delessert. Copyright © 1980 by Oxford University Press./ Illustration by Trina Schart Hyman from *Little Red Riding Hood,* retold by Trina Schart Hyman. Copyright © 1983 by Trina Schart Hyman. Reprinted by permission of Oxford University Press.

PANTHEON BOOKS, INC. Illustration by Philip Smith from *Long Meg* by Rosemary Minard. Text copyright © 1982 by Rosemary Minard. Illustrations copyright © 1982 by Philip Smith. Reprinted by permission of Pantheon Books, Inc.

PARENTS MAGAZINE PRESS. Illustration by Yaroslava from *The Winter Child: An Old Russian Folktale,* retold by Lee Wyndham. Text copyright © 1970 by Lee Wyndham. Illustrations copyright © 1970 by Yaroslava Mills./ Illustration by Charles Mikolaycak from *Russian Tales of Fabulous Beasts and Marvels* by Lee Wyndham. Copyright © 1969 by Lee Wyndham./ Illustration by Charles Mikolaycak from *Mourka, the Mighty Cat* by Lee Wyndham. Text copyright © 1969 by Lee Wyndham. Illustrations copyright © 1969 by Charles Mikolaycak. All reprinted by permission of Parents Magazine Press.

PRENTICE-HALL, INC. Illustration by Daniel Pinkwater from *The Blue Thing* by Daniel Pinkwater. Copyright © 1977 by Daniel Manus Pinkwater./ Illustration by Daniel Pinkwater from *The Hoboken Chicken Emergency* by Daniel Pinkwater. Copyright © 1977 by D. Manus Pinkwater./ Jacket illustration by Stanley Wyatt from *Robert Penn Warren: A Collection of Critical Essays,* edited by Richard Gray. Copyright © 1980 by Prentice-Hall, Inc. All reprinted by permission of Prentice-Hall, Inc.

THE PUTNAM PUBLISHING GROUP, INC. Illustration by Lorinda Bryan Cauley from *The Town Mouse and the Country Mouse,* retold by Lorinda Bryan Cauley. Copyright © 1984 by Lorinda Bryan Cauley./ Illustration by Trina Schart Hyman from *The Man Who Loved Books* by Jean Fritz. Text copyright © 1981 by Jean Fritz. Illustrations copyright © 1981 by Trina Schart Hyman./ Illustration by Trina Schart Hyman from *On to Widecombe Fair* by Patricia Lee Gauch. Text copyright © 1978 by Patricia Lee Gauch. Illustrations copyright © 1978 by Trina Schart Hyman. All reprinted by permission of The Putnam Publishing Group, Inc.

RAINTREE PUBLISHERS, INC. Illustration by Jay Blair from *Diana: Alone against the Sea* by Valjean McLenighan. Copyright © 1980 by Raintree Publishers, Inc. Reprinted by permission of Raintree Publishers, Inc.

ST. JAMES PRESS. Sidelight excerpts from an article "Betsy Byars" by Rachel Fordyce in *Twentieth-Century Children's Writers,* second edition, edited by D. L. Kirkpatrick. Copyright © 1983 by Macmillan Publishers Ltd. Reprinted by permission of St. James Press.

ST. MARTIN'S PRESS, INC. Sidelight excerpts from an article "Betsy Byars" by Rachel Fordyce in *Twentieth-Century Children's Writers,* second edition, edited by D. L. Kirkpatrick. Copyright © 1983 by Macmillan Publishers Ltd. Reprinted by permission of St. Martin's Press, Inc.

SCHOCKEN BOOKS, INC. Illustration by Sumiko from "The Little Mermaid" in *Hans Andersen's Fairy Tales.* Text copyright © 1979 by Ward Lock Ltd. Illustrations copyright © 1979 by Sumiko Davies. Reprinted by permission of Schocken Books, Inc.

SCHOLASTIC, INC. Illustration by Loretta Lustig from *Rich Mitch* by Marjorie Weinman Sharmat. Copyright © 1983 by Marjorie Weinman Sharmat. Reprinted by permission of Scholastic, Inc.

CHARLES SCRIBNER'S SONS. Illustration by Trina Schart Hyman from *Peter Pan* by J. M. Barrie. Text copyright 1911 by Charles Scribner's Sons. Copyright renewed 1939 by Lady Cynthia Asquith and Peter Llewelyn Davies. Illustrations copyright © 1980 by Trina Schart Hyman. Reprinted by permission of Charles Scribner's Sons.

SIMON & SCHUSTER, INC. Illustration by Reginald Birch from "The Cow" in *The Bad Parents' Garden of Verse* by Ogden Nash. Copyright 1936 by Ogden Nash. Reprinted by permission of Simon & Schuster, Inc.

VERLAG MIDDELHAUVE. Illustration by Etienne Delessert from *Die Maus und was ihr bleibt* [*Amelia Mouse and Her Great-Great-Grandchild*] by Anne van der Essen. Copyright © by Verlag Middelhauve. Reprinted by permission of Verlag Middelhauve.

VIKING KESTREL. Jacket illustration by Diane de Groat from *Cracker Jackson* by Betsy Byars. Jacket copyright © 1985 by Betsy Byars. Copyright © 1985 by Viking Penguin, Inc. Reprinted by permission of Viking Kestrel.

THE VIKING PRESS. Illustration by Ted CoConis from *The Summer of the Swans* by Betsy Byars. Copyright © 1970 by Betsy Byars./ Illustration by Gail Owens from *The Cybil War* by Betsy Byars. Text copyright © 1981 by Betsy Byars. Illustrations copyright © 1981 by The Viking Press./ Illustration by Ronald Himler from *After the Goat Man* by Betsy Byars. Copyright © 1974 by Betsy Byars. Illustrations copyright © 1974 by The Viking Press./ Illustration by Peggy Bacon from *Rama, the Gypsy Cat* by Betsy Byars. Text copyright © 1966 by Betsy C. Byars. Illustrations copyright © 1966 by Peggy Bacon./ Illustration by Harold Berson from *The Dancing Camel* by Betsy Byars. Text copyright © 1965 by Betsy C. Byars. Illustration copyright © 1965 by Harold Berson./ Illustration by Ann Grifalconi from *The Midnight Fox* by Betsy Byars. Copyright © 1968 by Betsy Byars./ Illustration by Robert Grossman from *The 18th Emergency* by Betsy Byars. Copyright © 1973 by Betsy Byars./ Illustration by Daniel Schwartz from *The House of Wings* by Betsy Byars. Copyright © 1972 by Betsy Byars./ Illustration by Richard Cuffari from *The Cartoonist* by Betsy Byars. Text copyright © 1978 by Betsy Byars. Illustrations copyright © 1978 by Viking Penguin, Inc./ Illustration by Betsy Byars from *The Lace Snail* by Betsy Byars. Copyright © 1975 by Betsy Byars./ Illustration by S. D. Schindler from *Fish Fry* by Susan Saunders. Text copyright © 1982 by Susan Saunders. Illustrations copyright © 1982 by S. D. Schindler. All reprinted by permission of The Viking Press.

ALBERT WHITMAN & CO. Illustration by Margot Apple from *Poppy and the Outdoors Cat* by Dorothy Haas. Text copyright © 1981 by Dorothy F. Haas. Illustrations copyright © 1981 by Margot Apple. Reprinted by permission of Albert Whitman & Co.

Sidelight excerpts from "Newbery Acceptance Speech" by Betsy Byars, August, 1971 in *Horn Book.* Copyright © 1971 by The Horn Book, Inc. Reprinted by permission of Betsy Byars./ Sidelight excerpts from *More Books by More People* by Lee Bennett Hopkins. Copyright © 1974 by Lee Bennett Hopkins. Reprinted by permission of Curtis Brown Ltd./ Sidelight excerpts from an article "Caldecott Medal Acceptance Speech" by Trina Schart Hyman, July/August, 1985 in *Horn Book.* Copyright © 1985 by Trina Schart Hyman. Reprinted by permission of Trina Schart Hyman./ Sidelight excerpts from an article "Betsy Byars—Writer for Today" by Ina Robertson in *Language Arts,* Volume 57, number 3. Copyright © 1980 by The National Council of Teachers of English. Reprinted by permission of *Language Arts.*/ Illustration by Manus Pinkwater from *Wizard Crystal* by Manus Pinkwater. Copyright © 1973 by Manus Pinkwater. Reprinted by permission of Daniel Pinkwater./ Photograph from *Battle of Britain* by G. C. Skipper. Copyright © 1980 by Regensteiner Publishing Enterprises, Inc. Reprinted by permission of United Press International./ Sidelight excerpts from an article "Writing for the Look 'n Listen Age" by Lee Wyndham, April 1960 in *The Writer.* Copyright © 1960 by The Writer, Inc. Reprinted by permission of The Writer, Inc./ Sidelight excerpts from *Writing for Children and Teen-agers* by Lee Wyndham. Copyright © 1968, 1972, 1980 by Writer's Digest Books. Reprinted by permission of Writer's Digest Books.

Appreciation also to the Performing Arts Research Center of the New York Public Library at Lincoln Center for permission to reprint the theater stills "One Touch of Venus" and "All the King's Men."

PHOTOGRAPH CREDITS

Otto Ludwig Bettmann: Peter Fink; Olga Cabral: Layle Silbert; Mary Higgins Clark: Copyright © 1984 by Helen Marcus; William Corlett: John H. Moore; William R. Cox: A Yeoman, Hollywood; Maurice Gee: Margaretha Garden; Dorcas Woodbury Haller: Copyright © by Harold Ryan; Joyce Hansen: A. Hansen Photography; Linda Heller: Michael Ayervais; Thacher Hurd: Liz Bordow; Charlotte Buel Johnson: Peter T. Muscato; Cornelia Lehn: Jim Stucky Photographics; Alison Lurie: Copyright © 1984 by Jim Kalett; Patrick McManus: Keith Jackson; Ogden Nash: Vandaman; Ogden Nash (at work): Abe Crank; Daniel Pinkwater (in Hoboken, New Jersey): Linda White; Alastair Reid: Layle Silbert; Susan Richards Shreve: Sally Stone Halvorson; Graham Tether: Ethel Holm; Robert Penn Warren: Nancy Crampton; Robert Penn Warren: Jim Caldwell; Melvyn Bernard Zerman: Joan Bingham.

something about the author

ABOLAFIA, Yossi

BRIEF ENTRY: Born in Israel, Abolafia has worked as an animation director in Israel, Canada, and the United States. He wrote and illustrated *My Three Uncles* (Greenwillow, 1984), the story of identical triplet uncles and their niece's efforts to tell them apart. The text tells only part of the story, as *School Library Journal* observed: "The rest is revealed by the breezy line drawings that are tinted with shades of blues, greens and yellows. Here, the uncles' personalities come to life, as do the little girl's feelings of agitation, bewilderment and finally smugness." Abolafia illustrated Barbara Ann Porte's *Harry's Visit* (Greenwillow, 1983), *Harry's Dog* (Greenwillow, 1984), which was listed as one of the American Library Association Notable Books in 1984, and *Harry's Mom* (Greenwillow, 1985). In *Harry's Dog* and *Harry's Visit*, he used flipbook drawings in the corners of the pages to create scenes of a dog moving toward a food dish and Harry playing basketball. Abolafia also provided cartoon drawings for Charlotte Pomerantz's *Buffy and Albert* (Greenwillow, 1982) as well as *It's Valentine's Day* (Greenwillow, 1983), and *What I Did Last Summer* (Greenwillow, 1984), and *My Parents Think I'm Sleeping* (Greenwillow, 1985), all written by Jack Prelutsky.

ADAMSON, Gareth   1925-1982

PERSONAL: Born May 10, 1925, in Liverpool, England; died in 1982 in Cambridge, England; son of William John (a manufacturer) and Isobel (Hughes) Adamson; married Jean Elizabeth Bailey (a free-lance artist), October 5, 1957; children: Leo, Gabrielle, Kate. *Education:* Attended Edinburgh College of Art and Architecture, 1944-46; Goldsmiths' College, London, National Diploma in Design (illustration), 1951. *Politics:* Liberal. *Religion:* Roman Catholic. *Residence:* Northumberland, England.

CAREER: Hunt Partners Ltd. (packaging company), London, England, research designer, 1952-53; Cravens Advertising Ltd., Newcastle upon Tyne, England, creative chief, 1953-57; free-lance author and illustrator of children's books, 1957-82. *Awards, honors:* First prize from British Broadcasting Corporation and North East Association for the Arts, 1965, for a television play.

WRITINGS—Self-illustrated, except as indicated: *Neighbours in the Park* (illustrated by wife, Jean Adamson), Harrap, 1962; *Old Man up a Tree*, Abelard, 1963; *Mr. Budge Builds a House*, Brockhampton Press, 1963, Chilton, 1968; *Mr. Budge Buys a Car*, Brockhampton Press, 1965; (with J. Adamson) *The Ahmed Story*, Whiting, 1966; *Three Discontented Clowns*, Abelard, 1966; *Harold, the Happy Handman*, Harvey House, 1968; (with J. Adamson) *Family Tree*, A Whitman, 1968; *Machines at Home*, Lutterworth, 1969; *People at Home*, Lutterworth, 1972; (with J. Adamson) *Hop Like Me*, A. Whitman, 1973; *Wheels for the Road*, Dent, 1973.

"Topsy and Tim" series; all with J. Adamson; all published by Blackie & Son: *Topsy and Tim's Monday Book*, 1959, reprinted, 1977; . . . *Tuesday Book*, 1959, reprinted, 1977; . . . *Wednesday Book*, 1960, reprinted, 1977; . . . *Thursday Book*, 1960, reprinted, 1977; . . . *Friday Book*, 1961, reprinted, 1977; . . . *Saturday Book*, 1961, reprinted, 1977; . . . *Sunday Book*, 1962, reprinted, 1977; . . . *Foggy Day*, 1962; *Topsy and Tim at the Football Match*, 1963; . . . *Go Fishing*, 1963; *Topsy and Tim's Bonfire Night*, 1964; . . . *Snowy Day*, 1964; *Topsy and Tim Go on Holiday*, 1965; . . . *at the Seaside*, 1965; . . . *at the Zoo*, 1968.

Hullo, Topsy and Tim!, 1971; *Surprises for Topsy and Tim*, 1971; *Happy Days with Topsy and Tim*, 1971; *Topsy and Tim*

GARETH ADAMSON

at School, 1971; . . . *and Their Friends*, 1971; . . . *Go to Hospital*, 1971; *Topsy and Tim's Birthday Party*, 1971; . . . *Paddling Pool*, 1971; *Topsy and Tim Go Pony-Trekking*, 1972; . . . *Go Safely*, 1972; *Topsy and Tim's Ups and Downs*, 1973; *Topsy and Tim Learn to Swim*, 1973; *Safety First with Topsy and Tim*, 1973; *Topsy and Tim Go Hill-Walking*, 1973; . . . *Take No Risks*, 1973; . . . *Cross the Channel*, 1974; . . . *Go Sailing*, 1974; . . . *in Belgium*, 1974; . . . *in Holland*, 1974; . . . *Out and About*, 1974; . . . *Visit Europe*, 1974.

Topsy and Tim's New Brother, 1975; *Topsy and Tim Visit the Dentist*, 1975; . . . *Visit the Doctor*, 1975; . . . *at the Wedding*, 1976; . . . *Visit the Tower of London*, 1976; *Topsy and Tim's New School*, 1976; . . . *Pet Show*, 1976; *Topsy and Tim at the Circus*, 1977; . . . *Go Camping*, 1977; . . . *Go Shopping*, 1977; . . . *on the Farm*, 1977; . . . *at the Fairground*, 1978; . . . *at the Library*, 1978; . . . *at the Vet*, 1978; . . . *Choose a Puppy*, 1978; . . . *Meet the Monsters*, 1978; *Topsy and Tim's Picnic*, 1978; . . . *School Outing*, 1978; . . . *Sports Day*, 1978; . . . *Train Journey*, 1978; . . . *Caravan Holiday*, 1979; *Topsy and Tim at the Hairdresser*, 1979; . . . *Go in an Aeroplane*, 1979; . . .*Have a Barbecue*, 1979; . . . *Move House*, 1979; . . . *at the Fire Station*, 1979; . . . *at the Jumble Sale*, 1979; . . . *at the Pantomime*, 1979.

Seven Days with Topsy and Tim, 1980; *Topsy and Tim Can Print in Colour*, 1980; . . . *Can Sing and Play*, 1980; . . . *Can Garden*, 1980; . . . *Can Cook*, 1981; . . . *Can Look after Pets*, 1981; . . . *Can Play Party Games*, 1981; . . . *Go to Play-*

school, 1981; *Topsy and Tim's Alphabet Frieze*, 1981; . . . *Birthday*, 1981; . . . *Country Day*, 1981; . . . *New Pet*, 1981; *Topsy and Tim Have Their Eyes Tested*, 1982; . . . *Can Help Birds*, 1982; *Topsy and Tim's A.B.C.*, 1982.

Also author of a television play.

Illustrator: Charles Hatcher, *What Shape Is It?*, Brockhampton Press, 1963, Duell, Sloan & Pearce, 1966; C. Hatcher, *What Size Is It?*, Brockhampton Press, 1964, Duell, Sloan & Pearce, 1966; Carol Adams, *How They Lived in a Medieval Castle*, Lutterworth, 1982.

SIDELIGHTS: Adamson's artistic interests included cartoon and animated puppet films (he and his wife Jean Adamson, devised a method of puppet animation they did not have time to develop) and architecture. The Adamsons lived in a house built in 1725 on the site of the old Baliff Gate, precisely ten paces from Alnwick Castle.

FOR MORE INFORMATION SEE—Obituaries: *AB Bookman's Weekly*, April 12, 1982.

AKABA, Suekichi   1910-

PERSONAL: Born May 3, 1910, in Tokyo, Japan; son of Fusajiro (an insurance company employee) and Natsu (a housewife; maiden name, Aota) Akaba; married Ryoko (a housewife), June 18, 1934; children: three sons, Kiichi, Kenzo, Daishiro. *Home:* Kamakura, Kanagawa Prefecture, Japan.

SUEKICHI AKABA

The young woman was modest and kind, and she served Yohei faithfully. ■ (From *The Crane Wife*, retold by Sumiko Yagawa. Illustrated by Suekichi Akaba.)

CAREER: Author, and illustrator of children's books. *Member:* Artists' Union for Juvenile Illustrated Publication. *Awards, honors:* Motai Takeschi Award of Japan, 1959; Shogakukan Bungakusho Illustration Award, 1961, for *Suho no shiroi uma* (title means "Suho and the White Horse: A Legend of Mongolia"), and 1975, for *Homan-Ike no Kappa;* Sankei Award for Children's Books and Publications, 1962, for *Daiku to Oniroku* (title means "Oniroku and the Carpenter"); Mainichi Cultural Prize for Publications, 1963, for *Yakaina Kicchomu San;* Ministry of Welfare Award for Children's Welfare and Culture, and Sankei Award for Children's Books and Publications, both 1968, both for *Suho no shiroi uma* (revised edi-

tion; title means "Suho and the White Horse: A Legend of Mongolia"); *Suho and the White Horse: A Legend of Mongolia* was one of Child Study Association's Children's Books of the Year, 1969, received the Brooklyn Art Books for Children Citation from the Brooklyn Museum and the Brooklyn Public Library, 1976, 1977, and 1978, was nominated for the Mildred Batchelder Award, 1971, and was selected as a notable children's trade book in the field of social studies by the joint committee of the National Council for Social Studies and the Children's Book Council, 1982; International Board on Books for Young People honor list, 1975, for *Homan-Ike no Kappa;* International Hans Christian Andersen Award, 1980, for his collected works; *The Crane Wife* was chosen one of *New York Times* Best Illustrated Children's Books, and one of *New York Times* Outstanding Books, both 1981.

WRITINGS: Okina okina oimo (title means "The Great Big Potato"), Fukuinkan, 1972; *Ehon Warabeuta,* Kaiseisha, 1977; *Sora Nigero,* Kaiseisha, 1978; *Hesotori Gorobe,* Doshinsha, 1978; *Ehon yomoyamabanashi* (biography; title means "Essays on Picture Books"), Kaiseisha, 1979.

Illustrator: Teiji Seta, *Kasajizo* (title means "Roku Jizo and the Braided Hats: An Old Tale of Japan"), Fukuinkan, 1960; Yuzo Otsuka, reteller, *Suho no shiroi uma,* Fukuinkan, 1961, revised edition, 1967, translation by Yasuko Hirawa published as *Suho and the White Horse: A Legend of Mongolia,* Bobbs-Merrill, 1969, new edition, adapted from the first translation by Ann Herring, Viking, 1981; Tadashi Matsui, *Daiku to Oniroku,* Fukuinkan, 1962, translation by Masako Matsuno published as *Oniroku and the Carpenter,* Prentice-Hall, 1963; Hirosuke Hamada, *Kojiki, Konjakumonogatari, Heike monogatari,* Kodansha, 1963; Toshio Nishiyhama, *Nihon no Minwa, Densetsu,* Kaiseisha, 1963; Yoshio Fujita, *Yukaina Kicchomu San,* Shikosha, 1963; T. Matsui, *Kobu Jii-sama,* Fukuinkan, 1964.

Yoshitomo Imae, *Esugata Nyobo,* Seikosha, 1965; Toshiko Knazawa, *Nuche no Boken,* Riron-sha, 1966; Y. Imae, *Futari Daimyo,* Komine, 1966; Yoshiki Akagi, *Yanagi no Wata Tobu Kuni,* Riron-sha, 1966; Joji Tsubota, *Tengu no Kakure Mino,* Heibonsha, 1967; Miyoko Matsutani, *Hanasaka Jiji,* Seikosha, 1967; Susumu Hani, *Yamata no Orochi,* Iwasaki, 1967; Shintaro Okuno, editor, *Ryosaishii,* Seikosha, 1967; Satoshi Kako, *Aruku Yama Ugoku Yama,* Doshinshu, 1968; Essei Okawa, *Kin-iro no Kitsune,* Populasha, 1968; T. Kanzawa, *Saru, to Kani,* Kodansha, 1968; Tomiko Inui, *Mienaku natta Akai Ski,* Daihihon Tosho, 1968; Nobuo Ishimori, *Inu no Ashiato,* Saerashobo, 1969; N. Ishimori, *Sengendake,* Toto-shobo, 1969; Hatoju Muku, *Chibizaru Kyodai,* Gakushu Kenkyusha, 1969; Hisako Kimishima, *Chiwan no Nishiki,* Populasha, 1969; Junji Kitamura, *Herakuresu no Boken,* Iwasaki, 1969; Taku Miki, *Horobita Kuni no Tabi,* Seikosha, 1969; Takashi Kawamura, *Saigo no Kujirabune,* Jitsugyo-no-nihonsha, 1969; E. Okawa, *Kintsuba jihei,* Populasha, 1969; Daiji Kawasaki, *Nihon no obake banashi* (title means "Japanese Folktales of Phantoms and Ghosts"), edited by Shimpachiro Matsumoto, Doshinsha, 1969; Kenji Miyazawa, *Suisenzuki no Yokka* (title means "The Fourth Day of the Narcissus Month"), Fukuinkan, 1969.

Yasuo Maekawa, *Danmari Oniju,* Flebel-kan, 1970; Kiyoto Fukuda, *Nihon no Shinwa,* Bunken Shuppan, 1970; Y. Otsuka, *Mongoru minwa ishi ni natta karyduo* (title means "The Great Brave Hunter Who Turned into a Stone"), Fukuinkan, 1970; Fumiko Koide, *Hayataro Inu,* Saero-shobo, 1971; M. Matsutani, *Kuroi Cho,* Kodansha, 1971; T. Kawamura, *Kujira to Shonen,* Jitsugyo-no-nihonsha, 1971; Haruko Akune, *Hinokami no Mago,* Seikosha, 1972; Seishi Horio, *Uriko Hime,* Flebel-kan, 1972; Nankichi Niimi, *Yama no Kyodai,* Akaneshobo, 1972; K. Fukuda, *Hakucho ni natta Omochi,* Bunken Shuppan, 1972; E. Okawa, *Yama no Kaasan to Juroppiki no Nezumi,* Populasha, 1972; H. Muku, *Hazukashi katta Monogatari,* Doshinsha, 1972; Sukeyuki Imanishi, *Kiso Yoshinaka* (title means "Kiso Yoshinaka [name of a famous warrior]"), Kaiseisha, 1972; S. Imanishi, *Minamoto Yoritomo,* Kaiseisha, 1972; Takashi Kawamura, *Morikui kujira,* Jitsugyo-no-nihonsha, 1972; T. Seta, *Ma no ii ryoshi* (title means "A Lucky Hunter: Old Japanese Tale"), Fukuinkan, 1973; Kaoruko Okano, *Shika no Dohjo,* Akane-shobo, 1973; T. Kawamura, *Amikake Kujira,* Jitsugyo-no-nihonsha, 1973.

Masako Matsuno, *Nakitaro,* Bunken Shuppan, 1974; Noboru Daita, *Koganeryu to Tennyo,* Gingasha, 1974; N. Daita and O. Masumura, editors, *Yume no Neshonben Yama,* Doshinsha, 1974; T. Kanzawa, *Saru to kani* (title means "A Monkey and a Crab"), Gingasha (Tokyo), 1974; H. Muku, *Homan-Ike no Kappa,* Gingasha, 1974; Yoshihiko Funazaki, *Oni Zorozoro,* Kaiseisha, 1978; S. Imanishi, *Gempei-Emake Monogatari,* ten volumes, revised edition, Kaiseisha, 1979; Sachiko Maki, *Haru no Wakare,* Kaiseisha, 1979; Sumiko Yagawa, reteller, *Tsurunyobo,* Fukuinkan, 1979, translation by Katherine Paterson published as *The Crane Wife,* Morrow, 1981; H. Kimishima, reteller, *Akari No Hana* (title means "The Flower of Fire"), Fukuinkan, 1985.

Also illustrator of more than fifteen additional books in Japan.

ADAPTATIONS: "Suho and the White Horse" (film), Weston Woods, 1982.

WORK IN PROGRESS: Illustrations for "Japanese Myth" series and *Japanese Folktale.*

SIDELIGHTS: "I illustrate other people's stories, but write and illustrate as well. My own books are mostly nonsense books with which I hope to give joy to children."

HOBBIES AND OTHER INTERESTS: Movies, drama, and reading.

ATKINSON, Allen

BRIEF ENTRY: Born and raised in rural Connecticut, where he still lives, Atkinson is an illustrator whose work appears in such books as Beatrix Potter's *The Tale of Peter Rabbit and Other Stories* (Knopf, 1982), Margery Williams's *The Velveteen Rabbit* (Knopf, 1983), *Mother Goose's Nursery Rhymes* (Knopf, 1984), and *Grimm's Fairy Tales* (Wanderer Books, 1982). Nine of Potter's tales have been collected and re-illustrated by Atkinson who, according to *Booklist,* "displays a soft, meticulous, literal style, more fully developed than Potter's cozy, fluid watercolors but similar in spirit." In *Mother Goose's Nursery Rhymes,* Atkinson uses animals to represent characters normally portrayed as humans: the Old Woman Who Lived in a Shoe is a rabbit, Little Jack Horner is a bear in a three-piece suit, and Jack Sprat and his wife appear as a giraffe and an elephant. The same magazine called the illustrations in this collection of over 100 rhymes "a lovely interpretation . . . firmly on the sentimental side of Mother Goose . . . a bridge into a never-never land of Old England." Atkinson also illustrated John Morressy's *The Windows of Forever* (Walker, 1975) and a 1985 edition of L. Frank Baum's *The Wizard of Oz.* In addition to illustrating, Atkinson designs toys for children. *Residence:* Connecticut.

AUGELLI, John P(at) 1921-

PERSONAL: Surname is pronounced *O*-jelly; born January 30, 1921, in Italy; children: John, Robert. *Education:* Clark University (Worcester, Mass.), B.A., 1943; Harvard University, M.A., Ph.D. *Home:* 1804 College St., Baldwin, Kan. 66006. *Office:* University of Kansas, Lawrence, Kan. 66045.

CAREER: University of Puerto Rico, Rio Piedras, assistant professor, later associate professor of geography, 1948-52; University of Maryland, College Park, associate professor,

1952-60, professor of geography, 1960-61; University of Kansas, Lawrence, professor of geography, 1961-70, and 1973—, director, Center of Latin America Area Studies, 1961-70, dean of International programs, 1971-73; University of Illinois, Urbana-Champaign, Ill., professor of geography and director, Center of Latin American Studies, 1970-71. Consultant at various times to U.S. Department of State, Ford Foundation, Foreign Area Fellowship Program, and publishing firms. Social Science Research Council, member of Joint Committee on Latin American Studies, 1964-67; U.S. National Committee for International Geographical Union, secretary, 1965-68; Pan American Institute of Geography and History, U.S. member, 1965-68; appointed by President Lyndon Johnson to the Board of Foreign Scholarships, 1967-70. *Military service:* U.S. Army Air Forces, 1943-45; U.S. Air Force Reserve, 1948-52; became lieutenant.

MEMBER: Association of American Geographers (chairman of Middle Atlantic division, 1960; national secretary, 1966), American Geographical Society, National Council for Geographic Education, Latin American Studies Association (president, Midwest Council 1963-64; national vice-president, 1968; national president, 1969). *Awards, honors:* Research and travel grants from governments of Brazil and Puerto Rico, University of Maryland, Organization of American States, Social Science Research Council, the University of Kansas, and American Council of Learned Societies; ''Master Teacher'' award from National Council for Geographic Education, 1979.

WRITINGS: (Contributor) *Symposium on the Geography of Puerto Rico,* edited by C. F. Jones and R. Pico, University of Puerto Rico Press, 1955; (geography editor) *The Great Plains States,* Fideler, 1963; (editor) *American Geography, 1960-63: Education, Employment, and Other Trends,* Association of American Geographers, 1964; (contributor) *Focus on Geographical Activity,* edited by R. Thomas and D. Patton, McGraw, 1964; *Caribbean Lands* (junior high text), Fideler, 1965; (with Robert West) *Geography of Middle America,* Prentice-Hall, 1966; *Puerto Rico,* Ginn, 1973; (with R. West) *Middle America: Its Lands and People,* Prentice-Hall, 1976; (editor) *American Neighbors* (with teacher's guide), revised edition, Fideler, 1982.

Author of five U.S. State Department monographs on West Indies, 1957-59. Contributor to *Encyclopedia Britannica, American Peoples Encyclopedia,* and *Collier's Encyclopedia;* also contributor of articles and reviews to professional journals. Geography editor, *Handbook of Latin American Studies,* 1961-64.

WORK IN PROGRESS: Preparation of third edition (with R. West) of *Middle America: Its Land and People,* for Prentice-Hall.

SIDELIGHTS: ''I author books because publishers ask me to translate my field experiences and interests into writings for young people. I have an enduring love of nature and the land. Perhaps this is why I am now a part-time farmer. I have never lost the deep curiosity about 'what is on the other side of the horizon.' This may explain why I have wandered (and continue to wander) over so much of the earth.

''My primary interest is teaching and writing about people, places and cultures, particularly those of Latin America.''

HOBBIES AND OTHER INTERESTS: Raising cattle.

AYRES, Patricia Miller   1923-1985

OBITUARY NOTICE: Born in 1923 in Tampico, Mexico; died of a cerebral hemorrhage, September 17, 1985, in New York, N.Y. Publishing executive, copywriter, and editor. A former vice-president and general manager of Parents' Magazine Enterprises, Ayres became rights and permissions editor for *Guideposts* magazine in 1981. In addition, she was a member of the Children's Book Council and lectured extensively on the topics of subsidiary rights and children's books.

FOR MORE INFORMATION SEE—Obituaries: *New York Times,* September 20, 1985; *Publishers Weekly,* October 4, 1985.

BARON, Virginia Olsen   1931-

PERSONAL: Born July 5, 1931, in Wilkes-Barre, Pa.; daughter of John Arthur (a controller) and Maxine (Spry) Olsen; married William J. Park (a professor), November 21, 1951; married second husband, Michael Riffaterre (a professor), February 10, 1956; married third husband, Richard W. Baron (a book publisher), February 15, 1963; children: (first marriage) Jonathan D. Park, Geoffrey W. Park; (second marriage) Lee K. Riffaterre; (third marriage) Amy R. Baron, Richard Thomas Baron. *Education:* Attended Beaver College, 1949-51. *Politics:* Democrat. *Religion:* ''Post-Christian.'' *Office:* Dial Press, 1 Dag Hammarskjold Plaza, 245 East 47th St., New York, N.Y. 10017.

CAREER: Riverside Radio WRVR-FM, New York City, radio producer, 1960-61; Dial Press, Inc., New York City, publicity

JOHN P. AUGELLI

director, 1962-64, member of board of directors, 1963—; Cambria Press, Inc. (division of Richard W. Baron Publishing Co.), New York City, publisher, beginning 1969. Columbia University, chairman of Children's Program series, 1956-58, president of Greenhouse Nursery School, 1957-58.

WRITINGS: (Compiler) *The Seasons of Time: Tanka Poetry of Ancient Japan* (ALA Notable Book; illustrated by Yashudie E. Kobashi), Dial, 1968; (compiler) *Here I Am! An Anthology of Poems Written by Young People in Some of America's Minority Groups* (illustrated by Emily Arnold McCully), Dutton, 1969; (editor) *Sunset in a Spider Web*, translation from the Korean by Chung S. Park, Holt, 1974.

WORK IN PROGRESS: Editing two books, *Mysticism in America*, for Dial, and *Songs from the Land Where the Cuckoo Sings in the Daytime: Sijo Poetry of Korea.*

FOR MORE INFORMATION SEE: Martha E. Ward and Dorothy A. Marquardt, *Authors of Books for Young People*, supplement to the 2nd edition, Scarecrow, 1979.

BAUER, Caroline Feller   1935-

BRIEF ENTRY: Born May 12, 1935, in Washington, D.C. Bauer, who earned a M.L.S. from Columbia University in 1958 and a Ph.D. from the University of Oregon in 1971, has written stories for children as well as handbooks for storytellers. During the late 1950s and early 1960s, she was employed as a children's librarian at the New York Public Library and as a public school librarian in Oregon; from 1972 to 1980, she served as producer of "Caroline's Corner" for the Oregon Educational Public Broadcasting System. An associate professor of library science at the University of Oregon from 1966 to 1979, Bauer received the Ersted Award for distinguished teaching in 1968. She also has worked as an educational consultant, a book reviewer for *Cricket*, and a lecturer.

Bauer's books for children include *My Mom Travels a Lot* (Warne, 1981), a *New York Times* best illustrated book of 1981 and recipient of the 1982 Christopher Award; *Too Many Books!* (Warne, 1984); and *Rainy Day: Stories and Poems* (Lippincott, 1986). In addition to educational aids such as teletexts and videocassettes, she has written *Handbook for Storytellers* (American Library Association, 1977). According to *Christian Science Monitor*, "It shows parents, teachers, librarians, or anyone else who enjoys books and storytelling how to use a variety of media effectively." Bauer is also the author of *This Way to Books* (H. W. Wilson, 1983), *Celebrations: Read-Aloud Holiday and Theme Book Programs* (H. W. Wilson, 1985), and "What's So Funny? Humor in Children's Literature," a sound recording. *Home:* 6892 Seaway Circle, Huntington Beach, Calif. 92648.

FOR MORE INFORMATION SEE: Contemporary Authors, Volumes 77-80, Gale, 1979; *Who's Who in Library and Information Services*, American Library Association, 1982; *Who's Who in the West*, 18th edition, Marquis, 1983; *Who's Who in the World*, 7th edition, Marquis, 1984; *Who's Who of American Women*, 14th edition, Marquis, 1984.

BENTLEY, Roy   1947-

PERSONAL: Born August 29, 1947, in London, England; son of David Parry (a policeman) and Marguerite (a post office clerk; maiden name, Clarke) Bentley; married Anne Elizabeth

ROY BENTLEY

Major (an author), July 5, 1969; children: Martyn Ian, Robert Alexander, Katie Anne. *Education:* University of Newcastle Upon Tyne, B.Sc. (with honors), 1968.

CAREER: Free-lance illustrator, 1978—; author, 1980—. *Exhibitions:* Museum of Space Technology, Manchester, England, 1984, 1985.

WRITINGS—All self-illustrated; all published by Deutsch: (With Jan Needle) *Rottenteeth*, 1980; (with wife, Anne Bentley) *The Groggs Have a Wonderful Summer*, 1980; (with A. Bentley) *The Groggs Day Out*, 1981; *Lift Off to Danger*, 1982; *Moonquake*, 1983; *Shuttleburn*, 1984; *Space Crash*, 1985; *Far from Earth*, 1986.

Illustrator: J. Needle, *The Size Spies*, Deutsch, 1980; Gyles Brandreth, *Frankenstein's Monster Fun Book*, Knight Books, 1981; J. Needle, *Another Fine Mess*, Deutsch, 1981; *Hey Presto* (anthology of songs), A. & C. Black, 1982; *The Jolly Herring* (anthology of songs), A. & C. Black, 1983; Michael Allaby, *2040*, Gollancz, 1985. Also illustrator of "Abracadabra Recorder" series, Volumes 1-7 (anthology of songs), A. & C. Black, 1984. Contributor of cartoons to magazines.

WORK IN PROGRESS: Writing text for *Spaceflight*, for Macdonald's "My First Library" series.

SIDELIGHTS: "I am a scientist come businessman who has developed an artistic side in parallel. At school whilst taking a full science course I also attended art school on Saturday mornings. At university whilst studying physics I was the art editor and cartoonist on the college newspaper.

"When I started work I was also pursuing my artistic ventures doing greeting cards. As my business career developed so did my artistic side, via magazine cartoons and general illustrating to book work. Initially as an illustrator and then as co-author and for the last five years as author also.

"Who knows what the future will bring, but it is my aim to eventually earn enough from writing and illustrating to make it a full time occupation."

BERRY, Joy Wilt

BRIEF ENTRY: Since 1980, when she founded both Living Skills Press and the Institute of Living Skills, Berry has written about two hundred self-help books for children. These books are designed to motivate children to take responsibility for their own lives and provide parents with helpful insight into child rearing. Formerly employed as a teacher, administrator, counselor, and recreation director, Berry now devotes her time to writing children's books and conducting Living Skills activities, such as lecturing, directing seminars, and making appearances on nationwide radio and television stations. Her books are divided into a number of series aimed at varying age groups, including the "Teach Me About" series (. . . *Mealtime*, . . . *Getting Dressed*, . . . *Potty Training*, . . . *Pretending*, etc.), for ages birth to four, the "Tuff Stuff" series (*Every Kid's Book about Going to the Hospital*, . . . *People Who Wear Glasses*, . . . *Spending the Night Away from Home*, etc.) for ages five to ten, and the "Survival" series (*What to Do When Your Mom or Dad Says Get Dressed!*, . . . *Stand Up Straight!*, . . . *Clean Your Room!*, etc.) for ages six to twelve. Other series include "Ready-Set-Grow," "You Can," "Let's Talk About," and "Danger Zones." In addition to the Institute of Living Skills, Berry is the sole producer of juvenile self-help material for ABC Broadcasting, Childrens Press, Grolier Enterprises, and Xerox Education Publications. *Office:* Living Skills Press, P.O. Box 83, Sebastopol, Calif. 95472.

OTTO LUDWIG BETTMANN

BETTMANN, Otto Ludwig   1903-

PERSONAL: Born October 15, 1903, in Leipzig, Germany; came to United States, 1935; naturalized, 1939; son of Hans (an orthopedic surgeon) and Charlotte (Frank) Bettmann; married Anne Clemens Gray, March 4, 1938. *Education:* University of Leipzig, Ph.D., 1927, M.S. in library science, 1932. *Politics:* Democrat. *Religion:* Jewish. *Home:* 2600 South Ocean Blvd., Boca Raton, Fla. 33432. *Office:* Boca Bank Building, 855 S. Federal Highway, Boca Raton, Fla. 33432.

CAREER: C. C. Peters (music publishers), Leipzig, Germany, associate editor, 1927-28; Axel Juncker, Publishers, Berlin, Germany, editor, 1928-30; State Art Library, Berlin, curator of rare books, 1930-33; The Bettmann Archive (a picture library on the history of civilization; now Kraus-Thomson Publishing Group), founder and director, 1936-80. Florida Atlantic University, visiting adjunct professor of history, 1976-82. *Awards, honors:* D.H.L., Florida Atlantic University, 1981.

WRITINGS: (With Bellamy Partridge) *As We Were: Family Life in America, 1850-1900*, Whittlesey House, 1946; (with John Durant) *A Pictorial History of American Sports*, A. S. Barnes, 1952; *A Pictorial History of Medicine*, C. C. Thomas, 1956; (with Van Wyck Brooks) *Our Literary Heritage*, Dutton, 1956; (with Paul H. Lang) *A Pictorial History of Music*, Norton, 1960; *Bettmann Portable Archive*, Picture House Press, 1966; *The Good Old Days: They Were Terrible*, Random House, 1974; *A Word from the Wise*, Crown, 1977; *The Bettmann Picture History of the World*, Random House, 1978; *The Wondrous World of Books*, Center for the Book at the Library of Congress, 1986. Also picture editor, *The New Pictorial Encyclopedia of the World*, 1954. Contributor of articles to *American Scholar*.

WORK IN PROGRESS: A psycho-biography of Bach.

SIDELIGHTS: The nucleus of Bettmann's famous picture library was a personal collection of 25,000 art, music, and medicine prints that accompanied him when he left Nazi Germany. It now consists of more than ten million items—its resources used worldwide by writers, publishers and the audio-visual media. Moving to Florida in 1981, he has made his avocation—music—his vocation with special emphasis on the music of Bach.

HOBBIES AND OTHER INTERESTS: Music.

FOR MORE INFORMATION SEE: Time, May 28, 1956, March 23, 1981; *Saturday Review*, February 11, 1961; *New York World Telegram*, March 4, 1961; *Publishers Weekly*, September 25, 1961; *Current Biography*, November, 1961, November, 1974; *New York Times Magazine*, October 18, 1981.

BLAIR, Anne Denton   1914-

PERSONAL: Born February 4, 1914, in Oakmont, Pa.; daughter of Hal Pomeroy (an editor and journalist) and Eliza Russell (Peachy) Denton; married Robert Farnham Blair, 1939 (divorced, 1947); children: Farnham Denton. *Education:* Attended Bryn Mawr College, 1931-32. *Politics:* Democrat. *Religion:* Episcopalian. *Home and office:* 3315 Dent Pl. N.W., Washington, D.C. 20007; and The Ark, Brooklin, Me. 04616 (summer).

CAREER: WQQW-Radio (now WGMS-Radio), Washington, D.C., woman's program director and commentator, 1948-62;

ANNE DENTON BLAIR

American National Red Cross, Washington, D.C., director of radio and television, 1959-62; Triangle Stations, Inc., Philadelphia, Pa., Washington bureau chief, 1962-73; Tele-Prompter Cable-TV, Washington, D.C., bureau chief, 1973-75; Environmental Protection Agency, Washington, D.C., radio and television consultant in Office of Public Affairs, 1975; *Programmer* magazine (formerly *PDCue*), Washington correspondent, 1975—. Press secretary for Rep. Lional Van Deerlin (D-Calif.) 1975. Commentator for "State Department Reports," 1970-75, and for "Capital Reading," "For and about Women," "Music for Moderns," "Window on Washington," and "Town and Country," which were produced and broadcast for syndication, 1962-73. Member of Board of Directors of Society for the Prevention of Blindness, St. John's Child Development Center, Travelers' Aid Society of Washington, and Smithsonian Associates Women's Committee; member of Public Relations Council of Episcopal Diocese of Washington, 1960-64.

MEMBER: American Women in Radio and Television, American Federation of Radio and Television Artists, Radio and Television Correspondents' Association, Washington Press Club, Washington Newswomen's Club (president, 1963-65), White House Correspondents' Association, Sulgrave Club, National Society of Colonial Dames, Bryn Mawr Club of Washington (past president), City Tavern Association (founding member), Center Harbor Yacht Club. *Awards, honors:* Distinguished Public Service Award from 21 Jewel Square Club, 1963, for coverage of President Kennedy's funeral; Alumna of the Year award, 1982, from Laurel School (Cleveland, Ohio).

WRITINGS: Rhymes with Little Reason, Mount Vernon Publishing, 1962; *Arthur, the White House Mouse* (juvenile; illustrated by Lily Spandorf), Media/America, 1975; *Where's Rachel? Another Adventure of Arthur, the White House Mouse* (juvenile; illustrated by Carol Watson), Acropolis Books, 1978; *Hurrah for Arthur! A Mount Vernon Birthday Party* (juvenile; illustrated by C. Watson), Seven Locks, 1982. Contributing editor, Washington *Dossier,* 1982—. Contributor to magazines and newspapers, including *Variety, Promenade, Programmer* and the *Washington Post.*

WORK IN PROGRESS: A novel; poems; research on Monticello and the Capitol building for new books about Arthur, the White House Mouse.

SIDELIGHTS: "Having covered the White House and its occupants through six administrations, I not only have a knowledge of the building but a remarkable respect for most of its occupants. I want young readers to sense not just the history but also the 'mystique' of what goes on in that building. When I took a six-and-a-half-year-old godson to see Lady Bird Johnson's Christmas tree (the one covered delectably with edible ornaments), he remarked that 'a mouse would like that.' I went home and wrote a story about the church mice from St. John's, 'The Church of the Presidents,' who came to the White House and nibbled on that famous tree. Several years later, after trying the story on my two granddaughters, I polished and found a publisher for *Arthur, the White House Mouse.*

"The other two stories, *Where's Rachel?* and *Hurrah for Arthur!* are written in the same vein. They are designed to instill in children respect for and a happy familiarity with the Executive Mansion and those who live there. I have covered presidential nominating conventions, inaugurals, and all state events as a newswoman and really *like* the White House and what it stands for, although some of its residents have disappointed us from time to time.

"I like mixing the *oral* word with the *written* one, and I therefore have great respect for *aural* English. That's why (I like to think) my books are good for reading aloud, and adult readers seem to enjoy them as much as their young listeners. *Aural* writing also spurs on young readers. I recently spoke to four fourth grades in a Virginia school, and they heartily confirmed this, as my two granddaughters did earlier."

SHIRLEY BLUMENTHAL

BLUMENTHAL, Shirley 1943-

PERSONAL: Born October 9, 1943, in New York, N.Y.; daughter of Max (a baker) and Lina (Katzenstein) Blumenthal. *Education:* City College of the City University of New York, B.A., 1964; University of Pennsylvania, M.A., 1966. *Residence:* New York, N.Y.

CAREER: Writer and producer for Educational Design, Inc., 1969-72; senior editor for Appleton-Century-Crofts, 1972-74; Macmillan Publishing Co., New York City, audiovisual product manager, 1974-77; free-lance writer, 1977-81; McGraw-Hill Productions, New York City, director of creative services, 1981-83; Arthur Young (public accounting and consulting firm), New York City, writer/consultant, 1984—.

WRITINGS: Black Cats and Other Superstitions, Raintree, 1977; (with Jerome S. Ozer) *Coming to America: Immigrants from the British Isles* (young adult), Delacorte, 1981; *Coming to America: Immigrants from Eastern Europe* (young adult), Delacorte, 1982.

SIDELIGHTS: "Writing is my means of understanding. I know things only by the handling of them. Writing, like speaking and thinking, is a tactile experience. Words, ideas, information are put this way, then that, tried, manipulated, until they create a block of meaning which sometimes, dazzlingly, is exactly what I mean to say, and sometimes comes only so close as the distance between two points that the philosopher says can never be crossed. And that's on a good day.

"My interest in immigration history comes partly from my family background (my parents being immigrants) but mostly from my desire to understand history and myself. Our lives and our times are products of history—the history of events, of cultural evolution, and of the personal realization made possible by the material and informational wealth of this modern age. I think a writer is someone who does not take these things as given but who wants to know, understand, and reflect, and ultimately express, in some way, what some of it may mean, not only for the edification of others, but mostly, I think, for the sheer pleasure of doing so.

"I'm also concerned with immigration history because most of human history is a history of struggle—and I don't mean the struggles of great names—but the struggle of people to survive, reasonably hale of body and spirit. I find this struggle heroic. It has nothing to do with great names and great events and everything to do with what matters—the lives of the great mass of us, what we suffer, what we endure, and what against all odds we can achieve. History tends to make me pessimistic; but the fortitude, courage, and grace with which some people can bear history is my source of hope."

BOORMAN, Linda (Kay) 1940-

PERSONAL: Born April 28, 1940, in Boston, Mass.; daughter of Felix M. (a farmer) and Grace (a homemaker; maiden name, Sledge) Eklund; married James R. Boorman (an electronics technician), August 24, 1963; children: Stephen, Bethany, Miriam. *Education:* Multnomah School of the Bible, diploma, 1961; Eastern Oregon State College, B.S., 1963. *Religion:* Evangelical Protestant. *Home:* 15660 Mill Creek Rd., Frenchtown, Mont. 59834.

CAREER: North Powder School District, North Powder, Ore., teacher of elementary school, 1963-64; full-time homemaker, 1964—; writer, 1974—.

LINDA BOORMAN

WRITINGS—Fiction for young adults: *The Mystery Man of Horseshoe Bend* (illustrated by Marilee Harrald), Scripture Press, 1980; *The Giant Tree Trunk Mystery* (illustrated by M. Harrald), Scripture Press, 1981; *The Drugstore Bandit of Horseshoe Bend* (illustrated by M. Harrald), Scripture Press, 1982.

Other: *Montana Bride* (illustrated by Garst), Accent Publications, 1985.

WORK IN PROGRESS: Another light-hearted romance similar to *Montana Bride* with a setting in Oregon during the 1880s.

SIDELIGHTS: "Anything from my typewriter reflects my interest in the history of Northwest America during the latter part of the nineteenth century. I attempt to present scriptural truths and historical facts accurately, while letting the characters and storyline take on a lighthearted mood. All of my writing portrays my concern for children, strong families, and love as revealed by God's Son—Jesus."

BOURDON, David 1934-

PERSONAL: Born October 15, 1934, in Glendale, Calif.; son of David and Marilyn (Casale) Bourdon. *Education:* Columbia University, B.S., 1961. *Home:* 315 West 23rd St., New York, N.Y. 10011. *Office: Vogue,* 350 Madison Ave., New York, N.Y. 10017.

CAREER: Life, New York City, assistant editor, 1966-71; *Saturday Review,* New York City, associate editor, 1972; *Smith-*

DAVID BOURDON

sonian, Washington, D.C., associate editor, 1972-74; *Arts Magazine*, New York City, associate editor, 1973-81; *GEO* (magazine), New York City, senior editor, 1981-83; *Vogue*, New York City, senior features editor, 1983—.

WRITINGS: Christo (adult), Abrams, 1971; (with Calvin Tomkins) *Christo: Running Fence* (adult), Abrams, 1979; *Calder: Mobilist, Ringmaster, Innovator* (young adult), Macmillan, 1980. Contributor of articles to numerous art and design magazines, including *Architectural Digest, Art in America, Art International,* and *New York*. Art critic for *Village Voice*, 1964-66 and 1974-77.

BRAGG, Michael 1948-

PERSONAL: Born October 24, 1948, in Croydon, England; son of Charles (a senior building officer) and Jacqueline (a homemaker; maiden name, Jackson) Bragg; married Christine Ann Scott Cumming (a homemaker), August 16, 1975; children: Cyan Alice Saskia, Cielle Amber Zoe. *Education:* Attended Croydon College of Art, 1965-67; Goldsmiths College, University of London, diploma in art and design, 1970, art teacher's certificate, 1971. *Home:* 9 Middle Lane, Ringwood, Hampshire BH24 1LE, England.

CAREER: Burgate School, Hampshire, England, head of art department, 1973-84; free-lance illustrator, 1984—. *Exhibitions:* Primrose Gallery, London, England, 1982; Andover Museum, Hampshire, England, 1983; Yeshiva Museum, New York, N.Y., 1984. *Member:* Society of Authors (London).

WRITINGS—Self-illustrated: The Pet Cellar, Methuen, 1986.

Illustrator: Leon Garfield, *King Nimrod's Tower*, Lothrop, 1982; L. Garfield, *The Writing on the Wall*, Lothrop, 1983; Alison Prince, *Haunted Children*, Methuen, 1983; Margaret Greaves, *Monster of Roundwater*, Methuen, 1984; Jules Older, *Jane and the Pirates*, Heinemann, 1984; L. Garfield, *The King in the Garden*, Methuen, 1984, Lothrop, 1985; Dick King-Smith, *Lightning Fred*, Heinemann, 1985.

WORK IN PROGRESS: Illustrations for *Candletree Walk* by Kenneth McLeish and Vallerie McLeish, for Heinemann.

SIDELIGHTS: "Making pictures seems always to have been a central part of my life. I went to art college and followed a fine art (painting) course. I experimented with different styles and approaches but had a strong tendency to figurative work. Interest in illustration, however, was not encouraged in a painting course and so I received no training as an illustrator. I had to learn about preparing work for reproduction later myself. After college I continued painting but supported myself by teaching.

"It was a suggestion from a friend that I try illustrating books—children's books. The idea grew—I prepared samples, approached a publisher, interest was shown and eventually commissions for picture books came.

"This was my introduction to illustration and I soon realised how much I liked this sort of work. I remembered how I had enjoyed the illustrations in books myself as a child—taking an interest even then in recognising different styles.

"I have usually illustrated other people's texts, sometimes being able to work in collaboration with the writer and I have

MICHAEL BRAGG

Everybody was looking at the wall; except Samuel, who was watching everybody to make sure they weren't watching him; and Mordecai the cat, who was watching Samuel.

"Hey there, you with the face! Cream, down here."

"Hey there, Mordecai! It's time for a cat!"

He lowered his dish, filled up a holy golden bowl from a holy silver jug, and put it on the floor under the table of Belshazzar, the King. Then he picked up his dish, and stood, stock-still, behind the mountain of strawberries, while tattered, one-eared, smelly old Mordecai finished off the cream and polished God's golden bowl with his rough pink tongue.

And all the while, Belshazzar, the King, and the rich and mighty of Babylon shook and trembled, and stared at the writing on the wall.

(From *The Writing on the Wall* by Leon Garfield. Illustrated by Michael Bragg.)

been lucky to be partnered with some very good writers and texts.

"Before I can start the artwork a good reading of the text is important—this means both a receptive and active state of mind. Fortunately reading is something I have always enjoyed.

"I am aware that in the artwork I often try to take many different visual viewpoints—like a camera moving to different vantage spots and angles. I try many alternatives in rough sketches and this helps develop my feeling and understanding of a whole scene.

"Most of my books have been for an age range where it has been suitable to build up quite complex scenes—a complete world in which subsidiary features can complement or contrast with the main action. Also, most of my pictures tend to be paintings as opposed to coloured drawings and so where the opportunity exists I will exploit lighting effects for dramatic purpose.

"I think one result of my teaching experience has been in some ways to broaden my interests and I quite enjoy the research necessary for some books, leading me to find out about things I would not otherwise have done.

"I am told I have a good visual memory and I like to think I have a sense of humour. These are the sort of things that make an important contribution to my work—as does working with a helpful, encouraging and understanding editor.

"I recently made the decision to leave teaching to pursue illustration full time—undertaking general illustration work as well as children's books—but children's work will always be something special as it offers one of the greatest opportunities for personal interpretation and imaginative input with which to reach eager and receptive young minds."

BRUCK, Lorraine 1921-
(Laurie Bridges)

BRIEF ENTRY: Born March 16, 1921, in Nebraska. Bruck earned a bachelor's of science degree in education from the University of Minnesota and a master's of science degree in education from the University of Bridgeport. Characterizing herself as an "inveterate entrepreneur" and claiming a major interest in the history of women, Bruck is writer, president, executive editor, and co-publisher with husband Marvin of the *Women's News,* a monthly newspaper for, by, and about professional women in Dallas and Fort Worth. In addition, she writes and works as projects coordinator for Southbury Press Inc. in Southbury, Conn., and acts as editor in chief for The Bruck Corporation in Lake Havasu City, Ariz.

Bruck's interest in feminist issues is reflected in some of the many organizations of which she is a member: Women in Communications, League of Women Voters, Dallas Women's Art Caucus, Ninety-Nines (international organization of women pilots), and Association of Women Entrepreneurs of Dallas. Bruck collects coins, flies—she has an active pilot's license with sea and land ratings—and holds a ham radio operator's license. "My interest in people, places and projects is insatiable, so my word processor is humming most of the time recording and writing and editing—life is a ball!"

Her juvenile works consist of four books in Bantam's "Dark Forces" series. Under the pseudonym Laurie Bridges, Bruck co-authored, with Paul Alexander, *The Swamp Witch, Magic Show,* and *Devil Wind* (all published in 1983). Bruck is sole author of a fourth "Dark Series" book, *The Ashton Horror* (1984).

These fast-moving, lightly romantic books portray high-school age protagonists who become enmeshed in supernatural and occult forces and battle the evil power of warlocks, voodoo, and monster worship. *Office:* TWN Communications Inc., Suite 101, 15790 Dooley Rd., Dallas, Tex. 75244.

BURKE, David 1927-

PERSONAL: Born May 17, 1927, in Melbourne, Australia; son of John William (an accountant) and Gertrude Olive (an opera singer; maiden name, Davies) Burke; married Helen Patricia Wane (a journalist), March 5, 1957; children: Mary, Anne, Margaret, Jane, Julia. *Education:* Attended school in South Brisbane, Queensland, Australia. *Residence:* Sydney, Australia. *Agent:* Curtis Brown Ltd., William St., Paddington, New South Wales, Australia. *Office address:* P.O. Box 82, Mosman, New South Wales 2088, Australia.

CAREER: Worked as radio scriptwriter and production assistant, Melbourne, Australia, 1948-50; *Melbourne Herald-Sun,* Melbourne, reporter, feature writer, and sub-editor, 1950-56; *Sydney Morning Sun-Herald,* Sydney, Australia, reporter and feature writer, 1956-62; free-lance author, 1965—; has also worked for Victorian Railways and in public relations. *Member:* Royal Australian Historical Society, Australian Railway Historical Society, Rail Transport Museum, Australian Society of Authors.

WRITINGS: (With C. C. Singleton) *Railways of Australia,* Angus & Robertson, 1936; *Monday at McMurdo* (novel), Muller, 1967; *Come Midnight Monday* (juvenile novel; illustrated by Janet Mare), Methuen, 1976; *Great Steam Trains of Australia,* Rigby, 1978; *Darknight* (novel), Methuen, 1979;

DAVID BURKE

Observer's Book of Steam Locomotives of Australia, Methuen, 1979; *Full Steam across the Mountains* (illustrated by Phil Belbin), Methuen, 1981; *Changing Trains,* Methuen, 1982; *Kings of the Iron House* (biography), Methuen, 1985; "Mary Ward, Then and Now" (30-minute video program), Loreto, Kirribilli (Australia), 1985; *Man of Steam* (biography), Iron Horse Productions (Australia), 1986.

ADAPTATIONS: "Come Midnight Monday" (seven-episode serial), Australian Broadcasting Commission, 1982.

WORK IN PROGRESS: Wings of Ice, a history of Antarctic aviation.

SIDELIGHTS: "I regard myself as a general free-lance writer, but my lifelong interest in railroads has led me to study the history of various Australian railways and their impact on the social and economic development of Australia. I tend to alternate between fact and fiction in my writing. I am almost constantly doing research at national and state libraries, archives, etc., and I maintain comprehensive files."

BURT, Jesse Clifton 1921-1976

PERSONAL: Born August 29, 1921, in Nashville, Tenn.; died November 20, 1976; son of Jesse Clifton and Agnes (Seals) Burt; married Eleanor Bales Jones (a librarian), September 27, 1947. *Education:* George Peabody College for Teachers, B.S., 1942, M.A., 1943; Vanderbilt University, Ph.D., 1950; Harvard University, Ed.M., 1961. *Religion:* Methodist.

CAREER: Presbyterian College, Clinton, S.C., instructor in history, 1943; Florence State College (now University of North Alabama), Florence, Ala., assistant professor of history, 1945-47; Vanderbilt University, Nashville, Tenn., teaching fellow, 1947-50; Lambuth College, Jackson, Tenn., dean, 1950-53; University of Tennessee, Nashville Center, extension division instructor in history, beginning 1956. Radio broadcaster, Nashville, Tenn., 1963. *Awards, honors:* Danforth Award, 1954, for youth writings; *Indians of the Southeast—Then and Now* was one of Child Association of America's Children's Books of the Year, 1973.

WRITINGS: Your Vocational Adventure, Abingdon, 1959; *Nashville: Its Life and Times,* Tennessee Book Co., 1959; (with Robert B. Ferguson) *So You Want To Be in Music,* Abingdon, 1970; (with Duane Allen) *The History of Gospel Music,* Silverline Music, 1971; (with R. B. Ferguson) *Indians of the Southeast—Then and Now* (illustrated by David Wilson), Abingdon, 1973; *Your Tennessee,* Steck, 1974, revised edition (with Robert M. McBride and James A. Crutchfield), 1979; *Chronicles of the Dixie Line: The First, and Only, Historical Story of a Famous Railroad* (monograph), Jandeco Press, 1976; *The Historic "Tennessee Line": The Nashville & Chattanooga Railroad Company, 1845-1873* (monograph), Jandeco Press, 1976; *Nashville, Chattanooga & St. Louis Railway from Railroad War to World War I* (monograph), Jandeco Press, 1976. Contributor to "The Illustrated Library of the Natural Sciences," American Museum of Natural History. Contributor of articles and over five hundred book reviews to various publications.

WORK IN PROGRESS: Science and Man's Hope; research on the achievements of William Tecumseh Sherman.

HOBBIES AND OTHER INTERESTS: Folk music, physical fitness, foreign films, and radio.

Aaron awoke. ■ (From *Aaron Awoke: An Alphabet Story* by Marilee Robin Burton. Illustrated by the author.)

BURTON, Marilee Robin   1950-

PERSONAL: Born December 27, 1950, in Los Angeles, Calif.; daughter of Joe (a chemical engineer) and Lillian (a teacher of adult education; maiden name, Weisman) Burton. *Education:* California State College, Sonoma, B.A., 1973, Pacific Oaks College, M.A., 1979. *Address:* c/o Burton, 4624 Varna Ave., Sherman Oaks, Calif. 91423.

CAREER: VBS Day School, Encino, Calif., kindergarten teacher, 1978-80; P.S.3 Manhattan, N.Y., kindergarten and first-grade teacher, 1981-84; author and illustrator of children's books, 1977—. *Member:* Society of Children's Book Writers.

WRITINGS—Juvenile; self-illustrated: *The Elephant's Nest: Four Wordless Stories,* Harper, 1979; *Aaron Awoke: An Alphabet Story,* Harper, 1982; *Oliver's Birthday,* Harper, 1986.

WORK IN PROGRESS: Moonlight Festival; a nonfiction book about shoes; and a second wordless picture book, all for children.

SIDELIGHTS: "Painting, drawing, making things—artwork—has always been a part of my life. My whole family was craft oriented and art projects were always a family concern, either individually or collectively.

"I often thought that illustrating children's books would be something I would like to do because my art style has always been a simple one. However, I knew very little, really, about the children's book field—or how to enter it.

"While I was studying to become a teacher, I did a language arts project with some kindergarten children. I was interested in wordless stories, drew some stories, and asked the children to tell me the words. I was pleased with the outcome and thought I would send the stories to a publisher. I did. They were accepted. And my career in the children's book field began.

"I am intrigued by the simple yet profound way children interpret and express their life experience. There is an innocence and truth in this vision and it is that which I attempt to capture in my own work."

MARILEE ROBIN BURTON

BYARS, Betsy (Cromer) 1928-

PERSONAL: Born August 7, 1928, in Charlotte, N.C.; daughter of George Guy (a cotton mill executive) and Nan (a housewife; maiden name, Rugheimer) Cromer; married Edward Ford Byars (a professor of engineering), June 24, 1950; children: Laurie, Betsy Ann, Nan, Guy. *Education:* Attended Furman University, 1946-48; Queens College, Charlotte, N.C., B.A., 1950. *Residence:* Clemson, S.C.

CAREER: Author of books for children. *Awards, honors:* Child Study Association of America's Book of the Year selection, 1968, for *The Midnight Fox,* 1969, for *Trouble River,* 1970, for *The Summer of the Swans,* 1972, for *The House of Wings,* 1973, for *The Winged Colt of Casa Mia* and *The 18th Emergency,* 1974, for *After the Goat Man,* 1975, for *The Lace Snail,* 1976, for *The TV Kid,* and 1980, for *The Night Swimmers;* Lewis Carroll Shelf Award, 1970, for *The Midnight Fox;* Newbery Medal, 1971, for *The Summer of the Swans; Go and Hush the Baby* was selected one of *School Library Journal*'s Best Books for Spring, 1971; *The House of Wings* was selected for *Library Journal*'s Book List, 1972, and was a National Book Award finalist, 1973; *New York Times* Outstanding Book of the Year, 1973, for *The Winged Colt of Casa Mia* and *The 18th Emergency,* 1979, for *Good-bye Chicken Little,* and 1982, for *The Two-Thousand-Pound Goldfish; After the Goat Man* was selected for the *School Library Journal* Book List, 1974.

Dorothy Canfield Fisher Memorial Book Award from Vermont Congress of Parents and Teachers, 1975, for *The 18th Emergency;* Woodward Park School Annual Book Award, 1977, one of *School Library Journal*'s Best Books of the Year, 1977, Child Study Children's Book Award from the Child Study Children's Book Committee at Bank Street College of Education, 1977, Hans Christian Andersen Honor List for Promoting Concern for the Disadvantaged and Handicapped, 1979, Georgia Children's Book Award, 1979, Charlie May Simon Book Award from the Arkansas Elementary School Council, 1980, Surrey School Book of the Year Award from the Surrey School Librarians of Surrey, British Columbia, 1980, Mark Twain Award from the Missouri Association of School Librarians, 1980, William Allen White Children's Book Award from Emporia State University (Kan.), 1980, Young Reader Medal from the California Reading Association, 1980, Nene Award runner up, 1981 and 1983, and Golden Archer Award from Department of Library Science of the University of Wisconsin—Oshkosh, 1982, all for *The Pinballs; Good-bye Chicken Little* was selected one of Library of Congress' Children's Books of Boston Globe-Horn Book fiction honor, 1980, *School Library Journal* Best Book of the Year, 1980, and American Book Award for Children's Fiction (hardcover), 1981, all for *The Night Swimmers; The Cybil War* was selected as a Notable Children's Book by *School Library Journal,* 1981, and as a Children's Choice by the International Reading Association, 1982, and received the Tennessee Children's Choice Book Award from the Tennessee Library Association, 1983 and the Sequoyah Children's Book Award, 1984; Parents' Choice Award for literature from Parents' Choice Foundation, 1982, named

BETSY BYARS

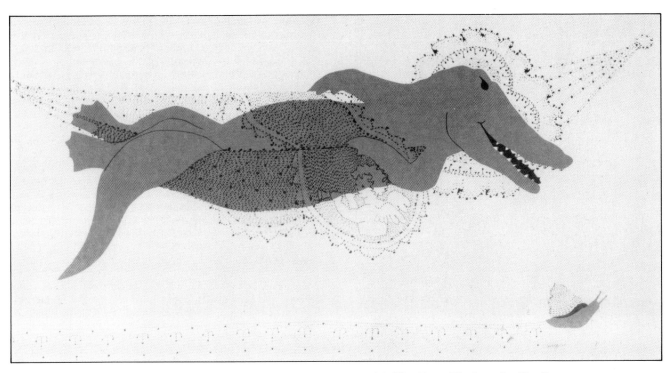

"...You can give me a push every time you go by, all right?" ■ (From *The Lace Snail* by Betsy Byars. Illustrated by the author.)

one of *School Library Journal*'s Best Children's Books of 1982, CRABbery Award from Oxon Hill Branch of Prince George's County Library (Md.), 1983, and Mark Twain Award, 1985, all for *The Animal, the Vegetable, and John D. Jones; The Two-Thousand-Pound Goldfish* was selected as a Notable Book of the Year by the *New York Times*, 1982.

WRITINGS: Clementine (illustrated by Charles Wilton), Houghton, 1962; *The Dancing Camel* (illustrated by Harold Berson), Viking, 1965; *Rama, the Gypsy Cat* (illustrated by Peggy Bacon), Viking, 1966; *The Groober* (self-illustrated), Harper, 1967; *The Midnight Fox* (illustrated by Ann Grifalconi), Viking, 1968; *Trouble River* (ALA Notable Book; illustrated by Rocco Negri), Viking, 1969.

The Summer of the Swans (Junior Literary Guild selection; ALA Notable Book, *Horn Book* honor list; illustrated by Ted CoConis), Viking, 1970; *Go and Hush the Baby* (illustrated by Emily A. McCully), Viking, 1971; *The House of Wings* (ALA Notable Book; illustrated by Daniel Schwartz), Viking, 1972; *The 18th Emergency* (illustrated by Robert Grossman), Viking, 1973; *The Winged Colt of Casa Mia* (illustrated by Richard Cuffari), Viking, 1973; *After the Goat Man* (ALA Notable Book; illustrated by Ronald Himler), Viking, 1974; *The Lace Snail* (self-illustrated), Viking, 1975; *The TV Kid* (illustrated by R. Cuffari), Viking, 1976; *The Pinballs* (ALA Notable Book; *Horn Book* honor list), Harper, 1977; *The Cartoonist* (*Horn Book* honor list; illustrated by R. Cuffari), Viking, 1978; *Good-bye, Chicken Little*, Harper, 1979.

The Night Swimmers (Junior Literary Guild selection; illustrated by Troy Howell), Delacorte, 1980; *The Cybil War* (ALA Notable Book; illustrated by Gail Owens), Viking, 1981; *The Animal, the Vegetable, and John D. Jones* (illustrated by Ruth Sanderson), Delacorte, 1982; *The Two-Thousand-Pound Goldfish* (ALA Notable Book), Harper, 1982; *The Glory Girl*, Viking, 1983; *The Computer Nut* (illustrated with computer graphics by son, Guy Byars), Viking, 1984; *Cracker Jackson* (*Horn Book* honor list), Viking, 1985; *The Not-Just-Anybody*

Family (illustrated by Jacqueline Rogers), Delacorte, 1986; *The Golly Sisters Go West* (illustrated by Sue Truesdale), Harper, 1986; *The Blossoms Meet the Vulture Lady* (illustrated by J. Rogers), Delacorte, 1986.

Also author of afterword of Margaret Sidney's *Five Little Peppers and How They Grew*, Dell, 1985. Contributor of articles to *Saturday Evening Post, TV Guide, Look,* and other magazines.

ADAPTATIONS—ABC Afterschool Specials; all broadcast on ABC-TV: "Pssst! Hammerman's After You" (based on *The 18th Emergency*), April, 1973; "Sara's Summer of the Swans" (based on *The Summer of the Swans*), produced by Martin Tahse Productions, 1974; "Trouble River," produced by Martin Tahse Productions, 1975; "The Winged Colt" (based on *The Winged Colt of Casa Mia*), produced by ABC Wide World of Learning, 1976; "The Pinballs," produced by Martin Tahse Productions, 1977; "Daddy I'm Their, Mamma Now" (based on *The Night Swimmers*), Martin Tahse Productions, 1981.

Other: "The Lace Snail" (filmstrip with cassette), Viking; "The Midnight Fox" (record or cassette), Miller-Brody; "The Summer of the Swans" (record or cassette), Miller-Brody; "Go and Hush the Baby" (cassette), Miller-Brody; "Sara's Summer of the Swans" (videocassette), Martin Tahse Productions, 1976; "The TV Kid" (record or cassette), 1977.

WORK IN PROGRESS: Another Blossom family book.

SIDELIGHTS: "I had a happy, uneventful childhood. I was born in Charlotte, N.C. in **1928,** during the depression, but I grew up with no feeling of being poor. My father had majored in civil engineering at the Citadel, but because times were hard, he had taken a job in the office of a small cotton mill. We lived part of the time in the city of Charlotte and part of the time out in the country, in the mill community. There I had goats and rabbits for pets, and I thought it was wonderful to have the best of both worlds—city life and country life.

The sun was warm on her back. ■ (From *The Animal, the Vegetable, and John D. Jones* by Betsy Byars. Illustrated by Ruth Sanderson.)

"My parents read a lot, and my earliest memory is of my father reading 'The Three Bears' to me. My older sister taught me to read when she was in first grade. I was about four. Because of this early, rigorous education, I was always ahead of my fellow students in reading ability, but in precious little else.

"I was a happy, busy child. I started sewing when I was very young because my father got free cloth."

"I was making my own clothes by the second grade, although I have a vague recollection of not being allowed to wear them out of the yard. I could make a gathered skirt in fifteen minutes. I sewed fast, without patterns, and with great hope and determination, and that is approximately the same way that I write.

"When I was young, I was mainly interested in having as much fun as possible. Adults were always saying to me, 'If only you would take your piano lessons seriously.' (I had to play 'The Spinning Song' three years in a row at my recital!) Or, 'If only you would take your math seriously—or your English.' Or whatever! Enjoying things was just more important to me than taking things seriously." [Lee Bennett Hopkins, *More Books by More People*, Citation, 1974.[1]]

1943. Attended local high school. "In all of my school years—from grade one through high school, not one single teacher

ever said to me, 'Perhaps you should consider becoming a writer.' Anyway, I didn't want to be a writer. Writing seemed boring. You sat in a room all day by yourself and typed. If I was going to be a writer at all, I was going to be a foreign correspondent like Claudette Colbert in "Arise My Love." I would wear smashing hats, wisecrack with the guys, and have a byline known round the world. My father wanted me to be a mathematician.

"I hit high school . . . and the important thing—the only important thing—was to look exactly like everybody else. We wore dirty saddle shoes, angora socks, pleated skirts, enormous sweaters (sometimes buttoned up the back) and pearls. If we were fortunate enough to be going with a high school athlete, we wore his sweater. We all had long hair with curved combs in the back so we could continuously comb our hair. We had mirrors taped inside our notebooks so we could check and make absolutely sure we looked exactly like everybody else.

"I spent a good part of my school day arranging to accidentally bump into some boy or other. I would rush out of science, tear up three flights of stairs, say a casual 'Hi' to a boy as he came out of English, and then tear back down three flights of stairs, rush into home ec and get marked tardy. I was tardy a lot."

1947. Entered college as a math major. "When I had gone away to college, I had not put up any real struggle against

He was drawing a comic strip called "Super Bird." ■ (From *The Cartoonist* by Betsy Byars. Illustrated by Richard Cuffari.)

majoring in math. The only thing I really loved to do was read, but I knew I couldn't get a job doing that. Besides, my sister whose actions I had been copying successfully for nineteen years was a math major, and I, like her, had always been very quick with those problems that start out, 'If one farmer can plow ten fields in one-and-a-half days, how many. . . .'

"Until I hit calculus and came upon sine and cosine and tangent and cotangent and secant and cosecant, I thought there was nothing in the world I could not master if I put my mind to it. This—no matter how hard I tried, and I tried hard—I could not get.

"It was a desperate semester for me. My father was paying hard-earned money for me to go to college and he expected me to do well. I had discovered early in life that things were easier all around if I lived up to my father's expectations. Even in high school when I was flitting through the halls, chasing boys, I made sure I never got a grade lower than B.

"Now calculus. My father had been disappointed at my mid-term calculus grade which had been, to my relief a C-. And here's the pathetic, desperate price I had paid for my C-.

"Dr. Bowen would pass out the tests. I would wait a moment and then go up to his desk. I would say, 'Dr. Bowen, would you please start me out on problem one? I've drawn an absolute blank. I know if you do the first line for me, I can finish.'

"I was the only girl in any of his classes and sort of a novelty. He would, in his enthusiasm for his own problem, work the whole thing.

"I would go back to my seat, and I could actually feel the scorn and resentment of the other students as I passed their desks. I couldn't help it. I had to keep up my C- average.

"I would try to do the next problem on my own. When I had a couple of meaningless rows of numbers and letters, I would go back to his desk and say, 'Is this right? It just doesn't look the way yours did on the board last week.'

"He'd say, 'Now, Miss Cromer, you know that's not right. Look at this.'

"And he'd work the second problem. The only calculus problems I ever got right were the ones he worked for me.

"It was the thought of more and more desperate years like this, more and more scorn from my classmates, that sent me into the living room where my father sat in his chair by the radio, smoking a Camel cigarette.

"Somehow I broke the bad news. I could not be a mathematician. Even worse, I was switching to English. There was not the terrible explosion that I had feared. To be honest, there usually wasn't.

"On my final calculus exam, when Dr. Bowen was working one last problem for me, he asked if I was planning to continue with my math.

"'No,' I said, 'I've decided not to be a mathematician.' 'Good,' he said.

"Nineteen forty-nine and fifty were great years. I was a senior at Queens College, just months away from getting out in the adult world where nobody could tell me what to do or what

time I had to be in, and I had just met the man I wanted to marry."

1950. Graduated from Queens College with a B.A. degree in English. Three weeks after graduating, Byars married husband Edward, a professor of engineering at Clemson College. "It is no longer fashionable to admit this, but I was very happy to be getting married instead of looking for a job. I had no work ambition. I had always wanted marriage and a family.

"For the next five years I was a young faculty wife at Clemson and married life agreed with me. Two of our daughters were born during those years—Laurie in October of **1951** and Betsy Ann in February of **1953.** I was extremely happy.

"My only writing consisted of letters and shopping lists.

"In **1955** Ed decided to go to graduate school at the University of Illinois. If he was going to remain in teaching—which he intended to do—he would have to have his Ph.D. degree.

"We rented our house, stored our furniture, loaned our dogs to Ed's mother, packed everything else in a red trailer and took off. It was a little like going West and I was excited about it.

The owl landed in the middle of the table and stood looking at Sammy. ■ (From *The House of Wings* by Betsy Byars. Illustrated by Daniel Schwartz.)

I was so interested in thinking about my discovery that I almost missed seeing the black fox. ■
(From *The Midnight Fox* by Betsy Byars. Illustrated by Ann Grifalconi.)

"When we pulled up two days later in front of the barracks where we would be living for the next two-and-a-half years, my excitement faded a little. When we went inside and I saw the barracks furniture, it faded even more.

"Well, I told myself, I can fix the place up with posters, and pillows and bright curtains. That took about a week. Now, I thought, I'm as settled as I'm ever going to be. I'm going to start making friends.

"As it turned out, every other wife in the barracks complex either worked or was going to school. The last thing any of them wanted was to come to my house to chat. I got lonelier and lonelier. Ed went to work early in the morning and came home late. The kids, after an initial period of being picked on daily, had gotten over being the new kids and were part of the gang. I alone was at loose ends. The highlight of my day was the arrival of the grocery truck after lunch.

"Now up until this point in my life, while I had never done any creative writing, I had always thought that I could write if I wanted to. I thought it couldn't be as hard as people say it is. I thought probably the reason professional writers claim it's so hard is because they don't want any more competition.

"I got a typewriter so old I had to press the keys down an inch to make a letter. The *i* stuck, all the circular letters were filled in, the *t*'s were noticably higher than the other letters. I was undaunted.

"My target was mainly the magazines. I would look through national magazines, see what they were publishing, write something similar and send it off. Sometimes this very amateurish approach worked.

"My first sale was a short article to the *Saturday Evening Post* and I got seventy-five dollars for it. I was elated. I had known all along there was nothing to writing! Seven months passed before I sold a second article.

"I was learning what most other writers have learned before me—that writing is a profession in which there is an apprenticeship period, oftentimes a very long one. In that, writing is like baseball or piano playing. You have got to practice if you want to be successful.

"In my last year at Illinois—by this time our third daughter, Nan, had been born—I had become aware that I needed some help. I was selling short articles with some regularity, but I had done a mystery novel I couldn't sell and some children's books."

Byars returned to Clemson, South Carolina with her family, and continued to write while rearing her children. Son, Guy, was born in April, **1958,** thus completing the family.

1962. First book published. Byars' husband had accepted a position as a professor of engineering at the University of West Virginia, which necessitated a move to that state. "*Clementine* . . . was not a success at all. It was panned terribly—got terrible reviews. I had put a lot of my own personality into the book and when that got panned so badly I thought, well, I'd better not do that quite so much; so I went back to writing books that anybody could have written, like *Rama, the Gypsy Cat*—very impersonal. And *Trouble River* was the same. *Trouble River* was written before *The Midnight Fox* but published after it. So when I wrote *The Midnight Fox* that was the first time I was getting myself back into a book.

"I did all of my writing . . . in West Virginia—all my children's books, that is. And I think it was very good for me. West Virginia is an area of individuals, of very strong people. I never got the feeling that people there want to be just like other people. They just 'did their own thing.' It was very good for me. The evening paper was filled with possibilities for books; there were always stories about what so-and-so was doing. I just wonder if I had stayed in South Carolina whether I could ever have written the books. . . . Not the books I did, of course—but whether I would have been successful. Now that I have moved back to South Carolina, I have shifted the locale of my current novel to the Carolina shore.

"I remember nothing of the locale of my childhood—of buildings and things like that—and so I use the streets, buildings, and settings of where I am when I'm writing." [Elizabeth Segel, "Betsy Byars: An Interview," *Children's Literature in Education,* winter, 1982.[2]]

1968. *The Midnight Fox* was published. "This is my favorite book, because it is very personal. A great deal of my own children and their activities went into it, and a great deal of myself. It came closer to what I was trying to do than any of my other books.''[1]

Although Byars' first goal was to write mystery stories, as her children grew she became more and more interested in writing books for children. ''I'm sure I would never have written my books if I had not had children. My kids not only read my books and gave me their very frank opinions, but they were also very communicative kids, always wanting to tell where they had been and who said what, and all of that was very helpful. I never followed them around with a pad and pencil taking down things to use in my books, but they certainly provided a good refresher course in childhood. . . .

''Ed has been my greatest source of encouragement over the years. He always believed I would eventually be successful, and in the periods when I got discouraged and went back to school to get a masters degree, or whatever, he would say, 'Just don't close the door on your writing.' However, I am convinced that our collaborating on a book would not only close the door on my writing forever, but also on a perfectly good marriage.'' [Ina Robertson, ''Betsy Byars—Writer for Today's Child,'' *Language Arts,* volume 57, number 3, March, 1980.[3]]

1970. *The Summer of the Swans* was published. Like most of her books, it grew out of everyday experiences. ''Several years ago I was asked to join a volunteer program to tutor some mentally retarded children. The novel came out of this experience. Although the character, Charlie, is not one of the children I tutored—he is purely a fictitious character—he was an outgrowth of the experience, and the book would never have been written if I had not come to know the children I was tutoring.

''The idea for the swans in the story came from an article in my college alumni magazine about the swans at Furman University in Greenville, South Carolina, who persist in leaving their beautiful lake and flying away to less desirable ponds. I took the liberty of moving the swans to West Virginia and the story began.''[1]

The book won numerous awards, including selection as a Junior Literary Club book, *Horn Book* honor book, and ALA Notable Book. ''I would like to be able to tell you exactly how *The Summer of the Swans* was written, because I myself like nothing better than to hear writers tell how they happened to write their books. Often this is the best part. And long after I have forgotten details of character and plot, I can remember that a specific book was written in the shade of an olive tree by a wheat field in Umbria with a number-two pencil.

''But I am like Jerome K. Jerome. He was asked how he wrote one of his books, and he said that actually he could not remember writing the book at all. He was not even sure he had written it. All he could remember was that he had felt very happy and pleased with himself that summer and that the view of London from his window at night had been beautiful.

''I am like that. I know I wrote *The Summer of the Swans,* because two of my daughters claim it is the size of their feet that plays an important role in the story, and also I have a three-inch-high stack of rewrites that could not be explained in any other way. But all I really remember about that winter

***Mouse* was lying on the sofa watching a cartoon. It was the kind of old cartoon that he particularly disliked. . . . ■** (From *The 18th Emergency* by Betsy Byars. Illustrated by Robert Grossman.)

is that I felt enormously fine, that none of the children had the flu, and that the West Virginia hills had looked beautiful when they were covered with snow.

"Since I cannot tell you exactly how *The Summer of the Swans* was written, I will tell you how I write in general, and perhaps you can imagine the rest.

"I write in four stages. In the first stage I mainly sit around and stare at a spot on the wall or at my thumbnail. This is a difficult stage for a writer who has children. Anytime my children see me sitting there staring at my thumbnail, they come running over with skirts that need hemming and blouses that need ironing and baskets of dirty clothes.

"I can protest for hours that I am working, that I am writing a book in my head, but they will not believe me. And the situation will end in bad feelings when one of the children says, 'You just don't *want* to wash these clothes!' And, of course, there is no denying that.

"The second stage is the best. At some point in this 'head writing' I become gripped with enthusiasm. There is nothing like my enthusiasm when I first begin writing. People who have seen me in this stage would never ask, 'How do you find time to write?' because it is obvious there is not time for anything else. I can hardly wait to get to the typewriter in the morning. I have even awakened in the middle of the night,

"His dog had a little aaaccident." ■ (From *The Cybil War* by Betsy Byars. Illustrated by Gail Owens.)

(Jacket illustration by Diane de Groat from *Cracker Jackson* by Betsy Byars.)

glanced at my desk, and wondered if it would disturb my husband if I got up and typed quietly in the dark.

"The third stage comes so gradually that I almost do not notice it, but soon the words which have been flying out of my typewriter in paragraphs, now start coming out in sentences. Then they start coming out in phrases, then one by one, and finally they do not come out at all.

"I look on this as a desperate situation, requiring great personal discipline. This is what works for me. I say to myself, 'All right, today you are either going to have to write pages or you are going to have to defrost the refrigerator.' Sometimes I do decide that the refrigerator is the lesser of the two evils. Sometimes I clean closets and wash cars, because writing at its worst is bad indeed. Sooner or later, however, I will find something that *is* worse. After all, there is always the attic.

"The last stage is the longest and the most trying. It involves reading what I have written and trying to make something of it. I have never read a manuscript in this stage without becoming aware again of the enormity of the gap which exists between the brain and a sheet of paper. I just do not know how it is possible to have something in your mind which is so hilarious you are all but chuckling as you write, and then when you read it over, it is completely flat.

"Or, there is a scene in your mind which is so sad, so touching, you can barely see the typewriter keys through your tears. And when you read it back, you find it is as touching and as moving as a recipe for corn bread.

"I do not know how this happens, but I do feel that the gap between the brain and a sheet of paper is at least as formidable as the generation gap. And whenever I read statistics on the number of books published in a month or a year, I never think of all those books. I think, 'That many authors conquered the gap this year!' And I am impressed.

"In this last stage I always ask my children to read my manuscript, even though they are my severest critics. They are not in the least tactful about what they do not like, either. If they find, for example, their interest is lagging, they draw a small arrow in the margin of the manuscript, pointing downward. A small, down-pointing arrow in the margin of a manuscript can be starkly eloquent. It can say more than a thousand words. In my most terrible and haunting nightmares, I open a magazine or a newspaper to read a review of one of my books and find that the review consists of a great blank space, no words at all, and in the center of the space is a small arrow—pointing down. The possibility is enough to make one tremble.

". . . On the night before my son's eighth birthday he was enormously excited because he was getting a bicycle. Sleep was impossible and he kept coming in my room where I was working at my desk to tell me how much trouble he was having falling asleep.

"Finally in desperation he said, 'You know, maybe it would help me get to sleep if I read some of your failures.'

"I asked after a moment if there was any particular failure that would induce sleep better than the others, and he named one. I opened my failure drawer—I had never thought of it as being that before, but in an instant that was what it had become—and handed it to him. He read for about three minutes, yawned, went into his room and fell fast asleep. It was a humbling moment." [Betsy Byars, "Newbery Award Acceptance Speech," *Horn Book,* August, 1971.[4]]

1971. Awarded the John Newbery Medal of the American Library Association for *The Summer of the Swans*. "When I first learned that I had won the Newbery Award, I became instantly overwhelmed with the thought, 'Now I'm going to be read!' I envisioned librarians all over the country pressing my book into readers' hands.

"This has been the worst summer of my life." ▪ (From *The Summer of the Swans* by Betsy Byars. Illustrated by Ted CoConis.)

Two men who were standing in a nearby doorway came forward. ▪ (From *The Dancing Camel* by Betsy Byars. Illustrated by Harold Berson.)

''The first letter that I got from a child, however, said:

'Dear Mrs. Byars,

'I'm dying to read your book that won the Newbery Medal, but our librarian has made a display of it and won't let anybody check it out.'

''It was something of a come-down, but since up until that time I had never even been a display, I really couldn't complain.

''One of the most interesting things that happened as a result of winning the award was the mail that I received. I got tapes from classes which I was supposed to retape and send back; I got letters; I got questionnaires.

''I recall a questionnaire in which one of the questions was, 'What do your children think of having a Newbery Award winning mother?' My husband was reading the questions at the table, and as he got to that one he turned to our fourteen year old daughter and said, 'Well, what do you think of having a Newbery Award winning mother?' And she gave that shrug that only fourteen year olds can give and said, 'Well, it's no big deal.'

''The Newbery Award ceremony remains something of a blur to me (I was very nervous about giving my speech), but I do recall two things clearly.

''The banquet was held in Dallas and the room was huge and elegant. Eighteen hundred people were there, and the people who were to sit at the head table formed a sort of procession through the tables. Leading us were two teenaged boys in kind of King Arthur page boy suits and they were bearing large banners. The boy preceding me had a banner on which there was a swan made of real swan feathers (hand sewn, one by one) and it was gorgeous. I almost felt I was back in medieval times. Then just before we were to enter the boy turned to me and said, 'I could just kill my mom for making me do this.' Instantly I was back in the twentieth century.

''My second and most poignant memory is the blueberry cheesecake. That is my favorite food in the world, and all during the banquet—and the food looked great—I was not able to take a bite. Indeed I considered myself fortunate to be able to get down a few glasses of wine. Then came the blueberry cheesecake and I could have wept because there was no way I could have even swallowed one berry.

''I got up to give my speech, fearful that a throat nervous enough not to accept cheesecake, might also be too nervous to form intelligible speech, but I got started all right. Toward the end, I began actually to relax a little, and at that moment a terrible hunger came over me. All I could think of was that cheesecake. I could see it in my mind waiting there for me. Later my husband told me that the only thing wrong with the way I gave my speech was that I talked too fast at the end.

''As soon as I delivered my last line, I was ravenous. I rushed back to my seat, ready to grab my fork, and the blueberry cheesecake was gone.

''Now, I have had many pieces of blueberry cheesecake in the intervening years, but I tell you I have never had one that would have been as good as the one I would have had if I could have delivered my whole speech at the same rapid pace that I delivered the last few lines.''[4]

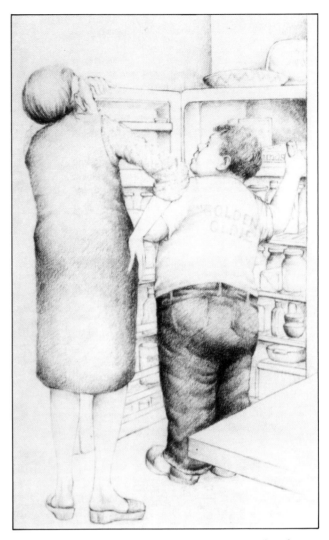

"I was *getting* a piece of *celery*." ■ (From *After the Goat Man* by Betsy Byars. Illustrated by Ronald Himler.)

After the notoriety of the Newbery Medal had subsided, Byars wrote, produced and directed an operetta for mentally retarded junior-high students. The project was undertaken with a music teacher whom she had met while tutoring a class of mentally retarded students, and, although it was never published, the operetta was a success with the special education classes.

The Summer of the Swans was followed by other books for children. ''My books usually begin with something that really happened, a newspaper story or an event from my children's lives. But, aside from this mutual starting-point, each book has been a different writing experience. My daughter once described one of my books by saying, 'Mom just made it up as she went along.' That was true, but in another book I wrote the end first and worked back.

''It takes me about a year to write a book, but I spend another year thinking about it and polishing it. Living with my own teenagers has taught me that not only must I not write down to my readers, I must write up to them. Boys and girls are very sharp today, and when I visit classrooms and talk with students I am always impressed to find how many of them are writing stories and how knowledgeable they are about writing.'' [Rachel Fordyce, ''Betsy Byars,'' *Twentieth-Century Children's Writers*, St. Martin's, 1978.[5]]

Byars' writing is done ''. . . during the winter months because my husband's hobby is gliding, and my summers are filled with putting a sailplane together, taking it apart, taping and polishing it and driving a thirty-five-foot trailer around the country.''

1975. Although many of Byars' books are contemporary realistic fiction, she departed from that genre with the picture book, *The Lace Snail,* which she wrote and illustrated. ''One of my editors pointed out to me that I wrote that book when I was planning my daughter's wedding! It's no wonder lace was predominant in my mind. I was taking a course in etching, not because I wanted to do any etching but because I wanted to know what good etchings are and how they're created. One of the assignments was to draw a little thing, and I drew a little snail. And then we were inventing things using dots and I drew some lace. After I got my plate back, I thought: hm . . . if I had moved the lace up a little higher, it would look like the snail was leaving the trail of lace. That was really the beginning. I've done about three picture books, and usually it's been because of a specific idea that wends its way rather than the way my other books are conceived.''[2]

Byars warned aspiring writers that they should not expect to support themselves immediately by their writing. ''My writing habits have changed a great deal in the past . . . years. When I first started writing, I wrote daily, beginning when my kids left for school in the morning and ending at three o'clock when

The claws of both cats were flexing in and out in readiness for battle. ■ (From *Rama, the Gypsy Cat* by Betsy Byars. Illustrated by Peggy Bacon.)

(Jacket illustration by Ruth Sanderson from *The Two-Thousand-Pound Goldfish* by Betsy Byars.)

they got home. I'm sure I would never have gotten published if I had not put in all those eight-hour days. Writing is something that has to be learned, like piano playing, and a writer has to put in many, many hours that seemingly never pay off. Today I write only when I have an idea and I write two or three hours a day. I still do a lot of rewriting and I don't think that will ever change.

''When I first began writing, I was insecure about my writing. My first real recognition was the Newbery Medal, and it seemed to me to be an enormous pat on the back, a sort of you're-on-the-right-track gesture. It encouraged me enormously, and since that time I have been more secure, more willing to try new things, more willing to fail.

''I still lead an unliterary life. . . . Writing is solitary, unglamorous work. My contact with my publishers is minimal—I have lunch with an editor about every other year. My contact with other authors is limited to meeting them at conventions where we both are speaking. So one of the most difficult questions to answer—and the one kids always ask—is, 'How does it feel to be an author?' . . . I still don't know.''[3]

1980s. Returned to South Carolina, after living and raising a family in West Virginia for twenty years. ''In the twenty years that I lived in West Virginia, I wrote in a corner of our bedroom. I had a huge L-shaped desk in front of a big window where I could look out over the beautiful West Virginia hills. Sometimes, even when I wasn't writing, I'd sit there.

"One of the things that bothered me most about moving was that I wouldn't have that corner and that desk and that view, and I didn't think I would be able to write without them. Also we were moving into a small, modern town house, and there wasn't any corner for my big desk. I didn't tell anybody, but I was absolutely certain I had written my last book.

"Two weeks later, in my new town house, I wrote the opening chapter of *The Animal, the Vegetable, and John D. Jones,* the first of my South Carolina books. I was back where I had started, once again on the kitchen table.

"I moved to a small desk upstairs with a beautiful view overlooking the lake and a new typewriter that could remember what I'd written and erase it. I started *The Two-Thousand-Pound Goldfish* on it. This book was a particular pleasure to write, not just because of the typewriter, but because I loved horror movies so much as a child that everyone said they would ruin my brain.

"Then I got a word processor and wrote *The Glory Girl,* my second South Carolina book. Then *The Computer Nut,* my first collaboration—with my son Guy. Then *Cracker Jackson.* [Then] *The Not Just Anybody Family.*

"I used to think, when I first started writing, that writers were like wells, and sooner or later we'd use up what had happened to us and our children and our friends and our dogs and cats, and there wouldn't be anything left. We'd go dry and have to quit.

"I imagine we would if it weren't for that elusive quality—creativity. I can't define it, but I have found from experience that the more you use it, the better it works.

"On April Fools' Day, **1983,** I took my first flying lesson. I had been flying with Ed for thirty-five years, but I had never tried it myself. My thought was that flying, like writing, couldn't possibly be as hard as everyone said it was.

"Like writing, it turned out to be harder. Months after I had learned how to take off and fly around and navigate, I still couldn't land. The ground was never exactly where I thought it was going to be. I made over a hundred landings before I did a good solid one, and then I made twenty before I did another.

"On **December 19, 1984,** I got my pilot's license, and I am as proud of that as of anything in my writing career.

"Uncle C. C. in *Good-Bye, Chicken Little* [1979] says, 'There's two parts to a man's life. Forget all the junk you've heard about youth, teenage, middle age, old age. There's two parts

(From the ABC Afterschool Special "The Winged Colt," based on the novel *The Winged Colt of Casa Mia* by Betsy Byars. Produced by ABC Wide World of Learning. Broadcast on ABC-TV, 1972.)

(From the ABC Afterschool Special "Sara's Summer of the Swans," based on the novel *The Summer of the Swans* by Betsy Byars. Produced by Martin Tahse Productions. Broadcast on ABC-TV, October 2, 1974.)

Byars, in her office.

to a man's life—up and down. Your life goes up like a fly ball and then, like it or not, it starts down. The people who are lucky have a long, long up and a quick down.'

"At age ninety-seven Uncle C. C. still felt he was on the way up. I, at [my age], feel I am too."

Byars' books have been translated into nine languages, many of her novels have been dramatized on national television, and she receives approximately 200 letters from children a week. "There is no activity in my life . . . which has brought me more pleasure than my writing. And the moment of receiving a package in the mail, opening it, and seeing the finished book for the first time is beyond description."

Byars' works are included in the Kerlan Collection at the University of Minnesota.

HOBBIES AND OTHER INTERESTS: Gliding, antique airplanes, reading, traveling, music, needlepoint, crosswords.

FOR MORE INFORMATION SEE: New York Times Book Review, September 14, 1969, April 23, 1972, June 4, 1972, November 5, 1972, June 10, 1973, August 19, 1973, November 4, 1973, October 13, 1974, December 15, 1974, May 2, 1976; *Library Journal,* July, 1970; *New York Times,* January 23, 1971; *Publishers Weekly,* February 22, 1971, September 6, 1971, July 25, 1977; *Horn Book,* February, 1971, August, 1971, December, 1978; *Top of the News,* April, 1971; Martha E. Ward and Dorothy A. Marquardt, *Authors of Books for Young People,* 2nd edition, Scarecrow Press, 1971; *Saturday Review,* May 20, 1972; Doris de Montreville and Donna Hill, editors, *Third Book of Junior Authors,* H. W. Wilson, 1972; *Christian Science Monitor,* October 3, 1973, November 7, 1973, June 10, 1975; *Psychology Today,* January 10, 1974; Lee Bennett Hopkins, *More Books by More People,* Citation,

1974; Lee Kingman, editor, *Newbery and Caldecott Medal Books: 1966-1975,* Horn Book, 1975.

"Meet the Newbery Author: Betsy Byars" (filmstrip with record or cassette), Miller-Brody, 1978; D. L. Kirkpatrick, *Twentieth-Century Children's Writers,* St. Martin's, 1978; Ina Robertson, "Profile: Betsy Byars—Writer for Today's Child," *Language Arts,* March, 1980; *Children's Literature in Education,* winter, 1982, spring, 1984; Betsy Byars, "Five Little Peppers and Me," *Dell Carousel,* fall/winter, 1985-86.

CABRAL, Olga 1909-
(O. M. Cabral)

PERSONAL: Born September 14, 1909, in Port of Spain, Trinidad, British West Indies; daughter of Anthony F. (an accountant) and Marie (Baptista) Cabral; married Aaron Samuel Kurtz (a Yiddish poet), June 27, 1951 (deceased). *Education:* Attended New School for Social Research, 1961-62. *Religion:* "Agnostic—Catholic childhood." *Home:* 463 West St., Apt. H-523, New York, N.Y. 10014.

CAREER: Poet and author. Little Art Center, Brooklyn, N.Y., co-owner and manager, 1950-56; French-American Gallery, Long Beach, N.Y., owner and manager, 1958-66. *Member:* Poetry Society of America, Authors Guild, Authors League of America, National Writers Union. *Awards, honors:* William Newman Poetry Prize, 1957, for poem, "O the White Towns"; Emily Dickinson Award, 1971, for poem, "Occupation: Spinster," and Lucille Medwick Memorial Award, 1976, for poem, "At the Jewish Museum," both from Poetry Society of America; *So Proudly She Sailed: Tales of Old Ironsides* was selected as a notable children's trade book in the field of social studies, 1982.

WRITINGS: The Seven Sneezes (juvenile), Simon & Schuster, 1948; *Four-in-One* (juvenile), World, 1948; *Tony the Tow Car* (juvenile), Capitol, 1949; *Cities and Deserts* (poetry), Roving Eye Press, 1959; (co-translator from the Yiddish) *Marc Chagall: A Poem by Aaron Kurtz,* French-American Gallery, 1961; *The Evaporated Man* (poetry), Olivant, 1968.

Tape Found in a Bottle (poetry), Olivant, 1971; *The Darkness in My Pockets* (poetry), Gallimaufry, 1976; *Occupied Country* (poetry), New Rivers Press, 1976; *In the Empire of Ice* (poetry), West End Press, 1980; *So Proudly She Sailed: Tales of Old Ironsides* (juvenile novel), Houghton, 1981.

Work has appeared in thirty-one anthologies, including: *We Become New: Poems by Contemporary American Women,* edited by Lucille Iverson and Kathryn Ruby, Bantam, 1976; *A Geography of Poets,* edited by Edward Field, Bantam, 1979; *The Poet Dreaming in the Artist's House,* edited by Emilie Buchwald and Ruth Roston, Mildweed Editions, 1984; *American Literature,* Macmillan, 1984. Contributor to pulp magazines under name O. M. Cabral, 1938-41; contributor to poetry magazines.

WORK IN PROGRESS: Such a Pretty Girl as I, a juvenile novel set in New England mills; poetry.

SIDELIGHTS: "I was born in the West Indies on the island of Trinidad in the year 1909. But when I was nine months old my parents moved to Canada and settled in the prairie city of Winnipeg, where I spent my early childhood until the age of ten. Both my parents were descended from Portuguese colonial families who were bilingual in English and Portuguese. My

OLGA CABRAL

maternal great-great grandparents had settled in the Caribbean area early in the nineteenth century.

"My Canadian childhood was serene, gentle. My father, an accountant, worked in the office of the City Comptroller. Besides myself and my parents the household consisted of my younger sister and two young uncles who had come to Canada from a Catholic college in England. We lived in a house with a large garden on a tree-lined suburban street.

"At the earliest possible age my father began teaching me to read and write. He taught me so well that when I began public school I went directly into third grade, skipping the first and second. My love affair with language, with the magic of words, had begun early.

"It was a childhood of story books—possible then when even radio did not as yet exist. I remember being allowed at age seven to go alone to the library to pick out my own fairy tale books. It had begun to snow very softly, and I had piled them on my sled, proud of the precious freight I was bringing home. And in my *Manitoba Reader* I had Robert Louis Stevenson's verses. 'My dear land of story books' meant exactly that to me.

"But there were other fascinations. My uncles had a neighborhood motion picture house, the 'Bijou.' On Saturday mornings I went with my sister to sit in lonely splendor in the box seats—which were cane-bottomed chairs cordoned off by vel-

vet ropes. There we eagerly followed the misadventures of Pearl White and saw all the early Chaplin films.

"World War I broke out when I was five. As it dragged on I became aware of feelings of bafflement and fear all around me. Newsboys would storm our quiet street shouting 'Extra! Extra!' People would rush from their homes to seize the papers and read about the latest mass slaughter. Something was happening that no one could explain or comprehend. I have a clear image of those huge black banner headlines, like mourning crepe, which I hated and feared, and of the equally black left-hand column running down the front page in boldface type—the endless listing of Canadians killed at the front.

"From early childhood we draw the deepest imagery about the world around us. That world remains intact in all of us, sharp and clear though distant in time. It is there for us to draw upon when we write for children.

"By the time of the Armistice my Canadian childhood had come to an end. The death of both my young uncles and the divorce of my parents meant beginning a new life in New York. I've been a New Yorker ever since except for various periods on the West Coast. New York was Whitman's city, and Melville's. I've always been conscious of that. I've loved it for that reason, for the terrific energy of its human tides. Unfortunately, like everything else around us it is less loveable today.

"I had started out to be a poet and published my verses in some of the little magazines of the 1930s. But coming to maturity in the beginning years of the Great Depression meant great hardships for the young, and I turned to other things. I wrote stories of adventure and fantasy for what was then known as the 'men's pulps.' I filled my life with art, social action. Women's lives tend to have discontinuities. It has been said by a writer who has made a study of such things (Tillie Olsen) that one woman in six who starts out to have a writing career manages to continue. In any case, I became a poet again later in life and married a Yiddish poet. I could not read or understand his poems then, but—again through the magic of words—I fell in love when I heard him declaim them.

"I literally sneezed my way into my first children's book, *The Seven Sneezes,* an early Golden Book. I had hay fever and the spasmodic sneezing made me so miserable I wished that I could sneeze myself into some other place. Without thinking about it, a procession of creatures, the characters in the story, passed before my eyes. They invented themselves. I had only to watch them. And children still love the story.

"Many poets have written for children, and more should do so. There is certainly a connection. The best of children's writing is in a sense poetry, a metaphor for childhood. Writing for children is an enjoyable experience because we get the opportunity to re-enter a pristine world, a world that may stand the real world completely on its head. A world that can still be remade, where words once again have the power of magic.

"But the warring world of banner headlines persists, while electronic media deliver atrocities to us at the dinner table. Children cannot escape the world around them because the television set never lets them forget it. But the land of story books—isn't that every child's birthright?

"'Beauty is truth, truth beauty'—as writers, what better can we offer to young readers? To tell the truth and to cherish beauty through the magic of words, words that have reclaimed their ancient art and purpose—to cast a spell.''

FOR MORE INFORMATION SEE: Choice, September, 1977; *New York Times Book Review,* November 15, 1981.

CAULEY, Lorinda Bryan   1951-

PERSONAL: Born July 2, 1951, in Washington, D.C.; daughter of Robert S. and Lucille E. Bryan; married Patrick Dennis Cauley (a painter), June 15, 1974; children: Ryan, Mackenzie. *Education:* Montgomery Junior College, associate degree, 1971; Rhode Island School of Design, B.F.A., 1974. *Home:* Philadelphia, Pa. *Agent:* Florence Alexander, 80 Park Ave., New York, N.Y. 10016.

CAREER: Illustrator and writer, 1976—.

WRITINGS—All self-illustrated, all children's books: *Things to Make and Do for Thanksgiving,* F. Watts, 1977; *Pease Porridge Hot: A Mother Goose Cookbook,* Putnam, 1977; *The Bake-Off,* Putnam, 1978; *The Animal Kids* (Junior Literary Guild selection), Putnam, 1979; (reteller) *The Ugly Duckling: A Tale from Hans Christian Andersen,* Harcourt, 1979; (reteller) *The Goose and the Golden Coins,* Harcourt, 1981; (reteller) *Goldilocks and the Three Bears,* Putnam, 1981; *The New House,* Harcourt, 1981; (reteller) *The Three Little Kittens,* Putnam, 1982; (reteller) *The Cock, the Mouse and the Little Red Hen,* Putnam, 1982; (reteller) *Jack and the Beanstalk,* Putnam, 1983; (reteller) *The Town Mouse and the Country Mouse,* Putnam, 1984; (reteller) *The Owl and the Pussycat,* Putnam, 1986; (reteller) *Puss in Boots,* Harcourt, 1986.

Illustrator: Sibyl Hancock, *Bill Picket: First Black Rodeo Star,* Harcourt, 1977; Mary Kwitz, *Rabbits' Search for a Little House,* Crown, 1977; Pauline Watson, *Curley Cat Baby-Sits,* Harcourt, 1977; Cynthia Jameson, *The House of Five Bears,* Putnam, 1978; Penny Pollock, *Ants Don't Get Sunday Off,* Putnam, 1978; William O. Steele, *The War Party,* Harcourt, 1978; Adelaide Holl, *Small Bear Solves a Mystery,* Garrard, 1979; Cecily Hogan, *Best of All!,* Western Publishing, 1979; Annabelle Sumera, *What Lily Goose Found,* Western Publishing, 1979; Joan Bowden, *Little Grey Rabbit,* Western Publishing, 1979; Dorothy A. Woolfolk, *The Teenage Surefire Diet Cookbook,* Watts, 1979.

She didn't see them. ■ (From *The Town Mouse and the Country Mouse,* retold and illustrated by Lorinda Bryan Cauley.)

LORINDA BRYAN CAULEY

P. Pollock, *The Slug Who Thought He Was a Snail,* Putnam, 1980; Joan L. Nixon, *If You Say So, Claude,* Warne, 1980; Joseph Jacobs, *The Story of the Three Little Pigs,* Putnam, 1980; Jan Wahl, *Old Hippo's Easter Egg,* Harcourt, 1980; Berniece Freschet, *Where's Henrietta's Hen,* Putnam, 1980; P. Pollock, *The Spit Bug Who Couldn't Spit,* Putnam, 1982; Rudyard Kipling, *The Elephant's Child,* Harcourt, 1983; Carolyn Lesser, *The Goodnight Circle,* Harcourt, 1984; Eve Bunting, *Clancy's Coat,* Warne, 1984; R. Kipling, *The Beginning of the Armadillos,* Harcourt, 1985.

ADAPTATIONS: "Goldilocks and the Three Bears" (filmstrip), Weston Woods, 1982.

SIDELIGHTS: "Even as a small child I realized that art was a major part of me. In school it helped me get better grades when I illustrated reports and projects, and it earned points with the teachers when I did their bulletin boards each month. At home it was a great way to keep busy and have fun. There was never any doubt in my mind that I would eventually have a career in the art field.

"After carefully selecting an art school, the Rhode Island School of Design, I studied painting, drawing, and sculpture the first three years then switched to illustration. I needed specific assignments and I preferred drawing pictures to tell a story rather than the vague, wide-open subjects used in painting. Commercial art was a bit too slick for me, but children's books seemed the perfect vehicle for my style of working—using my talents to the fullest.

"At the start of my career in children's books I wrote some of my own stories; but later, concentrated mainly on retelling and illustrating classic fairy tales. Recently, though, since I've had children of my own, I've become interested again in trying to write stories of my own telling.

"I find it intriguing to see how, time and again, children choose many of the same picture books to have read to them—whether the pictures are detailed or simple—something appeals to them. Certain things hold their interest and I want to write a book about a subject their little minds find particularly fascinating.

"I like to do books in which the animals are anatomically correct, yet still have human characteristics and feelings. I try to be accurate about details like landscapes, interiors, costumes, etc. because I think kids are pretty bright—they notice those things if they're not right. I also like to add small details and little things that may not be noticed on the first reading of the book, but show up as it's read again and again.

"Basically I try to do books that I would have enjoyed as a child. I try to fill the pages with rich and light colors that are appealing to the eye. I think what I really do best is to give my characters personality and life that the child reading can relate to."

HOBBIES AND OTHER INTERESTS: "My husband and I have two stores in Long Beach Island, N.J. during the summers. At them we sell clothes that we design and have hand-screened or embroidered with 'beachy' colorful prints."

CHAMBERLAIN, Margaret 1954-

PERSONAL: Born June 11, 1954, in London, England; daughter of Sidney George and Rose Myra (Farquhar) Chamberlain; married Ian Douglas Dicks (an illustrator), May 13, 1978. *Education:* Canterbury College of Art, B.A. (with honors), 1976; Royal College of Art, M.A., 1979. *Home:* 73, New Concordia Wharf, Mill St., London SE1 2BA, England. *Office:* Granary Building, Hope (Sufferance) Wharf, St. Mary Church St., London, SE16, England.

CAREER: Illustrator, 1979—. *Awards, honors:* National Federation of Children's Books Award, 1982, for *Fair's Fair.*

ILLUSTRATOR: Sid Fleischman, *The Man on the Moon-Eyed Horse,* Gollancz, 1980; S. Fleischman, *Humbug Mountain,* Gollancz, 1980; Leon Garfield, *Fair's Fair,* Macdonald & Janes, 1981; *Sing a Song of Sixpence,* Blackie, 1981, P. Be-

MARGARET CHAMBERLAIN

**Who wound up under lock and key
Where the gorilla used to be.**

■ (From *The Tale of Fearsome Fritz* by Jeanne Willis. Illustrated by Margaret Chamberlain.)

drick Books, 1984; Jeanne Willis, *The Tale of Georgie Grub,* Andersen, 1981, Holt, 1982; John Inman, *Curtain Up!,* Heinemann, 1981; J. Willis, *The Tale of Fearsome Fritz,* Andersen, 1982, Holt, 1983; Jasper Hood and Christopher Hood, *Contact with Maldonia,* Heinemann, 1982; Georgie Adams, *Mr. Bill and the Runaway Sausages,* Blackie & Son, 1983; Gwen Grant, *The Lily Pickle Band Book,* Heinemann, 1983, David & Charles, 1984; Margaret Mahy, *The Pirates' Mix-up Voyage,* Dent, 1984; J. Willis, *The Tale of Mucky Mabel,* Andersen, 1984; M. Mahy, *Leaf Magic and Five Other Favourites,* Dent, 1985; M. Mahy, *The Man Whose Mother Was a Pirate,* Dent, 1985. Also illustrator of educational books, comic strips, and posters for educational use.

SIDELIGHTS: ''Since my childhood I have really been interested in nothing but drawing, so it's just as well I have a talent and have been able to make a career of it. I believe my talent and use of it to be pretty unself-conscious. I direct my ideas towards nobody but myself. Ideas have always come to me straight from my imagination. I have always enjoyed escapist 'cosy' stories and have been very lucky to find authors whose vision of the world is similar to mine. I enjoy small, trivial, amusing detail. There is a side of my nature that revels in the grotesque and 'Victorianesque.' I illustrated a book by Leon Garfield who is a well-known and respected author of children's tales: he writes in a similar style to Dickens. I enjoyed capturing the poverty and absolute misery of life in Dickensian

London. This book won an award through votes from children of all ages for their favourite book, however 'grown-up' publishers and the U.S. market seem afraid of this type of uni-dealised thing and I have not been asked to work in this style again.

"I have always enjoyed the pathos of such writers as Hans Andersen and Grimm. These stories do not seem popular with publishers nowadays, although I believe children are still fascinated and moved by the misery of others. I think it is a shame that children are too protected by their parents and teachers who dread discussing the important things of life with children who are very interested in death, etc.

"These thoughts probably give the impression that I am a macabre illustrator which I definitely am not. I recently visited a school in a very poor part of London which really made me stop and think. The children I met, ages five through seven, lead lives very different from those featured in most idealised picture books. And although, they (like everyone else) enjoy escapism, they do appreciate what it's like to be poor and to live in a violent society.

"They also like to identify with characters illustrated in their books. I think it's very easy for illustrators to be too romantic in our ideas about what it is like to be a child. We forget how difficult it is and that it's not all easy.

"Apart from the picture books mentioned here I have worked on several educational books which have been interesting. This area of publishing has certainly improved since I was at primary school! (I have done comic strips and posters for educational use.) I have been very lucky that the self-indulgent flights of fancy I enjoy illustrating are enjoyed by enough other people for me to make my living from it."

CHAMBERS, John W.   1933-

BRIEF ENTRY: Born in 1933, in New York, N.Y. Educated at Yale and Columbia Universities, Chambers has taught English, history, and writing. His own writing includes novels, plays, short stories, and articles. For many years he has worked in the wine trade, frequently writing and lecturing on wine and teaching wine courses. Several of Chambers's books for middle-grade readers are set on Fire Island, located south of central Long Island, N.Y., where he and his family have had a summer home for many years. *Fritzi's Winter* (Atheneum, 1979) depicts a pet cat's winter alone on Fire Island in what *Publishers Weekly* described as "a dramatic adventure in survival." Mysteries abound on Fire Island for preteen Jenny Martin who makes her first appearance in *Finder* (Atheneum, 1981). While the Martin family vacations on the island for the summer, Jenny stumbles upon a young boy who turns out to be a kidnap victim. *Booklist* called the story a "nicely turned mystery. . . . A solid piece of writing in a genre beset by mediocrity."

The setting for *Showdown at Apple Hill* (Atheneum, 1982) is Dover Valley in western Connecticut, where Jenny and her family have recently moved from New York City. This time, she enlists the aid of her younger brother to solve a theft-and-murder mystery that dates back twelve years. Finally, in *Fire Island Forfeit* (Atheneum, 1984), Jenny finds herself back on the island and embroiled in a mystery that involves a dead model and a drug-smuggling operation. "[A] full-bodied story," again commented *Booklist,* "with smooth development and believable, childlike characters." Chambers's other books for

young readers include *Footlight Summer* (Atheneum, 1983) and *The Colonel and Me* (Atheneum, 1985).

CHRISTOPHER, Milbourne   1914(?)-1984

PERSONAL: Born about 1914, in Baltimore, Md.; died of post-surgical complications, June 17, 1984, in New York, N.Y.; married wife Maurine (a journalist). *Residence:* New York, N.Y.

CAREER: Magician and author. *Member:* Society of American Magicians (past president). *Awards, honors: Mediums, Mystics and the Occult* and *Houdini: A Pictorial Life* were each selected one of New York Public Library's Books for the Teen Age, 1980, 1981, and 1982, and *Search for the Soul,* 1980 and 1981.

WRITINGS—All published by Crowell, except as noted: (Compiler) *The Sphinx Golden Jubilee Book of Magic,* Sphinx Publishing, 1951; *Panorama of Magic,* Dover, 1962; *Houdini: The Untold Story,* 1969; *ESP, Seers, and Psychics,* 1970; *The Illustrated History of Magic,* 1973; *Mediums, Mystics and the Occult,* 1975; *Houdini: A Pictorial Life,* 1976; *Milbourne Christopher's Magic Book,* 1977; *Search for the Soul,* 1979; (editor and compiler) *Houdini's History of Magic in Boston 1792-1915,* Meyer Books, 1983.

SIDELIGHTS: Christopher's love of magic blossomed in his early childhood when his father broke a string and taught the youth to rejoin it. Later he established himself as one of the foremost American magicians, performing his act in more than seventy-two countries. In addition he is the author of books on illusionism, occultism, and mysticism, as well as volumes on the history of magic and the lives of magicians. Christopher was responsible for returning magic to the Broadway theatre after a lapse of twenty years and popularizing the art of deception on worldwide television.

Milbourne Christopher performing at Lincoln Center's Alice Tully Hall.

FOR MORE INFORMATION SEE: Variety, March 26, 1969, April 9, 1969, August 20, 1969, May 13, 1970; *Book World,* March 30, 1969; *Times Literary Supplement,* October 16, 1969; *Pittsburgh Press,* November 30, 1973; *New York Times Book Review,* December 16, 1973, July 8, 1978; *New York Times,* August 23, 1975; *Village Voice,* December 13, 1976.

Obituaries: *Chicago Tribune,* June 21, 1984; *Washington Post,* June 21, 1984; *Newsweek,* July 2, 1984.

CIARDI, John (Anthony)   1916-1986

OBITUARY NOTICE—See sketch in *SATA* Volume 1: Born June 24, 1916, in Boston, Mass.; died of a heart attack, March 30, 1986, in Edison, N.J. Poet, critic, educator, translator, editor, and lecturer. Ciardi was well known for his outspoken attempts to raise readers' interest in poetry in some forty books of verse and criticism. To this end, he consciously tried to address the average reader through much of his work. After earning a master's degree in 1939 from the University of Michigan, Ciardi taught English at the University of Kansas, Harvard University, and Rutgers University during the 1940s and 1950s; he also served as poetry editor of *Saturday Review* from 1956 to 1972. In 1954 he produced his internationally acclaimed translation of Dante's *Inferno*.

Ciardi left teaching in 1961 to pursue his writing career, producing collections of poetry such as *Homeward to America, Other Skies,* and *I Marry You: A Sheaf of Love Poems*. His prose includes *How Does a Poem Mean?* and *Poetry: A Closer Look*. Ciardi's interest in etymology is evident through works like *A Browser's Dictionary and Native's Guide to the Unknown American Language* and *A Second Browser's Dictionary*. He began writing poems for children as a way of playing games with his young nephews and, later, his own children. His first book of children's verse, *The Reason for the Pelican,* published in 1959, was followed by nearly a dozen others. These include *Scrappy the Pup, The Man Who Sang the Sillies, John J. Plenty and Fiddler Dan: A New Fable of the Grasshopper and the Ant,* and *The King Who Saved Himself from Being Saved*. Ciardi was the recipient of numerous awards for both his juvenile and adult works.

FOR MORE INFORMATION SEE: Contemporary Authors, New Revision Series, Volume 5, Gale, 1982; *Twentieth-Century Children's Writers,* 2nd edition, St. Martin's, 1983. Obituaries: *Facts on File,* April 4, 1986; *Newsweek,* April 14, 1986; *Time,* April 14, 1986; *Publishers Weekly,* April 18, 1986.

CLARK, Mary Higgins

PERSONAL: Born in New York, N.Y.; daughter of Luke Joseph (a restaurant owner) and Nora C. (a buyer; maiden name, Durkin) Higgins; married Warren F. Clark (an airline executive), December 26, 1949 (died, September 26, 1964); children: Marilyn, Warren, David, Carol, Patricia. *Education:* Attended Villa Maria Academy and Wood Secretarial School; Fordham University, B.A., 1978. *Religion:* Roman Catholic. *Home:* 2508 Cleveland Ave., Washington Township, N.J. 07675; and 200 Central Park South, New York, N.Y. 10019. *Agent:* McIntosh & Otis, 475 Fifth Ave., New York, N.Y. 10017.

CAREER: Writer. Worked for Remington Rand and as stewardess for Pan American Airlines. Partner and vice-president

MARY HIGGINS CLARK

of Aerial Communications. *Member:* Mystery Writers of America (member of board of directors), Authors Guild, American Society of Journalists and Authors. *Awards, honors:* New Jersey Author Award from the New Jersey Institute of Technology, 1969, for *Aspire to the Heavens: A Portrait of George Washington,* 1977, for *Where Are the Children?,* and 1978, for *A Stranger Is Watching;* Villanova University, honorary D.Litt., 1983.

WRITINGS: Aspire to the Heavens: A Portrait of George Washington (biography), Meredith Press, 1969; *Where Are the Children?,* Simon & Schuster, 1975; *A Stranger Is Watching,* Simon & Schuster, 1978; (contributor) *I, Witness,* Times Books, 1978; *The Cradle Will Fall,* Simon & Schuster, 1980; *A Cry in the Night,* Simon & Schuster, 1982; *Still Watch,* Simon & Schuster, 1984. Work anthologized in *The Best Saturday Evening Post Stories,* 1962. Also author of syndicated radio dramas. Contributor of stories to periodicals, including *Saturday Evening Post, Redbook, McCall's, Women's Day* and *Family Circle*.

ADAPTATIONS: "A Stranger Is Watching," Paramount, 1983; "The Cradle Will Fall," CBS Movie of the Week, CBS-TV, 1984; "Where Are the Children?" Columbia, 1986; "Still Watch," CBS Movie of the Week, CBS-TV, 1986.

WORK IN PROGRESS: Weep No More, My Lady.

SIDELIGHTS: "I feel a good suspense novel can and should hold a mirror up to society and make a social comment. For this reason, I've used the death penalty issue in *A Stranger Is Watching*." Elsewhere, Clark has commented on her novels and her desire to provide in them entertainment and romance. But, she noted: "I would like to get across a sense of values. I like nice, strong people confronting the forces of evil and vanquishing them.

"I believe reading a suspense novel should be like riding on a roller coaster. You're joyously terrified, you can't get off 'til the end and you're sorry when the ride is over.

"I believe that explicit sex and violence don't necessarily belong in suspense novels, and never use them in my books.

"The nicest compliment I can get is a reader writing, 'I was feeling rotten. A lot of things had been going wrong, but I forgot all about my problems when I read your book.'—It's what I like to find in other writers' books."

HOBBIES AND OTHER INTERESTS: Traveling, skiing, tennis.

(From the movie "A Stranger Is Watching," starring Shawn von Schreiber, based on the novel by Mary Higgins Clark. Copyright © 1982 by Heron Production Ltd.)

FOR MORE INFORMATION SEE: People, March 6, 1978; *New York Times Book Review,* May 14, 1978.

CORLETT, William   1938-

PERSONAL: Born October 8, 1938, in Darlington, Durham, England; son of Harold and Ida (Allen) Corlett. *Education:* Attended Royal Academy of Dramatic Art, London, 1956-58, diploma. *Agent:* Mark Lucas, Fraser & Dunlop Scripts Ltd., 91 Regent St., London W1R 8RU, England.

CAREER: Writer of fiction and drama; stage and television actor. *Member:* Screenwriters Guild, Society of Authors. *Awards, honors:* Pye television award, 1978, and 1981, for children's drama; New York film and television international award, 1980, for "Barriers."

WRITINGS—Fiction; all for young people: *The Gate of Eden,* Hamish Hamilton, 1974, Bradbury, 1975; *The I Deal Table,* Compton Russell, 1975; *The Land Beyond,* Hamish Hamilton, 1975, Bradbury, 1976; *Return to the Gate,* Hamish Hamilton, 1975, Bradbury, 1977; *The Dark Side of the Moon,* Hamish Hamilton, 1976, Bradbury, 1977; (with John H. Moore) *The Once and Forever Christmas,* Compton Russell, 1976; *Barriers,* Hamish Hamilton, 1981; *Bloxworth Blue,* MacRae, 1984, published in the U.S. as *The Bloxworth Blue,* Harper, 1985.

Nonfiction series; all with John H. Moore; all published by Hamish Hamilton: *The Question of Religion,* 1978, *The Christ Story,* 1978, *The Hindu Sound,* 1978, *The Judaic Law,* 1979, *The Buddha Way,* 1979, *The Islamic Space,* 1979, published under same titles as a six-volume series, "Questions of Human Existence As Answered by Major World Religions," Bradbury, 1980.

Published plays: *Another Round* (first produced in Farnham, England, 1962), Samuel French, 1963; *The Gentle Avalanche* (first produced in Farnham, 1962), Samuel French, 1964; *Return Ticket: A Comedy* (first produced in Farnham, 1962), English Theatre Guild, 1966; *Tinker's Curse* (first produced in Nottingham, England, 1968), Ungar, 1969.

Unpublished plays: "Flight of a Lone Sparrow," first produced in Farnham, 1965; "The Scallop Shell," first produced in Farnham, 1965; "The Scourging of Mathew Barrow," first produced in Leicester, England, 1966; "The Illusionist," first produced in Perth, Scotland, 1969; "We Never Went to Cheddar Gorge," first produced in Perth, 1969; "National Trust," first produced in Perth, 1970; "The Deliverance of Fanny Blaydon," first produced in Perth, 1971; "Orlando the Marmalade Cat Buys a Cottage" (juvenile; adapted from a story by Kathleen Hale), first produced in London, 1975; "Orlando's Camping Holiday," (juvenile; adapted from a story by Hale), first produced in London, 1976.

WILLIAM CORLETT

Also author of television plays, including: "Dead Set at Dream Boy," 1965; "We Never Went to Cheddar Gorge," 1968; "The Story Teller," 1969; "A Memory of Two Loves," 1972; "Conversations in the Dark," 1972; "Mr. Oddy" (adapted from a story by Hugh Walpole), 1975; "The Orsini Emeralds" (adapted from a story by G. B. Stern), 1975; "Emerdale Farm" series, 1975-77; "The Gate of Eden" (adapted from Corlett's own novel), 1979; "Barriers" series, 1980; "The Agatha Christie Hour" (four plays), Thames Television, 1982.

WORK IN PROGRESS: Adaptation of Corlett's own novel "Return to the Gate"; film adaptation of Jennifer Johnston's *The Christmas Tree;* film adaptation of *Dreams Lost, Dreams Found;* novel.

SIDELIGHTS: "I've been making a living from writing for the last twenty-five years, and still don't know why . . . or how I do it."

HOBBIES AND OTHER INTERESTS: Travel, food, reading, the company of friends, gardening.

FOR MORE INFORMATION SEE: Twentieth-Century Children's Writers, 2nd edition, St. Martin's, 1983.

When the first baby laughed for the first time, the laugh broke into a thousand pieces and they all went skipping about, and that was the beginning of fairies.
—Sir James Matthew Barrie
(From *Peter Pan*)

COX, William R(obert) (Joel Reeve)

PERSONAL: Born in Peapack, N.J.; son of William and Marion Grace (Wenz) Cox. *Agent:* Don Congdon Associates, Inc., 177 East 70th St., New York, N.Y. 10021.

CAREER: Professional writer. *Member:* Writers Guild of America (West), Western Writers of America.

WRITINGS—Young adult; published by Dodd, except as indicated: *Five Were Chosen: A Basketball Story,* 1956; *Gridiron Duel,* 1959; *The Wild Pitch,* 1963; *Tall on the Court,* 1964; *Third and Eight to Go,* 1964; *Big League Rookie,* 1965; *Trouble at Second Base,* 1966; *The Valley Eleven,* 1967; (under pseudonym Joel Reeve) *Goal Ahead,* S. G. Phillips, 1967; *Jump Shot Joe,* 1968; *Rookie in the Backcourt,* 1970; *Third and Goal,* 1971; *Five-Dollar Ballplayers,* 1971, published as *Big League Sandlotters,* 1971; *Playoff,* Bantam, 1972; *Gunner on the Court,* 1972; *The Backyard Five,* 1973; *The Unbeatable Five,* 1974; *The Running Back,* Bantam, 1974; *Game, Set, and Match,* 1977; *Battery Mates,* 1978; *Home Court Is Where You Find It,* 1980; *The Fourth-of-July Kid,* Tower Books, 1981.

Other: *Make My Coffin Strong,* Fawcett, 1954; *The Lusty Men,* Pyramid, 1957; *The Tycoon and the Tigress,* Fawcett, 1957; *Hell to Pay,* New American Library, 1958; *Comanche Moon: A Novel of the West,* McGraw, 1959; *Death Comes Early,* Dell, 1959; *The Duke,* New American Library, 1959; *Murder in Vegas,* New American Library, 1960; *Luke Short and His Era,* Doubleday, 1961 (published in England as *Luke Short, Famous Gambler of the Old West,* Fireside Press, 1962); *The Outlawed,* New American Library, 1961; *Death on Location,* New American Library, 1962; *Bigger Than Texas,* Fawcett, 1962; *The Mets Will Win the Pennant* (nonfiction), Putnam, 1964; (editor) *Rivers to Cross* (collection of stories by members of Western Writers of America), Dodd, 1966; *Moon of*

WILLIAM R. COX

Cobre, Bantam, 1969; *Chicago Cruz,* Bantam, 1972; *The Sixth Horseman,* Ballantine, 1972; *Jack O'Diamonds,* Dell, 1975; *Gunsharp,* Fawcett, 1976; *Johnny Bear,* Bantam, 1976; *Cemetery Jones,* Fawcett, 1985.

Contributor of more than one-thousand stories to magazines, including *Saturday Evening Post, Collier's, This Week, Argosy, American Pic, Blue Book,* and *Cosmopolitan.*

Author of several screenplays and of more than one-hundred television scripts for such shows as "Fireside Theater," "Broken Arrow," "Bonanza," "Zane Grey Theater," "The Virginian," "The Grey Ghost," "Alcoa Theater," "Wells Fargo," "Route 66," and other programs.

WORK IN PROGRESS: A novel; several untitled juveniles; screenplays and television scripts; another book in the "Cemetery Jones" series.

FOR MORE INFORMATION SEE: Martha E. Ward and Dorothy A. Marquardt, *Authors of Books for Young People,* Scarecrow, 1971.

CRAIG, Helen 1934-

BRIEF ENTRY: Born August 30, 1934, in London, England. Although a member of an artistic family, Craig did not begin her career as an author and illustrator of children's books until quite late in life. Her grandfather, Edward Gordon Craig, was known for his revolutionary ideas and designs for the theater, while both her father and brother are artists. Craig admits to feeling "rather overwhelmed by this wealth of talent around me"; it was not until she bought a copy of Maurice Sendak's *Where the Wild Things Are* for her young son that she found her calling as a children's book illustrator. Previously, Craig had worked as an apprentice for commercial photographers Gee & Watson in London, owner and operator of a photographic studio, sculptor and artist in southern Spain, and freelance photographer, potter, and Chinese wallpaper restorer.

Craig began illustrating children's books in 1969 and has since produced pictures for nearly twenty books, including Katharine Holabird's "Angelina Ballerina" series. In 1985 Craig received the Kentucky Blue Grass Award for her pastel illustrations of the mice characters in *Angelina Ballerina* (C. N. Potter, 1983). She is both author and illustrator of four small, foldout concertina books in "The Mouse House" series, beginning with *The Mouse House ABC* (Random House, 1978). *Publishers Weekly* commented on the "full color and really ingenious activities depicting the letters.... Mice children caricature a cat on a fence for C ... a serious scientist is at work on an experiment for E." The series also includes *The Mouse House 1, 2, 3* (Random House, 1980), a counting book; *The Mouse House Months of the Year* (Random House, 1981), picturing a tree through its annual cycle followed by a seasonal scene; and *The Mouse House: The Days of the Week* (Random House, 1982). Craig received an award from the Society of Illustrators in 1977 for *The Mouse House ABC.*

Craig also wrote and illustrated the "Susie and Alfred" series, which features the playful adventures of two little pigs. Among these tales are *Susie and Alfred in the Knight, the Princess, and the Dragon* (Random House, 1985), *Susie and Alfred in the Night of the Paper Bag Monsters* (Random House, 1985), and *Susie and Alfred in a Welcome for Annie* (Walker Books, 1985). Craig is working on another "Susie and Alfred" book as well as illustrations for two more "Angelina" books. Be-

sides writing and illustrating, she collects children's books and illustrated adult books and tries to find time for etching and ceramic sculpture. *Home:* Vine Cottage, Harroell, Long Crendon, Aylesbury, Buckinghamshire HP18 9AQ, England.

FOR MORE INFORMATION SEE: Contemporary Authors, Volume 117, Gale, 1986.

DANK, Gloria Rand 1955-

BRIEF ENTRY: Born October 5, 1955, in Toledo, Ohio. Dank graduated summa cum laude from Princeton University in 1977 and began graduate study at Cambridge University that same year. In 1979 she left her studies to work as a computer programmer and research analyst in Jenkintown, Pa. until 1981 when she became a free-lance writer. Dank writes fantasy and mystery novels for young adults, sometimes in collaboration with her father, Milton Dank, a physicist and writer. She describes her fantasy *The Forest of App* (Greenwillow, 1983) as "concerned with the fading of magic and the lives of those who are 'left behind' as it fades: the faeries, the bogles, the witches, the unicorns, and the Old Ones who are left hanging on...." The novel was chosen as a book of the month selection by the Philadelphia Children's Reading Round Table in 1984. Dank and her father are co-authors of a mystery series in which six boys and girls, members of the Galaxy Gang, solve mysteries involving computer games, ghosts, UFOs, and hidden treasures. All published by Delacorte, the series includes *The Computer Caper* (1983), *A UFO Has Landed* (1983), *The 3-D Traitor* (1984), *The Treasure Code* (1985), and *The Computer Game Murder* (1985). Dank is working on another fantasy novel, tentatively titled *The Changeling. Office:* c/o Greenwillow Books, 105 Madison Ave., New York, N.Y. 10016; and c/o Delacorte Press, 1 Dag Hammarskjold Plaza, 245 East 47th St., New York, N.Y. 10017.

FOR MORE INFORMATION SEE: Contemporary Authors, Volume 114, Gale, 1985.

DAVIES, Sumiko 1942-
(Sumiko)

PERSONAL: Born September 21, 1942, in Tokyo, Japan; daughter of Kunio (a doctor) and Kimiyo (Sato) Suzuki; married Derek Davies (a writer and editor), January 7, 1967; children: Ken, Hana. *Education:* Kuwazawa Design Institute, Tokyo, Japan, diploma in design and illustration, 1966. *Home:* 3E Robinson Road, 10/F Hong Kong.

CAREER: Free-lance illustrator. Marklin Advertising Agency, Thailand, art director, 1966-67. *Exhibitions:* Pinky Gallery, Tokyo, Japan, 1979; Museum of Modern Art, Oxford, England, 1984. *Member:* Foreign Correspondent's Club of Hong Kong.

WRITINGS—All self-illustrated; all under name Sumiko: *The Cat Who Thought He Was a Mouse,* Gakken, 1976; *Kittymouse,* Heinemann, 1978; *Little Red Riding Hood,* Shogakkan, 1977; *Hans Andersen's Fairy Tales,* Ward Lock, 1979, Schocken, 1980; *My Baby Brother Ned,* Heinemann, 1981, David & Charles, 1983; *My School,* Heinemann, 1983; *A Kiss on the Nose,* Heinemann, 1984.

WORK IN PROGRESS: Compiling a portfolio of drawings and paintings of Hong Kong; a third book in the "My" series, *My*

(From "The Little Mermaid" in *Hans Andersen's Fairy Tales*. Illustrated by Sumiko.)

SUMIKO DAVIES

Holiday; a set of stamps on traditional Chinese costume for the Hong Kong government.

SIDELIGHTS: "I was born in Tokyo in 1942 and I remember my childhood as being very happy with my family of six who were very close throughout the long and difficult postwar period. My father was a tuberculosis specialist working for the Double Red Cross organization. Though we never had much money we were a very active family and enjoyed hiking, skiing and ice-skating together as well as visiting museums and galleries.

"My first memories of paintings were of the French impressionists, particularly Monet. With the western influence after the war, we began to celebrate Christmas in 1949. My first Christmas present which impressed me was the book *Thumbelina,* illustrated by a Japanese painter. My mother used to read the stories of Hans Andersen (which had no illustrations) every night. I later illustrated some of Andersen's long time favourite stories. I used to love rainy days so I could stay quietly at home to draw. Paper was difficult to get and expensive in Japan at that time so my mother collected old calendars and I would draw on the backs of them.

"When I was nineteen I decided to go to design school to learn graphic design and illustration. I entered Kuwazawa Design Institute and graduated from there three years later. I then traveled in South East Asia and lived in Thailand for nearly two years where I worked as art director for an advertising

agency. I married Derek Davies (an English writer and editor) in 1967 in Hong Kong. We lived in Tokyo for two years before moving to London.

"While living in London I started illustrating children's books, which have been translated into many languages and published in Japan, Europe and the United States. My original drawings and paintings have been exhibited in Tokyo and at the Museum of Modern Art in Oxford.

"I now live with my family (including two young children) in Hong Kong where I continue to illustrate for children's books and magazines. During the past two years I have also been compiling a portfolio of drawings and paintings of Hong Kong."

FOR MORE INFORMATION SEE: South China Morning Post, December 14, 1984.

DAVIS, Gibbs 1953-

PERSONAL: Born November 16, 1953, in Milwaukee, Wis.; daughter of Price Morgan (a company president) and Margarett Kable (a writer; maiden name, Russell) Davis; *Education:* Attended Colorado College, 1972-74; University of California, Berkeley, B.A., 1976. *Residence:* New York, N.Y.; and Connecticut.

CAREER: K-Mart, Milwaukee, Wis., assistant advertising manager, 1977-78; Ozaukee Art Center, Cedarburg, Wis., public

GIBBS DAVIS

"Time for Show and Tell." ■ (From *The Other Emily* by Gibbs Davis. Illustrated by Linda Shute.)

relations coordinator, 1978-80; *Talk* (magazine), New York, N.Y., associate editor, 1980-81; free-lance writer, 1982—. *Member:* Society of Children's Book Writers.

WRITINGS—For children: *Maud Flies Solo,* Bradbury, 1981; *Swann Song,* Bradbury, 1982; *Fishman and Charly,* Houghton, 1983; *The Other Emily* (picture book; illustrated by Linda Shute), Houghton, 1984; *Katy's First Haircut* (illustrated by L. Shute), Houghton, 1985. Also author of ten controlled vocabulary stories for Macmillan, 1985-86.

WORK IN PROGRESS: A television film script; two picture books; a young adult novel.

SIDELIGHTS: "In junior high I kept a diary. Later, as an excuse to write, I wrote long letters to almost anyone who would read them. In college, I turned to poetry. It wasn't until I was living in New York City that I decided to take a workshop in writing for children. What could be easier than writing a picture book? Mistake number one—picture books, though shorter, are not necessarily easier to write. I was to discover the longer form that a novel allows came more naturally to me.

"One fateful evening our workshop had a guest speaker, the editor-in-chief of a children's publishing company. At the close of his visit, he invited the class to send our work to him for publication consideration. Too timid to even introduce myself after class I was certain I'd never send him my first few chapters. But I did—and I was encouraged with humorous weekly notes and nudgings to stretch my chapters into a novel.

"It wasn't long before I finished my first book. *Maud Flies Solo* was promptly accepted and published.

"Recently I decided to try my hand at writing scripts for television. Initially, my motivation was money. While writing books is personally rewarding (especially when I receive a letter from a young person touched in some special way by one of my books), it provides a meager income. I would never give up writing for children though. I know how very alone a young person can feel. I've been there and can only hope that the company of my books will help my readers realize that they are not truly alone in their thoughts and feelings.

"People talk about the difficulty of growing old gracefully. *Growing up* gracefully is the real trick.''

ETIENNE DELESSERT

DELESSERT, Etienne 1941-

PERSONAL: Born January 4, 1941, in Lausanne, Switzerland; son of Ferdinand (a minister) and Berengere (de Mestral) Delessert; married Rita Marshall (a graphic designer and art director), 1985. *Education:* Attended College Classique, Lausanne, 1951-56, and Gymnase Classique, Lausanne, 1957-58. *Religion:* Protestant. *Home:* Lausanne, Switzerland; and Lakeville, Conn.

CAREER: Painter, graphic designer, illustrator, film director, publisher and author. Free-lance graphic designer and illustrator in Lausanne, Switzerland and in Paris, France, 1962-65; author and illustrator of children's books, 1965—; co-founder with Herb Lubalin, Good Book (a publishing house), 1969—; co-founder with Anne van der Essen, Société Carabosse (production company of animated films), Lausanne, 1973. Art director, *Record* (children's magazine), Paris, 1975-76; co-founder of Editions Tournesol, 1977. *Exhibitions*—One man: Art Alliance Gallery, Philadelphia, Penn., 1970; California State College Gallery, 1972; Galerie Delpire, Paris, France, 1972; Galerie Melisa, Lausanne, Switzerland, 1974; Galerie Marquet, Paris, 1975; Le Musée des Arts décoratifs du Louvre, Paris, 1975; Musée des Arts décoratifs, Lausanne, 1976; Palais de l'Athénée, Geneva, Switzerland, 1976; Le Manoir, Martigny, 1985. Group: Galerie Wolfsberg, Zurich, Switzerland, 1970; Galerie Pauli, Lausanne, Switzerland, 1976; Centre Pompidou, 1985; Art Institute, Boston, Mass., 1985. *Military service:* Swiss Army, 1961.

AWARDS, HONORS: Gold Medal from the Society of Illustrators, 1967, for cover of *Graphis*, number 128, and 1972,

1976, and 1978; *Story Number One for Children under Three Years of Age* was selected one of *New York Times* Ten Best Illustrated Books of the Year, 1968, and *Just So Stories* was selected, 1972; Best Book of the Year, Germany, for *Story Number One for Children under Three Years of Age* and *Story Number Two for Children under Three Years of Age;* Priz Loisirs-Jeunes, Paris, for *Story Number One for Children under Three Years of Age, How the Mouse Was Hit on the Head by a Stone and So Discovered the World, Le Roman de Renart,* and *L'Eau* (title means "The Water"); *How the Mouse Was Hit on the Head by a Stone and So Discovered the World,* 1971, and *Just So Stories,* 1972 were both chosen one of American Institute of Graphic Arts Fifty Books of the Year, and for the Children's Book Show, 1971-72; Brooklyn Art Books for Children citation from the Brooklyn Museum and the Brooklyn Public Library, 1973, 1974, and 1975, for *How the Mouse Was Hit on the Head by a Stone and So Discovered the World.*

Premio Europeo Prize (best European book for children), Trente, Italy, for *Thomas et l'Infini,* 1977; Gold Plaque from the Biennale of Illustration of Bratislava, 1979, for both *Les sept familles du lac Pipple-Popple (The Seven Families from Lake Pipple-Popple)* and *Die Maus und was ihr bleibt (Amelia Mouse and Her Great-Great-Grandchild),* and 1985, for *La Belle et la Bête (Beauty and the Beast);* Hans Christian Andersen highly commended illustrator award, 1980, for entire body of work; First Graphic Prize of the International Exhibition of Bologna, 1981, for the "Yok-Yok" series; Prix Loisirs-Jeunes, Paris, 1981, for *Quinze gestes de Jésus.*

WRITINGS—For children: (With Eleonore Schmid) *The Endless Party* (self-illustrated), Quist, 1967, revised edition, retold by Jeffrey Tabberner, Oxford University Press, 1981; *How the Mouse Was Hit on the Head by a Stone and So Discovered the World* (self-illustrated), Doubleday, 1971; *Le Roman de Renart,* Gallimard, 1977; (with Anne van der Essen) *La souris s'en va-t'en en guerre,* Gallimard, 1978; (with Christophe Gallaz) *Petit Croque: L'Amour,* Tournesol-Gallimard, 1982. Author of animated films and children's films.

Illustrator; all for children: Eugene Ionesco, *Story Number One for Children under Three Years of Age,* Quist, 1968; Betty Jean Lifton, *The Secret Seller,* Norton, 1968; George Mendoza, *A Wart Snake in a Fig Tree,* Dial, 1968; E. Ionesco, *Story Number Two for Children under Three Years of Age,* Quist, 1969.

Rudyard Kipling, *Just So Stories,* anniversary edition, Doubleday, 1972; Gordon Lightfoot, *The Pony Man,* Harper Magazine Press, 1972; Joseph G. Raposo, *Being Green,* Western, 1973; Michel Déon, *Thomas et l'Infini* (title means "Thomas and the Infinite"), Gallimard, 1975; A. van der Essen, *La souris et les papillons* (title means "The Mouse and the Butterflies"), Gallimard, 1975; A. van der Essen, *La souris et les poisons,* Gallimard, 1975, translation published as *The Mouse and the Poisons,* Middelhauve, 1977.

A. van der Essen, *Die Maus und was ihr bleibt,* Middlehauve, 1977, translation published as *Amelia Mouse and Her Great-Great-Grandchild,* Evans, 1978; Oscar Wilde, *The Happy Prince,* Gallimard, 1977; Edgar Allan Poe, *The Gold-Bug,* Gallimard, 1978; Edward Lear, *Les sept familles du lac Pipple-Popple* (translation of *The Seven Families from Lake Pipple-Popple*), Gallimard, 1978; Andrienne Soutter-Perrot, *Les premiers livres de la nature* (title means "My First Nature Books"), Tournesol-Gallimard, 1979, Book 1: *The Earth,* Book 2: *The Water,* Book 3: *The Air,* Book 4: *The Worm;* Jacques Prévert, *Paroles,* Gallimard-Rombaldi, 1979.

Pierre-Marie Beaude and Jean Debruyne, *Quinze gestes de Jésus,* Centurion Jeunesse, 1981; Christophe Gallaz, Jean Touvet and Francois Baudier, *Petit Croque et ses amis,* Tournesol, 1982; Truman Capote, *A Christmas Memory,* Childrens Book, 1983; Marie Catherine D'Aulnoy, *La Belle et la Bête,* Editions Grasset, 1984, published in America as *The Beauty and the Beast,* Creative Education, 1985; Henri Dès, *Chanson pour mon chien,* Script (Switzerland), 1986; H. Dès, *La petite Charlotte,* Script, 1986; H. Dès, *On ne verra jamais,* Script, 1986.

"Yok-Yok" series; written by A. van der Essen; all published by Tournesol-Gallimard: *The Caterpillar,* 1979, Merrill, 1980; *The Magician,* 1979, Merrill, 1980; *The Night,* 1979, Merrill, 1980; *The Blackbird,* 1979, Merrill, 1980; *The Frog,* 1979, Merrill, 1980; *The Rabbit,* 1979, Merrill, 1980; *The Shadow,* 1981; *The Circus,* 1981; *The Cricket,* 1981; *The Snow,* 1981; *The Violin,* 1981; *The Cherry,* 1981; *Le grand livre de Yok-Yok,* 1981.

Illustrator; adult: Joël Jakubec, *Kafka contre l'absurde,* Cahiers, 1960; Maurice Chappaz, *Le Match Valais-Judée,* Cahiers, 1968; Jacques Chessex, *La confession du Pasteur Burg,* Le Livre du Mois, 1970; Francois Nourissier, *Le temps,* Le Verseau-Roth & Sauter, 1982; J. Chessex, *Les cinq sens,* Le Verseau-Roth & Sauter, 1982.

Contributor of editorial illustrations to *Atlantic Monthly, Fortune, Playboy, Punch, Redbook, McCall's, Fact, Elle,* and other magazines.

(From *La souris et les poisons* by Anne van der Essen. Illustrated by Etienne Delessert.)

The animals were not used to receiving mail, so the crows opened the envelopes for them with their beaks. ■ (From *The Endless Party* by Etienne Delessert. Illustrated by the author.)

WORK IN PROGRESS: Adult books; editorial work; work; paintings; watercolors.

SIDELIGHTS: **January 4, 1941.** Born in Lausanne, Switzerland. ''My mother died when I was fifteen days old. I was raised by my stepmother, who was a great storyteller, and who influenced my creative development tremendously. One of my earliest memories is of the day we met. I can still recall exactly what she wore and where I was standing when I first saw her, though I was only two years old. The stories she told were of her own invention; she was best at dialogue and situation. I'm

sure she would have made a fine playwright. We often acted out simple scenarios together which resembled Beckett plays—no sets, no props, no costumes—just long endless monologues in which I would attempt to become a tree or animal. If my stepmother had to stop this activity to run an errand, I would go on for hours by myself. It was very good training for my imagination, and as an only child, it taught me how to play by myself.

''As a small child I spent long summers in the countryside. I knew all about plants, animals, and insects and often went on

(From *La Belle et la Bête* [*The Beauty and the Beast*] by Marie Catherine D'Aulnoy. Illustrated by Etienne Delessert.)

walks through the forest accompanied by my father. He would sit still for hours and wait for birds and little mice to come and eat from his hand. These walks and my country summers made a strong impression on me. I learned about colors and smells and the feel of animals and landscape first-hand.

''I had profound respect for my father. An eminent Swiss minister, he was a great man, very open-minded and talented, able to discuss mechanics with a mechanic, law with a lawyer, medicine with a doctor. This impressed me deeply. He died when I was eighteen and only just beginning to find my own identity. I would have liked to have had more time to share with him.

''I started drawing Walt Disney characters, portraits and caricatures when I was eight years old. At fourteen, I came across a passage by Andre Malraux stating that 'in our century, the only possible art is abstract art.' Malraux, I then thought, could not be wrong. The truth is, I could never quite relate to that sentiment, and know what a stupid statement it was. Very early on, I became interested with the idea of visual communication, with the translation of ideas into visuals, with telling stories with art. I still have the same approach to my drawings that I had when I was twenty.

''I had classical training in Greek and Latin, but was always more interested in the fairy tales and fables of Northern Ger-

Poster for a French exhibition "The Magic and Wit of European Illustration," 1982.

"Now," said the Cat, "I will sing the Baby a song that shall keep him asleep for an hour." And he began to purr, loud and low, low and loud,…. ■ (From "The Cat That Walked by Himself" in *Just So Stories* by Rudyard Kipling. Illustrated by Etienne Delessert.)

many, Eastern Europe and Scandinavia. Much like in the northern fables, I have looked into the shadows and the fog for monsters and witches.''

1962. He was established in Paris, making a name for himself with a number of successful advertising campaigns and editorial illustrations which were published in leading European magazines. ''After high school, I worked at Studio Maffei in Lausanne for three years, learning the graphic trade. At twenty-one, I moved to Paris where I worked as an art director, conceiving and designing campaigns. I did editorial illustration for many magazines, ranging from *Fortune* to *Playboy*. I liked to read the story as a whole, and then try to sum it up with a visual interpretation.

''I'm a storyteller, and I love to tell stories. I was attracted to children's books because they are a medium in which I can develop a story through text and illustrations on several levels. Picture books are closely related to film, which also play with images and text.''

1965. Moved to the United States. ''I decided to come to the States to do more magazine illustration, work in advertising, and break into the field of children's books. Tomi Ungerer introduced me to some American publishers. Unfortunately, I was given manuscripts which I didn't care for, and to complicate matters, I was very unhappy about the idea of having to do my own color separations by hand, which was common at the time. So I waited for a year and a half until I could meet the art director at Quist, who was in the process of creating a line of children's books. I was excited by the prospect of working in full color with great freedom, and so became part of a group of six illustrators who were published in Quist's first line of children's books. It was an exciting endeavor and wonderful to be part of a small group of artists who pioneered new forms of children's book illustration. We later discovered, however, that Quist's Publishing House was mismanaged, and after two or three books, it was impossible for me to continue with him.

''In 1967, I suggested that Quist ask French 'playwright of the absurd' Eugene Ionesco to write a children's book. I had hoped that he would write a long piece, a sort of *Alice in Wonderland* of our time. I was surprised when I received four very short texts from him and didn't know how to approach them. I thought about it for more than a month and finally decided that since all of the characters were named Jacqueline, they should all look the same as well. When all of the Jacquelines started to wear the same kinds of jail stripes, the illustration became a social comment on conformity: it finally worked. Talking to Ionesco, I was amazed that his ideas about children's books were quite British, so proper and realistic. Still, he was very pleased with my surrealistic illustrations. At some point, I would like to reissue the two books we did together, since they disappeared with Quist.''

1969. ''I decided to send some of my books to the Swiss child psychologist Jean Piaget, to see what he felt about them. I was disturbed over the fact that some people regarded them beyond the grasp of children—too 'avant-garde.' I did not feel that they were in any way too sophisticated for children, and wrote to Piaget, asking his opinion. He understood and loved the books. We met, and after several hours of discussion, decided to work on a project together. Based on what five- and six-year-old children might know about natural phenomenon such as the sun, the moon, the rain, we were interested in investigating their interpretation of the world. This story eventually became the book *How the Mouse was Hit on the Head by a Stone and So Discovered the World.*

''Piaget was also interested in testing my drawings to see what children actually saw in them. He knew quite a bit about what children put in their own drawings, but had never explored how children *read* pictures by adults. We collaborated on setting up classes in different schools for months. I learned much from him and his assistant, Odile Mosimann, about the way children react. They read pictures differently than adults: they go from detail to detail, add them up, and see the final picture. Adults, on the other hand, see the complete picture and then go to the details.

''One of the most interesting discoveries was that five- and six-year-olds have their own interpretation of how the sun and moon rise and set, interpretations which are somewhat similar to some ancient Mexican and African legends. Big hands, for example, throw the sun into the sky at dawn, and catch it back at sunset. We asked children to make their own drawings illustrating the story we had built together. Without knowing it, the children made drawings very similar to my own.''

1973. Back in Europe, Delessert worked in Paris as art director for ''Record,'' a magazine for teenagers. He also founded in Lausanne, Switzerland the Carabosse Studios [Carabosse is the bad fairy who cast a spell on Sleeping Beauty]. At the studio he produced television commercials as well as animated films for children, some of which were created for ''Sesame Street.'' He also began work on an animated feature film ''Supersaxo,'' an adaptation of a Swiss novel by Maurice Chappaz, in which mythological heroes are pitted against the tycoons of industry and politics. ''I worked on designing characters and creating concepts and hired assistants to do the actual animation of my drawings.

''Along with highly skilled animators, I collaborated mostly with young illustrators who wanted to work with me and learn the trade. I tried to show them how to solve problems, how to visualize a text and how to come up with concepts for books, posters, magazine illustration and film. I had the responsibility of making things work with up to forty illustrators and animators, and it became very heavy structure. The positive aspect of having the studio was that it became like a school of illustration. Young illustrators worked with me and slowly created their own styles. Several have become fine artists.

''Some of the financial backers of the feature film had serious problems, and we had to interrupt production while two thirds of the material was completed. This sad and costly event made me decide to close Carabosse and to work by myself again.''

1977. Established Editions Tournesol [''Sunflower''] and published a line of children's books which won international acclaim. ''I did quite a bit of book designing and production and was involved in all other aspects of book publishing. This experience made me confident about starting my own company. I needed to work in association with a good distributor and approached French publisher Gallimard. The endeavor was a success, and some of the books, such as the 'Yok-Yok' or the 'Nature Books' series, eventually sold in many other countries.''

Delessert's character, Yok-Yok, has been featured in his animated films and in a series of books, which have been released in a dozen countries. ''The 'Yok-Yok' books were based on 150 ten-second animated films. When I first made the films for Swiss television I wanted to base them on nature. I wanted to answer such questions as 'Why does a woodpecker tap on a tree trunk?' and 'What do frogs eat?' with animation. We did pilots but felt that something was missing and created a

(From *Die Maus und was ihr bleibt* [*Amelia Mouse and Her Great-Great-Grandchild*] by Anne van der Essen. Illustrated by Etienne Delessert.)

character to link all the films. Yok-Yok was my first attempt to create a real 'character' and I feared at first that my drawings did not lend themselves to a cartoon style. Snoopy is not a real dog, and Mickey is not a mouse. They are animals which have been transformed into human caricatures. Yok-Yok is a magical character with a soft face, neither a boy nor a girl, a radical departure from the usual cartoon characters.

"I am interested by the whole concept of character creation, of what makes a character popular, successful, and enduring. I feel it has something to do with a combination of realistic, human qualities, and a decorative, intellectual creation of graphic forms. There is something unknown, some element which could be compared to the melody of a song. A great melody can withstand bad orchestration, it has a story line, which is equivalent to the essence of a successful character. It was wonderful to find that children in Swiss, German and French schools have asked their teachers to play Yok-Yok scenarios for school shows, or parades at Christmas. They made wonderful costumes with big red hats of different materials. I was also surprised to see how well the children related to the short, spontaneous format of the books and ten-second films; they would enter effortlessly into Yok-Yok's world. Perhaps it was the idea of bringing nature and animals to city life with fantasy."

1982. "American art director and designer Rita Marshall and I designed and produced a line of fairy tales for Swiss publisher Edipresse in collaboration with French publisher Grasset and Creative Education, a Minnesota publishing house with whom we have been collaborating for several years. I met Creative Education editor Ann Redpath at the Bologna International Bookfair where we presented the books of Editions Tournesol. She asked if we would be interested in becoming graphic consultants for Creative Education and discussed the possibility of doing a series of fairy tales. Rita and I selected a wonderful group of artists from the States and Europe, some of whom had never created a children's book. Our involvement was much more than merely art directing the project. We also co-edited and supervised the production of the twenty titles. Photographer Sarah Moon, for example, had worked mainly in advertising. We assigned her *Little Red Riding Hood,*

and her dark interpretation won the grand prize at the 1984 Bologna International Bookfair. Marshall Arisman works in editorial illustration. His images are usually violent, so we chose for him *Fitcher's Bird,* another version of *Bluebeard.* Many fairy tales are illustrated and interpreted too sweetly, even when the story itself is quite strong. I feel it is important to use visuals which are equivalent in strength to the text. Fairy tales usually work to open the reader up, to give him a kind of psychological help; while some images of the tale may be violent or bizarre, by the end, things are resolved and open. These great stories bring out the fears, loneliness and violence that a person must face in order to move into peace and harmony.

"*Little Red Riding Hood* ends with the girl being eaten by the wolf. I saw no reason to rewrite it, or to use other 'sweeter' versions such as the Brothers Grimm. We used the Perrault original text, and Sarah Moon set the story in Paris in the forties, using very disturbing, black and white photographs. You should not present children with sugar coated versions of reality. You have to expose them to all kinds of experiences, especially with a sense of humor and a sense of the bizarre with surrealistic situations which open them up to another kind of reality, another point of view. The more questions children ask, the more exposed they are to different points of view and different ways of solving problems, and the better they'll live a balanced adult life.

"The idea of shedding different light on a problem is important in children's books. As in *Rashomon*—the same story is told several times with a different perspective. After all, truth is not one sided, not only what you see on T.V. or read in the papers, or what your parents tell you, or what you learn in school: truth is also what *you* see and how you perceive the unknown forces of the world, how you face birth, life, decay and death. That has been, I believe, the essence of my books.

"I have always maintained control over the design of my books. Over the years, I have learned how to combine cold and warm colors in a precise way which is easy to color separate. I want even the smallest details to be clear, so I work usually at the

(From *Conte numéro 1 pour enfants de moins de trois ans* [*Story Number One for Children under Three Years of Age*] by Eugéne Ionesco. Illustrated by Etienne Delessert.)

same size. Rita Marshall and I collaborate closely with photoengravers and printers to insure a high quality reproduction. For most of the books we publish, we personally oversee the production every step of the way. Many aspects of the final printing are a matter of taste, and if you're not there to decide, for example, how light or dark you want the typography to be printed, the person in charge of the printing press will decide for you. It's similar to filmmaking, where the director has to follow every stage of the production.''

Delessert's own technique in creating a book is to ''begin with the story. I begin by reading or writing a text, then play visual games and make interpretations. I have to be completely calm and undistracted by music or noise during this part of the process. When I'm relaxed, it doesn't take too long to find an idea. Once I find an approach, I draw tiny sketches. Everything is included in the sketches—the design of the page, the proportions, and the atmosphere. Then I begin the actual illustration, usually working at the same size that the piece will eventually be printed. On tracing paper, I make quick sketches in pencil, then I transfer the sketch and redraw it on paper, using a fine pen to create outlines and details. I'll use watercolor, pencils and pen again. Sometimes I finish with several layers of varnish.

''Reference material is important for some subjects. I have books and files with reference material because I like to use elements of reality in my drawings. I think a drawing, even a surrealistic one, is richer when it is based on reality, a reality transformed and interpreted.

''I take at least two or three months to do a book. In some ways, I get more pleasure out of conceiving an idea than executing it. I love to make the little thumbnail sketches. But after that, there is a long period which is simply craft—slowly executing what you intended—which sometimes makes me impatient. The very last part of drawing, the polishing, the 'making it work,' interests me again, but I don't like that in-between, very technical and painstaking stage.''

Some of the books created by Delessert deal with environmental problems such as noise pollution, poison in food, and waste disposal. ''One of my deepest concerns is that people would begin to understand ecology and preservation, not as a trend, but as something of vital importance to everyone. The books I've done about pollution, toxins, the balance of life and death, are a way of expressing this concern. I'm interested in making little children aware of the balance and conservation of nature. It is a matter of survival.''

Delessert and his wife, Rita Marshall, live and work in Lakeville, Connecticut. A major part of his time is now devoted to painting and drawing. His work is represented in private collections in Europe and in the United States.

How the Mouse Was Hit on the Head by a Stone was adapted by Nathalie Nat into a play that was staged in Geneva, Switzerland, produced by the Amstramgram Theater Group. Delessert designed the costumes and settings.

HOBBIES AND OTHER INTERESTS: Work.

FOR MORE INFORMATION SEE: Idea (Japan), number 66, 1964, number 71, 1965; *Graphis,* number 128, 1967, number 208, 1979-80, number 235, 1985; *New York Times,* August 22, 1971; Jacques Chessex, *Les dessins d'Etienne Delessert,* Bertil Galland, 1974; *Catalogue du Musée des Arts décoratifs du Louvre,* Paris, 1975; *Novum gebrauchs graphik,* January 1, 1976; Lee Kingman and others, compilers, *Illustrators of*

Children's Books: 1967-1976, Horn Book, 1978; *Print,* April, 1986.

DENZEL, Justin F(rancis) 1917-

PERSONAL: Born January 15, 1917, in Clifton, N.J.; son of George and Alvina (Munzell) Denzel; married Josephine Ogazaly, 1947. *Education:* Attended New Jersey State Teachers College (now William Paterson College of New Jersey), 1939, and University of California, Los Angeles, 1940. *Politics:* Independent. *Religion:* Roman Catholic. *Home:* 73 Livingston St., Clifton, N.J. 07013.

CAREER: Has worked as a field naturalist for American Museum of Natural History, New York, N.Y., sailed on oceanographic vessel, *Atlantis,* collected marine life in Alaska, and as a scientific librarian with Hoffman La Roche in Nutley, N.J.; writer. *Military service:* U.S. Army, 1941-45; became sergeant; received Purple Heart. *Awards, honors:* New Jersey Association of Teachers of English Award, 1972, for *Genius with a Scalpel: Harvey Cushing,* and 1973, for *Jumbo: Giant Circus Elephant;* New Jersey Institute of Technology Award, 1971, for *Genius with a Scalpel: Harvey Cushing,* 1973 and 1975, for *Jumbo: Giant Circus Elephant,* 1975, for *Black Kettle: King of the Wild Horses,* 1976, for *Wild Wing: Great Hunting Eagle,* 1977, for *Snowfoot: White Reindeer of the Arctic,* 1978, for *Scat: The Movie Cat,* and 1981, for *Sampson: Yankee Stallion; Wild Wing: Great Hunting Eagle* was chosen as a Children's Book of the Year by the Child Study Association of America, 1976.

WRITINGS—Juvenile; published by Garrard, except as indicated: *Adventure North* (biography), Abelard, 1968; *Champion of Liberty* (biography), Messner, 1969; *Genius with a Scalpel: Harvey Cushing* (biography), Messner, 1971; *Jumbo:*

JUSTIN F. DENZEL

The boy ran after him, shouting and throwing handfuls of snow. ■ (From *Sampson: Yankee Stallion* by Justin F. Denzel. Illustrated by William Hutchinson.)

Giant Circus Elephant (illustrated by Richard Amundsen), 1973; *Black Kettle: King of the Wild Horses* (illustrated by R. Amundsen), 1974; *Wild Wing: Great Hunting Eagle* (illustrated by Herman B. Vestal), 1975; *Snowfoot: White Reindeer of the Arctic* (illustrated by Taylor Oughton), 1976; *Scat: The Movie Cat* (illustrated by H. B. Vestal), 1977; *Sampson: Yankee Stallion* (illustrated by William Hutchinson), 1980; *Hiboy: Young Devil Horse* (illustrated by Sam Svitt), 1980.

Contributor of more than one-hundred short stories and articles to periodicals, including *Coronet, American Mercury, Frontiers, Twelve/Fifteen, Catholic Boy, Venture,* and *Snowy Egret.*

WORK IN PROGRESS: A juvenile science-fiction novel, *The Secret of the Shining Stone.*

SIDELIGHTS: "As a boy I used to scribble long essays on nature, most of them glaring imitations of William Beebe or some other popular naturalist of the day. Years later, while in Alaska, I began writing with more serious intent, editing and writing for a little newspaper called *The Alaskan,* sponsored by the U.S. Forest Service. As a roving reporter I was free to tour the country turning out stories on whales, bears, eagles and other wildlife, plus articles on commercial and sports fishing, native Indians and the many and varied activities of the U.S. Forest Service. For almost two years I had a field day, living a foot-loose, freewheeling existence that any outdoor writer would envy.

"With the advent of World War II the gravy-train ended and I joined the army, serving as a tank gunner in Europe. At the same time I wrote combat news for regimental and divisional newspapers (84th Infantry's *The Railsplitter*), occasionally landing in *Stars and Stripes.*

"After the war I holed-up in a little cabin in the hills to write the 'Great American Novel,' mostly about Africa (I'd never been there). It's still sitting on the shelf.

"I gave up writing for a while then started again in the late fifties, writing for a few national magazines and many smaller ones. At that time there were dozens of denominational publications aimed at teenagers. A wonderful and avid market for short stories, 2000 to 2500 words, it demanded tight, concise writing with little room for fancy description of purple prose. Plot was essential, fast and realistic with plenty of action, both psychological and physical. Every word had to count. It was an excellent training ground. I wrote a hundred or more stories and became so imbued with its structure and style that, even now, after many years, I find it difficult to write any other way.

"At one time or another I've produced almost every genre on the market—biography, science, history, adventure, mystery, science fiction and more. I've occasionally written for adults but I seem to find my niche in the juveniles for the eight to twelve-year old age group. This is not to fault the adult world, it's merely that my concepts and values seemed to have remained at about that age level.

"I'm eternally grateful for what little talent I possess. Win, lose or draw I guess I'll go on plugging away until either I or my typewriter wear out completely.

"It's a crazy business, this writing. Just when you're sure you've written a best seller it comes flying back with a little note attached, 'No thanks.' Next time around you write something you're sure will be rejected and it sells fifteen to twenty thousand copies. (That's a best seller in my league.)

"But for anyone who likes to write, who likes to play with words and juggle ideas and characters, there's nothing more exciting, no trade, no craft or profession in the world that can beat it."

HOBBIES AND OTHER INTERESTS: Natural history.

DeWEESE, Thomas Eugene 1934- (Gene DeWeese; Jean DeWeese; Thomas Stratton, Victoria Thomas, joint pseudonyms)

PERSONAL: Born January 31, 1934, in Rochester, Ind.; son of Thomas Jacob and Alfreda (a print shop worker; maiden name, Henning) DeWeese; married Beverly Joanne Amers (a librarian), May, 1955. *Education:* Valparaiso Technical Institute, associate degree in electronic engineering, 1953; also attended University of Wisconsin—Milwaukee, Indiana University, and Marquette University. *Politics:* Independent. *Religion:* None. *Home and office:* 2718 North Prospect, Milwaukee, Wis. 53211. *Agent:* Booklength, Sharon Jarvis, Inc., 260 Willard Ave., Staten Island, N.Y. 10314; and Larry Sternig Literary Agency, 742 N. Robertson, Milwaukee, Wis. 53213.

CAREER: Delco Radio, Kokomo, Ind., technician, 1954-59; Delco Electronics, Milwaukee, Wis., technical writer, 1959-74; free-lance writer, 1974—. *Member:* Science Fiction Writers of America, Mystery Writers of America. *Awards, honors:*

THOMAS EUGENE DeWEESE

Award for the best novel, 1976, for *Jeremy Case,* and 1982, for *A Different Darkness,* and award for best juvenile book, 1979, for *Major Corby and the Unidentified Flapping Object,* all from Council for Wisconsin Writers; *Computers in Entertainment and the Arts* was selected as a Notable Science Book of the Year by the National Science Teachers of America, 1984.

WRITINGS—Novels; under name Gene DeWeese: (With Robert Coulson) *Gates of the Universe* (science fiction), Laser Books, 1975; (with R. Coulson) *Now You See It/Him/Them . . .* (science fiction), Doubleday, 1976, large print edition, G. K. Hall, 1976; *Jeremy Case* (science fiction), Laser Books, 1976; (with R. Coulson) *Charles Fort Never Mentioned Wombats* (science fiction), Doubleday, 1977; *Major Corby and the Unidentified Flapping Object* (juvenile science fiction), Doubleday, 1979.

The Wanting Factor (horror), Playboy Press, 1980; *Nightmares from Space* (juvenile science fiction; illustrated with photographs by Susan Kuklin), F. Watts, 1981; *A Different Darkness* (horror), PBJ Books, 1982; *Something Answered* (horror), Dell, 1983; *The Adventures of a Two-Minute Werewolf* (juvenile science fiction; illustrated by Ronald Fritz), Doubleday, 1983; (with R. Coulson) *Nightmare Universe* (science fiction, based on *Gates of the Universe*), TSR, 1985; *Black Suits from Outer Space* (juvenile science fiction), Putnam, 1985; *The Dandelion Caper* (juvenile science fiction; sequel to *Black Suits from Outer Space*), Putnam, 1986.

Novels; under pseudonym Jean DeWeese: *The Reimann Curse* (Gothic fantasy), Ballantine, 1975; *The Moonstone Spirit* (Gothic fantasy), Ballantine, 1975; *The Carnelian Cat* (Gothic fantasy), Ballantine, 1975; *Web of Guilt* (Gothic novel), Ballantine, 1976, large print edition, John Curley, 1977; *Cave of the Moaning Wind* (Gothic fantasy), Ballantine, 1976, large print edition, John Curley, 1977; *The Doll with Opal Eyes* (romantic suspense), Doubleday, 1976; *Nightmare in Pewter* (Gothic fantasy), Doubleday, 1978; *Hour of the Cat* (mystery), Doubleday, 1980; *The Backhoe Gothic* (Gothic mystery), Doubleday, 1981.

Science fiction; with R. Coulson, under joint pseudonym Thomas Stratton: *The Invisibility Affair: Man from U.N.C.L.E., No. 11,* Ace Books, 1967; *The Mind-Twisters Affair: Man from U.N.C.L.E., No. 12,* Ace Books, 1967; (contributor) L. Sprague de Camp and George Scithers, *The Conan Grimoire: Essays in Swordplay and Sorcery,* Mirage Press, 1972.

Romance novel; with Connie Kugi, under joint pseudonym Victoria Thomas: *Ginger's Wish,* Doubleday, in press.

Nonfiction; under name Gene DeWeese: *Fundamentals of Space Navigation* (four-volume programmed text), NASA, 1968; *Fundamentals of Digital Computers,* GM, 1972; *Fundamentals of Integrated Circuits* (two-volume programmed text), GM, 1972; (with Gini Rogowski) *Making American Folk Art Dolls,* Chilton, 1975; *Computers in Entertainment and the Arts* (juvenile nonfiction), F. Watts, 1984.

And when the mistball got within a dozen or so yards, we could see that something was swirling around inside the mist,.... ■ (Jacket illustration by Stephan Marchesi from *Major Corby and the Unidentified Flapping Object* by Gene DeWeese.)

Science fiction reviewer, *Milwaukee Journal*, 1980-84, *Science Fiction Review*, 1980—, *Comic Buyers Guide*, 1985—, *The Crazy Shepherd*, 1985—, and *Midwest Book Review*, 1985—. Contributor of short stories and articles to periodicals, including *Galileo, Stellar SF, Magazine of Fantasy and Science Fiction, Amazing Stories, Mike Shayne's Mystery Magazine, Woman's World*, and *Milwaukee Journal*, and in various anthologies.

ADAPTATIONS: "The Adventures of a Two-Minute Werewolf" (two-part ABC Weekend Special), ABC-TV, February-March, 1985.

WORK IN PROGRESS: A mystery novel.

SIDELIGHTS: "The first thing I remember writing was in grade school, something about Mickey Mouse, I think, inspired by one of his science-fictional adventures in Walt Disney comics. The first thing actually printed was probably an account of an ice storm in the high school paper, which was printed as an insert in the *Rochester News Sentinel*. The first money I ever got for anything I wrote was for a series of articles on local people and businesses and a science fiction column for the same *News Sentinel*. I was still in high school, and I got the magnificent sum of a nickel per column inch. Between that and my first 'professional fiction' sale were lots of 'payment-in-contributor's-copies' contributions to science fiction amateur magazines (fanzines) such as *Yandro, Indiana Fantasy, Fan-Fare*, and the *Chigger Patch of Fandom*.

"That first professional sale was a 'Man from U.N.C.L.E.' novel, a collaboration with Robert Coulson under the name Thomas Stratton. It was made primarily because the editor of the series happened to subscribe to a fanzine Coulson and his wife published and because she (Juanita Coulson, who had already sold a couple of science fiction novels) didn't really want to do an 'U.N.C.L.E.' novel when said editor offered her the chance. All of which partially explains why the dedication page reads, 'To Serendipity.'

"Incidentally, that book, *The Invisibility Affair*, may have the distinction of being the only book for which the text was accepted but the title, authors' names and dedication were all rejected. The original title, "The Invisible Dirigible Affair," was too long for their cover format (though it was restored in the French translation). Using two names was considered too confusing, no explanation given. Then, with only one author's name appearing on the cover, the original dedication, 'To my wives and child,' was considered too racy for the intended preteen audience, which I suppose shows how things have changed in the last twenty years.

"Since then I've plowed through twenty-odd books of various sorts and varying quality, with *Major Corby, Hour of the Cat, Jeremy Case, The Wanting Factor*, and *Something Answered* at the top of my own personal list of favorites. As you can tell from the books listed above, I've written in a number of fields, but one book, *The Doll with Opal Eyes*, may have established a record of sorts on its own, having been published in the U.S. as a hardcover 'romantic suspense,' in England as a straight crime novel, in France and Argentina as a romance, and again in the U.S. as a paperback occult horror.

"The science fiction, however, is usually the most rewarding, and in early 1986 it was doubly so. As one of the science-fiction writers invited to the Jet Propulsion Laboratory for the Uranus Voyager Encounter, I was able to watch the pictures as they came in from two billion miles in space. It was fascinating and a bit awesome, especially to someone who had

I guess I really lucked out the first time I turned into a werewolf. For one thing, it only lasted a couple of minutes. For another, the only person with me was Cindy Deardorf. ■ (From *The Adventures of a Two-Minute Werewolf* by Gene DeWeese. Illustrated by Ronald Fritz.)

been reading and writing about fictional space travel for over forty years.

"To close on a more down-to-earth note, the only 'advice' I've ever gotten that has been consistently helpful (and consistently difficult to follow) is simply, 'If you want to be a writer, sit down and *write!*' Don't dream about it or talk about it or read about it—do it. (Having a spouse with a steady job doesn't hurt, either.)"

DeWeese's works are included in the de Grummond Collection of the University of Southern Mississippi. His novels and short stories have been translated into other languages, including Japanese, French, Danish, Spanish, Italian, Dutch, and German.

FOR MORE INFORMATION SEE: Peter Nicholas, *The Encyclopedia of Science Fiction: An Illustrated A to Z*, Grenada, 1979.

A good tale is none the worse for being twice told.
—Proverb

DUANE, Diane (Elizabeth) 1952-

BRIEF ENTRY: Born May 18, 1952, in New York, N.Y. A former registered and psychiatric nurse, Duane has been a freelance novelist and television writer since 1978. She has worked as a staff writer for Filmation Studios and currently is the manager of Lioncelle Enterprises, a graphics company. As an author, Duane gained critics' notice with her science fiction and fantasy novels for young adults. Upon the publication of *The Door into Fire* (Dell, 1979), she was hailed by *Publishers Weekly* as a writer who "expands the limits of the sword and sorcery genre." The story follows the passage to adulthood of Herewiss, a young sorcerer who inhabits a world where bisexuality is the socially accepted form of interpersonal relationships and the worshipped deity is a goddess. In 1984 Duane produced *The Door into Shadow* (Bluejay Books). In this sequel, Herewiss is joined by Segnbora, a swordswoman and sorceress, in battle against the evil and threatening Shadow. A reviewer for *Kliatt,* although warning against the novel's unconventional and sometimes graphic sexuality, labeled the work "remarkable and well worth reading for the author's beautiful management of her fertile imagination."

Duane received similar praise for *So You Want to Be a Wizard?* (Delacorte, 1983), which features two novice wizards who set out to save all the light and goodness in the universe. "A splendid, unusual fantasy . . . ," observed *Horn Book,* "[that] stands between the works of Diana Wynne Jones . . . and those of Madeleine L'Engle." *School Library Journal* added that the "spells are complex, yet entirely logical. . . . [The] alternate world . . . is well structured and believable; the bridges between reality and fantasy are deftly handled." In a sequel, *Deep Wizardry* (Delacorte, 1985), the same young wizards assume the form of whales to partake of a powerful ceremony of sacrifice and redemption. "Deeply resonant, provocative, and moving," noted *Washington Post Book World.* "The descriptions of the world under water are precise, poetic, and masterful." The editors of *School Library Journal* chose *Deep Wizardry* one of the "Best Books 1985." In 1986 it appeared on *Voice of Youth Advocate*'s list of best science fiction and fantasy titles for young adults, along with *The Door into Shadow.*

Duane also wrote *The Wounded Sky* (Pocket/Timescape, 1983) and *My Enemy, My Ally* (Pocket, 1984), both based on the popular television series "Star Trek." *Booklist* called *The Wounded Sky* "a rare and wonderful thing—a Star Trek novel that . . . stands on its own . . . [with] brisk pacing, wit, intelligent characterizations, and an array of interesting aliens." *Home:* 617 Conshohocken State Rd., Bala Cynwyd, Pa. 19004.

FOR MORE INFORMATION SEE: Who's Who of American Women, 14th edition, Marquis, 1984.

DUNREA, Olivier 1953-

BRIEF ENTRY: Born September 22, 1953, in Virginia Beach, Va. An author and illustrator of picture books for children, Dunrea graduated from West Chester State College in 1975 with a B.A. in theater arts and music and did further study at Washington State University. Prior to the publication of his first book in 1983, Dunrea worked variously as a waiter, an administrative assistant, an artist-in-residence for the National Endowment for the Arts and Delaware State Arts Council, a management consultant, and a free-lance illustrator. Dunrea believes that "childhood should be a magical time. . . . The stories I write are fast paced, economically written, and present characters and adventures that I would have liked to have

experienced as a child." *Publishers Weekly* described him as an author-illustrator capable of creating "an aura of sweetness, feelings emanating from quaint characters that readers take to their hearts." In a review of *Eddy B, Pigboy* (Atheneum, 1983), *Wilson Library Bulletin* called the opening portraits "tender, candid characterizations of small-time farmers." Likewise, *Horn Book* labeled *Fergus and Bridey* (Holiday House, 1985) a "simple story . . . [with] uncluttered art, executed with a bright palette." Dunrea's other picture books are *Ravena* (Holiday House, 1984) and *Mogwogs on the March!* (Holiday House, 1985). His latest work is *Skara Brae: The Story of a Prehistoric Village* (Holiday House, 1986), the first in a planned series of books on prehistoric life. *Home and office:* 214 Wendover St., Philadelphia, Pa. 19128.

FOR MORE INFORMATION SEE: Philadelphia Inquirer, February 26, 1981, February 17, 1982; *Sunday News Journal* (Wilmington, Del.), December 12, 1982; *Bucks County* (Pa.) *Courier Times,* November 16, 1984.

EASTMAN, P(hilip) D(ey) 1909-1986

OBITUARY NOTICE—See sketch in *SATA* Volume 33: Born November 25, 1909, in Amherst, Mass.; died of pneumonia, January 7, 1986, in Cresskill, N.J. Film producer and author and illustrator of children's books. Eastman worked for Warner Brothers Cartoons and Disney Studios prior to World War II. As a member of the Army Signal Corps, he produced army orientation films. For seven years, he worked in the story department of United Productions of America in Hollywood, where he was one of the creators of the "Gerald McBoing Boing" film, the first non-Disney animated movie to win an Academy Award. Eastman, who attended Amherst College and Art School of the National Academy, began producing free-lance educational and commercial animated films in New York during the 1950s. In 1958 he wrote and illustrated his first children's book, *Sam and the Firefly.* His best-known work, *Are You My Mother?,* appeared two years later and has since sold over one-and-a-half million copies. Eastman's other self-illustrated books include *Big Dog . . . Little Dog: A Bedtime Story, The Alphabet Book, Go, Dog, Go!,* and *What Time Is It?* He also collaborated with Roy McKie on *Snow* and with Theodor Geisel on *The Cat in the Hat Beginner Book Dictionary by the Cat Himself.* Eastman's works have been translated into ten languages.

FOR MORE INFORMATION SEE: Illustrators of Children's Books: 1957-1966, Horn Book, 1968; *Authors of Books for Young People,* 2nd edition, Scarecrow, 1971; *Contemporary Authors,* Volume 107, Gale, 1983. Obituaries: *New York Times,* January 11, 1986; *Publishers Weekly,* January 31, 1986; *AB Bookman's Weekly,* February 17, 1986; *School Library Journal,* March, 1986.

FARQUHARSON, Alexander 1944-

PERSONAL: Born June 13, 1944, in Boston, Mass.; son of Malcolm W. (in the shipbuilding industry) and Clara L. (an artist; maiden name, Chapman) Farquharson; married Donna E. Gertler (a psychiatric counselor), August 21, 1977; children: Rachel. *Education:* Case Institute of Technology, B.S., 1966; attended School of the Museum of Fine Arts, Boston, Mass., 1969-73. *Home and office:* 16 Adams St., Marlborough, Mass. 01752.

CAREER: Boston Center for Adult Education, Boston, Mass., instructor, 1975—; DeCordova Museum School, Lincoln,

ALEXANDER FARQUHARSON

Mass., instructor, 1982—; School of the Worcester Art Museum, Worcester, Mass., instructor, 1982—; Lesley College, Cambridge, Mass., faculty member, 1985—. *Exhibitions:* Ainsworth Gallery, Boston, Mass., 1978; Gallery of World Art, Newton, Mass., 1980; Baak Gallery, Cambridge, Mass., 1982; Francesca Anderson Gallery, Boston, Mass., 1983. *Military service:* U.S. Army, 1967-69; achieved rank of E-4.

ILLUSTRATOR—Juvenile: George S. Fichter, *How the Plains Indians Lived,* McKay, 1980; George Laycock and Ellen Laycock, *How the Settlers Lived,* McKay, 1980; Stephen Krensky, *Conqueror and Hero: The Search for Alexander,* Little, Brown, 1981.

Contributor of illustrations to textbooks for Houghton Mifflin and Ginn, and to Houghton Mifflin "English" series, 1982. Also illustrator of adult and juvenile book jackets. Contributor of illustrations to periodicals.

WORK IN PROGRESS: The Best of the North End for Addison-Wesley; *The Dear Leap* by M. Grimes for Little, Brown; jacket illustration for *Her Majesty's Murder* by Beth Hilgartner, for Houghton.

SIDELIGHTS: "It's little wonder that with both my parents being artistically inclined, I decided early on to be an artist. My mother, a native of the Boston area, attended the Massachusetts School of Art and went on to work for a time in a greeting card studio. I can vividly remember how awe-struck my young eyes were when one day I secretly opened her school portfolio. My father was born in Glasgow, Scotland, and immigrated to the United States in 1923. His grandfather was a painter noted for his grazing sheep in the Scottish Highlands. Primarily self-taught, my father managed to take art correspondence courses and paint landscapes while working as a seaman on a steamship line and later in the ship building in-

dustry. His maxim 'draw it as you see it' has always served me well, and he ignited my early interest in painting. My one older brother, Colin, has found photography and the lore of the sea his main passions. We had a successful collaboration on an etching series of New England lighthouses.

"My ambition to be an artist took a temporary back seat to astronomy in my teens, and it was not until I began my undergraduate studies at Case Institute of Technology that my first love returned. The campus was surrounded by cultural stimuli, with the Cleveland Orchestra across the street and the Cleveland Art Museum close by. I can remember many an enchanted stroll through the art museum, and I'm sure it was there that my future in the arts began. Several years later this reawakening was further nourished by a year spent in Italy.

"My first children's book assignment, dealing with the life of the Plains Indians, was especially memorable. I knew virtually nothing about Indians at the outset, but by the end of the project I found myself buying many books on the subject. My wife and I were even seeking out pow-wows in our local area. This would be a pattern that repeated itself numerous times: my total immersion into the subject of my illustrations, whether it be pioneer living, Alexander the Great, or English mysteries.

The oracle was a woman who interpreted the will of the god Apollo through prophecies. ■ (From *Conqueror and Hero: The Search for Alexander* by Stephen Krensky. Illustrated by Alexander Farquharson.)

I guess I almost derive as much satisfaction from the researching as I do from the illustrating.

"Art also played a role in my first meeting with my wife. It was in an evening drawing class at Boston's Copley Society. In fact, we coincidentally met again at a Degas exhibit in Boston's Museum of Fine Arts, which led to our first date. Donna's interest and support of the arts has since been wonderful. During the summers, we try to get outside and paint together. Classical music concerts are also one of our favorite sources of entertainment. Our latest joy is our daughter, Rachel."

FUNAI, Mamoru (Rolland) 1932-

BRIEF ENTRY: Born June 7, 1932, in Kauai, Hawaii. Author and illustrator of books for children. Funai spent his childhood in Hawaii and was trained at the Honolulu Academy of Arts, Pittsburgh Institute of Art, and Cleveland Institute of Art. He graduated from the William Paterson College of New Jersey, then worked as a greeting card designer and a designer in advertising before moving to New York in 1962 to begin his career as a free-lance illustrator. Funai has illustrated over two dozen children's books, including Judy Delton's *On a Picnic* (Doubleday, 1979), which received the New Jersey Institute of Technology Award in 1980. The same award was conferred in 1973 for Funai's self-illustrated picture book *Moke and Poki in the Rain Forest* (Harper, 1972). The four tales about two menehunes, tiny people from Hawaiian folklore, and their animal friends are accompanied by three-color pictures of the rain forest. Funai's *Cartoons for Kids* (Prentice-Hall, 1977) contains twenty-two cartoon stories with simple themes in which, according to *School Library Journal,* "amusing drawings convey the humor well." Among his other illustrated works are Ishii Momoko's *The Dolls' Day for Yoshiko,* Roger Price's *The Last Little Dragon,* Catherine Woolley's *Mr. Turtle's Magic Glasses,* Robert A. Morris's *Dolphin,* Phyllis Krasilovsky's *The Man Who Cooked for Himself,* Betty Baker's *Rat Is Dead and Ant Is Sad,* and Nathaniel Benchley's *Running Owl the Hunter.*

FOR MORE INFORMATION SEE: Illustrators of Children's Books: 1957-1966, Horn Book, 1968.

MAURICE GEE

GEE, Maurice (Gough) 1931-

PERSONAL: Born August 22, 1931, in Whakatane, New Zealand; son of Leonard (a builder) and Lyndahl (Chapple) Gee; married Margaretha Hickman (a librarian), 1970; children: Nigel (from a previous marriage), Emily, Abigail. *Education:* Avondale College, M.A., 1949; University of Auckland, M.A., 1953; further study at Auckland Teachers College, 1954, and New Zealand Library School, 1966. *Home:* 125 Cleveland Tce., Nelson, New Zealand.

CAREER: Worked as teacher and at various odd jobs, 1955-65; Alexander Turnbull Library, Wellington, New Zealand, library assistant, 1967-69; Napier Public Library, Napier, New Zealand, city librarian, 1970-72; Teachers Colleges Library, Auckland, New Zealand, deputy librarian, 1974-75; writer, 1976—. *Member:* P.E.N., New Zealand Writers' Guild. *Awards, honors:* Scholarship from New Zealand Literary Fund, 1962, 1976, and 1986; Robert Burns Fellowship from University of Otago, 1964; award from New Zealand Literary Fund, 1965, for *A Special Flower,* and 1972, for *In My Father's Den;* Hubert Church Memorial Prize, 1972, for *In My Father's Den;* co-winner of New Zealand Book Award, 1975, for *A Glorious Morning, Comrade;* James Tait Black Memorial Prize, New Zealand Book Award, Buckland Literary Award, and Sir James Wattie New Zealand Book of the Year Award, all 1978, all for *Plumb;* New Zealand Book Award, and Buckland Literary Award, both 1981, both for *Meg;* New Zealand Children's Book of the Year Award, 1982, for *The Halfmen of O.*

WRITINGS: The Big Season (novel), Hutchinson, 1962; *A Special Flower* (novel), Hutchinson, 1965; *In My Father's Den* (novel), Faber, 1972; *A Glorious Morning, Comrade* (stories), Auckland University Press, 1975; *Games of Choice* (novel), Faber, 1976; *Plumb* (novel), Faber, 1978; *Under the Mountain* (juvenile), Oxford University Press, 1979, Merrimack, 1984; *The World around the Corner* (juvenile; illustrated by Gary Hebley), Oxford University Press, 1980, Merrimack, 1984; *Meg* (novel), Faber, 1981, St. Martin's, 1982; *The Halfmen of O* (juvenile), Oxford University Press, 1982, published as *The Halfmen of O,* Merrimack, 1983; *Sole Survivor* (novel), Faber, 1983, St. Martin's, 1984; *The Priests of Ferris* (juvenile), Oxford University Press, 1984; *Motherstone* (juvenile), Oxford University Press, 1985; *The Fire-raiser* (juvenile), Penguin (New Zealand), 1986; *Collected Stories,* Penguin, 1986.

Author of teleplays, including eight episodes of "Mortimer's Patch," and a filmplay, "Trespasses," 1984. Work represented in anthologies, including *New Authors Short Story I,* Hutchinson, 1961. Contributor to periodicals, including *Landfall, Mate,* and *Islands.*

ADAPTATIONS: "Under the Mountain" (seven-part serial), TVNZ (Television New Zealand), 1981; "The Fire-raiser" (five-part serial), TVNZ, 1986.

WORK IN PROGRESS: An adult novel.

SIDELIGHTS: "I grew up in a little town called Henderson, outside Auckland, a place of a dozen shops, a railway station, a boarding house, and not much more. Today Henderson has been swallowed by the city of Auckland, but then, in the thirties and forties, it was a place of farms, orchards, mushroom paddocks, blackberry patches, haystacks, draught horses, beehives—and, above all, the creek, Henderson creek. Looking back, I seem to have spent my boyhood swimming and eeling and sailing tin canoes and catching crayfish and diving from willow branches; and I suppose that's why creeks and streams keep coming into my stories.

"I went on from Henderson School to Avondale College, closer to the city, and then to Auckland University, and after that became a teacher—not because I wanted to but because I couldn't think of any other way to make a living. Secretly, I wanted to write, and I did write, all sorts of things, most of them pretty awful. I didn't write anything good until my mid-twenties, and that encouraged me to give up teaching and try to earn my living as a writer. So for ten years I did odd jobs—postman, window-cleaner, hospital porter, and so on—while writing stories. I didn't make much money but I learned a lot. Then I was married and had to get a regular job again, so I became a librarian. But somehow libraries had too many books, they seemed to stop me from writing my own. So we took a risk, my wife and I, and shifted with our two daughters to Nelson, a small city in the South Island of New Zealand, famous for its apple orchards, and I settled down to make my living as a writer. And here I am ten years later, still doing it, and loving it. And doing things I'd never attempted before—television plays, children's books.

"I came rather late to the writing of children's books, and to fantasy science fiction almost by accident. A friend lent me Alan Garner's *The Weirdstone of Brisingamen*. I read it with great enjoyment and decided it was the sort of thing I'd like to write myself. So my first children's book, *Under the Mountain*, had its beginning—and it's not really very much like Alan Garner's book after all. It's a book about Auckland—or rather, set in Auckland. There are extinct volcanic cones rising everywhere in that city, and also an explosion crater, a maar, filled with water, lying in the middle of the suburbs. Lake Pupuke is its name. I put them in the book because I used to walk past one of the hills, Mt. Eden, on my way to work; and, as I approached, it seemed to crouch behind the houses and hide itself, and then rear up and loom over the roofs—very sinister. I began to wonder if some strange creature, from another time, from another planet, might be hiding under the mountain. So the book began—and I had great fun writing it. It was very relaxing after writing adult novels.

"Since then I've kept on with children's books. My second, *The World around the Corner*, is set in Nelson, although it's part fantasy. If you look at Gary Hebley's illustrations you'll see Nelson and the river that runs below my house. The view from Caroline's lawn is the view from mine, and the hill, Botanical Hill, known locally as the Centre of New Zealand, is really there.

"Then I wrote the 'O' trilogy [includes *The Halfmen of O, The Priests of Ferris* and *Motherstone*], set on another planet. That brought me to the end of fantasy for a while. I'm trying to write something historical, about a man who burned down schools and shops in a little New Zealand town in 1915, and the children who set out to capture him. It's going along quite well. I hope you'll enjoy it."

The "O" trilogy has been translated into Japanese.

FOR MORE INFORMATION SEE: Times Literary Supplement, March 28, 1980.

A three-year-old child is a being who gets almost as much fun out of a fifty-six dollar set of swings as it does out of finding a small green worm.
—Bill Vaughan

GLASS, Andrew

BRIEF ENTRY: Author and illustrator. Glass attended Temple University, Philadelphia, and later studied at the School of Visual Arts in New York, where he now lives illustrating children's books and working at painting and collage. He has illustrated more than one dozen books—from Natalie Savage Carlson's *Spooky Night* (Lothrop, 1982), a Halloween fantasy for children, to Theodore Taylor's *Battle in the English Channel* (Avon, 1983) for young adults. Glass uses different art mediums, including water color drawings in Elizabeth Charlton's *Terrible Tyrannosaurus* (Elsevier/Nelson, 1981), black-and-white illustrations in Joan Lowery Nixon's *The Gift* (Macmillan, 1983), and shaded-gray drawings in Marilyn Singer's *The Fido Frame-Up* (Warne, 1983). He provided illustrations for Robert Newton Peck's *Banjo,* a testament to friendship and adventure story of two boys who fall into an abandoned mine silo and are rescued by a local hermit. "Glass' soft pencil drawings, with their cross-hatched backgrounds and exaggerated features, have a slightly eerie and yet humorous quality which suit well the story's tone," commented *School Library Journal.*

In addition, Glass has written and illustrated *Jackson Makes His Move* (Warne, 1982) and *My Brother Tries to Make Me Laugh* (Lothrop, 1984). Jackson, a raccoon, is unsatisfied with the realistic pictures he is painting and moves to the city where his style becomes abstract, but filled with feeling. *School Library Journal* noted that "Glass' use of pencil and diluted watercolors is particularly effective in making the transition from the bucolic green environment of Jackson's origins to the frenetic urban street scenes." *My Brother Tries to Make Me Laugh* introduces two purple space children with large heads, donkey ears, eyes on long antennae, and long pig-like snouts who try to amuse themselves on a space trip to earth. *Residence:* New York, N.Y.

GOBLE, Warwick (?)-1943

PERSONAL: Born in London, England; died in 1943. *Education:* Attended City of London Art School. *Residence:* Merstham, Surrey, England.

CAREER: Early in career, worked for a London printing firm; free-lance contributor of drawings to various magazines and newspapers, including *Pearson's Magazine, McClure's, Boy's Own Paper, Captain, Minister, World Wide Magazine,* and *Windsor Magazine;* also worked full-time on the staffs of the *Pall Mall Gazette* and the *Westminster Gazette.* Work has been exhibited at the Royal Academy, Walker Art Gallery, Brighton Fine Art Society, and Brook Street Art Gallery.

ILLUSTRATOR—All for children, except as indicated: Samuel R. Crockett, *Lads' Love* (adult), Bliss Sands, 1897; Alexander Van Millingen, *Constantinople,* A. & C. Black, 1906; Francis A. Gasquet, *The Greater Abbeys of England* (adult), Chatto & Windus, 1908; Jane Barlow, *Irish Ways* (adult), G. Allen, 1909; Charles Kingsley, *The Water Babies,* Macmillan (London), 1909; Grace James, *Green Willow, and Other Japanese Fairy Tales,* Macmillan, 1910, reprinted, Godfrey Cave, 1979; Giovanni B. Basile, *Stories from the Pentamerone,* edited by E. F. Strange, Macmillan, 1911; Julius R. Van Millingen, *Turkey,* A. & C. Black, 1911; Lal Behary Day, *Folk-Tales of Bengal,* Macmillan, 1912; Geoffrey Chaucer, *The Modern Reader's Chaucer: The Complete Poetical Works of Geoffrey Chaucer* (adult), edited by John S.P. Tatlock and Percy Mackaye, Macmillan (New York), 1912, reprinted, Free Press, 1966;

(From *The Water Babies* by Charles Kingsley. Illustrated by Warwick Goble.)

The star lovers. ■ (From *Green Willow, and Other Japanese Fairy Tales* by Grace James. Illustrated by Warwick Goble.)

Dinah M. Craik, *The Fairy Book,* Macmillan (London), 1913, reprinted, Mayflower, 1979; Donald A. MacKenzie, *Indian Myth and Legend,* Gresham, 1913.

D. Craik, *John Halifax Gentleman* (adult), Oxford University Press, 1914; Cornelia Sohrabji, *Indian Tales of the Great Ones among Men, Women, and Bird-People,* Blackie & Son, 1916; Joseph S. Fletcher, *The Cistercians in Yorkshire* (adult), S.P.C.K., 1919; Dora Owen, editor, *The Book of Fairy Poetry,* Longmans, 1920; Gordon Stables, *Young Peggy McQueen,* Collins, circa 1920; Robert Louis Stevenson, *Treasure Island,* Macmillan (New York), 1923; R. L. Stevenson, *Kidnapped: Being Memoirs of the Adventures of David Balfour in the Year 1751,* Macmillan, 1925; Washington Irving, *The Alhambra: Palace of Mystery and Splendor,* edited by Mabel Williams, Macmillan, 1926; Elinor Whitney, *Tod of the Fens,* Macmillan, 1928; George Griffith, *The Raid of "Le Vengeur," and Other Stories* (adult; illustrated with Henry Austin and Cyrus Cuneo), Ferret Fantasy, 1974.

SIDELIGHTS: Goble was born in London and educated there. After completing his education at the City of London School, he spent several years with a printing firm learning chromolithography and commercial designing, and studying art at night school.

For many years he worked on the staffs of *The Pall Mall Gazette* and *The Westminster Gazette* as a free-lance artist. He did numerous illustrations of books for children, including fairy and adventure stories. One of his earliest works was the illustrations for H. G. Wells' *War of the Worlds* for *Pearson's* magazine in England and *McClure's* in America.

Goble is probably best known for his illustrations of fairy tales in the early part of the twentieth century and for his illustrations of such children's classics as *Kidnapped* and *Treasure Island* by Robert Louis Stevenson, and *The Alhambra* by Washington Irving.

Besides his illustration work, Goble also exhibited his watercolor paintings at the Royal Academy, Corporation Galleries, and at other galleries. Although considered something of a hermit, he traveled widely during his lifetime. He was especially fond of the Far East, and was strongly influenced by Chinese paintings and Japanese art. His color washes are extremely subtle; his compositions consciously oriental. For many years he lived in Shepherd's Hill in Mertsham, Surrey, England.

FOR MORE INFORMATION SEE: Bertha E. Mahony and others, compilers, *Illustrators of Children's Books: 1744-1945,* Horn Book, 1947; B. E. Mahony and Elinor Whitney, compilers, *Contemporary Illustrators of Children's Books,* Bookshop for Boys and Girls, 1930, reprinted, Gale, 1978.

The things I want to know are in books; my best friend is the man who'll get me a book I ain't read.
—Abraham Lincoln

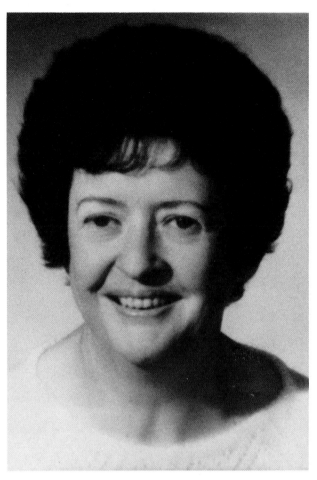

DOROTHY F. HAAS

HAAS, Dorothy F.
(Dee Francis)

PERSONAL: Born in Racine, Wis.; daughter of Allen L. (a pharmacist) and Elizabeth (Sweetman) Haas. *Education:* Marquette University, B.S., 1955. *Home:* 336 West Wellington Ave., Apt. 1502, Chicago, Ill. 60657.

CAREER: Author and editor, 1955—; Whitman Publishing Division, Western Publishing Co., Racine, Wis., became senior editor, 1955-68; Worldbook Childcraft, Chicago, Ill., senior editor, 1968-70; Rand McNally & Co., Chicago, Ill., editor, trade division, books for children and young adults, 1970-83. *Awards, honors:* Children's Reading Round Table Award, 1979, for "distinguished and continuing service" to children's books.

WRITINGS—Juvenile; all published by Western Publishing, except as indicated: *Little Joe's Puppy*, 1957; *Mimi, the Merry-Go-Round Cat*, 1958; *Christopher John's Fuzzy Blanket*, 1959; *Men of Science* (biography), 1959; *That Puppy!*, 1960; *Soda Pop*, 1960; *Oh, Look!*, 1961; *A Penny for Whiffles*, 1962; *Patrick and the Duckling*, 1963; *Especially from Thomas*, 1965; *Grandpapa and Me*, 1966; *A Special Place for Johnny*, 1966; *Maria, Everybody Has a Name*, 1966; *This Little Pony*, 1967; *The Bears Upstairs*, Greenwillow Books, 1978; *Poppy and the Outdoors Cat* (illustrated by Margot Apple), A. Whitman, 1980; *Tink in a Tangle* (illustrated by M. Apple), A. Whitman, 1984; *The Baby Hugs Bear and Baby Tugs Bear Counting Book* (illustrated by Tom Cooke), Parker Brothers, 1984; *Dor-*

othy and the Seven-Leaf Clover (illustrated by David Rose), Random House, 1985; *The Secret Life of Dilly McBean*, Bradbury Press, 1986; *Dorothy and Old King Crow* (picture book; illustrated by C. S. Ewing), Random House, 1986.

Original stories based on television or movie series; juvenile; all published by Western Publishing: *Corky and White Shadow*, 1956; (under pseudonym, Dee Francis) *Rinty and Pals for Rusty*, 1957; *Captain Kangaroo and the Too-Small House*, 1958; *Fury*, 1958; *Sir Lancelot*, 1958; *Quick Draw McGraw: Badmen Beware*, 1960; *National Velvet*, 1962; *Tom and Jerry: Goody Go-Round*, 1967.

Adaptations of movie scripts; juvenile; all published by Western Publishing: *Pinocchio*, 1961; (under pseudonym, Dee Francis) *Babes in Toyland*, 1961; (under pseudonym, Dee Francis) *The Sword in the Stone*, 1963.

Editor of "Tween-Age Books" (fiction for preteens), "Tell-a-Tale Books" (picture books), "Big Tell-a-Tale Books" (picture books), and "Tiny Tot Tales" (picture books), all published by Western Publishing.

WORK IN PROGRESS: My First Communion Book, for A. Whitman, and a junior novel for Random House, as yet untitled.

SIDELIGHTS: "Young readers sometimes ask why I write books for children. Adults occasionally ask when I intend to write a book for adults. And adult writers—who have known me primarily as an editor—have been known to ask why I want to write at all!

"The answer to children is, I write juvenile books simply because I enjoy them. The reply to adults asking about a possible adult book is, perhaps, someday. But the answer to why I write at all is—a writer writes because a writer must! Ideas come to me and I'm not comfortable until I've developed them into a story.

"I've been writing since fourth grade. A teacher talking to us about our stories gave the class sound bits of advice. They have become part of my writing style. I think of that wonderful teacher often, and I wonder if she went home to pen, paper, and characters she created to please herself.

"I've had tandem careers as an editor of books for children and as a writer. My first book, a picture book, was accepted for publication three months after my college graduation. *Little Joe's Puppy* was that book. Many picture books followed, most of them published by Western Publishing Company where I was a picture-book editor. I later moved on to World Book Childcraft where I was senior editor of factual books. After several years, I became editor of books for children at Rand McNally. In my many years as an editor, I worked with many talented writers and illustrators. Giving assistance to writers as they developed their books was highly satisfying. But my own writing continued as well, evenings, weekends. Now I spend my days full time at my typewriter.

"My early books, with the exception of a collection of biographies of famous scientists, were picture books. I finally felt the need to stretch myself, to develop characters and plots that were more complex than the limited space of a picture book permitted. *The Bears Upstairs*, a fantasy novel, was the result. Then I thought of all the children graduating out of picture books, looking for their first books with 'real chapters.' *Poppy and the Outdoors Cat* and *Tink in a Tangle* followed. Since

"Now everyone move in close to your mom." ▪ (From *Poppy and the Outdoors Cat* by Dorothy Haas. Illustrated by Margot Apple.)

that time, I've had the fun of creating new adventures in the Land of Oz, *Dorothy and the Seven Leaf Clover,* a short novel, and *Dorothy and Old King Crow,* a picture book. *The Secret Life of Dilly McBean* is an adventure-fantasy, aimed at the eleven to thirteen age group. *Dilly* was both harder to write, and more fun.

"One of the best questions ever asked of me was by a boy: 'How did you learn to think like a bear?' It was a good question because it told me that I had succeeded in creating real characters in *The Bears Upstairs.* The boy believed that Otto and Ursula Ma'am acted exactly as all bears do. I told the boy how I got to know the bears by making them my secret friends, by taking them with me in my imagination wherever I went, by looking at the city through their eyes, by considering the kind of language mountain bears could use to describe what they saw in the city. After a few weeks, I began to understand Otto as a very funny character, Ursula Ma'am as extremely shy. Their personalities became unique and they slipped easily into my story.

"As I said, a writer writes because a writer must. But not all writers have the fun of moving into worlds of fantasy, or of laughing as they write. I do. I count myself among the fortunate."

Haas' works are included in the de Grummond Collection at the University of Southern Mississippi.

HOBBIES AND OTHER INTERESTS: Music, art, travel. "And reading. I read omnivorously—children's books, adult literature, adult escape fiction, books on subjects that interest me such as art and life in the middle ages."

HALLER, Dorcas Woodbury 1946-

PERSONAL: Born July 31, 1946, in Concord, N.H.; married David Haller; children: two sons, Tristan and Tobias. *Education:* Received degree from Royal Danish School of Librarianship, 1980; attended University of Rhode Island. *Resi-*

DORCAS WOODBURY HALLER

dence: Rhode Island. *Agent:* International Children's Book Service, Skindergade 3B, DK-1159 Copenhagen K., Denmark.

CAREER: Librarian. Has also worked variously as a waitress, short-order cook, filing clerk, theatre carpenter, acting journeyman, au pair, ceramist's apprentice, carpenter, play group leader, and layout and production designer of filmstrips for Ibis (publisher), Copenhagen, Denmark.

AWARDS, HONORS: Bologna Fair Budding Critics' Prize, 1978; Boeken-Sleutel, Holland, 1979; German Youth Book Prize, Federal Ministry of Youth, Family, and Health, West Germany, 1979; Cestné Uznania Vydavatelstvam, Bratislava, Czechoslovakia, 1979; Suomen Nuorisokirjailijat, Finland, 1979; Prix Graphique Loisirs Jeunes, France, 1979; Janusz Korczak Honor List, Poland, 1981; Schönste Bücher aus aller Welt, Leipzig, East Germany, 1982; and European Prize for Children's Literature in Biennale, Padua, Italy, 1982, all for *What's That?,* also commended by both UNICEF and the Committee for International Year of the Child.

WRITINGS: (With Virginia Allen Jensen) *Hvad er det?* (picture book), Ibis (Copenhagen, Denmark), 1977, published as *What's That?,* Collins & World, 1978.

SIDELIGHTS: What's That?, the first printed picture book for blind children, has been published in a dozen countries, including Norway, Sweden, Finland, West Germany, Holland, France, Japan, Catalonia, and Venezuela. A special envelope featuring an illustration from the book was printed by the Czechoslovakian Post Office in 1981.

HAMPSON, Frank 1918(?)-1985

OBITUARY NOTICE: Born December 21 (one source cites December 22), 1918 (one source cites 1917), in Audenshaw, Manchester, England; died of cancer, July 8, 1985, in Epsom, Surrey, England. Civil servant, cartoonist, and author. Once credited with drawing the finest comics since World War II, Hampson created, among others, the science fiction cartoon character Dan Dare. Although his first career, begun at the age of fourteen, was as a civil servant with the British postal services, Hampson took art courses and eventually resigned his post to study art full time. He served for seven years in the Royal Army Service Corps, then resumed his art studies and began free-lance illustrating in 1947. He helped create the *Eagle,* a weekly comic tabloid for boys in 1950, and the strip "Dan Dare—Pilot of the Future" made its debut on the first two pages of the *Eagle's* premier issue. The Dan Dare strip became so popular that it inspired a variety of merchandise, which included playsuit uniforms and toy ray-guns. In addition to illustrating a number of educational color books for children in the 1960s, Hampson wrote several science fiction works, including *Dan Dare, Volume One: The Man from Nowhere, Dan Dare, Volume Two: Rogue Planet,* and *Reign of the Robots.*

FOR MORE INFORMATION SEE: Maurice Horn, editor, *The World Encyclopedia of Comics,* Chelsea House, 1976; *The Encyclopedia of Science Fiction: An Illustrated A to Z,* Grenada, 1979; Brigid Peppin and Lucy Micklethwait, *Book Illustrators of the Twentieth Century,* Arco, 1984. Obituaries: *Times* (London), July 10, 1985; *Facts on File,* July 19, 1985.

Even a child is known by his doings.
—Proverbs 20:11

JOYCE HANSEN

HANSEN, Joyce 1942-

PERSONAL: Born October 18, 1942, in New York, N.Y.; daughter of Austin Victor (a photographer) and Lillian (Dancy) Hansen; married Matthew Nelson (a musician), December 18, 1982. *Education:* Pace University, B.A., 1972; New York University, M.A., 1978. *Address:* 19 Dongan Pl., New York, N.Y. 10040.

CAREER: Board of Education, New York, N.Y., teacher of reading and language arts, 1973—; author of books for young people, 1980—. *Member:* Society of Children's Book Writers, Authors Guild.

WRITINGS: The Gift-Giver (juvenile), Houghton, 1980; *Home Boy* (young adult novel), Houghton, 1982; *Yellow Bird and Me* (juvenile), Houghton, 1986; *Which Way Freedom* (young adult), Walker, 1986.

SIDELIGHTS: "I was born in New York City and have lived here all of my life. I grew up in the Bronx at a time when New York City neighborhoods were thriving urban villages that children could grow and develop in. Though I write contemporary stories, my childhood experiences figure importantly in my themes.

"I write about what I know and/or what moves me deeply. My first novel, *The Gift-Giver,* was semi-autobiographical. The setting for the story was the Bronx neighborhood I grew up in.

"The setting for the second novel, *Home Boy,* was the Bronx and the Caribbean. I had to do research in order to create an 'authentic' Caribbean island, however, I knew my characters very well. The main character was a composite of the many young men I've met through teaching.

"In *The Gift-Giver* I tried to recreate some of the positive things that I experienced as a youngster. We forget that there are many people in our so called slums or ghettos that manage to raise whole and healthy families under extreme conditions. Not every story coming out of the black communities of New York City are horror stories.

"Another important influence on my writing was and is my family. My parents were stable and nurturing. We were rich in family love and caring. My love of books and writing came from my mother who wanted to be a journalist. She grew up in a large family during the depression and though she was intelligent and literate she couldn't even finish high school because she had to work; but she passed on to me her love of books and writing. She was my first teacher.

"From my father I learned how to tell stories. He entertained my brothers and me with stories about his boyhood in the West Indies and his experiences as a young man in the Harlem of the 20s and 30s. I also learned from him to see the beauty and poetry in the everyday scenes and 'just plain folks' he captured in his photographs.

"The people who lived in our old Bronx neighborhood and my extended family—cousins, uncles, aunts, grandmothers and grandfather—provided enough characters to populate many books and stories.

(Jacket illustration by Martha Perske from *The Gift-Giver* by Joyce Hansen.)

"I think of myself as a conduit through which information sifts and passes. I don't really create my characters and stories. They are given to me by the people I know—my family, friends and students. I may change some things—some of them don't even recognize themselves when they read my books. I'm not very good at fantasy—though I enjoyed reading fairy tales as a child. My stories come to me as tales of the real world—either as it is or as I'd like it to be.

"I take writing for children very seriously. So many children need direction—so many are floundering. I write for all children who need and can relate to the things I write about—the importance of family, maintaining a sense of hope, and responsibility for oneself and other living things.

"Writing for and teaching children are two of the most important things one can do. A literate society is maintained through its children. I hope one day to see children's literature recognized as an important literary genre, since children are our most important natural resource."

HARE, Norma Q(uarles) 1924-

PERSONAL: Born July 10, 1924, in Dadeville, Mo.; daughter of J. Norman (an educator) and Mary D. (Blakemore) Quarles; married John D. Hare II, June 27, 1944; children: J. Daniel III, Thomas Christopher. *Education:* Attended Southwest Missouri State University; California State University, Fresno, B.A., 1958, M.A., 1963. *Religion:* Presbyterian. *Home address:* P.O. Box 161, Millbrae, Calif. 94030.

CAREER: Teacher at schools in Parlier, Calif., 1956-57, in Sanger, Calif., 1958-66, and in South San Francisco, Calif., 1966-67; Hillside Elementary School, South San Francisco, principal, 1967-81. *Member:* National Association of Elementary School Principals, Society of Children's Book Writers, Association of California School Administrators, California Historical Society, Society of Mayflower Descendants, Parent-Teachers Association.

NORMA Q. HARE

WRITINGS—Juvenile: Who Is Root Beer? (illustrated by Rosalie Davidson), Garrard, 1977; *Wish Upon a Birthday* (illustrated by Diane Dawson), Garrard, 1979; *Mystery at Mouse House* (illustrated by Stella Ormai), Garrard, 1980. Contributor to *National Elementary Principal.*

WORK IN PROGRESS: An adult nonfiction, *Pilgrims, Pioneers and Planters,* a genealogy book "about seventy-five men who came to New England before the Revolutionary War. It traces their ancestors and descendants."

SIDELIGHTS: "'Play-like' was always my favorite game when I was growing up. Sometimes my sister and I would be circus riders in the center ring; other times we'd be fearless detectives on the trail of a crook; and sometimes we'd be famous movie stars or pirates sailing the seas. All it took was just the magic words, 'let's play-like.'

"Learning to read was undoubtedly the most exciting fun I'd ever had. Storybook characters became absolutely real to me. I could see the places they went, and I could feel exactly how they felt, and it was wonderful. Each week, I checked out as many books at the library as I was allowed, and I learned new ideas for our 'play-like' games.

"I believe the best gift I ever received as a child was a subscription to *Child Life* magazine. Through its stories, I met new people each month, and I reread every issue over and over.

"When I was ten, I wrote my first story that wasn't a school assignment. It was titled, 'The Extra Trip to Town.' I really wrote it only for myself, but I was so proud when I finished it, that I showed it to everyone. My mother's friend planned a garden party, and asked me to read it for her guests, and I immediately agreed. So, wearing a big straw hat to keep the sun out of my eyes, and with perspiration trickling down my spine, I stood in the center of the garden and read my story in a very loud voice to all the ladies sitting under huge umbrellas. They applauded when I finished, and I was almost famous. I also received a huge dish of strawberry ice cream and twenty-five cents!

"My father was superintendent of schools in the small Missouri town where I grew up. I'd always heard that you should write about things you knew something about, so I did. My first published article was called 'Observations of a Superintendent's Daughter.' It was printed in a magazine for school administrators when I was sixteen years old.

"At college I worked on the college newspaper. Later, I got married, moved to California, had children, began teaching, and finally became an elementary school principal. Always, I kept reading and writing. Most of my writing then was for school publications, local newspapers, or children's magazines.

"As a teacher, I really worried about the children who had trouble reading. Some of them struggled so hard to figure out the words, that they missed the whole point of the stories, and they hated reading. I believe that was terribly unfair, because I think reading should be fun for everyone.

"Then I decided that I'd try to write books for those struggling children, stories they could easily read and enjoy. I knew that some children have great difficulty with auditory discrimination, or hearing differences in the sound of the letters and words, and I decided to write a book just for them. *Who Is Root Beer?* uses basic sight words that don't need to be sounded out, and it tells the story of a bug and a bee who find a can with 'Root Beer' written on it. They want to know who Root Beer is, and an ant and a butterfly join them in trying to solve the mystery. I was pleased to learn that not only young readers in the primary grades enjoy the book, but that it was enthusiastically received by three and four-year-old listener-readers. It is also widely used in special education classes, to my great delight.

"One day at school, a second grade boy asked me, 'Why do we have cakes on our birthdays?' Now, I realize that school principals are supposed to be very smart and know nearly everything, but I didn't know the answer to that question. I thought about it a long time, and then I wrote *Wish Upon a Birthday*. It's my answer to that boy's question; at least, it's the way I think it might have been.

"Thanksgiving is one of my favorite holidays, maybe because my Pilgrim ancestors were there to help celebrate the very first one. I decided I wanted to write a Thanksgiving story. One night, while I was visiting a friend, I heard a mouse in her kitchen, and then *Mystery at Mouse House* came to life for me. It would be a Thanksgiving mystery story about a family of mice!

"Ideas for stories come from lots of places. When I get an idea, I start thinking about it, and then I play the 'play-like' game. I pretend that I am the character. I feel what's happening, and I see everything through the character's eyes. Then I put it down on paper, which is the hardest part, of course. But I can talk to my readers only through the words on the paper, so if I want them to enjoy my stories, they must read my words. Then, I hope they will be able to enjoy the 'play-like' game while they read the story."

HEATH, Charles D(ickinson) 1941-

PERSONAL: Born June 28, 1941, in Waterloo, Iowa; son of George C. (a trial judge) and Dorothy (a homemaker; maiden name, Dickinson) Heath; married Carilyn Cain (a teacher),

CHARLES D. HEATH

June 3, 1972. *Education:* University of Iowa, B.B.A., 1962, J.D., 1966; University of Arizona, M.B.A., 1963. *Residence:* Milwaukee, Wis.

CAREER: Admitted to the Bar of the State of Iowa, 1966, Pennsylvania, 1969, Indiana, 1970, Wisconsin, 1973, Arizona, 1975, Florida, 1979, and Michigan, 1979; and the Bar of the U.S. Supreme Court, 1971. Research attorney, 1966-68; corporate lawyer, 1968—. *Member:* American Bar Association.

WRITINGS—For young adults: *Your Future as a Legal Assistant,* Richards Rosen, 1979, revised edition, 1982; *Your Future in Big Business,* Richards Rosen, 1980.

WORK IN PROGRESS: A book about life inside a corporation.

SIDELIGHTS: "I have always been interested in writing and careers. These interests have been combined in my books."

HELLER, Linda 1944-

PERSONAL: Born September 14, 1944, in New York, N.Y. *Education:* Rhode Island School of Design, B.F.A., 1966. *Home:* 7 East 86th St., New York, N.Y. 10028.

CAREER: Free-lance illustrator and animator, 1967—; author and illustrator of books for children, 1979—. *Member:* Association of Children's Book Artists and Authors. *Awards, honors: A Picture Book of Jewish Holidays* was selected one of *School Library Journal*'s Notable Books, 1981; Parents' Choice Award for Illustration from Parents' Choice Foundation, 1982, and Children's Book Award from the Association of Jewish Libraries, 1983, both for *The Castle on Hester Street.*

WRITINGS—All self-illustrated: *Lily at the Table,* Macmillan, 1979; *Alexis and the Golden Ring,* Macmillan, 1980; *Horace Morris* (Junior Literary Guild selection), Macmillan, 1980; *Trouble at Goodewoode Manor,* Macmillan, 1981; *The Castle on Hester Street,* Jewish Publication Society, 1982.

Illustrator: David A. Adler, *A Picture Book of Jewish Holidays,* Holiday House, 1981; D. A. Adler, *A Picture Book of Passover,* Holiday House, 1982; D. A. Adler, *A Picture Book of Hanukkah,* Holiday House, 1982; Howard Schwartz, reteller, *Elijah's Violin and Other Jewish Fairy Tales,* Harper, 1982; Mirra Ginsburg, adapter, *The Magic Stove,* Coward, 1983.

WORK IN PROGRESS: Maybelle Dertz and Levon Hoover, a novel for eight- to ten-year-olds.

SIDELIGHTS: "As a child I loved reading and was proud of my record, a different book read every day, always taken out from the library. I drew and made my own books, trying various bindings, staples, tape and glue. But I never expected to actually write and illustrate children's books.

"I studied illustration in college. Later I had a hard time as a free-lance illustrator. An illustration might take two days to do, then I was unemployed again and forced to find work. Someone suggested I do children's books. It had never occurred to me. I thought one had to have children, but as soon as I started I knew I could do it. The child inside me is very close to the surface (or sometimes on top) and I write for her. Books take months or sometimes years to complete. No more daily searches for work.

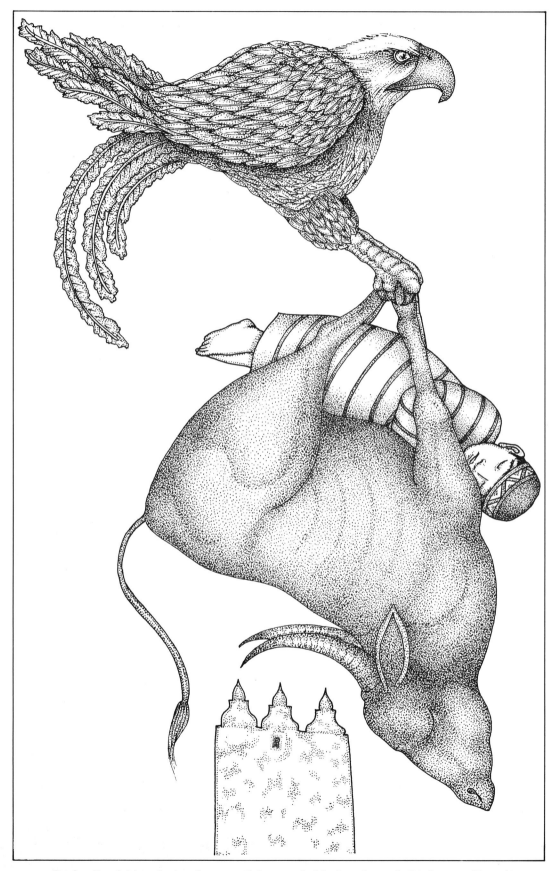

During the night, a giant eagle swooped down and picked up the ox in its claws, and bore it away, with Reuben still sleeping inside it. ■ (From "The Princess in the Tower" in *Elijah's Violin and Other Jewish Fairy Tales,* selected and retold by Howard Schwartz. Illustrated by Linda Heller.)

LINDA HELLER

"As a child during the 50s I felt I was different from children in books. They were either much happier or more noble when they suffered. Now, of course, the child that I was is in all of my books and I hope others can see themselves too.

"*Horace Morris* was inspired by the unexpected things one sees while living in New York. In Central Park last summer I saw a cow being led by two people dressed as vegetables, and a man playing the flute surrounded by an orchestra of wind-up toy monkeys. Just after I had decided to have Mrs. Potterton, in *Horace Morris*, meet a cockatoo on the bus, and was writing about her hearing something squawking, I began to hear similar sounds coming from the apartment next door. The squawking began each morning at 6:30 and continued all day, so although I didn't know my neighbor I decided it was time we met. I rang his bell and he asked me in. Perched on a small stepladder in the kitchen was a cockatoo, the first I had ever seen, and a baby parrot was standing in the bathtub with a look of happy expectation on its face. My neighbor said it loved to take showers and was waiting for the next one. Just as I was finishing *Horace Morris* my neighbor and his birds moved out. *Horace Morris* takes place in the 1930s because I wanted Horace and Emmaline to look like the photographs I have of my parents.

"For the past two years I've been writing a novel for children. I've never loved doing work more. The characters are part of my life. Friends ask, 'How's Levon? How's Maybelle?' I'll see a skinny girl dancing down the street. 'Excuse me,' I'll want to say, 'but you're the perfect child to play Maybelle.'"

HOWKER, Janni

BRIEF ENTRY: Author of books for young adults. Howker spent her childhood in the English counties of Norfolk, Suffolk, Lincolnshire, and Cumbria. She earned a B.A. from Lancaster University and, later, worked with the elderly and mentally handicapped as well as an assistant on an archeological site. About 1984, she returned to Lancaster University to study for a master's degree in creative writing. Howker's first book, *Badger on the Barge and Other Stories* (Greenwillow, 1985) is written "with sensitivity," according to *Bulletin of the Center for Children's Books*. "Her ear for dialogue is excellent, her settings and characters equally colorful." Each of the five short stories, set in England, involves an isolated young person

who gains support or insight from an old stranger. "The thoughtful reader (young or old) will find five gems—polished, smooth and sparkling—to treasure," noted *New York Times Book Review*.

Reviewers have acclaimed Howker's novel, *The Nature of the Beast* (Greenwillow, 1985), not only for its adventurous plot—a teenager determines to track down and kill a beast that has been attacking livestock and people—but also for its portrayal of the emotional upheaval caused by unemployment in a working-class, northern England town. "The adventure with the beast and the industrial conflicts are grim and terrifying . . . ," observed *Booklist*. "[The author] creates an authentic world in which the fierce and the battered struggle to survive." In 1985 Howker won the children's section of the Whitbread Literary Awards for *The Nature of the Beast*. The book also won the *Young Observer* Teenage Fiction Prize and was listed on *Horn Book*'s honor list. *Badger on the Barge* was a finalist for the 1984 Carnegie Medal, listed as one of *School Library Journal*'s "Best Books 1985," and included on the "YASD [Young Adult Services Division, ALA] Best Books—1986" list. *Residence:* Lancaster, England.

HURD, Thacher   1949-

PERSONAL: Born March 6, 1949, in Burlington, Vt.; son of Clement G. (an illustrator of children's books) and Edith (a writer of children's books; maiden name, Thacher) Hurd; married Olivia Scott (co-owner with husband of Peaceable King-

THACHER HURD

dom Press), June 12, 1976; children: Manton, Nicholas. *Education:* Attended University of California, Berkeley, 1967-68; California College of Arts and Crafts, B.F.A., 1972. *Home:* 2954 Hillegass Ave., Berkeley, Calif. 94705. *Agent:* Marilyn Marlow, Curtis Brown Ltd., 10 Astor Place, New York, N.Y. 10003.

CAREER: Grabhorn-Hoyem Press (now Arion Press), San Francisco, Calif., apprentice printer, 1967, 1969; self-employed builder, designer and cabinetmaker, 1972-78; writer and illustrator of children's books, 1974—; California College of Arts and Crafts, Oakland, teacher of writing and illustrating children's books, 1981—; Peaceable Kingdom Press (a children's book poster publishing company), co-owner with wife, Olivia Hurd, 1983—. Lecturer and guest speaker at seminars, conferences, and schools. *Member:* Society of Children's Book Writers. *Awards, honors: Boston Globe-Horn Book* Award for Illustration, 1985, for *Mama Don't Allow.*

WRITINGS—Juvenile: (With mother, Edith Thacher Hurd) *Little Dog Dreaming* (illustrated by father, Clement G. Hurd), Harper, 1965; *The Old Chair* (self-illustrated), Greenwillow, 1978; *The Quiet Evening* (self-illustrated), Greenwillow, 1978; *Hobo Dog* (self-illustrated), Scholastic Book Services, 1980; *Axle the Freeway Cat* (self-illustrated), Harper, 1981; *Mystery on the Docks* (self-illustrated), Harper, 1983; *Hobo Dog's Christmas Tree* (self-illustrated), Scholastic Book Services, 1983; *Mama Don't Allow* (self-illustrated picture book), Harper, 1984; *Hobo Dog in the Ghost Town* (self-illustrated), Scholastic, 1985; *The Pea Patch Jig* (self-illustrated), Crown, 1986; *A Night in the Swamp* (pop-up book), Harper, 1987.

ADAPTATIONS: "Mystery on the Docks," Reading Rainbow, PBS-TV, 1984; "Mama Don't Allow," Reading Rainbow, PBS-TV, 1986; "Mama Don't Allow" (filmstrip), Random House, 1986, CBS Storybreak, CBS-TV, 1986.

SIDELIGHTS: "When I was growing up, we lived in a big house by a river in North Ferrisburg, Vermont. The house and the land around it were magical to me, a warm and cosy world in which to live. The lawn went all the way around our house, down to the river where we swam in rock pools shaped like bathtubs. There was a barn attached to the house, with a schoolhouse bell on top which we rang when it was time for dinner, and a big freezer filled with all the summer vegetables we had grown.

"I feel very fortunate to have grown up in a household where both my parents worked on children's books. My parents, Edith Thacher Hurd and Clement Hurd, wrote and illustrated many books together, as well as collaborating with other authors and illustrators such as Margaret Wise Brown and Don Freeman.

"On the hill above our house in Vermont my father had a studio filled with his paintings and drawings and the children's books he was working on. I loved to just sit and watch him work and be in that atmosphere of paint smells, color and creativity. I think this was how I learned about children's books from my parents as I was growing up. My father never sat me down and said 'Learn this' or 'This is how you must draw.' I took everything in at my own pace, and when the time was right I started to do my own books.

"Although I grew up in the country I am fascinated with the city as a setting for picture books. To me the city is a place where anything can happen, where characters can be slightly crazy and still sympathetic. I remember visiting my aunt in New York with my parents when I was young and lying in bed at night listening to the sounds of the traffic noises in the street below. To me it was a lullaby of the city, something soothing and wonderful.

"I try to create characters in my books who are part of the tough, fast world of the city, but who are still able to make

(From *Mama Don't Allow* by Thacher Hurd. Illustrated by the author.)

their own cosy lives within that world. When I begin a book I start with a feeling, a mood or a setting. For *Mystery on the Docks* the mood was that of a foggy night, a dark pier and some nasty rats. The book grew out of those feelings and they were the basis for the plot and action of the story. My characters seem to be innocents in search of adventure in the big world and a place to call home.

"When I first became interested in children's books I had no idea that I could write as well as illustrate. My mother has written many children's books, but I thought of myself as exclusively an artist or illustrator. So at first I went looking for someone else's book to illustrate. But where were the writers who were looking for illustrators? I didn't know, and before I had found a book to illustrate, I found myself writing my own. At first my stories were tentative, slightly moralistic fairy tales, but slowly I began to find a voice and I began to be able to draw on my own experience.

"I find myself drawn to characters on the fringes of life: drifters, hoboes, short-order cooks, gangsters, litter-collectors. Music also seems to play an important part in my books. The rhythms of music spark the rhythms of a picture book, and music always seems to creep into my books. My book *Mama Don't Allow* is based on the traditional jazz song of the same name. The song's lyrics become a way for a 'possum named Miles to rebel against his parents and his town and everything staid and stuffy.' The music is a framework, a rhythm to weave the story around.

"To make a book exciting, to make the pages turn, to make a child laugh, to bring out a child's sense of wonder: these are what I am aiming at in my books. I believe that children's books should be for children, and not for the coffee tables of educators or librarians. I remember what I loved to read as a child, and I think I try to write something that I would have liked, something that could draw me into another world: an alive, vibrant world of energy and wild, bursting color."

FOR MORE INFORMATION SEE: Oakland Tribune, November 26, 1981; John Faucher, "A Fun, Rowdy Children's Book," *Berkeley Voice,* October 3, 1984; Barbara Kelley, "A Writer, an Illustrator, and a Peaceable Kingdom," *Christian Science Monitor,* December 10, 1984; *Horn Book,* February, 1986.

HYMAN, Trina Schart   1939-

PERSONAL: Born April 8, 1939, in Philadelphia, Pa.; daughter of Albert H. (a salesman) and Margaret Doris (Bruck) Schart; married Harris Hyman (a mathematician and engineer), 1959 (divorced, 1968); children: Katrin. *Education:* Studied at Philadelphia Museum College of Art, 1956-59, Boston Museum School of the Arts, 1959-60, and Konstfackskolan (Swedish State Art School), Stockholm, 1960-61. *Politics:* "Royalist." *Religion:* "Druid." *Home:* Brick Hill Rd., Lyme, N.H. 03768.

CAREER: Artist and illustrator; art director of *Cricket* (magazine), LaSalle, Ill., 1972-79. *Awards, honors: Boston Globe-Horn Book* honor for illustration, 1968, for *All in Free but Janey,* and 1978, for *On to Widecombe Fair; Book World*'s Spring Book Festival Award, 1969, for *A Walk out of the World,* and 1971, for *A Room Made of Windows; The Pumpkin Giant* was selected one of American Institute of Graphic Arts "Children's Books," 1970; *A Room Made of Windows* was selected one of *New York Times* Outstanding Books of the Year, 1971; *Boston Globe-Horn Book* Award for illustration, 1973, for *King Stork; Greedy Mariani and Other Folktales of*

the Antilles was included in Children's Book Council's "Children's Book Showcase," 1975, *Magic in the Mist,* 1976; Golden Kite Award for Illustration from Society of Children's Book Writers, and Parents' Choice Award for Illustration from Parents' Choice Foundation, both 1983, both for *Little Red Riding Hood;* Caldecott Honor Book from the American Library Association, 1984, for *Little Red Riding Hood; Saint George and the Dragon: A Golden Legend Adapted from Edmund Spenser's Faerie Queen* was selected one of *New York Times* Best Illustrated Books of the Year, 1984, and received the Caldecott Medal from the American Library Association, 1985.

WRITINGS—Self-illustrated: *How Six Found Christmas,* Little, Brown, 1969; (reteller) *The Sleeping Beauty, from the Brothers Grimm,* Little, Brown, 1977; *A Little Alphabet,* Little, Brown, 1980; *Self-Portrait: Trina Schart Hyman,* Addison-Wesley, 1981; (reteller) Jakob Grimm and Wilhelm Grimm, *Little Red Riding Hood* (ALA Notable Book), Holiday House, 1983; *The Enchanted Forest,* Putnam, 1984.

Illustrator: Hertha Von Gebhardt, *Toffe och den lilla bilen* (title means "Toffe and the Little Car"), Rabén & Sjögren, 1961; Carl Memling, *Riddles, Riddles, from A to Z,* Western, 1963; Melanie Bellah, *Bow Wow! Meow!,* Western, 1963; Sandol S. Warburg, *Curl Up Small,* Houghton, 1964; Eileen O'Faolain, *Children of the Salmon,* Little, Brown, 1965; *All Kinds of Signs,* Western, 1965.

Ruth Sawyer, *Joy to the World: Christmas Legends* (ALA Notable Book; *Horn Book* honor list), Little, Brown, 1966; Joyce Varney, *The Magic Maker,* Bobbs-Merrill, 1966; Vir-

Trina Schart Hyman. Photograph by Barbara Rogasky.

That winter, Katrin started nursery school in the town of Thetford, across the river. ■ (From *Self-Portrait: Trina Schart Hyman* by Trina Schart Hyman. Illustrated by the author.)

ginia Haviland, reteller, *Favorite Fairy Tales Told in Czechoslovakia,* Little, Brown, 1966; Edna Butler Trickey, *Billy Finds Out,* United Church Press, 1966; E. B. Trickey, *Billy Celebrates,* United Church Press, 1966; Jacob D. Townsend, *The Five Trials of the Pansy Bed,* Houghton, 1967; Elizabeth Johnson, *Stuck with Luck,* Little, Brown, 1967; Josephine Poole, *Moon Eyes,* Little, Brown, 1967; John T. Moore, *Cinnamon Seed,* Houghton, 1967; Paul Tripp, *The Little Red Flower,* Doubleday, 1968; Eve Merriam, reteller, *Epaminondas,* Follett, 1968, published as *That Noodle-Head Epaminondas,* Scholastic Book Services, 1972; J. Varney, *The Half-Time Gypsy,* Bobbs-Merrill, 1968; E. Johnson, *All in Free but Janey,* Little, Brown, 1968; Norah Smaridge, *I Do My Best,* Western, 1968; Betty M. Owen and Mary MacEwen, editors, *Wreath of Carols,* Scholastic Book Services, 1968; Tom McGowen, *Dragon Stew,* Follett, 1969; Susan Meyers, *The Cabin on the Fjord,* Doubleday, 1969; Peter Hunter Blair, *The Coming of Pout,* Little, Brown, 1969; Clyde R. Bulla, *The Moon Singer,* Crowell, 1969; Ruth Nichols, *A Walk out of the World,* Harcourt, 1969; Claudia Paley, *Benjamin the True,* Little, Brown, 1969.

P. Tripp, *The Vi-Daylin Book of Minnie the Mump,* Ross Laboratories, 1970; Donald J. Sobol, *Greta the Strong,* Follett, 1970; Blanche Luria Serwer, reteller, *Let's Steal the Moon:*

Jewish Tales, Ancient and Recent, Little, Brown, 1970; Mollie Hunter (pseudonym of Maureen Mollie Hunter McIlwraith), *The Walking Stones: A Story of Suspense,* Harper, 1970; T. McGowen, *Sir Machinery,* Follett, 1970; Phyllis Krasilovsky, *The Shy Little Girl,* Houghton, 1970; Ellin Greene, reteller, *The Pumpkin Giant,* Lothrop, 1970; Wylly Folk St. John, *The Ghost Next Door,* Harper, 1971; Osmond Molarsky, *The Bigger They Come,* Walck, 1971; O. Molarsky, *Take It or Leave It,* Walck, 1971; Carolyn Meyer, *The Bread Book: All about Bread and How to Make It,* Harcourt, 1971; E. Johnson, *Break a Magic Circle,* Little, Brown, 1971; E. Greene, reteller, *Princess Rosetta and the Popcorn Man* (from *The Pot of Gold* by Mary E. Wilkins), Lothrop, 1971; Eleanor Cameron, *A Room Made of Windows,* Little, Brown, 1971; Eleanor Clymer, *How I Went Shopping and What I Got,* Holt, 1972; Dori White, *Sarah and Katie,* Harper, 1972; R. Nichols, *The Marrow of the World,* Atheneum, 1972; Eva Moore, *The Fairy Tale Life of Hans Christian Andersen,* Scholastic Book Services, 1972; Jan Wahl, *Magic Heart,* Seabury, 1972; P. Krasilovsky, *The Popular Girls Club,* Simon & Schuster, 1972; Paula Hendrich, *Who Says So?,* Lothrop, 1972; Myra C. Livingston, editor, *Listen, Children, Listen: An Anthology of Poems for the Very Young,* Harcourt, 1972; Carol R. Brink, *The Bad Times of Irma Baumlein,* Macmillan, 1972; Howard Pyle, *King Stork* (ALA Notable Book; story first published in Pyle's collection, *The Wonder Clock*), Little, Brown, 1973; Hans Christian An-

He pushed him out over the thin ice until he could reach Caddie's groping hands. ■ (From *Caddie Woodlawn* by Carol Ryrie Brink. Illustrated by Trina Schart Hyman.)

"I have come to bring you home, dear brother!" said the child. ▪ (From *A Christmas Carol* by
Charles Dickens. Illustrated by Trina Schart Hyman.)

dersen, *The Ugly Duckling and Two Other Stories,* edited by Lilian Moore, Scholastic Book Services, 1973; Phyllis La Farge, *Joanna Runs Away,* Holt, 1973; E. Greene, compiler, *Clever Cooks: A Concoction of Stories, Recipes and Riddles,* Lothrop, 1973; C. R. Brink, *Caddie Woodlawn,* revised edition, Macmillan, 1973; Elizabeth Coatsworth, *The Wanderers,* Four Winds, 1974; Eleanor G. Vance, *The Everything Book,* Western, 1974; Doris Gates, *Two Queens of Heaven: Aphrodite and Demeter,* Viking, 1974; Dorothy S. Carter, editor, *Greedy Mariani and Other Folktales of the Antilles,* Atheneum, 1974; Charles Causley, *Figgie Hobbin* (poetry; *Horn Book* honor list), Walker, 1974; Charlotte Herman, *You've Come a Long Way, Sybil McIntosh: A Book of Manners and Grooming for Girls,* Philip J. O'Hara, 1974; J. Grimm and W. Grimm, *Snow White* (ALA Notable Book; *Horn Book* honor list), translated from the German by Paul Heins, Little, Brown, 1974; Jean

Fritz, *Why Don't You Get a Horse, Sam Adams?* (ALA Notable Book; *Horn Book* honor list), Coward, 1974.

Tobi Tobias, *The Quitting Deal,* Viking, 1975; Margaret Kimmel, *Magic in the Mist,* Viking, 1975; Jane Curry, *The Watchers,* Atheneum, 1975; Louise Moeri, *Star Mother's Youngest Child,* Houghton, 1975; J. Fritz, *Will You Sign Here, John Hancock?* (Junior Literary Guild selection), Coward, 1976; Daisy Wallace, editor, *Witch Poems,* Holiday House, 1976; Bill Sleator, *Among the Dolls,* Dutton, 1976; T. Tobias, *Jane, Wishing,* Viking, 1977; Spiridon Vangheli, *Meet Guguze,* Addison-Wesley, 1977; Norma Farber, *Six Impossible Things before Breakfast,* Addison-Wesley, 1977; Betsy Hearne, *South Star,* Atheneum, 1977; Patricia Gauch, *On to Widecombe Fair* (*Horn Book* honor list), Putnam, 1978; B. Hearne, *Home,* Atheneum, 1979; N. Farber, *How Does It Feel to Be Old?*

They rode through farmlands, where men and women working in their fields looked up.... ▪ (From *Saint George and the Dragon,* adapted by Margaret Hodges. Illustrated by Trina Schart Hyman.)

(*Horn Book* honor list), Dutton, 1979; Pamela Stearns, *The Mechanical Doll*, Houghton, 1979; Barbara S. Hazen, *Tight Times*, Viking, 1979.

D. Wallace, editor, *Fairy Poems*, Holiday House, 1980; J. M. Barrie, *Peter Pan*, Scribner, 1980; Elizabeth G. Jones, editor, *Ranger Rick's Holiday Book*, National Wildlife, 1980; Kathryn Lasky, *The Night Journey*, Warne, 1981; J. Fritz, *The Man Who Loved Books*, Putnam, 1981; J. Grimm and W. Grimm, *Rapunzel* (ALA Notable Book), retold by Barbara Rogasky, Holiday House, 1982; Margaret Mary Kimmel and Elizabeth Segel, *For Reading Out Loud! A Guide to Sharing Books with Children*, Delacorte, 1983; Mary Calhoun, *Big Sixteen*, Morrow, 1983; Astrid Lindgren, *Ronia, the Robber's Daughter*, Viking, 1983; Charles Dickens, *A Christmas Carol: In Prose, Being a Ghost Story of Christmas*, Holiday House, 1983; M. C. Livingston, *Christmas Poems*, Holiday House, 1984; (with Hilary Knight and others) Pamela Espeland and Marilyn Waniek, *The Cat Walked through the Casserole: And Other Poems for Children*, Carolrhoda, 1984; Margaret Hodges, *Saint George and the Dragon: A Golden Legend Adapted from Edmund Spenser's Faerie Queen*, Little, Brown, 1984; Elizabeth Winthrop, *The Castle in the Attic*, Holiday House, 1985; Dylan Thomas, *A Child's Christmas in Wales*, Holiday House, 1985; J. Grimm and W. Grimm, *The Water of Life*, retold by B. Rogasky, Holiday House, 1986; Vivian Vande Velde, *A Hidden Magic*, Crown, 1986.

Contributor of illustrations to textbooks.

ADAPTATIONS: "Dragon Stew" (filmstrip with record or cassette), BFA Educational Media, 1975; "Tight Times," Reading Rainbow, PBS-TV, 1983; "Little Red Riding Hood" (filmstrip with cassette), Listening Library, 1984.

WORK IN PROGRESS: Picture books and anthologies of folk tales; illustrations for *Cat Poems*, an anthology by Myra Cohn Livingston; illustrations for Chaucer's *Canterbury Tales*, retold by Barbara Cohen; illustrations for Mark Twain's *A Connecticut Yankee in King Arthur's Court*; illustrations for *Swan Lake*, retold by Margot Fonteyn.

SIDELIGHTS: **April 8, 1939.** Born in Philadelphia, Pennsylvania. "We lived in a rural area about twenty miles north of the city. Our house was in one of the very first housing developments built during the second World War. It was a little square brick house on a corner of new green grass. My father planted a tiny weeping willow tree and a golden ash in the front lawn, and my mother made a big garden in the backyard."

Hyman's house was located next to a farm, which she imagined to be owned by a king and queen. "The Queen wore farmer's overalls, heavy laced boots, faded flannel shirts, an old manure-stained sailor's hat, and beautiful old rings set with magic stones on her long fingers. She had an elegant bony face and a fierce smile with long white teeth. She was an artist, and she painted portraits of people who were as mysterious as she. One of the first drawings I can remember working on was of the Queen with a big basket of eggs on her arm. I didn't think her overalls were pretty, so I drew her in an elaborate long dress with lots of little egg-shaped polka dots.

"In the winter, we skated on the farm's pond. Everybody went—all the moms and dads and kids and everybody's dogs. Usually someone built a little bonfire at the far edge of the pond, and sometimes the Queen would come trudging through the snow with a huge coffee pot full of hot chocolate. It seemed then that it was always the week before Christmas: the sky was full of snowflakes ready to fall, and angels were perched on the barn along with the pigeons.

"As I grew up, the days of the King and Queen came to an end. . . . I still have dreams about the farm. It was my first kingdom, and in a way, my first real home.

"I was a really strange little kid. I was born terrified of anything and everything that moved or spoke. I was afraid of people, especially—kids my own age, all grownups, even my own family, dogs (until my parents bought me a puppy of my own), horses, trees, grass, cars, streets. I was afraid of the stars and the wind. Who knows why?

"My mother is a beautiful woman with red hair and the piercing blue gaze of a hawk. She never seemed afraid of anyone or anything. It was she who gave me the courage to draw and a love of books. She read to me from the time I was a baby, and once, when I was three or four and she was reading my favorite story, the words on the page, her spoken words, and the scenes in my head fell together in a blinding flash. I could read!

"The story was *Little Red Riding Hood*, and it was so much a part of me that I actually became Little Red Riding Hood. My mother sewed me a red satin cape with a hood that I wore almost every day, and on those days, she would make me a 'basket of goodies' to take to my grandmother's house. (My only grandmother lived in Rhode Island, three hundred miles away, but that didn't matter.) I'd take the basket and carefully negotiate the backyard, 'going to Grandmother's house.' My dog, Tippy, was the wolf. Whenever we met, which in a small backyard had to be fairly often, there was an intense confrontation. My father was the woodsman, and I greeted him when he came home each day with relief and joy.

"I was Red Riding Hood for a year or more. I think it's a great tribute to my mother that she never gave up and took

Hyman used her pipe-smoking great-grandmother as a model for the frontispiece of *Star Mother's Youngest Child*.

"Tut, Mother!" says the princess. "How you talk! Do you not see that there is nobody with me?"
■ (From *King Stork* by Howard Pyle. Illustrated by Trina Schart Hyman.)

me to a psychiatrist, and if she ever worried, she has never let me know.

"My father worked as a plumbing and heating supplies salesman. He loved music and singing, walking quietly in the woods, and fly-fishing. He could play almost any musical instrument, but the one he played most often was a concertina-accordian, decorated with inlaid mother-of-pearl and wood designs. He played the harmonica, too, and sometimes played both instruments at once, holding the harmonica on a brace around his neck. He also told the best stories. When I was a little girl and still afraid of the stars, he sometimes took me for walks at night and told me long magical stories of the origins of the stars and of the many gods who created the universe. My father's made-up mythology is still much more interesting to me than the stories the scientists have invented.

"I had to wear braces for nine years. Every Saturday morning, my father drove me into the city to the orthodontist. Some Saturdays after my appointment, I got to go to the Philadelphia Art Museum as a reward. I should have been afraid of that grand, imposing building, but I wasn't. I loved it. The museum's vast rooms and halls reminded me of a landscape. I loved the vales and glades and corridors full of paintings, and the period rooms which were full of tapestries and glass and wood and furniture that the artists who had done the paintings must have used or known!

"About the time I started with the braces, I also acquired a little sister—Karleen. I loved her dearly, even though I teased her a lot and we sometimes fought. Eventually, she became the main audience and accomplice for all of my imaginary kingdoms, complicated games and elaborate fantasies.

"Mostly, we loved fairies. They were more real to us than anything we could really see. But then Karleen started asking for a real fairy. One night, the moon gave me an idea: I'd make a real fairy for her! I bought a tiny celluloid doll at the five-and-ten, and when I got it home, I looked at it carefully. My mother gave me a piece of her long, red-gold hair, which I glued to the head. I painted the eyes big and blue and tried making dresses from cheesecloth and pieces of scarves. Meanwhile, I had started leaving tiny notes on Karleen's pillow. One day, after having left several tiny notes, I found a dead monarch butterfly on the ground at my feet. My father helped me take the wings off and glue them to Kloraine the fairy's shoulders. It was beautiful, and perfect! The next morning, Kloraine sat in all her splendor on Karleen's night table.

"Eventually, Lacey, another lost fairy, came to join Kloraine. She was a sarcastic, argumentative, troublemaking fairy, who always made Kloraine's life more difficult and exciting. The fairies stayed with us for many years and sat on the lowest, best branches of our Christmas tree even after we had both stopped believing in them. Kloraine and Lacey came to my sister's second wedding as well. They are just two messy little lumps after all these years, but we made fairy dresses for them and they sat in the apple tree and watched the garden ceremony. Later we put them on the wedding cake.

Old woman, enough!
Get up! It's late!
I will! But you'll have to wait
till I stretch these old, old, old, old knees—
I'm getting there, really I am.
One foot at a time I'm touching the floor.
Soon I'll be standing—
but not too fast
or I might fall down.
I might disgrace
this old, old self by landing—
silly old clown—
flat on my face.
I'm up at last!
Like sun! You see?
I'm up! (And only barely recalling
the youngster who long, long ago was me
with never a hint of a fear of falling.)

(From *How Does It Feel to Be Old?* by Norma Farber. Illustrated by Trina Schart Hyman.)

(From *Peter Pan* by J. M. Barrie. Illustrated by Trina Schart Hyman.)

"I figured out at four years old that *somebody* had made the pictures in my books and though I didn't know what these people were called, I knew *I* wanted to be a book illustrator. I remember when my parents gave me an edition of Grimm's *Fairy Tales* illustrated by Fritz Kredel (whose work I love now), I thought the pictures were hideous because the princesses didn't have long hair or pretty dresses. I knew I'd do better than that—at least I'd make my princesses pretty. I

began to make books from my own stories and drew pictures to illustrate them.

"I skipped first grade, but later became a terrible student. I couldn't concentrate on school work; all I wanted was to be left alone to read books, listen to music, or draw pictures of witches and princesses. Of course there were some kind and even inspiring teachers who did their best to 'draw me out.'

When she got there, she was amazed to find the door open, and she tiptoed in. ■ (From *Little Red Riding Hood,* retold and illustrated by Trina Schart Hyman.)

But in general I hated school, and was terrified and paralyzed by it. I do not learn, concentrate or perform well in a traditional classroom situation. Like many people, I learn best by *doing*. If I need to *use* what I have to learn, I learn it quickly and well, but I'm no scholar. Because I was an easily intimidated and daydreaming kid, I reacted in the worst way to the extroverted, structured atmosphere of a public school classroom and to the bullying of many of the teachers. (I still hate to even visit a school as 'visiting author'—my stomach sinks and my palms sweat with fear, just as they always did. Schools have changed somewhat, for the better—but not nearly enough to suit me. Too many of the teachers are still bullies—*unimaginative* and *stupid* bullies, at that.) The things that would have inspired me to learn as a child were flights of fancy, love, humor, drama, inspiration, excitement and concern for other human beings—and *Beauty*. And yet these elements were

In the next room, he found the most beautiful princess he had ever seen. ■ (From *The Water of Life,* retold by Barbara Rogasky. Illustrated by Trina Schart Hyman.)

A great argument arose. ■ (From *The Man Who Loved Books* by Jean Fritz. Illustrated by Trina Schart Hyman.)

and still are sadly lacking in our public schools. After eleven years, I came out of the public school system believing that I was a hopelessly stupid little creature who would never be able to learn or to think.

"I could draw, though, and after I graduated from high school, I went to art school in Philadelphia. Everything changed. Suddenly, I was not only *allowed* to draw all day long, I was *expected* to! I was surrounded by other artists, and we talked, ate, lived and dreamed about art. It was as though I had been living all my life in a strange country where I could never quite fit in, and now I had come home."

1959-61. Married Harris Hyman, a mechanical engineer. Studied art at Boston Museum School of the Arts, and Konstfackskolan (Swedish State Art School) in Stockholm, Sweden. "Harris and I lived in one big room in a big old house in Stockholm. Harris went to classes at the university and worked for IBM-Sweden part-time, while I went to art school. That spring, I got my first real job, illustrating a children's book, *Toffe och den lilla bilen* (Toffe and the Little Car). I had been taking my portfolio around to publishers, trying to get illustration work, ever since Philadelphia. Every month or so I did new pieces and went the rounds again. This time, author/editor Astrid Lindgren liked what she saw and gave me a book to do. Of course, the text was in Swedish, so it took nearly as

long for me to translate it as it did to draw the forty-six black and white illustrations."

Returned to Boston. "We bought a little house, right in the heart of downtown Boston, just two blocks from the Common. It was a mess when we bought it, and we worked hard to fix it up. In between tearing down walls and sanding floors, I got the old portfolio out and went looking for work. Nobody seemed to want a young brilliant illustrator, but I was pretty tough in those days, and my determination was fierce. Eventually I did get work—two little Golden Books and some textbook illustration. Not enough! I wanted to illustrate my beloved fairy tales, folk tales, and important, exciting children's books."

1963. Assigned a book of Irish folk tales, *Children of the Salmon*. "An art school friend of mine got the job of art director for adult books at Little, Brown and Co. She offered me the illustration job. It was an important favor in more ways than one. Because of the work I did on that book, another person at Little, Brown—Helen Jones, the children's book editor whom I had pestered often with my portfolio—decided to give me a book to do. That was the start of the most important relationship of my professional life and an important friendship, as well. I guess every young artist needs a special someone—a teacher, patron, relative, friend, or editor—who will say, 'I believe in you.' I loved and respected her with all

Samuel did as he was told. ■ (From *Why Don't You Get a Horse, Sam Adams?* by Jean Fritz. Illustrated by Trina Schart Hyman.)

"Come tell me, Brother Mouse, what news is abroad?" ■ (From *Joy to the World: Christmas Legends* by Ruth Sawyer. Illustrated by Trina Schart Hyman.)

my heart and listened to her carefully and learned a lot. She gave me courage and knocked some good sense into me at the same time.''

Daughter, Katrin, born. ''I had visions of a shy, little, pink fairy daughter who would stand by my drawing board and keep me company. Katrin Hyman was born, screaming her head off. She didn't stop screaming for a year and a half, until she learned to talk. A shy little fairy she certainly wasn't. I never saw a more stubborn, aggressive, opinionated baby in my whole life.''

1968. Divorced Harris Hyman. Moved to Lyme, New Hampshire. ''Nancie, my painter friend from Sweden, and her two-year-old twin daughters, Clea and Gaby, shared a little old stone house with Katrin and me on the northern bank of the Connecticut River. In the winter, Katrin started nursery school in the town of Thetford across the river. For fun, I wrote a little story about her called *How Six Found Christmas* and gave it to our landlord, Ed, as a birthday present. Helen Jones saw the story and liked it well enough to publish it. Now I was an author as well as an illustrator.

''During the next five years, I worked harder than I ever had before. With two adults and three children, bills piled up, and although I was getting more and more work to do, there were still many months when there wasn't enough money for groceries. Finally we worked out a system so that I could take on more books, with Nancie doing the layouts and color overlays. We worked long, late hours at our drawing boards, but were more secure and happy now. Friends came to visit from New York, Boston, Philadelphia, and even California; our lives were exciting and full of picnics and adventures.''

Purchased an old rambling farmhouse in Lyme. ''After nearly a year of looking at all the houses for sale in Vermont and New Hampshire, we found the house we were looking for right around the corner. On the coldest day of January, with the help of neighbors and friends, we moved our five-year collection of stuff out of the stone house and into the farmhouse. The next day, I set up my drawing board and went back to work.''

1972. Became art director for *Cricket* magazine. ''One day in June the publisher of a small Midwestern textbook company, his wife and two daughters came to see us at the farm. They wanted to start a magazine for children, and they wanted me to be the art director. As art director for *Cricket,* I wrote to every illustrator whose work I'd ever admired or loved as a child, art student or envious fellow illustrator. Word went out that unknown and aspiring artists should send me their portfolios, via letters, phone calls, taxis, and Volkswagens, whatever. Our farm was full of artists. We gave wonderful parties and produced and directed an occasional fairy tale.

"Is it possible, neighbor," said they, that kindly, "that ye'd lend us the mare for to go to Widecombe Fair?"

Tom went on walking his field but mumbled at last, "And when shall I see the grey mare again?"

"Aw," said Jan Stewer, that kindly, "by Friday noon or Saturday soon."

And Tom went on walking but nodded aye.

(From *On to Widecombe Fair* by Patricia Lee Gauch. Illustrated by Trina Schart Hyman.)

"Let's post Mr. Daniel a snowball through his letter box."

"Let's write things in the snow."

"Let's write, 'Mr. Daniel looks like a spaniel' all over his lawn."

Or we walked on the white shore. "Can the fishes see it's snowing?"

(From *A Child's Christmas in Wales* by Dylan Thomas. Illustrated by Trina Schart Hyman.)

"Working for *Cricket* magazine as an art director was terrific because it put me in contact with many working artists. It's nice to exchange ideas and opinions about art, to talk shop. Book illustration can be an isolating experience. You work at home for months, send off a finished set of illustrations, and unless the book is a howling success, you never get any real feedback. It's very lonely work, as I imagine writing is. On the other hand, when I'm in the middle of a book, I would love to be a solitary hermit on the top of a mountain in Tibet. Next year, I'm building a studio for myself, a healthy compromise—a 'room of my own.'"

Though Hyman has retold various classics and authored several books, she does not consider herself a writer. "I don't feel in control of the craft of writing, which makes me feel self-conscious about the act of writing. I do feel confident about retelling classics, such as *Sleeping Beauty* or *Little Red Riding Hood,* but that doesn't involve inventing a plot or characters. When I retell a classic, I gather all the versions and read them. I pick those I like best, and which I feel are suitable for today's readers. Then I sit down and write out the tale from beginning to end. Once I have my version, I go back to the others for details I may weave back in.

"I once had an editor tell me that violence was accepted in children's books, but that sex—meaning a princess in sexy clothes—was forbidden. Doesn't that say something about our culture? My work has been criticized in reviews and by librarians for my portrayal of gorgeous, vivacious female characters. For example, I received a lot of flack for *King Stork,* because I made the princess a real dish. The funny thing is that my daughter, Katrin, and the twins, Clea and Gaby, who were all six at the time, worked out the princess' clothes for me. I then illustrated their ideas of how a princess should look. I still receive letters from outraged librarians and school teachers about that book. However, one father wrote saying that he'd never be able to thank me enough. Apparently, his nine-year-old son had never succeeded in reading a book straight through until *King Stork.* I'm sure it had something to do with my princess.

"I don't like to show gruesome images in my illustration. In *Saint George and the Dragon,* the scene where George kills the dragon seemed very important to illustrate at first. In all the paintings of the legend I had studied, the artist had chosen to portray George slaying the dragon. I finally realized that these paintings all depicted George killing a dragon smaller than his horse. The Edmund Spenser version (retold by Margaret Hodges), which I was illustrating, described an enormous dragon. I couldn't figure out how to show George killing such a large dragon without making it a bloodbath. Margaret Hodges, bless her heart, finally suggested, 'Skip that image and show the dragon already dead.' It never would have occurred to me in a million years, but it was effective.

"Some books, like *Saint George* ... require not only a great deal of research, but some tough decisions. Our basic source, the Elizabethan era of Edmund Spenser, was too limiting. For our historical setting we chose the romantic pre-Arthurian period which I felt was more true to the feeling of the story. I researched the pre-Norman conquests, and though it had nothing to do with the story, I decided to use decorative borders of flowers and herbs indigenous to fourth-century England, an idea which grew out of a personal interest in herb lore and botany. Every Italian Renaissance painter did a 'Saint George and the Dragon,' but none of them painted Spenser's dragon and I had to be faithful to the text. I wanted a dragon with personality so I perused books on reptiles, lizards, even dinosaurs and then made a composite. I studied lizard scales

very carefully, as they have a notched shape quite different from snake scales, and used them in my illustration. My dragon's entire physiognomy is correct for a reptile, except for the wings, which were inspired by images of a pterodactyl."

Hyman was also inspired by a vision she had one morning of Spenser's dragon. "Every morning, unless the temperature is lower than ten degrees below zero, I take the same two-mile walk with the dogs. We go down to the river and then past Bernard Tullar's farm and back up the hill to our own road and then home. The landscape of our upper Connecticut River Valley is very like the west country of England and Wales— all sharp little grassy hills and wooded valleys and rocky fields. One misty morning in March, when I was taking this walk and thinking about what the dragon was thinking, I heard him coming toward me, across Bernard's cow pasture. I heard him first, like the sound of distant thunder, and then I saw him— I saw the huge shape of the dragon appear on the crest of the hill. And before I even had the chance to be frightened, he was gone." [Trina Schart Hyman, "Caldecott Medal Acceptance," *Horn Book,* July/August, 1985.[1]]

As part of the creative process, "to be left alone with the job is very important to me. I came into this world alone, and I'll go out of it alone, and each book I do is the same kind of birth and maybe the same kind of death on a smaller scale. I don't do sketches, or preliminaries. I think about it instead. I think about the story and about what it means and about how it can be brought to life in pictures. I think about the characters and what makes them tick and where they're coming from and where they might be going to. Who *are* these people? What do they like to eat for breakfast? How do they react in a situation that's *outside* this story? What are they *really* thinking while this story is happening to them? I think about the landscape. Where is this taking place? What time of year is it? What was the weather like? Was the sky in the fourth century the same as the sky we see now? Obviously, it wasn't. What was it like, then? Were the stars brighter, the light more pure, the colors clearer? What was this dragon like? *Were* there dragons? Of course there were. They still exist somewhere, I bet. So, what did he look like? What did *he* eat for breakfast?

"I think about all this a lot. I think about it so much that eventually I start to dream about it. And when my dreams start to become the dreams of the characters in the book, when their reality becomes a part of my subconscious, when I can live in their landscape, when I put on a little red cape with a hood and tie the red ribbons under my chin, then I know what to do with my pictures."[1]

"By contrast the Grimm's tale *The Water of Life* was not set in any particular time or place and didn't require much research, except for architectural details as well as saddles, bridles and other riding gear. These changed drastically over the centuries and my drawings of them had to be accurate and consistent.

"I feel like an actor preparing for a role when I'm working on a book. I need to get inside my characters and begin to think and feel their thoughts and feelings before I can succeed in my illustrations. In order to do that, I have to become them. I often get up from my drawing board and act out scenes. If I have to know the movements, for example, of a sword fight, I can't really see it in my mind's eye until I try the movement for myself. It's a way of finding gesture, and it's a necessary part of my process. I don't think an artist can create something that has truth or validity unless he or she is willing to be totally engaged in the work. I'm not very concerned with the surface of the picture, I'm not a stylist or an artist who simply decorates. I have to get into the story, the situation. And because I draw fairly realistically, it's absolutely necessary that the drawings be truthful. Illustration is theatre. You have to pick a setting, create characters, costumes, lighting. You even have to think about weather and how the weather creates mood. I often think I should have been a film director, because I see the imagery of a story in my mind as a film first, from which I pick out particular frames that I want to illustrate.

"It's important for me to live in the country for many reasons: one being that the light here is real. Although you can see light in cities, it has a different quality and is certainly not related to fairy or folk tales. If I were illustrating a book on inner city kids, I'd have to take a trip down to New York to see how the light acts in a big city.

"I really had to work at capturing light in my illustrations—and I'm still working at it. It's the hardest aspect of illustration and the older I get, the more convinced I am of its paramount importance. Light sets the mood, renders the images, and gives color its quality and intensity. Illustrator Garth Williams inspired me to think about light. I was illustrating *Snow White* when he came to Lyme for a visit. During his stay, he would often look over my shoulder while I worked. 'You must think more about and in *terms* of light and light source,' he told me one day. 'Light can create drama—light means *everything* in illustration.' He was right. I began to open my eyes, and study light. Winter light, for example, is quite amazing, especially up here and in the evening, when there is snow on the ground. The light from the sky reflected on the snow is magic—everything becomes peach, lavender and aquamarine and it feels as though you are living inside an opal. Now I set up problems

for myself: how would a lantern or a burning candle in a castle garden look in the morning when it's already light out? I worked on that particular problem for two weeks until I finally solved it.

"I think of myself as a black-and-white illustrator. Color was something I had to learn. My books are getting more and more colorful and I'm getting better at it. But working in black and white is always a joy—it's like writing a letter, whereas color is like writing a novel.

"I don't use models, I think about friends and relatives when I create a character. The man who lives across the road, an old Vermont farmer, has very strong features and I've used him endlessly in illustrations. He was the woodsman in *Little Red Riding Hood*. If I'm using him as a character and get stuck, I just walk over, pay him a visit, and study his face for an hour. It's fun to cast your friends as characters."

Asked which of her books were favorites, Hyman replied, "I'm still very fond of *Snow White,* which is technically one of my best books. *Little Red Riding Hood* was a very personal book and so much fun to illustrate that I'd love to do it all over again. But overall, I consider *How Does It Feel to Be Old?* by Norma Farber, to be my best book. Farber wrote the story to answer a child's questions about what it feels like to grow old. I used a very dear friend as the model for the grandmother, and Katrin at ten years old as the model for the child. Because I found the book very moving, my feelings about loss and cherished loved ones communicate through the illustrations."

Original brush drawing for *Witch Poems.*

"That is trade, is it not?" he said. "You get what you want and I get what I want." ■ (From *The Mechanical Doll* by Pamela Stearns. Illustrated by Trina Schart Hyman.)

Hyman traveled to Wales to study the landscape for *A Child's Christmas in Wales*. "I had always wanted to illustrate *A Child's Christmas in Wales* because it is one of my favorite stories and because I felt it had never been illustrated the right way. I love Dylan Thomas, an extraordinary writer. His text is so poetic and full of dreamlike imagery, but I felt that the story required my drawings to be precise and very real. I also did the book design on *A Child's Christmas in Wales,* and Dylan Thomas actually helped me design the book! I was having a hard time pacing the illustrations, until it dawned on me that I should listen to the recording of Thomas reading the story. Each time he paused, I made the page turn, and it worked out beautifully.

"I'd forgotten what a good writer Charles Dickens was until I illustrated *A Christmas Carol*. At first I thought I would illustrate it with radical differences from other versions I was familiar with, choosing different scenes than my predecessors had. In the end, I had to illustrate it the way *Dickens* told me to. He wrote so vividly and distinctly, it was as if he were standing behind my drawing board telling me what I had to draw. When I finished all the drawings, I looked back over the Arthur Rackham illustrations, which I had purposely avoided while I was working, only to discover that he and I had illustrated the same scenes! It was Dickens who told us how to illustrate his *Christmas Carol*. You can't be original when you're working with an author who has a mind of his own.

"Sometimes I like a text which will give me some room to play, a text which, unlike Dickens, needs definition and is crying out for pictures. But I must work from a good story. I

(Detail of a double-page spread by Trina Schart Hyman from *Snow White* by the Brothers Grimm.)

Trina Schart Hyman in her farmhouse kitchen in Lyme, New Hampshire. Photograph by Agnes Garrett.

prefer texts that stick to your ribs, and if a book doesn't move me, I won't illustrate it.

"Fairy tales are mythic and express great human drama, showing us how to work things out in life and giving us deep and vital information. I feel very strongly that as a culture, we are being fed too much visual junk food. We are bombarded by television, advertising and the media, and fine art no longer exists as we once knew it. Contemporary art—minimalist painting and color field—is not concerned with mythic images, and yet we *need* pictures we can think and dream about, relate to and experience. That's why book illustration is important. Books are one of the last places where we can find pictures. Children's books are carrying on the tradition of fine art, figurative painting, which I believe will re-emerge to replace minimalism. Meanwhile, somebody has to keep up the tradition, and it might as well be children's book illustrators."

Hyman is often said to be one of the better romantic illustrators of our time. "Romance and drama are interconnected for me. The great Romantic paintings had to do with symbolism and landscape and weather and storytelling. And while I love the grand mythic and symbolic elements of Romantic painting, I also enjoy contemporary realistic illustration because I love to draw people and their reactions, whether the story happens in fourth-century England or right now in Brooklyn.

"I do all my work on the same piece of paper, so my preliminary sketches *become* the finished piece of art work. First I make a pencil drawing, then I use India ink and brush followed by acrylic paint, which I dilute like watercolor and apply in thin glazes. I believe that because I work on the same piece of drawing board, the pictures are alive. My own struggle, underneath the final image, is what gives the picture its soul.

"When I run up against a technical difficulty, I study the illustrators I admire to see how they solved similar problems. Arthur Rackham, Edmund Dulac, Charles Robinson, N. C. Wyeth, Howard Pyle, Jessie Willcox Smith could all draw like demons, and although I never wind up adopting their strategies, looking at their work often gives me a jumping-off point. I also go back to painters such as Rembrandt and Goya for inspiration. They could do anything! That's my ambition, and though Rembrandt's talent is probably not in my genes, I'll still work hard to try and live up to his technical skill. I make progress with every book, but am still so frustrated by what I *can't* do, and become furious when I can't translate exactly what I see in terms of vantage point, color, light or composition.

"I also admire many of my contemporaries including Shirley Hughes, Wallace Tripp, David Macaulay, Jerry Pinkney, Chris Van Allsberg, Garth Williams, Margot Tomes, the Provensens, Barbara Cooney and Raymond Briggs. I have a special respect for illustrators who know how to understate, to underplay a scene. My instinct, because I love drama and romance, is to pull out the stops and show it all."

Hyman describes herself as a "life-affirming feminist-humanist. I was raised with very mixed signals. On the one hand, I

(From "Dame Hickory" by Walter De La Mare in *Fairy Poems*, edited by Daisy Wallace. Illustrated by Trina Schart Hyman.)

was told that the man is always right, and on the other, I was told that I could do anything I wanted. Women artists are still treated as second-class citizens and it's high time for this double standard to end. I hope through my work to give all young people the idea that women are wonderful, strong creatures. I believe that men and women are separate—that's why I don't see any point in putting one of my fairy tale princesses in blue jeans or a three-piece suit—but equal. One cannot have real beauty without intellect and wit, and my fairy princesses are gorgeous *and* strong as steel. I like masculine men and feminine women and all the people in between. I believe kids should be given images of a wide variety of people, a spectrum of humanity.''

To young people interested in becoming artists, Hyman notes, ''You have to be dedicated down to your bones to be an artist. It's a vocation and you must believe in it, and in yourself. It's much more competitive now than when I started out, so you must be either very lucky or equipped with an ego of iron.''

Hyman won the 1985 Caldecott medal for *Saint George and the Dragon.* In her acceptance speech, she reflected, ''I've always longed to be the sort of artist who simply paints pictures—big, mysterious, grown-up paintings on canvas—with oil paint. But I can't. I can't because there are too many stories in the world, too many books waiting to be illustrated, and not enough time to illustrate them all or to learn how to do it well enough. Besides, I have this consuming, fatal passion for books—the books themselves, the way they look and smell, the feel of them, and of course the stories that they have to tell. When I'm upset or depressed or unhappy, I go to a bookstore for comfort, the way other people go to a church or to a therapist. Books and illustrations are part of me: They're not just what I do; they're what I *am.*''[1]

HOBBIES AND OTHER INTERESTS: Kids, animals, weather, food, pictures, stories, and music.

FOR MORE INFORMATION SEE: Lee Kingman and others, compilers, *Illustrators of Children's Books: 1957-1966,* Horn Book, 1968; *Horn Book,* December, 1969, August, 1973, July/August, 1985; *Cricket,* September, 1975; *Wilson Library Bulletin,* October, 1977; L. Kingman and others, compilers, *Illustrators of Children's Books: 1967-1976,* Horn Book, 1978; Doris de Montreville and Elizabeth D. Crawford, editors, *Fourth Book of Junior Authors and Illustrators,* H. W. Wilson, 1978; *American Artist,* May, 1979; Trina Schart Hyman, *Self-Portrait: Trina Schart Hyman,* Addison-Wesley, 1981.

HYNDMAN, Jane Andrews 1912-1978 (Lee Wyndham)

PERSONAL: Born December 16, 1912, in Melitopol, Ukraine, Russia (now U.S.S.R.); came to the United States in 1923, became naturalized U.S. citizen, 1942; died March 18, 1978, in Morristown, N.J.; daughter of Andrew and Alexandra Levchenko; married Robert Hyndman (a writer and editor under pseudonym Robert Wyndham), 1933 (died 1973); children: William Lee, Jane Elizabeth. *Education:* Attended schools in the United States and Turkey; studied singing and painting. *Politics:* Republican. *Religion:* Episcopalian. *Residence:* Morristown, N.J.

CAREER: Author. *Morristown Daily Record,* Morristown, N.J., children's book editor, 1949-58; *Philadelphia Inquirer,* Philadelphia, Pa., children's book editor, 1950-63; New York University, New York, N.Y., lecturer on writing for children

and teenagers, 1958-72; author of syndicated children's book column in five New Jersey area newspapers, beginning 1963. Consultant, and director of the Masters Program, Institute of Children's Literature, Redding Ridge, Conn. Lecturer, book critic, free-lance editor, and project consultant. Conducted writing seminars at universities and writers' conferences, including Syracuse University, Fairleigh Dickinson University, Colorado Woman's College, New Hampshire Writers' Seminar, and First International Christian Writers' Conference, Green Lake, Wis., 1962. Did professional fashion modeling in New York. *Member:* Authors Guild of the Authors League of America, Women's National Book Association (New York), Society of Children's Book Writers (served on board of directors).

AWARDS, HONORS: A Dance for Susie was listed among the Best Books of the Year, 1953, by the *New York Times, Saturday Review of Literature,* and *Chicago Tribune;* New Jersey Institute of Technology Author Award, 1961, for *Beth Hilton, Model,* 1970, for *Russian Tales of Fabulous Beasts and Marvels, Tales the People Tell in Russia* and *The Winter Child: An Old Russian Folktale,* and 1976, for *Holidays in Scandinavia;* New Jersey Institute of Technology New Jersey Author Award Special Citation, 1969, for Husband and Wife Writers of Children's Books; *Russian Tales of Fabulous Beasts and Marvels* and *Florence Nightingale: Nurse to the World* were both chosen as a Children's Book of the Year by the Child Study Association of America, 1969, *The Winter Child: An Old Russian Folktale* and *Tales the People Tell in Russia,* 1970.

WRITINGS—All under pseudonym, Lee Wyndham: *Sizzling Pan Ranch* (illustrated by Robert Logan), Crowell, 1951; *Slipper under Glass* (illustrated by Vera Bock; Junior Literary Guild selection), Longmans, Green, 1952; *Golden Slippers* (illustrated by V. Bock; Junior Literary Guild selection), Longmans, Green, 1953; *Silver Yankee* (illustrated by Janet Smalley), Winston, 1953; *A Dance for Susie* (illustrated by Jane Miller), Dodd, 1953; (with Louise Barnes Gallagher) *Buttons and Beaux,* Dodd, 1953; *Showboat Holiday* (illustrated by Jean MacDonald Porter; Junior Literary Guild selection), Winston, 1954; *Susie and the Dancing Cat* (illustrated by J. Miller), Dodd, 1954; *Binkie's Billions* (illustrated by Raymond Abel), Knopf, 1954.

Susie and the Ballet Family (illustrated by J. Miller), Dodd, 1955; (with Thalia Mara) *First Steps in Ballet* (illustrated by George Bobrizsky), Doubleday, 1955, published in England as *Ballet: Home Practice for Beginners,* Constable, 1955; *Camel Bird Ranch* (illustrated by Bob Riger; Junior Literary Guild selection), Dodd, 1955; *Ballet Teacher,* Messner, 1956; *The Lost Birthday Present* (illustrated by Paul Brown), Dodd, 1957; *Lady Architect,* Messner, 1957; *On Your Toes, Susie!* (illustrated by J. Miller), Dodd, 1958; *Dance to My Measure,* Messner, 1958; *Candy Stripers,* Messner, 1958; *Ballet for You* (illustrated by Catherine Scholz), Grosset, 1959.

The Timid Dragon (illustrated by Kurt Werth), Lothrop, 1960; *Bonnie* (illustrated by Nina Albright), Doubleday, 1960; (with husband, Robert Wyndham) *The Little Wise Man* (illustrated by Anthony D'Adamo), Bobbs-Merrill, 1960; *Chip Nelson and the Contrary Indians* (illustrated by David Stone), F. Watts, 1960; *Susie and the Ballet Horse* (illustrated by J. M. Porter), Dodd, 1961; *Beth Hilton, Model,* Messner, 1961; *The How and Why Wonderbook of Ballet* (illustrated by Rafaello Busoni), Grosset, 1961; (editor) *Dancers, Dancers, Dancers!,* F. Watts, 1961; (editor) *Acting, Acting, Acting!,* F. Watts, 1962; *The Family at Seven Chimneys House* (illustrated by Jo Polseno), F. Watts, 1963; *Thanksgiving* (illustrated by Hazel Hoecker), Garrard, 1963.

(Compiler with R. Wyndham) *The Complete Birthday Book,* F. Watts, 1967; *Writing for Children and Teen-agers* (adult), Writer's Digest, 1968, 2nd revised edition, 1980; *Mourka, the Mighty Cat* (illustrated by Charles Mikolaycak), Parents Magazine Press, 1969; *Russian Tales of Fabulous Beasts and Marvels* (illustrated by C. Mikolaycak), Parents Magazine Press, 1969; *Florence Nightingale: Nurse to the World* (illustrated by Richard Cuffari), World Publishing, 1969, published as *The Lady with the Lamp: The Story of Florence Nightingale,* Scholastic Book Services, 1972.

Tales the People Tell in Russia (illustrated by Andrew Antal), Messner, 1970; *The Winter Child: An Old Russian Folktale* (illustrated by Yaroslava), Parents Magazine Press, 1970; (with R. Wyndham) *Tales the People Tell in China,* Messner, 1971; *Holidays in Scandinavia* (illustrated by Gordon Laite), Garrard, 1975; (editor) *The Favorites: A Collection of Stories and Articles Selected by Editors of Children's Magazines,* Institute of Children's Literature, 1976.

Adapter: Daphne du Maurier, *The King's General,* Doubleday, 1954; (author of revision) *Games and Stunts for All Occasions,* Lippincott, 1957; (author of revision) *Year 'Round Party Book,* Lippincott, 1957; Enid Bagnold, *National Velvet* (illustrated by Al Brule), Grosset, 1961; (from Walt Disney's screenplay) Mark Twain, *The Prince and the Pauper,* Whitman, 1962; *Folk Tales of India,* Bobbs-Merrill, 1962; (author of condensation) Charles Dickens, *A Tale of Two Cities,* Prentice-Hall, 1962; *Folk Tales of China,* Bobbs-Merrill, 1963; *Tales from the Arabian Nights* (illustrated by Robert J. Lee),

Whitman, 1965. Also adapter (from M-G-M motion picture script) with R. Wyndham of *Ben Hur,* Books Unlimited. Contributor of articles to *Writer* and *Writer's Digest* and of stories and articles to national magazines. Author of syndicated newspaper column, "The Junior Book Shelf."

SIDELIGHTS: **December 16, 1912.** "I was born four thousand miles away from where I live today—in the country house of my Russian grandfather, outside the small city of Melitopol, near the Sea of Azov, in the Ukraine.

"My grandfather was a dear scholarly gentleman who lectured in a university and also conducted a school for the village children near his home. I have a loving though fuzzy memory of my bearded grandfather, fused with a benign portrait of Tolstoy that hung somewhere in his house. Probably in the 'book room' which was filled with huge, gilt-edged tomes I used to haul out and lug about the house long before I learned to read. It was here that the first seeds for my own story telling were planted, for having no playmates, I made up stories and imaginary friends.

"I learned to read Russian, more or less under grandpa's beard, while he perused his daily paper, with me in his lap. I don't remember ever learning to read in any other way. Years later I learned to read English in similar fashion—by sight. Never by sounding out syllables. The words came to me whole. When I was nine, I read Charles Dickens' *David Copperfield* in Russian, while seated on a Turkish bench high above the minarets of Constantinople, and looking down upon the Golden Horn— the crescent-shaped inlet of the Bosporus that formed the harbor for this city. At thirteen I read the same book in English,

JANE ANDREWS HYNDMAN

"But I am real!" a tiny voice said. "I am a real Snow Girl. See?" ■ (From *The Winter Child: An Old Russian Folktale*, retold by Lee Wyndham. Illustrated by Yaroslava.)

in a park outside the Yonkers (New York) public library. I had come a long, long, way.

"My father was a White Russian Officer in the Tsar's army. He left to take up his commission a week after I was born. My earliest memory of him includes a spanking—after I had kicked him—because I found him, a total stranger! kissing *my* mother. I must have been all of two and a half at that time, when he came home on leave.

"When I was five, the Russian Revolution was upon us, and mother decided to join my father behind the lines at the fighting front. For two years we careened behind the army retreating from the Bolsheviks. Sometimes we commandeered plush quarters, more often we slept in barns—but always on the run. Then we were in a seaport on the Crimea—with oil tanks and ammunition dumps being blown up at our backs. I can still hear the booms and see the billowing smoke and almost feel the heat of the flames. We boarded a small Turkey-bound ship in the Harbor, leaving all of our possessions behind—even my teddy bear.

"When we sailed into Constantinople, which is built on beautiful green hillsides, the people waved sheets and tablecloths from the windows in sympathetic greeting.

"We lived in Turkey's picturesque setting for three years. I was put into various boarding schools—between hospital stays,

where I lay close to death on several occasions. At an island school, in a marvelously spooky old Greek monastery, I almost managed to drown in the Sea of Marmora. I survived everything—to come to the United States with the aid of the Red Cross."

1923. Attended school in the United States. "I learned to speak English fluently within two years, but was very shy and made few friends, so the making up of stories continued. Later I studied painting and music and was a fashion model in New York City, and developed a love for ballet, opera, the theatre and research reading—all of which proved useful when I did turn to writing professionally."

1933. Married writer-editor Robert Hyndman. "I did not begin to write seriously until after I was married (to a Mayflower American, descended from William Brewster) and had a son and daughter to enjoy my stories.

"In **1947** I fell down our back steps and broke my leg. During the enforced 'rest' I scribbled out a story and sold it to *Story Parade*, a leading children's magazine at the time. I haven't stopped scribbling since, but I do it all on an electric typewriter now."

1949. Began working as a children's book editor for a New Jersey newspaper. Hyndman's husband helped her to rewrite

Soon there was a crowd gazing on this marvel of marvels—a horseless sled speeding along by itself. And with none other than foolish Emilyan sitting inside it. ■ (From *Russian Tales of Fabulous Beasts and Marvels* by Lee Wyndham. Illustrated by Charles Mikolaycak.)

her stories and to develop her writing style. "At our house writing is a family affair and, in one way or another, everyone takes part in my creative efforts.

"Book reviewing is a family project, too. We have five columns. To supply them with reviews, we have to read hundreds of books each year. Bob handles the technical books and most of the books for boys, while I do all the rest, with help from Bill and Janie-Beth. . . ." [Lee Wyndham, "We All Work Together," *Young Wings*, October, 1952.[1]]

1951. First book for children was published. "Writing for young people is a great responsibility because their minds are impressionable and what they read can affect not only their current lives but even their futures. Writing for them should be approached with a serious regard for the possible influence of your words. Do not plan to write for children because you think it is easy, or the writing does not need to be as good as that in books for grownups. Requirements for good juvenile writing are far more strict than they are for adult fiction, and there are many dedicated people on guard to see that they are observed, for the very reasons mentioned above.

". . . You can train yourself to write even in the snippets of time available—and under almost any circumstances. I know.

"You don't *need* a book-lined, air-conditioned study, either. I have one now, but my first eight books were written in an all-purpose room filled with two children, a big black and white collie, two cats, and a TV set. I wrote right through the most gripping episodes of the Lone Ranger and Captain Video. My 'desk' was a rickety typing table and my typewriter an aged portable. My husband was a recording engineer then, and many of his sessions were run at night. So I wrote at night, too, and lullabyed the children with the sound of my tapping keys.

"Women are the interruptible, the adaptable sex, and must be able to adjust to circumstances. I had to adapt myself to my husband's odd hours until we were both able to work at home; to the children's needs (with one foot on the gas pedal); to what seemed to be overwhelming problems at times. And I know many other writers who managed to work in spite of unfavorable conditions. Successful books and stories have been written laboriously in bed by ailing men and women; and in attics and jails, concentration camps and at the bottom of the sea in submarines. They have been written at kitchen tables on brown paper sacks. There's no such thing as 'no place to write' just as there is no such thing as 'no time to write.'

". . . I broke into the juvenile writing field as a short-story writer—and I'm glad I did. In writing short fiction you can learn all the basic fundamentals of the writing craft and at the same time sharpen your ability to tell a story in relatively few words. The brisk pace becomes such a habit that when you graduate to booklengths, you will have overcome the tendency to ramble and will instead leap right into your plot and carry it along with lively action.

"Grownups, more patient than children, will bear with a slow-paced author who does not really begin his tale until page fifty. But a child's story must begin immediately—and never at any point slow down. Once you have learned to tell a story in 2,000 words—or less—you have also learned to free yourself of unnecessary details. Your stories will move ahead in the manner the modern reader has come to expect. In the course of a year you can write a great many short stories—and very possibly start to earn even as you learn how to write for children.

"A full-length book, on the other hand, must be from 30,000 to 60,000 words long. It requires much more preparation and time to write, and for a beginner, is just too much to tackle.

"I had fifty shorts and serials published before my first book was accepted. *The first book had ten rejections before it found a buyer on the eleventh submission.* It sold also as a five-part first-rights serial, made a book club, and was re-sold for second serial rights to another magazine.

"However, if I had not already had the short-story and three-and four-part serial training—and a baptism in rejection slips—I doubt if I'd have had the courage to continue submitting this book. So the short stories serve another purpose: they help to toughen a writer's skin." [Lee Wyndham, *Writing for Children and Teen-agers*, Writer's Digest, 1968.[2]]

1953. *A Dance for Susie* was listed on the *New York Times* "Best Books" list for that year. Hyndman wrote several books about ballerinas for young girls, including Junior Literary Guild selections, *Slipper under Glass* and *Golden Slippers*. "Ever since my first teen-age ballet book, *Slipper under Glass*, was published, letters have been coming in from all over the country, asking what happened next to Maggie, the heroine of the story. The only answer was to write a second book about her.

"By that time I had been fortunate in meeting the American prima ballerina, Patricia Bowman, and several of her men partners. Besides, Thalia Mara and Arthur Mahoney, teacher-directors of the Ballet Repertory School in New York, had become my friends, and so had several professional dancers and students. I asked innumerable questions, studied what they did, and visited theaters, rehearsal halls, dance studios, TV ballet broadcasts, and even a motion picture studio. This way I soon acquired reams of background material—and 'what happened next' began to grow into a book.

"The character of Alison Wells in *Golden Slippers* is patterned on Patricia Bowman, who took ballet lessons originally to build up her frail little body and her low resistance to colds. The character of the tiny, temperamental ballerina, Nadia Naladova, grew from the story of a former ballet dancer who was so tiny that she had special problems to overcome. You see, in the ballet world you cannot be too tall nor too short. Five feet six inches is a danger point for height, and a girl under five feet tall must be practically a soloist to succeed.

"I met some extremely interesting men dancers, too. They were beautifully developed athletes who took their work seriously. . . .

"All the dancers I met seemed to be bubbling over with youth and enthusiasm, even those who had been dancing for many years." [Lee Wyndham, "What Happened Next to Maggie?," *Young Wings*, November, 1953.[3]]

1954. *Showboat Holiday*, a Junior Literary Guild selection, was published. "The idea for my *Showboat Holiday* came from an illustration in a book I was reviewing (Holling C. Holling's *Min of the Mississippi*). A wrecked paddle-wheeler was shown washed up on land, with laundry flapping from a line between the smoke stacks: someone was living aboard. I transferred my paddle-wheeler to the inland waterway of the New Jersey coast, put a modern family of kids aboard, surrounded them with plenty of obstacles, and let them solve their problems. The book was a Junior Literary Guild selection, as well as a ten-part serial in *Trailblazer*."[2]

The crown is heavy and Lucia must be careful of the flickering flames. ■ (From "The Christmas Season in Scandinavia" in *Holidays in Scandinavia* by Lee Wyndham. Illustrated by Gordon Laite.)

Ever since he could remember, Mourka had lived by his wits. Once he had belonged to a peddler who went from village to village in Old Russia, selling his goods to the country people. Mourka rode in the peddler's wagon and slept in the straw among the pots and pans. His food was the scraps the peddler threw him from his own skimpy meals.

Whenever the peddler stopped to do business, Mourka jumped out to explore.

(From *Mourka, the Mighty Cat* by Lee Wyndham. Illustrated by Charles Mikolaycak.)

1957. A book for young children, aged three to four, entitled *The Lost Birthday Present,* was published. "For the very young child, . . . the story must be short and must come to a satisfying conclusion at one sitting. It must not bore the adult reading it, either! When writing picture books, your reader is two people, and you must work to please both.

"The humor in young children's stories has to be direct and obvious, must hinge on situations which are within the child's range of understanding. It must not involve experiences and situations with which a child in normal circumstances is not likely to be familiar. This is the area in which 'adult whimsey' goes astray most frequently, with a story that is completely over the child's head.

". . . *The Lost Birthday Present* . . . strikes a note of drama with the title, and goes on to depict the twins, Ginny and Peter, whose loving grandparents try to find 'an exactly right super special birthday present' for them. They find it on a ranch in Arizona—Tiny Timmie, a miniature burro, which they have shipped east. Almost at his destination, the tiny creature escapes. About half the book is devoted to Timmie's adventures before he is happily found just in time for the birthday celebration.

"In this book, and in all my 'Susie' picture books, I have utilized a 'grownup' touch—chapters, only three to five hundred words long, but enough to break the book up into interesting sections. This appeals especially to the six- and seven-year olds. The animals involved in *The Lost Birthday Present,* incidentally, 'seem' to talk to each other. They *never* talk to people, so this is a 'real' story.

"The picture book is one of the hardest things to write. It requires the sternest discipline of writing skill—not a word wasted. Rewrite it time and again—four, five, ten times—for the desired effect.

"Walter de la Mare said: 'Only the rarest kind of best in anything can be good enough for the young.' And so, the picture book writer must be a perfectionist, for the production of a lasting children's book is a specialized and highly developed art.

"But think—a novel may be forgotten in three months. Even the best ones are seldom read more than once by their buyers. A good children's book, on the other hand, should sell for at least ten years, usually longer, and once beloved; it will be read again and again, first by the parent to the child, and then so thoroughly memorized, the child will 'read' it to himself!

"Is it worth the effort? Of course it is!" [Lee Wyndham, "Writing for the 'Look 'n' Listen Age,'" *Writer,* April, 1960.[4]]

1963. Started a newspaper column on children's books, which was syndicated in five New Jersey newspapers. "Writing for young people is a great responsibility. An author can help mold character and even influence a young person's choice of and training for a career. I feel that young people make the most responsive and satisfying audience of all. My aim in writing stories for them is to create reading matter they will enjoy, and to foster the idea that reading is fun. I keep my backgrounds and all factual information as authentic as personal experience and research can make them. In my book talks—and I have addressed assemblies of as many as 750 youngsters—I stress the thought that in books they can find answers to anything they want to know, and that librarians are their friends, eager and ready to help them. Books have always been magic carpets to me, and I hope mine prove to be magic carpets for my readers."

1968. Published a practical guide for would-be writers entitled *Writing for Children and Teen-agers.* Hyndman, who wrote under the pseudonym Lee Wyndham, also lectured on writing for several years.

"There is much to learn about this special field. But if you have the qualifications, really love to write, and have the necessary spark of God-given talent, learn you can.

"Writing is an intensely personal form of communication. That is what gives it variety, freshness, interest, and surprise. No single method can be proclaimed *the* one to use. No writer should be forced to use another's method, no matter how successful that method is for that writer. Even the way a story is initially considered varies from writer to writer."[2]

Hyndman's textbook is widely used in schools, universities and correspondence courses in the United States and abroad. With more than fifty books for children, Hyndman is well qualified to offer her ten "commandments" to would-be writers:

"1 Love thy Subject.

"2 Love thy Reader.

"3 Thou shalt not Begin without Prior Meditation.

"4 Thou shalt Know thy Characters as well as thou knowest thyself—even better!

"5 Thou shalt not Begin until thou Knowest Whither Thou Goest, and have a well-thought-out Plan for the Journey.

"6 Thou shalt STOP when thy story is finished.

"7 Thou shalt not Worship thy Words as Images Graven in Precious Marble.

"8 Thou shalt make a Clear, Dark-ribbon copy of thy Work.

"9 Thou shalt Study thy Markets diligently, and ONLY THEN send thy Manuscript into the world.

"10 Thou shalt not brood upon its fate, but set about the Workings of thy Next Project, with good will and a high heart."[2]

1969. *Florence Nightingale: Nurse to the World* was illustrated by Richard Cuffari. "When I first began to think of a biography of the Lady with the Lamp, I didn't dare call her anything but *Miss* Nightingale, accompanied by a mental genuflection that threw all sensible perspective out of focus. She seemed to float above the ground in a luminescent halo. If I had started to write then, F. N. would have emerged as a disembodied ghost with about as much substance.

"I collected and read avidly everything I could on F. N. here, then wrote for material available only in England. Soon letters were flying between my sister-in-law, who undertook to do the leg work there, and my home. Before long, we had discovered and embroiled in our project 'Flo's' nephew, Sir Harry Verney. He was eighty-four at the time—and twenty-nine when his famous aunt died. He had known her well. Now Sir Harry did everything to help locate necessary material and data. Oddly enough, on this side of the ocean, I had found out something *he* didn't know! and our friendship deepened as we started to track down a mystery—a small notebook that had been pilfered from an exhibit. That may yet have a happy ending!

"One clue led to another, chipping away at the plaster cast of sainthood I had built around my subject, until the real extraordinary and warmly human person began to emerge. But it wasn't until she comfortably became 'Flo' to me, as she was to her friends and family in her lifetime, that I felt I knew her well enough to write about her.

"Biographies should never be written in haste. To bring them back *alive* takes time.

"The story should usually be told in strict chronology, taking the subject up from childhood through youth to adulthood, showing his character development and motivation toward what he ultimately became."[2]

March 18, 1978. Died after a long illness in Morristown, New Jersey. ". . . Writing is a vocation so compelling that even after you know all the hard work involved, there is still nothing else you'd rather do. You cannot give it up—at least not for long. There's heady stuff in being a maker and shaker of worlds of your own creation. You can *be* anything and anyone in any time or place or occupation. And, when you are writing for the young, you are doubly blessed because you form the habit of viewing everything around you with the fresh eyes of youth. Yours is always a big, wide, shining world—regardless of the headlines."[2]

Hyndman's works are included in the de Grummond Collection at the University of Southern Mississippi and her manuscript collection is at the University of Oregon Library in Eugene.

FOR MORE INFORMATION SEE: Young Wings, October, 1952, November, 1953; Lee Wyndham, "Writing for the 'Look 'n' Listen Age,'" *Writer,* April, 1960; Muriel Fuller, editor, *More Junior Authors,* H. W. Wilson, 1963; Lee Wyndham, *Writing for Children and Teen-agers,* Writer's Digest, 1968; *Writer's Digest,* August, 1969, November, 1970; Martha E. Ward and Dorothy A. Marquardt, *Authors of Books for Young People,* 2nd edition, Scarecrow, 1971; D. L. Kirkpatrick, editor, *Twentieth-Century Children's Writers,* St. Martin's, 1978. Obituaries: *Publishers Weekly,* April 10, 1978.

JEPPSON, J(anet) O(pal)   1926-
   (Janet Asimov)

BRIEF ENTRY: Born August 6, 1926, in Ashland, Pa. Physician and author. Since 1969 Jeppson has worked as a training and supervisory analyst at the William A. White Psychoanalytic Institute in New York City, becoming director of training from 1974 to 1982. The wife of author Isaac Asimov, Jeppson revealed that she had "read science fiction and tried to write it long before I met him." Since their marriage in 1973, Jeppson has produced three science fiction works for young adults: *The Second Experiment* (Houghton, 1974), *The Last Immortal* (Houghton, 1980), and *The Mysterious Cure and Other Stories of Pshrinks Anonymous* (Doubleday, 1985). Under the name Janet Asimov, Jeppson has collaborated with her husband on a series of science fiction books for middle-grade readers. These stories are set in a futuristic world and highlight the relationship between Norby, a robot with unusual abilities, and Jeff Wells, his human owner. First introduced in *Norby, the Mixed-Up Robot* (Walker, 1983), the pair continue their adventures in *Norby's Other Secret* (Walker, 1984), *Norby and the Lost Princess* (Walker, 1985), *Norby and the Invaders* (Walker, 1985), and *The Norby Chronicles* (Ace Science Fiction & Fan-

tasy, 1986). The Asimovs are also co-editors of *Laughing Space* (Houghton, 1982), an anthology of humorous science fiction stories and cartoons. *Home and office:* 10 West 66th St., New York, N.Y. 10023.

FOR MORE INFORMATION SEE: Contemporary Authors, Volumes 49-52, Gale, 1975; *Biographical Directory of the American Psychiatric Association,* Cattell, 1977; *Science Fiction and Fantasy Literature,* Volume 2, Gale, 1979; *Who's Who in the East,* 19th edition, 1983; *The Writers Directory: 1984-1986,* Macmillan, 1983.

JOHNSON, Charlotte Buel   1918-1982

PERSONAL: Born July 21, 1918, in Syracuse, N.Y.; died February 11, 1982, in Buffalo, N.Y.; daughter of Edward Sullivan and Mary Frances (Power) Johnson; married Henry von Wodtke. *Education:* Barnard College, B.A., 1941; New York University, M.A., 1951. *Residence:* Hamburg, N.Y.

CAREER: Vincent Smith School, Port Washington, N.Y., teacher, 1941-42; St. Mary's School for Girls, Peekskill, N.Y., art teacher, 1942-45; Calhoun School, New York, N.Y., art teacher, 1946-47; Hollins College, Hollins College, Va., instructor in art history, 1947-48; Maryville College, Maryville, Tenn., 1948-52, began as instructor, became assistant professor of art history; Worcester Art Museum, Worcester, Mass., museum instructor, 1952-57; Albright-Knox Art Gallery, Buffalo, N.Y., lecturer and research assistant, 1957-58, curator of education, 1959-82. Visiting lecturer in art history, Clark University, summer, 1957; part-time lecturer in American studies, University of Buffalo, 1957-68. *Member:* College Art Association of America, American Association of Museums, International Council of Museums, Barnard College Club of

CHARLOTTE BUEL JOHNSON

Western New York (former president). *Awards, honors:* Kinnicutt travel award to Greece, summer, 1954.

WRITINGS: Color and Shape (juvenile), Buffalo Fine Arts Academy, 1971; *Contemporary Art: Exploring Its Roots and Development,* Davis Publications, 1973. Contributor of articles to professional journals, including *School Arts, Art in America,* and *Instructor.* Contributing editor, *School Arts,* 1963-70.

JOHNSON, Maud Battle   1918(?)-1985

OBITUARY NOTICE: Born about 1918; died of cancer, September 5, 1985, in Richmond, Va.; buried in Pineview Cemetery, Rocky Mount, N.C. Journalist and author. After ten years of working for various North Carolina newspapers, including four years as managing editor of the Rocky Mount *Evening Telegram,* Johnson became a best-selling author of books for teenaged girls. She is best remembered for her series of books about the troubles of a Virginia girl growing up; titles include *I'm Christy, Christy's Choice, Christy's Love,* and *Christy's Senior Year.* Johnson's most recent book, *Dating Blues,* was posthumously published.

FOR MORE INFORMATION SEE—Obituaries: *Washington Post,* September 9, 1985.

JOYCE, William   1959(?)-

BRIEF ENTRY: Born about 1959. Author and illustrator of books for children. Joyce is a graduate of Southern Methodist University where he studied filmmaking and illustrating. The first book he illustrated was *Tammy and the Gigantic Fish* (Harper, 1983), by Catherine and James Gray. *Booklist* commended his "charming pen-and-ink drawings that show a light touch in their feathery details and sure sense of composition." In this story of Tammy's fishing trip with her father and grandfather, everything goes wrong for her at first—she catches crawdads instead of fish, and her roasting hotdog falls in the fire. Just as they are about to leave, Tammy catches a gigantic fish—one of Joyce's illustrations shows her leaning against it—but takes one look at its sad eyes and pushes it back into the lake. In a review of *My First Book of Nursery Tales: Five Favorite Bedtime Tales* (Random House, 1983), retold by Marianna Mayer, *School Library Journal* observed: "Joyce's pictures faithfully depict and expand on events described in the text, and his use of color and texture gives the book an appealing, cozy quality." He also illustrated *Mother Goose* (Random House, 1984) and Bethany Roberts' *Waiting-for-Spring-Stories* (Harper, 1984).

Joyce made his debut as an author/illustrator with *George Shrinks* (Harper, 1985), the story of a boy who awakens to find himself the size of a mouse. According to a note left by his parents, who have gone out, George must do his chores before they return. He harnesses his baby brother to a wagon to take out the garbage and dons a diving helmet to feed the fish. His chores ingeniously completed, George miraculously returns to normal size just as his parents arrive home. "The understated text . . . is counterpointed by paintings with realistic detail in cartoon colors," again noted *School Library Journal,* "and—outstandingly—by their perspective." *Residence:* Shreveport, La.

KRAUZE, Andrzej   1947-

BRIEF ENTRY: Born May 7, 1947, in Dawidy Bankowe, Poland. Political cartoonist, graphic designer, and author and illustrator of children's books. Krauze graduated from Warsaw's Academy of Fine Art in 1973. From 1970 to 1977 he contributed to the satirical magazine *Szpilki,* during which time he produced hundreds of cartoons and won six prizes for best cartoon of the year; beginning in 1974, he was a regular contributor of cartoons to the weekly Warsaw journal *Kultura.* In Warsaw, he also worked for the National Theatre; the film distribution company, ZRF; and the publishing company, Czytelnik, among others. In 1979 Krauze left Poland for London, leaving behind a reputation as a noted cartoonist, poster designer, and illustrator of children's books. Throughout his career, he has held one-man exhibitions in Poland, France, and Great Britain, and has participated in exhibitions of Polish posters in Europe, Japan, and Brazil.

Andrzej Krauze's Poland (Nina Karsov, 1981) is a selection of more than eighty of his cartoons with captions in Polish, Russian, and English. In a review of the book, *Times Literary Supplement* observed: "His cartoons deal with such aspects of the Polish situation as bureaucratic corruption; the pusillanimity of the press; economic chaos; censorship. . . . The tense and anxious relationship between the Party and Solidarity is a crucial theme." As both author and illustrator of the children's book *What's So Special about Today?* (Lothrop, 1984), Krauze portrays animal characters preparing for a birthday party: Freddy Frog presses his suit, Granny Owl spends all night baking a cake. *Booklist* called the illustrations "elaborate, full-color, pen-and-wash spreads containing a generous array of animal figures."

Krauze also wrote and illustrated a series of books based on the theme that a hard day's work earns an evening of rest and fun among friends. Aimed at beginning readers, these titles include *Ellie Elephant Builds a House, Reggie Rabbit Plants a Garden,* and *Christopher Crocodile Cooks a Meal* (all Macmillan, 1985). *Address:* c/o George Snow, 1 St. Andrews Rd., London W14, England.

FOR MORE INFORMATION SEE: Times Literary Supplement, January 22, 1982; *Who's Who in Graphic Art,* De Clivo Press, 1982.

LANGONE, John (Michael)   1929-

PERSONAL: Surname is pronounced Lan-*goh*-neh; born December 23, 1929, in Cambridge, Mass.; son of Joseph (a furrier) and Josephine (Consolazio) Langone; married Dolores de Nobrega (a general contractor), September 29, 1956; children: Matthew, Gia, Lisa. *Education:* Boston University, B.S., 1953; Harvard University, special student at School of Medicine, 1969. *Politics:* Democrat. *Religion:* Roman Catholic. *Home:* 33-46 92nd St., Jackson Heights, N.Y. 11372. *Office: Discover* Magazine, Time-Life Bldg., New York, N.Y. 10020.

CAREER: Worcester Gazette, Worcester, Mass., reporter, 1954-55; United Press (UP), Boston, Mass., reporter, 1955-56; *Worcester Telegram,* Worcester, Mass., reporter, 1956-57; United Press International (UPI), Providence, R.I., bureau chief, 1957-61, editor at national radio headquarters in Chicago, Ill., 1961-62; *Boston Herald-Traveler,* Boston, medical writer, 1962-66; *Psychiatric Opinion,* Framingham, Mass., editor, 1966-68; *Boston Herald-American,* Boston, editor of medical news and author of column ''Medical Beat,'' 1968-80; *Discover* Magazine, Time, Inc., New York, N.Y., senior editor, 1980—. Member of ethics committee, Advisory Council, Radcliffe Programs in Health Care. Harvard University, lecturer in department of preventive and social medicine, 1975—, instructor in journalism for University extension program, 1976-80. Consulting science writer, Worcester Foundation for Experimental Biology, 1966-68. *Military service:* U.S. Navy, 1948-51; U.S. Air Force Reserve, 1953-62, became first lieutenant.

MEMBER: National Association of Science Writers, American Public Health Association (fellow), Harvard Medical School Alumni Association (honorary associate member). *Awards, honors:* National journalism award, American Osteopathic Association, 1966, for series on osteopathy; citation for meritorious service, U.S. Veterans Administration, 1971, for series on Veterans Administration hospitals; Kennedy fellowship in medical ethics, Harvard University, 1974-75; Center for Advanced Study in the Behavioral Sciences fellowship in science writing, Stanford University, 1978-79; Fulbright Fellowship, 1981-82; Blakeslee Award from the American Heart Association, 1985; Science Writer Award from the American Dental Association, 1985.

WRITINGS—Published by Little, Brown, except as indicated: *Death Is a Noun: A View of the End of Life,* 1972; *Goodbye to Bedlam: Understanding Mental Illness and Retardation,* 1974; *Vital Signs: The Way We Die in America,* 1974; *Bombed, Buzzed, Smashed, or . . . Sober: A Book about Alcohol,* 1976; *Life at the Bottom: The People of Antarctica,* 1978; *Long Life,* 1978; *Human Engineering: Marvel or Menace?,* 1978.

Like, Love, Lust: A View of Sex and Sexuality, 1980; *Women Who Drink,* Addison-Wesley, 1980; *Thorny Issues: How Ethics and Morality Affect the Way We Live,* 1981; *Chiropractors: A Consumer's Guide,* Addison-Wesley, 1982; *Violence! Our Fastest-Growing Public Health Problem,* 1984; *Dead End: A Book about Suicide,* 1986. Executive editor of *Journal of Abdominal Surgery,* 1963—; member of editorial board of *American Journal of Public Health,* 1971-75.

WORK IN PROGRESS: A book about Japanese youth; a book about acquired immune deficiency syndrome (AIDS).

SIDELIGHTS: ''I am, I suppose, a compulsive writer who has been nurtured in the deadline world of daily newspaper and wire service reporting; and while I cannot honestly point to any special motivating factors and circumstances, I do know that I've wanted to be a journalist since my early high school days. My motivation to be a science journalist is a bit clearer: I grew up in a family with three scientist-members, and I used to spend a good deal of time during my adolescence playing in the biology and physiology laboratories at Harvard University where they worked. I'd wash bottles, get to talk to researchers, memorize the chemical formulas on the bottle labels. Eventually, I built my own home laboratory, which became a hobby I still pursue on occasion.''

Langone has written books for teenagers, each of which concerns ''a subject rarely discussed for this age group—death and dying, genetic manipulation, love and lust, mental illness, crime and violence, responsible drinking—and each raises ethical and moral questions which I feel have too long been neglected when dealing with junior and senior high school students. I am committed to nonfiction of this genre for teenagers and am, frankly, quite impatient with the attention that fiction—which deals only obliquely, if at all, with these issues—receives. I write about the real world, and not about furry animals who talk. [My books concern such subjects as] murder and rape, euthanasia and suicide, pornography and prostitution, and recombinant DNA and the issue of science's responsibility.

''My adult books have attempted to deal with a variety of scientific and behavioral issues [such as] the biology of aging and the prolongation of life, behavior in the isolation of Antarctica, the attitudes of dying patients and their caretakers, and medical ethics.

''When writing about purely scientific subjects, I try to translate as much as possible, always bearing in mind that the readers I am most interested in [reaching] are ordinary readers who have as much right to know about esoteric laboratory research as the scientists who do that research. Science writers who have forgotten their audience and write turgid prose in an attempt to impress their scientist-colleagues trouble me, just as do the scientists who refuse to discuss their work with a journalist on the grounds that it cannot be understood by an average reader.

''My writing biases are, obviously, the product of my years as a journalist, but I feel strongly about clarity and accuracy, about writing with one's senses, and am influenced, I will admit it, by the newspaper dictum, 'You cannot send your reader to the dictionary on a crowded bus.'''

Langone traveled with the National Science Foundation to Antarctica and the South Pole in 1972, and to Israel in 1973, to report on twenty-five years in the fields of science and medicine.

FOR MORE INFORMATION SEE: New England Journal of Medicine, April 9, 1970; *New York Times Book Review,* October 22, 1972, November 5, 1972, July 21, 1974; *Kirkus Reviews,* April 1, 1974, June 15, 1976; *Psychology Today,* February, 1979; *Choice,* April, 1979.

LEHN, Cornelia 1920-

PERSONAL: Born December 15, 1920, in Leonidavka, U.S.S.R.; became a Canadian citizen; daughter of Gerhard G. (a farmer) and Sara (Ens) Lehn. *Education:* Bethel College, North Newton, Kan., B.A., 1957; attended Mennonite Biblical Seminary, 1958-59; University of Iowa, M.A., 1969. *Religion:* Mennonite. *Home:* 9103 Hazel St. S., Chilliwack, British Columbia, Canada V2P 5N5.

CAREER: Did relief work under the Mennonite Central Committee for four years, working in Germany, 1950, 1951; General Conference Mennonite Church Central Office, Commission on Education, Newton, Kan., editor, 1959-70, director of children's work, 1970-82; free-lance writer, 1982—.

WRITINGS—Juvenile; all published by Faith & Life: *God Keeps His Promise: A Bible Story Book for Young Children* (illustrated by Beatrice Darwin), 1970; *Peace Be with You* (illustrated by Keith R. Neely), 1980; *Involving Children and Youth in Congregational Worship,* 1982; (reteller) *The Sun and the Wind* (illustrated by Robert Regier), 1983; *I Heard Good News Today* (illustrated by Ralph A. Schlegel), 1983; *Leaders Guide for Peace Be with You,* 1984. Editor of kindergarten curriculum materials published by Faith & Life and Herald Press. Co-editor of ''Foundation'' series, published by Evangel, Faith & Life, Mennonite Publishing House, and Mennonite Brethren Publishing. Editor of *Der Kinderboote* and *Junior Messenger.*

WORK IN PROGRESS: A biography of Dr. Mary Percy Jackson, who came to the wilds of Northern Alberta from England when she was twenty-five and who started her medical work on horseback.

SIDELIGHTS: "Often, when I was a child, my father and I sat on an old rocker in front of the fire. As we watched the moon come up over the Saskatchewan prairie, we talked about many things. But sooner or later I would say, 'Now tell me about the time when you were a little boy.'

"And so my father told me about life as he had known it in Russia. He told me about his great-grandparents who had come from Germany because of the militarism of the kaisers; he told me about his own experiences as a conscientious objector in World War I, taking the wounded from the battlefront to hospitals in the interior; he told me about the horrors of the revolution in Russia and about members of his family and friends who had been killed during that time; but above all, he told me about the lives of those who had gone before us—people who had dared to follow Christ in the way of peace and love.

"My father was not the only one who told me stories. My oldest sister, who was an adult at that time, told me Bible stories. Another sister recited ballads from literature to me. And my third sister told stories of every kind. She sometimes made up stories as she went.

"Since I grew up with storytelling, I thought it was a natural way of life. I, too, soon told stories.

CORNELIA LEHN

He gave a signal, and in a moment the soldiers with swords in their hands came out of their hiding and surrounded the Jews. ■ (From *Peace Be with You* by Cornelia Lehn. Illustrated by Keith R. Neely.)

"In 1967, I was asked to write a Bible story book for young children. *God Keeps His Promise* later became part of my thesis for a master's degree in journalism. In 1978, I was asked by the Peace and Social Concerns Committee of the General Conference Mennonite Church to write a book of stories for young people. They felt that history had been generous in providing us with a legacy of war stories; what we needed now was stories about peace heroes—people who had met violence with non-violence, and whose courage and convictions had surpassed that of the combatant soldier. *Peace Be with You,* and the picture storybook for children, *The Sun and the Wind,* were the result. *I Heard Good News Today* was commissioned by the Women in Mission organization of the General Conference Mennonite Church.

"In all my writing, I am sure I was greatly influenced by my childhood experiences. I told stories long before I wrote them, and tried to write them so that other people could tell them more easily. I believe that storytelling is an ancient art that we need to cultivate in order to pass on the wisdom of the human race to the next generation."

God Keeps His Promise and *Peace Be with You* have been translated into German.

LEIGH, Tom 1947-

PERSONAL: Born February 14, 1947, in Princeton, N.J.; son of Charles E. (a teacher) and Ruth (a nurse; maiden name, Miller) Leigh; married Susanna Barlow (an illustrator), De-

TOM LEIGH

cember 4, 1975. *Education:* Attended Ringling School of Art, 1965-68. *Residence:* Sheffield, Mass.

CAREER: Hallmark Cards, Kansas City, Mo., greeting card illustrator, 1968-71; free-lance illustrator, 1971—. *Exhibitions:* Photo exhibit in City Hall, Pittsfield, Mass., 1985. *Member:* Graphic Artists Guild. *Awards, honors:* American Institute of Graphic Arts Award, 1980, for *The Haunted House;* received various awards from Kansas City Ad Club.

ILLUSTRATOR: The Haunted House, Scholastic, 1978; *Sesame Street: What's Inside,* Golden Books, 1980; L. Hayward, *Early Bird on Sesame Street,* Western Publishing, 1980; L. Hayward, *Going Up!,* Western Publishing, 1980; *Grover's Book of Cute Little Baby Animals,* Western Publishing, 1980; Sarah Roberts, *Don't Cry Big Bird,* Random House, 1981; Pat Relf, *Muppet Manners (or the Night Gonzo Gave a Party),* Random House, 1981; *The Sesame Street Word Book,* Golden Books, 1983; Dina Anastasio, *Big Bird Can Share,* Golden Books, 1985.

WORK IN PROGRESS: Illustrations for *It's Not Fair* for Random House and for another Sesame Street "Start-to-Read" book.

LESTER, Helen 1936-

PERSONAL: Born June 12, 1936, in Evanston, Ill.; daughter of William Howard (a businessman) and Elizabeth (Sargent) Doughty; married Robin Lester (a headmaster of a private school), August 26, 1967; children: Robin Debevoise, James Robinson. *Education:* Bennett Junior College, A.A.S., 1956; Wheelock College, B.S., 1959. *Religion:* Protestant. *Residence:* San Francisco, Calif.

CAREER: Elementary school teacher in Lexington, Mass., 1959-62; Francis W. Parker School, Chicago, Ill., second-grade teacher, 1962-69; writer, 1979—. Volunteer worker in New York City soup kitchen.

WRITINGS—Juvenile: *Cora Copycat* (self-illustrated), Dutton, 1979; *The Wizard, the Fairy, and the Magic Chicken* (illustrated by Lynn Munsinger), Houghton, 1983; *It Wasn't My Fault* (illustrated by L. Munsinger), Houghton, 1985; *A Porcupine Named Fluffy* (illustrated by L. Munsinger), Houghton, 1986.

WORK IN PROGRESS: The Revenge of the Magic Chicken, illustrated by L. Munsinger.

SIDELIGHTS: "I am usually moved to write a book when an idea pops into my head, and an idea pops into my head usually when I'm in the middle of an unexciting task—doing such things as standing in bank lines or washing spinach. I also enjoy hatching ideas when I'm out on my daily two mile run, as it makes the time pass quickly.

"My books are written for the three- to six-year-old age group. As a mother of young children I felt a need for more short but satisfying bedtime stories, and that need spurred me into writing. My stories are humorous approaches to a message. *The Wizard* involves cooperation; *It Wasn't My Fault* is about guilt and is written for the clumsy of the world; *A Porcupine Named Fluffy* addresses the struggle of the young against barriers erected by their elders (in this case an impossible name). Life's pretty serious sometimes, and I feel the heavier concepts are better received if given a lighter touch.

"Once an idea comes into my head it usually takes one or two days until the story is completed. From then on it's in the lap of my wonderful illustrator, Lynn Munsinger. While we never

HELEN LESTER

"That's nothing," said the Fairy. "I can kiss a bicycle and turn it into a bowl of soup." ■ (From *The Wizard, the Fairy and the Magic Chicken* by Helen Lester. Illustrated by Lynn Munsinger.)

confer she has a sense of my stories and draws what I would if I could.

"After teaching for ten years, then having my two sons, and now being closely attached to the liveliness of a school as a headmaster's wife, I'm seldom at a loss for inspiration and new ideas."

HOBBIES AND OTHER INTERESTS: Cooking, running, tennis, writing country and western songs.

LEWIS, Alice C.   1936-

PERSONAL: Born October 7, 1936, in Walla Walla, Wash.; daughter of Julius Bode (a security guard) and Ellen (a housewife; maiden name, Yeatts) Hardy; married Delbert R. Lewis (a nursing assistant), June 2, 1963; children: Robert, Linda, David, Deborah, Jonathan, Rebecca. *Education:* Walla Walla College, B.A., 1959. *Politics:* Non-partisan. *Religion:* Seventh-Day Adventist. *Address:* 5738 N.E. 262nd Ave., Vancouver, Wash. 98662.

CAREER: Fresno Union Academy, Fresno, Calif., English teacher, 1959-60; Miramonte School, Mountain View, Calif., elementary school teacher, 1960-61; Upper Columbia Conference of Seventh-Day Adventists, Spokane, Wash., elementary school teacher, 1961-63; homemaker and writer, 1966—; Hewitt

Child Development Center, Washougal, Wash., educational counselor, 1985—. Active in community action agencies at the state and local levels; member of board at local volunteer center.

WRITINGS: Something Wonderful (primer), Southern Publishing, 1976. Also author of kindergarten Bible lessons for General Conference of Seventh-Day Adventists, 1981.

WORK IN PROGRESS: Miscellaneous short stories for a children's paper; *My Friend Sally,* a biography of a garden spider.

SIDELIGHTS: "Most of my motivation were my own children. I felt there was a lack of good material for reading aloud to small children, especially of a spiritual nature. *Something Wonderful* was written to help my children understand where they came from and where they are headed from a biblical viewpoint. I wrote *Something Wonderful* about ten years before it was published. I haven't done much for several years, but am able to think creatively again after a long dry spell."

'Never had any mother? What do you mean? Where were you born?' 'Never was born!' persisted Topsy; 'never had no father, nor mother, nor nothin'. I was raised by a speculator.'

—Harriet Elizabeth Beecher Stowe
(From *Uncle Tom's Cabin*)

ALICE C. LEWIS

LINDGREN, Barbro 1937-

BRIEF ENTRY: Born March 18, 1937, in Stockholm, Sweden. Lindgren is the author of over two dozen children's books, many of which have been translated from her native Swedish into English. Among these are *Hilding's Summer* (Macmillan, 1967), *Let's Be Gorillas!* (Clamshell Press, 1976), *The Wild Baby* (Greenwillow, 1981), its sequel, *The Wild Baby Goes to Sea* (Greenwillow, 1983), and a series of six books that feature a toddler named Sam. *The Wild Baby,* adapted by Jack Prelutsky, was described by *School Library Journal* as "reckless, loud and wild fun." *Horn Book* called the main character, Ben, "a bustling bundle of energy, one of the most deliciously naughty children to appear since [Maurice] Sendak's Pierre." Aimed at preschoolers and beginning readers, Lindgren's "Sam" books include *Sam's Car, Sam's Cookie, Sam's Teddy Bear* (all Morrow, 1982), *Sam's Bath, Sam's Ball,* and *Sam's Lamp* (all Morrow, 1983). *Booklist* labeled them "simple stories," while *School Library Journal* again observed: "[The author] obviously knows what makes little ones tick, and there is no attempt to sentimentalize the innocence of childhood." Now a full-time writer and the mother of two sons, Lindgren has worked as a commercial artist and designer. She is the recipient of several Swedish awards, including the Expressens Heffaklump, the Astrid Lindgren Prize, and the Nils Holgersson Plaque, Sweden's highest award for children's literature. *Residence:* Sweden.

With a tale forsooth he cometh unto you, with a tale which holdeth children from play, and old men from the chimney corner.

—Sir Philip Sidney
(From *The Defense of Poesy*)

LURIE, Alison 1926-

PERSONAL: Born September 3, 1926, in Chicago, Ill.; daughter of Harry (a social work executive) and Bernice (Stewart) Lurie; married Jonathan Peale Bishop, Jr. (a professor), September 10, 1948 (separated, 1976); children: John, Jeremy, Joshua. *Education:* Radcliffe College, A.B., 1947. *Office:* Department of English, Cornell University, Ithaca, N.Y. 14850.

CAREER: Author. Oxford University Press, New York, N.Y., manuscript reader, 1947-48; Cornell University, Ithaca, N.Y., lecturer, 1969-73, associate professor, 1973-76, professor of English, 1976—. *Awards, honors:* Yaddo Foundation fellowship, 1963, 1964, 1966; Guggenheim grant, 1965-66; Rockefeller Foundation grant, 1967-68; New York State Cultural Council Foundation grant, 1972-73; American Academy of Arts and Letters award in literature, 1978; American Book Award nomination in fiction, and National Book Critics Circle Award nomination for best work of fiction, both 1984, and Pulitzer Prize, 1985, all for novel, *Foreign Affairs.*

WRITINGS: V. R. Lang: A Memoir, privately printed, 1959; *Love and Friendship,* Macmillan, 1962; *The Nowhere City,* Coward, 1965; *Imaginary Friends,* Coward, 1967; *Real People,* Random House, 1969; *The War between the Tates,* Random House, 1974; *V. R. Lang: Poems and Plays,* Random House, 1975; *Only Children,* Random House, 1979; *The Heavenly Zoo: Legends and Tales of the Stars* (juvenile; illustrated by Monika Beisner), Farrar, Straus, 1980; *Clever Gretchen and Other Forgotten Folktales* (juvenile; illustrated by Margot Tomes), Crowell, 1980; *The Language of Clothes* (nonfic-

ALISON LURIE

The vegetable lamb or Barometz....though it resembles a young sheep ... grows out of the earth from a seed. ■ (From *Fabulous Beasts* by Alison Lurie. Illustrated by Monika Beisner.)

tion), Random House, 1981; *Fabulous Beasts* (juvenile; illustrated by Monika Beisner), Farrar, Straus, 1981; *Foreign Affairs,* Random House, 1984.

Editor, with Justin G. Schiller, of "Classics of Children's Literature, 1631-1932" series, Garland Publishing. Contributor of articles and reviews to *New York Review of Books, New York Times Book Review, New Statesman, New Review, Children's Literature, Harper's, New Republic, Ms.,* and other periodicals.

ADAPTATIONS: "The War between the Tates" (television movie), starring Richard Crenna and Elizabeth Ashley, NBC-TV, 1977.

SIDELIGHTS: **September 3, 1926.** Born in Chicago, Illinois. Family moved to Westchester, New York before Lurie began school. Her father was a sociology professor who became a Jewish-welfare administrator, and her mother was a former journalist. "I was encouraged to be creative past the usual age because I didn't have much else going for me. I was a skinny, plain, odd-looking little girl, deaf in one badly damaged ear from a birth injury, and with a resulting atrophy of the facial muscles that pulled my mouth sideways whenever I opened it to speak and turned my smile into a sort of sneer. I was clever, or, as one of my teachers put it, 'too clever for her own good,' but not especially charming or affectionate or helpful. I couldn't seem to learn to ride a bike or sing in tune, and I was always the last person chosen for any team.

"By the time I was eight or nine I was aware of these disadvantages, and it was my belief that as a result of them nobody would wish to marry me and I would never have any of the children whose names and sexes I had chosen at an earlier and more ignorant age. I would be an ugly old maid, the card in the pack that everyone tried to get rid of.

"I knew all about Old Maids from the Victorian and Edwardian children's books that were my favorite reading. Old Maids wore spectacles and old-fashioned clothes and lived in cottages with gardens, where they entertained children and other Old Maids to tea. They were always odd in some way: absent-minded or timid or rude or fussy. Sometimes they taught school, but most of their time was devoted to making wonderful walnut cake and blackberry jam and dandelion wine, to telling tales and painting watercolors, to embroidery and knitting and crocheting, and to growing prize cabbages and roses. Occasionally they shared their cottage with another Old Maid, but mostly they lived alone, often with a cat. Sometimes the cat was their familiar, and they were really witches. You could tell which ones were witches, according to one of my children's books, because there was always something wrong with them. . . .

"Just as with the Old Maids, all that I produced was praised: my school compositions, my drawings, my fudge brownies, my rag rugs and especially my stories. 'Charming!' 'Really beautiful.' 'Perfectly lovely, dear.' Nobody ever told me that *I* was perfectly lovely, though, as they did other little girls. Very well, then: perfection of the work." [Alison Lurie, "Nobody Asked Me to Write a Novel," *New York Times Book Review,* June 6, 1982.[1] Amended by Alison Lurie.]

From a very early age, Lurie liked making up stories and poems to entertain herself and her family. "Making up stories, for instance, was what I did for fun. With a pencil and paper I could revise the world. I could move mountains; I could fly over Westchester at night in a winged clothes basket; I could call up a brown-and-white-spotted milk-giving dragon to eat

"Well, Molly," said the king. "You are a clever girl." ■
(From "Molly Whuppie" in *Clever Gretchen and Other Forgotten Folktales,* retold by Alison Lurie. Illustrated by Margot Tomes.)

the neighbor who had told me and my sister not to walk through her field and bother her cows. And a little later, when I tried nonfiction, I found that without actually lying I could describe events and persons in such a way that my readers would think of them as I chose. 'Dear Parents—We have a new English teacher. He has a lovely wild curly brown beard and he gets really excited about poetry and ideas.' Or, if he had written an unfavorable comment on my latest paper: 'He is a small man with yellow teeth and a lot of opinions.' Or any of two, three, twenty other versions of him, all of them the truth—if I said so, the whole truth. That was what you could do with just a piece of paper and a pencil; writing was a kind of witch's spell."[1]

1940s. While in college, Lurie sold three poems and a short story, thus beginning her professional career as an author. "In my late teens . . . two things happened to disturb my contract with the world. First, adults stopped saying how wonderful my work was, and I had to admit that they were right. I had by then read enough classic European and American literature to realize that by comparison my stories and poems were not worth noticing. Clumsy apprentice spells, they seemed, when set beside the works of the great magicians—even when, as happened occasionally over the next few years, they managed to appear in print.

"The other thing that occurred about the same time was that a few young men began to show an interest in me, in spite of my looks. Maybe I wouldn't have to be an Old Maid after all, or at least not just yet.

"I didn't stop writing; I had got into the habit of it, as someone else might get into the habit of singing in the shower.'"[1]

1947. Graduated from Radcliff with a B.A. in English. "For Radcliffe students in my time the salient fact about Harvard was that it so evidently was not ours. Our position was like that of poor relations living just outside the walls of some great estate: patronized by some of our grand relatives, tolerated by others and snubbed or avoided by the rest.

"Almost every detail of our lives proclaimed our second-class status. Like poor relations, who might carry some contagious disease, we were housed at a sanitary distance of over a mile from the main campus, in comfortable but less grand quarters than those of our male contemporaries. Just to get to Harvard meant a long walk—and during the icy Cambridge winters a very chilling one, since slacks were forbidden outside the dormitory. These were also the days before fleece-lined boots and tights: instead we wore buckled or zippered rubber galoshes over our saddle shoes, and wool knee socks or heavy, baggy cotton stockings that left many inches of frozen thigh exposed under one's skirt.

"Though we took the same courses from the same professors, officially we were not attending Harvard, and we would not receive a Harvard degree. For the first year or two we would be taught in segregated classes in a Radcliffe building. Later we might be allowed into Harvard lectures, but once there we were invisible to many of our instructors, who continued to address the class as 'Gentlemen' and might not see our raised hands during the question period. Possibly as a result, few female hands—or voices—were ever raised in a Harvard course. We supported the status quo by keeping our hands in our laps. When a classmate attempted to attract the lecturer's attention we raised our eyebrows or shook our heads; we considered such behavior rather pushy, possibly a sign of emotional imbalance.

"For, like most poor relations, we knew our place and accepted it with only occasional murmurs of dissatisfaction. It didn't strike us as strange that there were no women on the Harvard faculty or that all our textbooks were written and edited by men. We didn't protest because we could not use the Harvard libraries, join the Dramatic Club or work on the *Crimson;* rather we were grateful for organizations like Choral and the Folk Dance Society that were, for practical reasons, coed. In midnight heart-to-heart sessions we decided (and I recorded in my journal) that though girls were 'just as important to the world' as men, they were somehow 'not really equal.' But semantics says it all: we were 'girls' and would be girls at forty, while every weedy Harvard freshman was an honorary 'man.'

"Despite these disadvantages my friends and I were not unhappy in Cambridge. Most of the time we were in a mild state of euphoria.

"History and Literature majors at Harvard in the 1940s . . . got to hear some of the most famous professors of the time. This was the age of the bravura lecture, and we went to our classes as if to a combination of theatrical performance, sermon and political oration—to be entertained and inspired as well as informed. Our teachers were larger-than-life, even heroic figures who provided not only interpretations of books and events, but dramatic examples of different world views and intellectual styles. . . .

"Not all our courses were theatrical events. At times we sought out odd and recondite subjects, partly out of an interest in them, partly because it meant that the classes would be small. One term, for instance, my best friend and I studied the folk tale ('Fairy Tales 101' in our jargon) with the celebrated Celtic leprechaun Kenneth Jackson, and cartography with the celebrated Hungarian gnome Erwin Raisz. As a result, I still know how to protect myself from witches and how to tell which way a river is flowing from an aerial photograph, should either necessity arise.

"Being unable to see into the future, just as I had no desire for a career in cartography, I had no expectation of ever teaching either folklore or English. Like most of my classmates I did not want to go on to graduate school (if we had, most of us would have been disappointed, since quotas for women were tiny or nonexistent). When I arrived in Cambridge I was already determined to be a writer—without, of course, having any idea of the difficulty of the task. Harvard compelled me to read the best poetry and prose of the past, in comparison with which my own efforts suddenly looked very shallow and shabby; only the optimism of extreme youth prevented despair. As for the writing of the present, it was not covered in Harvard courses: in our anthology of English literature the fiction of 'The Contemporary Period' ended in 1922 with Aldous Huxley. . . . Though fashions have changed, I think we were lucky not to have the writers of our own time predigested for us. We could feel that they belonged to us rather than to academia.

"Even less attention was paid at Harvard to teaching the writing of fiction. . . . In my final year, however, Albert Guerard, who had just come to teach at Harvard, began to give what was to be one of the best fiction seminars in the country, and I was lucky enough to be in it. Among his first students were future novelists Alice Adams, Stephen Becker, Robert Crichton and John Hawkes; I am sure that Guerard's advice and encouragement had a lot to do with the fact that so many of us in that small seminar ended up as professional writers." [Alison Lurie, "Their Harvard," in *My Harvard, My Yale,* edited by Diana Dubois, Random House, 1982.[2] Amended by A. Lurie.]

1947-48. Worked as manuscript reader for Oxford University Press upon completion of her Radcliffe education. ". . . Once I was out of college, with a full-time job, writing gradually got to seem more like smoking or biting one's nails or listening to soap operas: a bad habit, a waste of time. It was something my friends and lovers thought I really oughtn't to do too much of, especially since I got so upset when rejection letters came, as seemed to happen more and more often.'"[1]

1948. Married Jonathan Peale Bishop. The couple returned to Cambridge while he earned his Ph.D. at Harvard. Lurie continued to write. "Twice in my life I deliberately tried to break the habit of writing. The first time I was 26; I hadn't had a manuscript accepted for five years, and my first novel had been turned down by six publishers. Whenever I thought of this, which was several times a day, I felt as if I had an incurable toothache; and every day the toothache got worse.

"On the other hand, I had not only found someone who wanted to marry me, I now had a two-month-old baby. My graduate-student husband, seeing how depressed and distracted I was, suggested that I should cut my losses. 'After all, Alison, nobody is asking you to write a novel' was the way he put it that late-spring day after breakfast, as he shoved a stack of

It is known that those who wear the damasked skins of the Gulon become little by little fierce, cruel and greedy for the things of the world.... ■ (From *Fabulous Beasts* by Alison Lurie. Illustrated by Monika Beisner.)

Lurie cloaked for success in Ithaca, New York. Photograph copyright © 1986 by Thomas Victor.

corrected freshman themes into his briefcase, closed it and set out for Harvard Square.

"These words continued to echo inside my head while I did the dishes, and while I changed the baby, tucked him into his carriage and pushed him down toward the river so that he could, as the phrase went then, 'get some fresh air.' It was a hazy warm May day. The lilacs were out along the fence, bundles of dark-purple peppercorns opening into pale-mauve stars. Nobody is asking you to write a novel, I repeated to myself. You don't have to make up stories now. You're part of the real world; you have a real baby and a real husband and a real house. Look how pretty the world is, and all you have to do is live in it.

"I parked the carriage beside a bench and sat down on the grassy, sloping riverbank. The sun shimmered on the flowing water, and a white fishnet of cloud slid up behind the trees on the other shore. The words 'fishnet' and 'slid' crossed my mind, but I didn't try to stop them or scribble them down on the back of an envelope as I would have before, when I was a writer. There was no point in saving ingredients for new spells; I wouldn't need them anymore. Two people strolled by along the path: an oddly assorted couple, one very tall, taking long strides; the other much shorter and hop-skipping to keep up. I didn't speculate about them; I deliberately inhibited myself from imagining who they were or what their relationship was. You needn't bother; you are free of all that now, I told myself. You are normal, you are happy.

"I sat there by the water waiting to experience my new condition, to feel my freedom and normality and happiness, to be filled with it, to flow naturally as the river flowed and enter fully into Being.

"But instead another sensation, very much stronger, came over me. It was a sensation of intense boredom. Now that I wasn't a writer the world looked flat and vacant, emptied of possibility and meaning; the spring day had become a kind of glossy, banal calendar photograph: View of the Charles River. 'This is stupid,' I said aloud. I stood up and pushed the baby home and changed him and nursed him and put him down for a nap—and went back to the typewriter.

"The second time I stopped writing was more serious. It was two years later; I now had two unpublished novels and a batch of stories in a rejected condition. I also had two children in diapers and no household help. I had to write in the evening, when I was always tired and often miserable—miserable twice over because of guilt, for this was in the 50s when having a family was supposed to make a woman perfectly contented unless she was very immature, selfish or neurotic.

"This time it wasn't just my husband who suggested that I cut my losses, but many of my friends and relatives. Poor Alison, the consensus was, nearly 30, hasn't had anything published in seven years. . . .

"So I gave up being a writer. I really did it this time: not experimentally for an hour, but deliberately and for over a year. Instead of writing, I threw myself into togetherness the way I might have thrown a bone to a nasty dog I had to make friends with. I organized family picnics and parties and trips; I baked animal cookies and tuna-fish casseroles; I took my children to the supermarket and to the playground; I played monotonously simple board games with the older one and read monotonously simple books aloud; I entertained my husband's superiors and flirted with his colleagues and gossiped with their wives.

"I told myself that my life was rich and full. Everybody else seemed to think so. Only I knew that, right at the center, it was false and empty. I wasn't what I was pretending to be. I didn't like staying home and taking care of little children; I was restless, impatient, ambitious. Somehow, because I was clever, or because they were stupid, I had fooled people into forgetting my appearance. I passed in public as a normal woman, wife and mother; but inside I was still peculiar, skewed, maybe even wicked or crazy.''[1]

1959. First book, *V. R. Lang: A Memoir*, was privately printed.

1962. *Love and Friendship* was published by Macmillan.

1965. Awarded a Guggenheim fellowship. For three successive years prior to the Guggenheim, Lurie had been awarded Yaddo Foundation fellowships.

1969. Joined the English department of Cornell University.

1974. *The War between the Tates* published. The book became her best-known novel. "After *The War between the Tates* came out, my own sons wanted to know if those adolescents were based on them. If they had been that bad. I reassured them they hadn't been. I told them I had just used the worst parts of all the adolescents I knew as a way of piling up the difficulties for my heroine.

"And in the reviews, I began reading that I *hated* children. Gore Vidal compared me to some tyrant [Queen Herod] who actually murdered children. Which is not true. I *like* children. And I'm actually much sweeter—less mean—than the reviewers think. . . .'' [Larry Van Dyne, "Exploring the Worlds of Novelist Alison Lurie," *Chronicle Review of Higher Education*, April 30, 1979.[3] Amended by A. Lurie.]

1980. First juvenile, *The Heavenly Zoo*, was published. Lurie has also taught a course in children's literature at Cornell University since 1969. "I don't think children are a monolithic mass. Some children see a lot; some see very little. . . .

"Children—almost like foreigners—sometimes see things because they don't have a stake in everything being respectable or correct. They're not affected by the grown-up reasons for doing things. Adults go to a political speech and see a man discussing this issue and that issue. Children go to the same speech, and think: 'There's a man standing up in front of all these other people shouting and waving his arms.''[3]

1985. Won the Pulitzer Prize for fiction for her novel, *Foreign Affairs*. Lurie explained how she starts a novel: "I usually sit down and just think about each character for a few days, making lots of notes. I write down everything about them that occurs to me, until I sort of know what they look like, their backgrounds, the sounds of their voices. Then I have other notes about what's going to happen in the book. And notes about what the places look like.''[3]

Lurie divides her time between homes in Ithaca, New York; Key West, Florida; and London, England. "Not all writers are born with their feet on backward, but most of them, in my experience, sometimes feel themselves to be witches or warlocks, somehow wicked, somehow peculiar, somehow damaged. At least until recently, this has been especially true of women, who, in order to go on writing, have had to struggle not only with the ordinary evil spirits of economic necessity, editorial indifference and self-doubt, but also with the fear that they are not 'normal'—however this word is currently defined. In the past it meant staying home and keeping house; today, more often, it means having an absorbing job. But in both cases the underlying demand is the same, just as it is for most men. It is a demand that is always fatal to a writer: work, conform, accept, succeed; forget your childish impulse to play with words, to reimagine the world.''[1]

Lurie's manuscript collection is at Radcliffe College Library.

FOR MORE INFORMATION SEE: Newsweek, January 10, 1966, November 6, 1967, August 5, 1974, December 30, 1974, April 23, 1979, September 24, 1984; *Time,* March 4, 1966, June 6, 1969, June 11, 1979, November 30, 1981, October 15, 1984; *Book World,* September 24, 1967, August 11, 1974, September 7, 1975, July 13, 1980; *New York Times Book Review,* October 15, 1967, July 28, 1974, April 27, 1980, June 6, 1982, September 16, 1984; *Wall Street Journal,* October 30, 1967; *Life,* November 24, 1967, May 23, 1969; *Ithaca Journal* (New York), December 2, 1967, August 1, 1974, June 13, 1977, April 25, 1985; *Commonweal,* January 12, 1968; *New Yorker,* March 23, 1968, October 11, 1969, August 19, 1974, May 14, 1979, November 5, 1984; *Christian Science Monitor,* May 22, 1969, September 18, 1974, May 14, 1979, May 12, 1980; *New York Times,* May 27, 1969, November 18, 1981, September 13, 1984.

Times Literary Supplement, February 19, 1970, July 18, 1980, May 14, 1982, February 1, 1985; *Books & Bookmen,* April, 1970; *Listener,* June 20, 1974, April 19, 1979, May 6, 1982; *Village Voice,* August 8, 1974; *New Republic,* August 10, 1974, April 30, 1980, December 23, 1981, October 8, 1984; Barbara A. Bannon, ''Alison Lurie,'' *Publishers Weekly,* August 19, 1974; *Atlantic,* September, 1974, May, 1979, December, 1981; *New Leader,* September 2, 1974; *London Magazine,* December, 1974-January, 1975.

Contemporary Literary Criticism, Gale, Volume IV, 1975, Volume V, 1976; *Commentary,* January, 1975; *Progressive,* April, 1975, September, 1979; Jeffrey Helterman and Richard Layman, editors, *Dictionary of Literary Biography,* Volume 2, Gale, 1978; Larry Van Dyne, ''Exploring the Worlds of Novelist Alison Lurie,'' *Chronicle Review of Higher Education,* April 30, 1979; *Harper's,* July, 1979; *People,* November 30, 1981, December 3, 1984; *New York Times Biographical Service,* June, 1982; Diana Dubois, editor, *My Harvard, My Yale,* Random House, 1982; *Chicago Tribune Book World,* November 4, 1984; *Washington Post,* April 25, 1985.

LUSTIG, Loretta 1944-

PERSONAL: Born April 9, 1944, in New York, N.Y.; daughter of Otto (a servo-mechanic designer and engineer) and Elizabeth (a homemaker; maiden name, Beck) Lustig. *Education:* Pratt Institute, B.F.A., 1966. *Home and office:* 330 Clinton Ave., Brooklyn, N.Y. 11205. *Agent:* Ascuitto Art Representative, 19 East 48th St., New York, N.Y. 10017.

CAREER: Redmond, Marcus & Shure, New York, N.Y., assistant art director, 1966-70; free-lance illustrator, 1970-73, 1975—; Ogilvy & Mather, New York, N.Y., art director, 1973-75. *Member:* Society of Illustrators. *Awards, honors: Spaces, Shapes, and Sizes* was named an Outstanding Science Book for Children, 1980, by the National Science Teachers Association and Children's Book Council Joint Committee.

ILLUSTRATOR—All for children: Lillian Morrison, *Best Wishes, Amen,* Crowell, 1974; *Baby Animals,* Random House, 1974; *The Pop-Up Book of Trucks,* Random House, 1974; Paul

We've got about one minute to get rid of these gross detergent boxes. ■ (From *Rich Mitch* by Marjorie Weinman Sharmat. Illustrated by Loretta Lustig.)

Showers, *Where Does the Garbage Go?,* Crowell, 1974; Franklyn M. Branley, *Measure with Metric,* Crowell, 1975; Brenda Seabrooke, *The Best Burglar Alarm,* Morrow, 1978; Linda Allen, *Mr. Simkin's Grandma,* Morrow, 1979; *The Pop-Up Book of the Circus,* Random House, 1979; L. Allen, *Mrs. Simkin's Bed,* Morrow, 1980; Jane Jonas Srivastava, *Spaces, Shapes, and Sizes,* Crowell, 1980; Marjorie Weinman Sharmat, *Rich Mitch,* Morrow, 1983; M. W. Sharmat, *Get Rich Mitch,* Morrow, 1985.

SIDELIGHTS: Born in New York City, Lustig spent part of her childhood in Baltimore in a Jewish community. ''What I best remember is a neighbor Pearl who used to say, 'Well boobala, y'all come back, now!' As a kid, I read comic books. Donald Duck was my favorite; Mickey Mouse was too much of a goody-goody.

''From Baltimore we moved to Plainview, a suburb on Long Island. My father was an artist who met my mother while giving painting lessons—she was his student. They married, and he went into design and engineering. He was supportive of my going into art.

"I was definitely a closet artist in high school. Art had less prestige than home economics. My art teacher was a very bitter man—his hobby was deer hunting with a bow and arrow—and he had very little use for girls in his class. When I got accepted at both Pratt and Cooper Union in New York City, I had no idea that it was an honor . . . I was embarrassed. My friends were doing things like going to college to major in Russian, or to become astronomers, doctors . . . I thought I was going off to fingerpaint.

"Pratt was an enormous shock, a totally different world. I was very naive and knew almost nothing about art. For the first time, I met people with background and training, who were very competitive and serious about their art. It was a time of enormous growth.

"My favorite course at Pratt was taught by artist Richard Lindner, who was wonderful. His class was probably the best thing that ever happened to me. He'd give us great assignments: for example, to read the *National Enquirer* as a point of departure, something to work off. 'Even if you're a graphic artist, you don't have to work two-dimensionally on paper,' he'd say. I did some three-dimensional pieces, and it helped me, for the first time, to let go a little.

"At orientation, the dean announced, 'Look to the left of you. Look to the right of you. In four years, two of you will not be here. We are here to train you for a professional career.' My big disappointment at Pratt was that it did *not* adequately prepare me for a commercial art career, which is what the graphic arts program was supposed to do.

I painted it with some of Mother's enamel. ■ (From *Where Does the Garbage Go?* by Paul Showers. Illustrated by Loretta Lustig.)

If you cut up peeled potatoes to make French fries, you change their shape. Do you change their total volume?

(From *Spaces, Shapes, and Sizes* by Jane Jonas Srivastava. Illustrated by Loretta Lustig.)

"As students, we all learned a good deal about 'producing,' if you will, a creative piece of art, but I never saw a commercial printing press, or really understood the commercial reproduction of such graphic creations, until years later. This lack of knowledge led to some pretty embarrassing results in the beginning of my career. Nevertheless, the atmosphere, the guidance of the faculty and the excitement were irreplaceable, and would be for anyone wishing to go into art, fine or commercial (a slim line at best).

"My first job after Pratt was in the paste-up department of a small New York ad agency, now defunct. I had to learn everything on the job. I later worked as an art director at Ogilvy & Mather, a major ad agency, but that really wasn't for me. I'm a late-night person who is literally useless before noon. One summer I decided to take a trip across country. The trip had been so exciting, so mind-boggling, that when I got back, I wanted to make a big change in my life. I quit my job at the ad agency and began freelancing.

"I decided to freelance because I wanted to be able to manage my own time. I quickly learned that it's not as easy as it sounds. My bread and butter is artwork for educational materials such as textbooks and related matter.

"My style is very whimsical, and sometimes that has gotten me into trouble. For *Spaces, Shapes and Sizes,* I drew the 'kids,' who are shown carrying out various experiments with areas and volumes of different objects, as animals. That resulted in some bad reviews which claimed the drawings took away from the seriousness of the text. I didn't agree, for I enjoy humor, and think it involves, rather than distracts, especially in educational material. You can't do anything even a little saucy. For instance, kids aren't supposed to have crotches. If you happen to draw a little too much shadow in the crotch, you've got to take it out. If you have a kid falling, for example, it has to be at a certain angle so the crotch does not show. It doesn't make sense to me—I mean, kids are aware that there are crotches and underpants in the world. In another instance, I had to draw a cow, and was asked to erase the udder. A cow without an udder to me is a silly idea. I realized I couldn't draw the cow without an udder, and changed the position of the animal so that the udder would be out of the viewer's line of vision. I have since drawn an udderless cow, to my shame.

"It's parents, school teachers and school boards who buy books for children and, as a result, some publishers issue what they think will appeal to grown-ups, rather than to kids. I was happy to read that California decided that there was not enough representation of evolution in the textbooks being used in many of their school systems—an example of how adults can have very rigid ideas about what children should read.

"I really like projects that call for a bit of fancy, that let you inject something of yourself. I enjoyed illustrating *Mrs. Simkin's Bed* and *Mr. Simkin's Grandma* for that reason. I especially liked drawing the old people—old women carrying barbells, others with spider collections, and a guy in a wheelchair motorized with rockets. My favorite medium is gouache because you can paint with it, and I like to render, rather than do line drawings."

Lustig lives near the Brooklyn Navy Yard in an apartment filled with plants and antiques. "I finally had to say to myself, 'No more antiques!' I simply ran out of room—there was no place left for *me* in my apartment. But I do love collecting, and someday when I have more room, I'll go back to it. I love to find weird things and bring them home. I'm rarely in the market for something specific—it's the joy of the hunt. I used

to go to the Salvation Army every day just to see what they'd gotten in. I also enjoy flea markets, particularly the big one on Canal Street, but also the smaller ones scattered throughout Greenwich Village. Only really unusual things catch my eye. One of my favorite finds is a barber pole. Another favorite piece is a music box with the Christ Child lying in the manger. As it plays Italian music, the Baby Jesus' head rolls from side to side and His eyes move up and down. My undoing was the antiques show at the 67th Street Armory. There was a highboy—a glorious carved piece—mounted on a dais and cordoned off with scarlet roping. I'll start collecting again when I can have things as splendid as that!"

When she's not working, Lustig likes to read and watch movies. "I'll read anything. I've gone on a Stephen King kick. His books are great fun. Wonderful stories, horror stories that really get your imagination going. More than anything, I love a good story. My all-time favorite children's book is Tomi Ungerer's *The Beast of Monsieur Racine.* I also love Maurice Sendak. I tend to watch a lot of TV; I'm one of those people who will watch just about any movie that's on. But I hate going to the theatre; I'm so short I usually can't see the screen. The one exception I made was for *2001*—and for that I sat in the front row.

"My favorite artist is still Norman Rockwell. I say 'still' because when I applied to Pratt, I had to write on my application

It was hard to tell what the room was supposed to be. It was covered with *toys!* ■ (From *Get Rich Mitch* by Marjorie Weinman Sharmat. Illustrated by Loretta Lustig.)

which artist I most admired, and I chose Rockwell. When I got to school, I quickly learned that Rockwell was considered *déclassé*. I was terribly embarrassed about my preference and for years kept it a deep dark secret. But I always go back to Rockwell—he had humor, and he really could render. And now, lots of people are singing his praises again. What goes around comes around.''

Lustig spends most of her time in New York City, but during the summer visits a friend's farm in Maine. ''I always think I'll get lots of work done in the country, but it's awfully easy to just lay back and say, 'Oh well, the clouds are beautiful, the trees are lovely, the grass is green, now what was it I was supposed to be doing?' Essentially, I'm a city person.''

Her advice to prospective and beginning illustrators is to ''stick to what you want to do right from the start. It sounds cornball, I know, but it's the only way. I say this, because I didn't do that. When I first started out, upon graduating from Pratt, I was going around with my portfolio—as everyone must. I was told that everything I had was too grotesque—I was doing a lot of little monsters, and I guess they were a little grotesque. But I wish I had just kept at it. I spent years trying to accommodate what others wanted of illustrators. I spent years trying to be cute as a button, and now I am, and I don't like it. My advice is, don't give in. It's hard to stand firm, especially at the beginning of your career—you learn fast that good illustrators are a dime a dozen, and it seems everyone knows much more than you do. But if you find you have given in—and regret it—remember what they tell you about quicksand. If you find you've trodden into quicksand, don't panic, but lie down, and start to wade; eventually you'll get to a safe spot. That's what I must do now. I've resolved to write my own books and to illustrate them. I want my illustrations to express my vision, not someone else's. . . . ''

MACAULAY, David (Alexander) 1946-

PERSONAL: Born December 2, 1946, in Burton-on-Trent, England; came to the United States in 1957; son of James (a designer of textile machines) and Joan (Lowe) Macaulay; married Janice Elizabeth Michel (an organist and choir director), June 13, 1970 (divorced); married Ruth Marris, August 19, 1978 (divorced); married Charlotte Valerie; children: (first marriage) Elizabeth Alexandra. *Education:* Rhode Island School of Design, B.Arch., 1969. *Home:* 27 Rhode Island Ave., Providence, R.I. 02906.

CAREER: Rhode Island School of Design, Providence, instructor in interior design, 1969-73, instructor in two-dimensional design, 1974-76, adjunct faculty, department of illustration, 1976-77, head of department of illustration, 1977-79; free-lance illustrator and writer, 1979—. Public school teacher of art in Central Falls, R.I., 1969-70, and Newton, Mass., 1972-74; designer, Morris Nathanson Design, 1969-72.

AWARDS, HONORS: Cathedral: The Story of Its Construction was named one of the Ten Best Illustrated Books by the *New York Times,* 1973, was included in the American Institute of Graphic Arts Children's Book Show, 1973-74, was a Caldecott honor book and a Children's Book Showcase title, both 1974, received the Jugendbuchpreis (Germany) and the Silver Slate Pencil Award (Holland), both 1975; *City: A Story of Roman Planning and Construction* was a Children's Book Showcase title, 1975; *Pyramid* received the Christopher Award and was named an Outstanding Children's Book of the Year by the *New York Times,* both 1975, and was named a *Boston*

Globe-Horn Book honor book, and was a Children's Book Showcase title, both 1976.

Underground was named an Outstanding Children's Book of the Year by the *New York Times,* 1976, was a Children's Book Showcase title, and was included on *School Library Journal*'s ''Best of the Best 1966-1976'' list, 1978; *Castle* was named an Outstanding Book of the Year, 1977, by *New York Times Book Review,* received honorable mention from New York Academy of Sciences Children's Science Book Awards, was a Caldecott honor book and was named a *Boston Globe-Horn Book* honor book, all 1978; Washington Children's Book Guild Award for a body of work, 1977; American Institute of Architects Medal, 1978, for his contribution as ''an outstanding illustrator and recorder of architectural accomplishment''; *Motel of the Mysteries* was chosen one of American Library Association's Best Books for Young Adults, 1979, and one of New York Public Library's Books for the Teen Age, 1980.

Unbuilding was named one of the Ten Best Illustrated Books by the *New York Times,* and received the Parents' Choice Award for illustration in children's books, both 1980, received honorable mention from New York Academy of Sciences Awards, 1981, and was chosen an Ambassador of honor book by the English-Speaking Union Books-Across-the-Sea, 1982; *Help! Let Me Out!* was named a Notable Book of the Year by *New York Times Book Review,* 1982; *Mill* was selected one of *School Library Journal*'s Best Books, and one of New York Public Library's Children's Books, both 1983; nominated for Hans Christian Andersen Illustrator Medal, 1984.

WRITINGS—All self-illustrated; all published by Houghton: *Cathedral: The Story of Its Construction* (ALA Notable Book), 1973; *City: A Story of Roman Planning and Construction* (ALA

DAVID MACAULAY

***BAAA* vans were familiar to everyone. ■** (From *BAAA* by David Macaulay. Illustrated by the author.)

Notable Book; *Horn Book* honor list), 1974; *Pyramid* (ALA Notable Book), 1975; *Underground* (ALA Notable Book; *Horn Book* honor list), 1976; *Castle* (ALA Notable Book), 1977; *Great Moments in Architecture* (Book-of-the-Month Club selection), 1978; *Motel of the Mysteries,* 1979; *Unbuilding* (*Horn Book* honor list), 1980; *Mill* (ALA Notable Book; *Horn Book* honor list), 1983; *BAAA,* 1985.

Illustrator: David L. Porter, *Help! Let Me Out!,* Houghton, 1982; Robert Ornstein and Richard F. Thompson, *The Amazing Brain,* Houghton, 1984. Contributor of illustrated articles to magazines, including *Washington Post.*

ADAPTATIONS: ''Castle,'' PBS-TV, October, 1983; ''Cathedral,'' PBS-TV, 1985.

As an extra precaution the hoardings were installed around the tops of all the walls and towers.
■ (From *Castle* by David Macaulay. Illustrated by the author.)

WORK IN PROGRESS: ''Pyramid,'' a film for PBS-TV; *The Way Things Work* for Houghton in the U.S. and Dorling Kindersley in London, England.

SIDELIGHTS: Born **December 2, 1946,** in Burton-on-Trent, England. ''I grew up in England and I lived there until I was eleven. One of the great things about Bolton, Lancashire, where I lived, was the twenty-minute walk to school each day through woods past a stream. I was very familiar with the area, since it was my playground when not in school, and it allowed a chance to let the mind wander.

''Whenever the opportunity presented itself for me to daydream, I did. I remember one birthday when my parents gave me a real leather soccer ball. I took it to school, turned it over to the other kids during recess, and let them play with it. They had a terrific time. Even though I liked playing soccer, I had no desire to join in, preferring instead to spend all my recess pretending, inventing, and becoming lost with my imagina-

tion. I'd imagine myself riding a horse or flying. Those experiences of playing alone are remembered as some of the best and happiest times of my childhood.''

Macaulay allowed his imagination free reign at home as well. ''I would take my little soldiers into the sitting room—a room where nobody went except on Sundays or when company came—put them in the flower pots, and with threads and spools construct cable cars from the top of the curtain rods down to the corner of the room—a crazy spider web of threads on which I occasionally tied up soldiers, taking them for terrifying rides.

''My first eleven years were filled with play. I can recall some drawings I did in school, but I think of myself as having a more three-dimensionally oriented imagination. Drawing was a later development. My parents, both particularly good at making things, instilled in me an appreciation for craftsmanship. My mother would amaze me with her wonderful draw-

Many rooms contained jungle scenes full of wild animals and exotic plants. ■ (From *City: A Story of Roman Planning and Construction* by David Macaulay. Illustrated by the author.)

(From *Mill* by David Macaulay. Illustrated by the author.)

ings from *Cinderella* and any other fairy tale I requested. It was wonderful to watch someone draw—from nothing, something emerged.

"I came to America in September, 1957, because my father, who had been in textiles since he was fourteen, was offered a job in Bloomfield, New Jersey. We sailed from Southampton to New York. Being able to see the same movie on the ship three times a day without paying was an unprecedented luxury. I was soon to wear long pants for the first time in my life. Moving to the States was an incredible shock.

"The sixth grade in Bloomfield, New Jersey, was intellectually fairly easy for me, perhaps because the English system was more advanced, but by junior high school, things got tougher. I felt much younger than the kids around me. Life

was faster and my contemporaries seemed more mature. Looking back I wonder how many of them had the benefit of an extended childhood which I had had. My childhood came to an end between the sixth and seventh grades, but my imagination never stopped protecting me, coming back into play when I needed it.

"After five years in New Jersey, we moved to Rhode Island where I finished my last two years of high school. Now I drew all the time. I must have copied every photograph ever taken of the Beatles. I'd come home from school, would race through my homework, and then do another Beatles portrait, knowing that the next day at school everyone would rave over my effort, making me feel terrific—a totally self-serving endeavor, but why else would anybody draw? Rhode Island was more like England, a slower pace of life.

By midsummer of 1338, the last pieces of sculpture had been hoisted into their niches. The cathedral was finished. On August 19 the bishop and the chapter led a great procession through the narrow streets of Chutreaux, returning to the grand, new cathedral with the entire population of the city for a service of thanksgiving.

(From *Cathedral: The Story of Its Construction* by David Macaulay. Illustrated by the author.)

"I enjoyed high school, but realized that it was not going to last forever, and I had to make some plans. I applied for engineering at the University of Rhode Island and to the Rhode Island School of Design to study architecture because architecture seemed a 'safe' art oriented profession. It never even entered my mind to study painting or illustration. I was accepted by the School of Design first. Otherwise I may have ended up studying engineering and building bridges. In retrospect it looks predetermined and logical. At the time I kept my fingers crossed hoping for the best. I tend to make decisions by not making decisions. It is not such a bad thing because if you make decisions all the time, you tend to eliminate the opportunity for surprises, which are such an important part of a creative life. About half way through the course of study—it's a five-year program—I began to wonder what I was doing there. Not in terms of actually studying the design process, but in terms of the other avenues it opened to me.

"Architecture teaches you how to devise a way of thinking that allows you to believe you can tackle any problem of any scale. It fueled and educated my desire to understand how things work. Since then, I have realized that what I was learning in architecture—how to break down an immense problem into its smallest parts and put it back together logically with knowledge, expertise, and imagination—could also be applied to making books.

"In **1969** I taught junior high school art to avoid being yanked off to Vietnam. Had I been drafted, I would have had to leave the country and I didn't want to do that. It was the toughest year I've ever spent. Teaching was a tremendous strain. I realized immediately how difficult it would be to replenish myself and come back caring every day. It was impossible."

Macaulay took a job in an interior design office for two years, designing restaurants and shops. "The work was okay but it was not giving me everything I wanted—something was missing.

"Delessert is one illustrator whose work I found tremendously inspiring. His *Endless Party* made me want to make illustrations for books as well. The design of some of the pages is absolutely exquisite. Delessert, Sendak, and Milton Glaser were probably the three most powerful influences on my trying to make the move from architecture to books and design."

Left the interior design job to freelance for one year for a publisher of textbooks, illustrating a series of reading books. "Fortunately the reading series was never published. It wasn't very good. But that was when I started to put the pressure on my friends to write stories that I could illustrate. Whenever I finished a sequence of drawings for picture books, I put them in cellophane pages, typed the text, stuck it in, and actually created books. All of which I still have, none of which were published, but all of which got me in touch with publishers, and more important, provided me with practice at putting words and pictures together.

"I started to write stories as well. One was about a gargoyle beauty pageant. I produced an illustration which eventually

Macaulay on location during the making of "Cathedral," which was broadcast on PBS-TV, April 30, 1986.

(From *Unbuilding* by David Macaulay. Illustrated by the author.)

led to my book *Cathedral*. I wanted to draw gargoyles flying around in a fairy land. It was quite by accident that Houghton Mifflin looked at this illustration, and inasmuch as they didn't think the story terrific, they liked the illustration, especially the buildings.

"I spent the summer reading *Construction of the Gothic Vault*. I became extremely excited because I could visualize what [the author] was saying. I did some sketches, showing the sequences of cathedral construction from the foundation up. I realized that this was a story in itself."

In **1973** Houghton Mifflin gave Macaulay an advance towards the publication of *Cathedral: The Story of Its Construction*. "I decided to go to France and spend some serious time looking at buildings. The Cathedral of Amiens I regarded as the most perfect in terms of gothic architecture, the basic structure so unified and harmonious.

"I flew to Paris on my advance, and took the train to Amiens. I had never made a business trip further than Atlantic City before this, never mind to Amiens. In Amiens I walked around and through the cathedral, photographing and sketching. I would then work on one of the finished drawings. I did some drawings of the vaulting from inside, then removed the vaulting and tried to imagine what the roof looked like. Three of the illustrations for the book were done in Amiens on French paper with French ink.

"*Cathedral* was written in Amiens as well. I spent a couple of nights working on it, becoming acquainted with muscadet for the first time in my life—half a bottle with lunch, half a bottle with dinner. I was very loose during those two weeks, totally unintimidated by the process of writing this book. It was very difficult in the beginning since I'm not a 'natural' writer, and was not a reader. Now after thirteen years, writing is as much fun and as much of a challenge as making the pictures for the book.

"I try to develop pictures and words simultaneously. They are both part of the same thing, both contributing to the same ultimate conclusion which is to tell a story, to entertain and to teach. I have the opportunity to express myself in pictures rather than words. But if I become aware of words, there are times when I can express myself in a paragraph or in a sentence without a picture. It would be redundant to create a picture of something you've just described. Also by thinking the pictures and the words simultaneously, I avoid that awful situation where I've described something on one page, and the illustration appears three pages later."

During the actual writing process "I produce what amounts to a rough draft of words and pictures. Once I have a firm outline of text, I can separate the two. I can concentrate on producing something that holds both together, and on refining some of the little sketches into pieces of finished art. At this point most of the excitement of the process has ended for me, and when it comes to an end it's a wonderful feeling of relief that I can get on to something else, or do nothing at all for a while. The fun lies in developing the idea and creating a fluid framework for both words and pictures.

"One of the things I always try to do in a picture is to make the reader more of a participant than a spectator. I want him up on the roof of the building, and I want him to feel slightly sick because it's a long way up. If a reader can share that experience of being involved in a process, he will remember it. If I have any expertise at all, it is in that kind of communication."

1974. *City: A Story of Roman Planning and Construction* published. "I feel much more at home in a city like Rome. There is a pace and a quality of life in a European environment which are inseparable from a sense of history and tradition. Try as they may in America to create a sense of the past, the country is simply not old enough. It has not been tested. In a city like New York, for example, dynamic and exciting as it may be, it has ended up with a physical environment that reflects our greed, ambition and selfishness rather than other human qualities. There is a flimsy foundation on which life seems to continue. On the good side this means that if you get an idea and want to do something, you are encouraged to give it a shot. Some days I'm ready to pack up and go back to England. But when I'm away, I look forward to returning. At this stage of my life, flexibility is more important than perhaps trying to pick one place to settle down and be happy forever. I'm beginning to think that the most important thing for me is to be able to travel because no place is all good or all bad.

"I taught the Freshman Foundation Program at the Rhode Island School of Design and have been there on and off since. Getting out of the studio and talking to people about what you like to do is great. I have to teach. It forces me to focus my ideas—an invaluable discipline, which influences my drawings. I go into each class as if it was the first time. To keep the process fresh and spontaneous, I don't teach a lot, one or two courses each semester at most." Macaulay has also taught at Brown University and is presently teaching at Wellesley College.

"Education is working at its best when you create an environment in which there can be tension, conflicts and resolution; when you have to organize your ideas, present them and defend them. What could be more illuminating than that? It is an incredibly rich and valuable process for everybody involved. I learned a lot from my students. If teaching doesn't go both ways, it is not working."

1975. *Pyramid* published. "I wanted to travel to Egypt, and realized that to justify a trip to Cairo, I would have to do a book. So, I set off with my sketch book and my camera and visited the Pyramids every day.

"One of the most exciting things was climbing the Great Pyramid, something that I felt I wanted and needed to do in order to draw it more convincingly. I had to have a sense of what it feels like as well as what it looks like. It is critical for an illustrator to feel his subject matter. It's illegal to climb the Great Pyramid. Too many people have come down the 'fast' way. I had to persuade the necessary people, and by seven o'clock in the morning I was on top of it. The single most impressive image was the length of the shadow it cast. The sun was just coming up and the shadow went on forever across the desert. It was spectacular.

"*Castle* [1977] was hard to do because at that point I felt as though I was just plugging new information into an old formula. I knew the formula would work. I knew the material was interesting enough for most people, but I needed a break. It was then that I did *Great Moments in Architecture*—a series of drawings made for the fun of it.

"In *Motel of the Mysteries* I used myself as a model for the main character. I slicked my hair down and posed for some new photographs. I had some fun but it's all totally derivative. The drawings of the characters are not very lively, but they are okay because they're based on photographs. I can't draw people very well. It's a gift that I do not have, and a skill that I have not developed. I can draw buildings with my eyes closed,

The creation of the Empire State Building was a masterpiece of organization. ■ (From *Unbuilding* by David Macaulay. Illustrated by the author.)

The building filled with beautiful sounds and the people, most of them grandchildren of the men who laid the foundation, were filled with tremendous awe and a great joy. ■ (From *Cathedral: The Story of Its Construction* by David Macaulay. Illustrated by the author.)

but the better I get at drawing buildings, however, the worse my people look. I drew an ox in *City* which looks like a walking refrigerator—box-like and bulky. When I invent people and animals, you can tell right away. They are like the creation of an extra-terrestrial construction outfit specializing in imitation people.

"*Great Moments* and *Motel* constituted something of a two-year vacation. Then I thought it was time to get serious again. I went back to the building books and did *Unbuilding*, a combination of a serious book and parody. The book unbuilds the Empire State Building. Building it from the ground up was too much like earlier building books. It was not a particularly brilliant insight but allowed me to have fun while still making a series."

1982. "*Help! Let Me Out!* is my only book in color. A friend David L. Porter wrote the story and I illustrated it. The drawings were done with magic markers on tracing paper—the first time I used that technique to make finished art.

"My nonfiction books require much work with constant cross-checking. Every time I finish a picture I have to go back and check it with the previous ten pictures to make sure there are no inconsistencies. You become the continuity person as well as the creator and the illustrator. That's exhausting because it goes on for the entire process of making the book, which could be as long as six months. Technical accuracy is important to me and requires making lots of preliminary sketches—not just to determine the design of the page but also to make sure that the proportion details, such as sequence and so on are right. I always like my sketches much more than the finished art. They're looser, more spontaneous, and are mostly drawn with magic marker or felt-tip pen—anything I can get my hands on. But then I sit down with a sheet of white paper, a bottle of ink, a pen, and start scratching away. It is easy in large pen and ink drawings of great detail to lose the spontaneity of the sketches. It becomes automatically a sort of manufacturing process, which has always made me dissatisfied with my finished art.

"I look at architectural drawings all the time and I've always admired those drawings which maintain some crudeness. The drawings which are smooth and technically perfect become cold and leave me feeling indifferent. Somewhere between the two is what I'd like to achieve. I started to look at illustrations by people like Ernest Shepard as well. He could do amazing things with very few lines. I am driven to achieve maximum economy. I think the more you can do with less, the better the drawings because it leaves more room for the imagination of the reader. Learning the balance is the difficult part. If you show too little, the reader cannot figure out what you are trying to say. If you give too much, you deny him the opportunity of becoming creatively involved in the picture. With a few gestures, a few marks, you can create a mood, an action. Shepard did it brilliantly."

Macaulay can work in almost any kind of space as long as it is "comfortable and occasionally clean. I need the illusion of order before I can start working effectively. By the end of the task the studio is usually an absolute mess. One of the pleasures of finishing a project is spending an entire day cleaning the studio. It is tremendously satisfying to throw out all the junk, to clean up and say good-bye to the project."

FOR MORE INFORMATION SEE: Top of the News, April, 1974; *New York Times Book Review*, October 6, 1974, October 5, 1975, December 9, 1979, November 9, 1980, December 5, 1982; *Time*, December 8, 1975, November 21, 1977,

June 19, 1978; *Children's Literature Review*, Volume 3, Gale, 1978; *Times Literary Supplement*, April 7, 1978, September 15, 1978; "PW Interviews: David Macaulay," *Publishers Weekly*, April 10, 1978; Lee Kingman, editor, *The Illustrator's Notebook*, Horn Book, 1978; Lee Kingman and others, compilers, *Illustrators of Children's Books: 1967-1976*, Horn Book, 1978; *Washington Post Book World*, October 7, 1979, November 9, 1980; *Newsweek*, December 10, 1979; *Chicago Tribune Book World*, December 7, 1980; *Art Express*, May-June, 1981; Betsy Hearne and Marilyn Kaye, editors, *Celebrating Children's Books: Essays on Children's Literature in Honor of Zena Sutherland*, Lothrop, 1981; *Print*, February, 1982; *Language Arts*, April, 1982; *Contemporary Authors, New Revision Series*, Volume 5, Gale, 1982; Sally Holmes Holtze, editor, *Fifth Book of Junior Authors and Illustrators*, H. W. Wilson, 1983.

MacMASTER, Eve (Ruth) B(owers)   1942-

PERSONAL: Born September 24, 1942, in Baltimore, Md.; daughter of Quentin Homer (a civil engineer) and Ruth (a teacher; maiden name, Garratt) Bowers; married Richard K. MacMaster (a historian), February 3, 1968; children: Samuel, Thomas, Sarah. *Education:* Pennsylvania State University, B.A., 1963; George Washington University, M.A., 1968. Also attended Harvard University, 1961, and Eastern Mennonite Seminary, 1976-78. *Religion:* United Methodist. *Home:* 105 West College St., Bridgewater, Va. 22812.

EVE B. MacMASTER

CAREER: U.S. Peace Corps, Washington, D.C., volunteer worker in Turkey, 1963-65, recruiter, 1965-66; George Washington University, Washington, D.C., graduate assistant, 1967-68; free-lance writer, 1975—; Eastern Mennonite College, Harrisonburg, Va., instructor in Bible, 1978-79; James Madison University, Harrisonburg, instructor in history, 1981-82. Member of board of directors of Choice Books International Committee, 1979-82. *Member:* Sigma Tau Delta, Phi Alpha Theta, Pi Gamma Mu.

WRITINGS—"Story Bible" series; all illustrated by James Converse; all published by Herald Press: *God's Family,* 1981; *God Rescues His People,* 1982; *God Gives the Land,* 1983; *God's Chosen King,* 1983; *God's Wisdom and Power,* 1984; *God's Justice,* 1984; *God Comforts His People,* 1985; *God Sends His Son,* 1986; *God's Suffering Servant,* 1986.

Co-author of adult church school curriculum materials. Contributor of stories, articles, and poems to religious and children's magazines, including *Highlights for Children, Christian Living* and *Gospel Herald.*

WORK IN PROGRESS: One more Bible storybook on the early church, for Herald Press; a novel based on personal experiences in the Peace Corps; a church history for children; with husband, Richard K. MacMaster, lives of six Christian women activists, for Morehouse-Barlow.

SIDELIGHTS: "I am in the midst of the ambitious, ten-volume Bible story series. This is a retelling of the whole Bible without moralizing, adding, or interpreting. It is written in a simple, lively style suitable for both children and adults. The series is being used in numerous churches and family groups by people of different denominations. It is unique in its respect for the literary quality of the original Hebrew and Greek stories. I have a passionate, life-long interest in the Bible and its literary, historical, and religious treasures. My love of children, my Peace Corps experience in the Middle East, and my interest in writing have all combined in this project, along with my graduate studies in Middle Eastern history.

"I wrote the book *I* would like to read—the one I couldn't find for my children. It is generally classified as a juvenile series because its vocabulary is simple, but it is suitable for all ages.

"The Bible itself does not moralize. I try to respect the text and not impose my own notions on it. The *point* of the stories comes through the narrative itself—more subtle, more profound than tacked-on moralizing.

"I hope this series will lead its readers to the original, for no retelling is a substitute for the Bible itself. The Bible is actually a collection of books written over a long period of time in a variety of forms. It has been translated and retold in every generation, because people everywhere want to know what God is like.

"When this project is finished, I hope to write a novel and some interpretive books on the Bible for adults."

How dear to this heart are the scenes of my childhood,
When fond recollection presents them to view:—
The orchard, the meadow, the deep-tangled wildwood,
And every lov'd spot which my infancy knew.
—Samuel Woodworth

VIVIENNE MARGOLIS

MARGOLIS, Vivienne 1922-
(Vivienne Eisner)

PERSONAL: Born January 11, 1922, in Dayton, Ohio; daughter of Sol and Celia Margolis; married Leonard Eisner (a physicist), June 13, 1942 (divorced); children: Charna, Andrew, Jon. *Education:* George Washington University, B.A., 1944; Southern Connecticut State College, M.S. (with honors), 1964; California Western University, Ph.D., 1980. *Religion:* Jewish. *Home:* 5911 Edsall Rd., #713, Alexandria, Va. 22304. *Office:* 810 18th St. N.W., Washington, D.C. 20006.

CAREER: Teacher at several schools, including Norwalk Community College, Norwalk, Conn., 1975, Fairfield University, Fairfield, Conn., 1975, and Hackensack Medical Center, 1976-81; Empowerment Associates, Margolis & Smith, Washington, D.C., therapist, 1981—. *Awards, honors:* New Jersey Institute of Technology Award, 1978, for *Crafting with Newspapers.*

WRITINGS—Of interest to young readers; all under name Vivienne Eisner: (With Adelle Weiss) *The Newspaper Everything Book: How to Make 150 Useful Objects from Old Newspapers* (illustrated by A. Weiss), Dutton, 1975; (with William Shisler) *Crafting with Newspapers* (illustrated by Guy Brison-Stack), Sterling, 1976; (with A. Weiss) *A Boat, a Bat, and a Beanie: Things to Make from Newspaper* (illustrated by A. Weiss and with photographs by Daniel Dorn, Jr.), Lothrop, 1977; *Quick and Easy Holiday Costumes* (illustrated by Carolyn Bentley), Lothrop, 1977.

WORK IN PROGRESS: The New Newspaper Book and *Extraordinary Ordinary Women.*

No Arbor Day would be complete without mentioning Johnny Appleseed. ■ (From *Quick and Easy Holiday Costumes* by Vivienne Eisner. Illustrated by Carolyn Bentley.)

SIDELIGHTS: "I grew up in the Midwest, the youngest of four sisters. My mother, a painter and a singer, gave all of us private art and music lessons. The Depression hit us hard and we all had to learn to do without our home, car, meat, and private lessons. Yet, I can't remember the quality of our family life being anything but good. I think the Depression era inspired my interest in using free material, such as newspaper, to make useful products of all kinds which appear in my books."

Boys and girls come out to play,
The moon doth shine as bright as day.
                   —Nursery rhyme

MAY, Robert Stephen 1929-
(Robin May)

PERSONAL: Born December 26, 1929, in Deal, Kent, England; son of Robert Cyril (a naval surgeon) and Mary (Robertson) May; married Dorothy Joan Clarke, June 7, 1958 (died August 8, 1975); married Maureen Frances Filipkiewicz, December 4, 1976; children: (first marriage) Michael Robert, Elizabeth Magda, David Peter. *Education:* Attended Central School of Speech and Drama, 1950-53. *Religion:* Church of England. *Home:* 5 Ridgway Place, Wimbledon, London SW19 4EW, England. *Agent:* Rupert Crew Ltd., Kings Mews, London WC1N 2JA, England.

CAREER: Actor, under name Robin May, in British Isles, 1953-63; commercial artists' agent in London, England, 1963-66; free-lance writer and journalist in London, 1966—; I.P.C. Magazines Ltd., London, feature writer and sub-editor of *Look and Learn*, 1970-76. *Military service:* Royal Artillery, 1948-50; became second lieutenant. *Member:* National Union of Journalists, Society of Authors, Western Writers of America, English Westerners, Kansas Historical Society, Wyoming Historical Society, Company of Military Historians, Western History Association, Arizona Historical Society, New Mexico Historical Society, New York State Historical Association, South Dakota Historical Society.

WRITINGS—Under name Robin May: *Operamania,* Vernon & Yates, 1966; *Theatremania,* Vernon & Yates, 1967; (compiler) *The Wit of the Theatre,* Frewin, 1969.

Who's Who in Shakespeare, Elm Tree, 1972, Taplinger, 1973; *A Companion to the Theatre,* Lutterworth, 1973, published as *A Companion to the Theatre: The Anglo-American Stage From 1920,* Hippocrene, 1975; (with G. A. Embleton) *The American West,* Almark, 1973, Silver, 1983; *Who Was Shakespeare?,* David & Charles, 1974; *Wolfe's Army,* Osprey, 1974; (with Joseph G. Rosa) *The Pleasure of Guns,* Octupus, 1974; *The British Army in the American Revolution,* Osprey, 1974; *The Wild West,* Look-In, 1975; *The Gold Rushes,* Luscombe, 1977, Hippocrene, 1978; *A Companion to the Opera,* Hippocrene, 1977; *Opera,* Teach Yourself Books, 1977; *True Adventures of the Wild West,* Beaver, 1978; (with J. G. Rosa) *Gunlaw,* Contemporary Books, 1977, published in England as *Gunsmoke,* New English Library, 1978; *Show-Biz Quiz,* Beaver, 1978; *Warriors of the West,* ITV Books, 1978; *The Story of the Wild West,* Hamlyn, 1978; *Facts and Feats of the Wild West,* Beaver, 1979; *History Quiz,* Beaver, 1979; *Discovering Ballet,* Marshall Cavendish, 1979; *Looking at Theatre,* Marshall Cavendish, 1979.

Ballet, Macmillan, 1980, Granada, 1983; *The Quiz Book of Crime,* Futura, 1980; *Danger Girls,* Beaver, 1980; (with J. G. Rosa) *Cowboy: The Man and the Myth,* New English Library, 1980; *The World of Ballet,* Macmillan, 1981, Simon & Schuster, 1984; *Holiday Quiz,* Beaver, 1981; *Behind the Baton,* Muller, 1981, published as *Behind the Baton: A Who's Who of Conductors,* Merrimack, 1983; *Indians,* Bison Books, 1982; *Gunfighters,* Bison Books, 1983; *Pressure Groups,* Wayland, 1983; *Julius Caesar and the Romans,* F. Watts, 1984; *Canute and the Vikings,* Wayland, 1984, F. Watts, 1985; *Crazy History,* Beaver, 1984; *Alfred the Great and the Saxons,* F. Watts, 1984; *Plains Indians of North America,* Wayland, 1984; *History of the American West,* Deans, 1984; *William the Conqueror and the Normans,* Wayland, 1984, F. Watts, 1985; *Hallowe'en,* Wayland, 1984.

WORK IN PROGRESS: A biography of the Mohawk Indian, Joseph Brant, for University of Oklahoma Press; a biography

ROBERT STEPHEN MAY

of Buffalo Bill Cody, with Joseph G. Rosa, for the University of Nebraska Press.

SIDELIGHTS: "I became interested in writing because I had strong opinions on opera and theatre and wanted to voice them. I am a most fortunate writer because most of my books—for adults as well as for young readers—are about my two great enthusiasms, the American West (and American history in general) and the performing arts. Most of the rest are about general history which I love. People ask me if I miss being an actor. The answer is no, for though I enjoyed my time on the stage, it is so insecure a profession. Writing can be, but at least you can always get on with it, with or without a commission.

"My writing has enabled me to visit America every year since 1974, also Canada on several occasions. I have visited twenty states of the Union so far.... The generosity of American friends and colleagues is unending, partly, I believe, because they know I'm truly hooked on American history. Back in 1944, I was one of the first British school children to study American history for an exam of those days called School Certificate. I was superbly taught, and was hooked for life. As for the arts, my chief passions are opera and Shakespeare.

"I'm sometimes asked for whom I like writing best, adults or young people. The answer is both, though I prefer the nine- to fourteen-year-old range. I have written for the five- to eight-year-olds, but never feel too happy. A bonus when writing for the nine- to fourteen-year-olds is that you have to write good clear English, which does your adult writing a power of good. Give or take a few words, difficult or unsuitable, there is not much difference. Good writing is good writing period, and we all have to strive to achieve it."

FOR MORE INFORMATION SEE: Variety, December 10, 1969.

McINERNEY, Judith Whitelock   1945-

BRIEF ENTRY: Born June 1, 1945, in Chicago, Ill. McInerney grew up in the small, southern Illinois town of Metropolis, a safe, quiet place where she "could take the long way home from school and find more flowers, pet more stray dogs, look for more lost pennies." McInerney's first published work appeared when she was seven—her Brownie troop minutes were printed in the *Metropolis News.* As a teenager, she continued her affiliation with the same newspaper as the author of "Judy's Journal," a column of teenage news and opinions. McInerney's interest in writing led her to pursue a bachelor's degree in journalism at Marquette University where she graduated in 1967. She again contributed to the *Metropolis News* from 1966 to 1967 as editor of the centennial edition. Marriage and four children followed, along with the acquisition of Judge Benjamin, a 200-pound St. Bernard. Besides being a wife and mother, McInerney has acted as treasurer of her husband's commercial glazing business since 1970. Her writing was put on hold for a time, but "as the kids gained independence and my husband no longer needed me as an active partner at his business, creativity fever took hold again."

McInerney's home life has served as the inspiration for her "Judge Benjamin" series. Featuring her own Judge Benjamin, the books are written from the St. Bernard's point of view as custodian of the fictional O'Riley family. All published by Holiday House, the series includes *Judge Benjamin: Superdog* (1982), *Judge Benjamin: The Superdog Secret* (1983), *Judge Benjamin: The Superdog Rescue* (1984), and *Judge Benjamin: The Superdog Surprise* (1985). McInerney stated, "Now that I've rediscovered writing, I may never stop." In addition to the fifth book in her current series, *Judge Benjamin: The Superdog Gift,* she is working on a comic mystery for another possible series. *Home and office:* 3254 North University Ave., Decatur, Ill. 62526.

FOR MORE INFORMATION SEE: Holiday House: The First Fifty Years, Holiday House, 1985.

McLENIGHAN, Valjean   1947-

PERSONAL: Born December 28, 1947, in Chicago, Ill.; daughter of James Joseph (an accountant) and Wanda (a legal secretary; maiden name, Gawel) McLenighan. *Education:* Knox College, B.A., 1967. *Home and office:* 2125 West Cortez St., Chicago, Ill. 60622.

CAREER: Reilly & Lee Books, Chicago, Ill., editor, 1970-73; Follett Publishing Co., Chicago, associate editorial director in children's book department, 1974-77; free-lance writer, producer, and editorial consultant in Chicago, 1977—. Founding member of Chicago Editing Center (now Center for New Television) and Bissell Street Block Club; business communications consultant and computer-assisted learning consultant, 1982—. *Member:* Chicago Women in Publishing (founding member; vice-president, 1973).

WRITINGS—For children: *I Know You Cheated* (illustrated with photographs by Brent Jones), Raintree, 1977; *New Wheels,* Raintree, 1977; *You Can Go Jump* (illustrated by Jared D. Lee), Follett, 1977; *You Are What You Are* (illustrated by Jack Reilly), Follett, 1977; *International Games* (illustrated by Yoshi Miyake), Raintree, 1978; *Women and Science* (illustrated by Jane Palecek), Raintree, 1979; *Ernie's Work of Art,* Golden Books, 1979.

It's one painful stroke after another, hour after agonizing hour. ■ (From *Diana: Alone against the Sea* by Valjean McLenighan. Illustrated by Jay Blair.)

Six Who Dared (illustrated by Jackie Denison), Raintree, 1980; *Alone against the Sea: Diana Nyad* (illustrated by Jay Blair), Raintree, 1980, published as *Diana: Alone against the Sea*, 1982; (reteller) *What You See Is What You Get* (illustrated by Dev Appleyard), Follett, 1980; (reteller) *Know When to Stop* (illustrated by Jack Haesly), Follett, 1980; *Special Delivery*, Western Publishing, 1980; *Three Strikes and You're Out*, Follett, 1981; *Turtle and Rabbit* (illustrated by Vernon McKissack), Follett, 1981; *Stop-Go, Fast-Slow* (illustrated by Margrit Fiddle), Childrens Press, 1982; *One Whole Doughnut, One Doughnut Hole* (illustrated by Steven R. Cole), Childrens Press, 1982; *China: A History to 1949*, Childrens Press, 1983; *The People's Republic of China*, Childrens Press, 1984.

Videotapes: "Election Day, 1976," first broadcast by WTTW-TV, November, 1976; "Busia and Cioc," first broadcast by WSNS-TV, June, 1977; "The Bums," first broadcast by WTTW-TV, November, 1978; "Solar House," first broadcast by WTTW-TV, June, 1979; "The Aces," first broadcast by WTTW-TV, 1979-80.

Filmstrips: "Learning about Economics," Encyclopaedia Britannica, 1981; "The Pythagorean Theorem," Denoyer-Geppert, 1981; "Tracheophytes," Denoyer-Geppert, 1981; "Land Transportation," Denoyer-Geppert, 1981.

Screenplays: "Circus Kids," Encyclopaedia Britannica Educational Corp., 1985; "Wondering about Air," Encyclopaedia Britannica Educational Corp., 1986.

Also author of audiocassette series, "Arab Folk Tales," released by Denoyer-Geppert in 1978; of "World Book-Childcraft Reading Readiness Program," 1981; and of teacher's guides. Feature writer for *Chicago Daily News, Reader*, and Lerner Home Newspapers, 1974. Theatre critic for *Reader*, 1978.

SIDELIGHTS: "I was prompted to write books for kids when I was employed as a children's book editor and knew that I could write better manuscripts than those I was being paid to edit. The first book I wrote—on a dare from my boss—was for beginning readers, first-graders. For that one I had the good fortune of remembering quite clearly how exciting it was for me to learn to read at the age of five and how awful it was to have very little available but Dick and Jane. I was a born English major.

"Unless an interested, intelligent adult is on hand to reinforce whatever educational content is available in kids' programming, most children, in my opinion, would be better off doing almost anything else rather than watching television. The economics of broadcast television and cable TV provide little incentive for producing quality programming and often work against that goal. This is not to suggest that good programs are not available—they are. But even the most wonderful programs in the world, broadcast to a passive audience—whether kids or adults—are defused, sterilized, simply by being broadcast, pumped out through a box. My money is on *interactive* television."

McMANUS, Patrick (Francis) 1933-

PERSONAL: Born August 26, 1933, in Sandpoint, Idaho; son of Francis Edward (a sawmill worker) and Mabel (an elementary school teacher; maiden name, Klaus) McManus; married Darlene Keough (a business manager), February 3, 1954; children: Kelly McManus Walkup, Shannon McManus Bayfield, Peggy McManus Ferrie, Erin. *Education:* Washington State University, B.A., 1956, M.A., 1962, further study, 1965-67. *Home and office:* P.O. Box 13237, Spokane, Wash. 99206. *Agent:* Phyllis Westberg, Harold Ober Agency, 40 East 49th St., New York, N.Y. 10017.

CAREER: Daily Olympian, Olympia, Wash., news reporter, 1956; Washington State University, Pullman, editor, 1956-59; Eastern Washington University, Cheney, instructor, 1959-67, assistant professor, 1967-71, associate professor, 1971-74, codirector of journalism and English, 1973-83, professor of journalism and English, 1974-83, professor emeritus, 1983—. News reporter for KREM-TV, 1960-62. *Member:* Authors Guild, Outdoor Writers of America, Sigma Delta Chi.

WRITINGS: A Fine and Pleasant Misery (humor), edited by Jack Samson, Holt, 1978; *Kid Camping from Aaaaiiii! to Zip* (juvenile humor; illustrated by Roy Doty), Lothrop, 1979; *They Shoot Canoes, Don't They?* (humor), Holt, 1981; *Never Sniff a Gift Fish* (humor), Holt, 1983; *The Grasshopper Trap* (humor), Holt, 1985. Associate editor of *Field and Stream*, 1976-81; contributing editor of *Spokane*, 1979-82; editor-at-large of *Outdoor Life*, 1981—.

WORK IN PROGRESS: Research for a novel set in the early inland Pacific Northwest; new humor collection.

SIDELIGHTS: "Most of my stories are based on actual experiences, although some are purely imaginative. There are many standard devices humor writers can use to get laughs, but the best humor arises naturally out of the personalities of the characters in the stories and the comic situation in which they are placed. Although I may base a story on an actual

PATRICK McMANUS

GASP

Upon returning from a camping trip, you should never allow your mother to open your pack and look inside. ■ (From *Kid Camping from Aaaaiiii! to Zip* by Patrick F. McManus. Illustrated by Roy Doty.)

experience I've had, I usually will use characters who will produce the best comic effect from that particular situation. I use many characters repeatedly, and regular readers become familiar with them. This helps the humor writer, because he doesn't have much space in which to develop characters fully in a 2500-word story. Many of my characters have long histories, developed through dozens of stories.

"I have been influenced by the writing of James Thurber, Mark Twain and S. J. Perelman and dozens of other writers.

"I direct my humor at a broad audience, and have been particularly pleased in recent years to find so many young reading my books. Many of my stories are based on my own youth, and since everyone was young once, people of all ages seem to identify with the boy Pat and all his weird friends. Apparently, everybody has had weird friends.

"I find writing to be mostly hard work, but occasionally it is very exciting, particularly when a story comes to life and seems almost to write itself. Humor is particularly difficult, because its main purpose is to be funny. The writer never knows if other people will think the story is funny. Probably the very worst writing is a comic story that isn't funny, and the humor writer constantly worries that he may be writing that kind of story. Writing can be a very scary business, but that may be what makes it exciting, too."

HOBBIES AND OTHER INTERESTS: Fishing, hunting, traveling, photography.

MEYER, Kathleen Allan 1918-

BRIEF ENTRY: Born February 25, 1918, in Dunellen, N.J. Author of books for children and preschool director. Meyer became interested in writing when still a child in the sixth or seventh grade. She worked on her junior and senior high school newspapers, and spent the summer following graduation writing feature articles and a gossip column, "Over the Bridge Table," for her hometown newspaper. Meyer studied journalism at New York University, where she became the first woman to be chosen literary editor of the university yearbook. After earning her B.S. degree in 1940, Meyer found she was unable to afford the cost of Columbia University's Graduate School of Journalism; instead, she went to work for the script editor of a radio advertising agency. She later received a nursery school certificate from San Jose State University. Meyer has been employed as a preschool director since 1956, first at Grace Church in New York and then at St. Matthew's Episcopal Day School in San Mateo, Calif., where she has also taught creative writing to third graders.

Meyer initially began writing stories to amuse her two young daughters. However, not until both girls were out of college did she begin writing in earnest, selling her first piece to *Jack and Jill* in 1969. Shortly after, a poem was published in *Ranger Rick.* Meyer has since contributed articles to *Accent on Youth,* fiction to *Wee Wisdom,* and educational materials to *First Teacher* and *Instructor.* Some of her contributions to *Jack and Jill* were reprinted by Houghton Mifflin in a second-grade language arts textbook. Her first book, a teachers' manual entitled *Kindergarten Guide* (Hayes Publishing, 1977), was followed by several children's books, including *The Time-to-Sleep Book* (Western Publishing, 1978), *Ishi: The Story of an American Indian* (Dillon, 1980), *God Sends the Seasons* (Our Sunday Visitor, 1981), *Ireland: Land of Mist and Magic* (Dillon, 1983), and *God's Gifts* (Abingdon, 1985). *Ishi: The Story of an American Indian,* a factual book about the last known survivor of the Yahi tribe, was included by the Education Department of the State of California on the approved supplementary reading list for all its schools.

MILLER, Frances A. 1937-

BRIEF ENTRY: Born October 15, 1937, in New York, N.Y. Author of novels for young adults. The mother of four children, the first of which appeared in 1959, Miller described motherhood as "the toughest, most challenging job I'd ever had." Through the years, she found the time to tutor her chil-

dren's classmates in reading and math, run book fairs, and work as a library aide—aside from leading Cub Scouts and Girl Scouts, working on PTA and community newsletters, and cheering on her children at Little League, swim meets, horse shows, and band concerts. About 1974, with a B.A. in English from Wellesley College and a K-12 reading credential from California State University at Hayward, Miller began to pursue a three-year goal of becoming a reading specialist. However, in 1979, two-thirds of the way toward obtaining that goal, she was sidetracked when her husband's job moved the family to Australia. There she became a tutor with the Adult Literacy Program in Sydney, also acting as a member of the executive board. Returning to California in 1985, Miller has since visited junior high and elementary schools as an author/speaker.

The central character in each of Miller's three young adult novels, Matt McKendrick, came to life in her mind sometime between 1974 and 1975. Beginning in *The Truth Trap* (Dutton, 1980), Matt's story continues in *Aren't You the One Who . . .?* (Atheneum, 1983) and *Losers and Winners* (Fawcett Juniper, 1986). According to Miller, she has written several books about the same character because "like so many of Matt's fans, I too want to know 'what happens next.' Perhaps because people don't stop growing and changing or living in real life, and I don't want to leave readers with the impression that Matt's life—or theirs—will end because of one terrible event that happens when he—or they—are too young to prevent it." In 1984, *Aren't You the One Who . . .?* was the top choice on the *English Journal*'s Young Adult Poll; the following year, Miller received the California Young Reader Medal for *The Truth Trap.* She is currently working on "a fourth and probably final" novel in the McKendrick series, tentatively titled *Summer to Remember.* At the same time, she is writing an account of her family's life in Australia for adults, tentatively titled *Say Something in Australian. Home:* 50 Deer Meadow Lane, Daneville, Calif. 94526.

MITCHELL, Gladys (Maude Winifred) 1901-1983 (Stephen Hockaby, Malcolm Torrie)

PERSONAL: Born April 19, 1901, in Cowley, Oxford, England; died July, 1983; daughter of James and Annie Julia Maude (Simmonds) Mitchell. *Education:* Attended Goldsmith's College, 1919-21; University of London, diploma in history, 1926. *Politics:* Conservative. *Religion:* Agnostic. *Home:* Corfe Mullen, Dorsetshire, England. *Agent:* Curtis Brown Ltd., 1 Craven Hill, London W2 3EW, England.

CAREER: Author of mystery novels. Teacher of English and history at elementary schools in Middlesex, England, 1921-61. *Member:* Society of Authors, Crime Writers' Association, Ancient Monuments Society (fellow), Detection Club. *Awards, honors:* Silver Dagger Award from Crime Writers' Association, 1976.

WRITINGS—Juvenile: *The Three Fingerprints,* Heinemann, 1940; *Holiday River,* Evans Brothers, 1948; *The Seven Stones Mystery,* Evans Brothers, 1949; *The Malory Secret,* Evans Brothers, 1950; *Pam at Storne Castle,* Evans Brothers, 1951; *Caravan Creek,* Blackie & Son, 1954; *On Your Marks,* Heinemann, 1954, new revised edition, Parrish, 1964; *The Light Blue Hills,* Bodley Head, 1959.

Mystery novels; all published by M. Joseph, except as indicated: *Speedy Death,* Dial, 1929; *The Mystery of a Butcher's Shop,* Gollancz, 1929, Dial, 1930.

The Longer Bodies, Gollancz, 1930; *The Saltmarsh Murders*, Gollancz, 1932, Macrae Smith, 1933; (with Anthony Berkeley, Milward Kennedy, John Rhode, Dorothy Sayers, and Helen Simpson) *Ask a Policeman*, Arthur Barker, 1933; *Death in the Wet*, Macrae Smith, 1934 (published in England as *Death at the Opera*, Grayson & Grayson, 1934); *The Devil at Saxon Wall*, Grayson & Grayson, 1935; *Dead Men's Morris*, 1936; *Come Away, Death*, 1937; *St. Peter's Finger*, 1938; *Printer's Error*, 1939.

Brazen Tongue, 1940; *Hangman's Curfew*, 1941; *When Last I Died*, 1941, Knopf, 1942; *Laurels Are Poison*, 1942; *The Worsted Viper*, 1943; *Sunset over Soho*, 1943; *My Father Sleeps*, 1944; *The Rising of the Moon*, 1945; *Here Comes a Chopper*, 1946; *Death and the Maiden*, 1947, reissued, Lythway Press, 1973; *The Dancing Druids*, 1948, reissued, Severn House, 1975; *Tom Brown's Body*, 1949.

Groaning Spinney, 1950; *The Devil's Elbow*, 1951, reissued, Sheldon House, 1977; *The Echoing Strangers*, 1952, reissued, Severn House, 1975; *Merlin's Furlong*, 1953, reissued, Hutchinson, 1972; *Faintly Speaking*, 1954, reissued, Magna Print Books, 1979; *Watson's Choice*, 1955, reissued, Dell, 1981; *Twelve Horses and the Hangman's Noose*, 1956, reissued, Magna Print Books, 1977; *The Twenty-Third Man*, 1957; *Spotted Hemlock*, 1958, reissued, St. Martin's, 1985; *The Man Who Grew Tomatoes*, 1959, London House, 1960, reissued, Severn House, 1976.

Say It with Flowers, 1960; *The Nodding Canaries*, 1961; *My Bones Will Keep*, 1962, reissued, Magna Print Books, 1978; *Adders on the Heath*, London House, 1963; *Death of a Delft Blue*, 1964, London House, 1965; *Pageant of Murder*, London House, 1965; *The Croaking Raven*, 1966; *Skeleton Island*, 1967; *Three Quick and Five Dead*, 1968; *Dance to Your Daddy*, 1969.

Gory Dew, 1970; *Lament for Leto*, 1971; *A Hearse on May-Day*, 1972; *The Murder of Busy Lizzie*, 1973; *A Javelin for Jonah*, 1974; *Winking at the Brim*, McKay, 1974; *Convent on Styx*, 1975; *Late, Late in the Evening*, 1976; *Noonday and Night*, 1977; *Fault in the Structure*, 1977; *Wraiths and Changelings*, 1978; *Mingled with Venom*, 1978; *Nest of Vipers*, 1979; *The Mudflats of the Dead*, 1979.

Uncoffin'd Clay, 1980; *The Whispering Knights*, 1980; *The Death-Cap Dancers*, 1981; *Lovers, Make Moan*, 1981; *Here Lies Gloria Mundy*, 1982; *Death of a Burrowing Mole*, 1982; *The Greenstone Griffins*, 1983; *Cold, Lone and Still*, 1983.

Under pseudonym Stephen Hockaby: *Marsh Hay*, Grayson & Grayson, 1933; *Seven Stars and Orion*, Grayson & Grayson, 1934; *Gabriel's Hold*, Grayson & Grayson, 1935; *Shallow Brown*, M. Joseph, 1936; *Outlaws of the Border*, Pitman, 1936; *Grand Master*, M. Joseph, 1939.

Under pseudonym Malcolm Torrie; all published by M. Joseph: *Heavy as Lead*, 1966; *Late and Cold*, 1967; *Your Secret Friend*, 1968; *Churchyard Salad*, 1969; *Shades of Darkness*, 1970; *Bismarck Herrings*, 1971.

SIDELIGHTS: English educator and author, Gladys Mitchell wrote mystery novels for adults and children. She began her career as a teacher of English and history in 1921 and her writing career in 1929. Besides being the author of eight children's books, Mitchell, who was recognized in England as a mystery novelist, wrote over seventy books for adults. Her most famous character was Dame Beatrice Lestrange Bradley, a female sleuth who was the protagonist in over sixty of her

crime novels. Several of her books showed the influence of her Scottish heritage, and several were set in all girls' schools similar to those in which Mitchell taught for many years. "My vocational [writing] interests are governed by British Ordnance Survey maps, as a definite, real setting is usually necessary to the formation of my plots."

HOBBIES AND OTHER INTERESTS: Athletics, swimming, architecture (from Roman to eighteenth-century English).

FOR MORE INFORMATION SEE: Books, April 2, 1933, February 4, 1934; *Saturday Review of Literature*, February 10, 1934; *Times Literary Supplement*, March 29, 1934, August 8, 1980, April 17, 1981, October 29, 1982; *New Statesman*, August 30, 1958, December 3, 1960; *Manchester Guardian*, October 9, 1958; *New York Herald Tribune Book Review*, December 7, 1958; *New York Times Book Review*, December 11, 1960; *Observer Review*, September 1, 1968, May 9, 1970; *Punch*, September 11, 1968, May 28, 1969; *Books and Bookmen*, June, 1970; *Encyclopedia of Mystery and Detection*, McGraw, 1976; *Washington Post Book World*, February 15, 1981. Obituaries: *Times* (London), July 29, 1983.

MITCHELL, Joyce Slayton   1933-

PERSONAL: Born August 13, 1933, in Hardwick, Vt.; daughter of George Dix (an automobile dealer) and Sarah (Arkin) Slayton; married William E. Mitchell (an anthropologist), July 4, 1959; children: Edward Slayton, Elizabeth Dix. *Education:* Denison University, A.B., 1955; University of Bridgeport, M.S., 1958; Columbia University, further graduate study, 1960-62. *Politics:* Republican. *Religion:* Presbyterian. *Home and office:* 150 East 93rd St., New York, N.Y. 10128.

CAREER: West Rocks Junior High School, Norwalk, Conn., teacher of physical education, 1955-58; Amity Regional High School, Woodbridge, Conn., counselor, 1958-59; Greenwich High School, Greenwich, Conn., counselor, 1959-62; consultant in education, 1962—; author, 1965—. Visiting lecturer at Johnson State College, 1975. Member of advisory council of Harvard University's Divinity School, 1974-75.

MEMBER: American Personnel and Guidance Association (member of board of directors of Women's Caucus, 1976), National Vocational Guidance Association (professional member), American School Counselor Association, National Association of College Admissions Counselors, National Organization for Women (founder and coordinator of Vermont chapter, 1973-74), Vermont Guidance Association, Author's Guild. *Awards, honors: Free to Choose: Decision Making for Young Men* was selected one of New York Public Library's Books for the Teen Age, 1980, *Be a Mother and More: Career and Life Planning for Young Women* and *See Me More Clearly: Career and Life Planning for Teens with Physical Disabilities*, 1981 and 1982.

WRITINGS: The Guide to College Life, Prentice-Hall, 1969; *The Guide to Canadian Universities*, Simon & Schuster, 1970; (contributor) Mordica Pollack, editor, *N.O.W. Anthology*, Know, Inc., 1973; (editor) *Other Choices for Becoming a Woman*, Know, Inc., 1974, revised edition, Delacorte, 1975; *I Can Be Anything: Careers and Colleges for Young Women*, College Entrance Examination Board, 1975, 3rd edition published as *I Can Be Anything: A Career Book for Women*, 1982.

(Editor) *Free to Choose: Decision Making for Young Men*, Delacorte, 1976; *Tokenism: The Opiate of the Oppressed*, Know,

JOYCE SLAYTON MITCHELL

Inc., 1976; *Stopout! Working Ways to Learn,* Garrett Park Press, 1978; *The Work Book: A Guide to Skilled Jobs,* Sterling, 1978; *The Classroom Teacher's Workbook for Career Education,* Avon, 1979; *What's Where: The Official Guide to College Majors,* Avon, 1979; *The Men's Career Book: Work and Life Planning for a New Age,* Bantam, 1979.

See Me More Clearly: Career and Life Planning for Teens with Physical Disabilities, Harcourt, 1980; *Be a Mother and More: Career and Life Planning for Young Women,* Bantam, 1980; *Taking on the World: Empowering Strategies for Parents of Children with Disabilities,* Harcourt, 1982; *Choices and Changes: A Career Book for Men,* College Entrance Examination Board, 1982; *My Mommy Makes Money* (juvenile; illustrated by True Kelley), Little, Brown, 1984; *Computer-Age Jobs: The Computer Skills You Will Need to Get the Job You Want,* Scribner, 1984; *Cooking on Wheels: Trailer Folks Favorite Recipes,* RVer Annie, 1984; *From College to Career,* College Entrance Examination Board, 1986; *How to Make Ends Meet: Fifty-Five Special Job-Hunting Strategies for Retirees,* Prentice-Hall, 1986.

Contributor to educational and counseling journals, and to *Seventeen* and *Ms.* Member of editorial board of *School Counselor,* 1975-78.

WORK IN PROGRESS: 18-Wheeler! Tractor-Trailer Trucker; How to Cheer Up Your Family: The Official Guide to Becoming a Practical Joker.

SIDELIGHTS: "I was born and raised in a small village of 1200 people in Vermont. When I left home at seventeen to go to college, I had no idea of what the rest of the country was like. I thought everything outside of Vermont was a city. To my great surprise and disappointment, the Ohio town where I chose to go to college turned out to be a small village, and they liked to call it New England!

"After receiving my master's degree I started work as a school counselor in Connecticut, near New York City. I met a fascinating man in New York, an anthropologist, who loved the city so much that he didn't want to come to Connecticut to be with me. He wanted me to take the train and meet him in the city. I fell in love with the man and with the city.

"We were married in Vermont, a place he had never been to before. He fell in love with me and Vermont! So back to Vermont I went. This time, seven miles from where I was born, and in even a smaller place—a farm with a nearby village of 300! What could I do here! The only thing I could think to do was to write. To write about the questions students had when I was a counselor. 'What's it like in college?' 'What's it like in a city, in a village, in the suburbs?' 'What's it like to go to an intellectual college, a collegiate college, a business college, an artistic or community-centered college?' 'What's it like to be a banker? a promotion manager? a stockbroker? a computer graphics technician?'

"After all the surprises I got in college and working and marriage and motherhood, the main question I want to write about for young people is: What's it like?

"As a feminist and an educator, my work reflects the importance of decision-making on the basis of a student's abilities and interests rather than from a stereotypic expectation of what 'girls should do' or what 'boys should do.' My books are designed to help high school students understand the many choices open in developing all facets of their lives, so that they are not bound by traditional views of women and men.

"I write all the time. Early in the day, about six a.m. till noon. If I'm in Vermont I take a jogging or cross-country skiing break—right in my own pasture, then write some more till my children are home from school. Now that my son and daughter have gone off to universities of their own . . . I am back where I wanted to be in the first place—in the BIG APPLE, New York City!"

HOBBIES AND OTHER INTERESTS: Tennis, skiing, jogging, biking, studying French, theatre, movies, living in Paris every August.

MOORE, Jack (William) 1941-

PERSONAL: Born November 14, 1941, in Macon, Ga.; son of Cole L. and Avis Lanelle (Bolton) Moore; married Joan Linda Ballard, June 26, 1975; children: Tracy Ann. *Education:* Attended University of Maryland, 1959-60, and Maryland Institute of Art, 1960-61. *Office:* c/o MG Publishing, 1231 South Hill St., Oceanside, Calif. 92054.

CAREER: Baltimore (Morning) Sun, Baltimore, Md., editor of college edition, 1964-75; author and artist of the syndicated cartoon "Kelly and Duke," 1972-81. *Military service:* U.S. Army, 1961-64.

WRITINGS: What Is God's Area Code?: A Kelly-Duke Book (juvenile cartoons), afterword by Andrew M. Greeley, Sheed & Ward, 1974. Also author of *Furlong Deep,* 1977, and *Toledo Grand,* 1980.

Books are the treasured wealth of the world and the fit inheritance of generations and nations. . . . Their authors are a natural and irresistible aristocracy in every society, and, more than kings or emperors, exert an influence on mankind.

—Henry David Thoreau

MORGAN, Geoffrey 1916-

PERSONAL: Born October 13, 1916, in Essex, England; son of Robert (an employee of Bank of England) and Eleanor (Kine) Morgan; wife deceased. *Education:* Attended Clark's Commercial College and The Polytechnic, London, England. *Residence:* Bildeston, Suffolk, England.

CAREER: As a young man, worked for various newspapers in London as a reporter; after the war worked six months as a part-time public relations consultant. Full-time professional writer. *Military service:* Royal Air Force, 1941-46. *Member:* Society of Authors, Royal Yachting Association, Press Club, Wig and Pen Club (all London), Royal Harwich Yacht Club. *Awards, honors: A Small Piece of Paradise* was chosen as a Children's Book of the Year by the Children's Book Committee of the Child Study Association, 1968.

WRITINGS: Murderer's Moon (fiction), Jenkins, 1942; *Pig Keeping* (illustrated by D. G. Sibley), W. G. Foyle, 1951; *No Crest for the Wicked* (fiction), Forbes Robertson, 1952; (editor with Michael Hastings) *Guide to English Inns* (nonfiction), Elek, c. 1952; *Heavenly Body* (fiction), Forbes Robertson, 1953; *Cameras on the Conways* (juvenile fiction; illustrated by Peter Kay), Lutterworth, 1954; *Conways Ahoy* (juvenile fiction; illustrated by P. Kay), Lutterworth, 1955; *Small Boat Sailing* (nonfiction), W. G. Foyle, 1961; *Run for Cover* (juvenile fiction), Parrish, 1964; *Tea with Mr. Timothy* (juvenile fiction; illustrated by Nicholas Fisk), Parrish, 1964, Little, Brown, 1966.

The Small Wish (juvenile fiction; illustrated by N. Fisk), Parrish, 1965; (with Pamela Tucker) *The Yachtswoman's Pocket Book* (nonfiction), Parrish, 1965; *A Small Piece of Paradise* (juvenile fiction; illustrated by David Knight), Collins, 1967, Knopf, 1968; *A Touch of Magic* (juvenile fiction; illustrated by D. Knight), Collins, 1968; *A Window of Sky* (juvenile fiction; illustrated by D. Knight), Collins, 1969; (with Wieslaw Lasocki) *Soldier Bear* (nonfiction; illustrated by Biro), Collins, 1970; *The View from Prospect* (fiction), Collins, 1972; *Boy Dominic,* Fontana, 1974; *Summer of the Seals* (fiction), Collins, 1975; (with Judy Eron) *Charlie Rich* (juvenile biography; illustrated by John Keeley), Creative Education, 1975; *Lame Duck* (juvenile fiction; illustrated by Joanna Shibbs), Abelard, 1977; *Bailey's Bird* (fiction), Armada, 1977; *Flip: The Story of a Seal* (fiction; illustrated by Peter Reddick), Collins, 1979.

Has also adapted many of his books and other scripts for British Broadcasting Corp. Contributor of short stories and articles on sailing to women's magazines.

SIDELIGHTS: Morgan related that there is "too much sex, sadism and violence in so many books of today," and that "there is a place for the book that tells a story with simplicity, with feeling, about ordinary people in interesting and sometimes extraordinary circumstances, without resort to microscopic detail of their sex lives." Many of Morgan's books have been serialized in magazines.

HOBBIES AND OTHER INTERESTS: Sailing and golf.

FOR MORE INFORMATION SEE: Trade News, November, 1964; W.O.G. Lofts and D. J. Adley, *The Men behind Boy's Fiction,* Howard Baker, 1970; Martha E. Ward and Dorothy A. Marquardt, *Authors of Books for Young People,* Scarecrow, 1971.

MORTON, Miriam 1918(?)-1985

OBITUARY NOTICE—See sketch in *SATA* Volume 9: Born June 14, 1918 (one source cites 1916), in Kishinev, Rumania (now U.S.S.R.); died of cancer, September 22, 1985, in Washington, D.C. Social worker, educator, editor, translator, and author. Morton began her career as a nursery school teacher and social worker, then worked as a script reader for Twentieth Century-Fox and a manuscript editor for two university presses. In 1963 she became a full-time translator and editor of books written for, by, and about children. To promote an awareness of other cultures in American youth, Morton translated and edited poetry, plays, and tales from France and the Soviet Union, among them works by such prominent authors as Anton Chekhov, Leo Tolstoy, and Guy de Maupassant as well as collections such as *Voices from France: Ten Stories by French Nobel Laureates* and the award-winning *The Moon Is Like a Silver Sickle: A Celebration of Poetry by Soviet Children.* Morton, who immigrated to the United States as a child, also wrote books about fostering peace between children of different countries and about life in the Soviet Union. Her last book, *Growing Up in the Soviet Union: From Cradle to Career,* was published in 1982.

FOR MORE INFORMATION SEE: Contemporary Authors, New Revision Series, Volume 2, Gale, 1981; *Who's Who of American Women,* 13th edition, Marquis, 1983. Obituaries: *New York Times,* October 15, 1985.

MYRA, Harold L(awrence) 1939-

PERSONAL: Born July 19, 1939, in Camden, N.J.; son of John S. and Esther (Christensen) Myra; married Jeanette Austin (a registered nurse), May 7, 1966; children: Michelle, Todd,

HAROLD L. MYRA

Gregory. *Education:* East Stroudsburg State College, B.S., 1961. *Home:* 1737 Marion Ct., Wheaton, Ill. 60187. *Office:* Christianity Today, Inc., 465 Gundersen Dr., Carol Stream, Ill. 60188.

CAREER: Campus Life, Wheaton, Ill., began as editorial assistant, became vice-president of the literature division and publisher, 1961-75; *Christianity Today,* Carol Stream, Ill., president and publisher, 1975—; author. Instructor, Wheaton Graduate School, 1975—. *Military service:* U.S. Marine Corps Reserve, 1957-62. *Awards, honors:* Honorary doctorate, John Wesley College, 1977, Biola University, 1983.

WRITINGS: No Man in Eden, Word, Inc., 1969; *Michelle, You Scallawag, I Love You,* John T. Benson, 1972; *The New You: Questions about This Fresh Newborn Way of Life Now That You Believe,* Zondervan, 1972; *Is There a Place I Can Scream?,* Doubleday, 1975; *Elsbeth,* Revell, 1976; *Santa, Are You for Real?,* Thomas Nelson, 1977; *Love Notes to Jeanette,* Victor Books, 1979; *Easter Bunny, Are You for Real?,* Thomas Nelson, 1979; *The Choice,* Tyndale House, 1981; *Halloween, Is It for Real?* (illustrated by Dwight Walles), Thomas Nelson, 1982; *Today Is Your Super-Terrific Birthday,* Nelson Communications, 1985.

SIDELIGHTS: "I was born in Camden, New Jersey, and went to school there until the third grade; then we moved to the Pocono Mountains in Pennsylvania where I completed my schooling, including college.

"I always wanted to write. When I was in the second and third grades I would write funny little poems in which the words would rhyme—like tree, me, see, free. All through high school and then college, I just kept on writing and practicing. Frankly, I wasn't very good, but I kept at it, and kept at it, and kept at it and kept learning. In college, I sent a lot of short stories to a magazine and won a prize. That encouraged me!

"I meet many interesting people in my job as a publisher—businessmen, writers, speakers. I find most interesting of all the many editors of the magazines I work with, who constantly stimulate my thinking."

HOBBIES AND OTHER INTERESTS: Writing, reading.

NASH, (Frederic) Ogden   1902-1971

PERSONAL: Born August 19, 1902, in Rye, N.Y.; died May 19, 1971, in Baltimore, Md.; son of Edmund Strudwick (in the naval stores business) and Mattie (Chenault) Nash; married Frances Rider Leonard, June 6, 1931; children: Linell Chenault (Mrs. J. Marshall Smith), Isabel Jackson (Mrs. Frederick Eberstadt). *Education:* Attended Harvard University, 1920-21. *Residence:* Baltimore, Md.

CAREER: Poet, author; began writing light verse about 1925. Teacher, St. George's School, Providence, R.I., 1921-22; Dillon, Read & Company, New York, N.Y., began as mail clerk, became bond salesman; Barron Collier (advertising agency), New York, N.Y., copywriter for streetcar ads; worked in the editorial and publicity departments of Doubleday, Doran & Co., 1925-31, and Farrar & Rinehart, 1931-33; member of *New Yorker* editorial staff for a short time, then became a full-time writer. Gave frequent lectures and readings, 1949-71. Appeared on radio shows, including "Information, Please!" and the Bing Crosby and Rudy Vallee hours, and on television panel shows, including "Masquerade Party." *Member:* Na-

OGDEN NASH

tional Institute of Arts and Letters. *Awards, honors: New York Herald Tribune*'s Children's Spring Book Festival Picture Book Honor, 1962, for *The New Nutcracker Suite, and Other Innocent Verses; The Scroobious Pip* was selected as one of the American Institute of Graphic Arts Children's Books, 1967-68.

WRITINGS: (With Joseph Alger) *The Cricket of Carador,* Doubleday, 1925; (with Christopher Morley and Cleon Throckmorton) *Born in a Beer Garden; or, She Troupes to Conquer,* Rudge, 1930; *Hard Lines,* Simon & Schuster, 1931; *Free Wheeling,* Simon & Schuster, 1931; (editor) Pelham Granville Wodehouse, *Nothing But Wodehouse,* Doubleday, 1932; *Happy Days,* Simon & Schuster, 1933; *Four Prominent So and So's* (music by Robert Armbruster), Simon & Schuster, 1934; *The Primrose Path,* Simon & Schuster, 1935; *The Bad Parents' Garden of Verse,* Simon & Schuster, 1936; *I'm a Stranger Here Myself,* Little, Brown, 1938.

The Face Is Familiar: The Selected Works of Ogden Nash, Little, Brown, 1940; *Good Intentions,* Little, Brown, 1942, revised edition, Dent, 1956; *The Ogden Nash Pocket Book,* Blakiston, 1944; *Many Long Years Ago,* Little, Brown, 1945; *The Selected Verse of Ogden Nash,* Modern Library, 1946; *Ogden Nash's Musical Zoo* (music by Vladimire Dukelsky), Little, Brown, 1947; *Versus,* Little, Brown, 1949.

Family Reunion, Little, Brown, 1950; *Parents Keep Out: Elderly Poems for Youngerly Readers* (illustrated by Barbara Corrigan), Little, Brown, 1951; *The Private Dining Room, and Other New Verses,* Little, Brown, 1953; (editor) *The Moon is Shining Bright as Day: An Anthology of Good-Humored Verse,* Lippincott, 1953; *The Pocket Book of Ogden Nash,* Pocket Books, 1954; *You Can't Get There from Here,* Little, Brown, 1957; *The Boy Who Laughed at Santa Claus* (keepsake edition), printed by Cooper & Beatty Ltd. (London), 1957; *The Christmas That Almost Wasn't* (illustrated by daughter, Linell Nash), Little, Brown, 1957; (editor) *I Couldn't Help*

Laughing: Stories Selected and Introduced by Ogden Nash, Lippincott, 1957; *Verses from 1929 On,* Little, Brown, 1959 (published in England as *Collected Verse from 1929 On,* Dent, 1961); *Custard, the Dragon* (illustrated by L. Nash), Little, Brown, 1959.

Beastly Poetry, Hallmark Editions, 1960; *A Boy Is a Boy: The Fun of Being a Boy,* F. Watts, 1960; (editor) *Everybody Ought to Know: Verses Selected and Introduced by Ogden Nash,* Lippincott, 1961; *Custard, the Dragon and the Wicked Knight,* Little, Brown, 1961; *The New Nutcracker Suite, and Other Innocent Verses* (illustrated by Ivan Chermayeff), Little, Brown, 1962; *Girls Are Silly,* F. Watts, 1962; *Everyone But Thee and Me,* Little, Brown, 1962; *A Boy and His Room,* F. Watts, 1963; *The Adventures of Isabel,* Little, Brown, 1963; *The Untold Adventures of Santa Claus,* Little, Brown, 1964; *An Ogden Nash Bonanza* (five volumes; contains *Good Intentions, I'm a Stranger Here Myself, Many Long Years Ago, The Private Dining Room,* and *Versus*), Little, Brown, 1964; *Marriage Lines: Notes of a Student Husband,* Little, Brown, 1964 (published in England as *Notes of a Student Husband,* Dent, 1964).

The Animal Garden (illustrated by Hilary Knight), M. Evans, 1965; *Santa Go Home: A Case History for Parents,* Little, Brown, 1967; *The Cruise of the Aardvark,* M. Evans, 1967; *The Mysterious Ouphe,* Hale, 1967; *There's Always Another Windmill,* Little, Brown, 1968; *Funniest Verses of Ogden Nash: Light Lyrics by One of America's Favorite Humorists,* selected by Dorothy Price, Hallmark Editions, 1968; (with others) *New Comic Limericks: Laughable Poems,* compiled by Ivanette Dennis, Roger Schlesinger, 1969.

Bed Riddance: A Posy for the Indisposed, Little, Brown, 1970; *The Old Dog Barks Backwards,* Little, Brown, 1972; *Custard, the Dragon and the Wendigo* (illustrated by J. Astrop), Warne, 1978; *Custard and Company* (selected and illustrated by Quentin Blake), Kestrel, 1979, Little, Brown, 1980.

Completed *The Scroobious Pip* (ALA Notable Book; illustrated by Nancy E. Burkert), by Edward Lear, Harper, 1968.

"O Aardvark, Aardvark," chanted he, "How happy am I that thou art me...." ■ (From *The Cruise of the Aardvark* by Ogden Nash. Illustrated by Wendy Watson.)

(From the Broadway musical "One Touch of Venus," for which Nash co-authored the script and wrote the lyrics. Starring Mary Martin, it premiered at the Imperial Theatre, October 7, 1943.)

Wrote lyrics for Broadway musical, "One Touch of Venus," 1943, for off-Broadway production, "The Littlest Revue," and for television show, "Art Carney Meets Peter and the Wolf." Wrote adaptation of Otto A. Harbach's *The Firefly*, produced under same title, MGM, 1937; author of screenplay with George Oppenheimer and Edmund L. Hartmann, "The Feminine Touch," Loew's, 1941. Wrote new verses to Camille Saint-Saens's "Carnival of the Animals," narrated by Noel

Equestriennes will never ride
As other people do, astride.

■ (From "The Big Tent under the Roof" in *Custard and Company* by Ogden Nash. Selected and illustrated by Quentin Blake.)

Coward, for Columbia; author of verses set to Serge Proko-fiev's "Peter and the Wolf," and Paul Dukas's "The Sorcer-er's Apprentice."

Contributor to *Cricket's Choice,* Open Court Publishing, 1974. Contributor of verse to periodicals, including *New Yorker, Life, Saturday Evening Post, Holiday, Look, House and Garden, Good Housekeeping, Saturday Review, Harper's, Atlantic, Vogue, McCall's,* and *New Republic.*

ADAPTATIONS: "Custard the Dragon" (filmstrip with cas-sette), Weston Woods, 1962, (motion picture) Weston Woods, 1964.

SIDELIGHTS: **August 19, 1902.** "I was born . . . in Rye, New York, and raised in a back-and-forth way between Rye and Savannah, Georgia, until I was fourteen. My father was a North Carolinian who, as a boy eleven or twelve years old toward the end of the Civil War, patrolled the grounds of the

(From the movie "One Touch of Venus," based on the Broadway musical for which Nash wrote most of the lyrics, including the haunting "Speak Low." Copyright 1948 by Universal Pictures Co., Inc.)

Venus comes to life. ■ (From the movie "One Touch of Venus," starring Robert Walker and Ava Gardner. Copyright 1948 by Universal Pictures Co., Inc.)

Well, he wasn't a goblin or gnome or elf, Old Abidan, he was just himself. ■ (From *The Animal Garden* by Ogden Nash. Illustrated by Hilary Knight.)

family estate with a shotgun to protect his mother and sisters from stragglers and looters. He came North as a young man, and got into the naval stores business—rosin and turpentine—and he had dual headquarters, New York and Savannah; that was why we spent winters in the South and summers at Rye.

"At that time Rye was a small country town with dirt roads. One of the main roads ran right outside our place, and my brother and I used to sit on the wall and count the number of cars traveling on the Boston Post Road. If we counted eight or ten we had a very high mark to be chalked up on the calendar.

"My education was rather varied. My mother came from a very scholarly family. Her father, Jason Chenault, of Louisville, Kentucky, had been a professor of classics—Greek and

Latin—and his high principles regarding the 'right' education had been passed along. The family's intent was to send me to very good boarding schools, but when I was twelve or thirteen my father's business began to rock due to a series of lawsuits brought by the government, so our lives were disturbed as the financial situation changed. I was too young to realize exactly what was going on, but I knew that things were not as they used to be or should be. I went to day school in Rye, for a bit, and there was one short period—I was about ten and my family had gone abroad—when I was sent to a small boy's boarding school. When I say small I *mean* small. The capacity was eight boys, and it was outside Groton, Massachusetts.

**I love the Baby Giant Panda;
I'd welcome one on my veranda.**

■ (From "The Panda" in *Custard and Company* by Ogden Nash. Selected and illustrated by Quentin Blake.)

Presumably it was a preparatory school for Groton itself. At any rate, I spent a year there; the first half of it I was very homesick, but I got over that. I learned some Latin—began my rather serious study of Latin, a language I've found very useful—and I spent a good deal of time riding a bicycle through the New England countryside.

"After that my eyes got very bad. My mother was quite disturbed about this and thought they were going to grow progressively worse, so two things of some significance resulted. She had me take a course in touch-typing which proved invaluable until my fingers curled up on me in later life. And she took me out of school and had me study at home. I did a great deal of reading with her; she was very widely read, a scholarly woman, and I think that most of my real education was gained in those years she tutored me." ["Ogden Nash," *Conversations* by Roy Newquist, Rand McNally, 1967.[1]]

1917. Sent to prep school. "Later on, when I was fifteen, the family fortunes had recouped sufficiently to send me off to boarding school again, so I went to St. George's in Newport, Rhode Island, where I spent three very happy years. I was lucky enough to encounter a few good masters who were extremely stimulating, particularly in history, Latin, and English. I can't value Latin enough in view of what it has given me in later life. Nor, for that matter, can I value the whole experience of boarding school enough. A boy gains so much, not only in the matter of a better education, but in self-reliance and the disciplines and the individualities needed to cope with life.

"After St. George's I entered Harvard, where I spent only a freshman year. By this time I knew the family finances were again in very bad shape, and I'm afraid that I didn't have enough intellectual curiosity, nor enough physical vigor and ambition, to work my way through the remaining three years, so at the end of my freshman year I left and attempted to make myself self-supporting."[1]

At school, Nash played football, a game that remained fascinating to him throughout his lifetime. "You can get an idea of how good I was from the fact that although we lost The Game 49-0, I didn't get to play a minute of it." ["Poet Laureate of the Colts," *Life,* December 13, 1968.[2]]

1921. "I bounced through a variety of jobs.... I went, as all young men of that day around New York seemed to do, down into Wall Street. Not willingly, but because there were friends of the family who could give me a job, and I spent a year in the mailroom of Dillon, Read and Company, working from four o'clock in the afternoon to twelve or one in the morning. I discovered what the downtown financial district looks like at midnight, with no one in the streets and cats prowling around the garbage cans. It was a lot like Don Marquis' *Mehitabel.* I also developed a deeper interest in writing. I always had been interested in writing; I started jotting down verse as a small child. When I was six or seven I started turning out verses, jingles, rhymes. Now, on Wall Street, I knew that I wanted to write, and I found myself trying to get closer to it. But I did not know at the time what or how I wanted to write.

"I must say for myself that I did not write to established authors to ask them how I should go about being a writer.

"I was thoroughly sick of Wall Street in short order, and began to try seriously to get a writing job. I got one—writing advertising copy for streetcar ads. There were still streetcars running on trolley tracks in cities and towns, and I worked for a firm that sold poster space. I did this for two or three years,

but I followed in good footsteps: Scott Fitzgerald had worked for the same firm some ten years before me, and John Held, Jr., had been one of the artists on the staff. While I did this I roomed with three or four other young men in a gas-heated cold-water flat in the sixties, under the Elevated on Third Avenue in New York."[1]

1925. "One of my roommates, a fellow named Joe Alger, had been two years ahead of me at prep school, and had been very prominent at Harvard in the Hasty Pudding and on the *Lampoon.* He was a brilliant fellow, and he and I decided to write a book. We thought that the easiest book to turn out would be a juvenile, so we did it, *The Cricket of Carador.* It was accepted for publication by Doubleday, Page and Company. During the process of publication, I met the head of the advertising department, Dan Longwell, who had just lost his assistant, Frank Chapman.... At any rate, Longwell hired me.

"Now, after two years in the streetcar advertising business I was getting $100.00 a month. Doubleday offered me $90.00 a month, and I netted rather less than that because I was living in New York City and Doubleday's offices were out in Garden City, Long Island, so I had to buy a commutation ticket out of my $90.00. But I wanted so badly to get into the publishing field, to become associated with writers in one way or another, that I jumped at the opportunity. I spent seven or eight years in publishing, almost as happy as anyone could be, working in the editorial and advertising departments.

"To me it was the exciting sort of job a young man would grab and work on eagerly, twelve and fourteen hours a day. I

Nash at work, 1953.

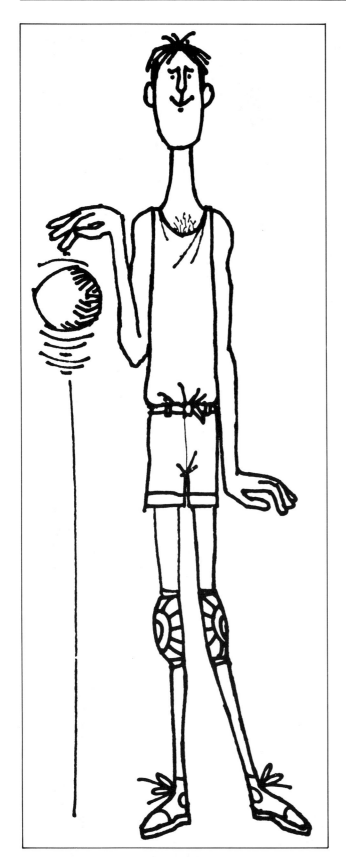

**By Dr. Naismith's monster child,
Basketball is not a sport,
Not even as a last resort—....**

■ (From "The Paid Attendance" in *Everyone But Thee and Me* by Ogden Nash. Illustrated by John Alcorn.)

used to get up at six o'clock to catch the Long Island out to Garden City, and I wouldn't get back to New York until eleven-thirty or twelve-thirty at night. Along about this time I began to stumble into the sort of thing I've been doing virtually ever since. As I said, I'd written a great deal of verse throughout my youth; I like to think of it as poetry, and it certainly was serious in conception and execution, but sometimes I was writing like Swinburne, sometimes like Browning, then like Kipling, then like Tennyson. But I finally realized that my imitations were not very good, and that I simply couldn't qualify as a serious poet. There was a ludicrous aspect to what I was trying to do; my emotional and naked-beauty stuff just didn't turn out as I intended.

"So I began to poke a little bit of fun at myself and these attempts, turning them upside down and accentuating the ludicrous side of which, at first, had been attempts at serious poetry. I kept working on these things at night after I got home from work, and eventually summoned up enough courage to send one of them to *The New Yorker*. To my great surprise and joy they liked it and asked for more. So I wrote more, at the same time keeping my job in editorial and advertising, and by 1931 enough of them had been assembled to encourage Simon and Schuster to ask me to make a book out of them. I did, and they published it, and it was extremely successful for a book of light verse. I think it sold about 40,000 copies rather quickly.

"I was launched. I still had no idea of devoting my life to being a writer; it was to be a sideline while publishing was my mainstay. But along came the Depression."[1]

George Stevens, a life-long friend, recalled the years that Nash and he spent in the advertising department of Doubleday. "Ogden was invariably entertaining to be with, as spontaneous in conversation as in those verses that I was not bright enough to recognize as more than unconsidered trifles; nor did I guess where his inexhaustible spontaneity was leading him. Between verses and asking me questions like 'Do you remember the names of Happy Hooligan's nephews?' (I did and do), he was a first-class copywriter. I remember a headline he wrote for an ad when *The Plutocrat* by Booth Tarkington was riding high on the best-seller lists: 'First in New York, First in Chicago, and First in the Hearts of His Countrymen.' One of the Doubleday vice presidents, a benign elderly gentleman, was a bit scandalized. Ogden could have had a successful career in advertising, but his celebrated first published poem ['Spring Comes to Murray Hill'] made it clear that he did not want to sit in an office at 244 Madison Avenue or anywhere else." [George Stevens, "Ogden Nash: A Memoir," *Saturday Review*, June 19, 1971.[3]]

Before becoming a full-time writer, Nash worked on the editorial staff of the *New Yorker*. "The Depression hit after I'd left Doubleday to do a three-month stint as managing editor of *The New Yorker* magazine. Harold Ross hired me under two misapprehensions: first, that he wanted a managing editor, and second, that I would be a good one. At that time the job of managing editor of that magazine was like being caught briefly in a revolving door. In my case the revolution of the door took ninety days which was, I believe, the usual period of tenure at the time.

"Ross was an astonishing man, worthy of all that has been written about him. He had superb taste, taste of an extremely sophisticated sort, yet he took great pains to present himself as an awkward, vulgar hick. I don't know if it was performance he enjoyed, or whether he was really a shy man hiding behind this facade; he certainly made a deplorable personal

The Scroobious Pip sat under a tree
By the silent shores of the Jellybolee—....

■ (From *The Scroobious Pip* by Edward Lear. Completed by Ogden Nash. Illustrated by Nancy Ekholm Burkert.)

appearance. But his energy and taste made *The New Yorker* a great magazine.''[1]

1931. Married Frances Rider Leonard.

1933. ''After my brief stay with Ross I went back into the publishing business, this time with a smaller firm, one that was just starting out. . . . The Depression had hit, and it was particularly rough for a young publishing house. Therefore my salary got cut and cut and cut until it was finally down to $25.00 a week. I was literally back to the $100.00 a month I'd earned in the streetcar advertising business eight or ten years before, and in the meantime I'd acquired a wife and one child and had another child on the way. Thus the new firm didn't seem to offer too bright a prospect. Fortunately, I knew most of the literary agents in New York through my job, and I approached one of them, a particularly good agent and also a dear and helpful friend. I asked him if he thought I could make a go of it as a free lance, and he scouted around amongst some magazine editors and finally said yes, he thought I could. The first thing he produced was a contract with *The Saturday Evening Post* for twenty-six verses a year during the next year, for which they would pay $100 each. That gave me a backbone

of $2,600 a year that I could count on, so I packed up my family and we moved out of New York and came down . . . to Baltimore, really as a temporary expedient. (As it turned out we stayed for twenty years.) And with that I became a free-lance writer.''[1]

1935. ''I supported myself completely by what I was writing, but at that time there were a great many more magazine and newspaper markets and even types of markets that don't exist anymore. I was extremely fortunate that I came along at a time when my sort of work had some novelty appeal and when there was a demand for it. In looking over my records I find that I sold 157 verses in 1935. A lot of them were very ephemeral stuff, some brief and topical, others done on assignment, but a good many of them seemed to qualify, in my own eyes, for inclusion in books. In fact, I can read them today without visibly flinching or wincing, and that says a great deal. A poet, whether he be serious or 'light,' often has a rough time reading his own stuff.

''This went on for a great many years until I made the mistake of going out to Hollywood, where I had the sort of experiences other writers have complained bitterly about, but which are no

Nash and the cast of the weekly television show, "Masquerade Party."

less bitter because they're duplicated. I was out there for two and one-half years under option, with my option being picked up every six months at a slight raise in salary, and I really had no work to do at all. I don't think I had more than four weeks of real work in that entire period and this was not good for me. Anything I could work on—well, I'd find myself engaged with four or five or six or seven other writers. Often you didn't even know that other writers were working on the job that had been assigned to you, so any sense of individuality, any sense of pride in what you were doing, was destroyed. Toward the end of that dreadful period I would often awaken in the night, then wake my wife to ask her who I was. I felt that I had become so merged in this vast conglomeration of writers that I didn't know whether I was me or somebody else or perhaps six other people. I had been used to being a sort of lone wolf.

"At any rate, it took me quite a while to recover from Hollywood. It wasn't until about a year and one-half after I'd come back East that I was able to stand on my own feet again. Since that time I've done some work in the theater, some on television, some on radio, but I made sure that writing was my main prop, my primary activity. I enjoy doing it.''[1]

1942. Collaborated on "A Touch of Venus," with S. J. Perelman and Kurt Weill. "I was 40 years old; the armed services and even the broadminded draft board had found me either mentally or physically deficient; perhaps both. Part of the time I spent as an air-raid warden patrolling the streets of suburban Baltimore looking for Nazi bombers that happily never showed up and part in touring the Eastern seaboard with a pride of such literary lions as Edna Ferber, Fannie Hurst, Louis Bromfield, and Dorothy Parker in an earnest if feeble attempt to sell War Bonds.

"I remember plumbing the depths of frustration in one large city where we sat at a long table after the speech-making, instructed and prepared to sign any Savings Stamps purchased at an adjacent booth for those thrifty patriots who might value our autographs. Sales seemed slower than usual, and at the end of the evening we found out why. The public apathy was due not to our collective lack of glamour but to the fact that the handsome and spellbinding mayor had established his pitch at the other end of the hall and was handing out autographed photographs of himself for free.

"Meanwhile my professional life was withering. I knew how to write light verse and sell enough of it to make a living, but it seemed to me that I had been writing such stuff forever, and facing the chore of writing light verse in a darkening world, I found that I had gone stale.

"Then I got a letter from Kurt Weill. He invited me to collaborate with him on the songs for a musical comedy he wanted to do, based on an old book by F. Anstey called *The Tinted Venus*. He had talked over the idea with his friend Marlene Dietrich, and she was eager to play the title role.

"I had never met Kurt, but I knew him as the composer of the scores for 'The Three-Penny Opera,' 'Knickerbocker Holiday,' and 'Lady in the Dark.' His success on the German stage had been at its height when Hitler seized the government. One night his plays were being performed in state theaters all over Germany, the next they were shut down by official edict, and Kurt, who could take a hint, was on his way to Paris, bound for the U.S. He had been shaping his new life here for about five years when he wrote me the letter that was to reshape my own.

"I took the next train to New York, carrying my clothes in a large stiff suitcase; not large because there were so many clothes

Nash in his garden, 1965.

or stiff to protect them but because a suitcase suitable for sitting on was a valuable adjunct to wartime travel. In the offices of Cheryl Crawford, the producer, I met Kurt and agreed to plunge into the perilous and, to me, unknown seas of the theater.

"You might say I was like a pitcher who has been pulled out of trouble by a brilliant double play; a unique double play started nearly 400 years ago by Shakespeare and completed by a tiny German émigré who knew Shakespeare better than I did.

"I hope that Kurt realized the inspiration that his patience, his kindness, and his continuing faith in me had given to me. I was out of the doldrums and ready once more to stand up and face the world with whatever abilities I possessed. My life since then has been a happy and creative one, and for that life I shall always be grateful to him.'' [Robert Fitzgibbon and

What's left on the plate, buy some swine and let them finish it. ■ (From "Go Ahead, It Will Do You Good or Her Eyes Are Bigger than His Stomach" in *You Can't Get There from Here* by Ogden Nash. Illustrated by Maurice Sendak.)

Ernest V. Heyn, editors, *My Most Inspiring Moment*, Doubleday, 1965.[4]]

"One Touch of Venus" became the Broadway hit of the 1943 season.

1949. To support himself, Nash took to the lecture circuit. Although his talks were primarily readings of his verse, he frequently embellished them with amusing observations. Hating airplanes, he scheduled his lecture dates so that he could travel by train. He wrote in one of his verses: "I think progress began to retrogress when Wilbur and Orville Wright started tinkering around in Dayton and Kitty Hawk, because I believe that two Wrights made a wrong." [Albin Krebs, "Ogden Nash, Master of Light Verse, Dies," *New York Times Biographical Edition*, New York Times, May 20, 1971.[5]]

Nash, who was famous for his unconventional rhymes and mangled verse, made an excellent living from his verse, producing twenty volumes. About his unusual format, the poet remarked: "I just stumbled on the idea when fooling around with light verse; and I suddenly discovered, that it gave me a chance to express my own ideas—which were not up to Plato or Santayana—in an inoffensive and unpretentious way. I've been in love with words all my life, and this particular style suddenly seemed to create an outlet for my own limited mentality.

"When you get right down to it, I suppose all this is really a cover-up for my naked self. It's my own private Society for the Prevention of Embarrassment. And I think it enables me to communicate with the ordinary human being without sounding like an Eddie Guest. In other words, I've got myself off the hook, and I'm able to have the best of two worlds." ["Trade Winds," *Saturday Review*, November 14, 1962.[6]]

Nash called himself a "worsifier" and his "worses" bore the mark of his unique style. "I like the style because it gives me a mask, a front behind which I can hide. I can't go straight to the point about anything emotionally valid; that's one of my faults, I get ponderous. By backing off I can make the point without belaboring it."

On how he wrote his verse, Nash remarked: "Sometimes I write from beginning to end, sometimes backwards and sometimes I start in the middle. When a pun comes to me, I usually work backward on how to lead people into the trap. I keep a pad and pencil near my bed, but the poems I write when I'm half asleep aren't much good. Though I do write some fair ones sitting up on the side of the bed. Usually I do a lot of rewriting—that sloppy appearance has to be carefully groomed.

"Sometimes I do get very pleased with myself and I'll show what I've done to my wife. If she doesn't laugh I become cross and go off and sulk. Later I make the revisions she suggested.

"My daughters appreciate my stuff more now than they did when they were younger. You see, I had the awful habit of

**A manifest magical, miracle mountain,
Cooling its toes in Saint Agnes' Fountain.**

■ (From *The Christmas That Almost Wasn't* by Ogden Nash. Illustrated by Linell Nash.)

writing about them then. I guess I was hoping to make the girls pay for themselves that way. I can still see the look of horror on their faces when they heard I was going to speak at a school they were attending.'' [Patricia Baum, ''Hear Your Heroes,'' *Seventeen*, January, 1963.[7]]

1951. Wrote *Parents Keep Out: Elderly Poems for Youngerly Readers,* which was followed by two of his Christmas books, *The Boy Who Laughed at Santa Claus,* and *The Christmas That Almost Wasn't.* ''I started writing verses for children many years ago when I did them for my own. I had no intention of making books out of them, but some did appear in one magazine or another and I found that certain verses I'd written twenty or twenty-five years previous still drew letters from schoolchildren. So my publishers and I started doing children's books. They took some of the verses I'd written long ago, made them into very handsome books and the books did surprisingly well. I found that I appreciated them, so it seemed logical to plan intervals here and there, between my other books when I needed a change of pace, to try my hand at writing new verse for children. So I've done quite a few books for youngsters; they've given me pleasure and they sell nicely. It's not a millionaire's investment, but the books sell year after year. The royalties are never high at any one time, but oddly enough, a book even ten or fifteen years old will bring in

The cow is of the bovine ilk;
One end is moo, the other, milk.

■ (From ''The Cow'' in *The Bad Parents' Garden of Verse* by Ogden Nash. Illustrated by Reginald Birch.)

pleasant royalties, and with six or seven going you end up with a little steady income.

''Now, the main thing I find in writing for children is to absolutely avoid the tendency to write down to them. I'm violently opposed to the trend in education today of trying to suit the books to the little mind instead of letting the little mind grow as it tackles the books. I think one of the reasons for the greatness of Churchill's oratory was that he would use a four or six-syllable word or a Latin quotation if he wanted to, and it suited his purpose. He wasn't thinking about whether the trash man or the beggar understood it or not; he simply swept them along with him through the power and grandeur of what he was saying. If they didn't understand the particular word they still got the idea; the context gave that to them.

''I think that's the way children learn; I do not think you can teach them by simply repeating hat, cat, rat, mat, vat. I think you have to sneak a few words in on them, and if they don't know them they'll either look them up or learn what they are from the context.

''I also think they love rhythm. I am much more careful about my rhythm and meter when I'm writing for children; I see that it has rollick and dance to it because I think they have a very keen ear, a deep appreciation of rhythm.

''Some of the things going on now in education horrify me. A few years ago we did a great deal of reading during the summer, reading aloud to one of my granddaughters and having her read to us. Well, she read a certain book—I forget whether it was *Lorna Doone* or *Treasure Island*—and her teacher was absolutely horrified to learn she had read it. She said, 'If you've read that now, what are you going to write your book report on next year?' Where are we when that kind of nonsense goes on?''[1]

1959. First ''Custard'' book for children, *Custard, the Dragon* was written. It was illustrated by daughter Linnell, who illustrated other books by her father as well. To would-be young authors, Nash prescribed a heavy diet of writing and reading. ''… Though I speak from personal experience, I recommend that the youngster try different forms of writing. I know that I was an imitator. I tried to write like Swinburne, like Tennyson, like the Elizabethans. None of it worked, but it was all experience. It gave me fluidity and facility. Good reading can't help but make an impression on the mind and give the youngster some idea of good taste and bad taste, what is fine and what is meretricious. Reading has to play a big part. It will send the young writer through phases; today he may be Hemingway, tomorrow Fitzgerald, the next day Mailer, the next Kerouac. But I think he'll go through all this until he finds something he's at home with, that fits him, that *is* him. It can't be done just by sitting down and saying, 'I want to be a writer.' Sounds lovely. They're probably thinking in terms of these package deals whereby they write a synopsis and the reprint is sold for five hundred thousand dollars before the manuscript is in, and the movie packet is included, and it all looks like the quick route to the James Bond automobiles and blondes. But I don't think they're the ones who are going to be writers. It's those who sweat it out by themselves and spend more hours working than dreaming that will make it.

''Between the ages of eight and twenty-five is when a person should gobble every book in sight. There are things you should read and enjoy when you're young that you just can't bear when you're older—Cooper, Walter Scott, most of George Eliot.

"Reading lists are another thing I have a tremendous quarrel with. The kind I see being brought home from school by my grandchildren make me think that teachers have gone completely mad in their idea of what is going to be of use, what will form tastes and bring experience.

"But I don't have required reading lists now. Just some required work I go at all too slowly."[1]

1968. Completed *The Scroobious Pip* by Edward Lear. Nash supplied two lines and three words—set off by brackets—to a nearly finished poem found among Lear's papers. Besides writing and lecturing, Nash also was a member of television panel shows and wrote verses to Saint-Saen's "Carnival of the Animals," Serge Prokofiev's "Peter and the Wolf," and Dukas' "The Sorcerer's Apprentice."

May 19, 1971. Died at the age of sixty-eight, in Baltimore, Maryland, of heart failure following stomach surgery. "I consider myself lucky to have been able to make a living doing something I really enjoy." [Laura Benét, *Famous American Humorists*, Dodd, 1959.[8]]

HOBBIES AND OTHER INTERESTS: "Looking at the ocean" in summertime, reading detective stories, some television programs, and his five grandchildren.

FOR MORE INFORMATION SEE: New York Times, November 9, 1940; *Life*, October 29, 1951, December 13, 1968; *Saturday Review*, April 11, 1953, November 24, 1962, June 19, 1971; *New York Times Book Review*, April 12, 1953; *New York Herald Tribune Book Review*, July 14, 1957; Laura Benét, *Famous American Humorists*, Dodd, 1959; *Seventeen*, January, 1963; Robert Fitzgibbon and Ernest V. Heyn, editors, *My Most Inspiring Moment*, Doubleday, 1965; *Holiday*, August, 1967; Roy Newquist, *Conversations*, Rand McNally, 1967; Martha E. Ward and Dorothy A. Marquardt, *Authors of Books for Young People*, 2nd edition, Scarecrow, 1971; L. B. Axford, *An Index to the Poems of Ogden Nash*, Scarecrow, 1972; Doris de Montreville and Elizabeth D. Crawford, editors, *Fourth Book of Junior Authors and Illustrators*, H. W. Wilson, 1978; David Stuart, *Ogden Nash: A Biography*, Stein and Day, 1985.

Obituaries: *New York Times*, May 20, 1971; *Washington Post*, May 21, 1971; *Variety*, May 26, 1971; *New Yorker*, May 29, 1971; *Newsweek*, May 31, 1971; *Time*, May 31, 1971; *Publishers Weekly*, May 31, 1971; *Antiquarian Bookman*, June 7-14, 1971.

NEWMAN, Gerald 1939-

PERSONAL: Born May 3, 1939, in New York, N.Y.; son of Harry and Lillie (Meyer) Newman; divorced; children: Aaron Roy. *Education:* Brooklyn College of the City University of New York, B.A., 1962, M.F.A., 1975. *Home and office:* 300 West 23rd St., New York, N.Y. 10011.

CAREER: New York City Board of Education, New York, N.Y., teacher of art and creative writing, 1962-83; Mark Twain Junior High School for the Gifted and Talented, Brooklyn, N.Y., teacher of English, 1983—; author of books for young people, 1976—; free-lance graphic artist, 1980—. *Awards, honors:* The Concise Encyclopedia of Sports was chosen one of New York Public Library's Books for the Teen Age, 1980, 1981, and 1982.

WRITINGS: (With Joe Bivona) *Elton John*, New American Library, 1976; (editor) *Encyclopedia of Health and the Human Body*, F. Watts, 1977; (editor) *The Concise Encyclopedia of Sports* (juvenile), 2nd revised edition, F. Watts, 1978; *Lebanon* (juvenile), F. Watts, 1978; *Eskimoes* (juvenile), F. Watts (England), 1978, published in the U.S. as *The Changing Eskimos*, F. Watts, 1979; *How to Write a Report* (juvenile), F. Watts, 1981; *Equatorial Africa* (juvenile), F. Watts, 1981; *Zaire, Gabon and the Congo* (juvenile), F. Watts, 1981.

Films; all produced by American Film Foundation: "The Iron Mountain," 1978; "Bogota: Fragments of a City," 1979; "A Tree Falls," 1980; "Graciella in Ecuador," 1980.

SIDELIGHTS: "I find it fascinating to be able to translate sophisticated concepts into easily understood information for children. The younger the age level of the book, the more difficult it is to write. When my son was younger, I used him as a sounding board. If I saw him diligently reading my manuscript, I knew all was well. If he lost interest, I was in trouble."

ORIOLO, Joseph 1913-1985
(Joe Oriolo)

OBITUARY NOTICE: Born February 21, 1913, in Union City, N.J.; died December 25, 1985, in Hackensack, N.J. A cartoonist since 1931, Oriolo was an animator on Popeye and Betty Boop cartoons and worked with Walt Disney studios before establishing his own studios in 1943. A year later, he created the character Casper the Friendly Ghost for his daughter, who was afraid of the dark. Oriolo produced and directed 254 episodes of "Felix the Cat" show for television in the 1960s and was the artist for the Felix newspaper comic strip and Felix comic books. He illustrated *A Surprise for Felix* (Wonder Books, 1959), written by Pat Sullivan. Oriolo created the Mighty Hercules television cartoon series and did voices for the Gulliver's Travels cartoons. He was working with his son on a revival of "Felix the Cat," Oriolo's first full-length theatrical film, at the time of his death. The Motion Picture Screen Cartoonists' Golden Award was awarded to Oriolo in 1984.

FOR MORE INFORMATION SEE: International Motion Picture Almanac, Quigley, 1985. Obituaries: *Detroit Free Press*, December 27, 1985; *Facts on File*, December 31, 1985.

PACE, Mildred Mastin 1907-

PERSONAL: Born June 8, 1907, in St. Louis, Mo.; daughter of Robert Thomas and Miriam (Norris) Mastin; married Clark Roberts Pace (an editor), May 26, 1935. *Education:* Cornell College, B.A., 1929. *Home:* Continental Towers, Apt. 1001, 2121 Nicholasville Rd., Lexington, Ky. 40503.

CAREER: Magazine writer in New York City, 1929-36; freelance radio writer for Mutual Broadcasting Co. and National Broadcasting Co., New York City, 1936-40; author of books for young people, 1940—; J. Walter Thompson (advertising agency), New York City, writer in publicity department, 1942-50. *Awards, honors:* New York Herald Tribune's Spring Book Festival Award for best book for older children, 1941, for *Clara Barton;* Dorothy Canfield Fisher Memorial Book Award from Vermont Congress of Parents and Teachers, 1957, for *Old Bones, the Wonder Horse;* New York Times Outstanding Book of the Year, 1974, and Children's Science Book Award honor from New York Academy of Sciences, 1975, both for *Wrapped for Eternity: The Story of the Egyptian Mummy.*

(From *Old Bones, the Wonder Horse* by Mildred Mastin Pace. Illustrated by Wesley Dennis.)

WRITINGS: Early American, Scribner, 1940; *Clara Barton* (illustrated by Robert Ball), Scribner, 1941; *Friend of Animals,* Scribner, 1942; *Juliette Low,* Scribner, 1947; *Home Is Where the Heart Is,* Whittlesey House, 1954; *Old Bones, the Wonder Horse* (illustrated by Wesley Dennis), Whittlesey House, 1955; (editor) Peggie Camman, *Black Fury,* Whittlesey House, 1956; (with Hiroko Nakamoto) *My Japan, 1930-1951,* McGraw, 1970; *Wrapped for Eternity: The Story of the Egyptian Mummy* (illustrated by Tom Huffman), McGraw, 1974; *The Pyramids: Tombs for Eternity,* McGraw, 1980.

WORK IN PROGRESS: A book about horses for young readers.

SIDELIGHTS: ''Though I will sorely miss the seclusion and beauty of my home in the woods, high above the Hudson River, I have moved to Kentucky, to the bluegrass country I have always loved. I spent most of my growing-up summers there, and have gone back all through the years to visit family. It was there I did most of the research for *Old Bones, the Wonder Horse,* a biography of the famous race horse 'Exterminator.' And not far away, in the mountains was the locale of the only fiction I've written (though based on fact), *Home Is Where the Heart Is.* I'll be living right in the heart of the

thoroughbred horse farms, and it shouldn't be difficult to find a good subject for my next book.''

HOBBIES AND OTHER INTERESTS: Community affairs, gardening, reading and writing, and ''just observing.''

FOR MORE INFORMATION SEE: New York Times Book Review, May 26, 1974; *School Library Journal,* September, 1978; Dorothy A. Marquardt and Martha E. Ward, *Authors of Books for Young People,* 2nd edition supplement, Scarecrow, 1979.

PINKWATER, Daniel Manus   1941-

PERSONAL: Born November 15, 1941, in Memphis, Tenn.; married Jill Schutz (an illustrator and author), October 12, 1969. *Education:* Bard College, B.A., 1964.

CAREER: Author and illustrator of children's books.

WRITINGS—All juvenile, except as noted; all self-illustrated, except as noted: *Wizard Crystal,* Dodd, 1973; *Magic Camera,* Dodd, 1974; *Lizard Music,* Dodd, 1976; (with wife, Jill Pinkwater) *Superpuppy: How to Choose, Raise, and Train the Best Possible Dog for You* (illustrated by J. Pinkwater), Clarion Books, 1976; *The Big Orange Splot*, Hastings House, 1977; *The Blue Thing*, Prentice-Hall, 1977; *The Hoboken Chicken Emergency*, Prentice-Hall, 1977; *Fat Men from Space* (Junior Literary Guild selection), Dodd, 1977; *The Last Guru*, Dodd, 1978; *Alan Mendelsohn, the Boy from Mars*, Dutton, 1979; *Return of the Moose*, Dodd, 1979; *Pickle Creature*, Four Winds, 1979; *Yobgorgle: Mystery Monster of Lake Ontario*, Clarion Books, 1979, revised edition, Bantam, 1981.

The Magic Moscow, Four Winds, 1980; (with Luqman Keele) *Java Jack*, Crowell, 1980; *The Wuggie Norple Story* (illustrated by Tomie de Paola), Four Winds, 1980; *Tooth-Gnasher Super Flash*, Four Winds, 1981; *Attila the Pun: A Magic Moscow Book*, Four Winds, 1981; *The Worms of Kukumlima*, Dutton, 1981; *Slaves of Spiegel: A Magic Moscow Story*, Four Winds, 1982; *Young Adult Novel*, Crowell, 1982; *Roger's Umbrella* (illustrated by James Marshall), Dutton, 1982; *The Snarkout Boys and the Avocado of Death*, Lothrop, 1982; *I Was a Second Grade Werewolf*, Dutton, 1983; *Ducks!*, Little, Brown, 1983; *The Snarkout Boys and the Baconburg Horror*, Lothrop, 1984; *Devil in the Drain*, Dutton, 1984; *Jolly Roger: A Dog of Hoboken*, Lothrop, 1984; *The Muffin Fiend*, Lothrop, 1986; *The Moospire*, Little, Brown, 1986; *The Frankenbagel Monster*, Dutton, 1986.

Juvenile; under name Manus Pinkwater: *The Terrible Roar*, Knopf, 1970; *Bear's Picture*, Holt, 1972; *Fat Elliot and the Gorilla*, Four Winds, 1974; *Blue Moose*, Dodd, 1975; *Three Big Hogs*, Seabury, 1975; *Wingman*, Dodd, 1975; *Around Fred's Bed* (illustrated by Robert Mertens), Prentice-Hall, 1976.

Other: *Young Adults*, Tor, 1985.

ADAPTATIONS: ''Wingman'' (cassette recording), Listening Library, 1981; ''Blue Moose'' (video cassette), Positive Images, 1982; ''The Hoboken Chicken Emergency'' (television movie), PBS-TV, 1984; ''I Was a Second Grade Werewolf'' (cassette recording), Live Oak Media, 1986.

WORK IN PROGRESS: ''Much.''

SIDELIGHTS: Pinkwater was interviewed by telephone on July 25, 1985: ''I grew up in Chicago, was taken away to Los Angeles for a number of years, and then reprieved back to Chicago. Upon my return I experienced a tremendous feeling of rising up, of getting back to a *real* place, and that excitement never wore off. When I later actually made it to the East Coast, which I like even better, I had that feeling all over again.

''Reading was in the air when I was young. The kids in the neighborhood played '20,000 Leagues under the Sea' and 'Mysterious Island' and 'Three Musketeers' games in their backyards. It was our older brothers and sisters who turned us on to good reading. Our teachers were merely functionaries— they didn't particularly want to be at school, and we didn't want to be there either. They forced us to learn to read anyway and then basically kept us indoors for the next few years. The

The author and his horses

DANIEL MANUS PINKWATER

librarians, without pretense of caring or understanding, simply told us not to get the book dirty. 'Here's your card, and there's a fine if you bring it back late.' This was fine with us. We heard about books by word of mouth—the kid next door had an older brother who told me about the *Three Musketeers*. I got to read good books, although mainly adventure stories, because there weren't as many books around at the time. What was around was not watered down, socially engineered monstrosities, which an overly fat publishing industry has produced to stock libraries in more recent times.

"My heroes back then, and now, are too many to mention, although I started and will finish with Mark Twain. I liked Mark Twain when I was seven and I like Mark Twain now and I'll like Mark Twain the day I die.

"My father was in the rag business, which is not a euphemism for the fashion industry. His business was selling the rags used to wipe off dip sticks. Somebody has to collect them and sell them to gas stations. He was from the old country, and was like one of Isaac Babel's father characters—just the kind of father a boy wants to have. What's that line of Babel's? 'A poppa like that, what does he think about? He thinks about drinking a big glass of vodka, he thinks about his horses, and he thinks about smashing someone's face in. A boy wants to live, and he makes him die ten times a day.' I loved my father. He toughened me.

(Jacket illustration by Daniel Pinkwater from *Slaves of Spiegel: A Magic Moscow Story* by Daniel Pinkwater.)

The people were whispering to one another about the moose, when he clumped back to the table. ■ (From *Blue Moose* by Manus Pinkwater. Illustrated by the author.)

"My mother is a nice lady. She lives in California, keeps her apartment nice and hopes that when I grow up, I will write some serious books for grown-ups. Whenever I speak to her, she asks, 'What are you doing?' I answer, 'Writing a book.' 'A real book, for adults?' she asks. She has a mainstream approach to the subject.

"It would be modest to the point of immodesty to claim that I wasn't brighter than the average kid, but when I was growing up, I used to pal around with other boys who were very much like me. We were like the 'Wild Dada Ducks' in my books and identified with each other. We had interests in common, and were able to form enough of a society so that we didn't feel especially alienated.

"I became a sculpture major in college with the hope of becoming a good writer. I had asked a friend whose writing I admired, 'How do you get to be a good writer?' 'You've got to understand form. I can't explain it, but you must understand it to be a good writer,' was his response. 'Form . . . form . . .' I thought. 'Maybe if I take sculpture courses I could learn about form.' I signed up for one sculpture course, and with that my father came to talk to me, 'You know, you've majored in everything they offer at this college. Pick something or I'm not going to pay any more bills.' Apparently, he didn't care what I chose, because, he pointed out, 'Whatever it is, you won't do it when you get out of college anyway.' So I got very involved in sculpture, and taking my father's advice, I did it to the exclusion of anything else—I ate, slept and breathed sculpture for two years.

"Up, Hercules. Up, you Malamute!" The dog snored.
■ (From *The Magic Moscow* by Daniel Pinkwater.
Illustrated by the author.)

"During and after college, I did a three-year apprenticeship
with a sculptor. At the end of that time, he shocked me by
admitting 'I never thought you'd be a sculptor. I've always
thought you'd be a writer.' 'No, no! I don't want to be a
writer. Writers are disgusting, and writing is a horrible un-
healthy activity. You get coffee nerves and a bad back, and
eye strain. You smoke, and you sit . . . it's terrible. I want to
be a sculptor! I want to make great big things out of stone and
eat spaghetti and sleep with fat women,' I responded. I had
forgotten that I ever wanted to be a writer. My teacher insisted
that I was going to be a writer. He was a pretty smart guy,
but I resisted for four more years.

"Most of the lessons I apply as a writer, I learned as a carver.
My work as a sculptor makes me a good writer, incisive,
strong, and daring, because when you carve wood or stone,
the moment comes when you've got to actually go *into* the
piece of material and start knocking hunks off of it. I was
trained to do that in a 'Zen way.' You put your whole life on
the line and dive in. My tendency to be extremely daring
results at times in sloppy work. Sometimes a piece just doesn't
look right, it gets out of hand, but there's nothing to do but
go on. When you read one of my books, and it seems to have
gotten away from itself—it has. Readers notice this. I invite
them to join me in the pleasure of trying to get the thing under
control.

"I've noticed that there are many books which start off with
a character biding his time, goofing off. What comes to mind
is *Moby Dick* or *A Study in Scarlet,* where the character—be
it Ishmael or Dr. Watson—is looking for something to happen.
This is really the writer, waiting to get himself into the story.
I like books where the author is included, where he is casting
about with his character while the reader waits for him to pick

up a scent. I take this a step further at times and actually lose
the scent. I get totally befuddled and the book goes to sleep,
but the reader doesn't, because there is a compression of time.
Somehow I come to the rescue and pull off improbable endings
that many writers wouldn't get away with. I approach a book
in the way a sculptor goes about his work, especially one who,
instead of making studies, *maquettes,* plans, and scale models,
sits around and looks at the hunk of stone for a year and then,
in one horrible moment, picks up his tools and makes a terrible
gash on it. Then he says, 'Oh God, I've ruined it now,' and
is forced, somehow, to save it.

"After my sculpting teacher told me to give up sculpting, to
accept that I was destined to be a writer, I told him to go to
hell, left town, and went to New York where I continued to
pursue a career in fine arts. Certain gallery people and museum
curators explained to me that I wasn't making it easy enough
for the viewer and although they respected what I had done,
they doubted my ever getting very far."

Traveled to Africa and joined a cooperative artists' workshop.
Pinkwater was the only participant who was not also a member
of the Wachagga tribe. "The first time I went to Africa, I was
engaged in a personal investigation which had a parallel to the
history of the race. I was also engaged in practices which
involved noting my dreams, and drawing pictures with related
intention. All of that led me to want to be in a place which
was reminiscent of a very early period in history. . . . My
desire came upon me one snowy February day. I looked at my
bankbook and discovered I had $1,500. 'I think this is enough
to go to Africa,' I said to myself. It was, and I went. I made
some important friendships, and I am still involved with some
of the people whom I met and worked with.

"I didn't decide to start doing children's books, I floated into
it. I was at a party where a pretty girl, an editor, was looking
for illustrations, specifically for examples of modern African
art. I had just returned from Tanzania, and after she saw my
work, suggested I try illustrating a story. I had to get a story

Mr. Pinkwater once lived in Hoboken, New Jersey.

The next morning, I looked in the mirror and noticed that I was not a werewolf. ■ (From *I Was a Second Grade Werewolf* by Daniel Pinkwater. Illustrated by the author.)

first, and not wishing to deal with writers, because I knew what *they* were like, I wrote one. Knopf published the book, and gave me money.

"For the first few books, I was more interested in creating vehicles for the illustration. Writing was a bit of a challenge. It was fun. I got the necessary tools, tried it, and discovered I could do it. Of course, I just went from bad to worse . . . right down hill. Paper was cheaper back then, so they published my stuff. But it was just a giggle, and I had no particular ambitions to continue. 'I'm going to stop doing art, and be a writer,' was never one of my thoughts. I was still teaching art, eking out a living, being a beatnik. The children's books were just another job. Then the stories became more interesting to me, and I began to come to grips with what my teacher had told me.

"I thought after two or three books I would have saturated my audience, whom I imagined as fat, bespectacled, intellectual boys. I often receive photographs from my readers, who to my surprise include good-looking blonde-haired kids, who are captains of their soccer teams. It's not just the sweaty, spotty, stinky, pimply kids who do college physics in middle school who read my work. Evidently, my audience is composed of mainstream kids who wouldn't stand out as being potential psychopaths, revolutionaries, homosexuals, geniuses, and anarchists (although they all write to me, too). And, many of my readers are girls, something which has troubled me, because I have always felt I could do better by my girl readers. But that's changing. I've got an engaging and highly popular girl character named Rat in *The Snarkout Boys and the Avocado of Death,* and *The Snarkout Boys and the Baconburg Horror.*

"I'm fairly scrupulous about not stealing the material my readers send me, although the temptation is tremendous at times. Before me right now are chapters of something called *The Chicken at the Edge of the Universe,* an ongoing piece of literature from, I believe, a fourteen-year-old reader of mine. The premise is that there is a chicken who is actually God who is actually a stand-up comedian. Its a mix of my stuff, the Douglas Adams books, *The Hitchhiker's Guide to the Galaxy,* with a little Kurt Vonnegut thrown in. This kid is not all that much more advanced than some of the other kids who write to me, and not all that different from me at his age. I submit that kids who achieve the power of reading and writing tend to be like that.

"I enjoy the fact that there are so many lively kids around, that they are as bright as they are and that they tend to choose me along with people whom I also respect as their favorites. I like that this kid is into Adams and Vonnegut and me. It's a nice combination of fun and good writers who will provide him with the necessary brain exercise to move on to writers like Dostoevski. The most gratifying type of letter from a kid says, 'I don't ordinarily like to read, but I've read five of your books and I'm looking for more.' That gladdens my heart, because I know I've caught another soul for the Master. I like making converts.

"Kids are more receptive to art because they don't have the kind of social overlay adults have, which forces a response even when none is called for. They are very matter of fact. They like something, or they don't, they can use something or they can't. Adults feel an obligation to consider what reflection their artistic preferences will make upon them as people of cultural breeding and intelligence. If they write saying, 'I really loved your book, I've read it fifteen times,' they really loved the book and they really have read it fifteen times. They

know it better than the author knows it. They don't care whether it reflects well upon them, or whether it contains 'beautiful' writing. I'm not one who does 'beautiful' writing. To me the beauty in writing is making it as clear as a pane of glass. That I can do, and I'm rather pleased because it took me years to learn how.

"I'm not literary. I'm a streetfighter and a subversive artist. I feel I'm in a different world from the arbitrators of what's good, the self-congratulatory types who are involved in literature for the 'betterment of children.' It is my intention to blow these people sky high, and I've done my very best in that direction. The readers are clear about what's synthetic and what's genuine and I'm honored by their choice.

"I have limited respect for my colleagues in the field of children's literature, both the people who write it and the people who publish it. I urge my readers to be suspicious of people who claim to be 'doing them good.' My advice is to use the library in a free and easy way. Don't limit yourselves to the children's section—I certainly haven't found that the nourishing things are likely to be there. Sometimes they are, but you stand a better chance going to the adult room, and most librarians, if you have brought your reading skills up to an advanced level, won't stop you."

Pinkwater has been called a surrealist writer. "Surrealism is certainly a noble appellation and a very valid notion. I regard myself as a realist—surrealism would be gilding the lily. I do object to being called zany and wacky—words which invariably appear in reviews simply because reviewers read them off book jackets."

Pinkwater once said that his book, *The Snarkout Boys and the Avocado of Death* was a celebration of dying cultural treasures. "I like urban life and I was turned on very early by used bookstores and other strange quarters in the city of Chicago, places which I found very rich and interesting. I'd been in a beer garden before I had any legal right to, and saw a whole kind of culture expressed there. In Chicago, there were

Pinkwater in Japan. Photograph courtesy of a passing tourist.

Author Pinkwater urges, "Wise up, before it's too late."

old Bohemian style beer gardens, and in the summertime, en-tire families would go there to pass the evening, drink beer, eat salami sandwiches, and sing songs while the kids ran around the tables. I was also a great prowler of back streets, a great walker and explorer (and still am) of the cities I lived in.

"Now we have evolved into something of a shopping center and freeway culture, so when I say my work is celebrating dying cultural treasures, I am referring to the fact that there are people who have *never been* in a beer garden. I want those people to know that such a thing existed, and may still exist somewhere. I want to expose my readers to some of these things. In my books I sometimes cite works of art which I admire. I get my characters interested in these works, or in works like them, and my readers take right off from there. One of my readers has now read everything in the library on dada and surrealism, and from there, has gone on to get a general notion of the history of modern art. That's a handy thing to have at fourteen. Now, I certainly wasn't setting him up to do this and I didn't give him any help, but I like to see that happen. It's not my main intention, but it *is* an intention of my books to present the sheer pleasure of the phenomena of civilized life.''

Feeling that the "problem novels" he had occasion to read were "sneaky" books, Pinkwater was inspired to write *Young Adult Novel.* "I had a contract with a publisher . . . I owed them a book. They sent me their catalogue, which was one-hundred percent 'problem novels.' I asked the editor to send me two or three of what she regarded as the best on her list.

I wanted to read them and perhaps write one. I read two, as did my wife, Jill, and we burned them in the stove. I thought that they were 'sneaky' books because the author had a char-acter experience tension, *sturm und drang,* and suffering, then just explained it away with a simplistic religious message. I felt it was both a cop out and an abuse of the reader. I wrote one. I liked mine. *Young Adult Novel* sold a little over 2,000 copies, which is interesting because so many people seem to know about it. I bought it back from the publisher and it has been published as part of an adult paperback entitled *Young Adults,* published by Tor Books, which includes *Young Adult Novel* and two sequels, *Dead-End Dada* and *The Dada Boys in Collitch,* as well as a scholarly afterword by a genius and some examples of avante-garde art.''

Pinkwater once described writing as "cheap psychotherapy." "Writing for kids has had an interesting effect on me—it has helped me to develop access to my own childhood. And since I'm writing the books for a specific kid, namely myself at different ages, I've gotten more and more expert at revisiting that person within me at different ages. I don't know that I'm a healthy person, but to the extent that I am, this practice has contributed to it.

"When I'm beginning a new book, I am almost like an actor getting into character. I listen to music, I watch television, I talk to people, I wander around eavesdropping, turn up at K-Mart, and go through all the motions of being an ordinary citizen.

That night I went out into the driveway and stood in the chariot. All of a sudden there was a really big duck attached to it.... ■ (From *Ducks!* by Daniel Pinkwater. Illustrated by the author.)

"When I start a novel, all I'm really doing is waiting for the characters to show up. I work on my notes, and every day, characters come. It's like the movie, 'Close Encounters. . . .' The people who have been 'selected' to be in this story show up. It's a very intriguing experience.

"There's always a gestation period at the beginning of a book and now that I'm working on a larger scale, huge stacks of notes accumulate. Those notes may never be looked at, and are basically a running commentary on the things I'm interested in while waiting. Then comes the moment, when I put a disc in the computer, and ruin it. Usually I start in some obscure corner of the story, where I didn't mean to start. Then I write sequentially, progressively trying to keep up with my characters. I'm good at getting my characters up and walking around very fast."

Though Pinkwater is prolific, he does not feel obligated to sit down and write every day. "I think that's terrible. If I had to work in that way I could have found some other field of work and gotten rich. I show up in my office every day in the event that something may want to happen, but if nothing happens, I don't feel that I have failed to perform. I show up, I sit around, if something gets started, fair enough. If it doesn't, and I feel I've given it enough time, I go to K-Mart. I showed up, the story didn't. There are some days when I know there's no point in bothering. . . . I don't work very hard but generally once I get into a project I stay with it until it goes to sleep. There's a standard pattern I've noticed again and again—I work on a book until the point that it just goes numb. Then I put it aside and when I pick it up again it has somehow seasoned and taken a different direction. When I'm working, I work every single day, and I usually get from four to twenty pages each session, which I consider good going.

"I love the story as it's being written. That's the absolute pleasure of the art, to be the first and only person to see the story coming into existence. Sometimes it's as though it were happening without my doing it. I'll go to bed, excited about what's going to happen tomorrow. I know something's got to happen because I've only got 175 pages done and I've got to do more.

"I hold the belief that the work I do as an artist may be better as art than I am as a person. Having confidence in that means you let the work itself take control, and I haven't been dis-

appointed too many times. This is why I allow a book to get out of hand, and in fact, _look_ for that to happen. The work is like a skateboard that suddenly gets away from me, and the anticipation is that somehow, miraculously, I will finish with the skateboard.

"I have a knack for getting characters to be vivid in very few lines. I try _not_ to employ description, and to limit it whenever possible because as a reader, I usually skip descriptions. Those things which are descriptive have to be salient. It amuses me to have very prosaic things described in the midst of wild happenings in the narrative. This 'connective tissue' in my books is sometimes what makes the experience of my characters seem real. For example, in one of my novels, there is a scene in which people are riding in an old car, through time and space, eating fig bars. Somehow, it's the fig bars that make it believeable."

Pinkwater writes on a computer. "The computer allows me to think in a different way. It helps me be a better, more daring writer, because I can try things that may not pan out without being penalized. I've come to feel a facility, a lightness on my feet that I never experienced on the typewriter. It was a breakthrough for me.

"Aside from the creative work, there's also the practical side of being an author. I have galleys coming constantly, as well as illustrations to do, and mail to answer. There's usually a few things aloft at once, which is good because it gives me something to do in between writing. A day in my office might consist of answering mail, conferring with one fine editor or another over some project that's going forth, as well as going over galleys or edited manuscripts.

"I'm not turned off with writing children's books and I'm certainly not turned off with my readers, who are wonderful and who write to me in great numbers. I'm turned off, however, by the way children's books are published, by the way they're edited, dealt with, distributed, and presented. I'd like to see all the people who have currently found their niche in children's publishing replaced by people with three digit IQs. I've observed after sixteen years in the field that children's books are generally written by people who aren't good enough to write for adults, and edited by people who aren't good enough to edit adult books. People who are good—and obviously there are some competent people in the field—are competing with and working with jerks and are obliged, by good manners and business useage, to take those jerks seri-

In a little house, in a little village, not far away from Thunderbolt City, lived a whistle fixer named Lunchbox Louie. He had a wife named Bigfoot the Chipmunk and a little son named King Waffle. Every day Lunchbox Louie would kiss Bigfoot the Chipmunk and King Waffle, and walk to his shop in Thunderbolt City.

(From _The Wuggie Norple Story_ by Daniel Pinkwater. Ilustrated by Tomie de Paola.)

The cow looked and wondered what it was. ■ (From *The Blue Thing* by Daniel Pinkwater. Illustrated by the author.)

ously. It would be irresponsible of me to say that everybody I've dealt with in children's books is a jerk, but I would say that too many of them are jerks.

"Some people I know, who for a time were interested in children's books, abandoned the field long before it occurred to them to be dissatisfied. They had to deal with such a poor mentality, both editorially and commercially, that ultimately they found something more gratifying to do. I have recently been writing adult fiction."

When asked to describe his notion of a masterpiece, Pinkwater responded, "I aspire to be second-rate. I reserve first-rate for Mozart, Shakespeare and a few other boys, whom I hope to meet later. I don't think we live in an age of giants. My intention and my hope is to try and make things as pure as I can. I'm not so different from a golfer who wants to improve his sport. I'm addicted to writing simply because I feel the possibility of actually bringing it off properly once in my lifetime. But something always goes wrong, and I always find that the work is not a fulfillment of what I had envisioned. I like the old notion of masterpieces being an exemplary piece done with exquisite care. I don't feel I've yet done a book that measures up to that. I sometimes feel fidgity and worry that I may die before I do it. I'd like to do it because of my profound respect for that kind of performance. The noblest thing I know is for someone to single-handedly do a work of art. It is what gives me the most excitement and delight. The work of various artists in various art forms causes me to cheer, applaud, feel elated, and, of course, inspires me to try it myself.

"I don't like any of my books. They all embarrass me because they all seem to be a little bit short of the mark. I like the book I'm *going* to write, or the one I'm writing, but by the time it gets into galleys, I feel the thing is a disaster. I've learned to ignore that sinking feeling, but each finished work seems a crude thing. Still, I've improved since the last failed attempt, and all I ask is a chance to redeem myself.

"I never took a writing course in my life. I strongly suspect you don't need them. I have no problem with the writing. Where I draw breath and get dry in the mouth is when I have to draw pictures, because I *know* about that. I even have a degree. I suffer from self-consciousness, and even though I'm opposed to that kind of thinking, it's hard to escape. I do think it's a good idea for someone interested in one art form to study a different art than that which they hope to pursue. It's like learning a foreign language. People who are able to learn languages tell me that it really changes the way they appreciate, and think in their native language. Where I went to school people were encouraged to dabble like crazy—physics majors were busy making woodcuts—and it had a tremendously good effect. I say, 'dabble,' but in fact there were some good people teaching, who wouldn't let you dabble, who'd get you really involved. I think that's a healthy practice. If I ever get into creative trouble, I'll just find somebody to teach me to play the violin and see what that does to me as a writer.

"I'm part of the history of culture, a tiny part. I hold to the theory that I have to be smarter than Socrates and a better writer than Shakespeare, because I *include* them, and they didn't include themselves, nor did they include all that I know, like Fats Waller or Schubert. In a sense, I can do things that Shakespeare, having never heard Fats Waller, couldn't possibly have done. Every time you add a generation, there's an enrichment, and in effect, one contributes his part to the cultural palimpsest, even if one is doing things like writing for more personal or immediate reasons. My theory on the function of art is just an extension of the eldest in the tribe, passing

At night the frogs would sing. ■ (From *Wizard Crystal* by Daniel Pinkwater. Illustrated by the author.)

on the old stories to keep certain things alive. I'm both re-telling and revising everything from the *Legend of the Flying Dutchman* to the history of pastrami, and at the same time, I'm making constructs that are personally meaningful to me, and which may be meaningful to others.

"I also believe it is impossible to make sense of life in this world except through art. That's always been so, but it's more true now than ever before. The only way we can deal with the proliferation of ideas and impetus is to make a story or a picture out of it. At present, there are things happening that I like, as well as things I don't like; by participating I'm able to put some weight on the side of the things I like.

"Living in a nuclear world, I feel a special responsibility, because my readers don't expect to reach my age. I agree with them that they probably won't, but I'm obliged, therefore, to put a lot of emphasis on the notion that they just might anyway. So far we haven't been blown up, and the reasonable thing to do in such a case is to project the future based on past performance. In the past we didn't destroy the world. At the same time, I have suspicions that this may be it, and the conviction that I have to proceed as though it weren't. That's according to Ghandi, who says we should live as though we are going to die tomorrow and study (or make art) as though we will live forever. This is why I don't think it particularly behooves one at this time in history to write in dreary tones for kids, or anybody for that matter. Being too serious is sometimes a good way to make a situation become even more serious. It's important that we are made to feel strong through humor or by knowing what others consider beautiful or precious. I am honestly trying to catalogue and record those things which are moving, or precious to me, like corner delicatessens and street life and people with exotic ideas. Because these

He looked very proud of his son and his chicken. ∎ (From *The Hoboken Chicken Emergency* by Daniel Pinkwater. Illustrated by the author.)

things are beautiful to me, they may actually retain and transmit some kind of beauty in the work.

"I set store by courage, and I try to be as brave as I can afford. Of course, I can be much braver on paper than I can in life. That's true of anybody, and it's why people turn to art. I want my readers to feel encouraged and *snarky*, because basically they are kids taking on a hostile and/or indifferent world. My books are about finding favoring signs in the world, about discovering riches—things which are not dead. My stories are about people prevailing."

After many years in Hoboken, New Jersey, Pinkwater and his writer-artist wife, Jill, moved to upstate New York. "I moved to the country because I'm a nice man and on a whim of my wife, who wanted a garden, I said 'Why not? Twelve years in Hoboken is long enough.' Our first move was to the suburbs of Long Island, where Jill began to acquire Icelandic horses. It then made sense to get a farm, so we moved up to Dutchess county. We bought a nice farm house, which is almost 200 years old and fixed it up. It's only two hours from New York City by train, so I can get some Chinese food once in a while. Jill likes her horses very much, which anyone who has read her novel, *Cloud Horse*, will know. For a year I turned into 'Dan the farmer,' and was out doing all the work. Then I discovered you can hire people to do that. I like the mountains up here and it's certainly pleasant observing the scenes. I don't need pavement under my feet to be happy."

The Pinkwaters at one time owned and ran a dog school. "That was short lived because it was turning into too much of an enterprise. We had a choice to make: to be writers or rich dog trainers. Taking the less honorable of the two, we decided to be writers. We still answer questions from the readers of *Superpuppy*, but I have forgotten everything I knew, so my answers have become more and more bizarre. I write letters to dog owners saying, 'Try reasoning with him.'"

FOR MORE INFORMATION SEE: Graphis 155, Volume 27, 1971-72; *Washington Post Book World*, November 5, 1972, June 10, 1984; *Christian Science Monitor*, May 1, 1974; *Publishers Weekly*, February 27, 1978, May 7, 1982; *New York Times Book Review*, April 29, 1979, February 24, 1980, April 25, 1982; *Children's Literature Review*, Volume 4, Gale, 1982.

PITMAN, (Isaac) James   1901-1985

OBITUARY NOTICE: Born August 14, 1901, in London, England; died September 1, 1985. Business executive, politician, educational reformer, and author. Perhaps best known for his work in developing and promoting a forty-two-character phonetic alphabet for teaching children to read, Pitman served for many years as chairman and managing director of his family's business firm. He also held a Conservative seat in Britain's House of Commons for nearly twenty years, retiring in 1964, a year after founding the Initial Teaching Alphabet Foundation. As chairman of the foundation and a committee member of the University of London Institute of Education-National Foundation for Educational Research, Pitman studied the processes and problems of learning to read and advocated the implementation of the forty-two-character initial teaching alphabet, often referred to as i.t.a., in schools. His books include *Alphabets and Reading: The Initial Teaching Alphabet*, which he wrote with John St. John. Pitman was a grandson of Sir Isaac Pitman, the inventor of the original system of shorthand.

FOR MORE INFORMATION SEE: Contemporary Authors, Permanent Series, Volume 2, Gale, 1978; *Who's Who*, 135th edition, St. Martin's, 1983. Obituaries: *Times* (London), September 3, 1985; *Facts on File*, September 9, 1985.

POLLOCK, Bruce   1945-

PERSONAL: Born July 24, 1945, in Brooklyn, N.Y.; son of Joseph and Rose (Prager) Pollock; married Barbara Hoffman (an art teacher, poet, and painter), December 19, 1970. *Education:* City College of the City University of New York, B.A., 1972. *Home:* 125 Sterling St., Fairfield, Conn. 06430.

CAREER: Managing editor, *Rock*, 1972-74; editor, *Contemporary Music*, 1974; managing editor, *Funny Papers*, 1975; senior editor, *Penthouse*, 1976; free-lance writer and editor, 1977—; *Guitar: For the Practicing Musician*, editor-in-chief, 1983. *Member:* American Society of Composers, Authors and Publishers, American Society of Journalists and Authors. *Awards, honors:* Dejur Award for fiction, 1971; Deems Taylor Award, 1973, for articles in *Rock;* Connecticut Commission on the Arts grant for fiction, 1978.

WRITINGS: In Their Own Words: Songs and Songwriters, 1955-1974, Macmillan, 1975; *Playing for Change* (novel), Houghton, 1977; *Me, Minsky and Max* (novel), Houghton, 1978; *The Face of Rock and Roll: Images of a Generation*, Holt, 1978; *The Disco Handbook*, Scholastic Book Services, 1979; *It's Only Rock and Roll* (novel), Houghton, 1980; *The Rock and Roll Fun Book*, Scholastic Book Services, 1980; *When Rock Was Young: A Nostalgic Review of the Top Forty Era*, Holt, 1981; *Housework for Men*, Greeting Books, 1982; *When the Music Mattered: Rock in the 60's*, Holt, 1983; *Popular Music: An Annotated Index of American Popular Songs*, Volumes 7-9, Gale, 1970-1984.

Columnist for *Viva*, 1977, Gannett Westchester Newspapers, 1978—, *USA Today*, and *Wilson Library Bulletin;* writer of celebrity profiles, *Family Weekly*, 1979—. Contributor to *Playboy*, *Saturday Review*, *Cosmopolitan*, *New York Times*, *TV Guide*, *Oui*, *Redbook*, *Panorama*, and *Us*. Contributing editor, *Modern Hi-Fi and Music*, 1975; editor, *Tomorrow's Music*, 1978-79.

FOR MORE INFORMATION SEE: Modern Hi-Fi and Music, July, 1975.

PRICE, Jonathan (Reeve)   1941-

PERSONAL: Born October 19, 1941, in Boston, Mass.; son of Robert DeMille (an entrepreneur and lawyer) and Newell (a teacher; maiden name, Potter) Price; married Elizabeth Deuchar (a software tester), February 15, 1981; children: Benjamin. *Education:* Harvard University, B.A. (cum laude), 1963; Yale University, D.F.A., 1968. *Politics:* Democrat. *Home:* 858 Neilson St., Berkeley, Calif. 94707. *Agent:* Writer's House, 21 West 26th St., New York, N.Y. 10010.

CAREER: New York University, New York City, assistant professor of English, 1968-70; WNET (Channel 13), New York City, video artist-in-residence, 1972-74; Association of Artist-Run Galleries, founder and director, 1974-78; Shakespeare Institute, University of Bridgeport, Bridgeport, Conn., director, 1974-78; Rutgers University, New Brunswick, N.J., assistant professor of English, 1978-79; University of California at

Berkeley, lecturer in extension studies, 1980—; Lucky Stores, Dublin, Calif., technical writer, 1981-82; Apple Computer, Cupertino, Calif., senior technical writer, 1982—.

WRITINGS: On Finnegan's Wake, Grove, 1972; (editor) *Critics on Robert Lowell,* University of Miami Press, 1972; (editor with John Lahr) *Life Show Anthology,* Bantam, 1973; (with J. Lahr) *Life Show: How to See Theater in Life and Life in Theater,* Viking, 1973; *Video-Visions: A Medium Discovers Itself,* New American Library, 1977; *The Best Thing on TV: Commercials,* Viking, 1978; (editor and translator) *Classic Scenes for Young Actors,* New American Library, 1979.

(Editor) *Three by Ben Jonson,* New American Library, 1980; *Thirty Days to More Powerful Writing,* Fawcett, 1981; *How to Find Work,* New American Library, 1982; (with Linda Urban) *The Definitive Word Processing Book,* Viking, 1984; *The Instant Expert's Guide to BASIC on the IBM PC,* Dell, 1984; *How to Write a Computer Manual,* Benjamin/Cummings, 1984; *Put That in Writing,* Viking, 1984; *Apple Presents AppleWorks* (training disk), Apple Computer, 1984.

WORK IN PROGRESS: A book on public speaking, for Viking; a book on using computers and electronic printers to do desktop publishing.

SIDELIGHTS: "I like pictures with my words. Recently, I've been playing with the device known as a mouse, drawing pictures on my Apple IIc and my Macintosh. When I write about writing, I think of myself as talking to you, sitting right next to you, watching as you get stuck; then I distract you. One of the ways I keep you from worrying about how hard it is to write is by drawing pictures. I show a picture of an old-fashioned locomotive. It's full of steam and fire and pipes and wheels. But one thing it's lacking is people. That's what I urge you to put in your own writing—people you see, people you talk to, people who mean a lot to you. Maybe you could even add their pictures. People make writing live."

FOR MORE INFORMATION SEE: Harper's, June, 1972, January, 1973, February, 1973, October, 1973; *Arts Magazine,* February, 1976, June, 1976; *New York Times,* June 11, 1976, September 21, 1976, December 18, 1977; *Washington Post,* November 22, 1978, December 21, 1978; *Minneapolis Tribune,* November 25, 1978; *Chicago Tribune,* December 3, 1978; *Reader's Digest,* March, 1979; *Softalk,* July, 1984.

REID, Alastair 1926-

PERSONAL: Born March 22, 1926, in Whithorn, Scotland; son of William Arnold (a minister) and Marian (Wilson) Reid; children: Jasper. *Education:* St. Andrews University, M.A. (with honors), 1949. *Residence:* Samaná, Dominican Republic. *Office:* c/o *New Yorker,* 25 West 43rd St., New York, N.Y. 10036.

CAREER: Sarah Lawrence College, Bronxville, N.Y., professor, 1951-55; *New Yorker,* New York, N.Y., staff writer, 1959—. Visiting professor of Latin American studies, Antioch College, 1969-70; summer instructor in Latin American literature, Oxford University and St. Andrew's University, 1972-73; visiting professor, Colorado College, 1977 and 1978, Yale University, 1979, and Dartmouth College, 1979. Lecturer for Association of American Colleges, 1966 and 1969. Translation judge, National Book Awards, 1979. Has given poetry readings at many colleges, universities, and cultural centers in the United States, Great Britain, Spain, and Latin

America. *Military service:* Royal Navy, 1943-46. *Awards, honors:* Guggenheim fellow, 1957 and 1958; *Once, Dice, Trice* and *Allth* were each selected one of the American Institute of Graphic Arts Children's Books, 1958-60; Columbia University fellow in writing, 1966.

WRITINGS—Juvenile: I Will Tell You of a Town, Houghton, 1955; *Fairwater,* Houghton, 1956; *A Balloon for a Blunderbuss,* Harper, 1957; *Allth* (illustrated by Walter H. Lorraine), Houghton, 1958; *Once, Dice, Trice* (illustrated by Ben Shahn), Atlantic-Little, Brown, 1958; *Supposing,* Atlantic-Little, Brown, 1960; *To Be Alive,* Macmillan, 1966; *Uncle Timothy's Traviata,* Dial, 1967; *La Isla Azul,* Editorial Lumen (Barcelona), 1973.

Other: *To Lighten My House* (poetry), Morgan, 1953; *Oddments Inklings Omens Moments* (poetry), Atlantic-Little, Brown, 1959; *Passwords: Places Poems Preoccupations* (poetry and prose), Atlantic-Little, Brown, 1963; (contributor) Dannie Abse, editor, *Corgi Modern Poets in Focus 3,* Corgi, 1971; *Weathering: New and Selected Poems,* Dutton, 1978; (editor with Emir R. Monegal) *Borges: A Reader,* Dutton, 1981; *Other People's Houses,* North Point, 1986.

Translator: (With others) Jorge Luis Borges, *Ficciones,* Grove, 1965; (with Anthony Kerrigan) *Mother Goose in Spanish,* Crowell, 1967; Pablo Neruda, *We Are Many,* J. Cape, 1967, Grossman, 1968; (with A. Kerrigan) *Jorge Luis Borges: A Personal Anthology,* Grove, 1967; (with Ben Belitt) P. Neruda, *A New Decade: Poems 1958-67,* Grove, 1968; (with others) P. Neruda, *Selected Poems: A Bilingual Edition,* J. Cape,

ALASTAIR REID

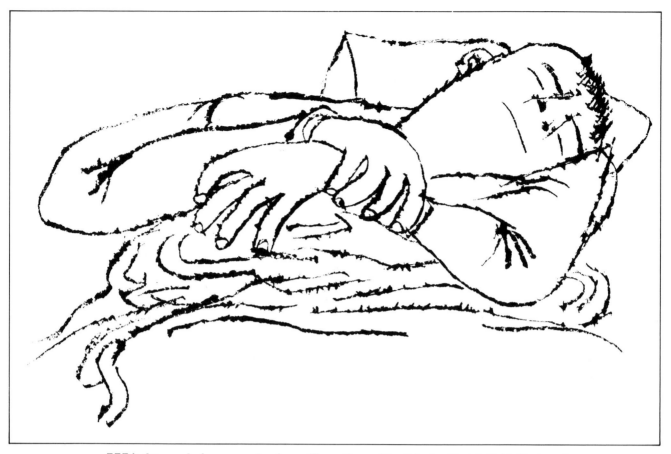

ZZZ is the sound of someone sleeping. ■ (From *Ounce Dice Trice* by Alastair Reid. Illustrated by Ben Shahn.)

1970, Delacorte, 1972; P. Neruda, *Extravagaria*, J. Cape, 1972, Farrar, Straus, 1974; (with others) J. L. Borges, *Selected Poems*, Delacorte, 1972; Mario Vargas Llasa, *Sunday Sunday*, Bobbs-Merrill, 1973; P. Neruda, *Fully Empowered*, Farrar, Straus, 1975; J. L. Borges, *Gold of the Tigers*, Dutton, 1977; Jose Emilio Pacheco, *Don't Ask Me How the Time Goes Past*, Columbia University Press, 1977; P. Neruda, *Isla Negra Notebook*, Farrar, Straus, 1981; (with Andrew Hurley) Heberto Padilla, *Legacies: Selected Poems*, Farrar, Straus, 1982.

WORK IN PROGRESS: New poems and translations; a collection of essays entitled *Hispanics*.

SIDELIGHTS: Reid—poet, translator, essayist, and author of books for children—sees nothing unusual in the fact that he has written in such a variety of genres throughout his career. Switching from one to the other, he told a *Publishers Weekly* interviewer, has "never involved a change of wavelength. . . . I never *felt* the division between prose and poetry, and now that I'm after writing prose with the same care and intensity that poetry asks for, I'm interested in just writing, putting-into-words-well. . . . But I am always grateful for the discipline and precision in language that poetry exacts. I'm grateful in a way to translation too, for it keeps the wheels turning. . . : But I have too many things I want to write myself to do much more translation.''

Scottish by birth, Reid has spent much of his life residing everywhere *but* Scotland, including Spain, Latin America, Greece, France, Morocco, Switzerland, and England. His strongest affinity, however, is reserved for the Hispanic countries. As he explains, "There's something in the Scottish at-titude I've always rejected, and still do, some leftover Calvin-ism which frowns on joy, on spontaneity, too cautious for me. . . . I found something in the Spanish wavelength, in its starkness and spontaneity, that felt like the antidote to Scotland for me. . . . I would emphatically rather live in a Latin country than any other.''

As for his itinerant lifestyle, Reid admits that it is possible only because "writing is the most portable occupation there is. . . . An itinerant existence has certain strange conse-quences, however—I have next to no possessions, and I never keep copies of my books or writings once they have come out. I look on my own writing always as something I've left be-hind, and am only interested in what I'm working on at the moment. . . . With all this talk about roots . . . , I feel some-what of an odd man out, for I've chosen to cut loose from my roots. It would make no sense at all to call me a Scottish writer. Mid-Atlantic, maybe. But I've elected, for most of my writing life, to live in a limbo, between countries and lan-guages, as interpreters, exiles and displaced persons do. I like the state of being a foreigner. It sharpens the ear and eye, and the kind of alienation it implies is not a bad wavelength for a writer to work on, as long as his nerve and curiosity are up to it, and as long as the mails still go through.''

FOR MORE INFORMATION SEE: Booklist, June 1, 1953; *San Francisco Chronicle,* August 23, 1953, September 21, 1958; *Christian Science Monitor,* May 10, 1956, September 29, 1958, October 9, 1958, April 27, 1959, December 5, 1963; *New York Times,* May 13, 1956, August 18, 1957, No-vember 2, 1958; *New York Herald Tribune Book Review,* May 20, 1956, May 12, 1957, September 28, 1958, November 2,

1958, May 8, 1960; *Saturday Review*, June 23, 1956, September 21, 1957, November 1, 1958, July 16, 1960; *Commonweal*, September 26, 1958; *New York Times Book Review*, November 2, 1958; *Christian Century*, February 25, 1959; *Yale Review*, June, 1959; *Atlantic*, July, 1959; *Poetry*, November, 1959; *Chicago Sunday Tribune*, May 8, 1960; *Poetry and Fiction*, Rutgers University Press, 1963; *Time*, September 20, 1963.

REINER, William B(uck) 1910-1976

PERSONAL: Born May 23, 1910, in New York, N.Y.; died January 24, 1976, in St. Thomas, Virgin Islands; son of Meyer (a tailor) and Mollie (Silver) Reiner; married Jeannette Ender, October 5, 1935 (died, 1970); married Myrtle Lifland (a professor), January 23, 1971; children: (first marriage) Albey M.; (second marriage) two stepsons. *Education:* City College (now City College of the City University of New York), B.S., 1931, M.S., 1932; New York University, Ph.D., 1942. *Religion:* Jewish. *Home:* New York, N.Y.

CAREER: New York City public schools, high school teacher of chemistry, 1934-49, Bureau of Educational Research, research assistant, 1949-54, research associate, 1954-63, Bureau of Curriculum Research, assistant director, 1963-65; Hunter College of the City University of New York, New York City, professor of education, beginning, 1965, director of Office of Institutional Research, 1966-68. Adjunct professor of research, Long Island University; lecturer at New York University and Brooklyn College of the City University of New York. *Member:* National Education Association, National Science Teachers Association, National Society for the Study of Education, National Council on Measurement in Education, American Educational Research Association, Doctorate Association of New York Educators.

WRITINGS: The Flying Rangers (juvenile science fiction), Messner, 1953; (with Don Wilcox and Helen Olos) *A Child's First Book of Outdoor Adventures,* Grosset, 1954; (wtih Frederic Shaw) *An Evaluation of the Pedagogic Staff Relations Plan, 1955,* Bureau of Administrative and Budgetary Research, New York (City) Board of Education, 1956; (contributing editor) J. Darrell Barnard, *Teaching High School Science* (pamphlet), American Educational Research Association, 1956; (contributor) Alice Crow and Lester Crow, editors, *Vital Issues in American Education,* Bantam, 1964; (contributor) Alfred de Grazia and David Sohn, editors, *Programs, Teachers, and Machines,* Bantam, 1964; (with Dale Scannell) *Tests of Academic Progress,* Houghton, 1965, revised edition, 1971; (with Charles Spiegler) *What to Do after High School,* Science Research Associates, 1971; (with wife, Myrtle Reiner) *Foundations of Educational Research,* Springer, 1974.

Also author of technical monographs, reports, and tests of academic progress; editor and co-author of "The Research Program in Our Schools," a radio script for WNYE-Radio, 1961. Co-editor, "Problems and Practices in New York City Schools," New York Society for the Experimental Study of Education, 1953, 1955, 1957, and 1959. Author of column "Spotlight on Research," *Science Teacher,* 1959-64. Contributor of more than sixty articles and reviews to education journals, including *Review of Educational Research, School Science and Mathematics, Education, Graduate School Record, Science Education,* and *Journal of Experimental Education.*

HOBBIES AND OTHER INTERESTS: Travel, sports.

FOR MORE INFORMATION SEE—Obituaries: *New York Times,* January 26, 1976.

RIEU, E(mile) V(ictor) 1887-1972

PERSONAL: Born in 1887, in London, England; died May 11, 1972, in London, England; son of C.P.H. Rieu; married Nelly Lewis, 1914; children: Richard, Christopher, Penelope, Rosamund Rieu Cowen. *Education:* Attended Balliol College, Oxford, 1906-08.

CAREER: Oxford University Press, Bombay, India, manager, 1912-19; Methuen & Co., Ltd., London, England, educational manager, 1923-33, managing director, 1933-36; Penguin Classics, London, editor, 1944-64. Member, Joint Churches Committee for New Translation of the Bible, 1951-72. *Military service:* British Army, Light Infantry, 1918, became major in Home Guard, 1943. *Member:* Virgil Society (president, 1941), Royal Society of Literature (vice-president, 1958), Athenaeum. *Awards, honors:* Litt.D., University of Leeds, 1949;

And the only sound he heard was the paradisal bird....
■ (From "Pirate Passes" in *The Flattered Flying Fish and Other Poems* by E. V. Rieu. Illustrated by E. H. Shepard.)

Commander, Order of the British Empire, 1953; Benson Medal, Royal Society of Literature, 1968; Golden Jubilee Medal from the Institute of Linguists, 1971.

WRITINGS: (Editor) *A Book of Latin Poetry from Ennius to Hadrian,* Methuen, 1925, 4th edition, St. Martins, 1953; *Cuckoo Calling* (children's verse), Methuen, 1933; (editor with Peter Wait) *Modern Masters of Wit and Laughter,* Methuen, 1938; (editor) *Essays by Divers Hands,* Volume XXIX, Royal Society of Literature, 1957; (co-author) *A Puffin Quartet of Poets,* Penguin, 1958; *The Flattered Flying Fish and Other Poems* (children's verse; illustrated by E. H. Shepard), Dutton, 1962; (editor with H. C. Bradby) *Lettres de mon moulin,* Clarendon Press, 1963.

Translator: *The Odyssey,* Methuen, 1946, reissued, Greenwich House, 1982; *The Pastoral Poems of Virgil,* Penguin, 1949, reissued, 1961; *The Four Gospels,* Penguin, 1952; *The Iliad,* Penguin, 1950, reissued, Folio Society, 1975; *Voyage of Argo,* Penguin, 1959; *The Word: A Synthesis of the Four Gospels,* Faith Press, 1965.

Contributor to *Penguin Reader's Guide* and *Cassell's Encyclopedia.*

SIDELIGHTS: Rieu was best known for making classical works of literature more accessible to the public by printing them as the paperback "Penguin Classics" series. As editor of Penguin Classics, he translated some of the works he published, such as *The Odyssey, The Pastoral Poems of Virgil* and *The Four Gospels.* Before working at Penguin, Rieu established and managed the Oxford University Press in India.

FOR MORE INFORMATION SEE: Anthology of Children's Literature, 4th edition, Houghton, 1970; Martha E. Ward and Dorothy A. Marquardt, *Authors of Books for Young People,* Scarecrow, 1971. Obituaries: *New York Times,* May 13, 1972.

SAUNDERS, Susan 1945-
(Sara Hughes)

PERSONAL: Born April 14, 1945, in San Antonio, Tex.; daughter of George S. (a rancher) and Brooksie (Hughes) Saunders; married John J. Cirigliano, September 7, 1969 (divorced, 1976). *Education:* Barnard College, B.A., 1966. *Home and office address:* P.O. Box 736, Westhampton, N.Y. 11977. *Agent:* Amy Berkower, Writer's House, Inc., 21 West 26th St., New York, N.Y. 10010.

CAREER: John Wiley, New York City, copy editor, 1966-67; CBS/Columbia House, New York City, 1967-70, began as proofreader and assistant to production manager, became copy editor, then staff writer; Greystone Press, New York City, copy editor, 1970-72; *Lighting Design and Application* (trade magazine), New York City, associate editor, 1972-76; Visual Information Systems (producer of radio programs and videotapes), New York City, editor, 1976-77; Random House (publisher), New York City, editor for Miller-Brody Productions, Inc., subsidiary, 1977-80; free-lance writer, scriptwriter, editor, copy editor, proofreader, and researcher for Harcourt Brace Jovanovich, *Psychology Today,* Random House, and the Rockefeller Foundation, 1980—. Professional ceramist. *Member:* Authors Guild. *Awards, honors: Fish Fry* was selected as a Notable Children's Trade Book by the National Council for Social Studies/Children's Book Council Joint Committee.

WRITINGS—Juvenile: *Wales' Tale* (illustrated by Marilyn Hirsh; Junior Literary Guild selection), Viking, 1980; *A Sniff in Time* (illustrated by Michael Mariano), Atheneum, 1982; *Fish Fry* (illustrated by S. D. Schindler), Viking, 1982; *The Green Slime: Choose Your Own Adventure,* Bantam, 1982; *The Creature from Miller's Pond: Choose Your Own Adventure,* Bantam, 1983; *Charles Rat's Picnic* (Junior Literary Guild selection; illustrated by Robert Byrd), Dutton, 1984; *The Tower of London: Choose Your Own Adventure* (illustrated by Lorna Tomei), Bantam, 1984; *Dorothy and the Magic Belt* (illustrated by David Rose), Random House, 1985; *The Get Along Gang and the Treasure Map* (illustrated by Carol Hudson), Scholastic, 1985; *Runaway Spaceship: Choose Your Own Adventure* (illustrated by Ted Enik), Bantam, 1985; *Ice Cave: Choose Your Own Adventure,* Bantam, 1985; *Dolly Parton: Country Goin' to Town, Women of Our Time,* Viking Kestrel, 1985; (under name Sara Hughes) *Morgan Swift and the Treasure of Crocodile Key,* Random House, 1985; (under name Sara Hughes) *Morgan Swift and the Kidnapped Goddess,* Random House, 1985; *Attack of the Monster Plants: Choose Your Own Adventure,* Bantam, 1986; *The Miss Liberty Caper: Choose Your Own Adventure,* Bantam, 1986; *Blizzard at Black Swan Inn: Choose Your Own Adventure,* Bantam, 1986; *The Haunted Halloween Party: Choose Your Own Adventure,* Bantam, 1986; *Light on Burro Mountain: Choose Your Own Adventure,* Bantam, 1986; *Sir Silver Swine and the Missing Rain,* Scholastic, 1986; *The Daring Rescue of Marlon the Swimming Pig,* Random House, 1986; *Mystery Cat and the Chocolate Trap,* Bantam, 1986; *The Bad News Bunny in Third Prize Surprise,* Simon & Schuster, 1986; *The Right House for Rabbit,* Western Publishing, 1986; *Mr. Nighttime and the Dream Machine,* Scholastic, 1986; (under name Sara Hughes) *Morgan Swift and the Lake of Diamonds,* Random House, 1986; *The Bad News Bunny in the Camping Trip,* Simon & Schuster, 1986.

WORK IN PROGRESS: A screenplay with Allen Coulter tentatively titled "Second Chance," set in south Texas and involving a stolen racehorse; a biography for children of Margaret Mead for Viking's "Women of Our Time" series; four more "Bad News Bunny" books; a series for Scholastic called "The Sleepover Club."

SIDELIGHTS: "I was bilingual (English and Spanish) until I started school, then my verbal Spanish drifted away until I studied it in high school, although I could always understand.

"I was an only child for a long time and books were my favorite entertainment, especially fairy tales from other lands, preferably with wizards, elves, dark forests, and rushing rivers. South Texas is semi-arid, so forests and rivers were as wonderful to me as elves.

"Animals were and are an important part of my life. I grew up with horses, lots of dogs, tame deer, tame—more or less—jackrabbits, and once an armadillo who really didn't work out as a pet. Since I've lived in Manhattan I've had to cut back, but I do have two cats and a cairn terrier.

"I have always loved children's books. There is a magic to them, especially picture books, that I think doesn't exist anywhere else in literature. I write in spurts: I can have an idea for a long time, but will only commit it to paper when it's almost all written in my head, or when the suspense is killing me."

HOBBIES AND OTHER INTERESTS: Avid gardener.

When Edith opened her eyes, the sun was already shining, warm on her face. ■ (From *Fish Fry* by Susan Saunders. Illustrated by S. D. Schindler.)

SCOTT, Bill   1920(?)-1985

OBITUARY NOTICE: Born about 1920; died of a heart attack, November 29, 1985, in Tunjunga, Calif. Producer, animated cartoon voice, and scriptwriter. Best known as the voice of such cartoon characters as Bullwinkle Moose and Dudley Do-Right in the animated cartoon series ''Rocky and His Friends,'' Scott began his career in animation in the mid-1940s. He worked as scriptwriter for Warner Brothers and United Productions of America before joining Jay Ward Productions—the home of the Rocky cartoon shows—in 1958. In addition to serving as many of the cartoon voices, Scott also worked as the series' head writer and coproducer. The program, noted for its spoofs and satires on topical issues, ran through 1973 and is still being rerun on television. Scott, who served on the board of governors of the Academy of Motion Picture Arts and Sciences, was also the voice behind several characters in the Disney cartoon production ''The Gummy Bears.''

FOR MORE INFORMATION SEE—Obituaries: *Chicago Tribune*, December 3, 1985; *New York Times*, December 3, 1985; *Washington Post*, January 2, 1985.

SEIDLER, Tor   1952-

BRIEF ENTRY: Born June 26, 1952, in New Hampshire. Author. Seidler earned a B.A. from Stanford University in 1972 and began writing children's books after working on elementary school readers for Harcourt, Brace, Jovanovich. He alternates between writing juvenile works and as yet unpublished adult fiction. ''I've been writing pretty much regularly for eleven years,'' he admits, ''and every once in a while I think I'm beginning to get the hang of it, but most of the time I really wonder.'' Seidler made his debut with *The Dulcimer Boy* (Viking, 1979), the story of orphaned twin boys and a silver-stringed dulcimer, their only possession. *New York Times Book Review* described it as ''a brilliant tale—half Dickens, half Thurber—that sparkles with imagination . . . woven [with] a thread of poetry and mysticism one rarely finds in children's books.'' Seidler also wrote *Terpin* (Farrar, Straus, 1982), listed as one of the *New York Times* Outstanding Books for 1982, and *A Rat's Tale* (Farrar, Straus), published in 1985. *Home:* 121 West 78th St., New York, N.Y. 10024.

Like author, like book.   —Proverb

SHREVE, Susan Richards 1939-

PERSONAL: Born May 2, 1939, in Toledo, Ohio; daughter of Robert Kenneth (a broadcaster and writer) and Helen Elizabeth (Greene) Richards; married Porter Gaylord Shreve (a family therapist), May 26, 1962; children: Porter Gaylord, Elizabeth Steward, Caleb Richards, Katharine Taylor. *Education:* University of Pennsylvania, B.A. (magna cum laude), 1961; University of Virginia, M.A., 1969. *Home:* 3518 35th St. N.W., Washington, D.C. 20016. *Agent:* Timothy Seldes, Russell & Volkening, Inc., 551 Fifth Ave., New York, N.Y. 10017. *Office:* Department of English, George Mason University, Fairfax, Va. 22030.

CAREER: Teacher of English in private schools in Cheshire, England, 1962-63, Rosemont, Pa., 1963-66, Washington, D.C., 1967-68, and Philadelphia, Pa., 1970-72; Community Learning Center (alternative school), Philadelphia, co-founder, 1972-75; George Mason University, Fairfax, Va., professor of literature, 1976—. *Member:* P.E.N., Author's Guild, Phi Beta Kappa. *Awards, honors: The Masquerade* was selected as an American Library Association Best Book for Young Adults, 1980; *Family Secrets: Five Very Important Stories* was chosen as a Notable Children's Trade Book in the field of social studies by the joint committee of the National Council for Social Studies and the Children's Book Council, 1980.

WRITINGS—Young adult; all published by Knopf, except as noted: *The Nightmares of Geranium Street,* 1977; *Loveletters,* 1978; *Family Secrets: Five Very Important Stories* (ALA Notable Book; illustrated by Richard Cuffari), 1979; *The Masquerade,* 1980; *The Revolution of Mary Leary,* 1982; *The Bad Dreams of a Good Girl* (illustrated by Diane De Groat), 1982; *The Flunking of Joshua T. Bates* (Junior Literary Guild selection; illustrated by D. De Groat), 1984; *How I Saved the World*

(Jacket illustration by Trina Schart Hyman from *The Nightmares of Geranium Street* by Susan Shreve.)

on Purpose (illustrated by Suzanne Richardson), Holt, 1985; *Lucy Forever and Miss Rosetree,* Holt, 1986.

Adult novels: *A Fortunate Madness,* Houghton, 1974; *A Woman Like That,* Atheneum, 1977; *Children of Power,* Macmillan, 1979; *Miracle Play,* Morrow, 1981; *Dreaming of Heroes,* Morrow, 1984; *Queen of Hearts,* Linden Press, 1986.

WORK IN PROGRESS: Sweet Promised Land, a novel; *The Girl Who Knew Secrets* for children.

SIDELIGHTS: "I grew up in a house full of stories.

"My father began as a crime reporter in Cincinnati, Ohio. By nature and profession he saw danger and excitement everywhere. One of the earliest family stories I remember comes of his crime reporter days. My parents were on their way to Cincinnati after their wedding on New Year's Day 1937. My father spotted a brown paper bag in the middle of the highway, and stopped the car. There was, he claimed in dead earnest, a baby in the paper bag.

"'A baby?' my mother asked incredulously. 'How do you know?'

"'Look, for heaven's sake,' he said to her, as though her sense of sight had failed her. 'Can't you tell?'

"She looked. It was nighttime, so there were lights on the highway and the car headlights were on, so she could see the

SUSAN RICHARDS SHREVE

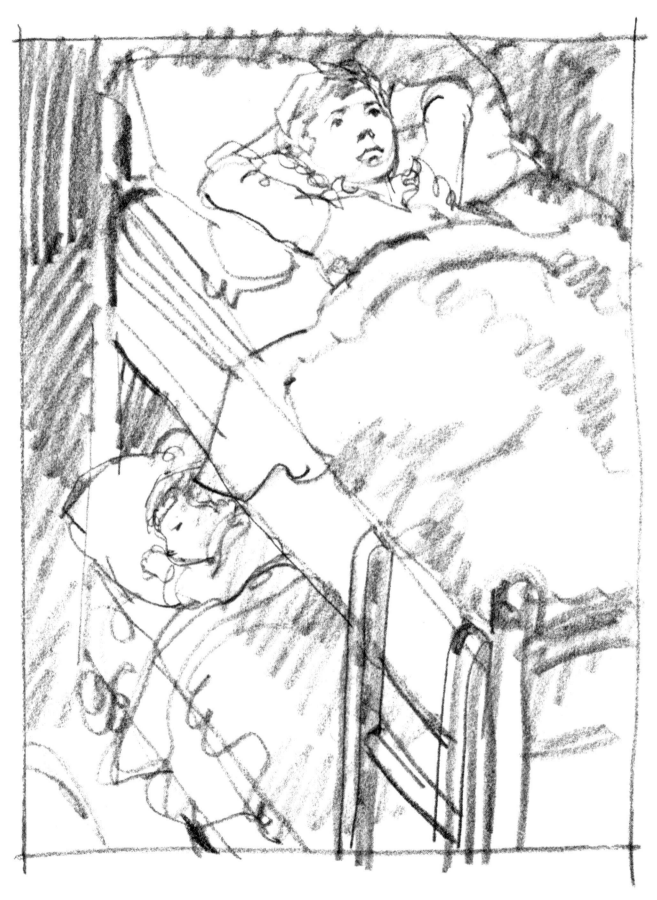

It's hard being the oldest. You get all the troubles. ∎ (From *Family Secrets: Five Very Important Stories* by Susan Shreve. Illustrated by Richard Cuffari.)

paper bag perfectly. It appeared to be a brown paper bag which gave no evidence of concealing a baby. But it did move, she noticed, as my father rushed to rescue it from the middle of the road.

"Filled with a sudden excitement, she began to believe that he was right and would return with a small baby which he'd dump from the paper bag onto her lap. She straightened her skirt in anticipation.

"'Well?' she asked as he opened the door by the driver's seat. 'What was it?'

"My father got in, tossed the paper bag in the back seat and turned on the engine.

"'Nothing,' he said and drove off into the night with his new bride, heading for Cincinnati.

"'Why,' my mother dared to ask sometime later, 'did you think there was a baby in the paper bag?'

"'There could have been a baby,' my father said simply.

"Anything, of course is possible, and so my reasonable mother agreed that 'yes,' there could have been a baby.

"'Besides,' my father later said. 'I couldn't imagine that it was simply an empty paper bag.'

"I loved being around the house when my father came home from work so I wouldn't miss my role in whatever high drama might be played out in our kitchen. It wasn't so much that he told us stories, although he did that, too, but that he made our lives into stories. I grew up believing that there could be a baby in an empty paper bag.

"My parents moved from Ohio to Washington, D.C., in 1943. I was three years old. I had rheumatic fever shortly after we arrived, followed by pneumonia. I'd already had polio before we left Ohio. I mention this not for itself but to say that my early life was attended by a certain amount of drama of which I was the center. It wasn't a bad time and I wasn't bored. I listened to soap operas on the console radio and played out melodramas of my own design on my bed. I used to make up events as if I were in the midst of them, turning them into stories in my mind, casting myself in the heroic role. Once, while waiting in a dress shop for my mother to try on suits, I spotted a child hiding under the dress racks. I pretended that the kidnapper of the Lindbergh baby was concealed in the dressing rooms, waiting for this child's mother to move out of sight so he could whisk the little girl away. I imagined warning the mother in the nick of time, and pulling the child, chewing Juicy Fruit gum, from under the dress rack.

"'That didn't happen,' my mother said to me in distress as we drove home that afternoon.

"'Yes it did,' I said. 'I was there. You were in the dressing room.'

"'You made it up,' my mother went on.

"'She tells lies,' my mother told my father at dinner time.

"'She exaggerates,' my father said.

"'Whatever,' my mother said, exasperated. 'She doesn't tell the truth.'

"Even now my mother will telephone about a book of mine that she's reading.

"'Look at page 96,' she'll say. 'Aunt Lucy isn't fat. She's going to be furious.'

"'The woman on page 96 isn't Aunt Lucy,' I say. 'I made her up.'

"'She has lavender hair,' she'll insist. 'What other woman do you know with lavender hair?'

"When I was nine, I started a theater for which I wrote the plays and directed the actors who performed for the neighborhood twice monthly in our living room. According to my brother, I often played the lead in these plays while he usually had a non-speaking role as a furry animal. The profits from the plays went to the Lollipop Patch, a small hideout where, I assured the children in the neighborhood, the other actors and I grew lollipops from seeds. Eventually, I incorporated a variation of this experience into one of my novels, *Loveletters*.

"I began to write books when I was a teenager. My first book, written when I was eighteen, was autobiographical. It was quite boring and, not surprisingly, did not sell. An editor in New York told me to go out and learn about the world and then write books. Instead I wrote another book, full of drama and romance which also did not sell. I got married right out of college and taught school in England for a while and then in Pennsylvania and rural Virginia. We had four children. . . . I went to graduate school, started a school in Philadelphia with my husband, and then moved to Houston, Texas, while my husband trained as a family therapist. I didn't try to write again until I was thirty when I wrote two books for adults. As my children got older, I began to write children's books, at first, by writing books for them.

"I write the kind of books I liked to read as a child—stories that could happen, often with a rebellious hero because that's the sort of child I was. They are family stories because my family, then as now, is the center of my life. I write every day for two hours, seldom more, and then I go to work teaching in a college because it allows me more time with my own children. I vary between writing books for children and books for adults.

"Recently I was looking through some of my old books and came upon a collection of opera stories which had been given to me one Christmas when I was small. On the last page of each opera, I had crossed out the tragic finale in black ink and over the print I had written: 'AND THEY ALL LIVED HAP-PILY EVER AFTER.'

"I do not believe in false promises but I do believe that in life as well as in books, we owe our children as well as ourselves the promise of a future."

FOR MORE INFORMATION SEE: New York Times Book Review, August 4, 1974, July 10, 1977, June 10, 1979, July 1, 1979; *Best Sellers,* December, 1977, June, 1980; *Washington Post Book World,* December 11, 1977, April 1, 1979, May 11, 1980, July 26, 1981; *Times Literary Supplement,* September 22, 1978; *Newsweek,* December 18, 1978; *Saturday Review,* May 12, 1979; *Books of the Times,* July, 1979; *Maclean's,* July 30, 1979; *Publishers Weekly,* July 23, 1982; *Wilson Library Bulletin,* February, 1983; *Ms.,* April, 1984.

On Labor Day, driving home from the beach, Joshua's mother told him that he was going to have to repeat third grade. ▪ (From *The Flunking of Joshua T. Bates* by Susan Shreve. Illustrated by Diane de Groat.)

SKIPPER, G. C. 1939-

PERSONAL: Born March 22, 1939, in Ozark, Ala.; son of G. C. (a railroad worker) and Ada (Price) Skipper; married Dorothy Wright (a secretary), March 26, 1960; children: Richard Craig (deceased), Lisa Ann. *Education:* University of Alabama, B.A., 1961. *Home:* 2344 Pleasant Ave., Glenside, Pa. 19038. *Office:* Al Paul Lefton Co., Philadelphia, Pa. 19106.

CAREER: Huntsville Times, Huntsville, Ala., reporter and columnist, 1961-65; United Airlines, Chicago, Ill., public relations representative, 1966-70; *Travel Weekly,* Chicago, Midwest news bureau chief, 1970-72; Hitchcock Publishing Co., Wheaton, Ill., executive editor, 1973-76; Al Paul Lefton Co., Philadelphia, Pa., vice-president of public relations, 1984—. Has also worked as folk and rock pianist.

WRITINGS—Books for children and young adults, except as indicated; published by Childrens Press, except as indicated: *And the Angels Rage* (adult novel), Touchstone Publishing, 1972; *The Ghost in the Church,* 1976; *A Night in the Attic,* 1977; *The Ghost at Manor House* (illustrated by Tom Dunnington), 1978.

"World at War" series; all published by Childrens Press: *Death of Hitler,* 1980; *Goering and the Luftwaffe,* 1980; *Mussolini: A Dictator Dies,* 1981; *Battle of Britain,* 1981; *Battle of the Atlantic,* 1981; *Battle of Stalingrad,* 1981; *Battle of Leyte Gulf,* 1981; *Battle of the Coral Sea,* 1981; *Battle of Midway,* 1981; *Invasion of Sicily,* 1981; *Fall of the Fox: Rommel,* 1981; *Submarines in the Pacific,* 1981; *MacArthur and the Philippines,* 1982; *Invasion of Poland* (maps illustrated by Len Meents), 1983; *D-Day,* 1983; *Pearl Harbor,* 1984.

Former editor of *Motor Service* magazine.

WORK IN PROGRESS: Southbound, a novel; *Triad Summer,* a novel.

SIDELIGHTS: "I've known since I was twelve years old that I not only wanted to write, but *had* to write. Some have labeled this obsession 'talent,' but in reality it's more like a disease. As to the reason why, I'm still trying to figure that out. Insanity helps a whole lot and if you keep your insanity you'll be okay. The worst thing in the world for a writer is to become a 'well-rounded individual.' Writers are an egotistical lot—they'd have to be to think they've got anything to say, much less believe people want to hear it. Whew!

"I grew up in Alabama, in the deep South, and I've seen how ridiculous other areas of the country have been in imagining what 'the South' is 'really like.' Now, like country music, suddenly it's 'in' to be Southern—and the worst thing in the world is a Professional Southerner. I believe all creativity springs out of an individual or a section of the country that has known defeat. The South is the only area of the United States that

"Pram Squad" children of London were allowed to collect firewood from damaged buildings. ■
(From *Battle of Britain* by G. C. Skipper. Photograph courtesy of United Press International.)

G. C. SKIPPER

has been defeated. I think that accounts, at least partially, for the Faulkners, the Weltys, the Jacksons, et cetera, et cetera. New York is getting there, too, in its own unique way—hence, the Mailers. In other words all this man-it's-a-rough-miserable-world-type-stuff is good fodder to sprout writers. Outside playing God, I think creativity—in this case in writing—is one of the most honorable, honest contributions Man can make. If it's really good, it survives everything. Any other profession, say a thousand years from now, will look just downright silly—if I can paraphrase Hemingway.

"There's only a handful of good writers around today, hidden among the mass of academic phonies. I mean good in the creative sense of Hemingway, Faulkner and Fitzgerald. Maybe these writers are hidden because the selling of fiction has been reduced to computerized marketing exercised by publishers. Yeah, I know all us word merchants can't be Hemingway and all editors can't be Max Perkins—but it sure would be refreshing to see a novel make it on merit rather than hype. There is a need now in the United States—not for entertainment (there's plenty of that)—but for literature. I'd like to contribute my limited amount toward filling that gap."

SMALL, David 1945-

BRIEF ENTRY: Born February 12, 1945, in Detroit, Mich. A B.A. graduate of Wayne State University, Small earned his M.F.A. at Yale University. Since 1978 he has been affiliated

with Kalamazoo College in Kalamazoo, Mich., first as an assistant art professor and then, beginning in 1983, as artist-in-residence. Earlier in his career, he also taught at Fredonia College of the State University of New York. A sickly child, Small remembers that he was "painfully shy, much abused by the world around me and unable for many years to be comfortable in it." As a result, his books are aimed at "the extraordinary children [who] often do not do well in school and are so different it's hard to accept them."

Small's self-illustrated picture book Eulalie and the Hopping Head (Macmillan/Collier, 1982) was described by Publishers Weekly as "a first in more ways than one . . . a frolic, enticingly illustrated by ingenious woodland scenes in pretty shades." Eulalie is a toddler toad, prone to misbehaving, while "the hopping head" is part of an abandoned doll. "[The] anthropomorphic actors," observed School Library Journal, "are endowed with a remarkable depth of feeling and body language." In Small's second book, Imogene's Antlers (Crown, 1985), also illustrated by the author, young Imogene awakens one morning to discover that she has sprouted wings. "Small maximizes the inherent humor of the absurd situation," again noted School Library Journal, "by allowing the imaginative possibilities . . . to run rampant." In addition to his own works, Small has provided illustrations for Maida Silverman's Anna and the Seven Swans, Burr Tilstrom's The Dragon Who Lived Downstairs, Eve Merriam's The Christmas Box, Nathan Zimelman's Mean Chickens and Wild Cucumbers, and a 1983 edition of Gulliver's Travels by Jonathan Swift. Home: 1815 W. Michigan, Kalamazoo, Mich. 49007.

SMITH, Joan 1933-

BRIEF ENTRY: Born January 11, 1933, in Birmingham, England. Author of books for children. Trained as a physiotherapist, Smith relinquished her career when her children, Caroline and twins Rachel and Matthew, were born. In 1971, after they had reached school age, she joined her husband's packaging firm as company secretary. The following year, she produced Just Like Corduroy (Hamish Hamilton, 1972), the first of a dozen books for children. Although Smith kept a journal from an early age, she claims that she is not a natural storyteller: "I never told my own children stories when they were young, although I read them plenty. My creative urge is to produce a character and to recreate atmosphere and emotion, or the feel of a place." According to Times Literary Supplement, Smith succeeds in November and the Truffle Pig (Hamish Hamilton, 1977), which "evokes the Périgord countryside and catches the cadence of the French language." Three of Smith's books are available in the United States, all published by Julia MacRae: The Gift of Umtal (1983), Grandmother's Donkey (1983), and We Three Kings from Pepper Street Prime (1985). Among her other works are The Folk Doll of Sion (Hamish Hamilton, 1973), The Hole in the Road (Hamish Hamilton, 1979), and Augusta (Dobson, 1979). Home: 14 Burlington Rd., Leicester LE2 3DD, England.

SMITH, Philip Warren 1936-

PERSONAL: Born November 18, 1936, in San Francisco, Calif.; son of John William Henry (a teamster) and Beulah Marie (a homemaker; maiden name, Phillips) Smith; married Linda Jean Gibson (divorced); married Susan Schellenger (divorced); children: Carrie Kathleen. Education: Attended California College

To everyone else, throughout Westminster and all around the countryside, she was known quite simply as Long Meg. ■ (From *Long Meg* by Rosemary Minard. Illustrated by Philip Smith.)

of Arts and Crafts, Oakland, 1958-61. *Home and office:* 3725 Mayette, #1D, Santa Rosa, Calif. 95405.

CAREER: Free-lance illustrator, 1960—. *Exhibitions:* Carmel, Calif.; Madrid, Spain; and Poland. *Military service:* U.S. Army, 1955-58. *Member:* American Wildlife Association.

ILLUSTRATOR: Muriel Stanek, *Growl When You Say R,* A. Whitman, 1979; Rosemary Minard, *Long Meg,* Pantheon, 1982. Illustrator of numerous text books.

WORK IN PROGRESS: Illustrating textbooks for Economy Co. and Houghton.

SIDELIGHTS: ''Most children's books undermine the child's ability to comprehend and understand both story content and pictures. If Dick, Jane and Spot seemed boring a few years ago, current efforts are running a close second. All things such as beauty, courage and honesty must be taught just as we teach fire burns and look both ways before you cross the street.

''Currently I am working with woodcuts and poster design.''

SPRINGSTUBB, Tricia 1950-

PERSONAL: Born September 15, 1950, in New York, N.Y.; daughter of Kenneth J. (an insurance manager) and Katherine (Hagerty) Carroll; married Paul Springstubb (a teacher), August 18, 1973; children: Zoe, Phoebe. *Education:* State University of New York at Albany, B.A., 1972. *Home:* 2399 Woodmere Dr., Cleveland Heights, Ohio 44106. *Address:* c/o

**Once upon a time
there was an old couple
named Minnie and Henry.**

■ (From *My Minnie Is a Jewel* by Tricia Springstubb. Illustrated by Jim Lamarche.)

Dell Publishing Co., Inc., 1 Dag Hammarskjold Plaza, New York, N.Y. 10017.

CAREER: Author of fiction for children and young adults, 1976—. *Member:* Authors Guild. *Awards, honors: Give and Take* was selected one of New York Public Library's Books for the Teen Age, 1982.

WRITINGS: My Minnie Is a Jewel (juvenile; illustrated by Jim Lamarche), Carolrhoda, 1980; *Give and Take* (young adult novel), Little, Brown, 1981; *The Blueberry Troll* (juvenile; illustrated by Jeannette Swofford), Carolrhoda, 1981; *The Magic Guinea Pig* (juvenile; illustrated by Bari Weissman), Morrow, 1982; *The Moon on a String* (young adult novel), Little, Brown, 1982; *Which Way to the Nearest Wilderness?* (juvenile; Junior Literary Guild selection), Little, Brown, 1984. Contributor of articles and stories to magazines, including *Redbook, Mc-Call's, Woman's Day, Ohio Review,* and *Writer.*

WORK IN PROGRESS: A novel tentatively titled *Eunice Gottlieb and the Unwhitewashed Truth about Life,* which takes Joy and Eunice ahead two years in their lives to junior high, when Joy finds herself a boyfriend and Eunice has to deal with the first real crack in their lifelong friendship; another novel entitled *Eunice, the Egg Salad, Gottlieb* which takes Joy and Eunice back in time to the fourth grade.

SIDELIGHTS: "A writer is one of the last things I ever expected to become. When I was growing up, in the New York suburb of Huntington, I wanted first to be a dog, then a cowgirl, then a nun, then an archaeologist—and settled at last, after four years at the State University of New York at Albany, on being a social worker. That career took me to the countryside a hundred miles north of Manhattan, lovely rolling farmland, where I worked with the retarded, with Headstart, and, with my husband, as a house-parent to troubled adolescents.

"All this time I was writing—long letters, a journal—and, of course, reading, reading, reading. But it wasn't until, suffering job burnout and encouraged by my husband, I submitted my first short story to *Redbook* and actually received a hand-written, friendly rejection, that I considered the possibility of being published. I continued to submit to *Redbook* and also to children's magazines and, lo and behold, eventually found myself being accepted. By then I had no desire to do anything else; I admitted to myself I was better suited to being an observer and cataloguer than a participator. I suppose that rather than confess I came to writing so haphazardly, I'd prefer to claim it was all I ever meant to do—yet so many of life's surprises aren't really surprises at all, but self-knowledge we've groped our way towards unconsciously.

"If I had to say what special incident in my life has been most significant I would choose meeting my husband, Paul, because without his encouragement and continuing support I'd never have begun showing anyone else my writing, and without writing I can't imagine, anymore, where I'd be.

"I am still pleased to find myself a writer except, of course, when the work isn't going well. The 'moral' of all my work so far seems to be the necessity of extending ourselves. Taking risks, letting life surprise you: these seem to me key ingredients of happiness and, happily, of my craft.

"These days I spend more time mothering than writing. We're expecting our third child. . . . While my daughters certainly rob me of time at my typewriter, they've given me another sort of time. Our lives together are a series of moments—discoverings, losses, ecstasies, cruelties. They keep me in the 'now,' where a writer certainly should be, as well as evoking memories of my own littleness and making me see how I still carry my childhood inside me."

TETHER, (Cynthia) Graham 1950-

PERSONAL: Born September 14, 1950, in White Plains, N.Y.; daughter of Willard L. (an investment counselor) and Doris A. (a public health nurse and teacher; maiden name, Bouton) Tether. *Education:* Mount Holyoke College, B.A. (with distinction) and teaching certificate, 1972; New York University, graduate study, 1974; Columbia University, M.B.A., 1980. *Religion:* Protestant. *Home:* 11 DeWitt Ave., Bronxville, N.Y. 10708. *Office:* International Business Machines Corp., 590 Madison Ave., New York, N.Y. 10022.

CAREER: Citibank, New York City, research assistant, 1971; News Election Service, New York City, assistant to payroll manager, 1972; free-lance writer, 1972-73; Harper & Row Publishers, Inc., New York City, editorial assistant in trade department, 1974-78; International Business Machines Corp., financial analyst, 1980-83; marketing representative, 1983—. Assistant concertmistress for All New York State Orchestra; violinist in chamber ensembles. *Member:* Daughters of the American Revolution. *Awards, honors:* Lincoln Center award for instrumental music, 1968; first prize from Society of Children's Book Writers, 1973, for "King Chub-Chub."

WRITINGS—Juvenile: Fudge Dream Supreme (illustrated by Carl Kock), J. Philip O'Hara, 1975; *The Hair Book* (illustrated by Roy McKie), Random House, 1979; *Skunk and Possum,* Houghton, 1979. Contributor to national magazines, including *My Weekly Reader* and *Golden* magazine of Western Publishing Co.

ADAPTATIONS: Fudge Dream Supreme was narrated on CBS-TV, 1977-78.

WORK IN PROGRESS: A book for children, *Danny Dunce.*

GRAHAM TETHER

Then she painted Possum's body and her long tail. ■ (From *Skunk and Possum* by Graham Tether. Illustrated by Lucinda McQueen.)

TRIVELPIECE, Laurel 1926-
(Hannah K. Marks)

BRIEF ENTRY: Born January 18, 1926, in Curtis, Neb. One of five children, Trivelpiece moved to California with her family in the 1930s after their Nebraska farm had succumbed to the dust storms of that period. In the San Joaquin Valley, Trivelpiece picked fruit and worked in the canneries. She earned an A.A. degree from Modesto Junior College and, with the aid of a small scholarship and several part-time jobs, attended the University of California at Berkeley. Always interested in

poetry, she signed up for a creative writing class, but was rejected. Although this considerably dampened her hopes of becoming a writer, she continued her English studies and earned a B.A. degree in 1948. Following a trip to Europe financed with secretarial work, Trivelpiece decided to enter the field of copywriting. She worked as an advertising copywriter for several companies in San Francisco and one in New York during the 1950s, and continued to write poetry on the side.

Trivelpiece has since produced novels, short fiction, and poetry, including three young adult novels set in California: *Dur-*

ing Water Peaches (Lippincott, 1979), *In Love and in Trouble* (Pocket Books, 1981), and *Trying Not to Love You* (Archway, 1985). As Hannah K. Marks, she wrote a novel entitled *Triad* (Pocket Books, 1980). Her short fiction has been published in periodicals such as *Denver Quarterly* and *Western Humanities Review,* and her poetry collection, *Legless in Flight* (Woolmer/Brotherson, 1978), was nominated for the William Carlos Williams Award. Trivelpiece is working on several projects, among them a young adult novel, *The Girl Is Lost;* an adult mystery, *My Father Sang That Song;* and a new collection of poems. *Home and office:* 23 Rocklyn Court, Corte Madera, Calif. 94925.

WARREN, Cathy

BRIEF ENTRY: Teacher and author of books for children. A former student at the University of St. Thomas in Houston, Tex., Warren teaches creative arts at the Children's Schoolhouse, a parent cooperative preschool in Davidson, N.C. She is also the author of three picture books, beginning with *The Ten-Alarm Camp-Out* (Lothrop, 1983), illustrated by Steven Kellogg. According to *School Library Journal,* Warren "cleverly weaves number concepts into her lighthearted selection" that follows the misadventures of Mama Armadillo and her nine offspring. *Booklist* agreed, noting that her "able storytelling helps pave the way" for "hilarious detail and sparkling color as only Kellogg can deliver." In *Victoria's ABC Adventure* (Lothrop, 1984), Warren teams up with illustrator Patience Brewster to create what *Publishers Weekly* called a "rousing adventure with enchanting pictures in summer-bright colors . . . a dazzler, brimful of fun." Letters of the alphabet are highlighted as Mamma Snake gives names to each of her twenty-six newborn daughters. Warren's third book, *Fred's Day* (Lothrop, 1984), explores a small black child's first day at nursery school and features illustrations by Pat Cummings.

WARREN, Elizabeth Avery   1916-
(Betsy Warren)

PERSONAL: Born January 27, 1916, in St. Louis, Mo.; daughter of Albert James (a coal merchant) and Ethel (Mitchell) Avery; married William Warren (news editor of *American Statesman*), March 18, 1942; children: William, Stephen, Mark, Melissa. *Education:* Miami University, Oxford, Ohio, B.S., 1937. *Politics:* Republican. *Religion:* Presbyterian. *Home:* 2409 Dormarion St., Austin, Tex. 78703.

CAREER: Teacher of organ and piano and free-lance artist, mainly as illustrator for children's books. Westminster Presbyterian Church, Austin, Tex., organist, 1951—. *Awards, honors:* Texas Institute of Letters Award, 1971, for *Indians Who Lived in Texas.*

WRITINGS—Under name Betsy Warren: *The Donkey Sat Down,* Steck, 1955; *Make a Joyful Noise,* Augsburg, 1963; *Papacito and His Family* (self-illustrated), Steck, 1969; *Indians Who Lived in Texas* (self-illustrated), Steck, 1970; *The Queen Cat,* Steck, 1972; *Let's Remember . . . Indians of Texas* (self-illustrated), Hendrick-Long, 1981; *Let's Remember When Texas Belonged to Spain* (self-illustrated), Hendrick-Long, 1982; *Texas in Historic Sites and Symbols* (self-illustrated), Hendrick-Long, 1982; *Let's Remember When Texas Was a Republic* (self-illustrated), Hendrick-Long, 1983; *Let's Remember Texas, the Twenty-Eighth State,* Hendrick-Long, 1984; *Twenty Texans, Historic Lives for Young Readers,* Hendrick-Long, 1985.

ELIZABETH AVERY WARREN

Illustrator; under name Betsy Warren: Louise K. Wilcox and Gordon E. Burks, *What Is Money,* Steck, 1959; Ruth Nordlie, *A Dog for Susie,* Childrens Press, 1960; Elsa Posell, *The True Book of Dogs,* Childrens Press, 1960; E. Posell, *The True Book of Horses,* Childrens Press, 1961; Robert L. Gilstrap, *Ten Texas Tales,* Steck, 1963; Eleanor Eisenberg, *The Pretty House That Found Happiness,* Steck, 1964, revised edition, 1974; Natalie Miller, *The Story of the Liberty Bell,* Children's Press, 1965; Dorothy E. Prince, *Speedy Gets Around,* Steck, 1965; Joan Potter Elwart, *Daisy Tells,* Steck, 1966; Doris J. Chaconas, *A Hat for Lilly,* Steck, 1967; Anne M. Halladay, *Secrets of White Owl,* Steck, 1967; David P. Butts, *Watermelon,* Steck, 1968; J. P. Elwart, *Right Foot, Wrong Foot,* Steck, 1968; Illa Podendorf, *The True Book of Spiders,* Childrens Press, 1972; Noel Grisham, *Buffalo and Indians on the Great Plains,* Eakin Publications, 1985.

WORK IN PROGRESS: Two books, *Wildflower Legends* and *Wilderness Walkers: Early Naturalists in Texas.*

The love of learning, the sequestered nooks,
And all the sweet serenity of books.
                              —Henry Wadsworth Longfellow

WARREN, Robert Penn 1905-

PERSONAL: Born April 24, 1905, in Guthrie, Ky.; son of Robert Franklin (a businessman) and Anna Ruth (Penn) Warren; married Emma Brescia, September 12, 1930 (divorced, 1950); married Eleanor Clark (a writer), December 7, 1952; children: (second marriage) Rosanna Phelps, Gabriel Penn. *Education:* Vanderbilt University, B.A. (summa cum laude), 1925; University of California, Berkeley, M.A., 1927; Yale University, graduate study, 1927-28; Oxford University, B.Litt., 1930. *Politics:* Democrat. *Home:* 2495 Redding Rd., Fairfield, Conn. 06430; and Vermont. *Agent:* Owen Laster, William Morris Agency, 1350 Avenue of the Americas, New York, N.Y. 10019. *Office:* Yale University, New Haven, Conn. 06520.

CAREER: Southwestern Presbyterian University (now Southwestern at Memphis), Memphis, Tenn., assistant professor of English, 1930-31; Vanderbilt University, Nashville, Tenn., acting assistant professor, 1931-34; Louisiana State University, Baton Rouge, assistant professor, 1934-36, associate professor, 1936-42; University of Minnesota, Minneapolis, professor of English, 1942-50; Yale University, New Haven, Conn., professor of playwrighting in School of Drama, 1950-56, professor of English, 1961-73, professor emeritus, 1973—. Visiting lecturer, State University of Iowa, 1941; Jefferson Lecturer, National Endowment for the Humanities, 1974. Staff member of writers conferences, University of Colorado, 1936, 1937, and 1940, and Olivet College, 1940. Consultant in poetry, Library of Congress, 1944-45. *Member:* American Academy of Arts and Letters (member of board), Academy of American Poets (chancellor), American Academy of Arts and Sciences, American Philosophical Society, Modern Language Association (honorary fellow), Century Club (New York).

ROBERT PENN WARREN

AWARDS, HONORS: Rhodes Scholar, Oxford University, 1928-30; Caroline Sinkler Prize, Poetry Society of South Carolina, 1936, 1937, and 1938; Levinson Prize, *Poetry* magazine, 1936; Houghton Mifflin literary fellowship, 1936; Guggenheim fellowship, 1939-40 and 1947-48; Shelley Memorial Prize, 1942, for *Eleven Poems on the Same Theme;* Pulitzer Prize for fiction, 1947, for *All the King's Men;* Southern Prize, 1947; Robert Meltzer Award, Screenwriters Guild, 1949; Union League Civic and Arts Foundation Prize, *Poetry* magazine, 1953; Sidney Hillman Award, 1957, Edna St. Vincent Millay Memorial Award, American Poetry Society, 1958, National Book Award, 1958, and Pulitzer Prize for poetry, 1958, all for *Promises: Poems, 1954-1956;* Irita Van Doren Award, *New York Herald Tribune,* 1965, for *Who Speaks for the Negro?;* Bollingen Prize in poetry, Yale University, 1967, for *Selected Poems: New and Old, 1923-1966;* National Endowment for the Arts Grant, 1968.

Van Wyck Brooks award for poetry, National Medal for Literature, and Henry A. Bellaman Prize, all 1970, all for *Audubon: A Vision;* award for literature, University of Southern California, 1973; Golden Rose Trophy, New England Poetry Club, 1975; Emerson-Thoreau Medal, American Academy of Arts and Sciences, 1975; Copernicus Prize, American Academy of Poets, 1976; Wilma and Robert Messing Award, 1977; Pulitzer Prize for poetry, 1979, for *Now and Then: Poems, 1976-1978;* Harriet Monroe Award for poetry, 1979, for *Selected Poems: 1923-1975;* MacArthur Foundation fellowship, 1980; Common Wealth Award for Literature, 1980; Hubbell Memorial Award, Modern Language Association, 1980; Connecticut Arts Council award, 1980; Presidential Medal of Freedom, 1980; National Book Critics Circle poetry award nomination, 1980, and American Book Award nomination, 1981, both for *Being Here: Poetry, 1977-1980; Los Angeles Times* poetry prize nomination, 1982, for *Rumor Verified: Poems, 1979-1980;* named the first poet laureate of the United States by the Library of Congress, 1986.

Recipient of honorary degrees from University of Louisville, 1949, Kenyon College, 1952, University of Kentucky, 1955, Colby College, 1956, Swarthmore College, 1958, Yale University, 1959, Bridgeport University, 1965, Fairfield University, 1969, Wesleyan University, 1970, Harvard University, 1973, Southwestern at Memphis, 1974, University of the South, 1974, University of New Haven, 1974, Johns Hopkins University, 1977, Monmouth College, 1979, New York University, 1983, and Oxford University, 1983.

WRITINGS—Poetry; published by Random House, except as indicated: *Thirty-Six Poems,* Alcestis Press, 1935; *Eleven Poems on the Same Theme,* New Directions, 1942; *Selected Poems: 1923-1943,* Harcourt, 1944; *Brother to Dragons: A Tale in Verse and Voices,* 1953, revised edition published as *Brother to Dragons: A Tale in Verse and Voices—A New Version,* 1979; *Promises: Poems, 1954-1956,* 1957; *You, Emperors and Others: Poems, 1957-1960,* 1960; *Selected Poems: New and Old, 1923-1966,* 1966; *Incarnations: Poems, 1966-1968,* 1968; *Audubon: A Vision,* 1969; *Or Else, Poem: Poems, 1968-1974,* 1974; *Selected Poems, 1923-1975,* 1976; *Now and Then: Poems, 1976-1978,* 1978; *Being Here: Poetry, 1977-1980,* 1980; *Rumor Verified: Poems, 1979-1980,* 1981; *Chief Joseph of the Nez Perce,* 1983.

Fiction; novels, except as indicated; published by Random House, except as indicated: *Night Rider,* Houghton, 1939, reprinted, Vintage Books, 1979, abridged edition, edited and introduced by George Mayberry, New American Library, 1950; *At Heaven's Gate,* Harcourt, 1943, reprinted, Random House, 1959, abridged edition, edited and introduced by Mayberry,

New American Library, 1949; *All the King's Men* (also see below), Harcourt, 1946, reprinted, Buccaneer, 1981; *Blackberry Winter* (novelette), Cummington Press, 1946; *The Circus in the Attic, and Other Stories* (short stories), Harcourt, 1947, reprinted, 1968; *World Enough and Time*, 1950, reprinted, Vintage Books, 1979; *Band of Angels*, 1955; *The Cave*, 1959; *The Gods of Mount Olympus* (adaptations of Greek myths for young readers), 1959; *Wilderness: A Tale of the Civil War*, 1961; *Flood: A Romance of Our Time*, 1964; *Meet Me in the Green Glen*, 1971; *A Place to Come To*, 1977.

Nonfiction; published by Random House, except as indicated: *John Brown: The Making of a Martyr*, Payson & Clarke, 1929, reprinted, Scholarly Press, 1970; (with others) *I'll Take My Stand: The South and the Agrarian Tradition*, Harper, 1930; (contributor) Herbert Agar and Allen Tate, editors, *Who Owns America?: A New Declaration of Independence*, Houghton, 1936; (author of critical essay) Samuel Taylor Coleridge, *The*

Rime of the Ancient Mariner, illustrated by Alexander Calder, Reynal & Hitchcock, 1946, reprinted, Folcroft, 1971; *Segregation: The Inner Conflict in the South*, 1956; *Remember the Alamo!*, 1958; *Selected Essays*, 1958; *How Texas Won Her Freedom: The Story of Sam Houston and the Battle of San Jacinto* (booklet), San Jacinto Museum of History, 1959; *The Legacy of the Civil War: Meditations on the Centennial*, 1961; *Who Speaks for the Negro?*, 1965; *A Plea in Mitigation: Modern Poetry and the End of an Era* (lecture), Wesleyan College, 1966; *Homage to Theodore Dreiser*, 1971; *Democracy and Poetry*, Harvard University Press, 1975; (contributor) *A Time to Hear and Answer: Essays for the Bicentennial Season*, University of Alabama Press, 1977; *Jefferson Davis Gets His Citizenship Back* (essay), University of Kentucky Press, 1980.

With Cleanth Brooks: (Editors with John T. Purser) *An Approach to Literature*, Louisiana State University Press, 1936, 5th edition, Prentice-Hall, 1975; (editors) *Understanding Po-*

(From the movie "All the King's Men," winner of several Academy Awards, one of which went to Broderick Crawford [center] for Best Actor, and one to Mercedes McCambridge [left] for Best Supporting Actress. Produced by Columbia Pictures Corp., 1950.)

(Jacket illustration "A Place to Come To" by Stanley Wyatt from *Robert Penn Warren: A Collection of Critical Essays,* edited by Richard Gray.)

etry: An Anthology for College Students, Holt, 1938, 4th edition, 1976; (editors) *Understanding Fiction,* Crofts, 1943, 2nd edition, Appleton-Century-Crofts, 1959, shortened version of 2nd edition published as *Scope of Fiction,* 1960, 3rd edition published under original title, Prentice-Hall, 1979; *Modern Rhetoric,* Harcourt, 1949, published as *Fundamentals of Good Writing: A Handbook of Modern Rhetoric,* 1950, 2nd edition published under original title, 1958, 4th edition, 1979; (editors) *An Anthology of Stories from the Southern Review,* Louisiana State University Press, 1953; (and R.W.B. Lewis) *American Literature: The Makers and the Making,* two volumes, St. Martin's, 1974.

Plays: "Proud Flesh" (in verse), produced in Minneapolis, Minn., 1947, revised prose version produced in New York City, 1948; (with Erwin Piscator) *Blut auf dem Mond: Ein Schauspiel in drei Akten* (adaptation of Warren's novel *All the King's Men;* produced in 1947, produced in Dallas, Tex., as "Willie Stark: His Rise and Fall," 1958, produced on Broadway, 1959), Lechte, 1956; *All the King's Men* (adaptation of Warren's novel of same title; produced at the Dramatic Workshop of the New School, New York City, 1948; produced Off-Broadway at East 74th St. Theatre; musical version by Vinette Carroll, Urban Arts Corps, 1974), Random House, 1960; *Ballad of a Sweet Dream of Piece: An Easter Charade* (produced in New York City at Cathedral of St. John the Divine), music by Alexei Haieff, Pressworks, 1981.

Editor: *A Southern Harvest: Short Stories by Southern Writers,* Houghton, 1937, reprinted, N. S. Berg, 1972; (with Albert

Erskine) *Short Story Masterpieces,* Dell, 1954, 2nd edition, 1958; (with Erskine) *Six Centuries of Great Poetry,* Dell, 1955; (with Erskine) *A New Southern Harvest,* Bantam, 1957; (with Allen Tate) Denis Devlin, *Selected Poems,* Holt, 1963; *Faulkner: A Collection of Critical Essays,* Prentice-Hall, 1966; *Randall Jarrell, 1914-1965,* Farrar, Straus, 1967; *John Greenleaf Whittier's Poetry: An Appraisal and a Selection,* University of Minnesota Press, 1971; *Selected Poems of Herman Melville,* Random House, 1971; *Katherine Anne Porter: A Collection of Critical Essays,* Prentice-Hall, 1979.

Contributor to numerous publications, including *Virginia Quarterly Review, Southern Review, Mademoiselle, Sewanee Review, New Republic, Poetry, American Review, Harvard Advocate, Nation, American Scholar, New York Times Book Review, Holiday, Fugitive, Botteghe Oscure, Yale Review,* and *Saturday Review.* Co-founding editor, *Fugitive,* 1922-25; founder and editor, with Cleanth Brooks, *Southern Review,* 1935-42; advisory editor, *Kenyon Review,* 1938-61.

ADAPTATIONS—Movies, except as noted: "All the King's Men," starring Broderick Crawford, Joanne Dru, John Ireland, John Derek, and Mercedes McCambridge, Columbia Pictures, 1950; "Band of Angels," starring Clark Gable, Yvonne DeCarlo, Sidney Poitier, and Efrem Zimbalist, Jr., Warner Brothers, 1957; "All the King's Men" (two-part television drama) was presented on Kraft Television Theatre, NBC-TV, 1958; "Willie Stark" (musical drama based on *All the King's Men*) was performed by the Houston Grand Opera, 1981, and broadcast on PBS-TV, 1984.

SIDELIGHTS: **April 24, 1905.** "To begin at the beginning, I was born at 7 A.M. . . . in Guthrie, in southern Kentucky, a town which has had about the same number of inhabitants—1,500, more or less—ever since I can remember.

"The country around, part of the Cumberland Valley, is a mixed country, fine rolling farmland breaking here and there into barrens, but with nice woodlands and plenty of water, a country well adapted to the proper pursuits of boyhood. The streams seem somewhat shrunken now and the woodlands denuded of their shadowy romance, but certain spots there and farther west, where I used to spend my summers on my grandfather's farm, are among my most vivid recollections.

"I recollect that grandfather very vividly, too—already an old man when I knew him, a Confederate veteran, a captain of cavalry who had ridden with Forrest, given to discussing the campaigns of Napoleon and, as well, of the immortal Nathan Bedford and to quoting bits of Byron and Scott and compositions like 'The Turk Lay in the Guarded Tent.' His daughters used to say that he was 'visionary,' by which they meant he was not practical. No doubt, in their sense, they were right. But in quite another sense, he was, I suppose, 'visionary' to me, too, looming much larger than life, the living symbol of the wild action and romance of the past. He was, whatever his own small part in great events may have been, 'history.' And I liked history. That was what my own father usually selected when he read aloud to his children." [Floyd C. Watkins and John T. Hiers, editors, *Robert Penn Warren Talking: Interviews 1950-1978,* Random House, 1980.[1]]

Attended public school in Guthrie and Clarksville, Kentucky. "Fortunately, that was before public education had suffered most of its present improvements, and so several years of Latin, at least two years of French, and four years of English literature were required in high school. One even had to do term papers on things like 'Lycidas'—the first poem (after

(From the movie "All the King's Men," starring Broderick Crawford, Mercedes McCambridge, and John Ireland. Copyright 1950 by Columbia Pictures Corp.)

(From the movie "Band of Angels," starring Clark Gable, Yvonne de Carlo, and Sidney Poitier. Copyright © 1957 by Warner Brothers Pictures, Inc.)

'Horatius at the Bridge,' at age six)—that I remember falling in love with, without at all understanding it.

"My family was quite bookish, and my father had the Victorian habit of reading to the children an hour before dinner. Mostly Greek and Roman history (in books adapted for children) and poems. He was very fond of poetry. I had lessons five nights a week under supervision.

"All my summers were spent on my maternal grandfather's remote farm. He was great company for a boy, full of tales of his own adventurous life, a reader of history, a head full of tales of poetry."

1921. "I had finished my original high school, but was too young for Annapolis, which was my goal. Then (just before or just after, I forget which), an accident prevented my taking an appointment, and so I went (at the age of sixteen) to Vanderbilt University, starting out to study chemistry, but quickly finding teachers and friends who were already making names for themselves as writers. Their influence and superlative teaching in English quickly switched my interest to writing, chiefly poetry. (I came to fiction rather late.)

"As a boy I spent a lot of time with one or two friends wandering the woods, and alone, read a great deal and tried to

paint birds and animals. No talent. Spent the summer when I was sixteen, before going to Vanderbilt, toting a Springfield rifle all around Fort Knox in the ROTC and CMTC camp, and fighting a sham battle. Which I thought fine, since nobody shot me. That ended my military career."

1925. "I went to school . . . by great good fortune, to Vanderbilt University. For this was the time of the Fugitives at Vanderbilt, a group of poets and arguers—including John Crowe Ransom, Donald Davidson, Allen Tate, Merrill Moore—and I imagine that more of my education came from those sessions than from the classroom. But aside from the Fugitives, writing poetry was almost epidemic at the university, and even an all-Southern center on the football team did some very creditable lyrics of a Housmanesque wistfulness.

"After Vanderbilt, graduate work at the University of California, Yale and Oxford (Rhodes Scholar). During those years I had been publishing a good deal of poetry in *The New Republic* and similar magazines, and in my last year at Oxford, at the invitation of Paul Rosenfeld, I did a novelette for *The American Caravan*. It is called *Prime Leaf*."[1] Warren found a "real need to write" from the time of his sophomore or junior year in college.

1928-1930. Lived in England and Paris while studying at Oxford University. "... I saw practically nothing of England during the years I was in England—I was always in France! I had friends who were in Paris and living on the Left Bank, the Tates and others, and they were great pals with Fitzgerald and Hemingway and the whole gang. So I fell right into that American group from the first meal in Paris on though I did go down to the Riviera for some weeks to swim. . . .

". . . It was a delightful time and a very romantic time for me. Another old friend was there, a young man who, as a student at Vanderbilt, was almost a one-man Left Bank. Many an evening he gave what amounted to seminars to friends—chiefly in Baudelaire. Tate's translations of Baudelaire came out of such evenings. . . .

"It's hard to say *what* effect that period had on me. For one thing you saw literature being written by people. In a strange way it was a projection of undergraduate Vanderbilt. I wasn't imitating the Left Bank people any more there than I was before or after. You're bound to be affected by a world you're growing up into, but I also kept one foot in Todd County, Kentucky, all the time."

1929. First book, *John Brown: The Making of a Martyr,* published. The following year, *I'll Take My Stand,* a collaborative book in which John Crowe Ransom, Allen Tate, Donald Davidson and Warren pleaded for a return to Southern country living. The group became known as the "Agarians." ". . . On the matter of what the Agarians stood for—as I look back, I see two sets of things, negatives and positives. And I think we were right on one set of those and very ignorant on the other. We were right on man and nature—the problems run to nature, not to man. Things have new names now. Ecology and such. People talk a great deal about man and nature—philosophers, hippies, retreats—but do they see the base? Of course, we didn't invent it either, but we had an early version of it—arrived at through experience, personal experience and Thomas Jefferson. It was the broad general idea of man's place in nature, his relationship to the whole natural world. . . .''[1]

Began a life-long career as an English teacher, teaching first as an assistant professor at Southwestern College in Memphis, Tennessee. "There are very fundamental compensations in teaching if you're in the right kind of place and have the right kind of students.

"I think the academic process, although on one side it has its comic aspects, on the other, produces truly profound and humanistic people who serve as a sort of buffer against the jittery fashionable kind of thing. A university has the failures and defects of institutions, just like government or the family or anything else. But I do think it gives certain perspectives in its better reaches that you'd not get if you were outside. The question doesn't come up in teaching, but it does in writing—whether it is a worthwhile activity: Is it really something to do? Is it a serious thing for a grown-up man to do? That sort of questioning today blanks out a lot of fellows.''[1]

1935. First collection of poetry published. ". . . Poetry is an exploration; the process of writing is an exploration. You may dimly envisage what a poem will be when you start it, but only as you wrangle through the process do you know your own meanings. In one way, it's a way of knowing what kind of poem you can write. And in finding that you find out yourself—I mean a lot about yourself. . . . I mean in the sense of what you can make available, poetically, is clearly something that refers to all of your living in very indirect and complicated ways. But you know more about yourself, not in a psychoanalytic way, but in another way of having dealt with yourself in a process. The poem is a way of knowing what kind of a

person you can be, getting your reality shaped a little bit better. And it's a way of living, and not a parlor trick even in its modest reaches; I mean, the most modest kind of effort that we make is a way of living.''[1]

1939. First novel, *Night Rider,* published. ". . . That isn't a historical novel. The events belonged to my early childhood. I remember the troops coming in when martial law was declared in that part of Kentucky. When I wrote the novel I wasn't thinking of it as history. For one thing, the world it treated still, in a way, survived. You could still talk to the old men who had been involved. In the 1930's I remember going to see a judge down in Kentucky—he was an elderly man then, a man of the highest integrity and reputation—who had lived through that period and who by common repute had been mixed up in it—his father had been a tobacco grower. He got to talking about that period in Kentucky. He said, 'Well, I won't say who was and who wasn't mixed up in some of those things, but I will make one observation: I have noticed that the sons of those who were opposed to getting a fair price for tobacco ended up as either bootleggers or brokers.' But he was an old-fashioned kind of guy, for whom bootlegging and brokerage looked very much alike. Such a man didn't look 'historical' thirty years ago. Now he looks like the thigh bone of a mastodon.

"I think I ought to say that behind *Night Rider* and my next novel, *At Heaven's Gate,* there was a good deal of the shadow not only of the events of that period but of the fiction of that period. I am more aware of that fact now than I was then. Of course, only an idiot could have not been aware that he was trying to write a novel about, in one sense, 'social justice' in *Night Rider* or, for that matter, *At Heaven's Gate.* But in some kind of a fumbling way I was aware, I guess, of trying to find the dramatic rub of the story at some point a little different from and deeper than the point of dramatic rub in some of the then current novels. But what I want to emphasize is the fact that I was fumbling rather than working according to plan and already arrived-at convictions. When you start any book, you don't know what, ultimately, your issues are. You try to write to find them. You're fiddling with the stuff, hoping to make sense, whatever kind of sense you can make.

"It never crossed my mind when I began writing fiction that I could write about anything except life in the South. It never crossed my mind that I knew about anything else; know, that is, at the level you know something to write about it. Nothing else ever nagged you enough to stir the imagination. But I stumbled into fiction rather late.

". . . When you try to write a book, even objective fiction, you have to write from the inside, not the outside—the inside of yourself—you have to find what's there—you can't predict it, just dredge for it, and hope you have something to work the dredging. That isn't 'confession'—that's just trying to use whatever the Lord lets you lay hand to. And of course you have to have common sense enough and structural sense enough to know what is relevant. You don't choose a story, it chooses you. You get together with that story somehow . . . you're stuck with it. There certainly is some reason it attracted you and you're writing it trying to find out that reason; justify, get at that reason. I can always look back and remember the exact moment when I encountered the germ of any story I wrote—a clear flash. . . .''[1]

Besides books and poetry, Warren also wrote reviews, which helped to financially support him. ". . . Every five dollars meant something for several years there, and reviewing was the way to get the five dollars. Now sonnets could get you as much as ten dollars, but it took a long time to write a sonnet. More often it got you fired!

"... In a classroom you are stuck with the idea of a point you are trying to put across to persuade your listeners. When you're trying to write a review, it's usually to make sense of the thing for yourself. The emphasis is different—at least it was for me. Writing about a poem for a review or for an essay, like on 'The Rime of the Ancient Mariner' or the Melville thing, I'm trying to make sense to myself; and as a textbook operation, the classroom is different. You have a fixed audience for a special purpose. That makes it different.

"Writing poems or novels I'm trying basically to make the thing right, put it that way—to create the thing as it should be, as I want it to be, as I hope it will be, rather than trying to think of how many copies it'll sell, or whom I'm writing for. You're bound to have a few people in mind that you respect, whom you know well, whose opinions mean something to you, who are there somehow as a possible audience. But that small, little bitty audience is all that you have to think about—that's my experience anyway. You want to make a thing that works, put it that way. How do you know whether it works? You don't know until you see it work on people. But you have to go with the nature of the thing in the process of writing the thing, it seems to me. It carries its own logic." ["Robert Penn Warren," *Conversations with Writers*, Gale, 1977.[2]]

1947. Won his first Pulitzer Prize for fiction for *All the King's Men*. His most celebrated political novel was made into a

movie in 1949. "... Poetry was my *central* interest for many years, up until the middle 1940's. I read it all the time and worked at it all the time, and fiction was definitely a secondary interest. Of course, when you are in the middle of a novel it *can't* be secondary, it becomes your life for a year or so. But behind this, the novels I was writing, came the notion that somehow they might be poems: the first conception of them. *All the King's Men* started as a verse play, ... and the other novels had very much the same background of feeling—came out of a sense that they might *be* poems if one wrote long poems like *that*. So the composition of novels didn't feel like a break between prose and poetry. Of course, there are obviously *great* differences, but they are tied to the poetic interest or commitment, or whatever you should call it, in a very definite way.

"Now, something happened about 1945. I got so I could not finish a short poem. I wrote, started many over that period of years. I never finished one—I lost the capacity for finishing a short poem. I'd write five lines, ten lines, twenty lines—it would die on me. I lost my sense of it. ..."[1]

1953. "... Some little time after I had finished *Brother to Dragons*, I felt a whole new sense of poetry. I felt freer than I had felt before. The narrative sense began to enter the short poem—as a germ, that is. ..."[1]

1958. Awarded the Edna St. Vincent Millay Memorial Award from the American Poetry Society, the National Book Award, and his second Pulitzer Prize for poetry, all for *Promises: Poems, 1954-1956*. "In general ... if a man's work does not

(From the 1981 Houston Grand Opera production of "Willie Stark," based on the novel *All the King's Men,* starring Timothy Nolen. Broadcast on PBS-TV in 1984.)

(From the stage production of "All the King's Men," presented by the New School's Dramatic Workshop [New York] in 1948.)

deliver something, there is no discussion about it that is going to make it deliver. Now, discussion, or background information, can sometimes make it possible to go beyond what had been written in the work. But you can't simply talk a good game of bridge; you have to *play* the game of bridge. Neither your intentions nor the theoretical assumptions behind your work are really relative to the work, in one sense. The work has to deliver itself. So you can't undertake to apologize for your work. All work does need context to be fully understood. But context doesn't necessarily make the work any better. It may lead to fuller understanding, but it may lead to a fuller understanding of the errors of your work, the failures of your work.

"... The books that I have written, for better or for worse, are a record of the various kinds of images of man that I have had at different times. Of course, I have changed my notions, or at least changed my feelings about my notions along the way.

"And this leads me to another point. I should think that, in most cases, anyway—I don't want to be dogmatic about this—the process of writing the novel or the poem is a process of trying to find out what the writer thinks. He is not working deductively from a highly articulated image, a careful scheme of values; he is trying to find the values, find the ideas, by a process of trial and error, as it were. Life is a process of trial and error about our own values. We may have certain assumptions about our values. We do have them. But at a certain age, say twenty-one, we feel one way; by the time we reach thirty-one, we feel quite different. Our ideas have changed. They may be more firmly established by experience; they may be completely blown up by experience. Certainly, they won't be the same; they can't be the same. They will have gone through, to a greater or lesser degree, the test of experience. They can't be the same after just a little bit of living."[1]

1959. Adapted Greek myths for young readers. Warren wrote several books for children for Random House at the request of Bennett Cerf. "He put a pistol to the heads of a lot of his authors when he decided to do a series of children's books. He said, 'You've got to write a child's book for me.' I just wrote those because of Bennett and his pistol. Fortunately it turned out that they were very salable."

About approaches to his writings, Warren commented: "The business of researching for a book strikes me as a sort of obscenity. What I mean is, researching for a book in the sense of trying to find a book to write. Once you are engaged by a subject, are in your book, have your idea, you may or may not want to do some investigating. But you ought to do it in the same spirit in which you'd take a walk in the evening air to think things over."

1970. *Audubon: A Vision* awarded the Van Wyck Brooks Award for poetry, the National Medal for Literature, and the Henry A. Bellman Prize. "*Audubon* started out to be a sort of narrative poem twenty years before I wrote the poem. I wrote another poem and gave up on it, miserable, because there's no narrative in *Audubon*, nothing to tell, except a whole thousand things. And so the poetry that became the little book called *Audubon* was written twenty years after I'd started serious work on a poem on Audubon. I didn't look at the manuscript at all, the whole manuscript, the time between. I just remembered one line one morning—'was not the lost Dauphin; was only'—and I started with that line, which wasn't the first line of the original one at all. I save all kinds of scraps of unfinished poems and poems that don't pan out; keep them for years. I go back now and then and read the old stuff, the

discards. Several times I've found some germ for a poem or some old line that starts a whole new poem. It's a kind of mine, something you have to mine later. Because a poem may be awful, but it may have one good line in it."

1979. Received his third Pulitzer Prize for poetry for *Now and Then: Poems, 1976-1978*. As a poet and novelist, Warren feels he has two obligations. "... One is not to lie. The other is to write as well as I can. You're trying, imaginatively, to set up a world that feels like truth to you. This is the way it really is. It must be that way. And you have to do it as well as you can. You're not going to whip out something worthwhile without feeling it through.

"I think your obligation begins at home, always, where you're trying to tell the truth as you see or feel it. And I'll make a remark on the side: I think that if more obligations began at home there would be fewer public troubles. If home truths were applied we'd have a great deal less trouble in the world." ["Eleanor Clark and Robert Penn Warren," Roy Newquist, *Conversations*, Rand McNally, 1967.[3]]

When asked to give advice to the young writer, Warren responded: "I'm not an advice-giver. I'm not even an advice-seeker. But I would above all, make him an honest man. If he's a genius, I suppose he can be a little crooked now and then. But anyone who wants to write is going to pay a price, a damned big price. The gamble is big. Anybody with common sense and a reasonably solid character and reasonably good health can make a comfortable living these days, but the aspiring writer has to put a lot more on the line. The gamble is bigger, and I suppose the reward can be bigger, too. If he's honest and he works, advice is beside the point. He'll merely do what he must do, and that is everything."[3]

1986. Named the first "poet laureate" of the United States. Warren's duties include opening the library season in October with a reading of his poetry, closing the season in May with a public lecture, advising the library on its literary programs and acquisition of literary material, and writing poetry for national ceremonies. "The best parts of a poem always come in bursts or in a flash. This has been said by many people—Frost said in a letter, 'My best poems are always my easiest.' My notion is this: that the poet is a hunter on the track of an unknown beast, and has only one shot in his gun. You don't know what the beast is, but when you see him, you've got to shoot him, and it has got to be instantaneous. You can labor on the pruning, and you can work at your technique, but you cannot labor the poem into being."[1]

Warren lives in Fairfield, Connecticut with his wife Eleanor Clark, who is also a writer. Throughout his long and distinguished career as a writer, poet, and teacher, he has received numerous prestigious awards, including the National Book Award, three Pulitzer Prizes, the Bollingen Prize, the National Medal for Literature, the Presidential Medal of Freedom, and is the recipient of over seventeen honorary degrees from universities and colleges. "I don't think about my audience when I'm working. This doesn't mean that the audience isn't important. It is, but not right then when I'm concerned with trying 'to make it right.' I've heard many writers say the same thing. Now, making it right, of course, means making your vision available to somebody. But if you see it's not being made available, if it's going off the rails, it's not because it isn't grasped by an audience but because the thing isn't right itself. You are your own audience, but because the thing you've written doesn't conform to what you think you wanted to express during the process, then it's wrong and you had better start over. No, I'm not saying what I mean. The question is

Robert Penn Warren with wife, Eleanor Clark. Photograph copyright © 1986 by Thomas Victor.

not whether the thing being done fails to conform to a preconceived notion. It is whether—and let me emphasize this—the thing being done is violating a logic implicit in the process of composing it. Or worse, because you have not discovered the internal logic."[1]

FOR MORE INFORMATION SEE—Books: John Bradbury, *The Fugitives*, University of North Carolina Press, 1958; Louise Cowan, *The Fugitive Group*, Louisiana State University Press, 1959; William Van O'Connor, editor, *Forms of Modern Fiction*, Indiana University Press, 1959; Malcolm Cowley, editor, *Writers at Work: The Paris Review Interviews*, Viking, 1959.

Leonard Casper, *Robert Penn Warren: The Dark and Bloody Ground*, University of Washington Press, 1960; Alfred Kazin, *Contemporaries*, Atlantic-Little, Brown, 1962; Cleanth Brooks, *The Hidden God*, Yale University Press, 1963; A. Walton Litz, editor, *Modern American Fiction: Essays in Criticism*, Oxford University Press, 1963; Louis D. Rubin, Jr., *Writers of the Modern South: The Faraway Country*, University of Washington Press, 1963; Charles H. Bohner, *Robert Penn Warren*, Twayne, 1964; Paul West, *Robert Penn Warren*, University of Minnesota Press, 1964; John L. Longley, Jr., editor, *Robert Penn Warren: A Collection of Critical Essays*, New York University Press, 1965; Roy Newquist, editor, *Conversations*, Rand McNally, 1967; James Dickey, *Babel to Byzantium*, Farrar, Straus, 1968.

Leslie Fiedler, *The Collected Essays of Fiedler*, Volume I, Stein & Day, 1971; *Contemporary Literary Criticism*, Gale, Volume I, 1973, Volume IV, 1975, Volume VI, 1976, Volume VIII, 1978, Volume X, 1979, Volume XIII, 1980, Volume XVIII, 1981; *Authors in the News*, Gale, Volume I, 1976; *Conversations with Writers*, Gale, 1977; Richard Gray, *The Literature of Memory: Modern Writers of the American South*, Johns Hopkins University Press, 1977; Victor H. Strandberg, *The Poetic Vision of Robert Penn Warren*, University Press of Kentucky, 1977; *Dictionary of Literary Biography*, Gale, Volume II: *American Novelists since World War II*, 1978, *Yearbook: 1980*, 1981; Gray, editor, *Robert Penn Warren: A Collection of Critical Essays*, Prentice-Hall, 1980; Floyd C. Watkins and John T. Hiers, editors, *Robert Penn Warren Talking: Interviews 1950-1978*, Random House, 1980; Neil Nakadate, editor, *Robert Penn Warren: Critical Perspectives*, University Press of Kentucky, 1981; Floyd C. Watkins, *Then and Now: The Personal Past in the Poetry of Robert Penn Warren*, University Press of Kentucky, 1982.

Periodicals: *Saturday Review of Literature*, August 17, 1946; *New York Times*, August 18, 1946, December 16, 1969, March 2, 1977, June 2, 1981, March 27, 1983, March 10, 1986; *San Francisco Chronicle*, August 18, 1946; *Nation*, August 24, 1946; *New Yorker*, August 24, 1946, December 29, 1980; *New Republic*, September 2, 1946; *Christian Science Monitor*, September 4, 1946; *Commonweal*, October 4, 1946; *Yale Review*, autumn, 1946; *Kenyon Review*, summer, 1948; *Saturday Review*, June 24, 1950, August 20, 1955, August, 1980; *New York Times Book Review*, June 25, 1950, January 9, 1977, November 2, 1980.

Sewanee Review, spring, 1970, spring, 1974, spring, 1975, summer, 1977, spring, 1979, summer, 1980; *Time*, August 18, 1975; *Parnassus: Poetry in Review*, fall/winter, 1975, summer, 1977, spring/summer, 1979; *London Magazine*, December, 1975/January, 1976; *Southern Review*, spring, 1976; *New Leader*, January 31, 1977; *Washington Post Book World*, March 6, 1977, October 22, 1978, September 30, 1979, August 31, 1980, October 4, 1981, June 26, 1983; *Hudson Review*, summer, 1977; *Virginia Quarterly Review*, summer, 1977;

Chicago Tribune, September 10, 1978; *Michigan Quarterly Review*, fall, 1978; *Chicago Tribune Book Review*, October 14, 1979, September 7, 1980, February 28, 1982.

Washington Post, May 2, 1980; *Newsweek*, August 25, 1980; *Los Angeles Times Book Review*, September 7, 1980, October 19, 1980, January 17, 1982; *Times Literary Supplement*, November 28, 1980, January 29, 1982; *Detroit News*, February 15, 1981; *Los Angeles Times*, March 19, 1981; *The Day* (New London, Conn.), February 2, 1986; *People Weekly*, March 17, 1986.

WATTS, Franklin (Mowry) 1904-1978

PERSONAL: Born June 11, 1904, in Sioux City, Iowa; died May 21, 1978, in New York, N.Y.; son of John Franklin (a minister) and Amanda (Mowry) Watts; married Helen Hoke (an editor), May 25, 1945. *Education:* Boston University, B.B.A., 1925.

CAREER: Book buyer for George Innes Co. and L. S. Ayers & Co., 1925-32; sales manager for the New York City publishing firms, Vanguard Press, Inc., 1932-34, Julian Messner, Inc., 1934-50, and Heritage Press, 1936-50; Franklin Watts, Inc. (publishers specializing in children's books), New York City, founder and president, 1942-70, vice-chairman, 1970-78; Franklin Watts Ltd. (a joint venture with Grolier publishers), London, England, founder and managing director, 1970-76; Frank Book Corporation, New York City, founder, 1976. A

FRANKLIN WATTS

director, Grolier Enterprises, Inc. Member of American Book Publishers Council and Government Book Program advisory committee; former member, U.S. Department of State international book projects and advisory committee. *Member:* Publishers Lunch Club.

WRITINGS: (Editor) *Voices of History,* F. Watts, 1941, 3rd edition, 1943; (editor) *The Complete Christmas Book,* F. Watts, 1958; *Let's Find Out about Christmas* (illustrated by Mary Ronin), F. Watts, 1967; *Let's Find Out about Easter,* F. Watts, 1969.

Published by Childrens Press: *Corn* (illustrated by Tom Dunnington), 1977; *Rice* (illustrated by Sam Shiromani), 1977; *Wheat* (illustrated by S. Shiromani), 1977; *Oranges,* 1978; *Peanuts,* 1978; *Tomatoes* (illustrated by Gene Sharp), 1978.

Editor, *Pocket Book Magazine,* 1954-56.

FOR MORE INFORMATION SEE—Obituaries: *New York Times,* May 23, 1978; *Publishers Weekly,* June 5, 1978.

WILD, Jocelyn   1941-

PERSONAL: Born October 21, 1941, in Mysore, India; daughter of Botha (a taxidermist) and Barbara (a photographer and artist; maiden name, Flaherty) Van Ingen; married Robin Ev-

ans Wild (an instructor of the mentally handicapped), July 22, 1963; children: Benjamin Daniel, Thomas Joseph. *Education:* Kings College, London, B.A. (with honors), 1963. *Home:* Lyes Farm, Barrington, near Ilminster, Somerset TA19 0JD, England.

CAREER: Author and illustrator of children's books.

WRITINGS—All written and illustrated with husband, Robin Wild; all fiction for children, except as indicated: *Little Pig and the Big Bad Wolf,* Heinemann, 1971, Coward, 1972; *The Mouse Who Stole a Zoo,* Coward, 1972; *Animals at Work* (nonfiction), Heinemann, 1973, published as *How Animals Work for Us,* Parents Magazine Press, 1974; *Dunmouse Monsters,* Heinemann, 1974, published as *Dunmousie Monsters,* Coward, 1975; *Monster Men and Beasts,* Heinemann, 1975; *Tiger Tree and Tyger Voyage,* Heinemann, 1976; *The Bears' ABC Book,* Lippincott, 1977; *The Bears' Counting Book,* Lippincott, 1978; *Spot's Dogs and the Alley Cats* (contains the stories "A Trip to the Sea," "A Day at the Fair," and "The Christmas Party"), Lippincott, 1979; *Spot's Dogs and the Kidnappers,* Lippincott, 1981; *Lady Agrippa's Unshuttable Caboodle Box,* Pavilion (London), 1984.

Illustrator: (With R. Wild) Aidan Chambers, *Fox Tricks* (fiction; based on Aesop's *Fables*), Heinemann, 1980.

Also contributor of illustrations to *Belles histoires* (title means "Lovely Stories"), Bayard Presse (Paris).

Robin and Jocelyn Wild with sons, Ben and Tom.

3
three beds

Those naughty bears bounced on the beds and hit each other with the pillows. ■ (From *The Bears' Counting Book* by Robin and Jocelyn Wild. Illustrated by Jocelyn Wild.)

WORK IN PROGRESS: Illustrations for *Belles histoires,* for Bayard Presse; *Illustrated Diary of Smallholder* (autobiographical; self-illustrated); series of short illustrated picture books about Florence and Eric—two little lambs—the first book entitled *Florence and Eric Take the Cake.*

SIDELIGHTS: ''I had no art training. I was influenced by my upbringing in India, by being in a family of naturalists, and by the encouragement of a mother who was a gifted artist. Artists whom I have always admired include cartoonists Ronald Searle and Steinberg; Rousseau; Indian Moghul painters; Thomas Bewick; and Hieronymus Bosch.

''My husband and I first thought about a career illustrating and writing children's books after I made a book for our son, aged one. We thought it was marvellous and were confident

They pulled out all the drawers and tried on some of the clothes. ■ (From *The Bears' Counting Book* by Robin and Jocelyn Wild. Illustrated by Jocelyn Wild.)

our future in children's books was assured. By pure luck we found a publisher, Heinemann, and worked for several years. But after awhile the need for a more regular income and a bigger one, to support ourselves and family and our property, forced my husband to look for other work, leaving me to continue writing and illustrating on my own. . . . After a period of great financial difficulty and no work, I am back doing children's books.

"When I am planning and thinking about a book, I do it entirely for myself, the publisher and the reader are not important to me at this stage. The book has to satisfy and entertain *me*. If it does, I know it will stand the scrutiny of others.

"We have generally worked in gouache with acrylic medium using a painterly technique. Lately we have been trying out crayon and pen, which involves fewer problems with printing and is much quicker. Curiously once a book is finished we immediately tend to lose interest in it, as we become absorbed in a new one.

"Ideas come fairly easily and any we think have a future are noted down. The ideas mainly come from our rural way of life, and animals play a large part in our books. We used to write for our children but now that they are leaving the picture book stage they are used as critics rather than an audience. The idea for a particular book is discussed at odd moments, then independently we work out very rough sketches and the story. We compare these, choosing the best, and constantly changing and developing them. Then we work out the roughs together, overlapping on different roles. The finished artwork is also done together, one leaving space for the other's work and pictures are passed backwards and forwards.

"We both feel that books for young children should offer an opportunity for quiet contemplation, away from the rush and pressure of the modern world. Ideally they should invite the child to study them at leisure and not spill their secrets at one quick flip through. We would like to do books with more and more detail so that the child can 'explore' them. We try to amuse but also like to feel there is some message woven into the story.

"So many of the beautifully produced books on the market now seem to appeal to the adult rather than the child, with a sophisticated technique that is too stylised for a child. We hope our books appeal firstly to children, that they will want to return to them and will remember them with affection."

HOBBIES AND OTHER INTERESTS: Gardening.

WILD, Robin (Evans)   1936-

PERSONAL: Born March 16, 1936, in Petersfield, U.K.; son of Reg (a grocer) and Gladys (Hawthorn) Wild; married Jocelyn Van Ingen (an author and illustrator), July 22, 1963; children: Benjamin Daniel, Thomas Joseph. *Education:* Received diploma in art from Worthing College of Art; received diploma in education from Manchester Teacher Training College. *Religion:* Church of England. *Home:* Lyes Farm, Barrington, near Ilminster, Somerset TA19 0JD, England.

CAREER: Instructor of the mentally handicapped. Former writer and illustrator of children's books. *Military service:* National Service, 1959-62.

WRITINGS—All written and illustrated with wife, Jocelyn Wild; all fiction for children, except as indicated: *Little Pig and the*

Big Bad Wolf, Heinemann, 1971, Coward, 1972; *The Mouse Who Stole a Zoo,* Coward, 1972; *Animals at Work* (nonfiction), Heinemann, 1973, published as *How Animals Work for Us,* Parents Magazine Press, 1974; *Dunmouse Monsters,* Heinemann, 1974, published as *Dunmousie Monsters,* Coward, 1975; *Monster Men and Beasts,* Heinemann, 1975; *Tiger Tree and Tyger Voyage,* Heinemann, 1976; *The Bears' ABC Book,* Lippincott, 1977; *The Bears' Counting Book,* Lippincott, 1978; *Spot's Dogs and the Alley Cats* (contains the stories "A Trip to the Sea," "A Day at the Fair," and "The Christmas Party"), Lippincott, 1979; *Spot's Dogs and the Kidnappers,* Lippincott, 1981; *Lady Agrippa's Unshuttable Caboodle Box,* Pavilion (London), 1984.

Illustrator: (With J. Wild) Aidan Chambers, *Fox Tricks* (fiction; based on Aesop's *Fables*), Heinemann, 1980.

WILSON, Christopher B.   1910(?)-1985

OBITUARY NOTICE: Born about 1910, in England; died in an automobile accident, October 3, 1985, near Waterford, Va. Educator, diplomat, and author of books for children, Wilson came to the United States in 1939 after graduating from Oxford University and teaching for a time at private schools in Britain. After settling in New York City, he accepted a position with the British Embassy there, and in 1941 he transferred to Washington, D.C., to direct an information service for British exporters. Wilson retired from the British Embassy in 1975. He was the author of children's books including *Hob Nob, Oliver at Sea, A Treasure Hunt,* and *Growing up with Daddy.*

FOR MORE INFORMATION SEE—Obituaries: *Washington Post,* October 7, 1985.

WILSON, Maurice (Charles John)   1914-

PERSONAL: Born March 15, 1914, in London, England; son of Charles Wilson; children: one son. *Education:* Attended Hastings School of Art, Royal College of Art, and Royal Academy. *Home:* 30 Woodland Way, Bidborough, Tunbridge Wells, Kent, England.

CAREER: Artist, author, and illustrator. Work has been exhibited at Royal Academy, Royal Institute of Painters in Water-colours, Society of Wildlife Artists, Royal Institute of Oil Painters, and Royal Society of Marine Artists. *Member:* Society of Wildlife Artists (vice-president), Tetropods Club, Thames Barge Sailing Club.

WRITINGS—All self-illustrated: *Just Monkeys,* Scribner, 1937; *Dogs* (juvenile), Penguin, 1946; *Coastal Craft,* N. Carrington, 1947; *Animals We Know,* Thomas Nelson, 1959; *Animals* (drawing book), Watson-Guptill, 1964; *Birds* (drawing book), Watson-Guptill, 1965; (with Barry Cox) *Prehistoric Animals* (juvenile), Lutterworth, 1976.

Illustrator; of interest to young people; all nonfiction, except as indicated: E. G. Boulenger, *Zoo Animals,* Penguin, 1948; David Seth Smith, *Zoo Birds,* Penguin, 1951; H. Mortimer Batten, *The Singing Forest* (storybook), W. Blackwood, 1955, Farrar, Straus, 1964; James Reeves, reteller, *Fables from Aesop,* Blackie & Son, 1961, Walck, 1962; Laurens Van der Post, *The Heart of the Hunter,* Hogarth, 1961; James Vance Marshall, *A River Ran Out of Eden* (fiction), Hodder & Stoughton, 1962, Morrow, 1963; Henry Gwynne Vevers, *Animals of the Arctic,* Bodley Head, 1964, McGraw-Hill, 1965;

Long ago, the Thule Eskimos used to hunt the huge Greenland whales, but these are nearly extinct. ■ (From *Eskimos* by Jill Hughes. Illustrated by Maurice Wilson.)

Felix Salten (pseudonym of Siegmund Salzmann), *Bambi: A Life in the Woods* (storybook; paperback), translated from the German by Whittaker Chambers, Knight Books, 1967 (Wilson was not associated with earlier or later editions); John Napier, *The Origins of Man*, Bodley Head, 1968, McGraw-Hill, 1969; Ben Masselink, *Green: The Story of a Caribbean Turtle's Struggle for Survival*, Little, Brown, 1969.

Eric John Barker and L. Williams, *First Interest in a Wider World* (textbook), 7 volumes, Ginn, 1972; E. J. Barker, *Deserts* (textbook), Ginn, 1972; E. J. Barker, *Hot Grasslands* (textbook), Ginn, 1972; Sandie Oram, *China Long Ago*, Macdonald & Co., 1972; (with Peter Duncan) Charles Higham, *The Earliest Farmers and the First Cities*, Cambridge University Press, 1974, Lerner, 1977; (with Jon Davis) George Beals, *The Quizzer Book about People*, Owlet Books, 1975; Frances Mann, *Oh Those Cats!* (textbook), Elek, 1975; (with Virginia Smith) F. W. Rawding, *The Buddha*, Cambridge University Press, 1975.

(With R. Coombs and D. Cordery) J. L. Hicks, *A Closer Look at Arctic Lands*, Hamish Hamilton, 1976, F. Watts, 1977; (with George Thompson) *A Closer Look at Plains Indians*, Hamish Hamilton, 1977, published as *Plains Indians*, Gloucester Press, 1978; Jill Hughes, *A Closer Look at Eskimos*, Hamish Hamilton, 1977, published as *Eskimos*, Gloucester Press, 1978; (with Tony Streek) Joyce Pope, *Ponies*, Scimitar, 1977; Adele Geras, *Beyond the Cross-Stitch Mountain*, Hamish Hamilton, 1978; Stephen Hugh-Jones, *A Closer Look at Amazonian Indians*, Hamish Hamilton, 1978, published as *Amazonian Indians*, Gloucester Press, 1979; (with Mike Woodhatch) Cathy Kilpatrick, *Birds of Prey*, Scimitar, 1978; Fidelity Lancaster, *The Bedouin*, Gloucester Press, 1978 (published in England as *A Closer Look at the Bedouin*, Hamish Hamilton, 1978); C. Everard Palmer, *A Dog Called Houdini* (fiction), Deutsch, 1978; Catherine Horton, *A Closer Look at Grasslands*, Gloucester Press, 1979; (with John Rignall) Henry Pluckrose, editor, *Birds*, Gloucester Press, 1979; (with Peter Barrett) Pluckrose, editor, *Horses*, Gloucester Press, 1979; (with Eric Tenney) Pluckrose, editor, *Lions and Tigers*, Gloucester Press, 1979; J. Hughes, *A Closer Look at Aborigines*, Hamish Ham-

ilton, 1979; J. Medawar, *Lifeclass*, Hamish Hamilton, 1980; Jane Heath, *Eskimos* (based on the 1978 edition by Jill Hughes), edited by H. Pluckrose, Gloucester Press, 1980; John Cunliffe, *The Daffiest Dog in the World*, Deutsch, 1980; J. Heath, *Plains Indians* (based on the 1978 edition by Christopher Davis), edited by Pluckrose, Gloucester Press, 1980; H. Pluckrose, editor, *Arctic Lands* (based on *A Closer Look at Arctic Lands* by J. L. Hicks), F. Watts, 1982; Rudyard Kipling, *The Jungle Book*, Schocken, 1984.

Other: Richard Carrington, *The Story of Our Earth*, Harper, 1956 (published in England as *A Guide to Earth History*, Chatto & Windus, 1956); Margery L.E. Fisher, compiler, *A World of Animals*, Brockhampton Press, 1962; Margaret Sharman, *Man, Civilization, and Conquest: From Prehistory to World Exploration*, Evans Brothers, 1971; Elizabeth Lee, selector, *A Quorum of Cats: An Anthology*, Elek, 1976 (Wilson was not associated with earlier edition).

All written by Doreen Tovey: *Cats in the Belfry*, Elek, 1957, Doubleday, 1958; *Cats in May*, Elek, 1959, published as *Cats in Cahoots*, Doubleday, 1960; *Donkey Work*, Elek, 1962, Doubleday, 1963; *Raining Cats and Donkeys*, M. Joseph, 1967, Norton, 1968; *The New Boy*, Norton, 1970; *Double Trouble*, Norton, 1972; *Making the Horse Laugh*, Norton, 1974; *The Coming of Saska*, St. Martin's, 1977; *A Comfort of Cats*, M. Joseph, 1979, St. Martin's, 1980.

WISLER, G(ary) Clifton 1950-

BRIEF ENTRY: Born May 15, 1950, in Oklahoma City, Okla. A teacher at Ben C. Jackson Middle School in Texas since 1974, Wisler writes juvenile western/adventure novels. Themes of Indians, the Civil War, hard times, and friendship recur in Wisler's books, which critics have noted as "suspenseful and involving." *Thunder on the Tennessee* (Lodestar, 1983), with its vividly recreated scenes of the Battle of Shiloh, won the Golden Spur Award for the Best Western Juvenile Book. In this story, sixteen-year-old Willie Delmar joins the Confederate army despite his father's efforts to dissuade him. He sees his first action at Shiloh and eventually watches his father and comrades fall under Northern gunfire. Willie's story continues in *The Trident Brand* (Doubleday, 1982) as he returns home after the war—only to be met by his ruthless, potentially murderous brother. Finally, *Buffalo Moon* (Lodestar, 1984), a companion novel to both *Thunder on the Tennessee* and *The Trident Brand*, tells of Willie's coming of age prior to his life as a soldier, during the summer he ran away from home to live with and learn the ways of a Comanche tribe.

Wisler's other works include *My Brother, the Wind* (Doubleday, 1979), featuring a mountain man named Bear who buys a nine-year-old boy from a band of Cheyennes and raises him as his son; *A Cry of Angry Thunder* (Doubleday, 1980), in which Johnny Whitelock and an Indian named Antelope Foot share their childhood together only to face each other in adversity as adults, during the battles of Black Kettle, Sand Creek, and the Little Big Horn; *Winter of the Wolf* (Elsevier/Nelson, 1980), a tale of friendship told in "campfire story" style; and *The Raid* (Lodestar, 1984), a chase-and-rescue adventure on the Texas frontier in the 1860s. Wisler, who earned a bachelor's of fine arts degree in journalism and a master's degree from Southern Methodist University, is a member of Western Writers of America. *Home:* 1806 Lyric Dr., Garland, Tex. 75040.

WORTH, Richard

BRIEF ENTRY: A native of Connecticut, Worth earned a master's degree in history from Trinity College. Producer of award-winning audiovisual programs, Worth has written educational materials and several sociological/historical books for young adults. *Poland: The Threat to National Renewal* (F. Watts, 1982) discusses the political history of the country, concentrating on Poland's struggles over the last thirty years. Ac-

cording to *School Library Journal, Israel and the Arab States* (F. Watts, 1983) is an "objective, concise, well researched and highly readable" work in which Worth surveys the history of Israel's tumultuous relations with her neighboring Arab states. Objective and informative, *The Third World Today* (F. Watts, 1983) provides an introductory overview to the Third World; problems such as economics, overpopulation and health care, and the relationship between the United States and Third World countries. *The American Family* (F. Watts, 1984) is an introduction to the family, how it has changed, and its impact on society. According to Worth, the family is "the most important institution in our lives." All four books have appended bibliographies and indexes. *Residence:* Fairfield, Conn.

ZERMAN, Melvyn Bernard   1930-

PERSONAL: Born July 10, 1930, in New York, N.Y.; son of Abraham (in real estate) and Ida (Belsky) Zirman; married Miriam Baron, September 14, 1952 (died January 9, 1985); children: Andrew, Jared, Lenore. *Education:* University of Michigan, B.A., 1952; Columbia University, M.A., 1953. *Politics:* Democrat. *Religion:* Jewish. *Home:* 110-37 68th Dr., Forest Hills, N.Y. 11375. *Office:* Limelight Editions, 118 East 30th St., New York, N.Y. 10016.

CAREER: Harper & Row Publishers, Inc., New York, N.Y., assistant to sales manager, 1959-64, sales department office manager, 1964-67, assistant director of sales, 1968-70, trade sales manager, 1970-77, administrative sales manager, 1977-79; Random House, Inc., New York, N.Y., administrative sales manager, 1979-83; Limelight Editions, New York, N.Y., founder, 1983—. *Awards, honors:* Freedom Foundation Award, 1981, for *Beyond a Reasonable Doubt: Inside the American Jury System*.

You have heard and seen all the evidence. The prosecution has rested its case and so, in turn, has the defense. ■ (From *Beyond a Reasonable Doubt: Inside the American Jury System* by Melvyn Bernard Zerman. Illustrated by John Caldwell.)

MELVYN BERNARD ZERMAN

WRITINGS—Nonfiction: *Call the Final Witness,* Harper, 1977; *Beyond a Reasonable Doubt: Inside the American Jury System* (young adult; illustrated by John Caldwell), Crowell, 1981; *Taking on the Press,* Crowell, 1986.

SIDELIGHTS: "In the almost-forgotten past I had thoughts of becoming a professional writer. Those thoughts were put aside for too many years until, in a very real sense, a subject discovered me. My experiences as a juror on a murder trial awakened a dormant ambition and eventually resulted in my first book. This in turn led to my being commissioned to write my second book. Now while still not my principal vocation, writing has become, by far, the source of my greatest personal satisfaction."

ZWINGER, Ann   1925-

PERSONAL: Born March 12, 1925, in Muncie, Ind.; daughter of William Thomas (an attorney) and Helen (Glass) Haymond; married Herman H. Zwinger (a photographer and pilot), June 18, 1952; children: Susan, Jane, Sara. *Education:* Wellesley College, B.A., 1946; Indiana University, M.A., 1950; additional graduate study at Radcliffe College, 1951-52. *Residence:* Colorado Springs, Colo. *Agent:* Marie Rodell-Frances Collin Literary Agency, 110 West 40th St., New York, N.Y. 10018.

CAREER: Smith College, Northampton, Mass., instructor in art history, 1950-51; Benet Hill Academy, Colorado Springs, Colo., instructor in art, 1963-66; currently director, American Electric Power Company, chairman, utility women's conference, 1985-88. Member of board of trustees, Colorado Springs School; member of board of directors, Friends of the Library, Penrose Public Library, Colorado Springs. *Member:* John Burroughs Memorial Association (director), Thoreau Society (president, 1982-84).

AWARDS, HONORS: Indiana Authors' Day Award, 1971, for nature and ecology writings; National Book Award nomination, 1972, for *Land above the Trees: A Guide to American Alpine Tundra;* John Burroughs Memorial Association Award and Friends of American Writers Award for nonfiction, 1976, for *Run, River, Run: A Naturalist's Journey Down One of the Great Rivers of the West;* D.H.L., Colorado College, 1976, and Carleton College, 1984; Alumnae Achievement Award, Wellesley College, 1977; Sara Chapman Francis Medal, Garden Club of America, 1977.

WRITINGS—Published by Harper, except as indicated: (Self-illustrated) *Beyond the Aspen Grove,* Random House, 1970; (with Beatrice Willard) *Land above the Trees: A Guide to American Alpine Tundra* (illustrated with photographs by husband, Herman H. Zwinger), 1972; (self-illustrated) *Run, River, Run: A Naturalist's Journey Down One of the Great Rivers of the West,* 1975; *Wind in the Rock,* 1978; (with Edwin Way Teale) *A Conscious Stillness: Two Naturalists on Thoreau's Rivers,* 1982; *A Desert Country Near the Sea,* 1983; *The Letters of John Xantus from Cabo San Lucas,* Glen Dawson, 1986; *The Letters of John Xantus from Fort Tejon, California, to Spencer Baird,* University of Arizona Press, 1986.

Illustrator: Edward R. Ricciuti, *Plants in Danger,* Harper, 1979.

WORK IN PROGRESS: A book on the natural history of the deserts of the contiguous U.S.

SIDELIGHTS: "I grew up on the banks of a river in Indiana and it was very much a part of my life although I was certainly no nature's child—I loathed camp and the outdoors. I loved

ANN ZWINGER

Pelican swallowing a fish. ■ (From *A Desert Country Near the Sea: A Natural History of the Cape Region of Baja, California* by Ann Zwinger. Photograph by Herman H. Zwinger.)

Gene Stratton Porter's books but shuddered at the thoughts of those dark woods she described. It strikes me as one of the miracles of my life that I have grown up to be an avid outdoors woman, rejoicing in all the remote places you can't get to from here.

"Drawing has been a part of my life ever since I can remember. I was trained as an art historian which is probably the best training possible for a nature writer. It teaches one how to look in a systematic and perceptive way. I suspect my love of detail stems from being myopic—when you can't see a lot far away, the immediate world becomes full of enchantment and meaning.

"Writing is inconceivable without drawing, as is drawing without writing. Each enhances the other: the more I learn the more I see, and the more I see the more I learn. Drawing comes easily; writing comes hard. Getting down the first draft is enough to make me clean closets and scrub floors instead. After that, it's all the editing and that's a joy, the refining and playing with words, balancing and exploring new ways of seeing and saying old things, old ways of seeing new.

"I did not come to writing until my children were all nearly grown; I could not write as I do had I not had that compan-ionship. I'm thankful: writing is such a consuming task that I could not have been both mother and writer.

"I do not consider myself an environmentalist nor a writer with an adversary stance. I believe that if you can just get someone to *look,* they will learn to enjoy, and if you enjoy you learn to care, and if you care you will never destroy.

"We live in the most beautiful of all possible worlds, that works impeccably well. Fitting into all the spinnings of that world makes nature writing a special kind of writing and observation, a special comfort. Yet, I envy the nature writers of a few decades ago who wrote in a time of greater innocence. I sometimes feel that those of us who write today are preserving a time and place that may never be again, leaving a description of fresh winds that clear the canyons, of rock walls that hold the heat and give it back, of a sky that stretches from horizon to horizon, and of a beetle that trundles across the sand and leaves scalloped footprints. Nature writing is in praise of the world around us. Difficult as it may be, there is nothing else I would rather do."

FOR MORE INFORMATION SEE: New York Times Book Review, July 12, 1970, October 12, 1975; *Harvard,* September, 1975; *Washington Post Book World,* November 7, 1982; *Los Angeles Times,* December 13, 1983; *Christian Science Monitor,* February 3, 1984; *Sierra Club,* March/April, 1984.

CUMULATIVE INDEX TO ILLUSTRATIONS AND AUTHORS

Illustrations Index

(In the following index, the number of the volume in which an illustrator's work appears is given *before* the colon, and the page on which it appears is given *after* the colon. For example, a drawing by Adams, Adrienne appears in Volume 2 on page 6, another drawing by her appears in Volume 3 on page 80, another drawing in Volume 8 on page 1, and another drawing in Volume 15 on page 107.)

YABC

Index citations including this abbreviation refer to listings appearing in *Yesterday's Authors of Books for Children,* also published by the Gale Research Company, which covers authors who died prior to 1960.

Aas, Ulf, *5:* 174
Abbé, S. van. *See* van Abbé, S.
Abel, Raymond, *6:* 122; *7:* 195; *12:* 3; *21:* 86; *25:* 119
Abrahams, Hilary, *26:* 205; *29:* 24-25
Abrams, Kathie, *36:* 170
Accorsi, William, *11:* 198
Acs, Laszlo, *14:* 156; *42:* 22
Adams, Adrienne, *2:* 6; *3:* 80; *8:* 1; *15:* 107; *16:* 180; *20:* 65; *22:* 134-135; *33:* 75; *36:* 103, 112; *39:* 74
Adams, John Wolcott, *17:* 162
Adamson, George, *30:* 23, 24
Adkins, Alta, *22:* 250
Adkins, Jan, *8:* 3
Adler, Peggy, *22:* 6; *29:* 31
Adler, Ruth, *29:* 29
Agard, Nadema, *18:* 1
Ahl, Anna Maria, *32:* 24
Aichinger, Helga, *4:* 5, 45
Aitken, Amy, *31:* 34
Akaba, Suekichi, *46:* 23
Akasaka, Miyoshi, *YABC 2:* 261
Akino, Fuku, *6:* 144
Alain, *40:* 41
Alajalov, *2:* 226
Albrecht, Jan, *37:* 176
Albright, Donn, *1:* 91
Alcorn, John, *3:* 159; *7:* 165; *31:* 22; *44:* 127; *46:* 23, 170
Alda, Arlene, *44:* 24
Alden, Albert, *11:* 103
Aldridge, Andy, *27:* 131
Alex, Ben, *45:* 25, 26
Alexander, Martha, *3:* 206; *11:* 103; *13:* 109; *25:* 100; *36:* 131
Alexeieff, Alexander, *14:* 6; *26:* 199
Aliki. *See* Brandenberg, Aliki
Allamand, Pascale, *12:* 9
Allan, Judith, *38:* 166
Alland, Alexander, *16:* 255
Alland, Alexandra, *16:* 255
Allen, Gertrude, *9:* 6
Allen, Graham, *31:* 145
Allison, Linda, *43:* 27

Almquist, Don, *11:* 8; *12:* 128; *17:* 46; *22:* 110
Aloise, Frank, *5:* 38; *10:* 133; *30:* 92
Althea. *See* Braithwaite, Althea
Altschuler, Franz, *11:* 185; *23:* 141; *40:* 48; *45:* 29
Ambrus, Victor G., *1:* 6-7, 194; *3:* 69; *5:* 15; *6:* 44; *7:* 36; *8:* 210; *12:* 227; *14:* 213; *15:* 213; *22:* 209; *24:* 36; *28:* 179; *30:* 178; *32:* 44, 46; *38:* 143; *41:* 25, 26, 27, 28, 29, 30, 31, 32; *42:* 87; *44:* 190
Ames, Lee J., *3:* 12; *9:* 130; *10:* 69; *17:* 214; *22:* 124
Amon, Aline, *9:* 9
Amoss, Berthe, *5:* 5
Amundsen, Dick, *7:* 77
Amundsen, Richard E., *5:* 10; *24:* 122
Ancona, George, *12:* 11
Anderson, Alasdair, *18:* 122
Anderson, Brad, *33:* 28
Anderson, C. W., *11:* 10
Anderson, Carl, *7:* 4
Anderson, Doug, *40:* 111
Anderson, Erica, *23:* 65
Anderson, Laurie, *12:* 153, 155
Anderson, Wayne, *23:* 119; *41:* 239
Andrew, John, *22:* 4
Andrews, Benny, *14:* 251; *31:* 24
Angelo, Valenti, *14:* 8; *18:* 100; *20:* 232; *32:* 70
Anglund, Joan Walsh, *2:* 7, 250-251; *37:* 198, 199, 200
Anno, Mitsumasa, *5:* 7; *38:* 25, 26-27, 28, 29, 30, 31, 32
Antal, Andrew, *1:* 124; *30:* 145
Apple, Margot, *33:* 25; *35:* 206; *46:* 81
Appleyard, Dev, *2:* 192
Araneus, *40:* 29
Archer, Janet, *16:* 69
Ardizzone, Edward, *1:* 11, 12; *2:* 105; *3:* 258; *4:* 78; *7:* 79; *10:* 100; *15:* 232; *20:* 69, 178; *23:* 223; *24:* 125; *28:* 25, 26, 27, 28, 29, 30, 31, 33, 34, 35, 36, 37;

31: 192, 193; *34:* 215, 217; *YABC 2:* 25
Arenella, Roy, *14:* 9
Armer, Austin, *13:* 3
Armer, Laura Adams, *13:* 3
Armer, Sidney, *13:* 3
Armitage, Eileen, *4:* 16
Armstrong, George, *10:* 6; *21:* 72
Arno, Enrico, *1:* 217; *2:* 22, 210; *4:* 9; *5:* 43; *6:* 52; *29:* 217, 219; *33:* 152; *35:* 99; *43:* 31, 32, 33; *45:* 212, 213, 214
Arnosky, Jim, *22:* 20
Arrowood, Clinton, *12:* 193; *19:* 11
Arting, Fred J., *41:* 63
Artzybasheff, Boris, *13:* 143; *14:* 15; *40:* 152, 155
Aruego, Ariane, *6:* 4
See also Dewey, Ariane
Aruego, Jose, *4:* 140; *6:* 4; *7:* 64; *33:* 195; *35:* 208
Asch, Frank, *5:* 9
Ashby, Gail, *11:* 135
Ashby, Gwynneth, *44:* 26
Ashley, C. W., *19:* 197
Ashmead, Hal, *8:* 70
Assel, Steven, *44:* 153
Astrop, John, *32:* 56
Atene, Ann, *12:* 18
Atherton, Lisa, *38:* 198
Atkinson, J. Priestman, *17:* 275
Atkinson, Wayne, *40:* 46
Attebery, Charles, *38:* 170
Atwood, Ann, *7:* 9
Augarde, Steve, *25:* 22
Austerman, Miriam, *23:* 107
Austin, Margot, *11:* 16
Austin, Robert, *3:* 44
Averill, Esther, *1:* 17; *28:* 39, 40, 41
Axeman, Lois, *2:* 32; *11:* 84; *13:* 165; *22:* 8; *23:* 49
Ayer, Jacqueline, *13:* 7
Ayer, Margaret, *15:* 12

B.T.B. *See* Blackwell, Basil T.
Babbitt, Bradford, *33:* 158

Babbitt, Natalie, *6:* 6; *8:* 220
Back, George, *31:* 161
Bacon, Bruce, *4:* 74
Bacon, Paul, *7:* 155; *8:* 121; *31:* 55
Bacon, Peggy, *2:* 11, 228; *46:* 44
Baker, Alan, *22:* 22
Baker, Charlotte, *2:* 12
Baker, Jeannie, *23:* 4
Baker, Jim, *22:* 24
Baldridge, Cyrus LeRoy, *19:* 69; *44:* 50
Balet, Jan, *11:* 22
Balian, Lorna, *9:* 16
Ballantyne, R. M., *24:* 34
Ballis, George, *14:* 199
Baltzer, Hans, *40:* 30
Bang, Molly Garrett, *24:* 37, 38
Banik, Yvette Santiago, *21:* 136
Banner, Angela. *See* Maddison, Angela Mary
Bannerman, Helen, *19:* 13, 14
Bannon, Laura, *6:* 10; *23:* 8
Baptist, Michael, *37:* 208
Bare, Arnold Edwin, *16:* 31
Bare, Colleen Stanley, *32:* 33
Bargery, Geoffrey, *14:* 258
Barker, Carol, *31:* 27
Barkley, James, *4:* 13; *6:* 11; *13:* 112
Barks, Carl, *37:* 27, 28, 29, 30-31, 32, 33, 34
Barling, Tom, *9:* 23
Barlow, Perry, *35:* 28
Barlowe, Dot, *30:* 223
Barlowe, Wayne, *37:* 72
Barner, Bob, *29:* 37
Barnes, Hiram P., *20:* 28
Barnett, Moneta, *16:* 89; *19:* 142; *31:* 102; *33:* 30, 31, 32; *41:* 153
Barney, Maginel Wright, *39:* 32, 33, 34; *YABC 2:* 306
Barnum, Jay Hyde, *11:* 224; *20:* 5; *37:* 189, 190
Barrauds, *33:* 114
Barrer-Russell, Gertrude, *9:* 65; *27:* 31
Barrett, Angela, *40:* 136, 137
Barrett, John E., *43:* 119
Barrett, Ron, *14:* 24; *26:* 35
Barron, John N., *3:* 261; *5:* 101; *14:* 220
Barrows, Walter, *14:* 268
Barry, Ethelred B., *37:* 79; *YABC 1:* 229
Barry, James, *14:* 25
Barry, Katharina, *2:* 159; *4:* 22
Barry, Robert E., *6:* 12
Barry, Scott, *32:* 35
Bartenbach, Jean, *40:* 31
Barth, Ernest Kurt, *2:* 172; *3:* 160; *8:* 26; *10:* 31
Barton, Byron, *8:* 207; *9:* 18; *23:* 66
Barton, Harriett, *30:* 71
Bartram, Robert, *10:* 42
Bartsch, Jochen, *8:* 105; *39:* 38
Bascove, Barbara, *45:* 73
Baskin, Leonard, *30:* 42, 43, 46, 47
Bassett, Jeni, *40:* 99
Batchelor, Joy, *29:* 41, 47, 48
Bate, Norman, *5:* 16
Bates, Leo, *24:* 35

Batet, Carmen, *39:* 134
Batherman, Muriel, *31:* 79; *45:* 185
Batten, John D., *25:* 161, 162
Battles, Asa, *32:* 94, 95
Bauernschmidt, Marjorie, *15:* 15
Baum, Allyn, *20:* 10
Baum, Willi, *4:* 24-25; *7:* 173
Baumann, Jill, *34:* 170
Baumhauer, Hans, *11:* 218; *15:* 163, 165, 167
Bayley, Dorothy, *37:* 195
Bayley, Nicola, *40:* 104; *41:* 34, 35
Baynes, Pauline, *2:* 244; *3:* 149; *13:* 133, 135, 137-141; *19:* 18, 19, 20; *32:* 208, 213, 214; *36:* 105, 108
Beame, Rona, *12:* 40
Beard, Dan, *22:* 31, 32
Beard, J. H., *YABC 1:* 158
Bearden, Romare, *9:* 7; *22:* 35
Beardsley, Aubrey, *17:* 14; *23:* 181
Bearman, Jane, *29:* 38
Beaton, Cecil, *24:* 208
Beaucé, J. A., *18:* 103
Beck, Charles, *11:* 169
Beck, Ruth, *13:* 11
Becker, Harriet, *12:* 211
Beckett, Sheilah, *25:* 5; *33:* 37, 38
Beckhoff, Harry, *1:* 78; *5:* 163
Beckman, Kaj, *45:* 38, 39, 40, 41
Beckman, Per, *45:* 42, 43
Bedford, F. D., *20:* 118, 122; *33:* 170; *41:* 220, 221, 230, 233
Bee, Joyce, *19:* 62
Beeby, Betty, *25:* 36
Beech, Carol, *9:* 149
Beek, *25:* 51, 55, 59
Beerbohm, Max, *24:* 208
Behr, Joyce, *15:* 15; *21:* 132; *23:* 161
Behrens, Hans, *5:* 97
Beisner, Monika, *46:* 128, 131
Belden, Charles J., *12:* 182
Belina, Renate, *39:* 132
Bell, Corydon, *3:* 20
Beltran, Alberto, *43:* 37
Bemelmans, Ludwig, *15:* 19, 21
Benda, Wladyslaw T., *15:* 256; *30:* 76, 77; *44:* 182
Bendick, Jeanne, *2:* 24
Bennett, F. I., *YABC 1:* 134
Bennett, Jill, *26:* 61; *41:* 38, 39; *45:* 54
Bennett, Rainey, *15:* 26; *23:* 53
Bennett, Richard, *15:* 45; *21:* 11, 12, 13; *25:* 175
Bennett, Susan, *5:* 55
Bentley, Carolyn, *46:* 153
Bentley, Roy, *30:* 162
Benton, Thomas Hart, *2:* 99
Berelson, Howard, *5:* 20; *16:* 58; *31:* 50
Berenstain, Jan, *12:* 47
Berenstain, Stan, *12:* 47
Berg, Joan, *1:* 115; *3:* 156; *6:* 26, 58
Berg, Ron, *36:* 48, 49
Berger, William M., *14:* 143; *YABC 1:* 204
Bering, Claus, *13:* 14
Berkowitz, Jeanette, *3:* 249

Bernadette. *See* Watts, Bernadette
Bernath, Stefen, *32:* 76
Bernstein, Ted, *38:* 183
Bernstein, Zena, *23:* 46
Berrill, Jacquelyn, *12:* 50
Berry, Erick. *See* Best, Allena.
Berry, William A., *6:* 219
Berry, William D., *14:* 29; *19:* 48
Berson, Harold, *2:* 17-18; *4:* 28-29, 220; *9:* 10; *12:* 19; *17:* 45; *18:* 193; *22:* 85; *34:* 172; *44:* 120; *46:* 42
Bertschmann, Harry, *16:* 1
Beskow, Elsa, *20:* 13, 14, 15
Best, Allena, *2:* 26; *34:* 76
Bethers, Ray, *6:* 22
Bettina. *See* Ehrlich, Bettina
Betts, Ethel Franklin, *17:* 161, 164-165; *YABC 2:* 47
Bewick, Thomas, *16:* 40-41, 43-45, 47; *YABC 1:* 107
Biamonte, Daniel, *40:* 90
Bianco, Pamela, *15:* 31; *28:* 44, 45, 46
Bible, Charles, *13:* 15
Bice, Clare, *22:* 40
Biggers, John, *2:* 123
Bileck, Marvin, *3:* 102; *40:* 36-37
Bimen, Levent, *5:* 179
Binks, Robert, *25:* 150
Binzen, Bill, *24:* 47
Birch, Reginald, *15:* 150; *19:* 33, 34, 35, 36; *37:* 196, 197; *44:* 182; *46:* 176; *YABC 1:* 84; *YABC 2:* 34, 39
Bird, Esther Brock, *1:* 36; *25:* 66
Birmingham, Lloyd, *12:* 51
Biro, Val, *1:* 26; *41:* 42
Bischoff, Ilse, *44:* 51
Bjorklund, Lorence, *3:* 188, 252; *7:* 100; *9:* 113; *10:* 66; *19:* 178; *33:* 122, 123; *35:* 36, 37, 38, 39, 41, 42, 43; *36:* 185; *38:* 93; *YABC 1:* 242
Blackwell, Basil T., *YABC 1:* 68, 69
Blades, Ann, *16:* 52; *37:* 213
Blair, Jay, *45:* 46; *46:* 155
Blaisdell, Elinore, *1:* 121; *3:* 134; *35:* 63
Blake, Quentin, *3:* 170; *9:* 21; *10:* 48; *13:* 38; *21:* 180; *26:* 60; *28:* 228; *30:* 29, 31; *40:* 108; *45:* 219; *46:* 165, 168
Blake, Robert J., *37:* 90
Blake, William, *30:* 54, 56, 57, 58, 59, 60
Blass, Jacqueline, *8:* 215
Blegvad, Erik, *2:* 59; *3:* 98; *5:* 117; *7:* 131; *11:* 149; *14:* 34, 35; *18:* 237; *32:* 219; *YABC 1:* 201
Bliss, Corinne Demas, *37:* 38
Bloch, Lucienne, *10:* 12
Bloom, Lloyd, *35:* 180; *36:* 149
Blossom, Dave, *34:* 29
Blumenschein, E. L., *YABC 1:* 113, 115
Blumer, Patt, *29:* 214
Blundell, Kim, *29:* 36
Boardman, Gwenn, *12:* 60
Bobri, *30:* 138

Bock, Vera, *1:* 187; *21:* 41
Bock, William Sauts, *8:* 7; *14:* 37; *16:* 120; *21:* 141; *36:* 177
Bodecker, N. M., *8:* 13; *14:* 2; *17:* 55-57
Boehm, Linda, *40:* 31
Bohdal, Susi, *22:* 44
Bolian, Polly, *3:* 270; *4:* 30; *13:* 77; *29:* 197
Bolognese, Don, *2:* 147, 231; *4:* 176; *7:* 146; *17:* 43; *23:* 192; *24:* 50; *34:* 108; *36:* 133
Bond, Arnold, *18:* 116
Bond, Barbara Higgins, *21:* 102
Bond, Felicia, *38:* 197
Bonn, Pat, *43:* 40
Bonners, Susan, *41:* 40
Bonsall, Crosby, *23:* 6
Booth, Franklin, *YABC 2:* 76
Booth, Graham, *32:* 193; *37:* 41, 42
Bordier, Georgette, *16:* 54
Boren, Tinka, *27:* 128
Borja, Robert, *22:* 48
Bornstein, Ruth, *14:* 44
Borten, Helen, *3:* 54; *5:* 24
Bossom, Naomi, *35:* 48
Boston, Peter, *19:* 42
Bosustow, Stephen, *34:* 202
Bottner, Barbara, *14:* 46
Boucher, Joelle, *41:* 138
Boulat, Pierre, *44:* 40
Bourke-White, Margaret, *15:* 286-287
Boutet de Monvel, M., *30:* 61, 62, 63, 65
Bowen, Richard, *42:* 134
Bowen, Ruth, *31:* 188
Bower, Ron, *29:* 33
Bowser, Carolyn Ewing, *22:* 253
Boyd, Patti, *45:* 31
Boyle, Eleanor Vere, *28:* 50, 51
Bozzo, Frank, *4:* 154
Bradford, Ron, *7:* 157
Bradley, Richard D., *26:* 182
Bradley, William, *5:* 164
Brady, Irene, *4:* 31; *42:* 37
Bragg, Michael, *32:* 78; *46:* 31
Braithwaite, Althea, *23:* 12-13
Bram, Elizabeth, *30:* 67
Bramley, Peter, *4:* 3
Brandenberg, Aliki, *2:* 36-37; *24:* 222; *35:* 49, 50, 51, 52, 53, 54, 56, 57
Brandi, Lillian, *31:* 158
Brandon, Brumsic, Jr., *9:* 25
Bransom, Paul, *17:* 121; *43:* 44
Brenner, Fred, *22:* 85; *36:* 34; *42:* 34
Brett, Bernard, *22:* 54
Brett, Harold M., *26:* 98, 99, 100
Brett, Jan, *30:* 135; *42:* 39
Brewer, Sally King, *33:* 44
Brewster, Patience, *40:* 68; *45:* 22, 183
Brick, John, *10:* 15
Bridge, David R., *45:* 28
Bridgman, L. J., *37:* 77
Bridwell, Norman, *4:* 37
Briggs, Raymond, *10:* 168; *23:* 20, 21
Brigham, Grace A., *37:* 148
Bright, Robert, *24:* 55

Brinckloe, Julie, *13:* 18; *24:* 79, 115; *29:* 35
Brisley, Joyce L., *22:* 57
Brock, Charles E., *15:* 97; *19:* 247, 249; *23:* 224, 225; *36:* 88; *42:* 41, 42, 43, 44, 45; *YABC 1:* 194, 196, 203
Brock, Emma, *7:* 21
Brock, Henry Matthew, *15:* 81; *16:* 141; *19:* 71; *34:* 115; *40:* 164; *42:* 47, 48, 49
Brodkin, Gwen, *34:* 135
Bromhall, Winifred, *5:* 11; *26:* 38
Brooke, L. Leslie, *16:* 181-183, 186; *17:* 15-17; *18:* 194
Brooker, Christopher, *15:* 251
Broomfield, Maurice, *40:* 141
Brotman, Adolph E., *5:* 21
Brown, Buck, *45:* 48
Brown, David, *7:* 47
Brown, Denise, *11:* 213
Brown, Judith Gwyn, *1:* 45; *7:* 5; *8:* 167; *9:* 182, 190; *20:* 16, 17, 18; *23:* 142; *29:* 117; *33:* 97; *36:* 23, 26; *43:* 184
Brown, Marc Tolon, *10:* 17, 197; *14:* 263
Brown, Marcia, *7:* 30; *25:* 203; *YABC 1:* 27
Brown, Margery W., *5:* 32-33; *10:* 3
Brown, Palmer, *36:* 40
Brown, Paul, *25:* 26; *26:* 107
Browne, Anthony, *45:* 50, 51, 52
Browne, Dik, *8:* 212
Browne, Gordon, *16:* 97
Browne, Hablot K., *15:* 65, 80; *21:* 14, 15, 16, 17, 18, 19, 20; *24:* 25
Browning, Coleen, *4:* 132
Browning, Mary Eleanor, *24:* 84
Bruce, Robert, *23:* 23
Brule, Al, *3:* 135
Bruna, Dick, *43:* 48, 49, 50
Brundage, Frances, *19:* 244
Brunhoff, Jean de, *24:* 57, 58
Brunhoff, Laurent de, *24:* 60
Brunson, Bob, *43:* 135
Bryan, Ashley, *31:* 44
Brychta, Alex, *21:* 21
Bryson, Bernarda, *3:* 88, 146; *39:* 26; *44:* 185
Buba, Joy, *12:* 83; *30:* 226; *44:* 56
Buchanan, Lilian, *13:* 16
Bucholtz-Ross, Linda, *44:* 137
Buchs, Thomas, *40:* 38
Buck, Margaret Waring, *3:* 30
Buehr, Walter, *3:* 31
Buff, Conrad, *19:* 52, 53, 54
Buff, Mary, *19:* 52, 53
Bull, Charles Livingston, *18:* 207
Bullen, Anne, *3:* 166, 167
Burbank, Addison, *37:* 43
Burchard, Peter, *3:* 197; *5:* 35; *6:* 158, 218
Burger, Carl, *3:* 33; *45:* 160, 162
Burgeson, Marjorie, *19:* 31
Burgess, Gelett, *32:* 39, 42
Burkert, Nancy Ekholm, *18:* 186; *22:* 140; *24:* 62, 63, 64, 65;

26: 53; *29:* 60, 61; *46:* 171; *YABC 1:* 46
Burn, Doris, *6:* 172
Burnett, Virgil, *44:* 42
Burningham, John, *9:* 68; *16:* 60-61
Burns, Howard M., *12:* 173
Burns, M. F., *26:* 69
Burns, Raymond, *9:* 29
Burns, Robert, *24:* 106
Burr, Dane, *12:* 2
Burra, Edward, *YABC 2:* 68
Burri, René, *41:* 143
Burridge, Marge Opitz, *14:* 42
Burris, Burmah, *4:* 81
Burroughs, John Coleman, *41:* 64
Burroughs, Studley O., *41:* 65
Burton, Marilee Robin, *46:* 33
Burton, Virginia Lee, *2:* 43; *44:* 49, 51; *YABC 1:* 24
Busoni, Rafaello, *1:* 186; *3:* 224; *6:* 126; *14:* 5; *16:* 62-63
Butterfield, Ned, *1:* 153; *27:* 128
Buzonas, Gail, *29:* 88
Buzzell, Russ W., *12:* 177
Byard, Carole M., *39:* 44
Byars, Betsy, *46:* 35
Byfield, Barbara Ninde, *8:* 18
Byfield, Graham, *32:* 29
Byrd, Robert, *13:* 218; *33:* 46

Caddy, Alice, *6:* 41
Cady, Harrison, *17:* 21, 23; *19:* 57, 58
Caldecott, Randolph, *16:* 98, 103; *17:* 32-33, 36, 38-39; *26:* 90; *YABC 2:* 172
Calder, Alexander, *18:* 168
Calderon, W. Frank, *25:* 160
Caldwell, Doreen, *23:* 77
Caldwell, John, *46:* 225
Callahan, Kevin, *22:* 42
Callahan, Philip S., *25:* 77
Cameron, Julia Margaret, *19:* 203
Campbell, Ann, *11:* 43
Campbell, Walter M., *YABC 2:* 158
Camps, Luis, *28:* 120-121
Canright, David, *36:* 162
Caras, Peter, *36:* 64
Caraway, James, *3:* 200-201
Carbe, Nino, *29:* 183
Carigiet, Alois, *24:* 67
Carle, Eric, *4:* 42; *11:* 121; *12:* 29
Carlson, Nancy L., *41:* 116
Carr, Archie, *37:* 225
Carrick, Donald, *5:* 194; *39:* 97
Carrick, Malcolm, *28:* 59, 60
Carrick, Valery, *21:* 47
Carroll, Lewis. *See* Dodgson, Charles L.
Carroll, Ruth, *7:* 41; *10:* 68
Carter, Harry, *22:* 179
Carter, Helene, *15:* 38; *22:* 202, 203; *YABC 2:* 220-221
Carty, Leo, *4:* 196; *7:* 163
Cary, *4:* 133; *9:* 32; *20:* 2; *21:* 143
Cary, Page, *12:* 41
Case, Sandra E., *16:* 2
Cassel, Lili. *See* Wronker, Lili Cassel

Cassel-Wronker, Lili.
    See also Wronker, Lili Cassel
Cassels, Jean, 8: 50
Castle, Jane, 4: 80
Cather, Carolyn, 3: 83; 15: 203;
    34: 216
Cauley, Lorinda Bryan, 44: 135;
    46: 49
Cayard, Bruce, 38: 67
Cellini, Joseph, 2: 73; 3: 35; 16: 116
Chabrian, Debbi, 45: 55
Chagnon, Mary, 37: 158
Chalmers, Mary, 3: 145; 13: 148;
    33: 125
Chamberlain, Christopher, 45: 57
Chamberlain, Margaret, 46: 51
Chambers, C. E., 17: 230
Chambers, Dave, 12: 151
Chambers, Mary, 4: 188
Chambliss, Maxie, 42: 186
Chandler, David P., 28: 62
Chapman, C. H., 13: 83, 85, 87
Chapman, Frederick T., 6: 27; 44: 28
Chapman, Gaynor, 32: 52, 53
Chappell, Warren, 3: 172; 21: 56;
    27: 125
Charles, Donald, 30: 154, 155
Charlip, Remy, 4: 48; 34: 138
Charlot, Jean, 1: 137, 138; 8: 23;
    14: 31
Charlton, Michael, 34: 50; 37: 39
Charmatz, Bill, 7: 45
Chartier, Normand, 9: 36
Chase, Lynwood M., 14: 4
Chastain, Madye Lee, 4: 50
Chauncy, Francis, 24: 158
Chen, Tony, 6: 45; 19: 131; 29: 126;
    34: 160
Cheney, T. A., 11: 47
Cheng, Judith, 36: 45
Cherry, Lynne, 34: 52
Chess, Victoria, 12: 6; 33: 42, 48, 49;
    40: 194; 41: 145
Chessare, Michele, 41: 50
Chesterton, G. K., 27: 43, 44, 45, 47
Chevalier, Christa, 35: 66
Chew, Ruth, 7: 46
Chin, Alex, 28: 54
Cho, Shinta, 8: 126
Chollick, Jay, 25: 175
Chorao, Kay, 7: 200-201; 8: 25;
    11: 234; 33: 187; 35: 239
Christelow, Eileen, 38: 44
Christensen, Gardell Dano, 1: 57
Christiansen, Per, 40: 24
Christy, Howard Chandler,
    17: 163-165, 168-169; 19: 186,
    187; 21: 22, 23, 24, 25
Chronister, Robert, 23: 138
Church, Frederick, YABC 1: 155
Chute, Marchette, 1: 59
Chwast, Jacqueline, 1: 63; 2: 275;
    6: 46-47; 11: 125; 12: 202;
    14: 235
Chwast, Seymour, 3: 128-129; 18: 43;
    27: 152
Cirlin, Edgard, 2: 168
Clark, Victoria, 35: 159
Clarke, Harry, 23: 172, 173

Claverie, Jean, 38: 46
Clayton, Robert, 9: 181
Cleaver, Elizabeth, 8: 204; 23: 36
Cleland, T. M., 26: 92
Clement, Charles, 20: 38
Clevin, Jörgen, 7: 50
Clifford, Judy, 34: 163; 45: 198
Coalson, Glo, 9: 72, 85; 25: 155;
    26: 42; 35: 212
Cober, Alan E., 17: 158; 32: 77
Cochran, Bobbye, 11: 52
CoConis, Ted, 4: 41; 46: 41
Coerr, Eleanor, 1: 64
Coes, Peter, 35: 172
Coggins, Jack, 2: 69
Cohen, Alix, 7: 53
Cohen, Vincent O., 19: 243
Cohen, Vivien, 11: 112
Colbert, Anthony, 15: 41; 20: 193
Colby, C. B., 3: 47
Cole, Herbert, 28: 104
Cole, Olivia H. H., 1: 134; 3: 223;
    9: 111; 38: 104
Collier, David, 13: 127
Collier, John, 27: 179
Colonna, Bernard, 21: 50; 28: 103;
    34: 140; 43: 180
Cone, Ferne Geller, 39: 49
Cone, J. Morton, 39: 49
Conklin, Paul, 43: 62
Connolly, Jerome P., 4: 128; 28: 52
Conover, Chris, 31: 52; 40: 184;
    41: 51; 44: 79
Converse, James, 38: 70
Cook, G. R., 29: 165
Cookburn, W. V., 29: 204
Cooke, Donald E., 2: 77
Coombs, Charles, 43: 65
Coombs, Patricia, 2: 82; 3: 52;
    22: 119
Cooney, Barbara, 6: 16-17, 50; 12: 42;
    13: 92; 15: 145; 16: 74, 111;
    18: 189; 23: 38, 89, 93; 32: 138;
    38: 105; YABC 2: 10
Cooper, Mario, 24: 107
Cooper, Marjorie, 7: 112
Copelman, Evelyn, 8: 61; 18: 25
Copley, Heather, 30: 86; 45: 57
Corbett, Grahame, 30: 114; 43: 67
Corbino, John, 19: 248
Corcos, Lucille, 2: 223; 10: 27; 34: 66
Corey, Robert, 9: 34
Corlass, Heather, 10: 7
Cornell, James, 27: 60
Cornell, Jeff, 11: 58
Corrigan, Barbara, 8: 37
Corwin, Judith Hoffman, 10: 28
Cory, Fanny Y., 20: 113
Cosgrove, Margaret, 3: 100
Costabel, Eva Deutsch, 45: 66, 67
Costello, David F., 23: 55
Courtney, R., 35: 110
Couture, Christin, 41: 209
Covarrubias, Miguel, 35: 118, 119,
    123, 124, 125
Coville, Katherine, 32: 57; 36: 167
Cox, 43: 93
Cox, Charles, 8: 20
Cox, Palmer, 24: 76, 77

Craft, Kinuko, 22: 182; 36: 220
Crane, Alan H., 1: 217
Crane, H. M., 13: 111
Crane, Jack, 43: 183
Crane, Walter, 18: 46-49, 53-54,
    56-57, 59-61; 22: 128; 24: 210,
    217
Crawford, Will, 43: 77
Credle, Ellis 1: 69
Crews, Donald, 32: 59, 60
Crofut, Susan, 23: 61
Crowell, Pers, 3: 125
Cruikshank, George, 15: 76, 83;
    22: 74, 75, 76, 77, 78, 79, 80,
    81, 82, 84, 137; 24: 22, 23
Crump, Fred H., 11: 62
Cruz, Ray, 6: 55
Cstari, Joe, 44: 82
Cuffari, Richard, 4: 75; 5: 98; 6: 56;
    7: 13, 84, 153; 8: 148, 155; 9: 89;
    11: 19; 12: 55, 96, 114; 15: 51,
    202; 18: 5; 20: 139; 21: 197;
    22: 14, 192; 23: 15, 106; 25: 97;
    27: 133; 28: 196; 29: 54; 30: 85;
    31: 35; 36: 101; 38: 171; 42: 97;
    44: 92, 192; 45: 212, 213; 46: 36,
    198
Cugat, Xavier, 19: 120
Cumings, Art, 35: 160
Cummings, Chris, 29: 167
Cummings, Pat, 42: 61
Cummings, Richard, 24: 119
Cunette, Lou, 20: 93; 22: 125
Cunningham, Aline, 25: 180
Cunningham, David, 11: 13
Cunningham, Imogene, 16: 122, 127
Curry, John Steuart, 2: 5; 19: 84;
    34: 36
Curtis, Bruce, 23: 96; 30: 88; 36: 22

Dabcovich, Lydia, 25: 105; 40: 114
Dain, Martin J., 35: 75
Dalton, Anne, 40: 62
Daly, Niki, 37: 53
Dalziel, Brothers, 33: 113
D'Amato, Alex, 9: 48; 20: 25
D'Amato, Janet, 9: 48; 20: 25; 26: 118
Daniel, Alan, 23: 59; 29: 110
Daniel, Lewis C., 20: 216
Daniels, Steve, 22: 16
Dann, Bonnie, 31: 83
Danska, Herbert, 24: 219
Danyell, Alice, 20: 27
Darley, F.O.C., 16: 145; 19: 79, 86,
    88, 185; 21: 28, 36; 35: 76, 77,
    78, 79, 80-81; YABC 2: 175
Darling, Lois, 3: 59; 23: 30, 31
Darling, Louis, 1: 40-41; 2: 63; 3: 59;
    23: 30, 31; 43: 54, 57, 59
Darrow, Whitney, Jr., 13: 25; 38: 220,
    221
Darwin, Beatrice, 43: 54
Darwin, Len, 24: 82
Dastolfo, Frank, 33: 179
Dauber, Liz, 1: 22; 3: 266; 30: 49
Daugherty, James, 3: 66; 8: 178;
    13: 27-28, 161; 18: 101; 19: 72;

29: 108; *32:* 156; *42:* 84;
    YABC 1: 256; *YABC 2:* 174
d'Aulaire, Edgar, *5:* 51
d'Aulaire, Ingri, *5:* 51
David, Jonathan, *19:* 37
Davidson, Kevin, *28:* 154
Davidson, Raymond, *32:* 61
Davis, Allen, *20:* 11; *22:* 45; *27:* 222;
    29: 157; *41:* 99
Davis, Bette J., *15:* 53; *23:* 95
Davis, Dimitris, *45:* 95
Davis, Jim, *32:* 63, 64
Davis, Marguerite, *31:* 38; *34:* 69, 70;
    YABC 1: 126, 230
Davisson, Virginia H., *44:* 178
Dawson, Diane, *24:* 127; *42:* 126
Dean, Bob, *19:* 211
de Angeli, Marguerite, *1:* 77; *27:* 62,
    j65, 66, 67, 69, 70, 72;
    YABC 1: 166
Deas, Michael, *27:* 219, 221; *30:* 156
de Bosschère, Jean, *19:* 252; *21:* 4
De Bruyn, M(onica) G., *13:* 30-31
De Cuir, John F., *1:* 28-29
Degen, Bruce, *40:* 227, 229
De Grazia, *14:* 59; *39:* 56, 57
de Groat, Diane, *9:* 39; *18:* 7; *23:* 123;
    28: 200-201; *31:* 58, 59; *34:* 151;
    41: 152; *43:* 88; *46:* 40, 200
de Groot, Lee, *6:* 21
Delacre, Lulu, *36:* 66
Delaney, A., *21:* 78
Delaney, Ned, *28:* 68
de Larrea, Victoria, *6:* 119, 204;
    29: 103
Delessert, Etienne, *7:* 140; *46:* 61, 62,
    63, 65, 67, 68; *YABC 2:* 209
Delulio, John, *15:* 54
Demarest, Chris L., *45:* 68-69, 70
De Mejo, Oscar, *40:* 67
Denetsosie, Hoke, *13:* 126
Dennis, Morgan, *18:* 68-69
Dennis, Wesley, *2:* 87; *3:* 111;
    11: 132; *18:* 71-74; *22:* 9;
    24: 196, 200; *46:* 178
Denslow, W. W., *16:* 84-87;
    18: 19-20, 24; *29:* 211
de Paola, Tomie, *8:* 95; *9:* 93; *11:* 69;
    25: 103; *28:* 157; *29:* 80; *39:* 52-
    53; *40:* 226; *46:* 187
Detmold, Edward J., *22:* 104, 105,
    106, 107; *35:* 120; *YABC 2:* 203
Detrich, Susan, *20:* 133
DeVelasco, Joseph E., *21:* 51
de Veyrac, Robert, *YABC 2:* 19
DeVille, Edward A., *4:* 235
Devito, Bert, *12:* 164
Devlin, Harry, *11:* 74
Dewey, Ariane, *7:* 64; *33:* 195;
    35: 208
    See also Aruego, Ariane
Dewey, Kenneth, *39:* 62
de Zanger, Arie, *30:* 40
Diamond, Donna, *21:* 200; *23:* 63;
    26: 142; *35:* 83, 84, 85, 86-87,
    88, 89; *38:* 78; *40:* 147; *44:* 152
Dick, John Henry, *8:* 181
Dickens, Frank, *34:* 131
Dickey, Robert L., *15:* 279

DiFate, Vincent, *37:* 70
DiFiori, Lawrence, *10:* 51; *12:* 190;
    27: 97; *40:* 219
Di Grazia, Thomas, *32:* 66; *35:* 241
Dillard, Annie, *10:* 32
Dillon, Corinne B., *1:* 139
Dillon, Diane, *4:* 104, 167; *6:* 23;
    13: 29; *15:* 99; *26:* 148; *27:* 136,
    201
Dillon, Leo, *4:* 104, 167; *6:* 23;
    13: 29; *15:* 99; *26:* 148; *27:* 136,
    201
DiMaggio, Joe, *36:* 22
Dinan, Carol, *25:* 169
Dines, Glen, *7:* 66-67
Dinesen, Thomas, *44:* 37
Dinnerstein, Harvey, *42:* 63, 64, 65,
    66, 67, 68
Dinsdale, Mary, *10:* 65; *11:* 171
Disney, Walt, *28:* 71, 72, 73, 76, 77,
    78, 79, 80, 81, 87, 88, 89, 90,
    91, 94
Dixon, Maynard, *20:* 165
Doares, Robert G., *20:* 39
Dobias, Frank, *22:* 162
Dobrin, Arnold, *4:* 68
Docktor, Irv, *43:* 70
Dodd, Ed, *4:* 69
Dodd, Lynley, *35:* 92
Dodgson, Charles L., *20:* 148;
    33: 146; *YABC 2:* 98
Dodson, Bert, *9:* 138; *14:* 195; *42:* 55
Dohanos, Stevan, *16:* 10
Dolesch, Susanne, *34:* 49
Dolson, Hildegarde, *5:* 57
Domanska, Janina, *6:* 66-67;
    YABC 1: 166
Domjan, Joseph, *25:* 93
Donahue, Vic, *2:* 93; *3:* 190; *9:* 44
Donald, Elizabeth, *4:* 18
Donna, Natalie, *9:* 52
Doré, Gustave, *18:* 169, 172, 175;
    19: 93, 94, 95, 96, 97, 98, 99,
    100, 101, 102, 103, 104, 105;
    23: 188; *25:* 197, 199
Doremus, Robert, *6:* 62; *13:* 90;
    30: 95, 96, 97; *38:* 97
Dorfman, Ronald, *11:* 128
Doty, Roy, *28:* 98; *31:* 32; *32:* 224;
    46: 157
Dougherty, Charles, *16:* 204; *18:* 74
Douglas, Aaron, *31:* 103
Douglas, Goray, *13:* 151
Dowd, Vic, *3:* 244; *10:* 97
Dowden, Anne Ophelia, *7:* 70-71;
    13: 120
Dowdy, Mrs. Regera, *29:* 100.
    See also Gorey, Edward
Doyle, Richard, *21:* 31, 32, 33;
    23: 231; *24:* 177; *31:* 87
Draper, Angie, *43:* 84
Drath, Bill, *26:* 34
Drawson, Blair, *17:* 53
Drescher, Joan, *30:* 100, 101; *35:* 245
Drew, Patricia, *15:* 100
Drummond, V. H., *6:* 70
du Bois, William Pène, *4:* 70; *10:* 122;
    26: 61; *27:* 145, 211; *35:* 243;
    41: 216

Duchesne, Janet, *6:* 162
Dudash, Michael, *32:* 122
Duer, Douglas, *34:* 177
Duffy, Joseph, *38:* 203
Duffy, Pat, *28:* 153
Duke, Chris, *8:* 195
Dulac, Edmund, *19:* 108, 109, 110,
    111, 112, 113, 114, 115, 117;
    23: 187; *25:* 152; *YABC 1:* 37;
    YABC 2: 147
Dulac, Jean, *13:* 64
Dunn, Harvey, *34:* 78, 79, 80, 81
Dunn, Phoebe, *5:* 175
Dunn, Iris, *5:* 175
Dunnington, Tom, *3:* 36; *18:* 281;
    25: 61; *31:* 159; *35:* 168
Dutz, *6:* 59
Duvoisin, Roger, *2:* 95; *6:* 76-77;
    7: 197; *28:* 125; *30:* 101, 102,
    103, 104, 105, 107
Dypold, Pat, *15:* 37

E.V.B. *See* Boyle, Eleanor Vere
    (Gordon)
Eachus, Jennifer, *29:* 74
Eagle, Michael, *11:* 86; *20:* 9; *23:* 18;
    27: 122; *28:* 57; *34:* 201; *44:* 189
Earle, Olive L., *7:* 75
Earle, Vana, *27:* 99
Eastman, P. D., *33:* 57
Easton, Reginald, *29:* 181
Eaton, Tom, *4:* 62; *6:* 64; *22:* 99;
    24: 124
Ebel, Alex, *11:* 89
Ebert, Len, *9:* 191; *44:* 47
Echevarria, Abe, *37:* 69
Ede, Janina, *33:* 59
Edgar, Sarah E., *41:* 97
Edrien, *11:* 53
Edwards, Freya, *45:* 102
Edwards, George Wharton, *31:* 155
Edwards, Gunvor, *2:* 71; *25:* 47;
    32: 71
Edwards, Jeanne, *29:* 257
Edwards, Linda Strauss, *21:* 134;
    39: 123
Eggenhofer, Nicholas, *2:* 81
Egielski, Richard, *11:* 90; *16:* 208;
    33: 236; *38:* 35
Ehlert, Lois, *35:* 97
Ehrlich, Bettina, *1:* 83
Eichenberg, Fritz, *1:* 79; *9:* 54;
    19: 248; *23:* 170; *24:* 200;
    26: 208; *YABC 1:* 104-105;
    YABC 2: 213
Einsel, Naiad, *10:* 35; *29:* 136
Einsel, Walter, *10:* 37
Einzig, Susan, *3:* 77; *43:* 78
Eitzen, Allan, *9:* 56; *12:* 212; *14:* 226;
    21: 194; *38:* 162
Eldridge, Harold, *43:* 83
Elgaard, Greta, *19:* 241
Elgin, Kathleen, *9:* 188; *39:* 69
Ellacott, S. E., *19:* 118
Elliott, Sarah M., *14:* 58
Emberley, Ed, *8:* 53
Emberley, Michael, *34:* 83
Engle, Mort, *38:* 64

Englebert, Victor, 8: 54
Enos, Randall, 20: 183
Enright, Maginel Wright, 19: 240, 243; 39: 31, 35, 36
Enrique, Romeo, 34: 135
Erhard, Walter, 1: 152
Erickson, Phoebe, 11: 83
Erikson, Mel, 31: 69
Escourido, Joseph, 4: 81
Esté, Kirk, 33: 111
Estoril, Jean, 32: 27
Estrada, Ric, 5: 52, 146; 13: 174
Etchemendy, Teje, 38: 68
Ets, Marie Hall, 2: 102
Eulalie, YABC 2: 315
Evans, Katherine, 5: 64
Ewing, Juliana Horatia, 16: 92

Falconer, Pearl, 34: 23
Falls, C. B., 1: 19; 38: 71, 72, 73, 74
Falter, John, 40: 169, 170
Farmer, Peter, 24: 108; 38: 75
Farquharson, Alexander, 46: 75
Farrell, David, 40: 135
Fatigati, Evelyn, 24: 112
Faul-Jansen, Regina, 22: 117
Faulkner, Jack, 6: 169
Fava, Rita, 2: 29
Fax, Elton C., 1: 101; 4: 2; 12: 77; 25: 107
Fay, 43: 93
Federspiel, Marian, 33: 51
Feelings, Tom, 5: 22; 8: 56; 12: 153; 16: 105; 30: 196
Fehr, Terrence, 21: 87
Feiffer, Jules, 3: 91; 8: 58
Feigeles, Neil, 41: 242
Feller, Gene, 33: 130
Fellows, Muriel H., 10: 42
Felts, Shirley, 33: 71
Fennelli, Maureen, 38: 181
Fenton, Carroll Lane, 5: 66; 21: 39
Fenton, Mildred Adams, 5: 66; 21: 39
Ferguson, Walter W., 34: 86
Fetz, Ingrid, 11: 67; 12: 52; 16: 205; 17: 59; 29: 105; 30: 108, 109; 32: 149; 43: 142
Fiammenghi, Gioia, 9: 66; 11: 44; 12: 206; 13: 57, 59
Field, Rachel, 15: 113
Fine, Peter K., 43: 210
Finger, Helen, 42: 81
Fink, Sam, 18: 119
Finlay, Winifred, 23: 72
Fiorentino, Al, 3: 240
Firmin, Charlotte, 29: 75
Fischel, Lillian, 40: 204
Fischer, Hans, 25: 202
Fisher, Leonard Everett, 3: 6; 4: 72, 86; 6: 197; 9: 59; 16: 151, 153; 23: 44; 27: 134; 29: 26; 34: 87, 89, 90, 91, 93, 94, 95, 96; 40: 206; YABC 2: 169
Fisher, Lois, 20: 62; 21: 7
Fisk, Nicholas, 25: 112
Fitschen, Marilyn, 2: 20-21; 20: 48
Fitzgerald, F. A., 15: 116; 25: 86-87

Fitzhugh, Louise, 1: 94; 9: 163; 45: 75, 78
Fitzhugh, Susie, 11: 117
Fitzsimmons, Arthur, 14: 128
Fix, Philippe, 26: 102
Flack, Marjorie, 21: 67; YABC 2: 122
Flagg, James Montgomery, 17: 227
Flax, Zeona, 2: 245
Fleishman, Seymour, 14: 232; 24: 87
Fleming, Guy, 18: 41
Floethe, Richard, 3: 131; 4: 90
Floherty, John J., Jr., 5: 68
Flora, James, 1: 96; 30: 111, 112
Florian, Douglas, 19: 122
Flory, Jane, 22: 111
Floyd, Gareth, 1: 74; 17: 245
Fluchère, Henri A., 40: 79
Flynn, Barbara, 7: 31; 9: 70
Fogarty, Thomas, 15: 89
Folger, Joseph, 9: 100
Folkard, Charles, 22: 132; 29: 128, 257-258
Foott, Jeff, 42: 202
Forberg, Ati, 12: 71, 205; 14: 1; 22: 113; 26: 22
Ford, George, 24: 120; 31: 70, 177
Ford, H. J., 16: 185-186
Ford, Pamela Baldwin, 27: 104
Foreman, Michael, 2: 110-111
Forrester, Victoria, 40: 83
Fortnum, Peggy, 6: 29; 20: 179; 24: 211; 26: 76, 77, 78; 39: 78; YABC 1: 148
Foster, Brad W., 34: 99
Foster, Genevieve, 2: 112
Foster, Gerald, 7: 78
Foster, Laura Louise, 6: 79
Foster, Marian Curtis, 23: 74; 40: 42
Fowler, Mel, 36: 127
Fox, Charles Phillip, 12: 84
Fox, Jim, 6: 187
Fracé, Charles, 15: 118
Frame, Paul, 2: 45, 145; 9: 153; 10: 124; 21: 71; 23: 62; 24: 123; 27: 106; 31: 48; 32: 159; 34: 195; 38: 136; 42: 55; 44: 139
Francois, André, 25: 117
Francoise. See Seignobosc, Francoise
Frank, Lola Edick, 2: 199
Frank, Mary, 4: 54; 34: 100
Franké, Phil, 45: 91
Frankel, Julie, 40: 84, 85, 202
Frankenberg, Robert, 22: 116; 30: 50; 38: 92, 94, 95
Franklin, John, 24: 22
Frascino, Edward, 9: 133; 29: 229; 33: 190
Frasconi, Antonio, 6: 80; 27: 208
Fraser, Betty, 2: 212; 6: 185; 8: 103; 31: 72, 73; 43: 136
Fraser, Eric, 38: 78; 41: 149, 151
Fraser, F. A., 22: 234
Frazetta, Frank, 41: 72
Freas, John, 25: 207
Freeman, Don, 2: 15; 13: 249; 17: 62-63, 65, 67-68; 18: 243; 20: 195; 23: 213, 217; 32: 155
Fregosi, Claudia, 24: 117
French, Fiona, 6: 82-83

Friedman, Judith, 43: 197
Friedman, Marvin, 19: 59; 42: 86
Frinta, Dagmar, 36: 42
Frith, Michael K., 15: 138; 18: 120
Fritz, Ronald, 46: 73
Fromm, Lilo, 29: 85; 40: 197
Frost, A. B., 17: 6-7; 19: 123, 124, 125, 126, 127, 128, 129, 130; YABC 1: 156-157, 160; YABC 2: 107
Fry, Guy, 2: 224
Fry, Rosalie, 3: 72; YABC 2: 180-181
Fry, Rosalind, 21: 153, 168
Fryer, Elmer, 34: 115
Fuchs, Erich, 6: 84
Fuchshuber, Annegert, 43: 96
Fufuka, Mahiri, 32: 146
Fujikawa, Gyo, 39: 75, 76
Fulford, Deborah, 23: 159
Fuller, Margaret, 25: 189
Funai, Mamoru, 38: 105
Funk, Tom, 7: 17, 99
Furchgott, Terry, 29: 86
Furukawa, Mel, 25: 42

Gaberell, J., 19: 236
Gackenbach, Dick, 19: 168; 41: 81
Gaetano, Nicholas, 23: 209
Gag, Flavia, 17: 49, 52
Gág, Wanda, YABC 1: 135, 137-138, 141, 143
Gagnon, Cécile, 11: 77
Gal, Laszlo, 14: 127
Galdone, Paul, 1: 156, 181, 206; 2: 40, 241; 3: 42, 144; 4: 141; 10: 109, 158; 11: 21; 12: 118, 210; 14: 12; 16: 36-37; 17: 70-74; 18: 111, 230; 19: 183; 21: 154; 22: 150, 245; 33: 126; 39: 136, 137; 42: 57
Gallagher, Sears, 20: 112
Galster, Robert, 1: 66
Galsworthy, Gay John, 35: 232
Gammell, Stephen, 7: 48; 13: 149; 29: 82; 33: 209; 41: 88
Gannett, Ruth Chrisman, 3: 74; 18: 254; 33: 77, 78
Gantschev, Ivan, 45: 32
Garbutt, Bernard, 23: 68
Garcia, 37: 71
Gardner, Earle, 45: 167
Gardner, Joan, 40: 87
Gardner, Joel, 40: 87, 92
Gardner, John, 40: 87
Gardner, Lucy, 40: 87
Gardner, Richard. See Cummings, Richard, 24: 119
Garland, Michael, 36: 29; 38: 83; 44: 168
Garnett, Eve, 3: 75
Garnett, Gary, 39: 184
Garraty, Gail, 4: 142
Garrett, Agnes, 46: 110
Garrett, Edmund H., 20: 29
Garrison, Barbara, 19: 133
Gates, Frieda, 26: 80
Gaughan, Jack, 26: 79; 43: 185
Gaver, Becky, 20: 61

Gay, Zhenya, *19:* 135, 136
Geary, Clifford N., *1:* 122; *9:* 104
Gee, Frank, *33:* 26
Geer, Charles, *1:* 91; *3:* 179; *4:* 201;
   6: 168; *7:* 96; *9:* 58; *10:* 72;
   12: 127; *39:* 156, 157, 158, 159,
   160; *42:* 88, 89, 90, 91
Gehm, Charlie, *36:* 65
Geisel, Theodor Seuss, *1:* 104-105,
   106; *28:* 108, 109, 110, 111, 112,
   113
Geldart, William, *15:* 121; *21:* 202
Genia, *4:* 84
Gentry, Cyrille R., *12:* 66
George, Jean, *2:* 113
Gérard, Jean Ignace, *45:* 80
Gérard, Rolf, *27:* 147, 150
Geritz, Franz, *17:* 135
Gerlach, Geff, *42:* 58
Gershinowitz, George, *36:* 27
Gerstein, Mordicai, *31:* 117
Gervase, *12:* 27
Getz, Arthur, *32:* 148
Gibbons, Gail, *23:* 78
Gibbs, Tony, *40:* 95
Gibran, Kahlil, *32:* 116
Giesen, Rosemary, *34:* 192-193
Giguère, George, *20:* 111
Gilbert, John, *19:* 184; *YABC 2:* 287
Gilbert, W. S., *36:* 83, 85, 96
Giles, Will, *41:* 218
Gill, Margery, *4:* 57; *7:* 7; *22:* 122;
   25: 166; *26:* 146, 147
Gillen, Denver, *28:* 216
Gillette, Henry J., *23:* 237
Gilliam, Stan, *39:* 64, 81
Gilman, Esther, *15:* 124
Giovanopoulos, Paul, *7:* 104
Githens, Elizabeth M., *5:* 47
Gladstone, Gary, *12:* 89; *13:* 190
Gladstone, Lise, *15:* 273
Glanzman, Louis S., *2:* 177; *3:* 182;
   36: 97, 98; *38:* 120, 122
Glaser, Milton, *3:* 5; *5:* 156; *11:* 107;
   30: 26; *36:* 112
Glass, Andrew, *36:* 38; *44:* 133
Glass, Marvin, *9:* 174
Glasser, Judy, *41:* 156
Glattauer, Ned, *5:* 84; *13:* 224; *14:* 26
Glauber, Uta, *17:* 76
Gleeson, J. M., *YABC 2:* 207
Glegg, Creina, *36:* 100
Gliewe, Unada, *3:* 78-79; *21:* 73;
   30: 220
Glovach, Linda, *7:* 105
Gobbato, Imero, *3:* 180-181; *6:* 213;
   7: 58; *9:* 150; *18:* 39; *21:* 167;
   39: 82, 83; *41:* 137, 251
Goble, Paul, *25:* 121; *26:* 86; *33:* 65
Goble, Warwick, *46:* 78, 79
Godal, Eric, *36:* 93
Godfrey, Michael, *17:* 279
Goembel, Ponder, *42:* 124
Goffstein, M. B., *8:* 71
Golbin, Andrée, *15:* 125
Goldfeder, Cheryl, *11:* 191
Goldsborough, June, *5:* 154-155;
   8: 92; *14:* 226; *19:* 139
Goldstein, Leslie, *5:* 8; *6:* 60; *10:* 106

Goldstein, Nathan, *1:* 175; *2:* 79;
   11: 41, 232; *16:* 55
Goodall, John S., *4:* 92-93; *10:* 132;
   YABC 1: 198
Goode, Diane, *15:* 126
Goodelman, Aaron, *40:* 203
Goodenow, Earle, *40:* 97
Goodwin, Harold, *13:* 74
Goodwin, Philip R., *18:* 206
Goor, Nancy, *39:* 85, 86
Goor, Ron, *39:* 85, 86
Gordon, Gwen, *12:* 151
Gordon, Margaret, *4:* 147; *5:* 48-49;
   9: 79
Gorecka-Egan, Erica, *18:* 35
Gorey, Edward, *1:* 60-61; *13:* 169;
   18: 192; *20:* 201; *29:* 90, 91,
   92-93, 94, 95, 96, 97, 98, 99,
   100; *30:* 129; *32:* 90; *34:* 200.
   See also Dowdy, Mrs. Regera
Gorsline, Douglas, *1:* 98; *6:* 13;
   11: 113; *13:* 104; *15:* 14; *28:* 117,
   118; *YABC 1:* 15
Gosner, Kenneth, *5:* 135
Gotlieb, Jules, *6:* 127
Gough, Philip, *23:* 47; *45:* 90
Govern, Elaine R., *26:* 94
Grabianski, *20:* 144
Grabiański, Janusz, *39:* 92, 93, 94, 95
Graboff, Abner, *35:* 103, 104
Graham, A. B., *11:* 61
Graham, L., *7:* 108
Graham, Margaret Bloy, *11:* 120;
   18: 305, 307
Grahame-Johnstone, Anne, *13:* 61
Grahame-Johnstone, Janet, *13:* 61
Grainger, Sam, *42:* 95
Gramatky, Hardie, *1:* 107; *30:* 116,
   119, 120, 122, 123
Grandville, J. J., *45:* 81, 82, 83, 84,
   85, 86, 87, 88
Granger, Paul, *39:* 153
Grant, Gordon, *17:* 230, 234; *25:* 123,
   124, 125, 126; *YABC 1:* 164
Grant, (Alice) Leigh, *10:* 52; *15:* 131;
   20: 20; *26:* 119
Graves, Elizabeth, *45:* 101
Gray, Harold, *33:* 87, 88
Gray, Reginald, *6:* 69
Green, Eileen, *6:* 97
Green, Michael, *32:* 216
Greenaway, Kate, *17:* 275; *24:* 180;
   26: 107; *41:* 222, 232;
   YABC 1: 88-89; *YABC 2:* 131,
   133, 136, 138-139, 141
Greenwald, Sheila, *1:* 34; *3:* 99; *8:* 72
Gregorian, Joyce Ballou, *30:* 125
Gregory, Frank M., *29:* 107
Greiffenhagen, Maurice, *16:* 137;
   27: 57; *YABC 2:* 288
Greiner, Robert, *6:* 86
Gretter, J. Clemens, *31:* 134
Gretz, Susanna, *7:* 114
Gretzer, John, *1:* 54; *3:* 26; *4:* 162;
   7: 125; *16:* 247; *18:* 117; *28:* 66;
   30: 85, 211; *33:* 235
Grey Owl, *24:* 41
Gri, *25:* 90
Grieder, Walter *9:* 84

Grifalconi, Ann, *2:* 126; *3:* 248;
   11: 18; *13:* 182; *46:* 38
Griffin, Gillett Good, *26:* 96
Griffin, James, *30:* 166
Griffiths, Dave, *29:* 76
Gringhuis, Dirk, *6:* 98; *9:* 196
Gripe, Harald, *2:* 127
Grisha, *3:* 71
Gropper, William, *27:* 93; *37:* 193
Grose, Helen Mason, *YABC 1:* 260;
   YABC 2: 150
Grossman, Nancy, *24:* 130; *29:* 101
Grossman, Robert, *11:* 124; *46:* 39
Groth, John, *15:* 79; *21:* 53, 54
Gruelle, Johnny, *35:* 107
Gschwind, William, *11:* 72
Guggenheim, Hans, *2:* 10; *3:* 37;
   8: 136
Guilbeau, Honoré, *22:* 69
Gundersheimer, Karen, *35:* 240
Gusman, Annie, *38:* 62
Gustafson, Scott, *34:* 111; *43:* 40
Guthrie, Robin, *20:* 122
Gwynne, Fred, *41:* 94, 95
Gyberg, Bo-Erik, *38:* 131

Haas, Irene, *17:* 77
Hader, Berta H., *16:* 126
Hader, Elmer S., *16:* 126
Hafner, Marylin, *22:* 196, 216; *24:* 44;
   30: 51; *35:* 95
Hague, Michael, *32:* 128
Halas, John, *29:* 41, 47, 48
Haldane, Roger, *13:* 76; *14:* 202
Hale, Irina, *26:* 97
Hale, Kathleen, *17:* 79
Haley, Gail E., *43:* 102, 103, 104, 105
Hall, Chuck, *30:* 189
Hall, Douglas, *15:* 184; *43:* 106, 107
Hall, H. Tom, *1:* 227; *30:* 210
Hall, Sydney P., *31:* 89
Hall, Vicki, *20:* 24
Hallinan, P. K., *39:* 98
Halpern, Joan, *10:* 25
Hamberger, John, *6:* 8; *8:* 32; *14:* 79;
   34: 136
Hamil, Tom, *14:* 80; *43:* 163
Hamilton, Bill and Associates, *26:* 215
Hamilton, Helen S., *2:* 238
Hamilton, J., *19:* 83, 85, 87
Hammond, Chris, *21:* 37
Hammond, Elizabeth, *5:* 36, 203
Hampshire, Michael, *5:* 187;
   7: 110-111
Hampson, Denman, *10:* 155; *15:* 130
Hampton, Blake, *41:* 244
Handforth, Thomas, *42:* 100, 101,
   102, 103, 104, 105, 107
Handville, Robert, *1:* 89; *38:* 76;
   45: 108, 109
Hane, Roger, *17:* 239; *44:* 54
Haney, Elizabeth Mathieu, *34:* 84
Hanley, Catherine, *8:* 161
Hann, Jacquie, *19:* 144
Hannon, Mark, *38:* 37
Hanson, Joan, *8:* 76; *11:* 139
Hardy, David A., *9:* 96
Hardy, Paul, *YABC 2:* 245

Harlan, Jerry, *3:* 96
Harnischfeger, *18:* 121
Harper, Arthur, *YABC 2:* 121
Harrington, Richard, *5:* 81
Harris, Susan Yard, *42:* 121
Harrison, Florence, *20:* 150, 152
Harrison, Harry, *4:* 103
Harrison, Jack, *28:* 149
Hart, William, *13:* 72
Hartelius, Margaret, *10:* 24
Hartshorn, Ruth, *5:* 115; *11:* 129
Harvey, Gerry, *7:* 180
Hassall, Joan, *43:* 108, 109
Hassell, Hilton, *YABC 1:* 187
Hasselriis, Else, *18:* 87; *YABC 1:* 96
Hauman, Doris, *2:* 184; *29:* 58, 59;
    32: 85, 86, 87
Hauman, George, *2:* 184; *29:* 58, 59;
    32: 85, 86, 87
Hausherr, Rosmarie, *15:* 29
Hawkinson, John, *4:* 109; *7:* 83;
    21: 64
Hawkinson, Lucy, *21:* 64
Haxton, Elaine, *28:* 131
Haydock, Robert, *4:* 95
Hayes, Geoffrey, *26:* 111; *44:* 133
Haywood, Carolyn, *1:* 112; *29:* 104
Healy, Daty, *12:* 143
Hearon, Dorothy, *34:* 69
Hechtkopf, H., *11:* 110
Hedderwick, Mairi, *30:* 127; *32:* 47;
    36: 104
Hefter, Richard, *28:* 170; *31:* 81, 82;
    33: 183
Heigh, James, *22:* 98
Heighway, Richard, *25:* 160
Heinly, John, *45:* 113
Hellebrand, Nancy, *26:* 57
Heller, Linda, *46:* 86
Hellmuth, Jim, *38:* 164
Helms, Georgeann, *33:* 62
Helweg, Hans, *41:* 118
Henderson, Keith, *35:* 122
Henkes, Kevin, *43:* 111
Henneberger, Robert, *1:* 42; *2:* 237;
    25: 83
Henriksen, Harold, *35:* 26
Henry, Everett, *29:* 191
Henry, Thomas, *5:* 102
Hensel, *27:* 119
Henstra, Friso, *8:* 80; *36:* 70; *40:* 222;
    41: 250
Hepple, Norman, *28:* 198
Herbert, Wally, *23:* 101
Herbster, Mary Lee, *9:* 33
Hergé. *See* Rémi, Georges
Hermanson, Dennis, *10:* 55
Herrington, Roger, *3:* 161
Heslop, Mike, *38:* 60; *40:* 130
Hess, Richard, *42:* 31
Hester, Ronnie, *37:* 85
Heustis, Louise L., *20:* 28
Heyduck-Huth, Hilde, *8:* 82
Heyer, Hermann, *20:* 114, 115
Heyman, Ken, *8:* 33; *34:* 113
Hickling, P. B., *40:* 165
Higginbottom, J. Winslow, *8:* 170;
    29: 105, 106
Hildebrandt, Greg, *8:* 191

Hildebrandt, Tim, *8:* 191
Hilder, Rowland, *19:* 207
Hill, Gregory, *35:* 190
Hillier, Matthew, *45:* 205
Himler, Ronald, *6:* 114; *7:* 162; *8:* 17,
    84, 125; *14:* 76; *19:* 145; *26:* 160;
    31: 43; *38:* 116; *41:* 44, 79;
    43: 52; *45:* 120; *46:* 43
Hinds, Bill, *37:* 127, 130
Hiroshige, *25:* 71
Hirsh, Marilyn, *7:* 126
Hitz, Demi, *11:* 135; *15:* 245
Hnizdovsky, Jacques, *32:* 96
Ho, Kwoncjan, *15:* 132
Hoban, Lillian, *1:* 114; *22:* 157;
    26: 72; *29:* 53; *40:* 105, 107, 195;
    41: 80
Hoban, Tana, *22:* 159
Hoberman, Norman, *5:* 82
Hockerman, Dennis, *39:* 22
Hodgell, P. C., *42:* 114
Hodges, C. Walter, *2:* 139; *11:* 15;
    12: 25; *23:* 34; *25:* 96; *38:* 165;
    44: 197; *45:* 95; *YABC 2:* 62-63
Hodges, David, *9:* 98
Hodgetts, Victoria, *43:* 132
Hofbauer, Imre, *2:* 162
Hoff, Syd, *9:* 107; *10:* 128; *33:* 94
Hoffman, Rosekrans, *15:* 133
Hoffman, Sanford, *38:* 208
Hoffmann, Felix, *9:* 109
Hofsinde, Robert, *21:* 70
Hogan, Inez, *2:* 141
Hogarth, Burne, *41:* 58
Hogarth, Paul, *41:* 102, 103, 104;
    YABC 1: 16
Hogarth, William, *42:* 33
Hogenbyl, Jan, *1:* 35
Hogner, Nils, *4:* 122; *25:* 144
Hogrogian, Nonny, *3:* 221; *4:* 106-107;
    5: 166; *7:* 129; *15:* 2; *16:* 176;
    20: 154; *22:* 146; *25:* 217;
    27: 206; *YABC 2:* 84, 94
Hokusai, *25:* 71
Holberg, Richard, *2:* 51
Holdcroft, Tina, *38:* 109
Holder, Heidi, *36:* 99
Holiday, Henry, *YABC 2:* 107
Holl, F., *36:* 91
Holland, Brad, *45:* 59, 159
Holland, Janice, *18:* 118
Holland, Marion, *6:* 116
Holldobler, Turid, *26:* 120
Holling, Holling C., *15:* 136-137
Hollinger, Deanne, *12:* 116
Holmes, B., *3:* 82
Holmes, Bea, *7:* 74; *24:* 156; *31:* 93
Holmgren, George Ellen, *45:* 112
Holt, Norma, *44:* 106
Holtan, Gene, *32:* 192
Holz, Loretta, *17:* 81
Homar, Lorenzo, *6:* 2
Homer, Winslow, *YABC 2:* 87
Honigman, Marian, *3:* 2
Honoré, Paul, *42:* 77, 79, 81, 82
Hood, Susan, *12:* 43
Hook, Frances, *26:* 188; *27:* 127
Hook, Jeff, *14:* 137
Hook, Richard, *26:* 188

Hoover, Carol A., *21:* 77
Hoover, Russell, *12:* 95; *17:* 2;
    34: 156
Hoppin, Augustus, *34:* 66
Horder, Margaret, *2:* 108
Horen, Michael, *45:* 121
Horvat, Laurel, *12:* 201
Horvath, Ferdinand Kusati, *24:* 176
Hotchkiss, De Wolfe, *20:* 49
Hough, Charlotte, *9:* 112; *13:* 98;
    17: 83; *24:* 195
Houlihan, Ray, *11:* 214
Housman, Laurence, *25:* 146, 147
Houston, James, *13:* 107
How, W. E., *20:* 47
Howard, Alan, *16:* 80; *34:* 58; *45:* 114
Howard, J. N., *15:* 234
Howard, John, *33:* 179
Howard, Rob, *40:* 161
Howe, Stephen, *1:* 232
Howell, Pat, *15:* 139
Howell, Troy, *23:* 24; *31:* 61; *36:* 158;
    37: 184; *41:* 76, 235
Howes, Charles, *22:* 17
Hudnut, Robin, *14:* 62
Huffaker, Sandy, *10:* 56
Huffman, Joan, *13:* 33
Huffman, Tom, *13:* 180; *17:* 212;
    21: 116; *24:* 132; *33:* 154; *38:* 59;
    42: 147
Hughes, Arthur, *20:* 148, 149, 150;
    33: 114, 148, 149
Hughes, David, *36:* 197
Hughes, Shirley, *1:* 20, 21; *7:* 3;
    12: 217; *16:* 163; *29:* 154
Hülsmann, Eva, *16:* 166
Hummel, Berta, *43:* 137, 138, 139
Hummel, Lisl, *29:* 109;
    YABC 2: 333-334
Humphrey, Henry, *16:* 167
Humphreys, Graham, *25:* 168
Hunt, James, *2:* 143
Hurd, Clement, *2:* 148, 149
Hurd, Peter; *24:* 30, 31, *YABC 2:* 56
Hurd, Thacher, *46:* 88-89
Hürlimann, Ruth, *32:* 99
Hustler, Tom, *6:* 105
Hutchins, Pat, *15:* 142
Hutchinson, William M., *6:* 3, 138;
    46: 70
Hutchison, Paula, *23:* 10
Hutton, Clarke, *YABC 2:* 335
Hutton, Kathryn, *35:* 155
Hutton, Warwick, *20:* 91
Huyette, Marcia, *29:* 188
Hyman, Trina Schart, *1:* 204; *2:* 194;
    5: 153; *6:* 106; *7:* 138, 145; *8:* 22;
    10: 196; *13:* 96; *14:* 114; *15:* 204;
    16: 234; *20:* 82; *22:* 133; *24:* 151;
    25: 79, 82; *26:* 82; *29:* 83; *31:* 37,
    39; *34:* 104; *38:* 84, 100, 128;
    41: 49; *43:* 146; *46:* 91, 92, 93,
    95, 96, 97, 98, 99, 100, 101, 102,
    103, 104-105, 108, 109, 111, 197

Ichikawa, Satomi, *29:* 152; *41:* 52
Ide, Jacqueline, *YABC 1:* 39

Ilsley, Velma, *3:* 1; *7:* 55; *12:* 109; *37:* 62; *38:* 184
Inga, *1:* 142
Ingraham, Erick, *21:* 177
Innocenti, Roberto, *21:* 123
Inoue, Yosuke, *24:* 118
Ipcar, Dahlov, *1:* 124-125
Irvin, Fred, *13:* 166; *15:* 143-144; *27:* 175
Irving, Jay, *45:* 72
Irving, Laurence, *27:* 50
Isaac, Joanne, *21:* 76
Isadora, Rachel, *43:* 159, 160
Ishmael, Woodi, *24:* 111; *31:* 99
Ives, Ruth, *15:* 257

Jackson, Michael, *43:* 42
Jacobs, Barbara, *9:* 136
Jacobs, Lou, Jr., *9:* 136; *15:* 128
Jacques, Robin, *1:* 70; *2:* 1; *8:* 46; *9:* 20; *15:* 187; *19:* 253; *32:* 102, 103, 104; *43:* 184; *YABC 1:* 42
Jagr, Miloslav, *13:* 197
Jakubowski, Charles, *14:* 192
Jambor, Louis, *YABC 1:* 11
James, Derek, *35:* 187; *44:* 91
James, Gilbert, *YABC 1:* 43
James, Harold, *2:* 151; *3:* 62; *8:* 79; *29:* 113
James, Will, *19:* 150, 152, 153, 155, 163
Janosch. *See* Eckert, Horst
Jansson, Tove, *3:* 90; *41:* 106, 108, 109, 110, 111, 113, 114
Jaques, Faith, *7:* 11, 132-33; *21:* 83, 84
Jaques, Frances Lee, *29:* 224
Jauss, Anne Marie, *1:* 139; *3:* 34; *10:* 57, 119; *11:* 205; *23:* 194
Jeffers, Susan, *17:* 86-87; *25:* 164-165; *26:* 112
Jefferson, Louise E., *4:* 160
Jeruchim, Simon, *6:* 173; *15:* 250
Jeschke, Susan, *20:* 89; *39:* 161; *41:* 84; *42:* 120
Jessel, Camilla, *29:* 115
Joerns, Consuelo, *38:* 36; *44:* 94
John, Diana, *12:* 209
John, Helen, *1:* 215; *28:* 204
Johns, Jeanne, *24:* 114
Johnson, Bruce, *9:* 47
Johnson, Crockett. *See* Leisk, David
Johnson, D. William, *23:* 104
Johnson, Harper, *1:* 27; *2:* 33; *18:* 302; *19:* 61; *31:* 181; *44:* 46, 50, 95
Johnson, Ingrid, *37:* 118
Johnson, James David, *12:* 195
Johnson, James Ralph, *1:* 23, 127
Johnson, John E., *34:* 133
Johnson, Margaret S., *35:* 131
Johnson, Milton, *1:* 67; *2:* 71; *26:* 45; *31:* 107
Johnson, Pamela, *16:* 174
Johnson, William R., *38:* 91
Johnstone, Anne, *8:* 120; *36:* 89
Johnstone, Janet Grahame, *8:* 120; *36:* 89
Jones, Carol, *5:* 131

Jones, Elizabeth Orton, *18:* 124, 126, 128-129
Jones, Harold, *14:* 88
Jones, Jeff, *41:* 64
Jones, Laurian, *25:* 24, 27
Jones, Robert, *25:* 67
Jones, Wilfred, *35:* 115; *YABC 1:* 163
Joyner, Jerry, *34:* 138
Jucker, Sita, *5:* 93
Judkis, Jim, *37:* 38
Juhasz, Victor, *31:* 67
Jullian, Philippe, *24:* 206; *25:* 203
Jupo, Frank, *7:* 148-149
Justice, Martin, *34:* 72

Kahl, M. P., *37:* 83
Kakimoo, Kozo, *11:* 148
Kalin, Victor, *39:* 186
Kalmenoff, Matthew, *22:* 191
Kalow, Gisela, *32:* 105
Kamen, Gloria, *1:* 41; *9:* 119; *10:* 178; *35:* 157
Kandell, Alice, *35:* 133
Kane, Henry B., *14:* 90; *18:* 219-220
Kane, Robert, *18:* 131
Kappes, Alfred, *28:* 104
Karalus, Bob, *41:* 157
Karlin, Eugene, *10:* 63; *20:* 131
Kasuya, Masahiro, *41:* 206-207
Katona, Robert, *21:* 85; *24:* 126
Kauffer, E. McKnight, *33:* 103; *35:* 127
Kaufman, Angelika, *15:* 156
Kaufman, Joe, *33:* 119
Kaufman, John, *13:* 158
Kaufmann, John, *1:* 174; *4:* 159; *8:* 43, 1; *10:* 102; *18:* 133-134; *22:* 251
Kaye, Graham, *1:* 9
Kazalovski, Nata, *40:* 205
Keane, Bil, *4:* 135
Keats, Ezra Jack, *3:* 18, 105, 257; *14:* 101, 102; *33:* 129
Keegan, Marcia, *9:* 122; *32:* 93
Keely, John, *26:* 104
Keen, Eliot, *25:* 213
Keeping, Charles, *9:* 124, 185; *15:* 28, 134; *18:* 115; *44:* 194, 196
Keith, Eros, *4:* 98; *5:* 138; *31:* 29; *43:* 220
Kelen, Emery, *13:* 115
Keller, Arthur I., *26:* 106
Keller, Dick, *36:* 123, 125
Keller, Holly, *45:* 79
Keller, Ronald, *45:* 208
Kelley, True, *41:* 114, 115; *42:* 137
Kellogg, Steven, *8:* 96; *11:* 207; *14:* 130; *20:* 58; *29:* 140-141; *30:* 35; *41:* 141; *YABC 1:* 65, 73
Kelly, Walt, *18:* 136-141, 144-146, 148-149
Kemble, E. W., *34:* 75; *44:* 178; *YABC 2:* 54, 59
Kemp-Welsh, Lucy, *24:* 197
Kennedy, Paul Edward, *6:* 190; *8:* 132; *33:* 120
Kennedy, Richard, *3:* 93; *12:* 179; *44:* 193; *YABC 1:* 57

Kent, Jack, *24:* 136; *37:* 37; *40:* 81
Kent, Rockwell, *5:* 166; *6:* 129; *20:* 225, 226, 227, 229
Kepes, Juliet, *13:* 119
Kerr, Judity, *24:* 137
Kessler, Leonard, *1:* 108; *7:* 139; *14:* 107, 227; *22:* 101; *44:* 96
Kesteven, Peter, *35:* 189
Ketcham, Hank, *28:* 140, 141, 142
Kettelkamp, Larry, *2:* 164
Key, Alexander, *8:* 99
Kiakshuk, *8:* 59
Kiddell-Monroe, Joan, *19:* 201
Kidder, Harvey, *9:* 105
Kidwell, Carl, *43:* 145
Kieffer, Christa, *41:* 89
Kiff, Ken, *40:* 45
Kilbride, Robert, *37:* 100
Kimball, Yeffe, *23:* 116; *37:* 88
Kincade, Orin, *34:* 116
Kindred, Wendy, *7:* 151
King, Robin, *10:* 164-165
King, Tony, *39:* 121
Kingman, Dong, *16:* 287; *44:* 100, 102, 104
Kingsley, Charles, *YABC 2:* 182
Kipling, John Lockwood, *YABC 2:* 198
Kipling, Rudyard, *YABC 2:* 196
Kipniss, Robert, *29:* 59
Kirchhoff, Art, *28:* 136
Kirk, Ruth, *5:* 96
Kirk, Tim, *32:* 209, 211
Kirmse, Marguerite, *15:* 283; *18:* 153
Kirschner, Ruth, *22:* 154
Klapholz, Mel, *13:* 35
Kleinman, Zalman, *28:* 143
Kliban, B., *35:* 137, 138
Knight, Ann, *34:* 143
Knight, Christopher, *13:* 125
Knight, Hilary, *1:* 233; *3:* 21; *15:* 92, 158-159; *16:* 258-260; *18:* 235; *19:* 169; *35:* 242; *46:* 167; *YABC 1:* 168-169, 172
Knotts, Howard, *20:* 4; *25:* 170; *36:* 163
Kobayashi, Ann, *39:* 58
Kocsis, J. C. *See* Paul, James
Koehn, Ilse, *34:* 198
Koering, Ursula, *3:* 28; *4:* 14; *44:* 53
Koerner, Henry. *See* Koerner, W.H.D.
Koerner, W.H.D., *14:* 216; *21:* 88, 89, 90, 91; *23:* 211
Koffler, Camilla, *36:* 113
Komoda, Kiyo, *9:* 128; *13:* 214
Konashevicha, V., *YABC 1:* 26
Konigsburg, E. L., *4:* 138
Korach, Mimi, *1:* 128-129; *2:* 52; *4:* 39; *5:* 159; *9:* 129; *10:* 21; *24:* 69
Koren, Edward, *5:* 100
Kossin, Sandy, *10:* 71; *23:* 105
Kostin, Andrej, *26:* 204
Kovacević, Zivojin, *13:* 247
Krahn, Fernando, *2:* 257; *34:* 206
Kramer, Anthony, *33:* 81
Kramer, Frank, *6:* 121
Krantz, Kathy, *35:* 83
Kraus, Robert, *13:* 217

Kredel, Fritz, *6:* 35; *17:* 93-96;
    22: 147; *24:* 175; *29:* 130; *35:* 77;
    YABC 2: 166, 300
Krementz, Jill, *17:* 98
Kresin, Robert, *23:* 19
Krush, Beth, *1:* 51, 85; *2:* 233; *4:* 115;
    9: 61; *10:* 191; *11:* 196;
    18: 164-165; *32:* 72; *37:* 203;
    43: 57
Krush, Joe, *2:* 233; *4:* 115; *9:* 61;
    10: 191; *11:* 196; *18:* 164-165;
    32: 72, 91; *37:* 203; *43:* 57
Kubinyi, Laszlo, *4:* 116; *6:* 113;
    16: 118; *17:* 100; *28:* 227; *30:* 172
Kuhn, Bob, *17:* 91; *35:* 235
Künstler, Mort, *10:* 73; *32:* 143
Kurchevsky, V., *34:* 61
Kurelek, William, *8:* 107
Kuriloff, Ron, *13:* 19
Kuskin, Karla, *2:* 170
Kutzer, Ernst, *19:* 249

LaBlanc, André, *24:* 146
Laboccetta, Mario, *27:* 120
Laceky, Adam, *32:* 121
La Croix, *YABC 2:* 4
Laimgruber, Monika, *11:* 153
Laite, Gordon, *1:* 130-131; *8:* 209;
    31: 113; *40:* 63; *46:* 117
Lamarche, Jim, *46:* 204
Lamb, Jim, *10:* 117
Lambert, J. K., *38:* 129; *39:* 24
Lambert, Saul, *23:* 112; *33:* 107
Lambo, Don, *6:* 156; *35:* 115; *36:* 146
Landa, Peter, *11:* 95; *13:* 177
Landau, Jacob, *38:* 111
Landshoff, Ursula, *13:* 124
Lane, John, *15:* 176-177; *30:* 146
Lane, John R., *8:* 145
Lang, Jerry, *18:* 295
Langner, Nola, *8:* 110; *42:* 36
Lantz, Paul, *1:* 82, 102; *27:* 88;
    34: 102; *45:* 123
Larrecq, John, *44:* 108
Larsen, Suzanne, *1:* 13
Larsson, Carl, *35:* 144, 145, 146, 147,
    148-149, 150, 152, 153, 154
Larsson, Karl, *19:* 177
La Rue, Michael D., *13:* 215
Lasker, Joe, *7:* 186-187; *14:* 55;
    38: 115; *39:* 47
Latham, Barbara, *16:* 188-189; *43:* 71
Lathrop, Dorothy, *14:* 117, 118-119;
    15: 109; *16:* 78-79, 81; *32:* 201,
    203; *33:* 112; *YABC 2:* 301
Lattimore, Eleanor Frances, *7:* 156
Lauden, Claire, *16:* 173
Lauden, George, Jr., *16:* 173
Laune, Paul, *2:* 235; *34:* 31
Lavis, Stephen, *43:* 143
Lawrence, John, *25:* 131; *30:* 141;
    44: 198, 200
Lawrence, Stephen, *20:* 195
Lawson, Carol, *6:* 38; *42:* 93, 131
Lawson, George, *17:* 280
Lawson, Robert, *5:* 26; *6:* 94; *13:* 39;
    16: 11; *20:* 100, 102, 103;

YABC 2: 222,
    224-225, 227-235, 237-241
Lazare, Jerry, *44:* 109
Lazarevich, Mila, *17:* 118
Lazarus, Keo Felker, *21:* 94
Lazzaro, Victor, *11:* 126
Lea, Tom, *43:* 72, 74
Leacroft, Richard, *6:* 140
Leaf, Munro, *20:* 99
Leander, Patricia, *23:* 27
Lear, Edward, *18:* 183-185
Lebenson, Richard, *6:* 209; *7:* 76;
    23: 145; *44:* 191
Le Cain, Errol, *6:* 141; *9:* 3; *22:* 142;
    25: 198; *28:* 173
Lee, Doris, *13:* 246; *32:* 183; *44:* 111
Lee, Manning de V., *2:* 200; *17:* 12;
    27: 87; *37:* 102, 103, 104;
    YABC 2: 304
Lee, Robert J., *3:* 97
Leech, John, *15:* 59
Leeman, Michael, *44:* 157
Lees, Harry, *6:* 112
Legrand, Edy, *18:* 89, 93
Lehrman, Rosalie, *2:* 180
Leichman, Seymour, *5:* 107
Leighton, Clare, *25:* 130; *33:* 168;
    37: 105, 106, 108, 109
Leisk, David, *1:* 140-141; *11:* 54;
    30: 137, 142, 143, 144
Leloir, Maurice, *18:* 77, 80, 83, 99
Lemke, Horst, *14:* 98; *38:* 117, 118,
    119
Lemke, R. W., *42:* 162
Lemon, David Gwynne, *9:* 1
Lenski, Lois, *1:* 144; *26:* 135, 137,
    139, 141
Lent, Blair, *1:* 116-117; *2:* 174;
    3: 206-207; *7:* 168-169; *34:* 62
Lerner, Sharon, *11:* 157; *22:* 56
Leslie, Cecil, *19:* 244
Levai, Blaise, *39:* 130
Levin, Ted, *12:* 148
Levine, David, *43:* 147, 149, 150,
    151, 152
Levit, Herschel, *24:* 223
Levy, Jessica Ann, *19:* 225; *39:* 191
Lewin, Betsy, *32:* 114
Lewin, Ted, *4:* 77; *8:* 168; *20:* 110;
    21: 99, 100; *27:* 110; *28:* 96, 97;
    31: 49; *45:* 55
Lewis, Allen, *15:* 112
Leydon, Rita Flodén, *21:* 101
Lieblich, Irene, *22:* 173; *27:* 209, 214
Liese, Charles, *4:* 222
Lightfoot, Norman R., *45:* 47
Lignell, Lois, *37:* 114
Lilly, Charles, *8:* 73; *20:* 127
Lilly, Ken, *37:* 224
Lim, John, *43:* 153
Lincoln, Patricia Henderson, *27:* 27
Lindberg, Howard, *10:* 123; *16:* 190
Linden, Seymour, *18:* 200-201;
    43: 140
Linder, Richard, *27:* 119
Lindman, Maj, *43:* 154
Lindsay, Vachel, *40:* 118
Line, Les, *27:* 143
Linell. See Smith, Linell

Lionni, Leo, *8:* 115
Lipinsky, Lino, *2:* 156; *22:* 175
Lippman, Peter, *8:* 31; *31:* 119, 120,
    160
Lisker, Sonia O., *16:* 274; *31:* 31;
    44: 113, 114
Lissim, Simon, *17:* 138
Little, Harold, *16:* 72
Little, Mary E., *28:* 146
Lively, Lorna, *19:* 216
Llerena, Carlos Antonio, *19:* 181
Lloyd, Errol, *11:* 39; *22:* 178
Lo, Koon-chiu, *7:* 134
Lobel, Anita, *6:* 87; *9:* 141; *18:* 248
Lobel, Arnold, *1:* 188-189; *5:* 12;
    6: 147; *7:* 167, 209; *18:* 190-191;
    25: 39, 43; *27:* 40; *29:* 174
Loefgren, Ulf, *3:* 108
Loescher, Ann, *20:* 108
Loescher, Gil, *20:* 108
Lofting, Hugh, *15:* 182-183
Loh, George, *38:* 88
Lonette, Reisie, *11:* 211; *12:* 168;
    13: 56; *36:* 122; *43:* 155
Long, Sally, *42:* 184
Longtemps, Ken, *17:* 123; *29:* 221
Looser, Heinz, *YABC 2:* 208
Lopshire, Robert, *6:* 149; *21:* 117;
    34: 166
Lord, John Vernon, *21:* 104; *23:* 25
Lorenz, Al, *40:* 146
Loretta, Sister Mary, *33:* 73
Lorraine, Walter H., *3:* 110; *4:* 123;
    16: 192
Loss, Joan, *11:* 163
Louderback, Walt, *YABC 1:* 164
Lousada, Sandra, *40:* 138
Low, Joseph, *14:* 124, 125; *18:* 68;
    19: 194; *31:* 166
Lowenheim, Alfred, *13:* 65-66
Lowitz, Anson, *17:* 124; *18:* 215
Lowrey, Jo, *8:* 133
Lubell, Winifred, *1:* 207; *3:* 15; *6:* 151
Lubin, Leonard B., *19:* 224; *36:* 79,
    80; *45:* 128, 129, 131, 132, 133,
    134, 135, 136, 137, 139, 140,
    141; *YABC 2:* 96
Ludwig, Helen, *33:* 144, 145
Lufkin, Raymond, *38:* 138; *44:* 48
Luhrs, Henry, *7:* 123; *11:* 120
Lupo, Dom, *4:* 204
Lustig, Loretta, *30:* 186; *46:* 134, 135,
    136, 137
Lydecker, Laura, *21:* 113; *42:* 53
Lynch, Charles, *16:* 33
Lynch, Marietta, *29:* 137; *30:* 171
Lyon, Elinor, *6:* 154
Lyon, Fred, *14:* 16
Lyons, Oren, *8:* 193
Lyster, Michael, *26:* 41

Maas, Dorothy, *6:* 175
Macaulay, David, *46:* 139, 140-141,
    142, 143, 144-145, 147, 149, 150
Macdonald, Alister, *21:* 55
MacDonald, Norman, *13:* 99
MacDonald, Roberta, *19:* 237
Macguire, Robert Reid, *18:* 67

Machetanz, Fredrick, *34:* 147, 148
MacInnes, Ian, *35:* 59
MacIntyre, Elisabeth, *17:* 127-128
Mack, Stan, *17:* 129
Mackay, Donald, *17:* 60
MacKaye, Arvia, *32:* 119
MacKenzie, Garry, *33:* 159
Mackinlay, Miguel, *27:* 22
MacKinstry, Elizabeth, *15:* 110;
    42: 139, 140, 141, 142, 143, 144,
    145
Maclise, Daniel, *YABC 2:* 257
Madden, Don, *3:* 112-113; *4:* 33, 108,
    155; *7:* 193; *YABC 2:* 211
Maddison, Angela Mary, *10:* 83
Maestro, Giulio, *8:* 124; *12:* 17;
    13: 108; *25:* 182
Magnuson, Diana, *28:* 102; *34:* 190;
    41: 175
Maguire, Sheila, *41:* 100
Mahony, Will, *37:* 120
Mahood, Kenneth, *24:* 141
Maik, Henri, *9:* 102
Maisto, Carol, *29:* 87
Maitland, Antony, *1:* 100, 176; *8:* 41;
    17: 246; *24:* 46; *25:* 177, 178;
    32: 74
Makie, Pam, *37:* 117
Malvern, Corinne, *2:* 13; *34:* 148, 149
Mandelbaum, Ira, *31:* 115
Manet, Edouard, *23:* 170
Mangurian, David, *14:* 133
Manham, Allan, *42:* 109
Manniche, Lise, *31:* 121
Manning, Samuel F., *5:* 75
Maraja, *15:* 86; *YABC 1:* 28;
    YABC 2: 115
Marcellino, Fred, *20:* 125; *34:* 222
Marchesi, Stephen, *34:* 140; *46:* 72
Marchiori, Carlos, *14:* 60
Margules, Gabriele, *21:* 120
Mariana. *See* Foster, Marian Curtis
Marino, Dorothy, *6:* 37; *14:* 135
Markham, R. L., *17:* 240
Marokvia, Artur, *31:* 122
Marriott, Pat, *30:* 30; *34:* 39; *35:* 164,
    165, 166; *44:* 170
Mars, W. T., *1:* 161; *3:* 115; *4:* 208,
    225; *5:* 92, 105, 186; *8:* 214;
    9: 12; *13:* 121; *27:* 151; *31:* 180;
    38: 102
Marsh, Christine, *3:* 164
Marsh, Reginald, *17:* 5; *19:* 89;
    22: 90, 96
Marshall, Anthony D., *18:* 216
Marshall, James, *6:* 160; *40:* 221;
    42: 24, 25, 29
Martin, David Stone, *23:* 232
Martin, Fletcher, *18:* 213; *23:* 151
Martin, René, *7:* 144; *42:* 148, 149,
    150
Martin, Ron, *32:* 81
Martin, Stefan, *8:* 68; *32:* 124, 126
Martinez, John, *6:* 113
Marx, Robert F., *24:* 143
Masefield, Judith, *19:* 208, 209
Mason, George F., *14:* 139
Massie, Diane Redfield, *16:* 194
Massie, Kim, *31:* 43

Mathieu, Joseph, *14:* 33; *39:* 206;
    43: 167
Matsubara, Naoko, *12:* 121
Matsuda, Shizu, *13:* 167
Matte, L'Enc, *22:* 183
Mattelson, Marvin, *36:* 50, 51
Matthews, F. Leslie, *4:* 216
Matulay, Laszlo, *5:* 18; *43:* 168
Matus, Greta, *12:* 142
Mauldin, Bill, *27:* 23
Mawicke, Tran, *9:* 137; *15:* 191
Max, Peter, *45:* 146, 147, 148-149,
    150
Maxie, Betty, *40:* 135
Maxwell, John Alan, *1:* 148
Mayan, Earl, *7:* 193
Mayer, Marianna, *32:* 132
Mayer, Mercer, *11:* 192; *16:* 195-196;
    20: 55, 57; *32:* 129, 130, 132,
    133, 134; *41:* 144, 248, 252
Mayhew, Richard, *3:* 106
Mayo, Gretchen, *38:* 81
Mays, Victor, *5:* 127; *8:* 45, 153;
    14: 245; *23:* 50; *34:* 155; *40:* 79;
    45: 158
Mazza, Adriana Saviozzi, *19:* 215
Mazzetti, Alan, *45:* 210
McBride, Angus, *28:* 49
McBride, Will, *30:* 110
McCaffery, Janet, *38:* 145
McCann, Gerald, *3:* 50; *4:* 94; *7:* 54;
    41: 121
McCay, Winsor, *41:* 124, 126, 128-
    129, 130-131
McClary, Nelson, *1:* 111
McClintock, Theodore, *14:* 141
McCloskey, Robert, *1:* 184-185;
    2: 186-187; *17:* 209; *39:* 139,
    140, 141, 142, 143, 146, 147, 148
McClung, Robert, *2:* 189
McClure, Gillian, *31:* 132
McConnel, Jerry, *31:* 75, 187
McCormick, A. D., *35:* 119
McCormick, Dell J., *19:* 216
McCrady, Lady, *16:* 198; *39:* 127
McCrea, James, *3:* 122; *33:* 216
McCrea, Ruth, *3:* 122; *27:* 102;
    33: 216
McCully, Emily, *2:* 89; *4:* 120-121,
    146, 197; *5:* 2, 129; *7:* 191;
    11: 122; *15:* 210; *33:* 23; *35:* 244;
    37: 122; *39:* 88; *40:* 103
McCurdy, Michael, *13:* 153; *24:* 85
McDermott, Beverly Brodsky, *11:* 180
McDermott, Gerald, *16:* 201
McDonald, Jill, *13:* 155; *26:* 128
McDonald, Ralph J., *5:* 123, 195
McDonough, Don, *10:* 163
McEntee, Dorothy, *37:* 124
McFall, Christie, *12:* 144
McGee, Barbara, *6:* 165
McGregor, Malcolm, *23:* 27
McHugh, Tom, *23:* 64
McIntosh, Jon, *42:* 56
McKay, Donald, *2:* 118; *32:* 157;
    45: 151, 152
McKeating, Eileen, *44:* 58
McKee, David, *10:* 48; *21:* 9
McKie, Roy, *7:* 44

McKillip, Kathy, *30:* 153
McKinney, Ena, *26:* 39
McLachlan, Edward, *5:* 89
McLean, Sammis, *32:* 197
McMahon, Robert, *36:* 155
McMillan, Bruce, *22:* 184
McMullan, James, *40:* 33
McNaught, Harry, *12:* 80; *32:* 136
McNaughton, Colin, *39:* 149; *40:* 108
McNicholas, Maureen, *38:* 148
McPhail, David, *14:* 105; *23:* 135;
    37: 217, 218, 220, 221
McPhee, Richard B., *41:* 133
McQueen, Lucinda, *28:* 149; *41:* 249;
    46: 206
McVay, Tracy, *11:* 68
McVicker, Charles, *39:* 150
Mead, Ben Carlton, *43:* 75
Mecray, John, *33:* 62
Meddaugh, Susan, *20:* 42; *29:* 143;
    41: 241
Melo, John, *16:* 285
Menasco, Milton, *43:* 85
Mendelssohn, Felix, *19:* 170
Meng, Heinz, *13:* 158
Mero, Lee, *34:* 68
Merrill, Frank T., *16:* 147; *19:* 71;
    YABC 1: 226, 229, 273
Meryman, Hope, *27:* 41
Meryweather, Jack, *10:* 179
Meth, Harold, *24:* 203
Meyer, Herbert, *19:* 189
Meyer, Renate, *6:* 170
Meyers, Bob, *11:* 136
Meynell, Louis, *37:* 76
Micale, Albert, *2:* 65; *22:* 185
Middleton-Sandford, Betty, *2:* 125
Mieke, Anne, *45:* 74
Mighell, Patricia, *43:* 134
Mikolaycak, Charles, *9:* 144; *12:* 101;
    13: 212; *21:* 121; *22:* 168;
    30: 187; *34:* 103, 150; *37:* 183;
    43: 179; *44:* 90; *46:* 115, 118-119
Miles, Jennifer, *17:* 278
Milhous, Katherine, *15:* 193; *17:* 51
Millais, John E., *22:* 230, 231
Millar, H. R., *YABC 1:* 194-195, 203
Millard, C. E., *28:* 186
Miller, Don, *15:* 195; *16:* 71; *20:* 106;
    31: 178
Miller, Edna, *29:* 148
Miller, Frank J., *25:* 94
Miller, Grambs, *18:* 38; *23:* 16
Miller, Jane, *15:* 196
Miller, Marcia, *13:* 233
Miller, Marilyn, *1:* 87; *31:* 69; *33:* 157
Miller, Mitchell, *28:* 183; *34:* 207
Miller, Shane, *5:* 140
Mills, Yaroslava Surmach, *35:* 169,
    170; *46:* 114
Minor, Wendell, *39:* 188
Mitsuhashi, Yoko, *45:* 153
Miyake, Yoshi, *38:* 141
Mizumura, Kazue, *10:* 143; *18:* 223;
    36: 159
Mochi, Ugo, *8:* 122; *38:* 150
Modell, Frank, *39:* 152
Mohr, Nicholasa, *8:* 139

Montresor, Beni, *2:* 91; *3:* 138; *38:* 152, 153, 154, 155, 156-157, 158, 159, 160

Moon, Carl, *25:* 183, 184, 185

Moon, Eliza, *14:* 40

Moon, Ivan, *22:* 39; *38:* 140

Moore, Agnes Kay Randall, *43:* 187

Moore, Mary, *29:* 160

Mora, Raul Mina, *20:* 41

Mordvinoff, Nicolas, *15:* 179

Morgan, Tom, *42:* 157

Morrill, Les, *42:* 127

Morrill, Leslie, *18:* 218; *29:* 177; *33:* 84; *38:* 147; *44:* 93

Morrison, Bill, *42:* 116

Morrow, Gray, *2:* 64; *5:* 200; *10:* 103, 114; *14:* 175

Morton, Lee Jack, *32:* 140

Morton, Marian, *3:* 185

Moses, Grandma, *18:* 228

Moskof, Martin Stephen, *27:* 152

Moss, Donald, *11:* 184

Moss, Geoffrey, *32:* 198

Moyers, William, *21:* 65

Moyler, Alan, *36:* 142

Mozley, Charles, *9:* 87; *20:* 176, 192, 193; *22:* 228; *25:* 205; *33:* 150; *43:* 170, 171, 172, 173, 174; *YABC 2:* 89

Mueller, Hans Alexander, *26:* 64; *27:* 52, 53

Mugnaini, Joseph, *11:* 35; *27:* 52, 53; *35:* 62

Müller, Jörg, *35:* 215

Muller, Steven, *32:* 167

Mullins, Edward S., *10:* 101

Munari, Bruno, *15:* 200

Munowitz, Ken, *14:* 148

Muñoz, William, *42:* 160

Munsinger, Lynn, *33:* 161; *46:* 126

Munson, Russell, *13:* 9

Murphy, Bill, *5:* 138

Murphy, Jill, *37:* 142

Murr, Karl, *20:* 62

Murray, Ossie, *43:* 176

Mussino, Attilio, *29:* 131

Mutchler, Dwight, *1:* 25

Myers, Bernice, *9:* 147; *36:* 75

Myers, Lou, *11:* 2

Nachreiner, Tom, *29:* 182

Nakai, Michael, *30:* 217

Nakatani, Chiyoko, *12:* 124

Nash, Linell, *46:* 175

Naso, John, *33:* 183

Nason, Thomas W., *14:* 68

Nast, Thomas, *21:* 29; *28:* 23

Natti, Susanna, *20:* 146; *32:* 141, 142; *35:* 178; *37:* 143

Navarra, Celeste Scala, *8:* 142

Naylor, Penelope, *10:* 104

Nebel, M., *45:* 154

Neebe, William, *7:* 93

Needler, Jerry, *12:* 93

Neel, Alice, *31:* 23

Neely, Keith R., *46:* 124

Negri, Rocco, *3:* 213; *5:* 67; *6:* 91, 108; *12:* 159

Neill, John R., *18:* 8, 10-11, 21, 30

Ness, Evaline, *1:* 164-165; *2:* 39; *3:* 8; *10:* 147; *12:* 53; *26:* 150, 151, 152, 153

Neville, Vera, *2:* 182

Newberry, Clare Turlay, *1:* 170

Newfeld, Frank, *14:* 121; *26:* 154

Newman, Ann, *43:* 90

Newsom, Carol, *40:* 159; *44:* 60

Ng, Michael, *29:* 171

Nicholson, William, *15:* 33-34; *16:* 48

Nicklaus, Carol, *45:* 194

Nickless, Will, *16:* 139

Nicolas, *17:* 130, 132-133; *YABC 2:* 215

Niebrugge, Jane, *6:* 118

Nielsen, Jon, *6:* 100; *24:* 202

Nielsen, Kay, *15:* 7; *16:* 211-213, 215, 217; *22:* 143; *YABC 1:* 32-33

Niland, Deborah, *25:* 191; *27:* 156

Niland, Kilmeny, *25:* 191

Ninon, *1:* 5; *38:* 101, 103, 108

Nissen, Rie, *44:* 35

Nixon, K., *14:* 152

Noble, Trinka Hakes, *39:* 162

Noguchi, Yoshie, *30:* 99

Nolan, Dennis, *42:* 163

Noonan, Julia, *4:* 163; *7:* 207; *25:* 151

Nordenskjold, Birgitta, *2:* 208

Norman, Mary, *36:* 138, 147

Norman, Michael, *12:* 117; *27:* 168

Numeroff, Laura Joffe, *28:* 161; *30:* 177

Nussbaumer, Paul, *16:* 219; *39:* 117

Nyce, Helene, *19:* 219

Nygren, Tord, *30:* 148

Oakley, Graham, *8:* 112; *30:* 164, 165

Oakley, Thornton, *YABC 2:* 189

Obligado, Lilian, *2:* 28, 66-67; *6:* 30; *14:* 179; *15:* 103; *25:* 84

Obrant, Susan, *11:* 186

O'Brien, John, *41:* 253

Odell, Carole, *35:* 47

O'Donohue, Thomas, *40:* 89

Oechsli, Kelly, *5:* 144-145; *7:* 115; *8:* 83, 183; *13:* 117; *20:* 94

Offen, Hilda, *42:* 207

Ogden, Bill, *42:* 59

Ogg, Oscar, *33:* 34

Ohlsson, Ib, *4:* 152; *7:* 57; *10:* 20; *11:* 90; *19:* 217; *41:* 246

Ohtomo, Yasuo, *37:* 146; *39:* 212, 213

O'Kelley, Mattie Lou, *36:* 150

Oliver, Jenni, *23:* 121; *35:* 112

Olschewski, Alfred, *7:* 172

Olsen, Ib Spang, *6:* 178-179

Olugebefola, Ademola, *15:* 205

O'Neil, Dan IV, *7:* 176

O'Neill, Jean, *22:* 146

O'Neill, Steve, *21:* 118

Ono, Chiyo, *7:* 97

Orbaan, Albert, *2:* 31; *5:* 65, 171; *9:* 8; *14:* 241; *20:* 109

Orbach, Ruth, *21:* 112

Orfe, Joan, *20:* 81

Ormsby, Virginia H., *11:* 187

Orozco, José Clemente, *9:* 177

Orr, Forrest W., *23:* 9

Orr, N., *19:* 70

Osborne, Billie Jean, *35:* 209

Osmond, Edward, *10:* 111

O'Sullivan, Tom, *3:* 176; *4:* 55

Otto, Svend, *22:* 130, 141

Oudry, J. B., *18:* 167

Oughton, Taylor, *5:* 23

Övereng, Johannes, *44:* 36

Overlie, George, *11:* 156

Owens, Carl, *2:* 35; *23:* 521

Owens, Gail, *10:* 170; *12:* 157; *19:* 16; *22:* 70; *25:* 81; *28:* 203, 205; *32:* 221, 222; *36:* 132; *46:* 40

Oxenbury, Helen, *3:* 150-151; *24:* 81

Padgett, Jim, *12:* 165

Page, Homer, *14:* 145

Paget, Sidney, *24:* 90, 91, 93, 95, 97

Pak, *12:* 76

Palazzo, Tony, *3:* 152-153

Palladini, David, *4:* 113; *40:* 176, 177, 178-179, 181, 224-225

Pallarito, Don, *43:* 36

Palmer, Heidi, *15:* 207; *29:* 102

Palmer, Jan, *42:* 153

Palmer, Juliette, *6:* 89; *15:* 208

Palmer, Lemuel, *17:* 25, 29

Palmquist, Eric, *38:* 133

Panesis, Nicholas, *3:* 127

Papas, William, *11:* 223

Papin, Joseph, *26:* 113

Papish, Robin Lloyd, *10:* 80

Paradis, Susan, *40:* 216

Paraquin, Charles H., *18:* 166

Paris, Peter, *31:* 127

Park, Seho, *39:* 110

Park, W. B., *22:* 189

Parker, Lewis, *2:* 179

Parker, Nancy Winslow, *10:* 113; *22:* 164; *28:* 47, 144

Parker, Robert, *4:* 161; *5:* 74; *9:* 136; *29:* 39

Parker, Robert Andrew, *11:* 81; *29:* 186; *39:* 165; *40:* 25; *41:* 78; *42:* 123; *43:* 144

Parks, Gordon, Jr., *33:* 228

Parnall, Peter, *5:* 137; *16:* 221; *24:* 70; *40:* 78

Parnall, Virginia, *40:* 78

Parrish, Anne, *27:* 159, 160

Parrish, Dillwyn, *27:* 159

Parrish, Maxfield, *14:* 160, 161, 164, 165; *16:* 109; *18:* 12-13; *YABC 1:* 149, 152, 267; *YABC 2:* 146, 149

Parry, David, *26:* 156

Parry, Marian, *13:* 176; *19:* 179

Partch, Virgil, *45:* 163, 165

Pascal, David, *14:* 174

Pasquier, J. A., *16:* 91

Paterson, Diane, *13:* 116; *39:* 163

Paterson, Helen, *16:* 93

Paton, Jane, *15:* 271; *35:* 176

Patterson, Robert, *25:* 118

Paul, James, *4:* 130; *23:* 161

Paull, Grace, *24:* 157

Payne, Joan Balfour, *1:* 118

Payson, Dale, *7:* 34; *9:* 151; *20:* 140; *37:* 22
Payzant, Charles, *21:* 147
Peake, Mervyn, *22:* 136, 149; *23:* 162, 163, 164; *YABC 2:* 307
Pearson, Larry, *38:* 225
Peat, Fern B., *16:* 115
Peck, Anne Merriman, *18:* 241; *24:* 155
Pederson, Sharleen, *12:* 92
Pedersen, Vilhelm, *YABC 1:* 40
Peek, Merle, *39:* 168
Peet, Bill, *2:* 203; *41:* 159, 160, 161, 162, 163
Peltier, Leslie C., *13:* 178
Pendle, Alexy, *7:* 159; *13:* 34; *29:* 161; *33:* 215
Pennington, Eunice, *27:* 162
Peppé, Mark, *28:* 142
Peppe, Rodney, *4:* 164-165
Perl, Susan, *2:* 98; *4:* 231; *5:* 44-45, 118; *6:* 199; *8:* 137; *12:* 88; *22:* 193; *34:* 54-55; *YABC 1:* 176
Perry, Patricia, *29:* 137; *30:* 171
Perry, Roger, *27:* 163
Perske, Martha, *46:* 83
Pesek, Ludek, *15:* 237
Petersham, Maud, *17:* 108, 147-153
Petersham, Miska, *17:* 108, 147-153
Peterson, R. F., *7:* 101
Peterson, Russell, *7:* 130
Petie, Haris, *2:* 3; *10:* 41, 118; *11:* 227; *12:* 70
Petrides, Heidrun, *19:* 223
Peyo, *40:* 56, 57
Peyton, K. M., *15:* 212
Pfeifer, Herman, *15:* 262
Phillips, Douglas, *1:* 19
Phillips, F. D., *6:* 202
Phillips, Thomas, *30:* 55
"Phiz." *See* Browne, Hablot K.
Piatti, Celestino, *16:* 223
Picarella, Joseph, *13:* 147
Pickard, Charles, *12:* 38; *18:* 203; *36:* 152
Picken, George A., *23:* 150
Pickens, David, *22:* 156
Pienkowski, Jan, *6:* 183; *30:* 32
Pimlott, John, *10:* 205
Pincus, Harriet, *4:* 186; *8:* 179; *22:* 148; *27:* 164, 165
Pinkney, Jerry, *8:* 218; *10:* 40; *15:* 276; *20:* 66; *24:* 121; *33:* 109; *36:* 222; *38:* 200; *41:* 165, 166, 167, 168, 169, 170, 171, 173, 174; *44:* 198
Pinkwater, Daniel Manus, *46:* 180, 181, 182, 185, 188, 189, 190
Pinkwater, Manus, *8:* 156; *46:* 180
Pinto, Ralph, *10:* 131; *45:* 93
Pitz, Henry C., *4:* 168; *19:* 165; *35:* 128; *42:* 80; *YABC 2:* 95, 176
Pitzenberger, Lawrence J., *26:* 94
Plummer, William, *32:* 31
Pogány, Willy, *15:* 46, 49; *19:* 222, 256; *25:* 214; *44:* 142, 143, 144, 145, 146, 147, 148
Poirson, V. A., *26:* 89
Polgreen, John, *21:* 44

Politi, Leo, *1:* 178; *4:* 53; *21:* 48
Polonsky, Arthur, *34:* 168
Polseno, Jo, *1:* 53; *3:* 117; *5:* 114; *17:* 154; *20:* 87; *32:* 49; *41:* 245
Ponter, James, *5:* 204
Poortvliet, Rien, *6:* 212
Portal, Colette, *6:* 186; *11:* 203
Porter, George, *7:* 181
Potter, Beatrix, *YABC 1:* 208-210, 212, 213
Potter, Miriam Clark, *3:* 162
Powers, Richard M., *1:* 230; *3:* 218; *7:* 194; *26:* 186
Powledge, Fred, *37:* 154
Pratt, Charles, *23:* 29
Price, Christine, *2:* 247; *3:* 163, 253; *8:* 166
Price, Edward, *33:* 34
Price, Garrett, *1:* 76; *2:* 42
Price, Hattie Longstreet, *17:* 13
Price, Norman, *YABC 1:* 129
Primavera, Elise, *26:* 95
Primrose, Jean, *36:* 109
Prince, Leonora E., *7:* 170
Prittie, Edwin J., *YABC 1:* 120
Provensen, Alice, *37:* 204, 215, 222
Provensen, Martin, *37:* 204, 215, 222
Pucci, Albert John, *44:* 154
Pudlo, *8:* 59
Purdy, Susan, *8:* 162
Puskas, James, *5:* 141
Pyk, Jan, *7:* 26; *38:* 123
Pyle, Howard, *16:* 225-228, 230-232, 235; *24:* 27; *34:* 124, 125, 127, 128

Quackenbush, Robert, *4:* 190; *6:* 166; *7:* 175, 178; *9:* 86; *11:* 65, 221; *41:* 154; *43:* 157
Quennell, Marjorie (Courtney), *29:* 163, 164
Quidor, John, *19:* 82
Quirk, Thomas, *12:* 81

Rackham, Arthur, *15:* 32, 78, 214-227; *17:* 105, 115; *18:* 233; *19:* 254; *20:* 151; *22:* 129, 131, 132, 133; *23:* 175; *24:* 161, 181; *26:* 91; *32:* 118; *YABC 1:* 25, 45, 55, 147; *YABC 2:* 103, 142, 173, 210
Rafilson, Sidney, *11:* 172
Raible, Alton, *1:* 202-203; *28:* 193; *35:* 181
Ramsey, James, *16:* 41
Rand, Paul, *6:* 188
Ransome, Arthur, *22:* 201
Rao, Anthony, *28:* 126
Raphael, Elaine, *23:* 192
Rappaport, Eva, *6:* 190
Raskin, Ellen, *2:* 208-209; *4:* 142; *13:* 183; *22:* 68; *29:* 139; *36:* 134; *38:* 173, 174, 175, 176, 177, 178, 179, 180, 181
Ratzkin, Lawrence, *40:* 143
Rau, Margaret, *9:* 157

Raverat, Gwen, *YABC 1:* 152
Ravielli, Anthony, *1:* 198; *3:* 168; *11:* 143
Ray, Deborah, *8:* 164; *29:* 238
Ray, Ralph, *2:* 239; *5:* 73
Raymond, Larry, *31:* 108
Rayner, Mary, *22:* 207
Raynor, Dorka, *28:* 168
Raynor, Paul, *24:* 73
Razzi, James, *10:* 127
Read, Alexander D. "Sandy," *20:* 45
Reed, Tom, *34:* 171
Reid, Stephen, *19:* 213; *22:* 89
Reinertson, Barbara, *44:* 150
Reiniger, Lotte, *40:* 185
Reiss, John J., *23:* 193
Relf, Douglas, *3:* 63
Relyea, C. M., *16:* 29; *31:* 153
Rémi, Georges, *13:* 184
Remington, Frederic, *19:* 188; *41:* 178, 179, 180, 181, 183, 184, 185, 186, 187, 188
Renlie, Frank, *11:* 200
Reschofsky, Jean, *7:* 118
Réthi, Lili, *2:* 153; *36:* 156
Reusswig, William, *3:* 267
Rey, H. A., *1:* 182; *26:* 163, 164, 166, 167, 169; *YABC 2:* 17
Reynolds, Doris, *5:* 71; *31:* 77
Rhead, Louis, *31:* 91
Rhodes, Andrew, *38:* 204
Ribbons, Ian, *3:* 10; *37:* 161; *40:* 76
Rice, Elizabeth, *2:* 53, 214
Rice, James, *22:* 210
Rice, Eve, *34:* 174, 175
Richards, George, *40:* 116, 119, 121; *44:* 179
Richards, Henry, *YABC 1:* 228, 231
Richardson, Ernest, *2:* 144
Richardson, Frederick, *18:* 27, 31
Richman, Hilda, *26:* 132
Richmond, George, *24:* 179
Rieniets, Judy King, *14:* 28
Riger, Bob, *2:* 166
Riley, Kenneth, *22:* 230
Ringi, Kjell, *12:* 171
Rios, Tere. *See* Versace, Marie
Ripper, Charles L., *3:* 175
Ritz, Karen, *41:* 117
Rivkin, Jay, *15:* 230
Rivoche, Paul, *45:* 125
Roach, Marilynne, *9:* 158
Robbin, Jodi, *44:* 156, 159
Robbins, Frank, *42:* 167
Roberts, Cliff, *4:* 126
Roberts, Doreen, *4:* 230; *28:* 105
Roberts, Jim, *22:* 166; *23:* 69; *31:* 110
Roberts, W., *22:* 2, 3
Robinson, Charles, *3:* 53; *5:* 14; *6:* 193; *7:* 150; *7:* 183; *8:* 38; *9:* 81; *13:* 188; *14:* 248-249; *23:* 149; *26:* 115; *27:* 48; *28:* 191; *32:* 28; *35:* 210; *36:* 37
Robinson, Charles [1870-1937], *17:* 157, 171-173, 175-176; *24:* 207; *25:* 204; *YABC 2:* 308-310, 331
Robinson, Jerry, *3:* 262
Robinson, Joan G., *7:* 184

Robinson, T. H., *17:* 179, 181-183; *29:* 254

Robinson, W. Heath, *17:* 185, 187, 189, 191, 193, 195, 197, 199, 202; *23:* 167; *25:* 194; *29:* 150; *YABC 1:* 44; *YABC 2:* 183

Roche, Christine, *41:* 98

Rocker, Fermin, *7:* 34; *13:* 21; *31:* 40; *40:* 190, 191

Rockwell, Anne, *5:* 147; *33:* 171, 173

Rockwell, Gail, *7:* 186

Rockwell, Harlow, *33:* 171, 173, 175

Rockwell, Norman, *23:* 39, 196, 197, 199, 200, 203, 204, 207; *41:* 140, 143; *YABC 2:* 60

Rodegast, Roland, *43:* 100

Rodriguez, Joel, *16:* 65

Roever, J. M., *4:* 119; *26:* 170

Roffey, Maureen, *33:* 142, 176, 177

Rogasky, Barbara, *46:* 90

Rogers, Carol, *2:* 262; *6:* 164; *26:* 129

Rogers, Frances, *10:* 130

Rogers, Walter S., *31:* 135, 138

Rogers, William A., *15:* 151, 153-154; *33:* 35

Rojankovsky, Feodor, *6:* 134, 136; *10:* 183; *21:* 128, 129, 130; *25:* 110; *28:* 42

Rorer, Abigail, *43:* 222

Rosamilia, Patricia, *36:* 120

Rose, Carl, *5:* 62

Rose, David S., *29:* 109

Rosenblum, Richard, *11:* 202; *18:* 18

Rosier, Lydia, *16:* 236; *20:* 104; *21:* 109; *22:* 125; *30:* 151, 158; *42:* 128; *45:* 214

Ross. *See* Thomson, Ross

Ross, Clare, *3:* 123; *21:* 45

Ross, Dave, *32:* 152

Ross, Herbert, *37:* 78

Ross, John, *3:* 123; *21:* 45

Ross, Johnny, *32:* 190

Ross, Tony, *17:* 204

Rossetti, Dante Gabriel, *20:* 151, 153

Roth, Arnold, *4:* 238; *21:* 133

Rotondo, Pat, *32:* 158

Roughsey, Dick, *35:* 186

Rouille, M., *11:* 96

Rounds, Glen, *8:* 173; *9:* 171; *12:* 56; *32:* 194; *40:* 230; *YABC 1:* 1-3

Rowe, Gavin, *27:* 144

Rowell, Kenneth, *40:* 72

Roy, Jeroo, *27:* 229; *36:* 110

Rubel, Nicole, *18:* 255; *20:* 59

Rubel, Reina, *33:* 217

Rud, Borghild, *6:* 15

Rudolph, Norman Guthrie, *17:* 13

Rue, Leonard Lee III, *37:* 164

Ruffins, Reynold, *10:* 134-135; *41:* 191, 192-193, 194-195, 196

Ruhlin, Roger, *34:* 44

Ruse, Margaret, *24:* 155

Rush, Peter, *42:* 75

Russell, E. B., *18:* 177, 182

Russo, Susan, *30:* 182; *36:* 144

Ruth, Rod, *9:* 161

Rutherford, Meg, *25:* 174; *34:* 178, 179

Rutland, Jonathan, *31:* 126

Ryden, Hope, *8:* 176

Rymer, Alta M., *34:* 181

Sabaka, Donna R., *21:* 172

Sabin, Robert, *45:* 35

Sacker, Amy, *16:* 100

Saffioti, Lino, *36:* 176

Sagsoorian, Paul, *12:* 183; *22:* 154; *33:* 106

Saint Exupéry, Antoine de, *20:* 157

St. John, J. Allen, *41:* 62

Saldutti, Denise, *39:* 186

Sale, Morton, *YABC 2:* 31

Sambourne, Linley, *YABC 2:* 181

Sampson, Katherine, *9:* 197

Samson, Anne S., *2:* 216

Sancha, Sheila, *38:* 185

Sand, George X., *45:* 182

Sandberg, Lasse, *15:* 239, 241

Sanders, Beryl, *39:* 173

Sanderson, Ruth, *21:* 126; *24:* 53; *28:* 63; *33:* 67; *41:* 48, 198, 199, 200, 201, 202, 203; *43:* 79; *46:* 36, 44

Sandin, Joan, *4:* 36; *6:* 194; *7:* 177; *12:* 145, 185; *20:* 43; *21:* 74; *26:* 144; *27:* 142; *28:* 224, 225; *38:* 86; *41:* 46; *42:* 35

Sandland, Reg, *39:* 215

Sandoz, Edouard, *26:* 45, 47

San Souci, Daniel, *40:* 200

Sapieha, Christine, *1:* 180

Sarg, Tony, *YABC 2:* 236

Sargent, Robert, *2:* 217

Saris, *1:* 33

Sarony, *YABC 2:* 170

Sasek, Miroslav, *16:* 239-242

Sassman, David, *9:* 79

Sätty, *29:* 203, 205

Sauber, Rob, *40:* 183

Savage, Steele, *10:* 203; *20:* 77; *35:* 28

Savitt, Sam, *8:* 66, 182; *15:* 278; *20:* 96; *24:* 192; *28:* 98

Say, Allen, *28:* 178

Scabrini, Janet, *13:* 191; *44:* 128

Scarry, Huck, *35:* 204-205

Scarry, Richard, *2:* 220-221; *18:* 20; *35:* 193, 194-195, 196, 197, 198, 199, 200-201, 202

Schaeffer, Mead, *18:* 81, 94; *21:* 137, 138, 139

Scharl, Josef, *20:* 132; *22:* 128

Scheel, Lita, *11:* 230

Scheib, Ida, *29:* 28

Schermer, Judith, *30:* 184

Schick, Joel, *16:* 160; *17:* 167; *22:* 12; *27:* 176; *31:* 147, 148; *36:* 23; *38:* 64; *45:* 116, 117

Schindelman, Joseph, *1:* 74; *4:* 101; *12:* 49; *26:* 51; *40:* 146

Schindler, Edith, *7:* 22

Schindler, S. D., *38:* 107; *46:* 196

Schlesinger, Bret, *7:* 77

Schmid, Eleanore, *12:* 188

Schmiderer, Dorothy, *19:* 224

Schmidt, Elizabeth, *15:* 242

Schneider, Rex, *29:* 64; *44:* 171

Schoenherr, Ian, *32:* 83

Schoenherr, John, *1:* 146-147, 173; *3:* 39, 139; *17:* 75; *29:* 72; *32:* 83; *37:* 168, 169, 170; *43:* 164, 165; *45:* 160, 162

Schomburg, Alex, *13:* 23

Schongut, Emanuel, *4:* 102; *15:* 186

Schoonover, Frank, *17:* 107; *19:* 81, 190, 233; *22:* 88, 129; *24:* 189; *31:* 88; *41:* 69; *YABC 2:* 282, 316

Schottland, Miriam, *22:* 172

Schramm, Ulrik, *2:* 16; *14:* 112

Schreiber, Elizabeth Anne, *13:* 193

Schreiber, Ralph W., *13:* 193

Schreiter, Rick, *14:* 97; *23:* 171; *41:* 247

Schroeder, E. Peter, *12:* 112

Schroeder, Ted, *11:* 160; *15:* 189; *30:* 91; *34:* 43

Schrotter, Gustav, *22:* 212; *30:* 225

Schucker, James, *31:* 163

Schulz, Charles M., *10:* 137-142

Schwartz, Charles, *8:* 184

Schwartz, Daniel, *46:* 37

Schwartzberg, Joan, *3:* 208

Schweitzer, Iris, *2:* 137; *6:* 207

Schweninger, Ann, *29:* 172

Scott, Anita Walker, *7:* 38

Scott, Art, *39:* 41

Scott, Frances Gruse, *38:* 43

Scott, Julian, *34:* 126

Scott, Roszel, *33:* 238

Scott, Trudy, *27:* 172

Scribner, Joanne, *14:* 236; *29:* 78; *33:* 185; *34:* 208

Scrofani, Joseph, *31:* 65

Seaman, Mary Lott, *34:* 64

Searle, Ronald, *24:* 98; *42:* 172, 173, 174, 176, 177, 179

Searle, Townley, *36:* 85

Sebree, Charles, *18:* 65

Sedacca, Joseph M., *11:* 25; *22:* 36

Ségur, Adrienne, *27:* 121

Seignobosc, Francoise, *21:* 145, 146

Sejima, Yoshimasa, *8:* 187

Selig, Sylvie, *13:* 199

Seltzer, Isadore, *6:* 18

Seltzer, Meyer, *17:* 214

Sempé, *YABC 2:* 109

Sendak, Maurice, *1:* 135, 190; *3:* 204; *7:* 142; *15:* 199; *17:* 210; *27:* 181, 182, 183, 185, 186, 187, 189, 190-191, 192, 193, 194, 195, 197, 198, 199, 203; *28:* 181, 182; *32:* 108; *33:* 148, 149; *35:* 238; *44:* 180, 181; *45:* 97, 99; *46:* 174; *YABC 1:* 167

Sengler, Johanna, *18:* 256

Seredy, Kate, *1:* 192; *14:* 20-21; *17:* 210

Sergeant, John, *6:* 74

Servello, Joe, *10:* 144; *24:* 139; *40:* 91

Seton, Ernest Thompson, *18:* 260-269, 271

Seuss, Dr. *See* Geisel, Theodor

Severin, John Powers, *7:* 62

Sewall, Marcia, *15:* 8; *22:* 170; *37:* 171, 172, 173; *39:* 73; *45:* 209

Seward, Prudence, *16:* 243

Sewell, Helen, *3:* 186; *15:* 308; *33:* 102; *38:* 189, 190, 191, 192
Shahn, Ben, *39:* 178; *46:* 193
Shalansky, Len, *38:* 167
Shanks, Anne Zane, *10:* 149
Sharp, William, *6:* 131; *19:* 241; *20:* 112; *25:* 141
Shaw, Charles, *21:* 135; *38:* 187
Shaw, Charles G., *13:* 200
Shearer, Ted, *43:* 193, 194, 195, 196
Shecter, Ben, *16:* 244; *25:* 109; *33:* 188, 191; *41:* 77
Shekerjian, Haig, *16:* 245
Shekerjian, Regina, *16:* 245; *25:* 73
Shenton, Edward, *45:* 187, 188, 189; *YABC 1:* 218-219, 221
Shepard, Ernest H., *3:* 193; *4:* 74; *16:* 101; *17:* 109; *25:* 148; *33:* 152, 199, 200, 201, 202, 203, 204, 205, 206, 207; *46:* 194; *YABC 1:* 148, 153, 174, 176, 180-181
Shepard, Mary, *4:* 210; *22:* 205; *30:* 132, 133
Sherman, Theresa, *27:* 167
Sherwan, Earl, *3:* 196
Shields, Charles, *10:* 150; *36:* 63
Shields, Leonard, *13:* 83, 85, 87
Shillabeer, Mary, *35:* 74
Shimin, Symeon, *1:* 93; *2:* 128-129; *3:* 202; *7:* 85; *11:* 177; *12:* 139; *13:* 202-203; *27:* 138; *28:* 65; *35:* 129; *36:* 130
Shinn, Everett, *16:* 148; *18:* 229; *21:* 149, 150, 151; *24:* 218
Shore, Robert, *27:* 54; *39:* 192, 193; *YABC 2:* 200
Shortall, Leonard, *4:* 144; *8:* 196; *10:* 166; *19:* 227, 228-229, 230; *25:* 78; *28:* 66, 167; *33:* 127
Shortt, T. M., *27:* 36
Shtainments, Leon, *32:* 161
Shulevitz, Uri, *3:* 198-199; *17:* 85; *22:* 204; *27:* 212; *28:* 184
Shute, Linda, *46:* 59
Siberell, Anne, *29:* 193
Sibley, Don, *1:* 39; *12:* 196; *31:* 47
Sidjakov, Nicolas, *18:* 274
Siebel, Fritz, *3:* 120; *17:* 145
Siegl, Helen, *12:* 166; *23:* 216; *34:* 185, 186
Sills, Joyce, *5:* 199
Silverstein, Alvin, *8:* 189
Silverstein, Shel, *33:* 211
Silverstein, Virginia, *8:* 189
Simon, Eric M., *7:* 82
Simon, Hilda, *28:* 189
Simon, Howard, *2:* 175; *5:* 132; *19:* 199; *32:* 163, 164, 165
Simont, Marc, *2:* 119; *4:* 213; *9:* 168; *13:* 238, 240; *14:* 262; *16:* 179; *18:* 221; *26:* 210; *33:* 189, 194; *44:* 132
Sims, Blanche, *44:* 116
Singer, Edith G., *2:* 30
Singer, Gloria, *34:* 56; *36:* 43
Singer, Julia, *28:* 190
Sivard, Robert, *26:* 124
Skardinski, Stanley, *23:* 144; *32:* 84

Slackman, Charles B., *12:* 201
Slater, Rod, *25:* 167
Sloan, Joseph, *16:* 68
Sloane, Eric, *21:* 3
Slobodkin, Louis, *1:* 200; *3:* 232; *5:* 168; *13:* 251; *15:* 13, 88; *26:* 173, 174, 175, 176, 178, 179
Slobodkina, Esphyr, *1:* 201
Small, W., *33:* 113
Smalley, Janet, *1:* 154
Smedley, William T., *34:* 129
Smee, David, *14:* 78
Smith, A. G., Jr., *35:* 182
Smith, Alvin, *1:* 31, 229; *13:* 187; *27:* 216; *28:* 226
Smith, Anne Warren, *41:* 212
Smith, Carl, *36:* 41
Smith, Doris Susan, *41:* 139
Smith, E. Boyd, *19:* 70; *22:* 89; *26:* 63; *YABC 1:* 4-5, 240, 248-249
Smith, Edward J., *4:* 224
Smith, Eunice Young, *5:* 170
Smith, Howard, *19:* 196
Smith, Jacqueline Bardner, *27:* 108; *39:* 197
Smith, Jessie Willcox, *15:* 91; *16:* 95; *18:* 231; *19:* 57, 242; *21:* 29, 156, 157, 158, 159, 160, 161; *34:* 65; *YABC 1:* 6; *YABC 2:* 180, 185, 191, 311, 325
Smith, L. H., *35:* 174
Smith, Lee, *29:* 32
Smith, Linell Nash, *2:* 195
Smith, Maggie Kaufman, *13:* 205; *35:* 191
Smith, Moishe, *33:* 155
Smith, Philip, *44:* 134; *46:* 203
Smith, Ralph Crosby, *2:* 267
Smith, Robert D., *5:* 63
Smith, Susan Carlton, *12:* 208
Smith, Terry, *12:* 106; *33:* 158
Smith, Virginia, *3:* 157; *33:* 72
Smith, William A., *1:* 36; *10:* 154; *25:* 65
Smollin, Mike, *39:* 203
Smyth, M. Jane, *12:* 15
Snyder, Andrew A., *30:* 212
Snyder, Jerome, *13:* 207; *30:* 173
Snyder, Joel, *28:* 163
Sofia, *1:* 62; *5:* 90; *32:* 166
Sokol, Bill, *37:* 178
Sokolov, Kirill, *34:* 188
Solbert, Ronni, *1:* 159; *2:* 232; *5:* 121; *6:* 34; *17:* 249
Solonevich, George, *15:* 246; *17:* 47
Sommer, Robert, *12:* 211
Sorel, Edward, *4:* 61; *36:* 82
Sotomayor, Antonio, *11:* 215
Soyer, Moses, *20:* 177
Spaenkuch, August, *16:* 28
Spanfeller, James, *1:* 72, 149; *2:* 183; *19:* 230, 231, 232; *22:* 66; *36:* 160, 161; *40:* 75
Sparks, Mary Walker, *15:* 247
Spence, Geraldine, *21:* 163
Spence, Jim, *38:* 89
Spiegel, Doris, *29:* 111
Spier, Jo, *10:* 30

Spier, Peter, *3:* 155; *4:* 200; *7:* 61; *11:* 78; *38:* 106
Spilka, Arnold, *5:* 120; *6:* 204; *8:* 131
Spivak, I. Howard, *8:* 10
Spollen, Christopher J., *12:* 214
Spooner, Malcolm, *40:* 142
Sprattler, Rob, *12:* 176
Spring, Bob, *5:* 60
Spring, Ira, *5:* 60
Springer, Harriet, *31:* 92
Spurrier, Steven, *28:* 198
Spy. *See* Ward, Leslie
Staffan, Alvin E., *11:* 56; *12:* 187
Stahl, Ben, *5:* 181; *12:* 91
Stair, Gobin, *35:* 214
Stamaty, Mark Alan, *12:* 215
Stanley, Diane, *3:* 45; *37:* 180
Steadman, Ralph, *32:* 180
Steichen, Edward, *30:* 79
Steig, William, *18:* 275-276
Stein, Harve, *1:* 109
Steinel, William, *23:* 146
Steiner, Charlotte, *45:* 196
Stephens, Charles H., *YABC 2:* 279
Stephens, William M., *21:* 165
Steptoe, John, *8:* 197
Stern, Simon, *15:* 249-250; *17:* 58; *34:* 192-193
Stevens, Janet, *40:* 126
Stevens, Mary, *11:* 193; *13:* 129; *43:* 95
Stevenson, James, *42:* 182, 183
Stewart, Arvis, *33:* 98; *36:* 69
Stewart, Charles, *2:* 205
Stiles, Fran, *26:* 85
Stillman, Susan, *44:* 130
Stinemetz, Morgan, *40:* 151
Stirnweis, Shannon, *10:* 164
Stobbs, William, *1:* 48-49; *3:* 68; *6:* 20; *17:* 117, 217; *24:* 150; *29:* 250
Stock, Catherine, *37:* 55
Stone, David, *9:* 173
Stone, David K., *4:* 38; *6:* 124; *9:* 180; *43:* 182
Stone, Helen, *44:* 121, 122, 126
Stone, Helen V., *6:* 209
Stratton, Helen, *33:* 151
Stratton-Porter, Gene, *15:* 254, 259, 263-264, 268-269
Streano, Vince, *20:* 173
Strong, Joseph D., Jr., *YABC 2:* 330
Ströyer, Poul, *13:* 221
Strugnell, Ann, *27:* 38
Stubis, Talivaldis, *5:* 182, 183; *10:* 45; *11:* 9; *18:* 304; *20:* 127
Stubley, Trevor, *14:* 43; *22:* 219; *23:* 37; *28:* 61
Stuecklen, Karl W., *8:* 34, 65; *23:* 103
Stull, Betty, *11:* 46
Suba, Susanne, *4:* 202-203; *14:* 261; *23:* 134; *29:* 222; *32:* 30
Sugarman, Tracy, *3:* 76; *8:* 199; *37:* 181, 182
Sugita, Yutaka, *36:* 180-181
Sullivan, Edmund J., *31:* 86
Sullivan, James F., *19:* 280; *20:* 192
Sumichrast, Jŏzef, *14:* 253; *29:* 168, 213

Sumiko, *46:* 57
Summers, Leo, *1:* 177; *2:* 273; *13:* 22
Svolinsky, Karel, *17:* 104
Swain, Su Zan Noguchi, *21:* 170
Swan, Susan, *22:* 220-221; *37:* 66
Sweat, Lynn, *25:* 206
Sweet, Darryl, *1:* 163; *4:* 136
Sweet, Ozzie, *31:* 149, 151, 152
Sweetland, Robert, *12:* 194
Swope, Martha, *43:* 160
Sylvester, Natalie G., *22:* 222
Szafran, Gene, *24:* 144
Szasz, Susanne, *13:* 55, 226; *14:* 48
Szekeres, Cyndy, *2:* 218; *5:* 185;
    8: 85; *11:* 166; *14:* 19; *16:* 57,
    159; *26:* 49, 214; *34:* 205

Taback, Simms, *40:* 207
Tafuri, Nancy, *39:* 210
Tait, Douglas, *12:* 220
Takakjian, Portia, *15:* 274
Takashima, Shizuye, *13:* 228
Talarczyk, June, *4:* 173
Tallon, Robert, *2:* 228; *43:* 200, 201,
    202, 203, 204, 205, 206, 207, 209
Tamas, Szecskó, *29:* 135
Tamburine, Jean, *12:* 222
Tandy, H. R., *13:* 69
Tanobe, Miyuki, *23:* 221
Tarkington, Booth, *17:* 224-225
Taylor, Ann, *41:* 226
Taylor, Isaac, *41:* 228
Teale, Edwin Way, *7:* 196
Teason, James, *1:* 14
Teeple, Lyn, *33:* 147
Tee-Van, Helen Damrosch, *10:* 176;
    11: 182
Tempest, Margaret, *3:* 237, 238
Temple, Herbert, *45:* 201
Templeton, Owen, *11:* 77
Tenggren, Gustaf, *18:* 277-279; *19:* 15;
    28: 86; *YABC 2:* 145
Tenney, Gordon, *24:* 204
Tenniel, John, *YABC 2:* 99
Thacher, Mary M., *30:* 72
Thackeray, William Makepeace,
    23: 224, 228
Thamer, Katie, *42:* 187
Thelwell, Norman, *14:* 201
Theobalds, Prue, *40:* 23
Theurer, Marilyn Churchill, *39:* 195
Thistlethwaite, Miles, *12:* 224
Thollander, Earl, *11:* 47; *18:* 112;
    22: 224
Thomas, Allan, *22:* 13
Thomas, Eric, *28:* 49
Thomas, Harold, *20:* 98
Thomas, Mark, *42:* 136
Thomas, Martin, *14:* 255
Thompson, Arthur, *34:* 107
Thompson, George, *22:* 18; *28:* 150;
    33: 135
Thompson, George, W., *33:* 135
Thompson, Julie, *44:* 158
Thomson, Arline K., *3:* 264
Thomson, Hugh, *26:* 88
Thomson, Ross, *36:* 179
Thorne, Diana, *25:* 212

Thorvall, Kerstin, *13:* 235
Thurber, James, *13:* 239, 242-245,
    248-249
Tibbles, Paul, *45:* 23
Tichenor, Tom, *14:* 207
Tiegreen, Alan, *36:* 143; *43:* 55, 56,
    58
Tilney, F. C., *22:* 231
Timbs, Gloria, *36:* 90
Timmins, Harry, *2:* 171
Tinkelman, Murray, *12:* 225; *35:* 44
Titherington, Jeanne, *39:* 90
Tolford, Joshua, *1:* 221
Tolkien, J. R. R., *2:* 243; *32:* 215
Tolmie, Ken, *15:* 292
Tomes, Jacqueline, *2:* 117; *12:* 139
Tomes, Margot, *1:* 224; *2:* 120-121;
    16: 207; *18:* 250; *20:* 7; *25:* 62;
    27: 78, 79; *29:* 81, 199; *33:* 82;
    36: 186, 187, 188, 189, 190;
    46: 129
Toner, Raymond John, *10:* 179
Toothill, Harry, *6:* 54; *7:* 49; *25:* 219;
    42: 192
Toothill, Ilse, *6:* 54
Topolski, Feliks, *44:* 48
Torbert, Floyd James, *22:* 226
Torrey, Marjorie, *34:* 105
Toschik, Larry, *6:* 102
Totten, Bob, *13:* 93
Tremain, Ruthven, *17:* 238
Tresilian, Stuart, *25:* 53; *40:* 212
Trez, Alain, *17:* 236
Trier, Walter, *14:* 96
Tripp, F. J., *24:* 167
Tripp, Wallace, *2:* 48; *7:* 28; *8:* 94;
    10: 54, 76; *11:* 92; *31:* 170, 171;
    34: 203; *42:* 57
Trnka, Jiri, *22:* 151; *43:* 212, 213,
    214, 215; *YABC 1:* 30-31
Troughton, Joanna, *37:* 186
Troyer, Johannes, *3:* 16; *7:* 18
Trudeau, G. B., *35:* 220, 221, 222
Tsinajinie, Andy, *2:* 62
Tsugami, Kyuzo, *18:* 198-199
Tuckwell, Jennifer, *17:* 205
Tudor, Bethany, *7:* 103
Tudor, Tasha, *18:* 227; *20:* 185, 186,
    187; *36:* 111; *YABC 2:* 46, 314
Tulloch, Maurice, *24:* 79
Tunis, Edwin, *1:* 218-219; *28:* 209,
    210, 211, 212
Turkle, Brinton, *1:* 211, 213; *2:* 249;
    3: 226; *11:* 3; *16:* 209; *20:* 22;
    YABC 1: 79
Turska, Krystyna, *12:* 103; *31:* 173,
    174-175
Tusan, Stan, *6:* 58; *22:* 236-237
Tzimoulis, Paul, *12:* 104

Uchida, Yoshiko, *1:* 220
Ulm, Robert, *17:* 238
Unada. *See* Gliewe, Unada
Underwood, Clarence, *40:* 166
Ungerer, Tomi, *5:* 188; *9:* 40; *18:* 188;
    29: 175; *33:* 221, 222-223, 225
Unwin, Nora S., *3:* 65, 234-235;
    4: 237; *44:* 173, 174; *YABC 1:* 59;
    YABC 2: 301

Utpatel, Frank, *18:* 114
Utz, Lois, *5:* 190

Van Abbé, S., *16:* 142; *18:* 282;
    31: 90; *YABC 2:* 157, 161
Van Allsburg, Chris, *37:* 205, 206
Vandivert, William, *21:* 175
Van Everen, Jay, *13:* 160;
    YABC 1: 121
Van Horn, William, *43:* 218
Van Loon, Hendrik Willem, *18:* 285,
    289, 291
Van Sciver, Ruth, *37:* 162
Van Stockum, Hilda, *5:* 193
Van Wely, Babs, *16:* 50
Varga, Judy, *29:* 196
Vasiliu, Mircea, *2:* 166, 253; *9:* 166;
    13: 58
Vaughn, Frank, *34:* 157
Vavra, Robert, *8:* 206
Vawter, Will, *17:* 163
Veeder, Larry, *18:* 4
Velasquez, Eric, *45:* 217
Vendrell, Carme Solé, *42:* 205
Ver Beck, Frank, *18:* 16-17
Verney, John, *14:* 225
Verrier, Suzanne, *5:* 20; *23:* 212
Versace, Marie, *2:* 255
Vestal, H. B., *9:* 134; *11:* 101; *27:* 25;
    34: 158
Vickrey, Robert, *45:* 59, 64
Victor, Joan Berg, *30:* 193
Viereck, Ellen, *3:* 242; *14:* 229
Vigna, Judith, *15:* 293
Vilato, Gaspar E., *5:* 41
Vimnèra, A., *23:* 154
Vincent, Eric, *34:* 98
Vincent, Félix, *41:* 237
Vip, *45:* 164
Vo-Dinh, Mai, *16:* 272
Vogel, Ilse-Margret, *14:* 230
Voigt, Erna, *35:* 228
Vojtech, Anna, *42:* 190
von Schmidt, Eric, *8:* 62
von Schmidt, Harold, *30:* 80
Vosburgh, Leonard, *1:* 161; *7:* 32;
    15: 295-296; *23:* 110; *30:* 214;
    43: 181
Voter, Thomas W., *19:* 3, 9
Vroman, Tom, *10:* 29

Wagner, John, *8:* 200
Wagner, Ken, *2:* 59
Waide, Jan, *29:* 225; *36:* 139
Wainwright, Jerry, *14:* 85
Waldman, Bruce, *15:* 297; *43:* 178
Waldman, Neil, *35:* 141
Walker, Charles, *1:* 46; *4:* 59; *5:* 177;
    11: 115; *19:* 45; *34:* 74
Walker, Dugald Stewart, *15:* 47;
    32: 202; *33:* 112
Walker, Gil, *8:* 49; *23:* 132; *34:* 42
Walker, Jim, *10:* 94
Walker, Mort, *8:* 213
Walker, Norman, *41:* 37; *45:* 58

Walker, Stephen, *12:* 229; *21:* 174
Wallace, Beverly Dobrin, *19:* 259
Waller, S. E., *24:* 36
Wallner, Alexandra, *15:* 120
Wallner, John C., *9:* 77; *10:* 188; *11:* 28; *14:* 209; *31:* 56, 118; *37:* 64
Wallower, Lucille, *11:* 226
Walters, Audrey, *18:* 294
Walther, Tom, *31:* 179
Walton, Tony, *11:* 164; *24:* 209
Waltrip, Lela, *9:* 195
Waltrip, Mildred, *3:* 209; *37:* 211
Waltrip, Rufus, *9:* 195
Wan, *12:* 76
Ward, John, *42:* 191
Ward, Keith, *2:* 107
Ward, Leslie, *34:* 126; *36:* 87
Ward, Lynd, *1:* 99, 132, 133, 150; *2:* 108, 158, 196, 259; *18:* 86; *27:* 56; *29:* 79, 187, 253, 255; *36:* 199, 200, 201, 202, 203, 204, 205, 206, 207, 209; *43:* 34
Ward, Peter, *37:* 116
Warner, Peter, *14:* 87
Warren, Betsy, *2:* 101
Warren, Marion Cray, *14:* 215
Warshaw, Jerry, *30:* 197, 198; *42:* 165
Washington, Nevin, *20:* 123
Washington, Phyllis, *20:* 123
Waterman, Stan, *11:* 76
Watkins-Pitchford, D. J., *6:* 215, 217
Watson, Aldren A., *2:* 267; *5:* 94; *13:* 71; *19:* 253; *32:* 220; *42:* 193, 194, 195, 196, 197, 198, 199, 200, 201; *YABC 2:* 202
Watson, Gary, *19:* 147; *36:* 68; *41:* 122
Watson, J. D., *22:* 86
Watson, Karen, *11:* 26
Watson, Wendy, *5:* 197; *13:* 101; *33:* 116; *46:* 163
Watts, Bernadette, *4:* 227
Watts, John, *37:* 149
Webber, Helen, *3:* 141
Webber, Irma E., *14:* 238
Weber, Florence, *40:* 153
Weber, William J., *14:* 239
Webster, Jean, *17:* 241
Wegner, Fritz, *14:* 250; *20:* 189; *44:* 165
Weidenear, Reynold H., *21:* 122
Weihs, Erika, *4:* 21; *15:* 299
Weil, Lisl, *7:* 203; *10:* 58; *21:* 95; *22:* 188, 217; *33:* 193
Weiner, Sandra, *14:* 240
Weisgard, Leonard, *1:* 65; *2:* 191, 197, 204, 264-265; *5:* 108; *21:* 42; *30:* 200, 201, 203, 204; *41:* 47; *44:* 125; *YABC 2:* 13
Weiss, Ellen, *44:* 202
Weiss, Emil, *1:* 168; *7:* 60
Weiss, Harvey, *1:* 145, 223; *27:* 224, 227
Weiss, Nicki, *33:* 229
Wells, Frances, *1:* 183
Wells, H. G., *20:* 194, 200
Wells, Rosemary, *6:* 49; *18:* 297
Wells, Susan, *22:* 43

Wendelin, Rudolph, *23:* 234
Wengenroth, Stow, *37:* 47
Werenskiold, Erik, *15:* 6
Werner, Honi, *24:* 110; *33:* 41
Werth, Kurt, *7:* 122; *14:* 157; *20:* 214; *39:* 128
Westerberg, Christine, *29:* 226
Weston, Martha, *29:* 116; *30:* 213; *33:* 85, 100
Wetherbee, Margaret, *5:* 3
Wheatley, Arabelle, *11:* 231; *16:* 276
Wheeler, Dora, *44:* 179
Wheelright, Rowland, *15:* 81; *YABC 2:* 286
Whistler, Rex, *16:* 75; *30:* 207, 208
White, David Omar, *5:* 56; *18:* 6
Whitear, *32:* 26
Whithorne, H. S., *7:* 49
Whitney, George Gillett, *3:* 24
Whittam, Geoffrey, *30:* 191
Wiberg, Harald, *38:* 127
Wiese, Kurt, *3:* 255; *4:* 206; *14:* 17; *17:* 18-19; *19:* 47; *24:* 152; *25:* 212; *32:* 184; *36:* 211, 213, 214, 215, 216, 217, 218; *45:* 161
Wiesner, David, *33:* 47
Wiesner, William, *4:* 100; *5:* 200, 201; *14:* 262
Wiggins, George, *6:* 133
Wikkelsoe, Otto, *45:* 25, 26
Wikland, Ilon, *5:* 113; *8:* 150; *38:* 124, 125, 130
Wilbur, C. Keith, M.D., *27:* 228
Wilcox, J.A.J., *34:* 122
Wilcox, R. Turner, *36:* 219
Wild, Jocelyn, *46:* 220-221, 222
Wilde, George, *7:* 139
Wildsmith, Brian, *16:* 281-282; *18:* 170-171
Wilkin, Eloise, *36:* 173
Wilkinson, Gerald, *3:* 40
Wilkoń, Józef, *31:* 183, 184
Wilks, Mike, *34:* 24; *44:* 203
Williams, Ferelith Eccles, *22:* 238
Williams, Garth, *1:* 197; *2:* 49, 270; *4:* 205; *15:* 198, 302-304, 307; *16:* 34; *18:* 283, 298-301; *29:* 177, 178, 179, 232-233, 241-245, 248; *40:* 106; *YABC 2:* 15-16, 19
Williams, Kit, *44:* 206-207, 208, 209, 211, 212
Williams, Maureen, *12:* 238
Williams, Patrick, *14:* 218
Williams, Richard, *44:* 93
Wilson, Charles Banks, *17:* 92; *43:* 73
Wilson, Dagmar, *10:* 47
Wilson, Edward A., *6:* 24; *16:* 149; *20:* 220-221; *22:* 87; *26:* 67; *38:* 212, 214, 215, 216, 217
Wilson, Forrest, *27:* 231
Wilson, Gahan, *35:* 234; *41:* 136
Wilson, Jack, *17:* 139
Wilson, John, *22:* 240
Wilson, Maurice, *46:* 224
Wilson, Patten, *35:* 61
Wilson, Peggy, *15:* 4
Wilson, Rowland B., *30:* 170
Wilson, Tom, *33:* 232

Wilson, W. N., *22:* 26
Wilwerding, Walter J., *9:* 202
Winchester, Linda, *13:* 231
Wind, Betty, *28:* 158
Windham, Kathryn Tucker, *14:* 260
Winslow, Will, *21:* 124
Winsten, Melanie Willa, *41:* 41
Winter, Milo, *15:* 97; *19:* 221; *21:* 181, 203, 204, 205; *YABC 2:* 144
Wise, Louis, *13:* 68
Wiseman, Ann, *31:* 187
Wiseman, B., *4:* 233
Wishnefsky, Phillip, *3:* 14
Wiskur, Darrell, *5:* 72; *10:* 50; *18:* 246
Wittman, Sally, *30:* 219
Woehr, Lois, *12:* 5
Wohlberg, Meg, *12:* 100; *14:* 197; *41:* 255
Woldin, Beth Weiner, *34:* 211
Wolf, J., *16:* 91
Wolf, Linda, *33:* 163
Wondriska, William, *6:* 220
Wonsetler, John C., *5:* 168
Wood, Grant, *19:* 198
Wood, Muriel, *36:* 119
Wood, Myron, *6:* 220
Wood, Owen, *18:* 187
Wood, Ruth, *8:* 11
Woodson, Jack, *10:* 201
Woodward, Alice, *26:* 89; *36:* 81
Wool, David, *26:* 27
Wooten, Vernon, *23:* 70
Worboys, Evelyn, *1:* 166-167
Worth, Jo, *34:* 143
Worth, Wendy, *4:* 133
Wosmek, Frances, *29:* 251
Wrenn, Charles L., *38:* 96; *YABC 1:* 20, 21
Wright, Dare, *21:* 206
Wright, George, *YABC 1:* 268
Wright, Joseph, *30:* 160
Wronker, Lili Cassel, *3:* 247; *10:* 204; *21:* 10
Wyatt, Stanley, *46:* 210
Wyeth, Andrew, *13:* 40; *YABC 1:* 133-134
Wyeth, Jamie, *41:* 257
Wyeth, N. C., *13:* 41; *17:* 252-259, 264-268; *18:* 181; *19:* 80, 191, 200; *21:* 57, 183; *22:* 91; *23:* 152; *24:* 28, 99; *35:* 61; *41:* 65; *YABC 1:* 133, 223; *YABC 2:* 53, 75, 171, 187, 317

Yang, Jay, *1:* 8; *12:* 239
Yap, Weda, *6:* 176
Yaroslava. *See* Mills, Yaroslava Surmach
Yashima, Taro, *14:* 84
Ylla. *See* Koffler, Camilla
Yohn, F. C., *23:* 128; *YABC 1:* 269
Young, Ed, *7:* 205; *10:* 206; *40:* 124; *YABC 2:* 242
Young, Noela, *8:* 221

Zacks, Lewis, *10:* 161

Zaffo, George, *42:* 208
Zaidenberg, Arthur, *34:* 218, 219, 220
Zalben, Jane Breskin, *7:* 211
Zallinger, Jean, *4:* 192; *8:* 8, 129;
    14: 273
Zallinger, Rudolph F., *3:* 245
Zeck, Gerry, *40:* 232
Zeiring, Bob, *42:* 130
Zelinsky, Paul O., *14:* 269; *43:* 56
Zemach, Margot, *3:* 270; *8:* 201;
    21: 210-211; *27:* 204, 205, 210;
    28: 185
Zemsky, Jessica, *10:* 62
Zepelinsky, Paul, *35:* 93
Zimmer, Dirk, *38:* 195
Zimnik, Reiner, *36:* 224
Zinkeisen, Anna, *13:* 106
Zoellick, Scott, *33:* 231
Zonia, Dhimitri, *20:* 234-235
Zweifel, Francis, *14:* 274; *28:* 187
Zwinger, Herman H., *46:* 227

Author Index

The following index gives the number of the volume in which an author's biographical sketch, Brief Entry, or Obituary appears.

This index includes references to all entries in the following series, which are also published by Gale Research Company.

YABC—*Yesterday's Authors of Books for Children: Facts and Pictures about Authors and Illustrators of Books for Young People from Early Times to 1960*, Volumes 1-2
CLR—*Children's Literature Review: Excerpts from Reviews, Criticism, and Commentary on Books for Children*, Volumes 1-10
SAAS—*Something about the Author Autobiography Series*, Volumes 1-3

A

Aardema, Verna 1911- 4
Aaron, Chester 1923- 9
Aaseng, Nate
   See Aaseng, Nathan
Aaseng, Nathan 1938-
   Brief Entry 38
Abbott, Alice
   See Borland, Kathryn Kilby
Abbott, Alice
   See Speicher, Helen Ross (Smith)
Abbott, Jacob 1803-1879 22
Abbott, Manager Henry
   See Stratemeyer, Edward L.
Abbott, Sarah
   See Zolotow, Charlotte S.
Abdul, Raoul 1929- 12
Abel, Raymond 1911- 12
Abell, Kathleen 1938- 9
Abercrombie, Barbara (Mattes)
   1939- 16
Abernethy, Robert G. 1935- 5
Abisch, Roslyn Kroop 1927- 9
Abisch, Roz
   See Abisch, Roslyn Kroop
Abodaher, David J. (Naiph)
   1919- 17
Abolafia, Yossi
   Brief Entry 46
Abrahall, C. H.
   See Hoskyns-Abrahall, Clare
Abrahall, Clare Hoskyns
   See Hoskyns-Abrahall, Clare
Abrahams, Hilary (Ruth)
   1938- 29
Abrahams, Robert D(avid)
   1905- 4
Abrams, Joy 1941- 16
Achebe, Chinua 1930- 40
   Brief Entry 38
Ackerman, Eugene 1888-1974 10
Acs, Laszlo (Bela) 1931- 42
   Brief Entry 32

Acuff, Selma Boyd 1924- 45
Ada, Alma Flor 1938- 43
Adair, Margaret Weeks
   (?)-1971 10
Adam, Cornel
   See Lengyel, Cornel Adam
Adams, Adrienne 1906- 8
Adams, Andy
   1859-1935 .... YABC 1
Adams, Dale
   See Quinn, Elisabeth
Adams, Harriet S(tratemeyer)
   1893(?)-1982 1
   Obituary 29
Adams, Harrison
   See Stratemeyer, Edward L.
Adams, Hazard 1926- 6
Adams, Laurie 1941- 33
Adams, Richard 1920- 7
Adams, Ruth Joyce 14
Adams, William Taylor
   1822-1897 28
Adamson, Gareth 1925-1982 46
   Obituary 30
Adamson, George Worsley
   1913- 30
Adamson, Graham
   See Groom, Arthur William
Adamson, Joy 1910-1980 11
   Obituary 22
Adamson, Wendy Wriston
   1942- 22
Addona, Angelo F. 1925- 14
Addy, Ted
   See Winterbotham, R(ussell)
   R(obert)
Adelberg, Doris
   See Orgel, Doris
Adelson, Leone 1908- 11
Adkins, Jan 1944- 8
   See also CLR 7
Adler, C(arole) S(chwerdtfeger)
   1932- 26
Adler, David A. 1947- 14

Adler, Irene
   See Penzler, Otto
   See Storr, Catherine (Cole)
Adler, Irving 1913- 29
   Earlier sketch in SATA 1
Adler, Larry 1939- 36
Adler, Peggy 22
Adler, Ruth 1915-1968 1
Adoff, Arnold 1935- 5
   See also CLR 7
Adorjan, Carol 1934- 10
Adrian, Mary
   See Jorgensen, Mary Venn
Adshead, Gladys L. 1896- 3
Aesop, Abraham
   See Newbery, John
Agapida, Fray Antonio
   See Irving, Washington
Agard, Nadema 1948- 18
Agle, Nan Hayden 1905- 3
Agnew, Edith J(osephine)
   1897- 11
Ahern, Margaret McCrohan
   1921- 10
Ahl, Anna Maria 1926- 32
Ahlberg, Allan
   Brief Entry 35
Ahlberg, Janet
   Brief Entry 32
Aichinger, Helga 1937- 4
Aiken, Clarissa (Lorenz)
   1899- 12
Aiken, Conrad (Potter)
   1889-1973 30
   Earlier sketch in SATA 3
Aiken, Joan 1924- 30
   Earlier sketch in SATA 2
   See also CLR 1
   See also SAAS 1
Ainsworth, Norma 9
Ainsworth, Ruth 1908- 7
Ainsworth, William Harrison
   1805-1882 24
Aistrop, Jack 1916- 14

Aitken, Amy 1952-
Brief Entry 40
Aitken, Dorothy 1916- 10
Akaba, Suekichi 1910- 46
Akers, Floyd
See Baum, L(yman) Frank
Alain
See Brustlein, Daniel
Albert, Burton, Jr. 1936- 22
Alberts, Frances Jacobs 1907- 14
Albion, Lee Smith 29
Albrecht, Lillie (Vanderveer)
1894- 12
Alcock, Gudrun
Brief Entry 33
Alcock, Vivien 1924- 45
Brief Entry 38
Alcorn, John 1935- 31
Brief Entry 30
Alcott, Louisa May
1832-1888 ....YABC 1
See also CLR 1
Alda, Arlene 1933- 44
Brief Entry 36
Alden, Isabella (Macdonald)
1841-1930 ....YABC 2
Alderman, Clifford Lindsey
1902- 3
Aldis, Dorothy (Keeley)
1896-1966 2
Aldiss, Brian W(ilson) 1925- 34
Aldon, Adair
See Meigs, Cornelia
Aldous, Allan (Charles) 1911- 27
Aldrich, Ann
See Meaker, Marijane
Aldrich, Thomas Bailey
1836-1907 17
Aldridge, Alan 1943(?)-
Brief Entry 33
Aldridge, Josephine Haskell 14
Alegria, Ricardo E. 1921- 6
Aleksin, Anatolii (Georgievich)
1924- 36
Alex, Ben [a pseudonym]
1946- 45
Alex, Marlee [a pseudonym]
1948- 45
Alexander, Anna Cooke 1913- 1
Alexander, Frances 1888- 4
Alexander, Jocelyn (Anne) Arundel
1930- 22
Alexander, Linda 1935- 2
Alexander, Lloyd 1924- 3
See also CLR 1, 5
Alexander, Martha 1920- 11
Alexander, Rae Pace
See Alexander, Raymond Pace
Alexander, Raymond Pace
1898-1974 22
Alexander, Sue 1933- 12
Alexander, Vincent Arthur 1925-1980
Obituary 23
Alexeieff, Alexandre A.
1901- 14
Alger, Horatio, Jr. 1832-1899 16
Alger, Leclaire (Gowans)
1898-1969 15

Aliki
See Brandenberg, Aliki
See also CLR 9
Alkema, Chester Jay 1932- 12
Allamand, Pascale 1942- 12
Allan, Mabel Esther 1915- 32
Earlier sketch in SATA 5
Allard, Harry
See Allard, Harry G(rover), Jr.
Allard, Harry G(rover), Jr.
1928- 42
Allee, Marjorie Hill
1890-1945 17
Allen, Adam [Joint pseudonym]
See Epstein, Beryl and Epstein,
Samuel
Allen, Alex B.
See Heide, Florence Parry
Allen, Allyn
See Eberle, Irmengarde
Allen, Betsy
See Cavanna, Betty
Allen, Gertrude E(lizabeth)
1888- 9
Allen, Jack 1899-
Brief Entry 29
Allen, Jeffrey (Yale) 1948- 42
Allen, Leroy 1912- 11
Allen, Linda 1925- 33
Allen, Marjorie 1931- 22
Allen, Maury 1932- 26
Allen, Merritt Parmelee
1892-1954 22
Allen, Nina (Strömgren)
1935- 22
Allen, Rodney F. 1938- 27
Allen, Ruth
See Peterson, Esther (Allen)
Allen, Samuel (Washington)
1917- 9
Allen, T. D. [Joint pseudonym]
See Allen, Terril Diener
Allen, Terril Diener 1908- 35
Allen, Terry D.
See Allen, Terril Diener
Allen, Thomas B(enton)
1929- 45
Allen, Tom
See Allen, Thomas B(enton)
Allerton, Mary
See Govan, Christine Noble
Alleyn, Ellen
See Rossetti, Christina (Georgina)
Allington, Richard L(loyd)
1947- 39
Brief Entry 35
Allison, Bob 14
Allison, Linda 1948- 43
Allmendinger, David F(rederick), Jr.
1938- 35
Allred, Gordon T. 1930- 10
Allsop, Kenneth 1920-1973 17
Almedingen, E. M.
1898-1971 3
Almedingen, Martha Edith von
See Almedingen, E. M.
Almquist, Don 1929- 11

Alsop, Mary O'Hara
1885-1980 34
Obituary 24
Earlier sketch in SATA 5
Alter, Robert Edmond
1925-1965 9
Althea
See Braithwaite, Althea 23
Altschuler, Franz 1923- 45
Altsheler, Joseph A(lexander)
1862-1919 ....YABC 1
Alvarez, Joseph A. 1930- 18
Ambler, C(hristopher) Gifford 1886-
Brief Entry 29
Ambrose, Stephen E(dward)
1936- 40
Ambrus, Gyozo (Laszlo)
1935- 41
Earlier sketch in SATA 1
Ambrus, Victor G.
See Ambrus, Gyozo (Laszlo)
Amerman, Lockhart
1911-1969 3
Ames, Evelyn 1908- 13
Ames, Gerald 1906- 11
Ames, Lee J. 1921- 3
Ames, Mildred 1919- 22
Amon, Aline 1928- 9
Amoss, Berthe 1925- 5
Anastasio, Dina 1941- 37
Brief Entry 30
Anckarsvard, Karin
1915-1969 6
Ancona, George 1929- 12
Andersdatter, Karla M(argaret)
1938- 34
Andersen, Hans Christian
1805-1875 ....YABC 1
See also CLR 6
Andersen, Ted
See Boyd, Waldo T.
Andersen, Yvonne 1932- 27
Anderson, Bernice G(oudy)
1894- 33
Anderson, Brad(ley Jay)
1924- 33
Brief Entry 31
Anderson, C(larence) W(illiam)
1891-1971 11
Anderson, Clifford [Joint pseudonym]
See Gardner, Richard
Anderson, Ella
See MacLeod, Ellen Jane (Anderson)
Anderson, Eloise Adell 1927- 9
Anderson, George
See Groom, Arthur William
Anderson, Grace Fox 1932- 43
Anderson, J(ohn) R(ichard) L(ane)
1911-1981 15
Obituary 27
Anderson, Joy 1928- 1
Anderson, LaVere (Francis Shoenfelt)
1907- 27
Anderson, (John) Lonzo
1905- 2
Anderson, Lucia (Lewis)
1922- 10
Anderson, Madelyn Klein 28

Anderson, Margaret J(ean)
  1931- 27
Anderson, Mary 1939- 7
Anderson, Mona 1910- 40
Anderson, Norman D(ean)
  1928- 22
Anderson, Poul (William) 1926-
  Brief Entry 39
Anderson, Rachel 1943- 34
Andre, Evelyn M(arie) 1924- 27
Andree, Louise
  See Coury, Louise Andree
Andrews, Benny 1930- 31
Andrews, F(rank) Emerson
  1902-1978 22
Andrews, J(ames) S(ydney)
  1934- 4
Andrews, Julie 1935- 7
Andrews, Laura
  See Coury, Louise Andree
Andrews, Roy Chapman
  1884-1960 19
Andrézel, Pierre
  See Blixen, Karen (Christentze
  Dinesen)
Andriola, Alfred J. 1912-1983
  Obituary 34
Andrist, Ralph K. 1914- 45
Angeles, Peter A. 1931- 40
Angell, Judie 1937- 22
Angell, Madeline 1919- 18
Angelo, Valenti 1897- 14
Angier, Bradford 12
Angle, Paul M(cClelland) 1900-1975
  Obituary 20
Anglund, Joan Walsh 1926- 2
  See also CLR 1
Angrist, Stanley W(olff)
  1933- 4
Anita
  See Daniel, Anita
Annett, Cora
  See Scott, Cora Annett
Annixter, Jane
  See Sturtzel, Jane Levington
Annixter, Paul
  See Sturtzel, Howard A.
Anno, Mitsumasa 1926- 38
  Earlier sketch in SATA 5
  See also CLR 2
Anrooy, Frans van
  See Van Anrooy, Francine
Antell, Will D. 1935- 31
Anthony, Barbara 1932- 29
Anthony, C. L.
  See Smith, Dodie
Anthony, Edward 1895-1971 21
Anticaglia, Elizabeth 1939- 12
Antolini, Margaret Fishback
  1904-1985
  Obituary 45
Anton, Michael (James) 1940- 12
Antonacci, Robert J(oseph)
  1916- 45
  Brief Entry 37
Aoki, Hisako 1942- 45
Apfel, Necia H(alpern) 1930-
  Brief Entry 41

Aphrodite, J.
  See Livingston, Carole
Appel, Benjamin 1907-1977 39
  Obituary 21
Appel, Martin E(liot) 1948- 45
Appel, Marty
  See Appel, Martin E(liot)
Appiah, Peggy 1921- 15
Apple, Margot
  Brief Entry 42
Applebaum, Stan 1929- 45
Appleton, Victor [Collective
  pseudonym] 1
Appleton, Victor II [Collective
  pseudonym] 1
  See also Adams, Harriet
  S(tratemeyer)
Apsler, Alfred 1907- 10
Aquillo, Don
  See Prince, J(ack) H(arvey)
Aragonés, Sergio 1937-
  Brief Entry 39
Arbuckle, Dorothy Fry 1910-1982
  Obituary 33
Arbuthnot, May Hill
  1884-1969 2
Archer, Frank
  See O'Connor, Richard
Archer, Jules 1915- 4
Archer, Marion Fuller 1917- 11
Archibald, Joseph S. 1898- 3
Arden, Barbie
  See Stoutenburg, Adrien
Arden, William
  See Lynds, Dennis
Ardizzone, Edward 1900-1979 28
  Obituary 21
  Earlier sketch in SATA 1
  See also CLR 3
Ardley, Neil (Richard) 1937- 43
Arehart-Treichel, Joan 1942- 22
Arenella, Roy 1939- 14
Arkin, Alan (Wolf) 1934-
  Brief Entry 32
Armer, Alberta (Roller) 1904- 9
Armer, Laura Adams
  1874-1963 13
Armitage, David 1943-
  Brief Entry 38
Armitage, Ronda (Jacqueline) 1943-
  Brief Entry 38
Armour, Richard 1906- 14
Armstrong, George D. 1927- 10
Armstrong, Gerry (Breen)
  1929- 10
Armstrong, Louise 43
  Brief Entry 33
Armstrong, Richard 1903- 11
Armstrong, William H. 1914- 4
  See also CLR 1
Arndt, Ursula (Martha H.)
  Brief Entry 39
Arneson, D(on) J(on) 1935- 37
Arnett, Carolyn
  See Cole, Lois Dwight
Arno, Enrico 1913-1981 43
  Obituary 28
Arnold, Caroline 1944- 36
  Brief Entry 34

Arnold, Elliott 1912-1980 5
  Obituary 22
Arnold, Oren 1900- 4
Arnoldy, Julie
  See Bischoff, Julia Bristol
Arnosky, Jim 1946- 22
Arnott, Kathleen 1914- 20
Arnov, Boris, Jr. 1926- 12
Arnow, Harriette (Louisa Simpson)
  1908- 42
Arnstein, Helene S(olomon)
  1915- 12
Arntson, Herbert E(dward)
  1911- 12
Aronin, Ben 1904-1980
  Obituary 25
Arora, Shirley (Lease) 1930- 2
Arquette, Lois S(teinmetz)
  1934- 1
  See Duncan, Lois S(teinmetz)
Arrowood, (McKendrick Lee) Clinton
  1939- 19
Arthur, Robert
  See Feder, Robert Arthur
Arthur, Ruth M(abel)
  1905-1979 7
  Obituary 26
Artis, Vicki Kimmel 1945- 12
Artzybasheff, Boris (Miklailovich)
  1899-1965 14
Aruego, Ariane
  See Dewey, Ariane
Aruego, Jose 1932- 6
  See also CLR 5
Arundel, Honor (Morfydd)
  1919-1973 4
  Obituary 24
Arundel, Jocelyn
  See Alexander, Jocelyn (Anne)
  Arundel
Asbjörnsen, Peter Christen
  1812-1885 15
Asch, Frank 1946- 5
Ash, Jutta 1942- 38
Ashabranner, Brent (Kenneth)
  1921- 1
Ashby, Gwynneth 1922- 44
Ashe, Geoffrey (Thomas)
  1923- 17
Asher, Sandy (Fenichel)
  1942- 36
  Brief Entry 34
Ashey, Bella
  See Breinburg, Petronella
Ashford, Daisy
  See Ashford, Margaret Mary
Ashford, Margaret Mary
  1881-1972 10
Ashley, Bernard 1935-
  Brief Entry 39
  See also CLR 4
Ashley, Elizabeth
  See Salmon, Annie Elizabeth
Ashton, Warren T.
  See Adams, William Taylor
Asimov, Issac 1920- 26
  Earlier sketch in SATA 1
Asimov, Janet
  See Jeppson, J(anet) O(pal)

Asinof, Eliot 1919- 6
Astley, Juliet
  See Lofts, Nora (Robinson)
Aston, James
  See White, T(erence) H(anbury)
Atene, Ann
  See Atene, (Rita) Anna
Atene, (Rita) Anna 1922- *12*
Atkinson, Allen
  Brief Entry *46*
Atkinson, M. E.
  See Frankau, Mary Evelyn
Atkinson, Margaret Fleming *14*
Atticus
  See Davies, (Edward) Hunter
  See Fleming, Ian (Lancaster)
Atwater, Florence (Hasseltine
  Carroll) *16*
Atwater, Montgomery Meigs
  1904- *15*
Atwater, Richard Tupper 1892-1948
  Brief Entry *27*
Atwood, Ann 1913- 7
Aubry, Claude B. 1914-1984 ..... *29*
  Obituary *40*
Augarde, Steve 1950- *25*
Augelli, John P(at) 1921- *46*
Ault, Phillip H. 1914- *23*
Ault, Rosalie Sain 1942- *38*
Ault, Roz
  See Ault, Rosalie Sain
Aung, (Maung) Htin 1910- *21*
Aung, U. Htin
  See Aung, (Maung) Htin
Auntie Deb
  See Coury, Louise Andree
Auntie Louise
  See Coury, Louise Andree
Austin, Elizabeth S. 1907- 5
Austin, Margot *11*
Austin, Oliver L., Jr. 1903- 7
Austin, Tom
  See Jacobs, Linda C.
Averill, Esther 1902- *28*
  Earlier sketch in SATA 1
Avery, Al
  See Montgomery, Rutherford
Avery, Gillian 1926- 7
Avery, Kay 1908- 5
Avery, Lynn
  See Cole, Lois Dwight
Avi
  See Wortis, Avi
Ayars, James S(terling) 1898- 4
Ayer, Jacqueline 1930- *13*
Ayer, Margaret *15*
Aylesworth, Jim 1943- *38*
Aylesworth, Thomas G(ibbons)
  1927- 4
  See also CLR 6
Aymar, Brandt 1911- *22*
Ayres, Patricia Miller 1923-1985
  Obituary *46*
Azaid
  See Zaidenberg, Arthur

B

B
  See Gilbert, W(illiam) S(chwenk)

B., Tania
  See Blixen, Karen (Christentze
  Dinesen)
BB
  See Watkins-Pitchford, D. J.
Baastad, Babbis Friis
  See Friis-Baastad, Babbis
Bab
  See Gilbert, W(illiam) S(chwenk)
Babbis, Eleanor
  See Friis-Baastad, Babbis
Babbitt, Natalie 1932- 6
  See also CLR 2
Babcock, Dennis Arthur
  1948- *22*
Bach, Alice (Hendricks)
  1942- *30*
  Brief Entry *27*
Bach, Richard David 1936- *13*
Bachman, Fred 1949- *12*
Bacmeister, Rhoda W(arner)
  1893- *11*
Bacon, Elizabeth 1914- 3
Bacon, Joan Chase
  See Bowden, Joan Chase
Bacon, Margaret Hope 1921- 6
Bacon, Martha Sherman
  1917-1981 .... *18*
  Obituary *27*
  See also CLR 3
Bacon, Peggy 1895- 2
Bacon, R(onald) L(eonard)
  1924- *26*
Baden-Powell, Robert (Stephenson
  Smyth) 1857-1941 .... *16*
Baerg, Harry J(ohn) 1909- *12*
Bagnold, Enid 1889-1981 .... *25*
  Earlier sketch in SATA 1
Bahr, Robert 1940- *38*
Bahti, Tom
  Brief Entry *31*
Bailey, Alice Cooper 1890- *12*
Bailey, Bernadine Freeman *14*
Bailey, Carolyn Sherwin
  1875-1961 .... *14*
Bailey, Jane H(orton) 1916- *12*
Bailey, Maralyn Collins (Harrison)
  1941- *12*
Bailey, Matilda
  See Radford, Ruby L.
Bailey, Maurice Charles
  1932- *12*
Bailey, Ralph Edgar 1893- *11*
Baird, Bil 1904- *30*
Baird, Thomas P. 1923- *45*
  Brief Entry *39*
Baity, Elizabeth Chesley
  1907- *1*
Bakeless, John (Edwin) 1894- 9
Bakeless, Katherine Little
  1895- 9
Baker, Alan 1951- *22*
Baker, Augusta 1911- 3
Baker, Betty (Lou) 1928- 5
Baker, Charlotte 1910- 2
Baker, Elizabeth 1923- 7
Baker, Gayle C(unningham)
  1950- *39*
Baker, James W. 1924- *22*

Baker, Janice E(dla) 1941- *22*
Baker, Jeannie 1950- *23*
Baker, Jeffrey J(ohn) W(heeler)
  1931- 5
Baker, Jim
  See Baker, James W.
Baker, Laura Nelson 1911- *3*
Baker, Margaret 1890- *4*
Baker, Margaret J(oyce)
  1918- *12*
Baker, Mary Gladys Steel
  1892-1974 .... *12*
Baker, (Robert) Michael
  1938- *4*
Baker, Nina (Brown)
  1888-1957 .... *15*
Baker, Rachel 1904-1978 .... *2*
  Obituary *26*
Baker, Samm Sinclair 1909- *12*
Baker, Susan (Catherine)
  1942- *29*
Balaam
  See Lamb, G(eoffrey) F(rederick)
Balch, Glenn 1902- *3*
Baldridge, Cyrus LeRoy 1889-
  Brief Entry *29*
Balducci, Carolyn Feleppa
  1946- 5
Baldwin, Anne Norris 1938- 5
Baldwin, Clara *11*
Baldwin, Gordo
  See Baldwin, Gordon C.
Baldwin, Gordon C. 1908- *12*
Baldwin, James 1841-1925 .... *24*
Baldwin, James (Arthur)
  1924- 9
Baldwin, Margaret
  See Weis, Margaret (Edith)
Baldwin, Stan(ley C.) 1929-
  Brief Entry *28*
Bales, Carol Ann 1940-
  Brief Entry *29*
Balet, Jan (Bernard) 1913- *11*
Balian, Lorna 1929- 9
Ball, Zachary
  See Masters, Kelly R.
Ballantine, Lesley Frost
  See Frost, Lesley
Ballantyne, R(obert) M(ichael)
  1825-1894 .... *24*
Ballard, Lowell Clyne 1904- *12*
Ballard, (Charles) Martin
  1929- *1*
Balogh, Penelope 1916-1975 ...... *1*
  Obituary *34*
Balow, Tom 1931- *12*
Baltzer, Hans (Adolf) 1900- *40*
Bamfylde, Walter
  See Bevan, Tom
Bamman, Henry A. 1918- *12*
Bancroft, Griffing 1907- 6
Bancroft, Laura
  See Baum, L(yman) Frank
Baner, Skulda V(anadis)
  1897-1964 .... *10*
Bang, Betsy (Garrett) 1912-
  Brief Entry *37*
Bang, Garrett
  See Bang, Molly Garrett

Bang, Molly Garrett 1943- 24
See also CLR 8
Banks, Laura Stockton Voorhees
1908(?)-1980
Obituary 23
Banks, Sara (Jeanne Gordon Harrell)
1937- 26
Banner, Angela
See Maddison, Angela Mary
Bannerman, Helen (Brodie Cowan
Watson) 1863(?)-1946 19
Banning, Evelyn I. 1903- 36
Bannon, Laura (?)-1963 6
Barbary, James
See Baumann, Amy (Brown)
Barbary, James
See Beeching, Jack
Barbe, Walter Burke 1926- 45
Barber, Antonia
See Anthony, Barbara
Barber, Linda
See Graham-Barber, Lynda
Barber, Richard (William)
1941- 35
Barbour, Ralph Henry
1870-1944 16
Barclay, Isabel
See Dobell, I.M.B.
Bare, Arnold Edwin 1920- 16
Bare, Colleen Stanley 32
Barish, Matthew 1907- 12
Barker, Albert W. 1900- 8
Barker, Carol (Minturn) 1938- 31
Barker, Cicely Mary 1895-1973
Brief Entry 39
Barker, Melvern 1907- 11
Barker, S. Omar 1894- 10
Barker, Will 1908- 8
Barkley, James Edward 1941- 6
Barks, Carl 1901- 37
Barnaby, Ralph S(tanton)
1893- 9
Barner, Bob 1947- 29
Barnes, (Frank) Eric Wollencott
1907-1962 22
Barnes, Malcolm 1909(?)-1984
Obituary 41
Barnett, Lincoln (Kinnear)
1909-1979 36
Barnett, Moneta 1922-1976 33
Barnett, Naomi 1927- 40
Barney, Maginel Wright
1881-1966 39
Brief Entry 32
Barnouw, Adriaan Jacob 1877-1968
Obituary 27
Barnouw, Victor 1915- 43
Brief Entry 28
Barnstone, Willis 1927- 20
Barnum, Jay Hyde
1888(?)-1962 20
Barnum, Richard [Collective
pseudonym] 1
Baron, Virginia Olsen 1931- 46
Brief Entry 28
Barr, Donald 1921- 20
Barr, George 1907- 2
Barr, Jene 1900-1985 16
Obituary 42

Barrer, Gertrude
See Barrer-Russell, Gertrude
Barrer-Russell, Gertrude
1921- 27
Barrett, Ethel
Brief Entry 44
Barrett, Judith 1941- 26
Barrett, Ron 1937- 14
Barrie, J(ames) M(atthew)
1860-1937 .... YABC 1
Barrol, Grady
See Bograd, Larry
Barry, James P(otvin) 1918- 14
Barry, Katharina (Watjen)
1936- 4
Barry, Robert 1931- 6
Barry, Scott 1952- 32
Bartenbach, Jean 1918- 40
Barth, Edna 1914-1980 7
Obituary 24
Barthelme, Donald 1931- 7
Bartholomew, Barbara 1941-
Brief Entry 42
Bartlett, Philip A. [Collective
pseudonym] 1
Bartlett, Robert Merrill 1899- 12
Barton, Byron 1930- 9
Barton, Harriett
Brief Entry 43
Barton, May Hollis [Collective
pseudonym] 1
See also Adams, Harriet
S(tratemeyer)
Bartos-Hoeppner, Barbara
1923- 5
Bartsch, Jochen 1906- 39
Baruch, Dorothy W(alter)
1899-1962 21
Bas, Rutger
See Rutgers van der Loeff, An(na)
Basenau
Bashevis, Isaac
See Singer, Isaac Bashevis
Baskin, Leonard 1922- 30
Brief Entry 27
Bason, Lillian 1913- 20
Bassett, Jeni 1960(?)-
Brief Entry 43
Bassett, John Keith
See Keating, Lawrence A.
Batchelor, Joy 1914-
Brief Entry 29
Bate, Lucy 1939- 18
Bate, Norman 1916- 5
Bates, Barbara S(nedeker)
1919- 12
Bates, Betty 1921- 19
Batey, Tom 1946-
Brief Entry 41
Batherman, Muriel
See Sheldon, Muriel
Batiuk, Thomas M(artin) 1947-
Brief Entry 40
Batson, Larry 1930- 35
Battaglia, Aurelius
Brief Entry 33
Batten, H(arry) Mortimer
1888-1958 25
Batten, Mary 1937- 5

Batterberry, Ariane Ruskin
1935- 13
Batterberry, Michael (Carver)
1932- 32
Battles, Edith 1921- 7
Baudouy, Michel-Aime 1909- 7
Bauer, Caroline Feller 1935-
Brief Entry 46
Bauer, Fred 1934- 36
Bauer, Helen 1900- 2
Bauer, Marion Dane 1938- 20
Bauernschmidt, Marjorie
1926- 15
Baum, Allyn Z(elton) 1924- 20
Baum, L(yman) Frank
1856-1919 18
Baum, Willi 1931- 4
Baumann, Amy (Brown)
1922- 10
Baumann, Elwood D.
Brief Entry 33
Baumann, Hans 1914- 2
Baumann, Kurt 1935- 21
Bawden, Nina
See Kark, Nina Mary
See also CLR 2
Bayer, Jane E. (?)-1985
Obituary 44
Bayley, Nicola 1949- 41
Baylor, Byrd 1924- 16
See also CLR 3
Baynes, Pauline (Diana)
1922- 19
Beach, Charles
See Reid, (Thomas) Mayne
Beach, Charles Amory [Collective
pseudonym] 1
Beach, Edward L(atimer)
1918- 12
Beach, Stewart Taft 1899- 23
Beachcroft, Nina 1931- 18
Bealer, Alex W(inkler III)
1921-1980 8
Obituary 22
Beals, Carleton 1893- 12
Beals, Frank Lee 1881-1972
Obituary 26
Beame, Rona 1934- 12
Beamer, (G.) Charles, (Jr.)
1942- 43
Beaney, Jan
See Udall, Jan Beaney
Beard, Charles Austin
1874-1948 18
Beard, Dan(iel Carter)
1850-1941 22
Bearden, Romare (Howard)
1914- 22
Beardmore, Cedric
See Beardmore, George
Beardmore, George
1908-1979 20
Bearman, Jane (Ruth) 1917- 29
Beatty, Elizabeth
See Holloway, Teresa (Bragunier)
Beatty, Hetty Burlingame
1907-1971 5
Beatty, Jerome, Jr. 1918- 5

Beatty, John (Louis)
  1922-1975 6
  Obituary 25
Beatty, Patricia (Robbins) 30
  Earlier sketch in SATA 1
Bechtel, Louise Seaman
  1894-1985 4
  Obituary 43
Beck, Barbara L. 1927- 12
Becker, Beril 1901- 11
Becker, John (Leonard) 1901- 12
Becker, Joyce 1936- 39
Becker, May Lamberton
  1873-1958 33
Beckett, Sheilah 1913- 33
Beckman, Gunnel 1910- 6
Beckman, Kaj
  See Beckman, Karin
Beckman, Karin 1913- 45
Beckman, Per (Frithiof) 1913- 45
Bedford, A. N.
  See Watson, Jane Werner
Bedford, Annie North
  See Watson, Jane Werner
Beebe, B(urdetta) F(aye)
  1920- 1
Beebe, (Charles) William
  1877-1962 19
Beeby, Betty 1923- 25
Beech, Webb
  See Butterworth, W. E.
Beeching, Jack 1922- 14
Beeler, Nelson F(rederick)
  1910- 13
Beers, Dorothy Sands 1917- 9
Beers, Lorna 1897- 14
Beers, V(ictor) Gilbert 1928- 9
Begley, Kathleen A(nne)
  1948- 21
Behn, Harry 1898-1973 2
  Obituary 34
Behnke, Frances L. 8
Behr, Joyce 1929- 15
Behrens, June York 1925- 19
Behrman, Carol H(elen) 1925- ... 14
Beiser, Arthur 1931- 22
Beiser, Germaine 1931- 11
Belair, Richard L. 1934- 45
Belaney, Archibald Stansfeld
  1888-1938 24
Belknap, B. H.
  See Ellis, Edward S(ylvester)
Bell, Corydon 1894- 3
Bell, Emily Mary
  See Cason, Mabel Earp
Bell, Gertrude (Wood) 1911- 12
Bell, Gina
  See Iannone, Jeanne
Bell, Janet
  See Clymer, Eleanor
Bell, Margaret E(lizabeth)
  1898- 2
Bell, Norman (Edward) 1899- 11
Bell, Raymond Martin 1907- 13
Bell, Robert S(tanley) W(arren)
  1871-1921
  Brief Entry 27
Bell, Thelma Harrington
  1896- 3

Bellairs, John 1938- 2
Belloc, (Joseph) Hilaire (Pierre)
  1870-1953 .... YABC 1
Bell-Zano, Gina
  See Iannone, Jeanne
Belpré, Pura 1899-1982 16
  Obituary 30
Belting, Natalie Maree 1915- 6
Belton, John Raynor 1931- 22
Beltran, Alberto 1923- 43
Belvedere, Lee
  See Grayland, Valerie
Bemelmans, Ludwig
  1898-1962 15
  See also CLR 6
Benary, Margot
  See Benary-Isbert, Margot
Benary-Isbert, Margot
  1889-1979 2
  Obituary 21
Benasutti, Marion 1908- 6
Benchley, Nathaniel (Goddard)
  1915-1981 25
  Obituary 28
  Earlier sketch in SATA 3
Benchley, Peter 1940- 3
Bender, Lucy Ellen 1942- 22
Bendick, Jeanne 1919- 2
  See also CLR 5
Bendick, Robert L(ouis)
  1917- 11
Benedict, Dorothy Potter
  1889-1979 11
  Obituary 23
Benedict, Lois Trimble
  1902-1967 12
Benedict, Rex 1920- 8
Benedict, Stewart H(urd)
  1924- 26
Benét, Laura 1884-1979 3
  Obituary 23
Benét, Stephen Vincent
  1898-1943 .... YABC 1
Benet, Sula 1903(?)-1982 21
  Obituary 33
Benezra, Barbara 1921- 10
Benjamin, Nora
  See Kubie, Nora (Gottheil) Benjamin
Bennett, Dorothea
  See Young, Dorothea Bennett
Bennett, Jay 1912- 41
  Brief Entry 27
Bennett, Jill (Crawford) 1934- 41
Bennett, John 1865-1956 ..... YABC 1
Bennett, Rachel
  See Hill, Margaret (Ohler)
Bennett, Rainey 1907- 15
Bennett, Richard 1899- 21
Bennett, Russell H(oradley)
  1896- 25
Benson, Sally 1900-1972 35
  Obituary 27
  Earlier sketch in SATA 1
Bentley, Judith (McBride)
  1945- 40
Bentley, Nicolas Clerihew 1907-1978
  Obituary 24

Bentley, Phyllis (Eleanor)
  1894-1977 6
  Obituary 25
Bentley, Roy 1947- 46
Berelson, Howard 1940- 5
Berends, Polly Berrien 1939-
  Brief Entry 38
Berenstain, Janice 12
Berenstain, Michael 1951-
  Brief Entry 45
Berenstain, Stan(ley) 1923- 12
Beresford, Elisabeth 25
Berg, Dave
  See Berg, David
Berg, David 1920- 27
Berg, Jean Horton 1913- 6
Berg, Joan
  See Victor, Joan Berg
Bergaust, Erik 1925-1978 20
Berger, Gilda
  Brief Entry 42
Berger, Josef 1903-1971 36
Berger, Melvin H. 1927- 5
  See also SAAS 2
Berger, Terry 1933- 8
Bergey, Alyce (Mae) 1934- 45
Berkebile, Fred D(onovan) 1900-1978
  Obituary 26
Berkey, Barry Robert 1935- 24
Berkowitz, Freda Pastor 1910- 12
Berliner, Don 1930- 33
Berliner, Franz 1930- 13
Berlitz, Charles L. (Frambach)
  1913- 32
Berman, Linda 1948- 38
Berna, Paul 1910- 15
Bernadette
  See Watts, Bernadette
Bernard, George I. 1949- 39
Bernard, Jacqueline (de Sieyes)
  1921-1983 8
  Obituary 45
Bernays, Anne
  See Kaplan, Anne Bernays
Bernstein, Joanne E(ckstein)
  1943- 15
Bernstein, Theodore M(enline)
  1904-1979 12
  Obituary 27
Berrien, Edith Heal
  See Heal, Edith
Berrill, Jacquelyn (Batsel)
  1905- 12
Berrington, John
  See Brownjohn, Alan
Berry, B. J.
  See Berry, Barbara J.
Berry, Barbara J. 1937- 7
Berry, Erick
  See Best, Allena Champlin
Berry, Jane Cobb 1915(?)-1979
  Obituary 22
Berry, Joy Wilt
  Brief Entry 46
Berry, William D(avid) 1926- 14
Berson, Harold 1926- 4
Berwick, Jean
  See Meyer, Jean Shepherd

Beskow, Elsa (Maartman)
1874-1953 20
Best, (Evangel) Allena Champlin
1892-1974 2
Obituary 25
Best, (Oswald) Herbert 1894- 2
Betancourt, Jeanne 1941-
Brief Entry 43
Beth, Mary
See Miller, Mary Beth
Bethancourt, T. Ernesto 1932- 11
See also CLR 3
Bethell, Jean (Frankenberry)
1922- 8
Bethers, Ray 1902- 6
Bethune, J. G.
See Ellis, Edward S(ylvester)
Betteridge, Anne
See Potter, Margaret (Newman)
Bettina
See Ehrlich, Bettina
Bettmann, Otto Ludwig 1903- 46
Betts, James [Joint pseudonym]
See Haynes, Betsy
Betz, Eva Kelly 1897-1968 10
Bevan, Tom
1868-1930(?) .... YABC 2
Bewick, Thomas 1753-1828 16
Beyer, Audrey White 1916- 9
Bialk, Elisa 1
Bianco, Margery (Williams)
1881-1944 15
Bianco, Pamela 1906- 28
Bibby, Violet 1908- 24
Bible, Charles 1937- 13
Bice, Clare 1909-1976 22
Bickerstaff, Isaac
See Swift, Jonathan
Biegel, Paul 1925- 16
Biemiller, Carl L(udwig)
1912-1979 40
Obituary 21
Bienenfeld, Florence L(ucille)
1929- 39
Bierhorst, John 1936- 6
Bileck, Marvin 1920- 40
Bill, Alfred Hoyt 1879-1964 44
Billings, Charlene W(interer)
1941- 41
Billington, Elizabeth T(hain)
Brief Entry 43
Billout, Guy René 1941- 10
Binkley, Anne
See Rand, Ann (Binkley)
Binzen, Bill 24
Binzen, William
See Binzen, Bill
Birch, Reginald B(athurst)
1856-1943 19
Birmingham, Lloyd 1924- 12
Biro, Val 1921- 1
Bischoff, Julia Bristol
1909-1970 12
Bishop, Bonnie 1943- 37
Bishop, Claire (Huchet) 14
Bishop, Curtis 1912-1967 6
Bishop, Elizabeth 1911-1979
Obituary 24
Bisset, Donald 1910- 7

Bitter, Gary G(len) 1940- 22
Bixby, William 1920- 6
Bjerregaard-Jensen, Vilhelm Hans
See Hillcourt, William
Bjorklund, Lorence F.
1913-1978 35
Brief Entry 32
Black, Algernon David 1900- 12
Black, Irma S(imonton)
1906-1972 2
Obituary 25
Black, Mansell
See Trevor, Elleston
Black, Susan Adams 1953- 40
Blackburn, Claire
See Jacobs, Linda C.
Blackburn, John(ny) Brewton
1952- 15
Blackburn, Joyce Knight
1920- 29
Blackett, Veronica Heath
1927- 12
Blackton, Peter
See Wilson, Lionel
Blades, Ann 1947- 16
Bladow, Suzanne Wilson
1937- 14
Blaine, John
See Goodwin, Harold Leland
Blaine, John
See Harkins, Philip
Blaine, Margery Kay 1937- 11
Blair, Anne Denton 1914- 46
Blair, Eric Arthur 1903-1950 29
Blair, Helen 1910-
Brief Entry 29
Blair, Jay 1953- 45
Blair, Ruth Van Ness 1912- 12
Blair, Walter 1900- 12
Blake, Olive
See Supraner, Robyn
Blake, Quentin 1932- 9
Blake, Robert 1949- 42
Blake, Walker E.
See Butterworth, W. E.
Blake, William 1757-1827 30
Bland, Edith Nesbit
See Nesbit, E(dith)
Bland, Fabian [Joint pseudonym]
See Nesbit, E(dith)
Blane, Gertrude
See Blumenthal, Gertrude
Blassingame, Wyatt Rainey
1909-1985 34
Obituary 41
Earlier sketch in SATA 1
Bleeker, Sonia 1909-1971 2
Obituary 26
Blegvad, Erik 1923- 14
Blegvad, Lenore 1926- 14
Blishen, Edward 1920- 8
Bliss, Corinne D(emas) 1947- 37
Bliss, Reginald
See Wells, H(erbert) G(eorge)
Bliss, Ronald G(ene) 1942- 12
Bliven, Bruce, Jr. 1916- 2
Blixen, Karen (Christentze Dinesen)
1885-1962 44
Bloch, Lucienne 1909- 10

Bloch, Marie Halun 1910- 6
Bloch, Robert 1917- 12
Blochman, Lawrence G(oldtree)
1900-1975 22
Block, Irvin 1917- 12
Blocksma, Mary
Brief Entry 44
Blood, Charles Lewis 1929- 28
Bloom, Freddy 1914- 37
Bloom, Lloyd
Brief Entry 43
Blos, Joan W(insor) 1928- 33
Brief Entry 27
Blough, Glenn O(rlando)
1907- 1
Blue, Rose 1931- 5
Blumberg, Rhoda 1917- 35
Blume, Judy (Sussman) 1938- 31
Earlier sketch in SATA 2
See also CLR 2
Blumenthal, Gertrude 1907-1971
Obituary 27
Blumenthal, Shirley 1943- 46
Blutig, Eduard
See Gorey, Edward St. John
Bly, Janet Chester 1945- 43
Bly, Stephen A(rthur) 1944- 43
Blyton, Carey 1932- 9
Blyton, Enid (Mary)
1897-1968 25
Boardman, Fon Wyman, Jr.
1911- 6
Boardman, Gwenn R. 1924- 12
Boase, Wendy 1944- 28
Boatner, Mark Mayo III
1921- 29
Bobbe, Dorothie 1905-1975 1
Obituary 25
Bobri
See Bobritsky, Vladimir
Bobri, Vladimir
See Bobritsky, Vladimir
Bobritsky, Vladimir 1898-
Brief Entry 32
Bock, Hal
See Bock, Harold I.
Bock, Harold I. 1939- 10
Bock, William Sauts
Netamux'we 14
Bodecker, N. M. 1922- 8
Boden, Hilda
See Bodenham, Hilda Esther
Bodenham, Hilda Esther
1901- 13
Bodie, Idella F(allaw) 1925- 12
Bodker, Cecil 1927- 14
Bodsworth, (Charles) Fred(erick)
1918- 27
Boeckman, Charles 1920- 12
Boegehold, Betty (Doyle) 1913-1985
Obituary 42
Boesch, Mark J(oseph) 1917- 12
Boesen, Victor 1908- 16
Boggs, Ralph Steele 1901- 7
Bograd, Larry 1953- 33
Bohdal, Susi 1951- 22
Boles, Paul Darcy 1916-1984 9
Obituary 38
Bolian, Polly 1925- 4

Bollen, Roger 1941(?)-
  Brief Entry 29
Bolliger, Max 1929- 7
Bolognese, Don(ald Alan)
  1934- 24
Bolton, Carole 1926- 6
Bolton, Elizabeth
  See Johnston, Norma
Bolton, Evelyn
  See Bunting, Anne Evelyn
Bond, Gladys Baker 1912- 14
Bond, J. Harvey
  See Winterbotham, R(ussell)
  R(obert)
Bond, Michael 1926- 6
  See also CLR 1
  See also SAAS 3
Bond, Nancy (Barbara) 1945- 22
Bond, Ruskin 1934- 14
Bonehill, Captain Ralph
  See Stratemeyer, Edward L.
Bonham, Barbara 1926- 7
Bonham, Frank 1914- 1
  See also SAAS 3
Bonn, Pat
  See Bonn, Patricia Carolyn
Bonn, Patricia Carolyn 1948- 43
Bonner, Mary Graham
  1890-1974 19
Bonsall, Crosby (Barbara Newell)
  1921- 23
Bontemps, Arna 1902-1973 44
  Obituary 24
  Earlier sketch in SATA 2
  See also CLR 6
Bonzon, Paul-Jacques 1908- 22
Booher, Dianna Daniels 1948- 33
Bookman, Charlotte
  See Zolotow, Charlotte S.
Boone, Pat 1934- 7
Boorman, Linda (Kay) 1940- 46
Booth, Ernest Sheldon
  1915-1984 43
Booth, Graham (Charles)
  1935- 37
Bordier, Georgette 1924- 16
Boring, Mel 1939- 35
Borja, Corinne 1929- 22
Borja, Robert 1923- 22
Borland, Hal 1900-1978 5
  Obituary 24
Borland, Harold Glen
  See Borland, Hal
Borland, Kathryn Kilby 1916- 16
Bornstein, Ruth 1927- 14
Borski, Lucia Merecka 18
Borten, Helen Jacobson 1930- 5
Borton, Elizabeth
  See Treviño, Elizabeth B. de
Bortstein, Larry 1942- 16
Bosco, Jack
  See Holliday, Joseph
Boshell, Gordon 1908- 15
Boshinski, Blanche 1922- 10
Bosse, Malcolm J(oseph)
  1926- 35
Bossom, Naomi 1933- 35

Boston, Lucy Maria (Wood)
  1892- 19
  See also CLR 3
Bosworth, J. Allan 1925- 19
Bothwell, Jean 2
Botkin, B(enjamin) A(lbert)
  1901-1975 40
Botting, Douglas (Scott)
  1934- 43
Bottner, Barbara 1943- 14
Boulle, Pierre (Francois Marie-Louis)
  1912- 22
Bourdon, David 1934- 46
Bourne, Leslie
  See Marshall, Evelyn
Bourne, Miriam Anne 1931- 16
Boutet De Monvel, (Louis) M(aurice)
  1850(?)-1913 30
Bova, Ben 1932- 6
  See also CLR 3
Bowden, Joan Chase 1925-
  Brief Entry 38
Bowen, Betty Morgan
  See West, Betty
Bowen, Catherine Drinker
  1897-1973 7
Bowen, David
  See Bowen, Joshua David
Bowen, Joshua David 1930- 22
Bowen, Robert Sidney 1900(?)-1977
  Obituary 21
Bowie, Jim
  See Stratemeyer, Edward L.
Bowler, Jan Brett
  See Brett, Jan
Bowman, James Cloyd
  1880-1961 23
Bowman, John S(tewart)
  1931- 16
Bowman, Kathleen (Gill) 1942-
  Brief Entry 40
Boyce, George A(rthur) 1898- 19
Boyd, Pauline
  See Schock, Pauline
Boyd, Selma
  See Acuff, Selma Boyd
Boyd, Waldo T. 1918- 18
Boyer, Robert E(rnst) 1929- 22
Boyle, Ann (Peters) 1916- 10
Boyle, Eleanor Vere (Gordon)
  1825-1916 28
Boylston, Helen (Dore)
  1895-1984 23
  Obituary 39
Boynton, Sandra 1953-
  Brief Entry 38
Boz
  See Dickens, Charles
Bradbury, Bianca 1908- 3
Bradbury, Ray (Douglas)
  1920- 11
Bradford, Ann (Liddell) 1917-
  Brief Entry 38
Bradford, Lois J(ean) 1936- 36
Bradley, Duane
  See Sanborn, Duane
Bradley, Virginia 1912- 23
Brady, Esther Wood 1905- 31
Brady, Irene 1943- 4

Brady, Lillian 1902- 28
Bragdon, Elspeth 1897- 6
Bragdon, Lillian (Jacot) 24
Bragg, Mabel Caroline
  1870-1945 24
Bragg, Michael 1948- 46
Braithwaite, Althea 1940- 23
Bram, Elizabeth 1948- 30
Brancato, Robin F(idler)
  1936- 23
Brandenberg, Aliki (Liacouras)
  1929- 35
  Earlier sketch in SATA 2
Brandenberg, Franz 1932- 35
  Earlier sketch in SATA 8
Brandhorst, Carl T(heodore)
  1898- 23
Brandon, Brumsic, Jr. 1927- 9
Brandon, Curt
  See Bishop, Curtis
Brandreth, Gyles 1948- 28
Brandt, Catharine 1905- 40
Brandt, Keith
  See Sabin, Louis
Branfield, John (Charles)
  1931- 11
Branley, Franklyn M(ansfield)
  1915- 4
Branscum, Robbie 1937- 23
Bransom, (John) Paul
  1885-1979 43
Bratton, Helen 1899- 4
Braude, Michael 1936- 23
Braymer, Marjorie 1911- 6
Brecht, Edith 1895-1975 6
  Obituary 25
Breck, Vivian
  See Breckenfeld, Vivian Gurney
Breckenfeld, Vivian Gurney
  1895- 1
Breda, Tjalmar
  See DeJong, David C(ornel)
Breinburg, Petronella 1927- 11
Breisky, William J(ohn) 1928- ... 22
Brennan, Joseph L. 1903- 6
Brennan, Tim
  See Conroy, Jack (Wesley)
Brenner, Barbara (Johnes)
  1925- 42
  Earlier sketch in SATA 4
Brenner, Fred 1920- 36
  Brief Entry 34
Brent, Hope 1935(?)-1984
  Obituary 39
Brent, Stuart 14
Brett, Bernard 1925- 22
Brett, Grace N(eff) 1900-1975 ... 23
Brett, Hawksley
  See Bell, Robert S(tanley) W(arren)
Brett, Jan 1949- 42
Brewer, Sally King 1947- 33
Brewster, Benjamin
  See Folsom, Franklin
Brewton, John E(dmund)
  1898- 5
Brick, John 1922-1973 10
Bridgers, Sue Ellen 1942- 22
  See also SAAS 1

Bridges, Laurie
  See Bruck, Lorraine
Bridges, William (Andrew)
  1901- 5
Bridwell, Norman 1928- 4
Brier, Howard M(axwell)
  1903-1969 8
Briggs, Katharine Mary 1898-1980
  Obituary 25
Briggs, Peter 1921-1975 39
  Obituary 31
Briggs, Raymond (Redvers)
  1934- 23
  See also CLR 10
Bright, Robert 1902- 24
Brightwell, L(eonard) R(obert) 1889-
  Brief Entry 29
Brimberg, Stanlee 1947- 9
Brin, Ruth F(irestone) 1921- 22
Brinckloe, Julie (Lorraine)
  1950- 13
Brindel, June (Rachuy) 1919- 7
Brindze, Ruth 1903- 23
Brink, Carol Ryrie 1895-1981 31
  Obituary 27
  Earlier sketch in SATA 1
Brinsmead, H(esba) F(ay)
  1922- 18
Briquebec, John
  See Rowland-Entwistle, (Arthur)
  Theodore (Henry)
Brisco, Pat A.
  See Matthews, Patricia
Brisco, Patty
  See Matthews, Patricia
Brisley, Joyce Lankester
  1896- 22
Britt, Albert 1874-1969
  Obituary 28
Britt, Dell 1934- 1
Brittain, William 1930- 36
Britton, Louisa
  See McGuire, Leslie (Sarah)
Bro, Margueritte (Harmon)
  1894-1977 19
  Obituary 27
Broadhead, Helen Cross
  1913- 25
Brochmann, Elizabeth (Anne)
  1938- 41
Brock, Betty 1923- 7
Brock, C(harles) E(dmund)
  1870-1938 42
  Brief Entry 32
Brock, Emma L(illian)
  1886-1974 8
Brock, H(enry) M(atthew)
  1875-1960 42
Brockett, Eleanor Hall
  1913-1967 10
Brockman, C(hristian) Frank
  1902- 26
Broderick, Dorothy M. 1929- 5
Brodie, Sally
  See Cavin, Ruth (Brodie)
Broekel, Rainer Lothar 1923- 38
Broekel, Ray
  See Broekel, Rainer Lothar
Bröger, Achim 1944- 31

Brokamp, Marilyn 1920- 10
Bromhall, Winifred 26
Brommer, Gerald F(rederick)
  1927- 28
Brondfield, Jerome 1913- 22
Brondfield, Jerry
  See Brondfield, Jerome
Bronson, Lynn
  See Lampman, Evelyn Sibley
Bronson, Wilfrid Swancourt
  1894-1985
  Obituary 43
Brooke, L(eonard) Leslie
  1862-1940 17
Brooke-Haven, P.
  See Wodehouse, P(elham)
  G(renville)
Brookins, Dana 1931- 28
Brooks, Anita 1914- 5
Brooks, Barbara
  See Simons, Barbara B(rooks)
Brooks, Charlotte K. 24
Brooks, Gwendolyn 1917- 6
Brooks, Jerome 1931- 23
Brooks, Lester 1924- 7
Brooks, Maurice (Graham)
  1900- 45
Brooks, Polly Schoyer 1912- 12
Brooks, Ron(ald George) 1948-
  Brief Entry 33
Brooks, Walter R(ollin)
  1886-1958 17
Brosnan, James Patrick 1929- 14
Brosnan, Jim
  See Brosnan, James Patrick
Broun, Emily
  See Sterne, Emma Gelders
Brower, Millicent 8
Brower, Pauline (York) 1929- 22
Browin, Frances Williams
  1898- 5
Brown, Alexis
  See Baumann, Amy (Brown)
Brown, Bill
  See Brown, William L.
Brown, Billye Walker
  See Cutchen, Billye Walker
Brown, Bob
  See Brown, Robert Joseph
Brown, Buck 1936- 45
Brown, Conrad 1922- 31
Brown, David
  See Myller, Rolf
Brown, Dee (Alexander)
  1908- 5
Brown, Eleanor Frances 1908- 3
Brown, Elizabeth M(yers)
  1915- 43
Brown, Fern G. 1918- 34
Brown, (Robert) Fletch 1923- 42
Brown, George Earl
  1883-1964 11
Brown, George Mackay 1921- 35
Brown, Irene Bennett 1932- 3
Brown, Irving
  See Adams, William Taylor
Brown, Ivor (John Carnegie)
  1891-1974 5
  Obituary 26

Brown, Joe David 1915-1976 44
Brown, Judith Gwyn 1933- 20
Brown, Lloyd Arnold
  1907-1966 36
Brown, Marc Tolon 1946- 10
Brown, Marcia 1918- 7
Brown, Margaret Wise
  1910-1952 .... YABC 2
  See also CLR 10
Brown, Margery 5
Brown, Marion Marsh 1908- 6
Brown, Myra Berry 1918- 6
Brown, Palmer 1919- 36
Brown, Pamela 1924- 5
Brown, Robert Joseph 1907- 14
Brown, Rosalie (Gertrude) Moore
  1910- 9
Brown, Roswell
  See Webb, Jean Francis (III)
Brown, Roy (Frederick) 1921-1982
  Obituary 39
Brown, Vinson 1912- 19
Brown, Walter R(eed) 1929- 19
Brown, Will
  See Ainsworth, William Harrison
Brown, William L(ouis)
  1910-1964 5
Browne, Anthony (Edward Tudor)
  1946- 45
  Brief Entry 44
Browne, Dik
  See Browne, Richard
Browne, Hablot Knight
  1815-1882 21
Browne, Matthew
  See Rands, William Brighty
Browne, Richard 1917-
  Brief Entry 38
Browning, Robert
  1812-1889 .... YABC 1
Brownjohn, Alan 1931- 6
Bruce, Dorita Fairlie 1885-1970
  Obituary 27
Bruce, Mary 1927- 1
Bruchac, Joseph III 1942- 42
Bruck, Lorraine 1921-
  Brief Entry 46
Bruna, Dick 1927- 43
  Brief Entry 30
  See also CLR 7
Brunhoff, Jean de 1899-1937 24
  See also CLR 4
Brunhoff, Laurent de 1925- 24
  See also CLR 4
Brustlein, Daniel 1904- 40
Brustlein, Janice Tworkov 40
Bryan, Ashley F. 1923- 31
Bryan, Dorothy (Marie) 1896(?)-1984
  Obituary 39
Bryant, Bernice (Morgan)
  1908- 11
Brychta, Alex 1956- 21
Bryson, Bernarda 1905- 9
Buba, Joy Flinsch 1904- 44
Buchan, Bryan 1945- 36
Buchan, John 1875-1940 .... YABC 2
Buchheimer, Naomi Barnett
  See Barnett, Naomi
Buchwald, Art(hur) 1925- 10

Buchwald, Emilie 1935- 7
Buck, Lewis 1925- *18*
Buck, Margaret Waring 1910- 3
Buck, Pearl S(ydenstricker)
    1892-1973 .... *25*
    Earlier sketch in SATA 1
Buckeridge, Anthony 1912- 6
Buckley, Helen E(lizabeth)
    1918- 2
Buckmaster, Henrietta 6
Budd, Lillian 1897- 7
Buehr, Walter 1897-1971 3
Buff, Conrad 1886-1975 .... *19*
Buff, Mary Marsh 1890-1970 .... *19*
Bugbee, Emma 1888(?)-1981
    Obituary *29*
Bulfinch, Thomas 1796-1867 .... *35*
Bull, Angela (Mary) 1936- *45*
Bull, Norman John 1916- *41*
Bull, Peter (Cecil) 1912-1984
    Obituary *39*
Bulla, Clyde Robert 1914- *41*
    Earlier sketch in SATA 2
Bunin, Catherine 1967- *30*
Bunin, Sherry 1925- *30*
Bunting, A. E.
    See Bunting, Anne Evelyn
Bunting, Anne Evelyn 1928- *18*
Bunting, Eve
    See Bunting, Anne Evelyn
Bunting, Glenn (Davison)
    1957- *22*
Burack, Sylvia K. 1916- *35*
Burbank, Addison (Buswell)
    1895-1961 .... *37*
Burch, Robert J(oseph) 1925- *1*
Burchard, Peter D(uncan) 5
Burchard, Sue 1937- *22*
Burchardt, Nellie 1921- 7
Burdick, Eugene (Leonard)
    1918-1965 .... *22*
Burford, Eleanor
    See Hibbert, Eleanor
Burger, Carl 1888-1967 9
Burgess, Anne Marie
    See Gerson, Noel B(ertram)
Burgess, Em
    See Burgess, Mary Wyche
Burgess, (Frank) Gelett
    1866-1951 .... *32*
    Brief Entry *30*
Burgess, Mary Wyche 1916- *18*
Burgess, Michael
    See Gerson, Noel B(ertram)
Burgess, Robert F(orrest)
    1927- 4
Burgess, Thornton W(aldo)
    1874-1965 .... *17*
Burgess, Trevor
    See Trevor, Elleston
Burgwyn, Mebane H. 1914- 7
Burke, David 1927- *46*
Burke, John
    See O'Connor, Richard
Burkert, Nancy Ekholm 1933- ... *24*
Burland, Brian (Berkeley)
    1931- *34*
Burland, C. A.
    See Burland, Cottie A.

Burland, Cottie A. 1905- 5
Burlingame, (William) Roger
    1889-1967 2
Burman, Alice Caddy 1896(?)-1977
    Obituary *24*
Burman, Ben Lucien
    1896-1984 6
    Obituary *40*
Burn, Doris 1923- *1*
Burnett, Constance Buel
    1893-1975 .... *36*
Burnett, Frances (Eliza) Hodgson
    1849-1924 .... *YABC 2*
Burnford, S. D.
    See Burnford, Sheila
Burnford, Sheila 1918-1984 3
    Obituary *38*
    See also CLR 2
Burningham, John (Mackintosh)
    1936- *16*
    See also CLR 9
Burns, Marilyn
    Brief Entry *33*
Burns, Paul C. 5
Burns, Raymond (Howard)
    1924- 9
Burns, William A. 1909- 5
Burroughs, Edgar Rice
    1875-1950 .... *41*
Burroughs, Jean Mitchell
    1908- *28*
Burroughs, Polly 1925- 2
Burroway, Janet (Gay) 1936- *23*
Burstein, John 1949-
    Brief Entry *40*
Burt, Jesse Clifton 1921-1976 .... *46*
    Obituary *20*
Burt, Olive Woolley 1894- 4
Burton, Hester 1913- 7
    See also CLR 1
Burton, Leslie
    See McGuire, Leslie (Sarah)
Burton, Marilee Robin 1950- *46*
Burton, Maurice 1898- *23*
Burton, Robert (Wellesley)
    1941- *22*
Burton, Virginia Lee
    1909-1968 2
Burton, William H(enry)
    1890-1964 .... *11*
Busby, Edith (?)-1964
    Obituary *29*
Busch, Phyllis S. 1909- *30*
Bushmiller, Ernie 1905-1982
    Obituary *31*
Busoni, Rafaello 1900-1962 ..... *16*
Butler, Beverly 1932- 7
Butler, Suzanne
    See Perreard, Suzanne Louise Butler
Butters, Dorothy Gilman
    1923- 5
Butterworth, Emma Macalik
    1928- *43*
Butterworth, Oliver 1915- *1*
Butterworth, W(illiam) E(dmund III)
    1929- 5
Byars, Betsy (Cromer) 1928- *46*
    Earlier sketch in SATA 4
    See also CLR 1
    See also SAAS 1

Byfield, Barbara Ninde 1930- 8
Byrd, Elizabeth 1912- *34*
Byrd, Robert (John) 1942- *33*

C

C.3.3.
    See Wilde, Oscar (Fingal O'Flahertie Wills)
Cable, Mary 1920- 9
Cabral, O. M.
    See Cabral, Olga
Cabral, Olga 1909- *46*
Caddy, Alice
    See Burman, Alice Caddy
Cadwallader, Sharon 1936- 7
Cady, (Walter) Harrison
    1877-1970 .... *19*
Cagle, Malcolm W(infield)
    1918- *32*
Cahn, Rhoda 1922- *37*
Cahn, William 1912-1976 .... *37*
Cain, Arthur H. 1913- 3
Cain, Christopher
    See Fleming, Thomas J(ames)
Caines, Jeanette (Franklin)
    Brief Entry *43*
Cairns, Trevor 1922- *14*
Caldecott, Moyra 1927- *22*
Caldecott, Randolph (J.)
    1846-1886 .... *17*
Caldwell, John C(ope) 1913- 7
Calhoun, Mary (Huiskamp)
    1926- 2
Calkins, Franklin
    See Stratemeyer, Edward L.
Call, Hughie Florence
    1890-1969 .... *1*
Callahan, Dorothy M. 1934- *39*
    Brief Entry *35*
Callahan, Philip S(erna) 1923- ... *25*
Callaway, Kathy 1943- *36*
Callen, Larry
    See Callen, Lawrence Willard, Jr.
Callen, Lawrence Willard, Jr.
    1927- *19*
Calmenson, Stephanie 1952-
    Brief Entry *37*
Calvert, John
    See Leaf, (Wilbur) Munro
Calvert, Patricia 1931- *45*
Cameron, Ann 1943- *27*
Cameron, Edna M. 1905- 3
Cameron, Eleanor (Butler)
    1912- *25*
    Earlier sketch in SATA 1
    See also CLR 1
Cameron, Elizabeth
    See Nowell, Elizabeth Cameron
Cameron, Elizabeth Jane
    1910-1976 .... *32*
    Obituary *30*
Cameron, Ian
    See Payne, Donald Gordon
Cameron, Polly 1928- 2
Camp, Charles Lewis 1893-1975
    Obituary *31*
Camp, Walter (Chauncey)
    1859-1925 .... *YABC 1*

Campbell, Ann R. 1925- *11*
Campbell, Bruce
  See Epstein, Samuel
Campbell, Camilla 1905- *26*
Campbell, Hope *20*
Campbell, Jane
  See Edwards, Jane Campbell
Campbell, Patricia J(ean)
  1930- *45*
Campbell, Patty
  See Campbell, Patricia J(ean)
Campbell, R. W.
  See Campbell, Rosemae Wells
Campbell, Rod 1945-
  Brief Entry *44*
Campbell, Rosemae Wells
  1909- *1*
Campion, Nardi Reeder 1917- *22*
Candell, Victor 1903-1977
  Obituary *24*
Canfield, Dorothy
  See Fisher, Dorothy Canfield
Canfield, Jane White
  1897-1984 .... *32*
  Obituary *38*
Cannon, Cornelia (James) 1876-1969
  Brief Entry *28*
Cannon, Ravenna
  See Mayhar, Ardath
Canusi, Jose
  See Barker, S. Omar
Caplin, Alfred Gerald 1909-1979
  Obituary *21*
Capp, Al
  See Caplin, Alfred Gerald
Cappel, Constance 1936- *22*
Capps, Benjamin (Franklin)
  1922- *9*
Captain Kangaroo
  See Keeshan, Robert J.
Carafoli, Marci
  See Ridlon, Marci
Caras, Roger A(ndrew) 1928- *12*
Carbonnier, Jeanne 1894-1974 .... *3*
  Obituary *34*
Care, Felicity
  See Coury, Louise Andree
Carew, Jan (Rynveld) 1925-
  Brief Entry *40*
Carey, Bonnie 1941- *18*
Carey, Ernestine Gilbreth
  1908- *2*
Carey, M. V.
  See Carey, Mary (Virginia)
Carey, Mary (Virginia) 1925- *44*
  Brief Entry *39*
Carigiet, Alois 1902- *24*
Carini, Edward 1923- *9*
Carle, Eric 1929- *4*
  See CLR 10
Carleton, Captain L. C.
  See Ellis, Edward S(ylvester)
Carley, V(an Ness) Royal 1906-1976
  Obituary *20*
Carlisle, Clark, Jr.
  See Holding, James
Carlisle, Olga A(ndreyev)
  1930- *35*

Carlsen, G(eorge) Robert
  1917- *30*
Carlsen, Ruth C(hristoffer) *2*
Carlson, Bernice Wells 1910- *8*
Carlson, Dale Bick 1935- *1*
Carlson, Daniel 1960- *27*
Carlson, Nancy L(ee) 1953-
  Brief Entry *45*
Carlson, Natalie Savage *2*
Carlson, Vada F. 1897- *16*
Carmer, Carl (Lamson)
  1893-1976 .... *37*
  Obituary *30*
Carmer, Elizabeth Black
  1904- *24*
Carmichael, Carrie *40*
Carmichael, Harriet
  See Carmichael, Carrie
Carol, Bill J.
  See Knott, William Cecil, Jr.
Caroselli, Remus F(rancis)
  1916- *36*
Carpelan, Bo (Gustaf Bertelsson)
  1926- *8*
Carpenter, Allan 1917- *3*
Carpenter, Frances 1890-1972 ..... *3*
  Obituary *27*
Carpenter, Patricia (Healy Evans)
  1920- *11*
Carr, Glyn
  See Styles, Frank Showell
Carr, Harriett Helen 1899- *3*
Carr, Mary Jane *2*
Carrick, Carol 1935- *7*
Carrick, Donald 1929- *7*
Carrick, Malcolm 1945- *28*
Carrighar, Sally *24*
Carris, Joan Davenport 1938- *44*
  Brief Entry *42*
Carroll, Curt
  See Bishop, Curtis
Carroll, Latrobe *7*
Carroll, Laura
  See Parr, Lucy
Carroll, Lewis
  See Dodgson, Charles Lutwidge
  See also CLR 2
Carse, Robert 1902-1971 .... *5*
Carson, Captain James
  See Stratemeyer, Edward L.
Carson, John F. 1920- *1*
Carson, Rachel (Louise)
  1907-1964 .... *23*
Carson, Rosalind
  See Chittenden, Margaret
Carson, S. M.
  See Gorsline, (Sally) Marie
Carter, Bruce
  See Hough, Richard (Alexander)
Carter, Dorothy Sharp 1921- *8*
Carter, Forrest 1927(?)-1979 ..... *32*
Carter, Helene 1887-1960 .... *15*
Carter, (William) Hodding
  1907-1972 .... *2*
  Obituary *27*
Carter, Katharine J(ones)
  1905- *2*
Carter, Nick
  See Lynds, Dennis

Carter, Phyllis Ann
  See Eberle, Irmengarde
Carter, Samuel III 1904- *37*
Carter, William E. 1926-1983 ..... *1*
  Obituary *35*
Cartlidge, Michelle 1950-
  Brief Entry *37*
Cartner, William Carruthers
  1910- *11*
Cartwright, Sally 1923- *9*
Carver, John
  See Gardner, Richard
Cary
  See Cary, Louis F(avreau)
Cary, Barbara Knapp 1912(?)-1975
  Obituary *31*
Cary, Louis F(avreau) 1915- *9*
Caryl, Jean
  See Kaplan, Jean Caryl Korn
Case, Marshal T(aylor) 1941- *9*
Case, Michael
  See Howard, Robert West
Casewit, Curtis 1922- *4*
Casey, Brigid 1950- *9*
Casey, Winifred Rosen
  See Rosen, Winifred
Cason, Mabel Earp 1892-1965 .... *10*
Cass, Joan E(velyn) *1*
Cassedy, Sylvia 1930- *27*
Cassel, Lili
  See Wronker, Lili Cassell
Cassel-Wronker, Lili
  See Wronker, Lili Cassell
Castellanos, Jane Mollie (Robinson)
  1913- *9*
Castillo, Edmund L. 1924- *1*
Castle, Lee [Joint pseudonym]
  See Ogan, George F. and Ogan,
  Margaret E. (Nettles)
Castle, Paul
  See Howard, Vernon (Linwood)
Caswell, Helen (Rayburn)
  1923- *12*
Cate, Dick
  See Cate, Richard (Edward Nelson)
Cate, Richard (Edward Nelson)
  1932- *28*
Cather, Willa (Sibert)
  1873-1947 .... *30*
Catherall, Arthur 1906- *3*
Cathon, Laura E(lizabeth)
  1908- *27*
Catlin, Wynelle 1930- *13*
Catton, (Charles) Bruce
  1899-1978 .... *2*
  Obituary *24*
Catz, Max
  See Glaser, Milton
Caudill, Rebecca 1899-1985 ...... *1*
  Obituary *44*
Cauley, Lorinda Bryan 1951- *46*
  Brief Entry *43*
Causley, Charles 1917- *3*
Cavallo, Diana 1931- *7*
Cavanagh, Helen (Carol) 1939-
  Brief Entry *37*
Cavanah, Frances 1899-1982 ...... *31*
  Earlier sketch in SATA 1

Cavanna, Betty 1909- *30*
Earlier sketch in SATA 1
Cavin, Ruth (Brodie) 1918- *38*
Cawley, Winifred 1915- *13*
Caxton, Pisistratus
See Lytton, Edward G(eorge) E(arle)
L(ytton) Bulwer-Lytton, Baron
Cazet, Denys 1938-
Brief Entry *41*
Cebulash, Mel 1937- *10*
Ceder, Georgiana Dorcas *10*
Celestino, Martha Laing
1951- *39*
Cerf, Bennett 1898-1971 .... *7*
Cerf, Christopher (Bennett)
1941- *2*
Cervon, Jacqueline
See Moussard, Jacqueline
Cetin, Frank (Stanley) 1921- *2*
Chadwick, Lester [Collective
pseudonym] *1*
Chaffee, Allen *3*
Chaffin, Lillie D(orton) 1925- *4*
Chaikin, Miriam 1928- *24*
Challans, Mary 1905-1983 .... *23*
Obituary *36*
Chalmers, Mary 1927- *6*
Chamberlain, Margaret 1954- *46*
Chambers, Aidan 1934- *1*
Chambers, Bradford 1922-1984
Obituary *39*
Chambers, Catherine E.
See Johnston, Norma
Chambers, John W. 1933-
Brief Entry *46*
Chambers, Margaret Ada Eastwood
1911- *2*
Chambers, Peggy
See Chambers, Margaret Ada
Eastwood
Chandler, Caroline A(ugusta)
1906-1979 .... *22*
Obituary *24*
Chandler, David Porter 1933- *28*
Chandler, Edna Walker
1908-1982 .... *11*
Obituary *31*
Chandler, Linda S(mith)
1929- *39*
Chandler, Robert 1953- *40*
Chandler, Ruth Forbes
1894-1978 .... *2*
Obituary *26*
Channel, A. R.
See Catherall, Arthur
Chapian, Marie 1938- *29*
Chapman, Allen [Collective
pseudonym] *1*
Chapman, (Constance) Elizabeth
(Mann) 1919- *10*
Chapman, Gaynor 1935- *32*
Chapman, Jean *34*
Chapman, John Stanton Higham
1891-1972
Obituary *27*
Chapman, Maristan [Joint pseudonym]
See Chapman, John Stanton Higham
Chapman, Vera 1898- *33*

Chapman, Walker
See Silverberg, Robert
Chappell, Warren 1904- *6*
Chardiet, Bernice (Kroll) *27*
Charles, Donald
See Meighan, Donald Charles
Charles, Louis
See Stratemeyer, Edward L.
Charlip, Remy 1929- *4*
See also CLR 8
Charlot, Jean 1898-1979 .... *8*
Obituary *31*
Charlton, Michael (Alan)
1923- *34*
Charmatz, Bill 1925- *7*
Charosh, Mannis 1906- *5*
Chase, Alice
See McHargue, Georgess
Chase, Mary (Coyle)
1907-1981 .... *17*
Obituary *29*
Chase, Mary Ellen 1887-1973 ..... *10*
Chastain, Madye Lee 1908- *4*
Chauncy, Nan 1900-1970 .... *6*
See also CLR 6
Chaundler, Christine
1887-1972 .... *1*
Obituary *25*
Chen, Tony 1929- *6*
Chenault, Nell
See Smith, Linell Nash
Chenery, Janet (Dai) 1923- *25*
Cheney, Cora 1916- *3*
Cheney, Ted
See Cheney, Theodore Albert
Cheney, Theodore Albert
1928- *11*
Cheng, Judith 1955- *36*
Chernoff, Dorothy A.
See Ernst, (Lyman) John
Chernoff, Goldie Taub 1909- *10*
Cherry, Lynne 1952- *34*
Cherryholmes, Anne
See Price, Olive
Chess, Victoria (Dickerson)
1939- *33*
Chessare, Michele
Brief Entry *42*
Chesterton, G(ilbert) K(eith)
1874-1936 .... *27*
Chetin, Helen 1922- *6*
Chevalier, Christa 1937- *35*
Chew, Ruth *7*
Chidsey, Donald Barr
1902-1981 .... *3*
Obituary *27*
Childress, Alice 1920- *7*
Childs, (Halla) Fay (Cochrane)
1890-1971 .... *1*
Obituary *25*
Chimaera
See Farjeon, Eleanor
Chinery, Michael 1938- *26*
Chipperfield, Joseph E(ugene)
1912- *2*
Chittenden, Elizabeth F.
1903- *9*
Chittenden, Margaret 1933- *28*
Chittum, Ida 1918- *7*

Choate, Judith (Newkirk)
1940- *30*
Chorao, (Ann Mc)Kay (Sproat)
1936- *8*
Chorpenning, Charlotte (Lee Barrows)
1872-1955
Brief Entry *37*
Chrisman, Arthur Bowie
1889-1953 .... *YABC 1*
Christelow, Eileen 1943- *38*
Brief Entry *35*
Christensen, Gardell Dano
1907- *1*
Christesen, Barbara 1940- *40*
Christgau, Alice Erickson
1902- *13*
Christian, Mary Blount 1933- *9*
Christie, Agatha (Mary Clarissa)
1890-1976 .... *36*
Christopher, John
See Youd, (Christopher) Samuel
See also CLR 2
Christopher, Matt(hew F.)
1917- *2*
Christopher, Milbourne
1914(?)-1984 .... *46*
Christy, Howard Chandler
1873-1952 .... *21*
Chu, Daniel 1933- *11*
Chukovsky, Kornei (Ivanovich)
1882-1969 .... *34*
Earlier sketch in SATA 5
Church, Richard 1893-1972 .... *3*
Churchill, E. Richard 1937- *11*
Chute, B(eatrice) J(oy) 1913- *2*
Chute, Marchette (Gaylord)
1909- *1*
Chwast, Jacqueline 1932- *6*
Chwast, Seymour 1931- *18*
Ciardi, John (Anthony)
1916-1986 .... *1*
Obituary *46*
Clair, Andrée *19*
Clampett, Bob
Obituary *38*
See Clampett, Robert
Clampett, Robert
1914(?)-1984 .... *44*
Clapp, Patricia 1912- *4*
Clare, Helen
See Hunter, Blair Pauline
Clark, Ann Nolan 1898- *4*
Clark, David
See Hardcastle, Michael
Clark, David Allen
See Ernst, (Lyman) John
Clark, Frank J(ames) 1922- *18*
Clark, Garel [Joint pseudonym]
See Garelick, May
Clark, Leonard 1905-1981 .... *30*
Obituary *29*
Clark, Margaret Goff 1913- *8*
Clark, Mary Higgins *46*
Clark, Mavis Thorpe *8*
Clark, Merle
See Gessner, Lynne
Clark, Patricia (Finrow) 1929- *11*
Clark, Ronald William 1916- *2*
Clark, Van D(eusen) 1909- *2*

Clark, Virginia
  See Gray, Patricia
Clark, Walter Van Tilburg
  1909-1971 8
Clarke, Arthur C(harles)
  1917- 13
Clarke, Clorinda 1917- 7
Clarke, Joan 1921- 42
  Brief Entry 27
Clarke, John
  See Laklan, Carli
Clarke, Mary Stetson 1911- 5
Clarke, Michael
  See Newlon, Clarke
Clarke, Pauline
  See Hunter Blair, Pauline
Clarkson, E(dith) Margaret
  1915- 37
Clarkson, Ewan 1929- 9
Claverie, Jean 1946- 38
Claypool, Jane
  See Miner, Jane Claypool
Cleary, Beverly (Bunn) 1916- 43
  Earlier sketch in SATA 2
  See also CLR 2, 8
Cleaver, Bill 1920-1981 22
  Obituary 27
  See also CLR 6
Cleaver, Carole 1934- 6
Cleaver, Elizabeth (Mrazik)
  1939-1985 23
  Obituary 43
Cleaver, Vera 22
  See also CLR 6
Cleishbotham, Jebediah
  See Scott, Sir Walter
Cleland, Mabel
  See Widdemer, Mabel Cleland
Clemens, Samuel Langhorne
  1835-1910 .... YABC 2
Clemens, Virginia Phelps
  1941- 35
Clements, Bruce 1931- 27
Clemons, Elizabeth
  See Nowell, Elizabeth Cameron
Clerk, N. W.
  See Lewis, C. S.
Cleveland, Bob
  See Cleveland, George
Cleveland, George 1903(?)-1985
  Obituary 43
Cleven, Cathrine
  See Cleven, Kathryn Seward
Cleven, Kathryn Seward 2
Clevin, Jörgen 1920- 7
Clewes, Dorothy (Mary)
  1907- 1
Clifford, Eth
  See Rosenberg, Ethel
Clifford, Harold B. 1893- 10
Clifford, Margaret Cort 1929- 1
Clifford, Martin
  See Hamilton, Charles H. St. John
Clifford, Mary Louise (Beneway)
  1926- 23
Clifford, Peggy
  See Clifford, Margaret Cort
Clifton, Harry
  See Hamilton, Charles H. St. John

Clifton, Lucille 1936- 20
  See also CLR 5
Clifton, Martin
  See Hamilton, Charles H. St. John
Climo, Shirley 1928- 39
  Brief Entry 35
Clinton, Jon
  See Prince, J(ack) H(arvey)
Clish, (Lee) Marian 1946- 43
Clive, Clifford
  See Hamilton, Charles H. St. John
Cloudsley-Thompson, J(ohn) L(eonard)
  1921- 19
Clymer, Eleanor 1906- 9
Clyne, Patricia Edwards 31
Coalson, Glo 1946- 26
Coates, Belle 1896- 2
Coates, Ruth Allison 1915- 11
Coats, Alice M(argaret) 1905- 11
Coatsworth, Elizabeth 1893- 2
  See also CLR 2
Cobb, Jane
  See Berry, Jane Cobb
Cobb, Vicki 1938- 8
  See also CLR 2
Cobbett, Richard
  See Pluckrose, Henry (Arthur)
Cober, Alan E. 1935- 7
Cobham, Sir Alan
  See Hamilton, Charles H. St. John
Cocagnac, A(ugustin) M(aurice-Jean)
  1924- 7
Cochran, Bobbye A. 1949- 11
Cockett, Mary 3
Coe, Douglas [Joint pseudonym]
  See Epstein, Beryl and Epstein,
  Samuel
Coe, Lloyd 1899-1976
  Obituary 30
Coen, Rena Neumann 1925- 20
Coerr, Eleanor 1922- 1
Coffin, Geoffrey
  See Mason, F. van Wyck
Coffman, Ramon Peyton
  1896- 4
Coggins, Jack (Banham)
  1911- 2
Cohen, Barbara 1932- 10
Cohen, Daniel 1936- 8
  See also CLR 3
Cohen, Jene Barr
  See Barr, Jene
Cohen, Joan Lebold 1932- 4
Cohen, Miriam 1926- 29
Cohen, Peter Zachary 1931- 4
Cohen, Robert Carl 1930- 8
Cohn, Angelo 1914- 19
Coit, Margaret L(ouise) 2
Colbert, Anthony 1934- 15
Colby, C(arroll) B(urleigh)
  1904-1977 35
  Earlier sketch in SATA 3
Colby, Jean Poindexter 1909- 23
Cole, Annette
  See Steiner, Barbara A(nnette)
Cole, Davis
  See Elting, Mary
Cole, Jack
  See Stewart, John (William)

Cole, Jackson
  See Schisgall, Oscar
Cole, Joanna 1944-
  Brief Entry 37
  See also CLR 5
Cole, Lois Dwight
  1903(?)-1979 10
  Obituary 26
Cole, Sheila R(otenberg)
  1939- 24
Cole, William (Rossa) 1919- 9
Coleman, William L(eRoy) 1938-
  Brief Entry 34
Coles, Robert (Martin) 1929- 23
Collier, Christopher 1930- 16
Collier, Ethel 1903- 22
Collier, James Lincoln 1928- 8
  See also CLR 3
Collier, Jane
  See Collier, Zena
Collier, Zena 1926- 23
Collins, David 1940- 7
Collins, Hunt
  See Hunter, Evan
Collins, Michael
  See Lynds, Dennis
Collins, Pat Lowery 1932- 31
Collins, Ruth Philpott 1890-1975
  Obituary 30
Collodi, Carlo
  See Lorenzini, Carlo
  See also CLR 5
Colloms, Brenda 1919- 40
Colman, Hila 1
Colman, Morris 1899(?)-1981
  Obituary 25
Colonius, Lillian 1911- 3
Colorado (Capella), Antonio J(ulio)
  1903- 23
Colt, Martin [Joint pseudonym]
  See Epstein, Beryl and Epstein,
  Samuel
Colum, Padraic 1881-1972 15
Columella
  See Moore, Clement Clarke
Colver, Anne 1908- 7
Colwell, Eileen (Hilda) 1904- 2
Combs, Robert
  See Murray, John
Comfort, Jane Levington
  See Sturtzel, Jane Levington
Comfort, Mildred Houghton
  1886- 3
Comins, Ethel M(ae) 11
Comins, Jeremy 1933- 28
Commager, Henry Steele
  1902- 23
Comus
  See Ballantyne, R(obert) M(ichael)
Conan Doyle, Arthur
  See Doyle, Arthur Conan
Condit, Martha Olson 1913- 28
Cone, Ferne Geller 1921- 39
Cone, Molly (Lamken) 1918- 28
  Earlier sketch in SATA 1
Conford, Ellen 1942- 6
  See also CLR 10
Conger, Lesley
  See Suttles, Shirley (Smith)

Conklin, Gladys (Plemon)
1903- 2
Conklin, Paul S. 43
Brief Entry 33
Conkling, Hilda 1910- 23
Conly, Robert Leslie
1918(?)-1973 23
Connell, Kirk [Joint pseudonym]
See Chapman, John Stanton Higham
Connelly, Marc(us Cook) 1890-1980
Obituary 25
Connolly, Jerome P(atrick)
1931- 8
Conover, Chris 1950- 31
Conquest, Owen
See Hamilton, Charles H. St. John
Conrad, Joseph 1857-1924 27
Conroy, Jack (Wesley) 1899- 19
Conroy, John
See Conroy, Jack (Wesley)
Constant, Alberta Wilson
1908-1981 22
Obituary 28
Conway, Gordon
See Hamilton, Charles H. St. John
Cook, Bernadine 1924- 11
Cook, Fred J(ames) 1911- 2
Cook, Joseph J(ay) 1924- 8
Cook, Lyn
See Waddell, Evelyn Margaret
Cooke, Ann
See Cole, Joanna
Cooke, David Coxe 1917- 2
Cooke, Donald Ewin
1916-1985 2
Obituary 45
Cookson, Catherine (McMullen)
1906- 9
Coolidge, Olivia E(nsor)
1908- 26
Earlier sketch in SATA 1
Coombs, Charles I(ra) 1914- 43
Earlier sketch in SATA 3
Coombs, Chick
See Coombs, Charles I(ra)
Coombs, Patricia 1926- 3
Cooney, Barbara 1917- 6
Cooney, Caroline B. 1947-
Brief Entry 41
Cooney, Nancy Evans 1932- 42
Coontz, Otto 1946- 33
Cooper, Gordon 1932- 23
Cooper, James Fenimore
1789-1851 19
Cooper, James R.
See Stratemeyer, Edward L.
Cooper, John R. [Collective
pseudonym] 1
Cooper, Kay 1941- 11
Cooper, Lee (Pelham) 5
Cooper, Lester (Irving)
1919-1985 32
Obituary 43
Cooper, Lettice (Ulpha) 1897- ... 35
Cooper, Susan 1935- 4
See also CLR 4
Copeland, Helen 1920- 4
Copeland, Paul W. 23

Copley, (Diana) Heather Pickering
1918- 45
Coppard, A(lfred) E(dgar)
1878-1957 ....YABC 1
Corbett, Grahame 43
Brief Entry 36
Corbett, Scott 1913- 42
Earlier sketch in SATA 2
See also CLR 1
See also SAAS 2
Corbett, W(illiam) J(esse) 1938-
Brief Entry 44
Corbin, Sabra Lee
See Malvern, Gladys
Corbin, William
See McGraw, William Corbin
Corby, Dan
See Catherall, Arthur
Corcoran, Barbara 1911- 3
Corcos, Lucille 1908-1973 10
Cordell, Alexander
See Graber, Alexander
Coren, Alan 1938- 32
Corey, Dorothy 23
Corfe, Thomas Howell 1928- 27
Corfe, Tom
See Corfe, Thomas Howell
Corlett, William 1938- 46
Brief Entry 39
Cormack, M(argaret) Grant
1913- 11
Cormack, Maribelle B.
1902-1984 39
Cormier, Robert (Edmund)
1925- 45
Earlier sketch in SATA 10
Cornelius, Carol 1942- 40
Cornell, J.
See Cornell, Jeffrey
Cornell, James (Clayton, Jr.)
1938- 27
Cornell, Jean Gay 1920- 23
Cornell, Jeffrey 1945- 11
Cornish, Samuel James 1935- 23
Cornwall, Nellie
See Sloggett, Nellie
Correy, Lee
See Stine, G. Harry 10
Corrigan, (Helen) Adeline
1909- 23
Corrigan, Barbara 1922- 8
Cort, M. C.
See Clifford, Margaret Cort
Corwin, Judith Hoffman
1946- 10
Cosgrave, John O'Hara II 1908-1968
Obituary 21
Cosgrove, Stephen E(dward) 1945-
Brief Entry 40
Coskey, Evelyn 1932- 7
Cosner, Shaaron 1940- 43
Costabel, Eva Deutsch 1924- 45
Costello, David F(rancis)
1904- 23
Cott, Jonathan 1942- 23
Cottam, Clarence 1899-1974 25
Cottler, Joseph 1899- 22
Cottrell, Leonard 1913-1974 24

The Countryman
See Whitlock, Ralph
Courlander, Harold 1908- 6
Courtis, Stuart Appleton 1874-1969
Obituary 29
Coury, Louise Andree 1895(?)-1983
Obituary 34
Cousins, Margaret 1905- 2
Cousteau, Jacques-Yves 1910- 38
Coville, Bruce 1950- 32
Cowen, Eve
See Werner, Herma
Cowie, Leonard W(allace)
1919- 4
Cowles, Kathleen
See Krull, Kathleen
Cowley, Joy 1936- 4
Cox, Donald William 1921- 23
Cox, Jack
See Cox, John Roberts
Cox, John Roberts 1915- 9
Cox, Palmer 1840-1924 24
Cox, Victoria
See Garretson, Victoria Diane
Cox, Wally 1924-1973 25
Cox, William R(obert) 1901- 46
Brief Entry 31
Coy, Harold 1902- 3
Craft, Ruth
Brief Entry 31
Craig, A. A.
See Anderson, Poul (William)
Craig, Alisa
See MacLeod, Charlotte (Matilda Hughes)
Craig, Helen 1934-
Brief Entry 46
Craig, John Eland
See Chipperfield, Joseph
Craig, John Ernest 1921- 23
Craig, M. Jean 17
Craig, Margaret Maze
1911-1964 9
Craig, Mary Francis 1923- 6
Craik, Dinah Maria (Mulock)
1826-1887 34
Crane, Barbara J. 1934- 31
Crane, Caroline 1930- 11
Crane, M. A.
See Wartski, Maureen (Ann Crane)
Crane, Roy
See Crane, Royston Campbell
Crane, Royston Campbell 1901-1977
Obituary 22
Crane, Stephen (Townley)
1871-1900 ....YABC 2
Crane, Walter 1845-1915 18
Crane, William D(wight)
1892- 1
Crary, Elizabeth (Ann) 1942-
Brief Entry 43
Crary, Margaret (Coleman)
1906- 9
Craven, Thomas 1889-1969 22
Crawford, Charles P. 1945- 28
Crawford, Deborah 1922- 6
Crawford, John E. 1904-1971 3
Crawford, Mel 1925- 44
Brief Entry 33

Crawford, Phyllis 1899- 3
Craz, Albert G. 1926- 24
Crayder, Dorothy 1906- 7
Crayder, Teresa
  See Colman, Hila
Crayon, Geoffrey
  See Irving, Washington
Crecy, Jeanne
  See Williams, Jeanne
Credle, Ellis 1902- 1
Cresswell, Helen 1934- 1
Cretan, Gladys (Yessayan)
  1921- 2
Crew, Helen (Cecilia) Coale
  1866-1941 ....YABC 2
Crews, Donald 1938- 32
  Brief Entry 30
  See also CLR 7
Crichton, (J.) Michael 1942- 9
Crofut, Bill
  See Crofut, William E. III
Crofut, William E. III 1934- 23
Croman, Dorothy Young
  See Rosenberg, Dorothy
Cromie, Alice Hamilton 1914- 24
Cromie, William J(oseph)
  1930- 4
Crompton, Anne Eliot 1930- 23
Crompton, Richmal
  See Lamburn, Richmal Crompton
Cronbach, Abraham
  1882-1965 11
Crone, Ruth 1919- 4
Cronin, A(rchibald) J(oseph)
  1896-1981
  Obituary 25
Crook, Beverly Courtney 38
  Brief Entry 35
Cros, Earl
  See Rose, Carl
Crosby, Alexander L.
  1906-1980 2
  Obituary 23
Crosher, G(eoffry) R(obins)
  1911- 14
Cross, Gillian (Clare) 1945- 38
Cross, Helen Reeder
  See Broadhead, Helen Cross
Cross, Wilbur Lucius III
  1918- 2
Crossley-Holland, Kevin 5
Crouch, Marcus 1913- 4
Crout, George C(lement)
  1917- 11
Crow, Donna Fletcher 1941- 40
Crowe, Bettina Lum 1911- 6
Crowe, John
  See Lynds, Dennis
Crowell, Grace Noll
  1877-1969 34
Crowell, Pers 1910- 2
Crowfield, Christopher
  See Stowe, Harriet (Elizabeth)
  Beecher
Crowley, Arthur M(cBlair)
  1945- 38
Crownfield, Gertrude
  1867-1945 ....YABC 1

Crowther, James Gerald 1899- 14
Cruikshank, George
  1792-1878 22
Crump, Fred H., Jr. 1931- 11
Crump, J(ames) Irving 1887-1979
  Obituary 21
Cruz, Ray 1933- 6
Ctvrtek, Vaclav 1911-1976
  Obituary 27
Cuffari, Richard 1925-1978 6
  Obituary 25
Cullen, Countee 1903-1946 18
Culliford, Pierre 1928- 40
Culp, Louanna McNary
  1901-1965 2
Cumming, Primrose (Amy)
  1915- 24
Cummings, Betty Sue 1918- 15
Cummings, Parke 1902- 2
Cummings, Pat 1950- 42
Cummings, Richard
  See Gardner, Richard
Cummins, Maria Susanna
  1827-1866 ....YABC 1
Cunliffe, John Arthur 1933- 11
Cunliffe, Marcus (Falkner)
  1922- 37
Cunningham, Captain Frank
  See Glick, Carl (Cannon)
Cunningham, Cathy
  See Cunningham, Chet
Cunningham, Chet 1928- 23
Cunningham, Dale S(peers)
  1932- 11
Cunningham, E.V.
  See Fast, Howard
Cunningham, Julia W(oolfolk)
  1916- 26
  Earlier sketch in SATA 1
  See also SAAS 2
Cunningham, Virginia
  See Holmgren, Virginia
  C(unningham)
Curiae, Amicus
  See Fuller, Edmund (Maybank)
Curie, Eve 1904- 1
Curley, Daniel 1918- 23
Curry, Jane L(ouise) 1932- 1
Curry, Peggy Simson 1911- 8
Curtis, Bruce (Richard) 1944- 30
Curtis, Patricia 1921- 23
Curtis, Peter
  See Lofts, Norah (Robinson)
Curtis, Richard (Alan) 1937- 29
Curtis, Wade
  See Pournelle, Jerry (Eugene)
Cushman, Jerome 2
Cutchen, Billye Walker 1930- 15
Cutler, (May) Ebbitt 1923- 9
Cutler, Ivor 1923- 24
Cutler, Samuel
  See Folsom, Franklin
Cutt, W(illiam) Towrie 1898- 16
Cuyler, Margery Stuyvesant
  1948- 39
Cuyler, Stephen
  See Bates, Barbara S(nedeker)

D

Dahl, Borghild 1890-1984 7
  Obituary 37
Dahl, Roald 1916- 26
  Earlier sketch in SATA 1
  See also CLR 1; 7
Dahlstedt, Marden 1921- 8
Dain, Martin J. 1924- 35
Dale, Jack
  See Holliday, Joseph
Dale, Margaret J(essy) Miller
  1911- 39
Dale, Norman
  See Denny, Norman (George)
Dalgliesh, Alice 1893-1979 17
  Obituary 21
Dalton, Anne 1948- 40
Daly, Jim
  See Stratemeyer, Edward L.
Daly, Kathleen N(orah)
  Brief Entry 37
Daly, Maureen 2
  See also SAAS 1
Daly, Nicholas 1946- 37
Daly, Niki
  See Daly, Nicholas
D'Amato, Alex 1919- 20
D'Amato, Janet 1925- 9
Damrosch, Helen Therese
  See Tee-Van, Helen Damrosch
Dana, Barbara 1940- 22
Dana, Richard Henry, Jr.
  1815-1882 26
Danachair, Caoimhin O.
  See Danaher, Kevin
Danaher, Kevin 1913- 22
D'Andrea, Kate
  See Steiner, Barbara A(nnette)
Dangerfield, Balfour
  See McCloskey, Robert
Daniel, Anita 1893(?)-1978 23
  Obituary 24
Daniel, Anne
  See Steiner, Barbara A(nnette)
Daniel, Hawthorne 1890- 8
Daniels, Guy 1919- 11
Dank, Gloria Rand 1955-
  Brief Entry 46
Dank, Leonard D(ewey)
  1929- 44
Dank, Milton 1920- 31
Danziger, Paula 1944- 36
  Brief Entry 30
Darby, J. N.
  See Govan, Christine Noble
Darby, Patricia (Paulsen) 14
Darby, Ray K. 1912- 7
Daringer, Helen Fern 1892- 1
Darke, Marjorie 1929- 16
Darley, F(elix) O(ctavius) C(arr)
  1822-1888 35
Darling, David J.
  Brief Entry 44
Darling, Kathy
  See Darling, Mary Kathleen
Darling, Lois M. 1917- 3
Darling, Louis, Jr. 1916-1970 3
  Obituary 23

Darling, Mary Kathleen 1943- *9*
Darrow, Whitney, Jr. 1909- *13*
Darwin, Len
  See Darwin, Leonard
Darwin, Leonard 1916- *24*
Dasent, Sir George Webbe 1817-1896
  Brief Entry *29*
Dauer, Rosamond 1934- *23*
Daugherty, Charles Michael
  1914- *16*
Daugherty, James (Henry)
  1889-1974 .... *13*
Daugherty, Richard D(eo)
  1922- *35*
Daugherty, Sonia Medwedeff (?)-1971
  Obituary *27*
d'Aulaire, Edgar Parin 1898- *5*
d'Aulaire, Ingri (Maartenson Parin)
  1904-1980 .... *5*
  Obituary *24*
Daveluy, Paule Cloutier 1919- *11*
Davenport, Spencer
  See Stratemeyer, Edward L.
Daves, Michael 1938- *40*
David, Jonathan
  See Ames, Lee J.
Davidson, Alice Joyce 1932-
  Brief Entry *45*
Davidson, Basil 1914- *13*
Davidson, Jessica 1915- *5*
Davidson, Judith 1953- *40*
Davidson, Margaret 1936- *5*
Davidson, Marion
  See Garis, Howard R(oger)
Davidson, Mary R.
  1885-1973 .... *9*
Davidson, R.
  See Davidson, Raymond
Davidson, Raymond 1926- *32*
Davidson, Rosalie 1921- *23*
Davies, Andrew (Wynford)
  1936- *27*
Davies, Bettilu D(onna) 1942- *33*
Davies, (Edward) Hunter 1936-
  Brief Entry *45*
Davies, Sumiko 1942- *46*
Davis, Bette J. 1923- *15*
Davis, Burke 1913- *4*
Davis, Christopher 1928- *6*
Davis, D(elbert) Dwight
  1908-1965 .... *33*
Davis, Daniel S(heldon) 1936- *12*
Davis, Gibbs 1953- *46*
  Brief Entry *41*
Davis, Hubert J(ackson) 1904- *31*
Davis, James Robert 1945- *32*
Davis, Jim
  See Davis, James Robert
Davis, Julia 1904- *6*
Davis, Louise Littleton 1921- *25*
Davis, Marguerite 1889- *34*
Davis, Mary L(ee) 1935- *9*
Davis, Mary Octavia 1901- *6*
Davis, Paxton 1925- *16*
Davis, Robert
  1881-1949 .... *YABC 1*
Davis, Russell G. 1922- *3*
Davis, Verne T. 1889-1973 .... *6*

Dawson, Elmer A. [Collective
  pseudonym] *1*
Dawson, Mary 1919- *11*
Day, Beth (Feagles) 1924- *33*
Day, Maurice 1892-
  Brief Entry *30*
Day, Thomas 1748-1789 ..... *YABC 1*
Dazey, Agnes J(ohnston) *2*
Dazey, Frank M. *2*
Deacon, Eileen
  See Geipel, Eileen
Deacon, Richard
  See McCormick, (George) Donald
  (King)
Dean, Anabel 1915- *12*
de Angeli, Marguerite 1889- *27*
  Earlier sketch in SATA 1
  See also CLR 1
DeArmand, Frances Ullmann
  1904(?)-1984 .... *10*
  Obituary *38*
Deary, Terry 1946-
  Brief Entry *41*
deBanke, Cecile 1889-1965 ...... *11*
De Bruyn, Monica 1952- *13*
de Camp, Catherine C(rook)
  1907- *12*
DeCamp, L(yon) Sprague
  1907- *9*
Decker, Duane 1910-1964 .... *5*
DeClements, Barthe 1920- *35*
Deedy, John 1923- *24*
Deegan, Paul Joseph 1937-
  Brief Entry *38*
Defoe, Daniel 1660(?)-1731 ...... *22*
deFrance, Anthony
  See Di Franco, Anthony (Mario)
DeGering, Etta 1898- *7*
De Grazia
  See De Grazia, Ted
De Grazia, Ted 1909-1982 .... *39*
De Grazia, Ettore
  See De Grazia, Ted
De Groat, Diane 1947- *31*
de Grummond, Lena Young *6*
Deiss, Joseph J. 1915- *12*
DeJong, David C(ornel)
  1905-1967 .... *10*
de Jong, Dola *7*
De Jong, Meindert 1906- *2*
  See also CLR 1
de Kay, Ormonde, Jr. 1923- *7*
de Kiriline, Louise
  See Lawrence, Louise de Kiriline
Dekker, Carl
  See Laffin, John (Alfred Charles)
Dekker, Carl
  See Lynds, Dennis
deKruif, Paul (Henry)
  1890-1971 .... *5*
Delacre, Lulu 1957- *36*
De Lage, Ida 1918- *11*
de la Mare, Walter 1873-1956 .... *16*
Delaney, Harry 1932- *3*
Delaney, Ned 1951- *28*
Delano, Hugh 1933- *20*
De La Ramée, (Marie) Louise
  1839-1908 .... *20*
Delaune, Lynne *7*

DeLaurentis, Louise Budde
  1920- *12*
Delderfield, Eric R(aymond)
  1909- *14*
Delderfield, R(onald) F(rederick)
  1912-1972 .... *20*
De Leeuw, Adele Louise
  1899- *30*
  Earlier sketch in SATA 1
Delessert, Etienne 1941- *46*
  Brief Entry *27*
Delmar, Roy
  See Wexler, Jerome (LeRoy)
Deloria, Vine (Victor), Jr.
  1933- *21*
Del Rey, Lester 1915- *22*
Delton, Judy 1931- *14*
Delulio, John 1938- *15*
Delving, Michael
  See Williams, Jay
Demarest, Chris(topher) L(ynn)
  1951- *45*
  Brief Entry *44*
Demarest, Doug
  See Barker, Will
Demas, Vida 1927- *9*
De Mejo, Oscar 1911- *40*
de Messières, Nicole 1930- *39*
Deming, Richard 1915- *24*
Dengler, Sandy 1939-
  Brief Entry *40*
Denmark, Harrison
  See Zelazny, Roger (Joseph
  Christopher)
Denney, Diana 1910- *25*
Dennis, Morgan 1891(?)-1960 .... *18*
Dennis, Wesley 1903-1966 .... *18*
Denniston, Elinore 1900-1978
  Obituary *24*
Denny, Norman (George)
  1901-1982 .... *43*
Denslow, W(illiam) W(allace)
  1856-1915 .... *16*
Denzel, Justin F(rancis) 1917- *46*
  Brief Entry *38*
Denzer, Ann Wiseman
  See Wiseman, Ann (Sayre)
de Paola, Thomas Anthony
  1934- *11*
de Paola, Tomie
  See de Paola, Thomas Anthony
  See also CLR 4
DePauw, Linda Grant 1940- *24*
deRegniers, Beatrice Schenk
  (Freedman) 1914- *2*
Derleth, August (William)
  1909-1971 .... *5*
Derman, Sarah Audrey 1915- *11*
de Roo, Anne Louise 1931- *25*
De Roussan, Jacques 1929-
  Brief Entry *31*
Derry Down Derry
  See Lear, Edward
Derwent, Lavinia *14*
Desbarats, Peter 1933- *39*
De Selincourt, Aubrey
  1894-1962 .... *14*
Desmond, Alice Curtis 1897- *8*

Detine, Padre
See Olsen, Ib Spang
Deutsch, Babette 1895-1982 1
Obituary 33
De Valera, Sinead 1870(?)-1975
Obituary 30
Devaney, John 1926- 12
Devereux, Frederick L(eonard), Jr.
1914- 9
Devlin, Harry 1918- 11
Devlin, (Dorothy) Wende
1918- 11
DeWaard, E. John 1935- 7
DeWeese, Gene
See DeWeese, Thomas Eugene
DeWeese, Jean
See DeWeese, Thomas Eugene
DeWeese, Thomas Eugene
1934- 46
Brief Entry 45
Dewey, Ariane 1937- 7
Dewey, Ken(neth Francis)
1940- 39
DeWit, Dorothy (May Knowles)
1916-1980 39
Obituary 28
Deyneka, Anita 1943- 24
Deyrup, Astrith Johnson
1923- 24
Diamond, Donna 1950- 35
Brief Entry 30
Dias, Earl Joseph 1916- 41
Dick, Cappy
See Cleveland, George
Dick, Trella Lamson
1889-1974 9
Dickens, Charles 1812-1870 15
Dickens, Frank
See Huline-Dickens, Frank William
Dickens, Monica 1915- 4
Dickerson, Roy Ernest 1886-1965
Obituary 26
Dickinson, Emily (Elizabeth)
1830-1886 29
Dickinson, Mary 1949-
Brief Entry 41
Dickinson, Peter 1927- 5
Dickinson, Susan 1931- 8
Dickinson, William Croft
1897-1973 13
Dickson, Helen
See Reynolds, Helen Mary
Greenwood Campbell
Dickson, Naida 1916- 8
Dietz, David H(enry)
1897-1984 10
Obituary 41
Dietz, Lew 1907- 11
Di Franco, Anthony (Mario)
1945- 42
Digges, Jeremiah
See Berger, Josef
D'Ignazio, Fred 1949- 39
Brief Entry 35
Di Grazia, Thomas (?)-1983 32
Dillard, Annie 1945- 10
Dillard, Polly (Hargis) 1916- ... 24
Dillon, Barbara 1927- 44
Brief Entry 39

Dillon, Diane 1933- 15
Dillon, Eilis 1920- 2
Dillon, Leo 1933- 15
Dilson, Jesse 1914- 24
Dines, Glen 1925- 7
Dinesen, Isak
See Blixen, Karen (Christentze Dinesen)
Dinnerstein, Harvey 1928- 42
Dinsdale, Tim 1924- 11
Dirks, Rudolph 1877-1968
Brief Entry 31
Disney, Walt(er Elias)
1901-1966 28
Brief Entry 27
DiValentin, Maria 1911- 7
Dixon, Dougal 1947- 45
Dixon, Franklin W. [Collective
pseudonym] 1
See also Adams, Harriet
S(tratemeyer); McFarlane, Leslie;
Stratemeyer, Edward L.; Svenson,
Andrew E.
Dixon, Jeanne 1936- 31
Dixon, Peter L. 1931- 6
Doane, Pelagie 1906-1966 7
Dobell, I(sabel) M(arian) B(arclay)
1909- 11
Dobie, J(ames) Frank
1888-1964 43
Dobkin, Alexander 1908-1975
Obituary 30
Dobler, Lavinia G. 1910- 6
Dobrin, Arnold 1928- 4
Dockery, Wallene T. 1941- 27
"Dr. A"
See Silverstein, Alvin
Dodd, Ed(ward) Benton 1902- 4
Dodd, Lynley (Stuart) 1941- 35
Dodge, Bertha S(anford)
1902- 8
Dodge, Mary (Elizabeth) Mapes
1831-1905 21
Dodgson, Charles Lutwidge
1832-1898 .... YABC 2
Dodson, Kenneth M(acKenzie)
1907- 11
Dodson, Susan 1941-
Brief Entry 40
Doherty, C. H. 1913- 6
Dolan, Edward F(rancis), Jr.
1924- 45
Brief Entry 31
Dolson, Hildegarde 1908- 5
Domanska, Janina 6
Domino, John
See Averill, Esther
Domjan, Joseph 1907- 25
Donalds, Gordon
See Shirreffs, Gordon D.
Donna, Natalie 1934- 9
Donovan, Frank (Robert) 1906-1975
Obituary 30
Donovan, John 1928-
Brief Entry 29
See also CLR 3
Donovan, William
See Berkebile, Fred D(onovan)

Doob, Leonard W(illiam)
1909- 8
Dor, Ana
See Ceder, Georgiana Dorcas
Doré, (Louis Christophe Paul) Gustave
1832-1883 19
Doremus, Robert 1913- 30
Dorian, Edith M(cEwen)
1900- 5
Dorian, Harry
See Hamilton, Charles H. St. John
Dorian, Marguerite 7
Dorman, Michael 1932- 7
Dorman, N. B. 1927- 39
Dorson, Richard M(ercer)
1916-1981 30
Doss, Helen (Grigsby) 1918- 20
Doss, Margot Patterson 6
dos Santos, Joyce Audy
Brief Entry 42
Dottig
See Grider, Dorothy
Dotts, Maryann J. 1933- 35
Doty, Jean Slaughter 1929- 28
Doty, Roy 1922- 28
Doubtfire, Dianne (Abrams)
1918- 29
Dougherty, Charles 1922- 18
Douglas, James McM.
See Butterworth, W. E.
Douglas, Kathryn
See Ewing, Kathryn
Douglas, Marjory Stoneman
1890- 10
Douglass, Barbara 1930- 40
Douglass, Frederick
1817(?)-1895 29
Douty, Esther M(orris)
1911-1978 8
Obituary 23
Dow, Emily R. 1904- 10
Dowdell, Dorothy (Florence) Karns
1910- 12
Dowden, Anne Ophelia 1907- 7
Dowdey, Landon Gerald
1923- 11
Dowdy, Mrs. Regera
See Gorey, Edward St. John
Downer, Marion 1892(?)-1971 ... 25
Downey, Fairfax 1893- 3
Downie, Mary Alice 1934- 13
Doyle, Arthur Conan
1859-1930 24
Doyle, Donovan
See Boegehold, Betty (Doyle)
Doyle, Richard 1824-1883 21
Draco, F.
See Davis, Julia
Dragonwagon, Crescent 1952- ... 41
Earlier sketch in SATA 11
Drake, Frank
See Hamilton, Charles H. St. John
Drapier, M. B.
See Swift, Jonathan
Drawson, Blair 1943- 17
Dresang, Eliza (Carolyn Timberlake)
1941- 19
Drescher, Joan E(lizabeth)
1939- 30

Drew, Patricia (Mary) 1938- *15*

Drewery, Mary 1918- *6*

Drial, J. E.
  See Laird, Jean E(louise)

Drucker, Malka 1945- *39*
  Brief Entry *29*

Drummond, V(iolet) H. 1911- *6*

Drummond, Walter
  See Silverberg, Robert

Drury, Roger W(olcott) 1914- *15*

Dryden, Pamela
  See Johnston, Norma

Duane, Diane (Elizabeth) 1952-
  Brief Entry *46*

du Blanc, Daphne
  See Groom, Arthur William

DuBois, Rochelle Holt
  See Holt, Rochelle Lynn

Du Bois, Shirley Graham
  1907-1977 .... *24*

Du Bois, W(illiam) E(dward)
  B(urghardt) 1868-1963 .... *42*

du Bois, William Pène 1916- *4*
  See also CLR 1

DuBose, LaRocque (Russ)
  1926- *2*

Du Chaillu, Paul (Belloni)
  1831(?)-1903 .... *26*

Duchesne, Janet 1930-
  Brief Entry *32*

Ducornet, Erica 1943- *7*

Dudley, Martha Ward 1909(?)-1985
  Obituary *45*

Dudley, Nancy
  See Cole, Lois Dwight

Dudley, Robert
  See Baldwin, James

Dudley, Ruth H(ubbell) 1905- *11*

Dueland, Joy V(ivian) *27*

Duff, Maggie
  See Duff, Margaret K.

Duff, Margaret K. *37*

Dugan, Michael (Gray) 1947- *15*

Duggan, Alfred Leo
  1903-1964 .... *25*

Duggan, Maurice (Noel)
  1922-1974 .... *40*
  Obituary *30*

du Jardin, Rosamond (Neal)
  1902-1963 .... *2*

Dulac, Edmund 1882-1953 .... *19*

Dumas, Alexandre (the elder)
  1802-1870 .... *18*

du Maurier, Daphne 1907- *27*

Dunbar, Paul Laurence
  1872-1906 .... *34*

Dunbar, Robert E(verett)
  1926- *32*

Duncan, Gregory
  See McClintock, Marshall

Duncan, Jane
  See Cameron, Elizabeth Jane

Duncan, Julia K. [Collective
  pseudonym] *1*

Duncan, Lois S(teinmetz)
  1934- *36*
  Earlier sketch in SATA 1
  See also SAAS 2

Duncan, Norman
  1871-1916 .... *YABC 1*

Duncombe, Frances (Riker)
  1900- *25*

Dunlop, Agnes M.R. *3*

Dunlop, Eileen (Rhona) 1938- *24*

Dunn, Harvey T(homas)
  1884-1952 .... *34*

Dunn, Judy
  See Spangenberg, Judith Dunn

Dunn, Mary Lois 1930- *6*

Dunnahoo, Terry 1927- *7*

Dunne, Mary Collins 1914- *11*

Dunnett, Margaret (Rosalind)
  1909-1977 .... *42*

Dunrea, Olivier 1953-
  Brief Entry *46*

Dupuy, T(revor) N(evitt)
  1916- *4*

Durant, John 1902- *27*

Durrell, Gerald (Malcolm)
  1925- *8*

Du Soe, Robert C.
  1892-1958 .... *YABC 2*

Dutz
  See Davis, Mary Octavia

Duvall, Evelyn Millis 1906- *9*

Duvoisin, Roger (Antoine)
  1904-1980 .... *30*
  Obituary *23*
  Earlier sketch in SATA 2

Dwiggins, Don 1913- *4*

Dwight, Allan
  See Cole, Lois Dwight

Dyer, James (Frederick) 1934- *37*

Dygard, Thomas J. 1931- *24*

Dyke, John 1935- *35*

E

E.V.B.
  See Boyle, Eleanor Vere (Gordon)

Eagar, Frances 1940- *11*

Eager, Edward (McMaken)
  1911-1964 .... *17*

Eagle, Mike 1942- *11*

Earle, Olive L. *7*

Earnshaw, Brian 1929- *17*

Eastman, Charles A(lexander)
  1858-1939 .... *YABC 1*

Eastman, P(hilip) D(ey)
  1909-1986 .... *33*
  Obituary *46*

Eastwick, Ivy O. *3*

Eaton, Anne T(haxter)
  1881-1971 .... *32*

Eaton, George L.
  See Verral, Charles Spain

Eaton, Jeanette 1886-1968 .... *24*

Eaton, Tom 1940- *22*

Ebel, Alex 1927- *11*

Eber, Dorothy (Margaret) Harley
  1930- *27*

Eberle, Irmengarde 1898-1979 .... *2*
  Obituary *23*

Eccles
  See Williams, Ferelith Eccles

Eckblad, Edith Berven 1923- *23*

Ecke, Wolfgang 1927-1983
  Obituary *37*

Eckert, Allan W. 1931- *29*
  Brief Entry *27*

Eckert, Horst 1931- *8*

Ede, Janina 1937- *33*

Edell, Celeste *12*

Edelman, Lily (Judith) 1915- *22*

Edens, (Bishop) David 1926- *39*

Edey, Maitland A(rmstrong)
  1910- *25*

Edgeworth, Maria 1767-1849 ..... *21*

Edmonds, I(vy) G(ordon)
  1917- *8*

Edmonds, Walter D(umaux)
  1903- *27*
  Earlier sketch in SATA 1

Edmund, Sean
  See Pringle, Laurence

Edsall, Marian S(tickney)
  1920- *8*

Edwards, Anne 1927- *35*

Edwards, Audrey 1947-
  Brief Entry *31*

Edwards, Bertram
  See Edwards, Herbert Charles

Edwards, Bronwen Elizabeth
  See Rose, Wendy

Edwards, Cecile (Pepin)
  1916- *25*

Edwards, Dorothy 1914-1982 ..... *4*
  Obituary *31*

Edwards, Gunvor *32*

Edwards, Harvey 1929- *5*

Edwards, Herbert Charles
  1912- *12*

Edwards, Jane Campbell
  1932- *10*

Edwards, Julie
  See Andrews, Julie

Edwards, Julie
  See Stratemeyer, Edward L.

Edwards, Linda Strauss
  Brief Entry *42*

Edwards, Monica le Doux Newton
  1912- *12*

Edwards, Olwen
  See Gater, Dilys

Edwards, Sally 1929- *7*

Edwards, Samuel
  See Gerson, Noel B(ertram)

Egan, E(dward) W(elstead)
  1922- *35*

Eggenberger, David 1918- *6*

Eggleston, Edward 1837-1902 ..... *27*

Egielski, Richard 1952- *11*

Egypt, Ophelia Settle
  1903-1984 .... *16*
  Obituary *38*

Ehlert, Lois (Jane) 1934- *35*

Ehrlich, Amy 1942- *25*

Ehrlich, Bettina (Bauer) 1903- *1*

Eichberg, James Bandman
  See Garfield, James B.

Eichenberg, Fritz 1901- *9*

Eichler, Margrit 1942- *35*

Eichner, James A. 1927- *4*

Eifert, Virginia S(nider)
  1911-1966 .... *2*

Einsel, Naiad *10*
Einsel, Walter 1926- *10*
Einzig, Susan 1922- *43*
Eiseman, Alberta 1925- *15*
Eisenberg, Azriel 1903- *12*
Eisenberg, Phyllis Rose 1924- *41*
Eisner, Vivienne
   See Margolis, Vivienne
Eisner, Will(iam Erwin) 1917- *31*
Eitzen, Allan 1928- *9*
Eitzen, Ruth (Carper) 1924- *9*
Elam, Richard M(ace, Jr.)
   1920- *9*
Elfman, Blossom 1925- *8*
Elgin, Kathleen 1923- *39*
Elia
   See Lamb, Charles
Eliot, Anne
   See Cole, Lois Dwight
Elisofon, Eliot 1911-1973
   Obituary *21*
Elkin, Benjamin 1911- *3*
Elkins, Dov Peretz 1937- *5*
Ellacott, S(amuel) E(rnest)
   1911- *19*
Elliott, Sarah M(cCarn) 1930- *14*
Ellis, Anyon
   See Rowland-Entwistle, (Arthur)
   Theodore (Henry)
Ellis, Edward S(ylvester)
   1840-1916 .... *YABC 1*
Ellis, Ella Thorp 1928- *7*
Ellis, Harry Bearse 1921- *9*
Ellis, Herbert
   See Wilson, Lionel
Ellis, Mel 1912-1984 .... *7*
   Obituary *39*
Ellison, Lucile Watkins 1907(?)-1979
   Obituary *22*
Ellison, Virginia Howell
   1910- *4*
Ellsberg, Edward 1891- *7*
Elmore, (Carolyn) Patricia
   1933- *38*
   Brief Entry *35*
Elspeth
   See Bragdon, Elspeth
Elting, Mary 1906- *2*
Elwart, Joan Potter 1927- *2*
Emberley, Barbara A(nne) *8*
   See also CLR 5
Emberley, Ed(ward Randolph)
   1931- *8*
   See also CLR 5
Emberley, Michael 1960- *34*
Embry, Margaret (Jacob)
   1919- *5*
Emerson, Alice B. [Collective
   pseudonym] *1*
Emerson, William K(eith)
   1925- *25*
Emery, Anne (McGuigan)
   1907- *33*
   Earlier sketch in SATA 1
Emmens, Carol Ann 1944- *39*
Emmons, Della (Florence) Gould
   1890-1983
   Obituary *39*

Emrich, Duncan (Black Macdonald)
   1908- *11*
Emslie, M. L.
   See Simpson, Myrtle L(illias)
Ende, Michael 1930(?)-
   Brief Entry *42*
Enderle, Judith (Ann) 1941- *38*
Engdahl, Sylvia Louise 1933- *4*
   See also CLR 2
Engle, Eloise Katherine 1923- *9*
Englebert, Victor 1933- *8*
English, James W(ilson)
   1915- *37*
Enright, D(ennis) J(oseph)
   1920- *25*
Enright, Elizabeth 1909-1968 ..... *9*
   See also CLR 4
Enright, Maginel Wright
   See Barney, Maginel Wright
Enys, Sarah L.
   See Sloggett, Nellie
Epp, Margaret A(gnes) *20*
Epple, Anne Orth 1927- *20*
Epstein, Anne Merrick 1931- *20*
Epstein, Beryl (Williams)
   1910- *31*
   Earlier sketch in SATA 1
Epstein, Perle S(herry) 1938- *27*
Epstein, Samuel 1909- *31*
   Earlier sketch in SATA 1
Erdman, Loula Grace *1*
Erdoes, Richard 1912- *33*
   Brief Entry *28*
Erhard, Walter 1920-
   Brief Entry *30*
Erickson, Russell E(verett)
   1932- *27*
Erickson, Sabra R(ollins)
   1912- *35*
Ericson, Walter
   See Fast, Howard
Erikson, Mel 1937- *31*
Erlanger, Baba
   See Trahey, Jane
Erlich, Lillian (Feldman)
   1910- *10*
Ernest, William
   See Berkebile, Fred D(onovan)
Ernst, (Lyman) John 1940- *39*
Ernst, Kathryn (Fitzgerald)
   1942- *25*
Ernst, Lisa Campbell 1957-
   Brief Entry *44*
Ervin, Janet Halliday 1923- *4*
Erwin, Will
   See Eisner, Will(iam Erwin)
Eshmeyer, R(einhart) E(rnst)
   1898- *29*
Espeland, Pamela (Lee) 1951-
   Brief Entry *38*
Espy, Willard R(ichardson)
   1910- *38*
Estep, Irene (Compton) *5*
Estes, Eleanor 1906- *7*
   See also CLR 2
Estoril, Jean
   See Allan, Mabel Esther
Etchemendy, Nancy 1952- *38*
Etchison, Birdie L(ee) 1937- *38*

Ets, Marie Hall *2*
Eunson, Dale 1904- *5*
Evans, Eva Knox 1905- *27*
Evans, Katherine (Floyd)
   1901-1964 .... *5*
Evans, Mari *10*
Evans, Mark *19*
Evans, Patricia Healy
   See Carpenter, Patricia
Evarts, Esther
   See Benson, Sally
Evarts, Hal G. (Jr.) 1915- *6*
Evernden, Margery 1916- *5*
Evslin, Bernard 1922- *45*
   Brief Entry *28*
Ewen, David 1907- *4*
Ewing, Juliana (Horatia Gatty)
   1841-1885 .... *16*
Ewing, Kathryn 1921- *20*
Eyerly, Jeannette Hyde 1908- *4*
Eyre, Dorothy
   See McGuire, Leslie (Sarah)
Eyre, Katherine Wigmore
   1901-1970 .... *26*
Ezzell, Marilyn 1937- *42*
   Brief Entry *38*

F

Fabe, Maxene 1943- *15*
Faber, Doris 1924- *3*
Faber, Harold 1919- *5*
Fabre, Jean Henri (Casimir)
   1823-1915 .... *22*
Facklam, Margery Metz 1927- *20*
Fadiman, Clifton (Paul) 1904- *11*
Fair, Sylvia 1933- *13*
Fairfax-Lucy, Brian (Fulke Cameron-
   Ramsay) 1898-1974 .... *6*
   Obituary *26*
Fairlie, Gerard 1899-1983
   Obituary *34*
Fairman, Joan A(lexandra)
   1935- *10*
Faithfull, Gail 1936- *8*
Falconer, James
   See Kirkup, James
Falkner, Leonard 1900- *12*
Fall, Thomas
   See Snow, Donald Clifford
Falls, C(harles) B(uckles)
   1874-1960 .... *38*
   Brief Entry *27*
Falstein, Louis 1909- *37*
Fanning, Leonard M(ulliken)
   1888-1967 .... *5*
Faralla, Dana 1909- *9*
Faralla, Dorothy W.
   See Faralla, Dana
Farb, Peter 1929-1980 .... *12*
   Obituary *22*
Farber, Norma 1909-1984 .... *25*
   Obituary *38*
Farge, Monique
   See Grée, Alain
Farjeon, (Eve) Annabel 1919- *11*
Farjeon, Eleanor 1881-1965 .... *2*
Farley, Carol 1936- *4*

Author Index

Farley, Walter 1920- 43
  Earlier sketch in SATA 2
Farmer, Penelope (Jane)
  1939- 40
  Brief Entry 39
  See also CLR 8
Farmer, Peter 1950- 38
Farnham, Burt
  See Clifford, Harold B.
Farquhar, Margaret C(utting)
  1905- 13
Farquharson, Alexander 1944- 46
Farquharson, Martha
  See Finley, Martha
Farr, Finis (King) 1904- 10
Farrar, Susan Clement 1917- 33
Farrell, Ben
  See Cebulash, Mel
Farrington, Benjamin 1891-1974
  Obituary 20
Farrington, Selwyn Kip, Jr.
  1904- 20
Farthing, Alison 1936- 45
  Brief Entry 36
Fassler, Joan (Grace) 1931- 11
Fast, Howard 1914- 7
Fatchen, Max 1920- 20
Father Xavier
  See Hurwood, Bernhardt J.
Fatigati, (Frances) Evelyn de Buhr
  1948- 24
Fatio, Louise 6
Faulhaber, Martha 1926- 7
Faulkner, Anne Irvin 1906- 23
Faulkner, Nancy
  See Faulkner, Anne Irvin
Fax, Elton Clay 1909- 25
Feagles, Anita MacRae 9
Feagles, Elizabeth
  See Day, Beth (Feagles)
Feague, Mildred H. 1915- 14
Fecher, Constance 1911- 7
Feder, Paula (Kurzband)
  1935- 26
Feder, Robert Arthur 1909-1969
  Brief Entry 35
Feelings, Muriel (Grey) 1938- 16
  See also CLR 5
Feelings, Thomas 1933- 8
Feelings, Tom
  See Feelings, Thomas
  See also CLR 5
Fehrenbach, T(heodore) R(eed, Jr.)
  1925- 33
Feiffer, Jules 1929- 8
Feig, Barbara Krane 1937- 34
Feikema, Feike
  See Manfred, Frederick F(eikema)
Feil, Hila 1942- 12
Feilen, John
  See May, Julian
Feldman, Anne (Rodgers)
  1939- 19
Félix
  See Vincent, Félix
Fellows, Muriel H. 10
Felsen, Henry Gregor 1916- 1
  See also SAAS 2
Felton, Harold William 1902- 1

Felton, Ronald Oliver 1909- 3
Felts, Shirley 1934- 33
Fenderson, Lewis H. 1907-1983
  Obituary 37
Fenner, Carol 1929- 7
Fenner, Phyllis R(eid)
  1899-1982 1
  Obituary 29
Fenten, Barbara D(oris) 1935- 26
Fenten, D. X. 1932- 4
Fenton, Carroll Lane
  1900-1969 5
Fenton, Edward 1917- 7
Fenton, Mildred Adams 1899- 21
Fenwick, Patti
  See Grider, Dorothy
Feravolo, Rocco Vincent
  1922- 10
Ferber, Edna 1887-1968 7
Ferguson, Bob
  See Ferguson, Robert Bruce
Ferguson, Cecil 1931- 45
Ferguson, Robert Bruce 1927- 13
Ferguson, Walter (W.) 1930- 34
Fergusson, Erna 1888-1964 5
Fermi, Laura (Capon)
  1907-1977 6
  Obituary 28
Fern, Eugene A. 1919- 10
Ferrier, Lucy
  See Penzler, Otto
Ferris, Helen Josephine
  1890-1969 21
Ferris, James Cody [Collective
  pseudonym] 1
  See also McFarlane, Leslie;
  Stratemeyer, Edward L.
Ferry, Charles 1927- 43
Fetz, Ingrid 1915- 30
Feydy, Anne Lindbergh
  Brief Entry 32
  See Sapieyevski, Anne Lindbergh
Fiammenghi, Gioia 1929- 9
Fiarotta, Noel 1944- 15
Fiarotta, Phyllis 1942- 15
Fichter, George S. 1922- 7
Fidler, Kathleen (Annie)
  1899-1980 3
  Obituary 45
Fiedler, Jean 4
Field, Edward 1924- 8
Field, Elinor Whitney 1889-1980
  Obituary 28
Field, Eugene 1850-1895 16
Field, Rachel (Lyman)
  1894-1942 15
Fife, Dale (Odile) 1910- 18
Fighter Pilot, A
  See Johnston, H(ugh) A(nthony)
  S(tephen)
Figueroa, Pablo 1938- 9
Fijan, Carol 1918- 12
Fillmore, Parker H(oysted)
  1878-1944 .... YABC 1
Filstrup, Chris
  See Filstrup, E(dward) Christian
Filstrup, E(dward) Christian
  1942- 43

Filstrup, Jane Merrill
  See Merrill, Jane
Filstrup, Janie
  See Merrill, Jane
Finder, Martin
  See Salzmann, Siegmund
Fine, Anne 1947- 29
Finger, Charles J(oseph)
  1869(?)-1941 42
Fink, William B(ertrand)
  1916- 22
Finke, Blythe F(oote) 1922- 26
Finkel, George (Irvine)
  1909-1975 8
Finlay, Winifred 1910- 23
Finlayson, Ann 1925- 8
Finley, Martha 1828-1909 43
Firmin, Charlotte 1954- 29
Firmin, Peter 1928- 15
Fischbach, Julius 1894- 10
Fischler, Stan(ley I.)
  Brief Entry 36
Fishback, Margaret
  See Antolini, Margaret Fishback
Fisher, Aileen (Lucia) 1906- 25
  Earlier sketch in SATA 1
Fisher, Barbara 1940- 44
  Brief Entry 34
Fisher, Clavin C(argill) 1912- ... 24
Fisher, Dorothy Canfield
  1879-1958 .... YABC 1
Fisher, John (Oswald Hamilton)
  1909- 15
Fisher, Laura Harrison 1934- 5
Fisher, Leonard Everett 1924- 34
  Earlier sketch in SATA 4
  See also SAAS 1
Fisher, Lois I. 1948- 38
  Brief Entry 35
Fisher, Margery (Turner)
  1913- 20
Fisk, Nicholas 1923- 25
Fitch, Clarke
  See Sinclair, Upton (Beall)
Fitch, John IV
  See Cormier, Robert (Edmund)
Fitschen, Dale 1937- 20
Fitzalan, Roger
  See Trevor, Elleston
Fitzgerald, Captain Hugh
  See Baum, L(yman) Frank
Fitzgerald, Edward Earl 1919- 20
Fitzgerald, F(rancis) A(nthony)
  1940- 15
Fitzgerald, John D(ennis)
  1907- 20
  See also CLR 1
Fitzhardinge, Joan Margaret
  1912- 2
Fitzhugh, Louise (Perkins)
  1928-1974 45
  Obituary 24
  Earlier sketch in SATA 1
  See also CLR 1
Flack, Marjorie
  1899-1958 .... YABC 2
Flack, Naomi John (White) 40
  Brief Entry 35

Flash Flood
 See Robinson, Jan M.
Fleischer, Max 1889-1972
 Brief Entry 30
Fleischhauer-Hardt, Helga
 1936- 30
Fleischman, Paul 1952- 39
 Brief Entry 32
Fleischman, (Albert) Sid(ney)
 1920- 8
 See also CLR 1
Fleishman, Seymour 1918-
 Brief Entry 32
Fleming, Alice Mulcahey
 1928- 9
Fleming, Ian (Lancaster)
 1908-1964 9
Fleming, Susan 1932- 32
Fleming, Thomas J(ames)
 1927- 8
Fletcher, Charlie May 1897- 3
Fletcher, Colin 1922- 28
Fletcher, Helen Jill 1911- 13
Fletcher, Richard E. 1917(?)-1983
 Obituary 34
Fletcher, Rick
 See Fletcher, Richard E.
Fleur, Anne 1901-
 Brief Entry 31
Flexner, James Thomas 1908- 9
Flitner, David P. 1949- 7
Floethe, Louise Lee 1913- 4
Floethe, Richard 1901- 4
Floherty, John Joseph
 1882-1964 25
Flood, Flash
 See Robinson, Jan M.
Flora, James (Royer) 1914- 30
 Earlier sketch in SATA 1
Florian, Douglas 1950- 19
Flory, Jane Trescott 1917- 22
Flowerdew, Phyllis 33
Floyd, Gareth 1940-
 Brief Entry 31
Fluchère, Henri A(ndré) 1914- 40
Flynn, Barbara 1928- 9
Flynn, Jackson
 See Shirreffs, Gordon D.
Flynn, Mary
 See Welsh, Mary Flynn
Fodor, Ronald V(ictor) 1944- 25
Foley, (Anna) Bernice Williams
 1902- 28
Foley, June 1944- 44
Foley, (Mary) Louise Munro 1933-
 Brief Entry 40
Foley, Rae
 See Denniston, Elinore
Folkard, Charles James 1878-1963
 Brief Entry 28
Follett, Helen (Thomas) 1884(?)-1970
 Obituary 27
Folsom, Franklin (Brewster)
 1907- 5
Folsom, Michael (Brewster)
 1938- 40
Fontenot, Mary Alice 1910- 34
Fooner, Michael 22
Forberg, Ati 1925- 22

Forbes, Bryan 1926- 37
Forbes, Cabot L.
 See Hoyt, Edwin P(almer), Jr.
Forbes, Esther 1891-1967 2
Forbes, Graham B. [Collective
 pseudonym] 1
Forbes, Kathryn
 See McLean, Kathryn (Anderson)
Ford, Albert Lee
 See Stratemeyer, Edward L.
Ford, Barbara
 Brief Entry 34
Ford, Elbur
 See Hibbert, Eleanor
Ford, George (Jr.) 31
Ford, Hilary
 See Youd, (Christopher) Samuel
Ford, Hildegarde
 See Morrison, Velma Ford
Ford, Marcia
 See Radford, Ruby L.
Ford, Nancy K(effer) 1906-1961
 Obituary 29
Foreman, Michael 1938- 2
Forest, Antonia 29
Forester, C(ecil) S(cott)
 1899-1966 13
Forman, Brenda 1936- 4
Forman, James Douglas 1932- 8
Forrest, Sybil
 See Markun, Patricia M(aloney)
Forrester, Marian
 See Schachtel, Roger
Forrester, Victoria 1940- 40
 Brief Entry 35
Forsee, (Frances) Aylesa 1
Fort, Paul
 See Stockton, Francis Richard
Fortnum, Peggy 1919- 26
Foster, Brad W. 1955- 34
Foster, Doris Van Liew 1899- 10
Foster, E(lizabeth) C(onnell)
 1902- 9
Foster, Elizabeth 1905-1963 10
Foster, Elizabeth Vincent
 1902- 12
Foster, F. Blanche 1919- 11
Foster, G(eorge) Allen
 1907-1969 26
Foster, Genevieve (Stump)
 1893-1979 2
 Obituary 23
 See also CLR 7
Foster, Hal
 See Foster, Harold Rudolf
Foster, Harold Rudolf 1892-1982
 Obituary 31
Foster, John T(homas) 1925- 8
Foster, Laura Louise 1918- 6
Foster, Margaret Lesser 1899-1979
 Obituary 21
Foster, Marian Curtis
 1909-1978 23
Fourth Brother, The
 See Aung, (Maung) Htin
Fowke, Edith (Margaret)
 1913- 14
Fowles, John 1926- 22
Fox, Charles Philip 1913- 12

Fox, Eleanor
 See St. John, Wylly Folk
Fox, Fontaine Talbot, Jr. 1884-1964
 Obituary 23
Fox, Fred 1903(?)-1981
 Obituary 27
Fox, Freeman
 See Hamilton, Charles H. St. John
Fox, Grace
 See Anderson, Grace Fox
Fox, Larry 30
Fox, Lorraine 1922-1975 11
 Obituary 27
Fox, Mary Virginia 1919- 44
 Brief Entry 39
Fox, Michael Wilson 1937- 15
Fox, Paula 1923- 17
 See also CLR 1
Fox, Petronella
 See Balogh, Penelope
Fox, Robert J. 1927- 33
Fradin, Dennis Brindel 1945- 29
Frame, Paul 1913-
 Brief Entry 33
Frances, Miss
 See Horwich, Frances R.
Franchere, Ruth 18
Francis, Charles
 See Holme, Bryan
Francis, Dee
 See Haas, Dorothy F.
Francis, Dorothy Brenner
 1926- 10
Francis, Pamela (Mary) 1926- 11
Franco, Marjorie 38
Francois, André 1915- 25
Francoise
 See Seignobosc, Francoise
Frank, Anne 1929-1945(?)
 Brief Entry 42
Frank, Josette 1893- 10
Frank, Mary 1933- 34
Frank, R., Jr.
 See Ross, Frank (Xavier), Jr.
Frankau, Mary Evelyn 1899- 4
Frankel, Bernice 9
Frankel, Edward 1910- 44
Frankel, Julie 1947- 40
 Brief Entry 34
Frankenberg, Robert 1911- 22
Franklin, Harold 1920- 13
Franklin, Max
 See Deming, Richard
Franklin, Steve
 See Stevens, Franklin
Franzén, Nils-Olof 1916- 10
Frascino, Edward 193(?)-
 Brief Entry 33
Frasconi, Antonio 1919- 6
Fraser, Antonia (Pakenham) 1932-
 Brief Entry 32
Fraser, Betty
 See Fraser, Elizabeth Marr
Fraser, Elizabeth Marr 1928- 31
Fraser, Eric (George)
 1902-1983 38
Frazier, Neta Lohnes 7
Freed, Alvyn M. 1913- 22
Freedman, Benedict 1919- 27

Freedman, Nancy 1920- 27
Freedman, Russell (Bruce)
1929- 16
Freeman, Barbara C(onstance)
1906- 28
Freeman, Don 1908-1978 17
Freeman, Ira M(aximilian)
1905- 21
Freeman, Lucy (Greenbaum)
1916- 24
Freeman, Mae (Blacker)
1907- 25
Freeman, Peter J.
See Calvert, Patricia
Freeman, Tony
Brief Entry 44
Fregosi, Claudia (Anne Marie)
1946- 24
French, Allen 1870-1946 ..... *YABC 1*
French, Dorothy Kayser 1926- 5
French, Fiona 1944- 6
French, Kathryn
See Mosesson, Gloria R(ubin)
French, Michael 1944-
Brief Entry 38
French, Paul
See Asimov, Isaac
Freund, Rudolf 1915-1969
Brief Entry 28
Frewer, Glyn 1931- 11
Frick, C. H.
See Irwin, Constance Frick
Frick, Constance
See Irwin, Constance Frick
Friedlander, Joanne K(ohn)
1930- 9
Friedman, Estelle 1920- 7
Friedman, Frieda 1905- 43
Friedman, Ina R(osen) 1926-
Brief Entry 41
Friedman, Marvin 1930- 42
Brief Entry 33
Friedrich, Otto (Alva) 1929- 33
Friedrich, Priscilla 1927- 39
Friendlich, Dick
See Friendlich, Richard J.
Friendlich, Richard J. 1909- 11
Friermood, Elisabeth Hamilton
1903- 5
Friis, Babbis
See Friis-Baastad, Babbis
Friis-Baastad, Babbis
1921-1970 7
Frimmer, Steven 1928- 31
Friskey, Margaret Richards
1901- 5
Fritz, Jean (Guttery) 1915- 29
Earlier sketch in SATA 1
See also CLR 2
See also SAAS 2
Froissart, Jean
1338(?)-1410(?) 28
Froman, Elizabeth Hull
1920-1975 10
Froman, Robert (Winslow)
1917- 8
Fromm, Lilo 1928- 29
Frommer, Harvey 1937- 41

Frost, A(rthur) B(urdett)
1851-1928 19
Frost, Erica
See Supraner, Robyn
Frost, Lesley 1899(?)-1983 14
Obituary 34
Frost, Robert (Lee) 1874-1963 14
Fry, Edward Bernard 1925- 35
Fry, Rosalie 1911- 3
Fuchs, Erich 1916- 6
Fuchshuber, Annegert 1940- 43
Fujikawa, Gyo 1908- 39
Brief Entry 30
Fujita, Tamao 1905- 7
Fujiwara, Michiko 1946- 15
Fuka, Vladimir 1926-1977
Obituary 27
Fuller, Catherine L(euthold)
1916- 9
Fuller, Edmund (Maybank)
1914- 21
Fuller, Iola
See McCoy, Iola Fuller
Fuller, Lois Hamilton 1915- 11
Fuller, Margaret
See Ossoli, Sarah Margaret (Fuller)
marchesa d'
Fults, John Lee 1932- 33
Funai, Mamoru (Rolland) 1932-
Brief Entry 46
Funk, Thompson
See Funk, Tom
Funk, Tom 1911- 7
Funke, Lewis 1912- 11
Furchgott, Terry 1948- 29
Furukawa, Toshi 1924- 24
Fyleman, Rose 1877-1957 21
Fyson, J(enny) G(race) 1904- 42

G

Gackenbach, Dick
Brief Entry 30
Gaddis, Vincent H. 1913- 35
Gadler, Steve J. 1905- 36
Gaeddert, Lou Ann (Bigge)
1931- 20
Gàg, Flavia 1907-1979
Obituary 24
Gàg, Wanda (Hazel)
1893-1946 .... *YABC 1*
See also CLR 4
Gage, Wilson
See Steele, Mary Q.
Gagliardo, Ruth Garver 1895(?)-1980
Obituary 22
Gal, Laszlo 1933-
Brief Entry 32
Galdone, Paul 1914- 17
Galinsky, Ellen 1942- 23
Gallant, Roy (Arthur) 1924- 4
Gallico, Paul 1897-1976 13
Galt, Thomas Franklin, Jr.
1908- 5
Galt, Tom
See Galt, Thomas Franklin, Jr.
Gamerman, Martha 1941- 15
Gannett, Ruth Chrisman (Arens)
1896-1979 33

Gannett, Ruth Stiles 1923- 3
Gannon, Robert (Haines)
1931- 8
Gans, Roma 1894- 45
Gantos, Jack
See Gantos, John (Bryan), Jr.
Gantos, John (Bryan), Jr.
1951- 20
Garbutt, Bernard 1900-
Brief Entry 31
Gard, Joyce
See Reeves, Joyce
Gard, Robert Edward 1910- 18
Gardam, Jane 1928- 39
Brief Entry 28
Garden, Nancy 1938- 12
Gardner, Dic
See Gardner, Richard
Gardner, Jeanne LeMonnier 5
Gardner, John (Champlin, Jr.)
1933-1982 40
Obituary 31
Gardner, Martin 1914- 16
Gardner, Richard 1931- 24
Gardner, Richard A. 1931- 13
Gardner, Robert 1929-
Brief Entry 43
Gardner, Sheldon 1934- 33
Garelick, May 19
Garfield, James B. 1881-1984 6
Obituary 38
Garfield, Leon 1921- 32
Earlier sketch in SATA 1
Garis, Howard R(oger)
1873-1962 13
Garner, Alan 1934- 18
Garnett, Eve C. R. 3
Garraty, John A. 1920- 23
Garret, Maxwell R. 1917- 39
Garretson, Victoria Diane
1945- 44
Garrett, Helen 1895- 21
Garrigue, Sheila 1931- 21
Garrison, Barbara 1931- 19
Garrison, Frederick
See Sinclair, Upton (Beall)
Garrison, Webb B(lack) 1919- 25
Garst, Doris Shannon 1894- 1
Garst, Shannon
See Garst, Doris Shannon
Garthwaite, Marion H. 1893- 7
Garton, Malinda D(ean) (?)-1976
Obituary 26
Gater, Dilys 1944- 41
Gates, Doris 1901- 34
Earlier sketch in SATA 1
See also SAAS 1
Gates, Frieda 1933- 26
Gathorne-Hardy, Jonathan G.
1933- 26
Gatty, Juliana Horatia
See Ewing, Juliana (Horatia Gatty)
Gatty, Margaret Scott 1809-1873
Brief Entry 27
Gauch, Patricia Lee 1934- 26
Gault, Clare S. 1925- 36
Gault, Frank 1926-1982 36
Brief Entry 30

Gault, William Campbell
   1910- 8
Gaver, Becky
   See Gaver, Rebecca
Gaver, Rebecca 1952- 20
Gay, Francis
   See Gee, H(erbert) L(eslie)
Gay, Kathlyn 1930- 9
Gay, Zhenya 1906-1978 19
Gee, H(erbert) L(eslie) 1901-1977
   Obituary 26
Gee, Maurice (Gough) 1931- 46
Geer, Charles 1922- 42
   Brief Entry 32
Gehr, Mary 32
Geipel, Eileen 1932- 30
Geis, Darlene 7
Geisel, Helen 1898-1967 26
Geisel, Theodor Seuss 1904- 28
   Earlier sketch in SATA 1
   See also CLR 1
Geldart, William 1936- 15
Gelinas, Paul J. 1911- 10
Gelman, Steve 1934- 3
Gemming, Elizabeth 1932- 11
Gendel, Evelyn W. 1916(?)-1977
   Obituary 27
Gentleman, David 1930- 7
George, Jean Craighead 1919- 2
   See also CLR 1
George, John L(othar) 1916- 2
George, S(idney) C(harles)
   1898- 11
George, W(illiam) Lloyd 1900(?)-1975
   Obituary 30
Georgiou, Constantine 1927- 7
Gérard, Jean Ignace Isidore
   1803-1847 45
Geras, Adele (Daphne) 1944- 23
Gergely, Tibor 1900-1978
   Obituary 20
Geringer, Laura 1948- 29
Gernstein, Mordicai
   Brief Entry 36
Gerrard, Roy 1935-
   Brief Entry 45
Gerson, Corinne 37
Gerson, Noel B(ertram) 1914- 22
Gesner, Clark 1938- 40
Gessner, Lynne 1919- 16
Gewe, Raddory
   See Gorey, Edward St. John
Gibbons, Gail 1944- 23
   See also CLR 8
Gibbs, Alonzo (Lawrence)
   1915- 5
Gibbs, (Cecilia) May 1877-1969
   Obituary 27
Gibbs, Tony
   See Gibbs, Wolcott, Jr.
Gibbs, Wolcott, Jr. 1935- 40
Giblin, James Cross 1933- 33
Gibson, Josephine
   See Joslin, Sesyle
Gidal, Sonia 1922- 2
Gidal, Tim N(ahum) 1909- 2
Giegling, John A(llan) 1935- 17
Giff, Patricia Reilly 1935- 33
Gifford, Griselda 1931- 42

Gilbert, Ann
   See Taylor, Ann
Gilbert, Harriett 1948- 30
Gilbert, (Agnes) Joan (Sewell)
   1931- 10
Gilbert, John (Raphael) 1926- 36
Gilbert, Miriam
   See Presberg, Miriam Goldstein
Gilbert, Nan
   See Gilbertson, Mildred
Gilbert, Sara (Dulaney) 1943- 11
Gilbert, W(illiam) S(chwenk)
   1836-1911 36
Gilbertson, Mildred Geiger
   1908- 2
Gilbreath, Alice (Thompson)
   1921- 12
Gilbreth, Frank B., Jr. 1911- 2
Gilfond, Henry 2
Gilge, Jeanette 1924- 22
Gill, Derek L(ewis) T(heodore)
   1919- 9
Gill, Margery Jean 1925- 22
Gillett, Mary 7
Gillette, Henry Sampson
   1915- 14
Gillham, Bill
   See Gillham, William Edwin Charles
Gillham, William Edwin Charles
   1936- 42
Gilliam, Stan 1946- 39
   Brief Entry 35
Gilman, Dorothy
   See Butters, Dorothy Gilman
Gilman, Esther 1925- 15
Gilmore, Iris 1900- 22
Gilson, Barbara
   See Gilson, Charles James Louis
Gilson, Charles James Louis
   1878-1943 ....YABC 2
Gilson, Jamie 1933- 37
   Brief Entry 34
Ginsburg, Mirra 6
Giovanni, Nikki 1943- 24
   See also CLR 6
Giovanopoulos, Paul 1939- 7
Gipson, Frederick B.
   1908-1973 2
   Obituary 24
Girard, Linda Walvoord 1942- 41
Girion, Barbara 1937- 26
Gittings, Jo Manton 1919- 3
Gittings, Robert 1911- 6
Gladstone, Gary 1935- 12
Gladstone, M(yron) J. 1923- 37
Gladwin, William Zachary
   See Zollinger, Gulielma
Glanville, Brian (Lester)
   1931- 42
Glanzman, Louis S. 1922- 36
Glaser, Dianne E(lizabeth) 1937-
   Brief Entry 31
Glaser, Milton 1929- 11
Glaspell, Susan
   1882-1948 ....YABC 2
Glass, Andrew
   Brief Entry 46
Glauber, Uta (Heil) 1936- 17
Glazer, Tom 1914- 9

Gleasner, Diana (Cottle)
   1936- 29
Gleason, Judith 1929- 24
Glendinning, Richard 1917- 24
Glendinning, Sally
   See Glendinning, Sara W(ilson)
Glendinning, Sara W(ilson)
   1913- 24
Glenn, Mel 1943-
   Brief Entry 45
Gles, Margaret Breitmaier
   1940- 22
Glick, Carl (Cannon)
   1890-1971 14
Glick, Virginia Kirkus 1893-1980
   Obituary 23
Gliewe, Unada 1927- 3
Glines, Carroll V(ane), Jr.
   1920- 19
Globe, Leah Ain 1900- 41
Glovach, Linda 1947- 7
Glubok, Shirley 6
   See also CLR 1
Gluck, Felix 1924(?)-1981
   Obituary 25
Glynne-Jones, William 1907- 11
Gobbato, Imero 1923- 39
Goble, Dorothy 26
Goble, Paul 1933- 25
Goble, Warwick (?)-1943 46
Godden, Rumer 1907- 36
   Earlier sketch in SATA 3
Gode, Alexander
   See Gode von Aesch, Alexander
   (Gottfried Friedrich)
Gode von Aesch, Alexander (Gottfried
   Friedrich) 1906-1970 14
Godfrey, Jane
   See Bowden, Joan Chase
Godfrey, William
   See Youd, (Christopher) Samuel
Goettel, Elinor 1930- 12
Goetz, Delia 1898- 22
Goffstein, M(arilyn) B(rooke)
   1940- 8
   See also CLR 3
Golann, Cecil Paige 1921- 11
Golbin, Andrée 1923- 15
Gold, Phyllis 1941- 21
Gold, Sharlya 9
Goldberg, Herbert S. 1926- 25
Goldberg, Stan J. 1939- 26
Goldfeder, Cheryl
   See Pahz, Cheryl Suzanne
Goldfeder, Jim
   See Pahz, James Alon
Goldfrank, Helen Colodny
   1912- 6
Goldin, Augusta 1906- 13
Goldsborough, June 1923- 19
Goldsmith, Howard 1943- 24
Goldsmith, Oliver 1728-1774 26
Goldstein, Philip 1910- 23
Goldston, Robert (Conroy)
   1927- 6
Goll, Reinhold W(eimar)
   1897- 26
Gonzalez, Gloria 1940- 23

Goodall, John S(trickland)
1908- *4*
Goodbody, Slim
See Burstein, John
Goode, Diane 1949- *15*
Goode, Stephen 1943-
Brief Entry *40*
Goodenow, Earle 1913- *40*
Goodman, Elaine 1930- *9*
Goodman, Walter 1927- *9*
Goodrich, Samuel Griswold
1793-1860 .... *23*
Goodwin, Hal
See Goodwin, Harold Leland
Goodwin, Harold Leland
1914- *13*
Goor, Nancy (Ruth Miller)
1944- *39*
Brief Entry *34*
Goor, Ron(ald Stephen) 1940- *39*
Brief Entry *34*
Goossen, Agnes
See Epp, Margaret A(gnes)
Gordon, Bernard Ludwig
1931- *27*
Gordon, Colonel H. R.
See Ellis, Edward S(ylvester)
Gordon, Donald
See Payne, Donald Gordon
Gordon, Dorothy 1893-1970 ...... *20*
Gordon, Esther S(aranga)
1935- *10*
Gordon, Frederick [Collective
pseudonym] *1*
Gordon, Hal
See Goodwin, Harold Leland
Gordon, John 1925- *6*
Gordon, John
See Gesner, Clark
Gordon, Lew
See Baldwin, Gordon C.
Gordon, Margaret (Anna)
1939- *9*
Gordon, Mildred 1912-1979
Obituary *24*
Gordon, Selma
See Lanes, Selma G.
Gordon, Shirley 1921-
Brief Entry *41*
Gordon, Sol 1923- *11*
Gordon, Stewart
See Shirreffs, Gordon D.
Gordons, The [Joint pseudonym]
See Gordon, Mildred
Gorelick, Molly C. 1920- *9*
Gorey, Edward St. John
1925- *29*
Brief Entry *27*
Gorham, Charles Orson
1911-1975 .... *36*
Gorham, Michael
See Folsom, Franklin
Gormley, Beatrice 1942- *39*
Brief Entry *35*
Gorog, Judith (Allen) 1938- *39*
Gorsline, Douglas (Warner)
1913-1985 .... *11*
Obituary *43*
Gorsline, (Sally) Marie 1928- *28*

Gorsline, S. M.
See Gorsline, (Sally) Marie
Goryan, Sirak
See Saroyan, William
Goscinny, René 1926-1977
Brief Entry *39*
Gottlieb, Bill
See Gottlieb, William P(aul)
Gottlieb, Gerald 1923- *7*
Gottlieb, William P(aul) *24*
Goudey, Alice E. 1898- *20*
Goudge, Elizabeth 1900-1984 ..... *2*
Obituary *38*
Gough, Catherine 1931- *24*
Gough, Philip 1908- *45*
Goulart, Ron 1933- *6*
Gould, Chester 1900-1985
Obituary *43*
Gould, Jean R(osalind) 1919- *11*
Gould, Lilian 1920- *6*
Gould, Marilyn 1923- *15*
Govan, Christine Noble 1898- *9*
Govern, Elaine 1939- *26*
Graber, Alexander *7*
Graber, Richard (Fredrick)
1927- *26*
Grabiański, Janusz 1929-1976 ..... *39*
Obituary *30*
Graboff, Abner 1919- *35*
Grace, F(rances Jane) *45*
Graeber, Charlotte Towner
Brief Entry *44*
Graff, Polly Anne
See Colver, Anne
Graff, (S.) Stewart 1908- *9*
Graham, Ada 1931- *11*
Graham, Brenda Knight 1942- *32*
Graham, Charlotte
See Bowden, Joan Chase
Graham, Eleanor 1896-1984 ...... *18*
Obituary *38*
Graham, Frank, Jr. 1925- *11*
Graham, John 1926- *11*
Graham, Kennon
See Harrison, David Lee
Graham, Lorenz B(ell) 1902- *2*
See also CLR 10
Graham, Margaret Bloy 1920- *11*
Graham, Robin Lee 1949- *7*
Graham, Shirley
See Du Bois, Shirley Graham
Graham-Barber, Lynda 1944- *42*
Graham-Cameron, M(alcolm) G(ordon)
1931-
Brief Entry *45*
Graham-Cameron, Mike
See Graham-Cameron, M(alcolm)
G(ordon)
Grahame, Kenneth
1859-1932 ....*YABC 1*
See also CLR 5
Gramatky, Hardie 1907-1979 ..... *30*
Obituary *23*
Earlier sketch in SATA 1
Grand, Samuel 1912- *42*
Grandville, J. J.
See Gérard, Jean Ignace Isidore
Grandville, Jean Ignace Isidore Gérard
See Gérard, Jean Ignace Isidore

Grange, Peter
See Nicole, Christopher Robin
Granger, Margaret Jane 1925(?)-1977
Obituary *27*
Granger, Peggy
See Granger, Margaret Jane
Granstaff, Bill 1925- *10*
Grant, Bruce 1893-1977 .... *5*
Obituary *25*
Grant, Cynthia D. 1950- *33*
Grant, Eva 1907- *7*
Grant, Evva H. 1913-1977
Obituary *27*
Grant, Gordon 1875-1962 .... *25*
Grant, (Alice) Leigh 1947- *10*
Grant, Matthew C.
See May, Julian
Grant, Maxwell
See Lynds, Dennis
Grant, Myrna (Lois) 1934- *21*
Grant, Neil 1938- *14*
Gravel, Fern
See Hall, James Norman
Graves, Charles Parlin
1911-1972 .... *4*
Graves, Robert (von Ranke)
1895-1985 .... *45*
Gray, Elizabeth Janet 1902- *6*
Gray, Genevieve S. 1920- *4*
Gray, Harold (Lincoln)
1894-1968 .... *33*
Brief Entry *32*
Gray, Jenny
See Gray, Genevieve S.
Gray, Marian
See Pierce, Edith Gray
Gray, Nicholas Stuart
1922-1981 .... *4*
Obituary *27*
Gray, Nigel 1941- *33*
Gray, Patricia *7*
Gray, Patsey
See Gray, Patricia
Grayland, V. Merle
See Grayland, Valerie
Grayland, Valerie *7*
Great Comte, The
See Hawkesworth, Eric
Greaves, Margaret 1914- *7*
Grée, Alain 1936- *28*
Green, Adam
See Weisgard, Leonard
Green, D.
See Casewit, Curtis
Green, Hannah
See Greenberg, Joanne (Goldenberg)
Green, Jane 1937- *9*
Green, Mary Moore 1906- *11*
Green, Morton 1937- *8*
Green, Norma B(erger) 1925- *11*
Green, Phyllis 1932- *20*
Green, Roger (Gilbert) Lancelyn
1918- *2*
Green, Sheila Ellen 1934- *8*
Greenaway, Kate
1846-1901 ....*YABC 2*
See also CLR 6
Greenbank, Anthony Hunt
1933- *39*

Greenberg, Harvey R. 1935- 5
Greenberg, Joanne (Goldenberg)
  1932- 25
Greenberg, Polly 1932-
  Brief Entry 43
Greene, Bette 1934- 8
  See also CLR 2
Greene, Carla 1916- 1
Greene, Carol
  Brief Entry 44
Greene, Constance C(larke)
  1924- 11
Greene, Ellin 1927- 23
Greene, Graham 1904- 20
Greene, Laura 1935- 38
Greene, Wade 1933- 11
Greenfeld, Howard 19
Greenfield, Eloise 1929- 19
  See also CLR 4
Greenhaus, Thelma Nurenberg
  1903-1984 45
Greening, Hamilton
  See Hamilton, Charles H. St. John
Greenleaf, Barbara Kaye
  1942- 6
Greenleaf, Peter 1910- 33
Greenwald, Sheila
  See Green, Sheila Ellen
Gregg, Walter H(arold) 1919- 20
Gregor, Arthur 1923- 36
Gregori, Leon 1919- 15
Gregorian, Joyce Ballou
  1946- 30
Gregorowski, Christopher
  1940- 30
Gregory, Diana (Jean) 1933-
  Brief Entry 42
Gregory, Stephen
  See Penzler, Otto
Greisman, Joan Ruth 1937- 31
Grendon, Stephen
  See Derleth, August (William)
Grenville, Pelham
  See Wodehouse, P(elham)
  G(renville)
Gretz, Susanna 1937- 7
Gretzer, John 18
Grey, Jerry 1926- 11
Grey Owl
  See Belaney, Archibald Stansfeld
Gri
  See Denney, Diana
Grice, Frederick 1910- 6
Grider, Dorothy 1915- 31
Gridley, Marion E(leanor)
  1906-1974 35
  Obituary 26
Grieder, Walter 1924- 9
Griese, Arnold A(lfred) 1921- 9
Grifalconi, Ann 1929- 2
Griffin, Gillett Good 1928- 26
Griffin, Judith Berry 34
Griffith, Helen V(irginia)
  1934- 39
Griffith, Jeannette
  See Eyerly, Jeanette
Griffiths, G(ordon) D(ouglas)
  1910-1973
  Obituary 20

Griffiths, Helen 1939- 5
Grimm, Cherry Barbara Lockett 1930-
  Brief Entry 43
Grimm, Jacob Ludwig Karl
  1785-1863 22
Grimm, Wilhelm Karl
  1786-1859 22
Grimm, William C(arey)
  1907- 14
Grimshaw, Nigel (Gilroy)
  1925- 23
Grimsley, Gordon
  See Groom, Arthur William
Gringhuis, Dirk
  See Gringhuis, Richard H.
Gringhuis, Richard H.
  1918-1974 6
  Obituary 25
Grinnell, George Bird
  1849-1938 16
Gripe, Maria (Kristina) 1923- 2
  See also CLR 5
Groch, Judith (Goldstein)
  1929- 25
Grode, Redway
  See Gorey, Edward St. John
Grohskopf, Bernice 7
Grol, Lini Richards 1913- 9
Grollman, Earl A. 1925- 22
Groom, Arthur William
  1898-1964 10
Gross, Alan 1947-
  Brief Entry 43
Gross, Ruth Belov 1929- 33
Gross, Sarah Chokla
  1906-1976 9
  Obituary 26
Grossman, Nancy 1940- 29
Grossman, Robert 1940- 11
Groth, John 1908- 21
Groves, Georgina
  See Symons, (Dorothy) Geraldine
Gruelle, John (Barton)
  1880-1938 35
  Brief Entry 32
Gruelle, Johnny
  See Gruelle, John
Gruenberg, Sidonie M(atsner)
  1881-1974 2
  Obituary 27
Guck, Dorothy 1913- 27
Gugliotta, Bobette 1918- 7
Guillaume, Jeanette G. (Flierl)
  1899- 8
Guillot, Rene 1900-1969 7
Gundersheimer, Karen
  Brief Entry 44
Gundrey, Elizabeth 1924- 23
Gunn, James E(dwin) 1923- 35
Gunston, Bill
  See Gunston, William Tudor
Gunston, William Tudor
  1927- 9
Gunterman, Bertha Lisette
  1886(?)-1975
  Obituary 27
Gunther, John 1901-1970 2
Gurko, Leo 1914- 9
Gurko, Miriam 9

Gustafson, Anita 1942-
  Brief Entry 45
Gustafson, Sarah R.
  See Riedman, Sarah R.
Gustafson, Scott 1956- 34
Guthrie, Anne 1890-1979 28
Gutman, Bill
  Brief Entry 43
Gutman, Naham 1899(?)-1981
  Obituary 25
Guy, Rosa (Cuthbert) 1928- 14
Gwynne, Fred(erick Hubbard)
  1926- 41
  Brief Entry 27

H

Haas, Carolyn Buhai 1926- 43
Haas, Dorothy F. 46
  Brief Entry 43
Haas, Irene 1929- 17
Haas, James E(dward) 1943- 40
Haas, Merle S. 1896(?)-1985
  Obituary 41
Habenstreit, Barbara 1937- 5
Haber, Louis 1910- 12
Hader, Berta (Hoerner)
  1891(?)-1976 16
Hader, Elmer (Stanley)
  1889-1973 16
Hadley, Franklin
  See Winterbotham, R(ussell)
  R(obert)
Hadley, Lee 1934-
  Brief Entry 38
Hafner, Marylin 1925- 7
Hager, Alice Rogers 1894-1969
  Obituary 26
Haggard, H(enry) Rider
  1856-1925 16
Haggerty, James J(oseph)
  1920- 5
Hagon, Priscilla
  See Allan, Mabel Esther
Hague, Kathleen
  Brief Entry 45
Hague, Michael (R.)
  Brief Entry 32
Hahn, Emily 1905- 3
Hahn, Hannelore 1926- 8
Hahn, James (Sage) 1947- 9
Hahn, (Mona) Lynn 1949- 9
Hahn, Mary Downing 1937-
  Brief Entry 44
Haig-Brown, Roderick (Langmere)
  1909-1976 12
Haight, Anne Lyon 1895-1977
  Obituary 30
Haines, Gail Kay 1943- 11
Haining, Peter 1940- 14
Halacy, D(aniel) S(tephen), Jr.
  1919- 36
Haldane, Roger John 1945- 13
Hale, Edward Everett
  1822-1909 16
Hale, Helen
  See Mulcahy, Lucille Burnett
Hale, Irina 1932- 26
Hale, Kathleen 1898- 17

Hale, Linda 1929- 6
Hale, Lucretia Peabody
  1820-1900 26
Hale, Nancy 1908- 31
Haley, Gail E(inhart) 1939- 43
  Brief Entry 28
Hall, Adam
  See Trevor, Elleston
Hall, Adele 1910- 7
Hall, Anna Gertrude
  1882-1967 8
Hall, Borden
  See Yates, Raymond F(rancis)
Hall, Brian P(atrick) 1935- 31
Hall, Caryl
  See Hansen, Caryl (Hall)
Hall, Donald (Andrew, Jr.)
  1928- 23
Hall, Douglas 1931- 43
Hall, Elvajean 6
Hall, James Norman
  1887-1951 21
Hall, Jesse
  See Boesen, Victor
Hall, Lynn 1937- 2
Hall, Malcolm 1945- 7
Hall, Marjory
  See Yeakley, Marjory Hall
Hall, Rosalys Haskell 1914- 7
Hallard, Peter
  See Catherall, Arthur
Hallas, Richard
  See Knight, Eric (Mowbray)
Hall-Clarke, James
  See Rowland-Entwistle, (Arthur)
  Theodore (Henry)
Haller, Dorcas Woodbury
  1946- 46
Halliburton, Warren J. 1924- 19
Hallin, Emily Watson 1919- 6
Hallinan, P(atrick) K(enneth)
  1944- 39
  Brief Entry 37
Hallman, Ruth 1929- 43
  Brief Entry 28
Hall-Quest, Olga W(ilbourne)
  1899- 11
Hallstead, William F(inn) III
  1924- 11
Hallward, Michael 1889- 12
Halsell, Grace 1923- 13
Halsted, Anna Roosevelt 1906-1975
  Obituary 30
Halter, Jon C(harles) 1941- 22
Hamalian, Leo 1920- 41
Hamberger, John 1934- 14
Hamblin, Dora Jane 1920- 36
Hamerstrom, Frances 1907- 24
Hamil, Thomas Arthur 1928- 14
Hamil, Tom
  See Hamil, Thomas Arthur
Hamill, Ethel
  See Webb, Jean Francis (III)
Hamilton, Alice
  See Cromie, Alice Hamilton
Hamilton, Charles Harold St. John
  1875-1961 13
Hamilton, Clive
  See Lewis, C. S.

Hamilton, Dorothy 1906-1983 12
  Obituary 35
Hamilton, Edith 1867-1963 20
Hamilton, Elizabeth 1906- 23
Hamilton, Morse 1943- 35
Hamilton, Robert W.
  See Stratemeyer, Edward L.
Hamilton, Virginia 1936- 4
  See also CLR 1
Hamley, Dennis 1935- 39
Hammer, Richard 1928- 6
Hammerman, Gay M(orenus)
  1926- 9
Hammond, Winifred G(raham)
  1899- 29
Hammontree, Marie (Gertrude)
  1913- 13
Hampson, (Richard) Denman
  1929- 15
Hampson, Frank 1918(?)-1985
  Obituary 46
Hamre, Leif 1914- 5
Hamsa, Bobbie 1944-
  Brief Entry 38
Hancock, Mary A. 1923- 31
Hancock, Sibyl 1940- 9
Handforth, Thomas (Schofield)
  1897-1948 42
Handville, Robert (Tompkins)
  1924- 45
Hane, Roger 1940-1974
  Obituary 20
Haney, Lynn 1941- 23
Hanff, Helene 11
Hanlon, Emily 1945- 15
Hann, Jacquie 1951- 19
Hanna, Paul R(obert) 1902- 9
Hano, Arnold 1922- 12
Hansen, Caryl (Hall) 1929- 39
Hansen, Joyce 1942- 46
  Brief Entry 39
Hanser, Richard (Frederick)
  1909- 13
Hanson, Joan 1938- 8
Hanson, Joseph E. 1894(?)-1971
  Obituary 27
Harald, Eric
  See Boesen, Victor
Harcourt, Ellen Knowles 1890(?)-1984
  Obituary 36
Hardcastle, Michael 1933-
  Brief Entry 38
Harding, Lee 1937- 32
  Brief Entry 31
Hardwick, Richard Holmes, Jr.
  1923- 12
Hardy, Alice Dale [Collective
  pseudonym] 1
Hardy, David A(ndrews)
  1936- 9
Hardy, Stuart
  See Schisgall, Oscar
Hardy, Thomas 1840-1928 25
Hare, Norma Q(uarles) 1924- 46
  Brief Entry 41
Harford, Henry
  See Hudson, W(illiam) H(enry)
Hark, Mildred
  See McQueen, Mildred Hark

Harkaway, Hal
  See Stratemeyer, Edward L.
Harkins, Philip 1912- 6
Harlan, Elizabeth 1945- 41
  Brief Entry 35
Harlan, Glen
  See Cebulash, Mel
Harman, Fred 1902(?)-1982
  Obituary 30
Harman, Hugh 1903-1982
  Obituary 33
Harmelink, Barbara (Mary) 9
Harmer, Mabel 1894- 45
Harmon, Margaret 1906- 20
Harnan, Terry 1920- 12
Harnett, Cynthia (Mary)
  1893-1981 5
  Obituary 32
Harper, Anita 1943- 41
Harper, Mary Wood
  See Dixon, Jeanne
Harper, Wilhelmina
  1884-1973 4
  Obituary 26
Harrah, Michael 1940- 41
Harrell, Sara Gordon
  See Banks, Sara (Jeanne Gordon
  Harrell)
Harries, Joan 1922- 39
Harrington, Lyn 1911- 5
Harris, Aurand 1915- 37
Harris, Christie 1907- 6
Harris, Colver
  See Colver, Anne
Harris, Dorothy Joan 1931- 13
Harris, Janet 1932-1979 4
  Obituary 23
Harris, Joel Chandler
  1848-1908 .... *YABC 1*
Harris, Lavinia
  See Johnston, Norma
Harris, Leon A., Jr. 1926- 4
Harris, Lorle K(empe) 1912- 22
Harris, Mark Jonathan 1941- 32
Harris, Rosemary (Jeanne) 4
Harris, Sherwood 1932- 25
Harrison, C. William 1913- 35
Harrison, David Lee 1937- 26
Harrison, Deloris 1938- 9
Harrison, Harry 1925- 4
Harrison, Molly 1909- 41
Harshaw, Ruth H(etzel)
  1890-1968 27
Hart, Bruce 1938-
  Brief Entry 39
Hart, Carole 1943-
  Brief Entry 39
Harte, (Francis) Bret(t)
  1836-1902 26
Hartley, Ellen (Raphael)
  1915- 23
Hartley, Fred Allan III 1953- 41
Hartley, William B(rown)
  1913- 23
Hartman, Evert 1937- 38
  Brief Entry 35
Hartman, Louis F(rancis)
  1901-1970 22
Hartshorn, Ruth M. 1928- 11

Harvey, Edith 1908(?)-1972
  Obituary 27
Harwin, Brian
  See Henderson, LeGrand
Harwood, Pearl Augusta (Bragdon)
  1903- 9
Haseley, Dennis
  Brief Entry 44
Haskell, Arnold 1903- 6
Haskins, James 1941- 9
  See also CLR 3
Haskins, Jim
  See Haskins, James
Hasler, Joan 1931- 28
Hassall, Joan 1906- 43
Hassler, Jon (Francis) 1933- .. 19
Hatch, Mary Cottam 1912-1970
  Brief Entry 28
Hatlo, Jimmy 1898-1963
  Obituary 23
Haugaard, Erik Christian
  1923- 4
Hauman, Doris 1898- 32
Hauman, George 1890-1961 32
Hauser, Margaret L(ouise)
  1909- 10
Hausman, Gerald 1945- 13
Hausman, Gerry
  See Hausman, Gerald
Hautzig, Deborah 1956- 31
Hautzig, Esther 1930- 4
Havenhand, John
  See Cox, John Roberts
Havighurst, Walter (Edwin)
  1901- 1
Haviland, Virginia 1911- 6
Hawes, Judy 1913- 4
Hawk, Virginia Driving
  See Sneve, Virginia Driving Hawk
Hawkesworth, Eric 1921- 13
Hawkins, Arthur 1903- 19
Hawkins, Quail 1905- 6
Hawkinson, John 1912- 4
Hawkinson, Lucy (Ozone)
  1924-1971 21
Hawley, Mable C. [Collective
  pseudonym] 1
Hawthorne, Captain R. M.
  See Ellis, Edward S(ylvester)
Hawthorne, Nathaniel
  1804-1864 .... YABC 2
Hay, John 1915- 13
Hay, Timothy
  See Brown, Margaret Wise
Haycraft, Howard 1905- 6
Haycraft, Molly Costain
  1911- 6
Hayden, Gwendolen Lampshire
  1904- 35
Hayden, Robert C(arter), Jr. 1937-
  Brief Entry 28
Hayden, Robert E(arl)
  1913-1980 19
  Obituary 26
Hayes, Carlton J. H.
  1882-1964 11
Hayes, Geoffrey 1947- 26
Hayes, John F. 1904- 11
Hayes, Will 7

Hayes, William D(imitt)
  1913- 8
Haynes, Betsy 1937-
  Brief Entry 37
Hays, H(offman) R(eynolds)
  1904-1980 26
Hays, Wilma Pitchford 1909- ... 28
  Earlier sketch in SATA 1
  See also SAAS 3
Hayward, Linda 1943-
  Brief Entry 39
Haywood, Carolyn 1898- 29
  Earlier sketch in SATA 1
Hazen, Barbara Shook 1930- 27
Head, Gay
  See Hauser, Margaret L(ouise)
Headley, Elizabeth
  See Cavanna, Betty
Headstrom, Richard 1902- 8
Heady, Eleanor B(utler) 1917- .. 8
Heal, Edith 1903- 7
Healey, Brooks
  See Albert, Burton, Jr.
Healey, Larry 1927- 44
  Brief Entry 42
Heaps, Willard (Allison)
  1909- 26
Hearne, Betsy Gould 1942- 38
Heath, Charles D(ickinson)
  1941- 46
Heath, Veronica
  See Blackett, Veronica Heath
Heaven, Constance
  See Fecher, Constance
Hecht, George J(oseph) 1895-1980
  Obituary 22
Hecht, Henri Joseph 1922- 9
Hechtkopf, Henryk 1910- 17
Heck, Bessie Holland 1911- 26
Hedderwick, Mairi 1939- 30
Hedges, Sid(ney) G(eorge)
  1897-1974 28
Hefter, Richard 1942- 31
Hegarty, Reginald Beaton
  1906-1973 10
Heide, Florence Parry 1919- ... 32
Heiderstadt, Dorothy 1907- 6
Hein, Lucille Eleanor 1915- ... 20
Heinemann, George Alfred 1918-
  Brief Entry 31
Heinlein, Robert A(nson)
  1907- 9
Heins, Paul 1909- 13
Heintze, Carl 1922- 26
Heinz, W(ilfred) C(harles)
  1915- 26
Heinzen, Mildred
  See Masters, Mildred
Helfman, Elizabeth S(eaver)
  1911- 3
Helfman, Harry 1910- 3
Hellberg, Hans-Eric 1927- 38
Heller, Linda 1944- 46
  Brief Entry 40
Hellman, Hal
  See Hellman, Harold
Hellman, Harold 1927- 4
Helps, Racey 1913-1971 2
  Obituary 25

Helweg, Hans H. 1917-
  Brief Entry 33
Hemming, Roy 1928- 11
Hemphill, Martha Locke
  1904-1973 37
Henderley, Brooks [Collective
  pseudonym] 1
Henderson, LeGrand
  1901-1965 9
Henderson, Nancy Wallace
  1916- 22
Henderson, Zenna (Chlarson)
  1917- 5
Hendrickson, Walter Brookfield, Jr.
  1936- 9
Henkes, Kevin 1960- 43
Henriod, Lorraine 1925- 26
Henry, Joanne Landers 1927- 6
Henry, Marguerite 11
  See also CLR 4
Henry, O.
  See Porter, William Sydney
Henry, Oliver
  See Porter, William Sydney
Henry, T. E.
  See Rowland-Entwistle, (Arthur)
  Theodore (Henry)
Henson, James Maury 1936- 43
Henson, Jim
  See Henson, James Maury
Henstra, Friso 1928- 8
Hentoff, Nat(han Irving)
  1925- 42
  Brief Entry 27
  See also CLR 1
Herald, Kathleen
  See Peyton, Kathleen (Wendy)
Herbert, Cecil
  See Hamilton, Charles H. St. John
Herbert, Don 1917- 2
Herbert, Frank (Patrick) 1920- . 37
  Earlier sketch in SATA 9
Herbert, Wally
  See Herbert, Walter William
Herbert, Walter William
  1934- 23
Hergé
  See Rémi, Georges
  See also CLR 6
Herkimer, L(awrence) R(ussell)
  1925- 42
Herman, Charlotte 1937- 20
Hermanson, Dennis (Everett)
  1947- 10
Hermes, Patricia 1936- 31
Herriot, James
  See Wight, James Alfred
Herrmanns, Ralph 1933- 11
Herron, Edward A(lbert)
  1912- 4
Hersey, John (Richard) 1914- .. 25
Hertz, Grete Janus 1915- 23
Hess, Lilo 1916- 4
Heuer, Kenneth John 1927- 44
Heuman, William 1912-1971 21
Hewes, Agnes Danforth
  1874-1963 35
Hewett, Anita 1918- 13

Hext, Harrington
  See Phillpotts, Eden
Hey, Nigel S(tewart) 1936- 20
Heyduck-Huth, Hilde 1929- 8
Heyerdahl, Thor 1914- 2
Heyliger, William
  1884-1955 .... *YABC 1*
Heyman, Ken(neth Louis)
  1930- 34
Heyward, Du Bose 1885-1940 21
Hibbert, Christopher 1924- 4
Hibbert, Eleanor Burford
  1906- 2
Hickman, Janet 1940- 12
Hickman, Martha Whitmore
  1925- 26
Hickok, Lorena A.
  1892(?)-1968 20
Hickok, Will
  See Harrison, C. William
Hicks, Eleanor B.
  See Coerr, Eleanor
Hicks, Harvey
  See Stratemeyer, Edward L.
Hieatt, Constance B(artlett)
  1928- 4
Hiebert, Ray Eldon 1932- 13
Higdon, Hal 1931- 4
Higginbottom, J(effrey) Winslow
  1945- 29
Highet, Helen
  See MacInnes, Helen
Hightower, Florence Cole
  1916-1981 4
  Obituary 27
Highwater, Jamake 1942- 32
  Brief Entry 30
Hildebrandt, Greg 1939-
  Brief Entry 33
Hildebrandt, Tim 1939-
  Brief Entry 33
Hilder, Rowland 1905- 36
Hildick, E. W.
  See Hildick, Wallace
Hildick, (Edmund) Wallace
  1925- 2
Hill, Donna (Marie) 24
Hill, Douglas (Arthur) 1935- 39
Hill, Elizabeth Starr 1925- 24
Hill, Grace Brooks [Collective
  pseudonym] 1
Hill, Grace Livingston
  1865-1947 .... *YABC 2*
Hill, Helen M(orey) 1915- 27
Hill, Kathleen Louise 1917- 4
Hill, Kay
  See Hill, Kathleen Louise
Hill, Lorna 1902- 12
Hill, Margaret (Ohler) 1915- 36
Hill, Meg
  See Hill, Margaret (Ohler)
Hill, Monica
  See Watson, Jane Werner
Hill, Robert W(hite)
  1919-1982 12
  Obituary 31
Hill, Ruth A.
  See Viguers, Ruth Hill

Hill, Ruth Livingston
  See Munce, Ruth Hill
Hillcourt, William 1900- 27
Hillerman, Tony 1925- 6
Hillert, Margaret 1920- 8
Hillman, Martin
  See Hill, Douglas (Arthur)
Hillman, Priscilla 1940-
  Brief Entry 39
Hills, C(harles) A(lbert) R(eis)
  1955- 39
Hilton, Irene (P.) 1912- 7
Hilton, James 1900-1954 34
Hilton, Ralph 1907- 8
Hilton, Suzanne 1922- 4
Him, George 1900-1982
  Obituary 30
Himler, Ann 1946- 8
Himler, Ronald 1937- 6
Hinckley, Helen
  See Jones, Helen Hinckley
Hines, Anna G(rossnickle) 1946-
  Brief Entry 45
Hinton, S(usan) E(loise)
  1950- 19
  See also CLR 3
Hinton, Sam 1917- 43
Hintz, (Loren) Martin 1945-
  Brief Entry 39
Hirsch, Phil 1926- 35
Hirsch, S. Carl 1913- 2
Hirschmann, Linda (Ann)
  1941- 40
Hirsh, Marilyn 1944- 7
Hirshberg, Al(bert Simon)
  1909-1973 38
Hiser, Iona Seibert 1901- 4
Hitchcock, Alfred (Joseph)
  1899-1980 27
  Obituary 24
Hitte, Kathryn 1919- 16
Hitz, Demi 1942- 11
Hnizdovsky, Jacques 1915- 32
Ho, Minfong 1951- 15
Hoare, Robert J(ohn)
  1921-1975 38
Hoban, Lillian 1925- 22
Hoban, Russell C(onwell)
  1925- 40
  Earlier sketch in SATA 1
  See also CLR 3
Hoban, Tana 22
Hobart, Lois 7
Hoberman, Mary Ann 1930- 5
Hobson, Burton (Harold)
  1933- 28
Hochschild, Arlie Russell
  1940- 11
Hockaby, Stephen
  See Mitchell, Gladys (Maude
  Winifred)
Hockenberry, Hope
  See Newell, Hope (Hockenberry)
Hodge, P(aul) W(illiam)
  1934- 12
Hodgell, P(atricia) C(hristine)
  1951- 42
Hodges, C(yril) Walter 1909- 2
Hodges, Carl G. 1902-1964 10

Hodges, Elizabeth Jamison 1
Hodges, Margaret Moore
  1911- 33
  Earlier sketch in SATA 1
Hodgetts, Blake Christopher
  1967- 43
Hoexter, Corinne K. 1927- 6
Hoff, Carol 1900- 11
Hoff, Syd(ney) 1912- 9
Hoffman, Phyllis M. 1944- 4
Hoffman, Rosekrans 1926- 15
Hoffmann, E(rnst) T(heodor)
  A(madeus) 1776-1822 27
Hoffmann, Felix 1911-1975 9
Hofsinde, Robert 1902-1973 21
Hogan, Bernice Harris 1929- 12
Hogan, Inez 1895- 2
Hogarth, Jr.
  See Kent, Rockwell
Hogarth, Paul 1917- 41
Hogg, Garry 1902- 2
Hogner, Dorothy Childs 4
Hogner, Nils 1893-1970 25
Hogrogian, Nonny 1932- 7
  See also CLR 2
  See also SAAS 1
Hoke, Helen (L.) 1903- 15
Hoke, John 1925- 7
Holbeach, Henry
  See Rands, William Brighty
Holberg, Ruth Langland
  1889- 1
Holbrook, Peter
  See Glick, Carl (Cannon)
Holbrook, Sabra
  See Erickson, Sabra R(ollins)
Holbrook, Stewart Hall
  1893-1964 2
Holden, Elizabeth Rhoda
  See Lawrence, Louise
Holding, James 1907- 3
Holisher, Desider 1901-1972 6
Holl, Adelaide (Hinkle) 8
Holland, Isabelle 1920- 8
Holland, Janice 1913-1962 18
Holland, John L(ewis) 1919- 20
Holland, Lys
  See Gater, Dilys
Holland, Marion 1908- 6
Hollander, John 1929- 13
Hollander, Phyllis 1928- 39
Holldobler, Turid 1939- 26
Holliday, Joe
  See Holliday, Joseph
Holliday, Joseph 1910- 11
Holling, Holling C(lancy)
  1900-1973 15
  Obituary 26
Hollingsworth, Alvin C(arl)
  1930- 39
Holloway, Teresa (Bragunier)
  1906- 26
Holm, (Else) Anne (Lise)
  1922- 1
Holman, Felice 1919- 7
Holme, Bryan 1913- 26
Holmes, Marjorie 1910- 43
Holmes, Oliver Wendell
  1809-1894 34

Holmes, Rick
  See Hardwick, Richard Holmes, Jr.
Holmgren, George Ellen
  See Holmgren, Helen Jean
Holmgren, Helen Jean 1930- *45*
Holmgren, Virginia C(unningham)
  1909- *26*
Holmquist, Eve 1921- *11*
Holt, Margaret 1937- *4*
Holt, Margaret Van Vechten
  (Saunders) 1899-1963 .... *32*
Holt, Michael (Paul) 1929- *13*
Holt, Rackham
  See Holt, Margaret Van Vechten
  (Saunders)
Holt, Rochelle Lynn 1946- *41*
Holt, Stephen
  See Thompson, Harlan H.
Holt, Victoria
  See Hibbert, Eleanor
Holton, Leonard
  See Wibberley, Leonard (Patrick
  O'Connor)
Holyer, Erna Maria 1925- *22*
Holyer, Ernie
  See Holyer, Erna Maria
Holz, Loretta (Marie) 1943- *17*
Homze, Alma C. 1932- *17*
Honig, Donald 1931- *18*
Honness, Elizabeth H. 1904- *2*
Hoobler, Dorothy *28*
Hoobler, Thomas *28*
Hood, Joseph F. 1925- *4*
Hood, Robert E. 1926- *21*
Hook, Frances 1912- *27*
Hook, Martha 1936- *27*
Hooker, Ruth 1920- *21*
Hooks, William H(arris)
  1921- *16*
Hooper, Byrd
  See St. Clair, Byrd Hooper
Hooper, Meredith (Jean)
  1939- *28*
Hoopes, Lyn Littlefield 1953-
  Brief Entry *44*
Hoopes, Ned E(dward) 1932- *21*
Hoopes, Roy 1922- *11*
Hoople, Cheryl G.
  Brief Entry *32*
Hoover, H(elen) M(ary) 1935- *44*
  Brief Entry *33*
Hoover, Helen (Drusilla Blackburn)
  1910-1984 .... *12*
  Obituary *39*
Hope, Laura Lee [Collective
  pseudonym] *1*
  See also Adams, Harriet
  S(tratemeyer)
Hope Simpson, Jacynth 1930- *12*
Hopf, Alice L(ightner) 1904- *5*
Hopkins, A. T.
  See Turngren, Annette
Hopkins, Clark 1895-1976
  Obituary *34*
Hopkins, Joseph G(erard) E(dward)
  1909- *11*
Hopkins, Lee Bennett 1938- *3*
Hopkins, Lyman
  See Folsom, Franklin

Hopkins, Marjorie 1911- *9*
Hoppe, Joanne 1932- *42*
Hopper, Nancy J. 1937- *38*
  Brief Entry *35*
Horgan, Paul 1903- *13*
Hornblow, Arthur (Jr.)
  1893-1976 .... *15*
Hornblow, Leonora (Schinasi)
  1920- *18*
Horne, Richard Henry
  1803-1884 .... *29*
Horner, Althea (Jane) 1926- *36*
Horner, Dave 1934- *12*
Hornos, Axel 1907- *20*
Horvath, Betty 1927- *4*
Horwich, Frances R(appaport)
  1908- *11*
Horwitz, Elinor Lander *45*
  Brief Entry *33*
Hosford, Dorothy (Grant)
  1900-1952 .... *22*
Hosford, Jessie 1892- *5*
Hoskyns-Abrahall, Clare *13*
Houck, Carter 1924- *22*
Hough, (Helen) Charlotte
  1924- *9*
Hough, Richard (Alexander)
  1922- *17*
Houghton, Eric 1930- *7*
Houlehen, Robert J. 1918- *18*
Household, Geoffrey (Edward West)
  1900- *14*
Houselander, (Frances) Caryll
  1900-1954
  Brief Entry *31*
Housman, Laurence
  1865-1959 .... *25*
Houston, James A(rchibald)
  1921- *13*
  See also CLR 3
Houton, Kathleen
  See Kilgore, Kathleen
Howard, Alan 1922- *45*
Howard, Elizabeth
  See Mizner, Elizabeth Howard
Howard, Prosper
  See Hamilton, Charles H. St. John
Howard, Robert West 1908- *5*
Howard, Vernon (Linwood)
  1918- *40*
Howarth, David 1912- *6*
Howe, Deborah 1946-1978 .... *29*
Howe, James 1946- *29*
  See also CLR 9
Howell, Pat 1947- *15*
Howell, S.
  See Styles, Frank Showell
Howell, Virginia Tier
  See Ellison, Virginia Howell
Howes, Barbara 1914- *5*
Howker, Janni
  Brief Entry *46*
Hoy, Nina
  See Roth, Arthur J(oseph)
Hoyle, Geoffrey 1942- *18*
Hoyt, Edwin P(almer), Jr.
  1923- *28*
Hoyt, Olga (Gruhzit) 1922- *16*
Hubbell, Patricia 1928- *8*

Hubley, John 1914-1977
  Obituary *24*
Hudson, Jeffrey
  See Crichton, (J.) Michael
Hudson, (Margaret) Kirsty
  1947- *32*
Hudson, W(illiam) H(enry)
  1841-1922 .... *35*
Huffaker, Sandy 1943- *10*
Huffman, Tom *24*
Hughes, Dean 1943- *33*
Hughes, (James) Langston
  1902-1967 .... *33*
  Earlier sketch in SATA 4
Hughes, Matilda
  See MacLeod, Charlotte (Matilda
  Hughes)
Hughes, Monica 1925- *15*
  See also CLR 9
Hughes, Richard (Arthur Warren)
  1900-1976 .... *8*
  Obituary *25*
Hughes, Sara
  See Saunders, Susan
Hughes, Shirley 1929- *16*
Hughes, Ted 1930-
  Brief Entry *27*
  See also CLR 3
Hughes, Thomas 1822-1896 .... *31*
Hughes, Walter (Llewellyn)
  1910- *26*
Huline-Dickens, Frank William
  1931- *34*
Hull, Eleanor (Means) 1913- *21*
Hull, Eric Traviss
  See Harnan, Terry
Hull, H. Braxton
  See Jacobs, Helen Hull
Hull, Katharine 1921-1977 .... *23*
Hülsmann, Eva 1928- *16*
Hults, Dorothy Niebrugge
  1898- *6*
Hume, Lotta Carswell *7*
Hume, Ruth (Fox) 1922-1980 ..... *26*
  Obituary *22*
Hummel, Berta 1909-1946 .... *43*
Hummel, Sister Maria Innocentia
  See Hummel, Berta
Humphrey, Henry (III) 1930- *16*
Humphreys, Graham 1945-
  Brief Entry *32*
Hungerford, Pixie
  See Brinsmead, H(esba) F(ay)
Hunt, Francis
  See Stratemeyer, Edward L.
Hunt, Irene 1907- *2*
  See also CLR 1
Hunt, Joyce 1927- *31*
Hunt, Linda Lawrence 1940- *39*
Hunt, Mabel Leigh 1892-1971 .... *1*
  Obituary *26*
Hunt, Morton 1920- *22*
Hunt, Nigel
  See Greenbank, Anthony Hunt
Hunter, Bernice Thurman 1922-
  Brief Entry *45*
Hunter, Clingham, M.D.
  See Adams, William Taylor

Hunter, Dawe
  See Downie, Mary Alice
Hunter, Edith Fisher 1919- *31*
Hunter, Evan 1926- 25
Hunter, Hilda 1921- 7
Hunter, Kristin (Eggleston)
  1931- *12*
  See also CLR 3
Hunter, Leigh
  See Etchison, Birdie L(ee)
Hunter, Mel 1927- 39
Hunter, Mollie
  See McIllwraith, Maureen
Hunter, Norman (George Lorimer)
  1899- 26
Hunter Blair, Pauline 1921- 3
Huntington, Harriet E(lizabeth)
  1909- *1*
Huntsberry, William E(mery)
  1916- 5
Hurd, Clement 1908- 2
Hurd, Edith Thacher 1910- 2
Hurd, Thacher 1949- 46
  Brief Entry 45
Hürlimann, Bettina 1909-1983 39
  Obituary 34
Hürlimann, Ruth 1939- 32
  Brief Entry 31
Hurwitz, Johanna 1937- 20
Hurwood, Bernhardt J. 1926- 12
Hutchens, Paul 1902-1977 .... *31*
Hutchins, Carleen Maley
  1911- 9
Hutchins, Pat 1942- *15*
Hutchins, Ross E(lliott) 1906- 4
Hutchmacher, J. Joseph 1929- 5
Hutto, Nelson (Allen) 1904- 20
Hutton, Warwick 1939- 20
Hyde, Dayton O(gden) 9
Hyde, Hawk
  See Hyde, Dayton O(gden)
Hyde, Margaret Oldroyd
  1917- *42*
  Earlier sketch in SATA 1
Hyde, Shelley
  See Reed, Kit
Hyde, Wayne F. 1922- 7
Hylander, Clarence J.
  1897-1964 7
Hyman, Robin P(hilip) 1931- *12*
Hyman, Trina Schart 1939- 46
  Earlier sketch in SATA 7
Hymes, Lucia M. 1907- 7
Hyndman, Jane Andrews
  1912-1978 46
  Obituary 23
  Earlier sketch in SATA 1
Hyndman, Robert Utley
  1906(?)-1973 18

I

Iannone, Jeanne 7
Ibbotson, Eva 1925- 13
Ibbotson, M. C(hristine)
  1930- 5
Ichikawa, Satomi
  Brief Entry 36
Ilowite, Sheldon A. 1931- 27

Ilsley, Dent [Joint pseudonym]
  See Chapman, John Stanton Higham
Ilsley, Velma (Elizabeth)
  1918- *12*
Immel, Mary Blair 1930- 28
Ingelow, Jean 1820-1897 .... *33*
Ingham, Colonel Frederic
  See Hale, Edward Everett
Ingraham, Leonard W(illiam)
  1913- *4*
Ingrams, Doreen 1906- 20
Inyart, Gene 1927- 6
Ionesco, Eugene 1912- 7
Ipcar, Dahlov (Zorach) 1917- *1*
Irvin, Fred 1914- 15
Irving, Alexander
  See Hume, Ruth (Fox)
Irving, Robert
  See Adler, Irving
Irving, Washington
  1783-1859 ....*YABC 2*
Irwin, Ann(abelle Bowen)
  1915- 44
  Brief Entry 38
Irwin, Constance Frick 1913- 6
Irwin, Hadley [Joint pseudonym]
  See Hadley, Lee and Irwin, Ann
Irwin, Keith Gordon
  1885-1964 11
Isaac, Joanne 1934- 21
Isaacs, Jacob
  See Kranzler, George G(ershon)
Isadora, Rachel 1953(?)-
  Brief Entry 32
  See also CLR 7
Isham, Charlotte H(ickox)
  1912- 21
Ish-Kishor, Judith 1892-1972 11
Ish-Kishor, Sulamith
  1896-1977 17
Ishmael, Woodi 1914- 31
Israel, Elaine 1945- 12
Israel, Marion Louise 1882-1973
  Obituary 26
Iwamatsu, Jun Atsushi 1908- 14

J

Jac, Lee
  See Morton, Lee Jack, Jr.
Jackson, Anne 1896(?)-1984
  Obituary 37
Jackson, C. Paul 1902- 6
Jackson, Caary
  See Jackson, C. Paul
Jackson, Jesse 1908- 29
  Earlier sketch in SATA 2
Jackson, O. B.
  See Jackson, C. Paul
Jackson, Robert B(lake) 1926- 8
Jackson, Sally
  See Kellogg, Jean
Jackson, Shirley 1919-1965 2
Jacob, Helen Pierce 1927- 21
Jacobi, Kathy
  Brief Entry 42
Jacobs, Flora Gill 1918- 5
Jacobs, Francine 1935- 43
  Brief Entry 42

Jacobs, Frank 1929- 30
Jacobs, Helen Hull 1908- 12
Jacobs, Joseph 1854-1916 25
Jacobs, Leland Blair 1907- 20
Jacobs, Linda C. 1943- *21*
Jacobs, Lou(is), Jr. 1921- 2
Jacobs, Susan 1940- 30
Jacobs, William Jay 1933- 28
Jacobson, Daniel 1923- *12*
Jacobson, Morris K(arl) 1906- *21*
Jacopetti, Alexandra 1939- *14*
Jacques, Robin 1920- 32
  Brief Entry 30
Jaffee, Al(lan) 1921-
  Brief Entry 37
Jagendorf, Moritz (Adolf)
  1888-1981 2
  Obituary 24
Jahn, (Joseph) Michael 1943- 28
Jahn, Mike
  See Jahn, (Joseph) Michael
Jahsmann, Allan Hart 1916- 28
James, Andrew
  See Kirkup, James
James, Dynely
  See Mayne, William
James, Edwin
  See Gunn, James E(dwin)
James, Harry Clebourne 1896- *11*
James, Josephine
  See Sterne, Emma Gelders
James, T. F.
  See Fleming, Thomas J(ames)
James, Will(iam Roderick)
  1892-1942 .... *19*
Jane, Mary Childs 1909- 6
Janes, Edward C. 1908- 25
Janeway, Elizabeth (Hall)
  1913- *19*
Janice
  See Brustlein, Janice Tworkov
Janosch
  See Eckert, Horst
Jansen, Jared
  See Cebulash, Mel
Janson, Dora Jane 1916- *31*
Janson, H(orst) W(oldemar)
  1913- 9
Jansson, Tove (Marika) 1914- *41*
  Earlier sketch in SATA 3
  See also CLR 2
Janus, Grete
  See Hertz, Grete Janus
Jaques, Faith 1923- *21*
Jaques, Francis Lee 1887-1969
  Brief Entry 28
Jarman, Rosemary Hawley
  1935- 7
Jarrell, Mary von Schrader
  1914- 35
Jarrell, Randall 1914-1965 7
  See also CLR 6
Jauss, Anne Marie 1907- 10
Jayne, Lieutenant R. H.
  See Ellis, Edward S(ylvester)
Jaynes, Clare [Joint pseudonym]
  See Mayer, Jane Rothschild
Jeake, Samuel, Jr.
  See Aiken, Conrad

Jefferies, (John) Richard
1848-1887 .... *16*
Jeffers, Susan *17*
Jefferson, Sarah
See Farjeon, Annabel
Jeffries, Roderic 1926- *4*
Jenkins, Marie M. 1909- *7*
Jenkins, William A(twell)
1922- *9*
Jennings, Gary (Gayne) 1928- *9*
Jennings, Robert
See Hamilton, Charles H. St. John
Jennings, S. M.
See Meyer, Jerome Sydney
Jennison, C. S.
See Starbird, Kaye
Jennison, Keith Warren 1911- *14*
Jensen, Niels 1927- *25*
Jensen, Virginia Allen 1927- *8*
Jeppson, J(anet) O(pal) 1926-
Brief Entry *46*
Jeschke, Susan *42*
Brief Entry *27*
Jessel, Camilla (Ruth) 1937- *29*
Jewell, Nancy 1940-
Brief Entry *41*
Jewett, Eleanore Myers
1890-1967 .... *5*
Jewett, Sarah Orne 1849-1909 .... *15*
Jezard, Alison 1919-
Brief Entry *34*
Jiler, John 1946- *42*
Brief Entry *35*
Jobb, Jamie 1945- *29*
Joerns, Consuelo *44*
Brief Entry *33*
John, Naomi
See Flack, Naomi John (White)
Johns, Avery
See Cousins, Margaret
Johnson, A. E. [Joint pseudonym]
See Johnson, Annabell and Johnson, Edgar
Johnson, Annabell Jones
1921- *2*
Johnson, Benj. F., of Boone
See Riley, James Whitcomb
Johnson, Charles R. 1925- *11*
Johnson, Charlotte Buel
1918-1982 .... *46*
Johnson, Chuck
See Johnson, Charles R.
Johnson, Crockett
See Leisk, David (Johnson)
Johnson, D(ana) William
1945- *23*
Johnson, Dorothy M(arie)
1905-1984 .... *6*
Obituary *40*
Johnson, E(ugene) Harper *44*
Johnson, Edgar Raymond
1912- *2*
Johnson, Elizabeth 1911-1984 ..... *7*
Obituary *39*
Johnson, Eric W(arner) 1918- *8*
Johnson, Evelyne 1932- *20*
Johnson, Gaylord 1884- *7*

Johnson, Gerald White
1890-1980 .... *19*
Obituary *28*
Johnson, Harper
See Johnson, E(ugene) Harper
Johnson, James Ralph 1922- *1*
Johnson, James Weldon
See Johnson, James William
Johnson, James William
1871-1938 .... *31*
Johnson, John E(mil) 1929- *34*
Johnson, LaVerne B(ravo)
1925- *13*
Johnson, Lois S(mith) *6*
Johnson, Lois W(alfrid) 1936- *22*
Johnson, Margaret S(weet)
1893-1964 .... *35*
Johnson, Mary Frances K.
1929(?)-1979
Obituary *27*
Johnson, Maud Battle 1918(?)-1985
Obituary *46*
Johnson, Milton 1932- *31*
Johnson, Natalie
See Robison, Nancy L(ouise)
Johnson, (Walter) Ryerson
1901- *10*
Johnson, Shirley K(ing) 1927- *10*
Johnson, Siddie Joe 1905-1977
Obituary *20*
Johnson, Spencer 1938-
Brief Entry *38*
Johnson, William R. *38*
Johnson, William Weber
1909- *7*
Johnston, Agnes Christine
See Dazey, Agnes J.
Johnston, Annie Fellows
1863-1931 .... *37*
Johnston, H(ugh) A(nthony) S(tephen)
1913-1967 .... *14*
Johnston, Johanna
1914(?)-1982 .... *12*
Obituary *33*
Johnston, Norma *29*
Johnston, Portia
See Takakjian, Portia
Johnston, Tony 1942- *8*
Jonas, Ann
Brief Entry *42*
Jones, Adrienne 1915- *7*
Jones, Diana Wynne 1934- *9*
Jones, Elizabeth Orton 1910- *18*
Jones, Evan 1915- *3*
Jones, Geraldine 1951- *43*
Jones, Gillingham
See Hamilton, Charles H. St. John
Jones, Harold 1904- *14*
Jones, Helen Hinckley 1903- *26*
Jones, Helen L. 1904(?)-1973
Obituary *22*
Jones, Hettie 1934- *42*
Brief Entry *27*
Jones, Hortense P. 1918- *9*
Jones, Jessie Mae Orton 1887(?)-1983
Obituary *37*
Jones, Margaret Boone
See Zarif, Margaret Min'imah
Jones, Mary Alice *6*

Jones, McClure *34*
Jones, Penelope 1938- *31*
Jones, Rebecca C(astaldi)
1947- *33*
Jones, Weyman 1928- *4*
Jonk, Clarence 1906- *10*
Jordan, Don
See Howard, Vernon (Linwood)
Jordan, E(mil) L(eopold) 1900-
Brief Entry *31*
Jordan, Hope (Dahle) 1905- *15*
Jordan, Jael (Michal) 1949- *30*
Jordan, June 1936- *4*
See also CLR 10
Jordan, Mildred 1901- *5*
Jorgensen, Mary Venn *36*
Jorgenson, Ivar
See Silverberg, Robert
Joseph, Joan 1939- *34*
Joseph, Joseph M(aron)
1903-1979 .... *22*
Joslin, Sesyle 1929- *2*
Joyce, J(ames) Avery *11*
Joyce, William 1959(?)-
Brief Entry *46*
Joyner, Jerry 1938- *34*
Jucker, Sita 1921- *5*
Judd, Denis (O'Nan) 1938- *33*
Judd, Frances K. [Collective
pseudonym] *1*
Judson, Clara Ingram
1879-1960 .... *38*
Brief Entry *27*
Jukes, Mavis
Brief Entry *43*
Jumpp, Hugo
See MacPeek, Walter G.
Jupo, Frank J. 1904- *7*
Juster, Norton 1929- *3*
Justus, May 1898- *1*
Juvenilia
See Taylor, Ann

K

Kabdebo, Tamas
See Kabdebo, Thomas
Kabdebo, Thomas 1934- *10*
Kabibble, Osh
See Jobb, Jamie
Kadesch, Robert R(udstone)
1922- *31*
Kahl, M(arvin) P(hilip) 1934- *37*
Kahl, Virginia (Caroline) 1919-
Brief Entry *38*
Kahn, Roger 1927- *37*
Kakimoto, Kozo 1915- *11*
Kalashnikoff, Nicholas
1888-1961 .... *16*
Kalb, Jonah 1926- *23*
Kaler, James Otis 1848-1912 ..... *15*
Kalnay, Francis 1899- *7*
Kalow, Gisela 1946- *32*
Kamen, Gloria 1923- *9*
Kamerman, Sylvia E.
See Burack, Sylvia K.
Kamm, Josephine (Hart)
1905- *24*
Kandell, Alice S. 1938- *35*

Kane, Henry Bugbee
  1902-1971 .... *14*
Kane, Robert W. 1910- *18*
Kanetzke, Howard W(illiam)
  1932- *38*
Kanzawa, Toshiko
  See Furukawa, Toshi
Kaplan, Anne Bernays 1930- *32*
Kaplan, Bess 1927- *22*
Kaplan, Boche 1926- *24*
Kaplan, Irma 1900- *10*
Kaplan, Jean Caryl Korn
  1926- *10*
Karageorge, Michael
  See Anderson, Poul (William)
Karasz, Ilonka 1896-1981
  Obituary *29*
Karen, Ruth 1922- *9*
Kark, Nina Mary 1925- *4*
Karl, Jean E(dna) 1927- *34*
Karlin, Eugene 1918- *10*
Karp, Naomi J. 1926- *16*
Kashiwagi, Isami 1925- *10*
Kästner, Erich 1899-1974 .... *14*
  See also CLR 4
Katchen, Carole 1944- *9*
Kathryn
  See Searle, Kathryn Adrienne
Katona, Robert 1949- *21*
Katsarakis, Joan Harries
  See Harries, Joan
Katz, Bobbi 1933- *12*
Katz, Fred 1938- *6*
Katz, Jane 1934- *33*
Katz, Marjorie P.
  See Weiser, Marjorie P(hillis) K(atz)
Katz, William Loren 1927- *13*
Kaufman, Joe 1911- *33*
Kaufman, Mervyn D. 1932- *4*
Kaufmann, Angelika 1935- *15*
Kaufmann, John 1931- *18*
Kaula, Edna Mason 1906- *13*
Kavaler, Lucy 1930- *23*
Kay, Helen
  See Goldfrank, Helen Colodny
Kay, Mara *13*
Kaye, Geraldine 1925- *10*
Keane, Bil 1922- *4*
Keating, Bern
  See Keating, Leo Bernard
Keating, Lawrence A.
  1903-1966 .... *23*
Keating, Leo Bernard 1915- *10*
Keats, Ezra Jack 1916-1983 ...... *14*
  Obituary *34*
  See also CLR 1
Keegan, Marcia 1943- *9*
Keen, Martin L. 1913- *4*
Keene, Carolyn [Collective
  pseudonym]
  See Adams, Harriet S.
Keeping, Charles (William James)
  1924- *9*
Keeshan, Robert J. 1927- *32*
Keir, Christine
  See Pullein-Thompson, Christine
Keith, Carlton
  See Robertson, Keith
Keith, Hal 1934- *36*

Keith, Harold (Verne) 1903- *2*
Keith, Robert
  See Applebaum, Stan
Kelen, Emery 1896-1978 .... *13*
  Obituary *26*
Kelleam, Joseph E(veridge)
  1913-1975 .... *31*
Keller, B(everly) L(ou) *13*
Keller, Charles 1942- *8*
Keller, Dick 1923- *36*
Keller, Gail Faithfull
  See Faithfull, Gail
Keller, Holly
  Brief Entry *42*
Keller, Irene (Barron) 1927- *36*
Kelley, Leo P(atrick) 1928- *32*
  Brief Entry *31*
Kelley, True Adelaide 1946- *41*
  Brief Entry *39*
Kellin, Sally Moffet 1932- *9*
Kelling, Furn L. 1914- *37*
Kellogg, Gene
  See Kellogg, Jean
Kellogg, Jean 1916- *10*
Kellogg, Steven 1941- *8*
  See also CLR 6
Kellow, Kathleen
  See Hibbert, Eleanor
Kelly, Eric P(hilbrook)
  1884-1960 .... *YABC 1*
Kelly, Martha Rose
  1914-1983 .... *37*
Kelly, Marty
  See Kelly, Martha Rose
Kelly, Ralph
  See Geis, Darlene
Kelly, Regina Z. *5*
Kelly, Rosalie (Ruth) *43*
Kelly, Walt(er Crawford)
  1913-1973 .... *18*
Kelsey, Alice Geer 1896- *1*
Kemp, Gene 1926- *25*
Kempner, Mary Jean
  1913-1969 .... *10*
Kempton, Jean Welch 1914- *10*
Kendall, Carol (Seeger) 1917- ... *11*
Kendall, Lace
  See Stoutenburg, Adrien
Kenealy, James P. 1927-
  Brief Entry *29*
Kenealy, Jim
  See Kenealy, James P.
Kennedy, John Fitzgerald
  1917-1963 .... *11*
Kennedy, Joseph 1929- *14*
Kennedy, Paul E(dward)
  1929- *33*
Kennedy, (Jerome) Richard
  1932- *22*
Kennedy, T(eresa) A. 1953- *42*
  Brief Entry *35*
Kennedy, X. J.
  See Kennedy, Joseph
Kennell, Ruth E(pperson)
  1893-1977 .... *6*
  Obituary *25*
Kenny, Ellsworth Newcomb
  1909-1971
  Obituary *26*

Kenny, Herbert A(ndrew)
  1912- *13*
Kenny, Kathryn
  See Bowden, Joan Chase
  See Krull, Kathleen
Kenny, Kevin
  See Krull, Kathleen
Kent, Alexander
  See Reeman, Douglas Edward
Kent, Deborah Ann 1948-
  Brief Entry *41*
Kent, Jack
  See Kent, John Wellington
Kent, John Wellington
  1920-1985 .... *24*
  Obituary *45*
Kent, Margaret 1894- *2*
Kent, Rockwell 1882-1971 .... *6*
Kent, Sherman 1903- *20*
Kenward, Jean 1920- *42*
Kenworthy, Leonard S. 1912- *6*
Kenyon, Ley 1913- *6*
Kepes, Juliet A(ppleby) 1919- ... *13*
Kerigan, Florence 1896- *12*
Kerman, Gertrude Lerner
  1909- *21*
Kerr, Jessica 1901- *13*
Kerr, (Anne) Judith 1923- *24*
Kerr, M. E.
  See Meaker, Marijane
  See also SAAS 1
Kerry, Frances
  See Kerigan, Florence
Kerry, Lois
  See Duncan, Lois S(teinmetz)
Ker Wilson, Barbara 1929- *20*
Kessel, Joyce Karen 1937- *41*
Kessler, Ethel 1922- *44*
  Brief Entry *37*
Kessler, Leonard P. 1921- *14*
Kesteven, G. R.
  See Crosher, G(eoffry) R(obins)
Ketcham, Hank
  See Ketcham, Henry King
Ketcham, Henry King 1920- *28*
  Brief Entry *27*
Kettelkamp, Larry 1933- *2*
  See also SAAS 3
Kevles, Bettyann 1938- *23*
Key, Alexander (Hill)
  1904-1979 .... *8*
  Obituary *23*
Keyes, Daniel 1927- *37*
Keyes, Fenton 1915- *34*
Keyser, Marcia 1933- *42*
Keyser, Sarah
  See McGuire, Leslie (Sarah)
Khanshendel, Chiron
  See Rose, Wendy
Kherdian, David 1931- *16*
Kidd, Ronald 1948- *42*
Kiddell, John 1922- *3*
Kidwell, Carl 1910- *43*
Kiefer, Irene 1926- *21*
Kiesel, Stanley 1925- *35*
Kikukawa, Cecily H. 1919- *44*
  Brief Entry *35*
Kilgore, Kathleen 1946- *42*
Kilian, Crawford 1941- *35*

Killilea, Marie (Lyons) 1913- 2
Kilreon, Beth
  See Walker, Barbara K.
Kimball, Yeffe 1914-1978 37
Kimbrough, Emily 1899- 2
Kimmel, Eric A. 1946- 13
Kimmel, Margaret Mary
  1938- 43
  Brief Entry 33
Kindred, Wendy 1937- 7
Kines, Pat Decker 1937- 12
King, Adam
  See Hoare, Robert J(ohn)
King, Arthur
  See Cain, Arthur H.
King, Billie Jean 1943- 12
King, (David) Clive 1924- 28
King, Cynthia 1925- 7
King, Frank O. 1883-1969
  Obituary 22
King, Marian 23
King, Martin
  See Marks, Stan(ley)
King, Martin Luther, Jr.
  1929-1968 14
King, Reefe
  See Barker, Albert W.
King, Stephen 1947- 9
King, Tony 1947- 39
Kingman, Dong (Moy Shu)
  1911- 44
Kingman, (Mary) Lee 1919- 1
  See also SAAS 3
Kingsland, Leslie William
  1912- 13
Kingsley, Charles
  1819-1875 .... YABC 2
Kingsley, Emily Perl 1940- 33
King-Smith, Dick 1922-
  Brief Entry 38
Kinney, C. Cle 1915- 6
Kinney, Harrison 1921- 13
Kinney, Jean Stout 1912- 12
Kinsey, Elizabeth
  See Clymer, Eleanor
Kipling, (Joseph) Rudyard
  1865-1936 .... YABC 2
Kirk, Ruth (Kratz) 1925- 5
Kirkup, James 1927- 12
Kirkus, Virginia
  See Glick, Virginia Kirkus
Kirtland, G. B.
  See Joslin, Sesyle
Kishida, Eriko 1929- 12
Kisinger, Grace Gelvin
  1913-1965 10
Kissin, Eva H. 1923- 10
Kjelgaard, James Arthur
  1910-1959 17
Kjelgaard, Jim
  See Kjelgaard, James Arthur
Klagsbrun, Francine (Lifton) 36
Klaperman, Gilbert 1921- 33
Klaperman, Libby Mindlin
  1921-1982 33
  Obituary 31
Klass, Morton 1927- 11
Klass, Sheila Solomon 1927- 45
Kleberger, Ilse 1921- 5

Klein, Aaron E. 1930- 45
  Brief Entry 28
Klein, Gerda Weissmann
  1924- 44
Klein, H. Arthur 8
Klein, Leonore 1916- 6
Klein, Mina C(ooper) 8
Klein, Norma 1938- 7
  See also CLR 2
  See also SAAS 1
Klein, Robin 1936-
  Brief Entry 45
Klemm, Edward G., Jr. 1910- 30
Klemm, Roberta K(ohnhorst)
  1884- 30
Klevin, Jill Ross 1935- 39
  Brief Entry 38
Kliban, B. 1935- 35
Klimowicz, Barbara 1927- 10
Klug, Ron(ald) 1939- 31
Knapp, Ron 1952- 34
Knebel, Fletcher 1911- 36
Knickerbocker, Diedrich
  See Irving, Washington
Knifesmith
  See Cutler, Ivor
Knight, Anne (Katherine)
  1946- 34
Knight, Damon 1922- 9
Knight, David C(arpenter) 14
Knight, Eric (Mowbray)
  1897-1943 18
Knight, Francis Edgar 14
Knight, Frank
  See Knight, Francis Edgar
Knight, Hilary 1926- 15
Knight, Mallory T.
  See Hurwood, Bernhardt J.
Knight, Ruth Adams 1898-1974
  Obituary 20
Knott, Bill
  See Knott, William Cecil, Jr.
Knott, William Cecil, Jr.
  1927- 3
Knotts, Howard (Clayton, Jr.)
  1922- 25
Knowles, Anne 1933- 37
Knowles, John 1926- 8
Knox, Calvin
  See Silverberg, Robert
Knox, (Mary) Eleanor Jessie
  1909- 30
Knox, James
  See Brittain, William
Knudsen, James 1950- 42
Knudson, Richard L(ewis)
  1930- 34
Knudson, R. R.
  See Knudson, Rozanne
Knudson, Rozanne 1932- 7
Koch, Dorothy Clarke 1924- 6
Kocsis, J. C.
  See Paul, James
Koehn, Ilse
  See Van Zwienen, Ilse (Charlotte
  Koehn)
Koerner, W(illiam) H(enry) D(avid)
  1878-1938 21

Kohler, Julilly H(ouse) 1908-1976
  Obituary 20
Kohn, Bernice (Herstein)
  1920- 4
Kohner, Frederick 1905- 10
Kolba, Tamara 22
Komisar, Lucy 1942- 9
Komoda, Beverly 1939- 25
Komoda, Kiyo 1937- 9
Komroff, Manuel 1890-1974 2
  Obituary 20
Konigsburg, E(laine) L(obl)
  1930- 4
  See also CLR 1
Koning, Hans
  See Koningsberger, Hans
Koningsberger, Hans 1921- 5
Konkle, Janet Everest 1917- 12
Koob, Theodora (Johanna Foth)
  1918- 23
Korach, Mimi 1922- 9
Koren, Edward 1935- 5
Korinetz, Yuri (Iosifovich)
  1923- 9
  See also CLR 4
Korman, Gordon 1963-
  Brief Entry 41
Korty, Carol 1937- 15
Kossin, Sandy (Sanford)
  1926- 10
Kotzwinkle, William 1938- 24
  See also CLR 6
Koutoukas, H. M.
  See Rivoli, Mario
Kouts, Anne 1945- 8
Krahn, Fernando 1935-
  Brief Entry 31
  See also CLR 3
Kramer, Anthony
  Brief Entry 42
Kramer, George
  See Heuman, William
Kramer, Nora 1896(?)-1984 26
  Obituary 39
Krantz, Hazel (Newman)
  1920- 12
Kranzler, George G(ershon)
  1916- 28
Kranzler, Gershon
  See Kranzler, George G(ershon)
Krasilovsky, Phyllis 1926- 38
  Earlier sketch in SATA 1
Kraske, Robert
  Brief Entry 36
Kraus, Robert 1925- 4
Krauss, Ruth (Ida) 1911- 30
  Earlier sketch in SATA 1
Krautter, Elisa
  See Bialk, Elisa
Krauze, Andrzej 1947-
  Brief Entry 46
Kredel, Fritz 1900-1973 17
Krementz, Jill 1940- 17
  See also CLR 5
Krensky, Stephen (Alan) 1953-
  Brief Entry 41
Kripke, Dorothy Karp 30
Kristof, Jane 1932- 8

Kroeber, Theodora (Kracaw)
1897- 1
Kroll, Francis Lynde
1904-1973 10
Kroll, Steven 1941- 19
Kropp, Paul (Stephen) 1948- 38
Brief Entry 34
Krull, Kathleen 1952-
Brief Entry 39
Krumgold, Joseph 1908-1980 1
Obituary 23
Krush, Beth 1918- 18
Krush, Joe 1918- 18
Krüss, James 1926- 8
See also CLR 9
Kubie, Nora (Gottheil) Benjamin
1899- 39
Kubinyi, Laszlo 1937- 17
Kuh, Charlotte 1892(?)-1985
Obituary 43
Kujoth, Jean Spealman 1935-1975
Obituary 30
Kullman, Harry 1919-1982 35
Kumin, Maxine (Winokur)
1925- 12
Kunhardt, Dorothy Meserve
1901(?)-1979
Obituary 22
Künstler, Morton 1927- 10
Kupferberg, Herbert 1918- 19
Kuratomi, Chizuko 1939- 12
Kurelek, William 1927-1977 8
Obituary 27
See also CLR 2
Kurland, Gerald 1942- 13
Kuskin, Karla (Seidman)
1932- 2
See also CLR 4
See also SAAS 3
Kuttner, Paul 1931- 18
Kuzma, Kay 1941- 39
Kvale, Velma R(uth) 1898- 8
Kyle, Elisabeth
See Dunlop, Agnes M. R.
Kyte, Kathy S. 1946-
Brief Entry 44

L

Lacy, Leslie Alexander 1937- 6
Ladd, Veronica
See Miner, Jane Claypool
Lader, Lawrence 1919- 6
Lady, A
See Taylor, Ann
Lady Mears
See Tempest, Margaret Mary
Lady of Quality, A
See Bagnold, Enid
La Farge, Oliver (Hazard Perry)
1901-1963 19
La Farge, Phyllis 14
Laffin, John (Alfred Charles)
1922- 31
La Fontaine, Jean de
1621-1695 18
Lagercrantz, Rose (Elsa)
1947- 39

Lagerlöf, Selma (Ottiliana Lovisa)
1858-1940 15
See also CLR 7
Laiken, Deirdre S(usan) 1948-
Brief Entry 40
Laimgruber, Monika 1946- 11
Laing, Martha
See Celestino, Martha Laing
Laird, Jean E(louise) 1930- 38
Laite, Gordon 1925- 31
Laklan, Carli 1907- 5
la Mare, Walter de
See de la Mare, Walter
Lamb, Beatrice Pitney 1904- 21
Lamb, Charles 1775-1834 17
Lamb, Elizabeth Searle 1917- 31
Lamb, G(eoffrey) F(rederick) 10
Lamb, Lynton 1907- 10
Lamb, Mary Ann 1764-1847 17
Lamb, Robert (Boyden) 1941- 13
Lambert, Janet (Snyder)
1894-1973 25
Lambert, Saul 1928- 23
Lamburn, Richmal Crompton
1890-1969 5
Lamorisse, Albert (Emmanuel)
1922-1970 23
Lamplugh, Lois 1921- 17
Lampman, Evelyn Sibley
1907-1980 4
Obituary 23
Lamprey, Louise
1869-1951 ....YABC 2
Lancaster, Bruce 1896-1963 9
Lancaster, Matthew 1973(?)-1983
Obituary 45
Land, Barbara (Neblett) 1923- 16
Land, Jane [Joint pseudonym]
See Borland, Kathryn Kilby and
Speicher, Helen Ross (Smith)
Land, Myrick (Ebben) 1922- 15
Land, Ross [Joint pseudonym]
See Borland, Kathryn Kilby and
Speicher, Helen Ross (Smith)
Landau, Elaine 1948- 10
Landau, Jacob 1917- 38
Landeck, Beatrice 1904- 15
Landin, Les(lie) 1923- 2
Landshoff, Ursula 1908- 13
Lane, Carolyn 1926- 10
Lane, Jerry
See Martin, Patricia Miles
Lane, John 1932- 15
Lane, Margaret 1907-
Brief Entry 38
Lane, Rose Wilder 1886-1968 29
Brief Entry 28
Lanes, Selma G. 1929- 3
Lang, Andrew 1844-1912 16
Lange, John
See Crichton, (J.) Michael
Lange, Suzanne 1945- 5
Langley, Noel 1911-1980
Obituary 25
Langner, Nola 1930- 8
Langone, John (Michael)
1929- 46
Brief Entry 38

Langstaff, John 1920- 6
See also CLR 3
Langstaff, Launcelot
See Irving, Washington
Langton, Jane 1922- 3
Lanier, Sidney 1842-1881 18
Lansing, Alfred 1921-1975 35
Lantz, Paul 1908- 45
Lantz, Walter 1900- 37
Lappin, Peter 1911- 32
Larom, Henry V. 1903(?)-1975
Obituary 30
Larrecq, John M(aurice)
1926-1980 44
Obituary 25
Larrick, Nancy G. 1910- 4
Larsen, Egon 1904- 14
Larson, Eve
See St. John, Wylly Folk
Larson, Norita D. 1944- 29
Larson, William H. 1938- 10
Larsson, Carl (Olof)
1853-1919 35
Lasell, Elinor H. 1929- 19
Lasell, Fen H.
See Lasell, Elinor H.
Lash, Joseph P. 1909- 43
Lasher, Faith B. 1921- 12
Lasker, David 1950- 38
Lasker, Joe 1919- 9
Lasky, Kathryn 1944- 13
Lassalle, C. E.
See Ellis, Edward S(ylvester)
Latham, Barbara 1896- 16
Latham, Frank B. 1910- 6
Latham, Jean Lee 1902- 2
Latham, Mavis
See Clark, Mavis Thorpe
Latham, Philip
See Richardson, Robert S(hirley)
Lathrop, Dorothy P(ulis)
1891-1980 14
Obituary 24
Lathrop, Francis
See Leiber, Fritz
Lattimore, Eleanor Frances
1904- 7
Lauber, Patricia (Grace) 1924- 33
Earlier sketch in SATA 1
Laugesen, Mary E(akin)
1906- 5
Laughbaum, Steve 1945- 12
Laughlin, Florence 1910- 3
Lauré, Jason 1940-
Brief Entry 44
Laurence, Ester Hauser 1935- 7
Laurin, Anne
See McLaurin, Anne
Lauritzen, Jonreed 1902- 13
Lavine, David 1928- 31
Lavine, Sigmund A. 1908- 3
Lawrence, Ann (Margaret)
1942- 41
Lawrence, Isabelle (Wentworth)
Brief Entry 29
Lawrence, J. T.
See Rowland-Entwistle, (Arthur)
Theodore (Henry)
Lawrence, John 1933- 30

Lawrence, Josephine 1890(?)-1978
  Obituary *24*
Lawrence, Linda
  See Hunt, Linda Lawrence
Lawrence, Louise 1943- *38*
Lawrence, Louise de Kiriline
  1894- *13*
Lawrence, Mildred 1907- *3*
Lawson, Carol (Antell) 1946- *42*
Lawson, Don(ald Elmer)
  1917- *9*
Lawson, Marion Tubbs 1896- *22*
Lawson, Robert
  1892-1957 .... *YABC 2*
  See also CLR 2
Laycock, George (Edwin)
  1921- *5*
Lazare, Gerald John 1927- *44*
Lazare, Jerry
  See Lazare, Gerald John
Lazarevich, Mila 1942- *17*
Lazarus, Keo Felker 1913- *21*
Lea, Alec 1907- *19*
Lea, Richard
  See Lea, Alec
Leach, Maria 1892-1977 .... *39*
  Brief Entry *28*
Leacroft, Helen 1919- *6*
Leacroft, Richard 1914- *6*
Leaf, (Wilbur) Munro
  1905-1976 .... *20*
Leaf, VaDonna Jean 1929- *26*
Leakey, Richard E(rskine Frere)
  1944- *42*
Leander, Ed
  See Richelson, Geraldine
Lear, Edward 1812-1888 .... *18*
  See also CLR 1
Leavitt, Jerome E(dward)
  1916- *23*
LeBar, Mary E(velyn)
  1910-1982 .... *35*
LeCain, Errol 1941- *6*
Lee, Benjamin 1921- *27*
Lee, Betsy 1949- *37*
Lee, Carol
  See Fletcher, Helen Jill
Lee, Dennis (Beynon) 1939- *14*
  See also CLR 3
Lee, Doris (Emrick)
  1905-1983 .... *44*
  Obituary *35*
Lee, (Nelle) Harper 1926- *11*
Lee, John R(obert) 1923-1976 ..... *27*
Lee, Manning de V(illeneuve)
  1894-1980 .... *37*
  Obituary *22*
Lee, Marian
  See Clish, (Lee) Marian
Lee, Mary Price 1934- *8*
Lee, Mildred 1908- *6*
Lee, Robert C. 1931- *20*
Lee, Robert J. 1921- *10*
Lee, Roy
  See Hopkins, Clark
Lee, Tanith 1947- *8*
Leekley, Thomas B(riggs)
  1910- *23*

Leeming, Jo Ann
  See Leeming, Joseph
Leeming, Joseph 1897-1968 .... *26*
Leeson, R. A.
  See Leeson, Robert (Arthur)
Leeson, Robert (Arthur) 1928- *42*
Lefler, Irene (Whitney) 1917- *12*
Le Gallienne, Eva 1899- *9*
Legg, Sarah Martha Ross Bruggeman
  (?)-1982
  Obituary *40*
LeGrand
  See Henderson, LeGrand
Le Guin, Ursula K(roeber)
  1929- *4*
  See also CLR 3
Legum, Colin 1919- *10*
Lehn, Cornelia 1920- *46*
Lehr, Delores 1920- *10*
Leiber, Fritz 1910- *45*
Leichman, Seymour 1933- *5*
Leigh, Tom 1947- *46*
Leigh-Pemberton, John 1911- *35*
Leighton, Clare (Veronica Hope)
  1900(?)- *37*
Leighton, Margaret 1896- *1*
Leipold, L. Edmond 1902- *16*
Leisk, David (Johnson)
  1906-1975 .... *30*
  Obituary *26*
  Earlier sketch in SATA 1
Leister, Mary 1917- *29*
Leitch, Patricia 1933- *11*
LeMair, H(enriette) Willebeek
  1889-1966
  Brief Entry *29*
Lemke, Horst 1922- *38*
Lenanton, C.
  See Oman, Carola (Mary Anima)
Lenard, Alexander 1910-1972
  Obituary *21*
L'Engle, Madeleine 1918- *27*
  Earlier sketch in SATA 1
  See also CLR 1
Lengyel, Cornel Adam 1915- *27*
Lengyel, Emil 1895-1985 .... *3*
  Obituary *42*
Lens, Sidney 1912- *13*
Lenski, Lois 1893-1974 .... *26*
  Earlier sketch in SATA 1
Lent, Blair 1930- *2*
Lent, Henry Bolles 1901-1973 .... *17*
Leodhas, Sorche Nic
  See Alger, Leclaire (Gowans)
Leokum, Arkady 1916(?)- *45*
Leonard, Constance (Brink)
  1923- *42*
  Brief Entry *40*
Leonard, Jonathan N(orton)
  1903-1975 .... *36*
Leong Gor Yun
  See Ellison, Virginia Howell
Lerner, Aaron B(unsen) 1920- *35*
Lerner, Carol 1927- *33*
Lerner, Marguerite Rush
  1924- *11*
Lerner, Sharon (Ruth)
  1938-1982 .... *11*
  Obituary *29*

LeRoy, Gen
  Brief Entry *36*
Lerrigo, Marion Olive 1898-1968
  Obituary *29*
LeShan, Eda J(oan) 1922- *21*
  See also CLR 6
LeSieg, Theo
  See Geisel, Theodor Seuss
Leslie, Robert Franklin 1911- *7*
Leslie, Sarah
  See McGuire, Leslie (Sarah)
Lesser, Margaret 1899(?)-1979
  Obituary *22*
Lester, Helen 1936- *46*
Lester, Julius B. 1939- *12*
  See also CLR 2
Le Sueur, Meridel 1900- *6*
Leutscher, Alfred (George)
  1913- *23*
Levai, Blaise 1919- *39*
Levin, Betty 1927- *19*
Levin, Marcia Obrasky 1918- *13*
Levin, Meyer 1905-1981 .... *21*
  Obituary *27*
Levine, David 1926- *43*
  Brief Entry *35*
Levine, Edna S(imon) *35*
Levine, I(srael) E. 1923- *12*
Levine, Joan Goldman *11*
Levine, Joseph 1910- *33*
Levine, Rhoda *14*
Levinson, Nancy Smiler
  1938- *33*
Levitin, Sonia 1934- *4*
  See also SAAS 2
Levoy, Myron
  Brief Entry *37*
Levy, Elizabeth 1942- *31*
Lewees, John
  See Stockton, Francis Richard
Lewin, Betsy 1937- *32*
Lewin, Hugh (Francis) 1939-
  Brief Entry *40*
  See also CLR 9
Lewin, Ted 1935- *21*
Lewis, Alfred E. 1912-1968
  Brief Entry *32*
Lewis, Alice C. 1936- *46*
Lewis, Alice Hudson 1895(?)-1971
  Obituary *29*
Lewis, (Joseph) Anthony
  1927- *27*
Lewis, C(live) S(taples)
  1898-1963 .... *13*
  See also CLR 3
Lewis, Claudia (Louise) 1907- *5*
Lewis, E. M. *20*
Lewis, Elizabeth Foreman
  1892-1958 .... *YABC 2*
Lewis, Francine
  See Wells, Helen
Lewis, Hilda (Winifred) 1896-1974
  Obituary *20*
Lewis, Lucia Z.
  See Anderson, Lucia (Lewis)
Lewis, Marjorie 1929- *40*
  Brief Entry *35*
Lewis, Paul
  See Gerson, Noel B(ertram)

Lewis, Richard 1935- 3
Lewis, Roger
  See Zarchy, Harry
Lewis, Shari 1934- 35
  Brief Entry 30
Lewis, Thomas P(arker) 1936- 27
Lewiton, Mina 1904-1970 2
Lexau, Joan M. 36
  Earlier sketch in SATA 1
Ley, Willy 1906-1969 2
Leydon, Rita (Flodén) 1949- 21
Leyland, Eric (Arthur) 1911- 37
L'Hommedieu, Dorothy K(easley)
  1885-1961
  Obituary 29
Libby, Bill
  See Libby, William M.
Libby, William M. 1927-1984 5
  Obituary 39
Liberty, Gene 1924- 3
Liebers, Arthur 1913- 12
Lieblich, Irene 1923- 22
Liers, Emil E(rnest)
  1890-1975 37
Lietz, Gerald S. 1918- 11
Lifton, Betty Jean 6
Lightner, A. M.
  See Hopf, Alice L.
Lignell, Lois 1911- 37
Lillington, Kenneth (James)
  1916- 39
Lilly, Charles
  Brief Entry 33
Lilly, Ray
  See Curtis, Richard (Alan)
Lim, John 1932- 43
Liman, Ellen (Fogelson)
  1936- 22
Limburg, Peter R(ichard)
  1929- 13
Lincoln, C(harles) Eric 1924- 5
Lindbergh, Anne
  See Sapieyevski, Anne Lindbergh
Lindbergh, Anne Morrow (Spencer)
  1906- 33
Lindbergh, Charles A(ugustus, Jr.)
  1902-1974 33
Lindblom, Steven (Winther)
  1946- 42
  Brief Entry 39
Linde, Gunnel 1924- 5
Lindgren, Astrid 1907- 38
  Earlier sketch in SATA 2
  See also CLR 1
Lindgren, Barbro 1937-
  Brief Entry 46
Lindman, Maj (Jan)
  1886-1972 43
Lindop, Edmund 1925- 5
Lindquist, Jennie Dorothea
  1899-1977 13
Lindquist, Willis 1908- 20
Lindsay, Norman (Alfred William)
  1879-1969
  See CLR 8
Lindsay, (Nicholas) Vachel
  1879-1931 40
Line, Les 1935- 27
Linfield, Esther 40

Lingard, Joan 8
Link, Martin 1934- 28
Lionni, Leo 1910- 8
  See also CLR 7
Lipinsky de Orlov, Lino S.
  1908- 22
Lipkind, William 1904-1974 15
Lipman, David 1931- 21
Lipman, Matthew 1923- 14
Lippincott, Bertram 1898(?)-1985
  Obituary 42
Lippincott, Joseph Wharton
  1887-1976 17
Lippincott, Sarah Lee 1920- 22
Lippman, Peter J. 1936- 31
Lipsyte, Robert 1938- 5
Lisker, Sonia O. 1933- 44
Lisle, Seward D.
  See Ellis, Edward S(ylvester)
Lisowski, Gabriel 1946-
  Brief Entry 31
Liss, Howard 1922- 4
Lissim, Simon 1900-1981
  Brief Entry 28
List, Ilka Katherine 1935- 6
Liston, Robert A. 1927- 5
Litchfield, Ada B(assett)
  1916- 5
Litowinsky, Olga (Jean) 1936- 26
Little, A. Edward
  See Klein, Aaron E.
Little, (Flora) Jean 1932- 2
  See also CLR 4
Little, Mary E. 1912- 28
Littledale, Freya (Lota) 2
Lively, Penelope 1933- 7
  See also CLR 7
Liversidge, (Henry) Douglas
  1913- 8
Livingston, Carole 1941- 42
Livingston, Myra Cohn 1926- 5
  See also CLR 7
  See also SAAS 1
Livingston, Richard R(oland)
  1922- 8
Llerena-Aguirre, Carlos Antonio
  1952- 19
Llewellyn, Richard
  See Llewellyn Lloyd, Richard
  Dafydd Vyvyan
Llewellyn, T. Harcourt
  See Hamilton, Charles H. St. John
Llewellyn Lloyd, Richard Dafydd
  Vyvyan 1906-1983 11
  Obituary 37
Lloyd, Errol 1943- 22
Lloyd, Norman 1909-1980
  Obituary 23
Lloyd, (Mary) Norris 1908- 10
Lobel, Anita 1934- 6
Lobel, Arnold 1933- 6
  See also CLR 5
Lobsenz, Amelia 12
Lobsenz, Norman M. 1919- 6
Lochak, Michèle 1936- 39
Lochlons, Colin
  See Jackson, C. Paul
Locke, Clinton W. [Collective
  pseudonym] 1

Locke, Lucie 1904- 10
Lockwood, Mary
  See Spelman, Mary
Lodge, Bernard 1933- 33
Lodge, Maureen Roffey
  See Roffey, Maureen
Loeb, Robert H., Jr. 1917- 21
Loeper, John J(oseph) 1929- 10
Loescher, Ann Dull 1942- 20
Loescher, Gil(burt Damian)
  1945- 20
Loewenstein, Bernice
  Brief Entry 40
Löfgren, Ulf 1931- 3
Lofting, Hugh 1886-1947 15
Lofts, Norah (Robinson)
  1904-1983 8
  Obituary 36
Logue, Christopher 1926- 23
Loken, Newton (Clayton)
  1919- 26
Lomas, Steve
  See Brennan, Joseph L.
Lomask, Milton 1909- 20
London, Jack 1876-1916 18
London, Jane
  See Geis, Darlene
London, John Griffith
  See London, Jack
Lonergan, (Pauline) Joy (Maclean)
  1909- 10
Lonette, Reisie (Dominee)
  1924- 43
Long, Helen Beecher [Collective
  pseudonym] 1
Long, Judith Elaine 1953- 20
Long, Judy
  See Long, Judith Elaine
Long, Laura Mooney 1892-1967
  Obituary 29
Longfellow, Henry Wadsworth
  1807-1882 19
Longman, Harold S. 1919- 5
Longsworth, Polly 1933- 28
Longtemps, Kenneth 1933- 17
Longway, A. Hugh
  See Lang, Andrew
Loomis, Robert D. 5
Lopshire, Robert 1927- 6
Lord, Athena V. 1932- 39
Lord, Beman 1924- 5
Lord, (Doreen Mildred) Douglas
  1904- 12
Lord, John Vernon 1939- 21
Lord, Nancy
  See Titus, Eve
Lord, Walter 1917- 3
Lorenz, Lee (Sharp) 1932(?)-
  Brief Entry 39
Lorenzini, Carlo 1826-1890 29
Lorraine, Walter (Henry)
  1929- 16
Loss, Joan 1933- 11
Lot, Parson
  See Kingsley, Charles
Lothrop, Harriet Mulford Stone
  1844-1924 20
Louie, Ai-Ling 1949- 40
  Brief Entry 34

Louisburgh, Sheila Burnford
 See Burnford, Sheila
Lourie, Helen
 See Storr, Catherine (Cole)
Love, Katherine 1907- 3
Love, Sandra (Weller) 1940- 26
Lovelace, Delos Wheeler
 1894-1967 7
Lovelace, Maud Hart
 1892-1980 2
 Obituary 23
Lovett, Margaret (Rose) 1915- 22
Low, Alice 1926- 11
Low, Elizabeth Hammond
 1898- 5
Low, Joseph 1911- 14
Lowe, Jay, Jr.
 See Loper, John J(oseph)
Lowenstein, Dyno 1914- 6
Lowitz, Anson C.
 1901(?)-1978 18
Lowitz, Sadyebeth (Heath)
 1901-1969 17
Lowrey, Janette Sebring
 1892- 43
Lowry, Lois 1937- 23
 See also CLR 6
 See also SAAS 3
Lowry, Peter 1953- 7
Lowther, George F. 1913-1975
 Obituary 30
Lozier, Herbert 1915- 26
Lubell, Cecil 1912- 6
Lubell, Winifred 1914- 6
Lubin, Leonard B. 1943- 45
 Brief Entry 37
Lucas, E(dward) V(errall)
 1868-1938 20
Lucas, Jerry 1940- 33
Luce, Celia (Geneva Larsen)
 1914- 38
Luce, Willard (Ray) 1914- 38
Luckhardt, Mildred Corell
 1898- 5
Ludden, Allen (Ellsworth)
 1918(?)-1981
 Obituary 27
Ludlam, Mabel Cleland
 See Widdemer, Mabel Cleland
Ludwig, Helen 33
Lueders, Edward (George)
 1923- 14
Lufkin, Raymond H. 1897- 38
Lugard, Flora Louisa Shaw
 1852-1929 21
Luger, Harriett M(andelay)
 1914- 23
Luhrmann, Winifred B(ruce)
 1934- 11
Luis, Earlene W. 1929- 11
Lum, Peter
 See Crowe, Bettina Lum
Lund, Doris (Herold) 1919- 12
Lunn, Janet 1928- 4
Lurie, Alison 1926- 46
Lustig, Loretta 1944- 46
Luther, Frank 1905-1980
 Obituary 25
Luttrell, Guy L. 1938- 22

Luttrell, Ida (Alleene) 1934- 40
 Brief Entry 35
Lutzker, Edythe 1904- 5
Luzzati, Emanuele 1912- 7
Luzzatto, Paola (Caboara)
 1938- 38
Lydon, Michael 1942- 11
Lyfick, Warren
 See Reeves, Lawrence F.
Lyle, Katie Letcher 1938- 8
Lynch, Lorenzo 1932- 7
Lynch, Marietta 1947- 29
Lynch, Patricia (Nora)
 1898-1972 9
Lynds, Dennis 1924-
 Brief Entry 37
Lynn, Mary
 See Brokamp, Marilyn
Lynn, Patricia
 See Watts, Mabel Pizzey
Lyon, Elinor 1921- 6
Lyon, Lyman R.
 See De Camp, L(yon) Sprague
Lyons, Dorothy 1907- 3
Lyons, Grant 1941- 30
Lystad, Mary (Hanemann)
 1928- 11
Lyttle, Richard B(ard) 1927- 23
Lytton, Edward G(eorge) E(arle)
 L(ytton) Bulwer-Lytton, Baron
 1803-1873 23

M

Maar, Leonard (F., Jr.) 1927- 30
Maas, Selve 14
Mac
 See MacManus, Seumas
Mac Aodhagáin, Eamon
 See Egan, E(dward) W(elstead)
MacArthur-Onslow, Annette
 (Rosemary) 1933- 26
Macaulay, David (Alexander)
 1946- 46
 Brief Entry 27
 See also CLR 3
MacBeth, George 1932- 4
MacClintock, Dorcas 1932- 8
MacDonald, Anson
 See Heinlein, Robert A(nson)
MacDonald, Betty (Campbell Bard)
 1908-1958 ....YABC 1
Macdonald, Blackie
 See Emrich, Duncan
Macdonald, Dwight
 1906-1982 29
 Obituary 33
MacDonald, George
 1824-1905 33
Mac Donald, Golden
 See Brown, Margaret Wise
Macdonald, Marcia
 See Hill, Grace Livingston
Macdonald, Mary
 See Gifford, Griselda
Macdonald, Shelagh 1937- 25
Macdonald, Zillah K(atherine)
 1885- 11
Mace, Elisabeth 1933- 27

MacFarlan, Allan A.
 1892-1982 35
MacFarlane, Iris 1922- 11
MacGregor, Ellen 1906-1954 39
 Brief Entry 27
MacGregor-Hastie, Roy 1929- 3
Machetanz, Frederick 1908- 34
Machin Goodall, Daphne
 (Edith) 37
MacInnes, Helen 1907-1985 22
 Obituary 44
MacIntyre, Elisabeth 1916- 17
Mack, Stan(ley) 17
Mackay, Claire 1930- 40
MacKaye, Percy (Wallace)
 1875-1956 32
MacKellar, William 1914- 4
Macken, Walter 1915-1967 36
Mackenzie, Dr. Willard
 See Stratemeyer, Edward L.
MacKenzie, Garry 1921-
 Brief Entry 31
MacKinstry, Elizabeth
 1879-1956 42
MacLachlan, Patricia
 Brief Entry 42
MacLean, Alistair (Stuart)
 1923- 23
MacLeod, Beatrice (Beach)
 1910- 10
MacLeod, Charlotte (Matilda Hughes)
 1922- 28
MacLeod, Ellen Jane (Anderson)
 1916- 14
MacManus, James
 See MacManus, Seumas
MacManus, Seumas
 1869-1960 25
MacMaster, Eve (Ruth) B(owers)
 1942- 46
MacMillan, Annabelle
 See Quick, Annabelle
MacPeek, Walter G.
 1902-1973 4
 Obituary 25
MacPherson, Margaret 1908- 9
MacPherson, Thomas George
 1915-1976
 Obituary 30
Macrae, Hawk
 See Barker, Albert W.
MacRae, Travi
 See Feagles, Anita (MacRae)
Macumber, Mari
 See Sandoz, Mari
Madden, Don 1927- 3
Maddison, Angela Mary
 1923- 10
Maddock, Reginald 1912- 15
Madian, Jon 1941- 9
Madison, Arnold 1937- 6
Madison, Winifred 5
Maestro, Betsy 1944-
 Brief Entry 30
Maestro, Giulio 1942- 8
Magorian, James 1942- 32
Maguire, Anne
 See Nearing, Penny
Maguire, Gregory 1954- 28

Maher, Ramona 1934- 13
Mählqvist, (Karl) Stefan
  1943- 30
Mahon, Julia C(unha) 1916- 11
Mahony, Elizabeth Winthrop
  1948- 8
Mahood, Kenneth 1930- 24
Mahy, Margaret 1936- 14
  See also CLR 7
Maidoff, Ilka List
  See List, Ilka Katherine
Maik, Henri
  See Hecht, Henri Joseph
Maiorano, Robert 1946- 43
Maitland, Antony (Jasper)
  1935- 25
Major, Kevin 1949- 32
Makie, Pam 1943- 37
Malcolmson, Anne
  See Storch, Anne B. von
Malcolmson, David 1899- 6
Mali, Jane Lawrence 1937-
  Brief Entry 44
Mallowan, Agatha Christie
  See Christie, Agatha (Mary Clarissa)
Malmberg, Carl 1904- 9
Malo, John 1911- 4
Malory, (Sir) Thomas 1410(?)-1471(?)
  Brief Entry 33
Maltese, Michael 1908(?)-1981
  Obituary 24
Malvern, Corinne 1905-1956 34
Malvern, Gladys (?)-1962 23
Manchel, Frank 1935- 10
Manes, Stephen 1949- 42
  Brief Entry 40
Manfred, Frederick F(eikema)
  1912- 30
Mangione, Jerre 1909- 6
Mangurian, David 1938- 14
Maniscalco, Joseph 1926- 10
Manley, Deborah 1932- 28
Manley, Seon 15
  See also CLR 3
  See also SAAS 2
Mann, Peggy 6
Mannheim, Grete (Salomon)
  1909- 10
Manniche, Lise 1943- 31
Manning, Rosemary 1911- 10
Manning-Sanders, Ruth 1895- 15
Manson, Beverlie 1945-
  Brief Entry 44
Manton, Jo
  See Gittings, Jo Manton
Manushkin, Fran 1942- 7
Mapes, Mary A.
  See Ellison, Virginia Howell
Mara, Barney
  See Roth, Arthur J(oseph)
Mara, Jeanette
  See Cebulash, Mel
Marais, Josef 1905-1978
  Obituary 24
Marasmus, Seymour
  See Rivoli, Mario
Marcellino
  See Agnew, Edith J.

Marchant, Bessie
  1862-1941 .... YABC 2
Marchant, Catherine
  See Cookson, Catherine (McMulen)
Marcher, Marion Walden
  1890- 10
Marcus, Rebecca B(rian)
  1907- 9
Margaret, Karla
  See Andersdatter, Karla M(argaret)
Margolis, Richard J(ules)
  1929- 4
Margolis, Vivienne 1922- 46
Mariana
  See Foster, Marian Curtis
Marino, Dorothy Bronson
  1912- 14
Maris, Ron
  Brief Entry 45
Mark, Jan 1943- 22
Mark, Pauline (Dahlin) 1913- 14
Mark, Polly
  See Mark, Pauline (Dahlin)
Markins, W. S.
  See Jenkins, Marie M.
Markle, Sandra L(ee) 1946-
  Brief Entry 41
Marko, Katherine D(olores) 28
Marks, Burton 1930-
  Brief Entry 43
Marks, Hannah K.
  See Trivelpiece, Laurel
Marks, J
  See Highwater, Jamake
Marks, J(ames) M(acdonald)
  1921- 13
Marks, Margaret L. 1911(?)-1980
  Obituary 23
Marks, Mickey Klar 12
Marks, Peter
  See Smith, Robert Kimmel
Marks, Stan(ley) 1929- 14
Marks-Highwater, J
  See Highwater, Jamake
Markun, Patricia M(aloney)
  1924- 15
Marlowe, Amy Bell [Collective
  pseudonym] 1
Marokvia, Artur 1909- 31
Marokvia, Mireille (Journet)
  1918- 5
Marrin, Albert 1936-
  Brief Entry 43
Marriott, Alice Lee 1910- 31
Marriott, Pat(ricia) 1920- 35
Mars, W. T.
  See Mars, Witold Tadeusz J.
Mars, Witold Tadeusz J.
  1912- 3
Marsh, J. E.
  See Marshall, Evelyn
Marsh, Jean
  See Marshall, Evelyn
Marshall, Anthony D(ryden)
  1924- 18
Marshall, (Sarah) Catherine
  1914-1983 2
  Obituary 34

Marshall, Douglas
  See McClintock, Marshall
Marshall, Evelyn 1897- 11
Marshall, James 1942- 6
Marshall, James Vance
  See Payne, Donald Gordon
Marshall, Kim
  See Marshall, Michael (Kimbrough)
Marshall, Michael (Kimbrough)
  1948- 37
Marshall, Percy
  See Young, Percy M(arshall)
Marshall, S(amuel) L(yman) A(twood)
  1900-1977 21
Marsten, Richard
  See Hunter, Evan
Marston, Hope Irvin 1935- 31
Martignoni, Margaret E. 1908(?)-1974
  Obituary 27
Martin, Ann M(atthews)
  1955- 44
  Brief Entry 41
Martin, Bill, Jr.
  See Martin, William Ivan
Martin, David Stone 1913- 39
Martin, Eugene [Collective
  pseudonym] 1
Martin, Frances M(cEntee)
  1906- 36
Martin, Fredric
  See Christopher, Matt
Martin, J(ohn) P(ercival)
  1880(?)-1966 15
Martin, Jeremy
  See Levin, Marcia Obransky
Martin, Lynne 1923- 21
Martin, Marcia
  See Levin, Marcia Obransky
Martin, Nancy
  See Salmon, Annie Elizabeth
Martin, Patricia Miles 1899- 43
  Earlier sketch in SATA 1
Martin, Peter
  See Chaundler, Christine
Martin, René 1891-1977 42
  Obituary 20
Martin, Rupert (Claude) 1905- 31
Martin, Stefan 1936- 32
Martin, Vicky
  See Storey, Victoria Carolyn
Martin, William Ivan 1916-
  Brief Entry 40
Martineau, Harriet
  1802-1876 .... YABC 2
Martini, Teri 1930- 3
Marx, Robert F(rank) 1936- 24
Marzani, Carl (Aldo) 1912- 12
Marzollo, Jean 1942- 29
Masefield, John 1878-1967 19
Mason, Edwin A. 1905-1979
  Obituary 32
Mason, F. van Wyck
  1901-1978 3
  Obituary 26
Mason, Frank W.
  See Mason, F. van Wyck
Mason, George Frederick
  1904- 14

Mason, Miriam (Evangeline)
  1900-1973 2
  Obituary 26
Mason, Tally
  See Derleth, August (William)
Mason, Van Wyck
  See Mason, F. van Wyck
Masselman, George
  1897-1971 19
Massie, Diane Redfield 16
Masters, Kelly R. 1897- 3
Masters, Mildred 1932- 42
Masters, William
  See Cousins, Margaret
Matchette, Katharine E. 1941- 38
Math, Irwin 1940- 42
Mathews, Janet 1914- 41
Mathews, Louise
  See Tooke, Louise Mathews
Mathiesen, Egon 1907-1976
  Obituary 28
Mathieu, Joe
  See Mathieu, Joseph P.
Mathieu, Joseph P. 1949- 43
  Brief Entry 36
Mathis, Sharon Bell 1937- 7
  See also CLR 3
  See also SAAS 3
Matson, Emerson N(els)
  1926- 12
Matsui, Tadashi 1926- 8
Matsuno, Masako 1935- 6
Matte, (Encarnacion) L'Enc
  1936- 22
Matthews, Ann
  See Martin, Ann M(atthews)
Matthews, Ellen 1950- 28
Matthews, Jacklyn Meek
  See Meek, Jacklyn O'Hanlon
Matthews, Patricia 1927- 28
Matthews, William Henry III
  1919- 45
  Brief Entry 28
Matthias, Catherine 1945-
  Brief Entry 41
Matthiessen, Peter 1927- 27
Mattingley, Christobel (Rosemary)
  1931- 37
Matulay, Laszlo 1912- 43
Matulka, Jan 1890-1972
  Brief Entry 28
Matus, Greta 1938- 12
Mauser, Patricia Rhoads
  1943- 37
Maves, Mary Carolyn 1916- 10
Maves, Paul B(enjamin)
  1913- 10
Mawicke, Tran 1911- 15
Max, Peter 1939- 45
Maxon, Anne
  See Best, Allena Champlin
Maxwell, Arthur S.
  1896-1970 11
Maxwell, Edith 1923- 7
May, Charles Paul 1920- 4
May, Julian 1931- 11
May, Robert Lewis 1905-1976
  Obituary 27
May, Robert Stephen 1929- 46

May, Robin
  See May, Robert Stephen
Mayberry, Florence V(irginia
  Wilson) 10
Mayer, Albert Ignatius, Jr. 1906-1960
  Obituary 29
Mayer, Ann M(argaret) 1938- 14
Mayer, Jane Rothschild 1903- 38
Mayer, Marianna 1945- 32
Mayer, Mercer 1943- 32
  Earlier sketch in SATA 16
Mayerson, Charlotte Leon 36
Mayhar, Ardath 1930- 38
Maynard, Chris
  See Maynard, Christopher
Maynard, Christopher 1949-
  Brief Entry 43
Maynard, Olga 1920- 40
Mayne, William 1928- 6
Maynes, Dr. J. O. Rocky
  See Maynes, J. Oscar, Jr.
Maynes, J. O. Rocky, Jr.
  See Maynes, J. Oscar, Jr.
Maynes, J. Oscar, Jr. 1929- 38
Mayo, Margaret (Mary) 1935- 38
Mays, (Lewis) Victor, (Jr.)
  1927- 5
Mazer, Harry 1925- 31
Mazer, Norma Fox 1931- 24
  See also SAAS 1
Mazza, Adriana 1928- 19
McBain, Ed
  See Hunter, Evan
McCaffery, Janet 1936- 38
McCaffrey, Anne 1926- 8
McCain, Murray (David, Jr.)
  1926-1981 7
  Obituary 29
McCall, Edith S. 1911- 6
McCall, Virginia Nielsen
  1909- 13
McCallum, Phyllis 1911- 10
McCann, Gerald 1916- 41
McCannon, Dindga Fatima
  1947- 41
McCarthy, Agnes 1933- 4
McCarty, Rega Kramer 1904- 10
McCaslin, Nellie 1914- 12
McCaughrean, Geraldine
  See Jones, Geraldine
McCay, Winsor 1869-1934 41
McClintock, Marshall
  1906-1967 3
McClintock, Mike
  See McClintock, Marshall
McClintock, Theodore
  1902-1971 14
McClinton, Leon 1933- 11
McCloskey, (John) Robert
  1914- 39
  Earlier sketch in SATA 2
  See also CLR 7
McClung, Robert M. 1916- 2
McClure, Gillian Mary 1948- 31
McConnell, James Douglas
  (Rutherford) 1915- 40
McCord, Anne 1942- 41

McCord, David (Thompson Watson)
  1897- 18
  See also CLR 9
McCord, Jean 1924- 34
McCormick, Brooks
  See Adams, William Taylor
McCormick, Dell J.
  1892-1949 19
McCormick, (George) Donald (King)
  1911- 14
McCormick, Edith (Joan)
  1934- 30
McCourt, Edward (Alexander)
  1907-1972
  Obituary 28
McCoy, Iola Fuller 3
McCoy, J(oseph) J(erome)
  1917- 8
McCoy, Lois (Rich) 1941- 38
McCrady, Lady 1951- 16
McCrea, James 1920- 3
McCrea, Ruth 1921- 3
McCullers, (Lula) Carson
  1917-1967 27
McCulloch, Derek (Ivor Breashur)
  1897-1967
  Obituary 29
McCullough, Frances Monson
  1938- 8
McCully, Emily Arnold 1939- 5
McCurdy, Michael 1942- 13
McDearmon, Kay 20
McDermott, Beverly Brodsky
  1941- 11
McDermott, Gerald 1941- 16
  See also CLR 9
McDole, Carol
  See Farley, Carol
McDonald, Gerald D.
  1905-1970 3
McDonald, Jamie
  See Heide, Florence Parry
McDonald, Jill (Masefield)
  1927-1982 13
  Obituary 29
McDonald, Lucile Saunders
  1898- 10
McDonnell, Christine 1949- 34
McDonnell, Lois Eddy 1914- 10
McEntee, Dorothy (Layng)
  1902- 37
McEwen, Robert (Lindley) 1926-1980
  Obituary 23
McFall, Christie 1918- 12
McFarland, Kenton D(ean)
  1920- 11
McFarlane, Leslie 1902-1977 31
McGaw, Jessie Brewer 1913- 10
McGee, Barbara 1943- 6
McGiffin, (Lewis) Lee (Shaffer)
  1908- 1
McGill, Marci
  See Ridlon, Marci
McGinley, Phyllis 1905-1978 44
  Obituary 24
  Earlier sketch in SATA 2
McGinnis, Lila S(prague)
  1924- 44

McGough, Elizabeth (Hemmes) 1934- ... 33
McGovern, Ann ... 8
McGowen, Thomas E. 1927- ... 2
McGowen, Tom
See McGowen, Thomas
McGrady, Mike 1933- ... 6
McGrath, Thomas 1916- ... 41
McGraw, Eloise Jarvis 1915- ... 1
McGraw, William Corbin 1916- ... 3
McGregor, Craig 1933- ... 8
McGregor, Iona 1929- ... 25
McGuire, Edna 1899- ... 13
McGuire, Leslie (Sarah) 1945-
Brief Entry ... 45
McGurk, Slater
See Roth, Arthur J(oseph)
McHargue, Georgess ... 4
See also CLR 2
McHugh, (Berit) Elisabet 1941-
Brief Entry ... 44
McIlwraith, Maureen 1922- ... 2
McInerney, Judith Whitelock 1945-
Brief Entry ... 46
McKay, Donald 1895- ... 45
McKay, Robert W. 1921- ... 15
McKeever, Marcia
See Laird, Jean E(louise)
McKenzie, Dorothy Clayton 1910-1981
Obituary ... 28
McKillip, Patricia A(nne) 1948- ... 30
McKinley, (Jennifer Carolyn) Robin
Brief Entry ... 32
See also CLR 10
McKown, Robin ... 6
McLaurin, Anne 1953- ... 27
McLean, Kathryn (Anderson) 1909-1966 ... 9
McLeish, Kenneth 1940- ... 35
McLenighan, Valjean 1947- ... 46
Brief Entry ... 40
McLeod, Emilie Warren 1926-1982 ... 23
Obituary ... 31
McLeod, Kirsty
See Hudson, (Margaret) Kirsty
McLeod, Margaret Vail
See Holloway, Teresa (Bragunier)
McMahan, Ian
Brief Entry ... 45
McManus, Patrick (Francis) 1933- ... 46
McMeekin, Clark
See McMeekin, Isabel McLennan
McMeekin, Isabel McLennan 1895- ... 3
McMillan, Bruce 1947- ... 22
McMullen, Catherine
See Cookson, Catherine (McMullen)
McMurtrey, Martin A(loysius) 1921- ... 21
McNair, Kate ... 3
McNamara, Margaret C(raig) 1915-1981
Obituary ... 24
McNaught, Harry ... 32

McNaughton, Colin 1951- ... 39
McNeely, Jeannette 1918- ... 25
McNeer, May ... 1
McNeill, Janet 1907- ... 1
McNickle, (William) D'Arcy 1904-1977
Obituary ... 22
McNulty, Faith 1918- ... 12
McPhail, David M(ichael) 1940-
Brief Entry ... 32
McPharlin, Paul 1903-1948
Brief Entry ... 31
McPhee, Richard B(yron) 1934- ... 41
McPherson, James M. 1936- ... 16
McQueen, Mildred Hark 1908- ... 12
McShean, Gordon 1936- ... 41
McSwigan, Marie 1907-1962 ... 24
McVicker, Charles (Taggart) 1930- ... 39
McVicker, Chuck
See McVicker, Charles (Taggart)
McWhirter, Norris (Dewar) 1925- ... 37
McWhirter, (Alan) Ross 1925-1975 ... 37
Obituary ... 31
Mead, Margaret 1901-1978
Obituary ... 20
Mead, Russell (M., Jr.) 1935- ... 10
Mead, Stella (?)-1981
Obituary ... 27
Meade, Ellen (Roddick) 1936- ... 5
Meade, Marion 1934- ... 23
Meader, Stephen W(arren) 1892- ... 1
Meadow, Charles T(roub) 1929- ... 23
Meadowcroft, Enid LaMonte
See Wright, Enid Meadowcroft
Meaker, M. J.
See Meaker, Marijane
Meaker, Marijane 1927- ... 20
Means, Florence Crannell 1891-1980 ... 1
Obituary ... 25
Medary, Marjorie 1890- ... 14
Meddaugh, Susan 1944- ... 29
Medearis, Mary 1915- ... 5
Mee, Charles L., Jr. 1938- ... 8
Meek, Jacklyn O'Hanlon 1933-
Brief Entry ... 34
Meek, S(terner St.) P(aul) 1894-1972
Obituary ... 28
Meeker, Oden 1918(?)-1976 ... 14
Meeks, Esther MacBain ... 1
Meggendorfer, Lothar 1847-1925
Brief Entry ... 36
Mehdevi, Alexander 1947- ... 7
Mehdevi, Anne (Marie) Sinclair ... 8
Meighan, Donald Charles 1929- ... 30
Meigs, Cornelia Lynde 1884-1973 ... 6
Meilach, Dona Z(weigoron) 1926- ... 34

Melcher, Daniel 1912-1985
Obituary ... 43
Melcher, Frederic Gershom 1879-1963
Obituary ... 22
Melcher, Marguerite Fellows 1879-1969 ... 10
Melin, Grace Hathaway 1892-1973 ... 10
Mellersh, H(arold) E(dward) L(eslie) 1897- ... 10
Meltzer, Milton 1915- ... 1
See also SAAS 1
Melville, Anne
See Potter, Margaret (Newman)
Melwood, Mary
See Lewis, E. M.
Melzack, Ronald 1929- ... 5
Memling, Carl 1918-1969 ... 6
Mendel, Jo [House pseudonym]
See Bond, Gladys Baker
Mendonca, Susan 1950-
Brief Entry ... 45
Mendoza, George 1934- ... 41
Brief Entry ... 39
Meng, Heinz (Karl) 1924- ... 13
Menotti, Gian Carlo 1911- ... 29
Menuhin, Yehudi 1916- ... 40
Mercer, Charles (Edward) 1917- ... 16
Meredith, David William
See Miers, Earl Schenck
Meriwether, Louise 1923-
Brief Entry ... 31
Merriam, Eve 1916- ... 40
Earlier sketch in SATA 3
Merrill, Jane 1946- ... 42
Merrill, Jean (Fairbanks) 1923- ... 1
Merrill, Phil
See Merrill, Jane
Merwin, Decie 1894-1961
Brief Entry ... 32
Messmer, Otto 1892(?)-1983 ... 37
Metcalf, Suzanne
See Baum, L(yman) Frank
Metos, Thomas H(arry) 1932- ... 37
Meyer, Carolyn 1935- ... 9
Meyer, Edith Patterson 1895- ... 5
Meyer, F(ranklyn) E(dward) 1932- ... 9
Meyer, Jean Shepherd 1929- ... 11
Meyer, Jerome Sydney 1895-1975 ... 3
Obituary ... 25
Meyer, June
See Jordan, June
Meyer, Kathleen Allan 1918-
Brief Entry ... 46
Meyer, Louis A(lbert) 1942- ... 12
Meyer, Renate 1930- ... 6
Meyers, Susan 1942- ... 19
Meynier, Yvonne (Pollet) 1908- ... 14
Mezey, Robert 1935- ... 33
Micale, Albert 1913- ... 22
Michel, Anna 1943-
Brief Entry ... 40
Micklish, Rita 1931- ... 12

Miers, Earl Schenck
  1910-1972 .... *1*
  Obituary *26*
Miklowitz, Gloria D. 1927- *4*
Mikolaycak, Charles 1937- *9*
Mild, Warren (Paul) 1922- *41*
Miles, Betty 1928- *8*
Miles, Miska
  See Martin, Patricia Miles
Miles, (Mary) Patricia 1930- *29*
Miles, Patricia A.
  See Martin, Patricia Miles
Milgrom, Harry 1912- *25*
Milhous, Katherine 1894-1977 .... *15*
Militant
  See Sandburg, Carl (August)
Millar, Barbara F. 1924- *12*
Miller, Albert G(riffith)
  1905-1982 .... *12*
  Obituary *31*
Miller, Alice P(atricia
  McCarthy) *22*
Miller, Don 1923- *15*
Miller, Doris R.
  See Mosesson, Gloria R(ubin)
Miller, Eddie
  See Miller, Edward
Miller, Edna (Anita) 1920- *29*
Miller, Edward 1905-1974 .... *8*
Miller, Elizabeth 1933- *41*
Miller, Eugene 1925- *33*
Miller, Frances A. 1937-
  Brief Entry *46*
Miller, Helen M(arkley) *5*
Miller, Helen Topping 1884-1960
  Obituary *29*
Miller, Jane (Judith) 1925- *15*
Miller, John
  See Samachson, Joseph
Miller, Margaret J.
  See Dale, Margaret J(essy) Miller
Miller, Marilyn (Jean) 1925- *33*
Miller, Mary Beth 1942- *9*
Miller, Natalie 1917-1976 .... *35*
Miller, Ruth White
  See White, Ruth C.
Miller, Sandy (Peden) 1948- *41*
  Brief Entry *35*
Milligan, Spike
  See Milligan, Terence Alan
Milligan, Terence Alan 1918- *29*
Mills, Claudia 1954- *44*
  Brief Entry *41*
Mills, Yaroslava Surmach
  1925- *35*
Millstead, Thomas Edward *30*
Milne, A(lan) A(lexander)
  1882-1956 ....*YABC 1*
  See also CLR 1
Milne, Lorus J. *5*
Milne, Margery *5*
Milonas, Rolf
  See Myller, Rolf
Milotte, Alfred G(eorge)
  1904- *11*
Milton, Hilary (Herbert)
  1920- *23*
Milton, John R(onald) 1924- *24*

Milton, Joyce 1946-
  Brief Entry *41*
Milverton, Charles A.
  See Penzler, Otto
Minarik, Else Holmelund
  1920- *15*
Miner, Jane Claypool 1933- *38*
  Brief Entry *37*
Miner, Lewis S. 1909- *11*
Minier, Nelson
  See Stoutenburg, Adrien
Mintonye, Grace *4*
Mirsky, Jeannette 1903- *8*
Mirsky, Reba Paeff
  1902-1966 .... *1*
Miskovits, Christine 1939- *10*
Miss Francis
  See Horwich, Francis R.
Miss Read
  See Saint, Dora Jessie
Mister Rogers
  See Rogers, Fred (McFeely)
Mitchell, Cynthia 1922- *29*
Mitchell, (Sibyl) Elyne (Keith)
  1913- *10*
Mitchell, Gladys (Maude Winifred)
  1901-1983 .... *46*
  Obituary *35*
Mitchell, Joyce Slayton 1933- *46*
  Brief Entry *43*
Mitchell, Yvonne 1925-1979
  Obituary *24*
Mitchison, Naomi Margaret (Haldane)
  1897- *24*
Mitchnik, Helen 1901- *41*
  Brief Entry *35*
Mitsuhashi, Yoko *45*
  Brief Entry *33*
Mizner, Elizabeth Howard
  1907- *27*
Mizumura, Kazue *18*
Moché, Dinah (Rachel) L(evine)
  1936- *44*
  Brief Entry *40*
Mochi, Ugo (A.) 1889-1977 ...... *38*
Modell, Frank B. 1917- *39*
  Brief Entry *36*
Moe, Barbara 1937- *20*
Moeri, Louise 1924- *24*
Moffett, Martha (Leatherwood)
  1934- *8*
Mofsie, Louis B. 1936-
  Brief Entry *33*
Mohn, Peter B(urnet) 1934- *28*
Mohn, Viola Kohl 1914- *8*
Mohr, Nicholasa 1935- *8*
Molarsky, Osmond 1909- *16*
Mole, John 1941- *36*
Molloy, Anne Baker 1907- *32*
Molloy, Paul 1920- *5*
Momaday, N(avarre) Scott 1934-
  Brief Entry *30*
Moncure, Jane Belk *23*
Monjo, F(erdinand) N.
  1924-1978 .... *16*
  See also CLR 2
Monroe, Lyle
  See Heinlein, Robert A(nson)

Monroe, Marion 1898-1983
  Obituary *34*
Monsell, Helen (Albee)
  1895-1971 .... *24*
Montana, Bob 1920-1975
  Obituary *21*
Montgomerie, Norah Mary
  1913- *26*
Montgomery, Constance
  See Cappell, Constance
Montgomery, Elizabeth Rider
  1902-1985 .... *34*
  Obituary *41*
  Earlier sketch in SATA 3
Montgomery, L(ucy) M(aud)
  1874-1942 ....*YABC 1*
  See also CLR 8
Montgomery, R(aymond) A., (Jr.)
  1936- *39*
Montgomery, Rutherford George
  1894- *3*
Montgomery, Vivian *36*
Montresor, Beni 1926- *38*
  Earlier sketch in SATA 3
Moody, Ralph Owen 1898- *1*
Moon, Carl 1879-1948 .... *25*
Moon, Grace 1877(?)-1947 .... *25*
Moon, Sheila (Elizabeth)
  1910- *5*
Moor, Emily
  See Deming, Richard
Moore, Anne Carroll
  1871-1961 .... *13*
Moore, Clement Clarke
  1779-1863 .... *18*
Moore, Eva 1942- *20*
Moore, Fenworth
  See Stratemeyer, Edward L.
Moore, Jack (William) 1941- *46*
  Brief Entry *32*
Moore, Janet Gaylord 1905- *18*
Moore, Jim 1946- *42*
Moore, John Travers 1908- *12*
Moore, Lamont 1909-
  Brief Entry *29*
Moore, Margaret Rumberger
  1903- *12*
Moore, Marianne (Craig)
  1887-1972 .... *20*
Moore, Patrick (Alfred) 1923-
  Brief Entry *39*
Moore, Ray (S.) 1905(?)-1984
  Obituary *37*
Moore, Regina
  See Dunne, Mary Collins
Moore, Rosalie
  See Brown, Rosalie (Gertrude)
  Moore
Moore, Ruth *23*
Moore, Ruth Nulton 1923- *38*
Moore, S. E. *23*
Mooser, Stephen 1941- *28*
Mordvinoff, Nicolas
  1911-1973 .... *17*
More, Caroline [Joint pseudonym]
  See Cone, Molly Lamken and
  Strachan, Margaret Pitcairn
Morey, Charles
  See Fletcher, Helen Jill

Morey, Walt 1907- *3*
Morgan, Alfred P(owell)
  1889-1972 .... *33*
Morgan, Alison Mary 1930- *30*
Morgan, Geoffrey 1916- *46*
Morgan, Helen (Gertrude Louise)
  1921- *29*
Morgan, Helen Tudor
  See Morgan, Helen (Gertrude
  Louise)
Morgan, Jane
  See Cooper, James Fenimore
Morgan, Lenore 1908- *8*
Morgan, Louise
  See Morgan, Helen (Gertrude
  Louise)
Morgan, Shirley 1933- *10*
Morgan, Tom 1942- *42*
Morgenroth, Barbara
  Brief Entry *36*
Morrah, Dave
  See Morrah, David Wardlaw, Jr.
Morrah, David Wardlaw, Jr.
  1914- *10*
Morressy, John 1930- *23*
Morrill, Leslie H.
  Brief Entry *33*
Morris, Desmond (John)
  1928- *14*
Morris, Robert A. 1933- *7*
Morris, William 1913- *29*
Morrison, Bill 1935-
  Brief Entry *37*
Morrison, Dorothy Nafus *29*
Morrison, Gert W.
  See Stratemeyer, Edward L.
Morrison, Lillian 1917- *3*
Morrison, Lucile Phillips
  1896- *17*
Morrison, Roberta
  See Webb, Jean Francis (III)
Morrison, Velma Ford 1909- *21*
Morrison, William
  See Samachson, Joseph
Morriss, James E(dward)
  1932- *8*
Morrow, Betty
  See Bacon, Elizabeth
Morse, Carol
  See Yeakley, Marjory Hall
Morse, Dorothy B(ayley) 1906-1979
  Obituary *24*
Morse, Flo 1921- *30*
Mort, Vivian
  See Cromie, Alice Hamilton
Mortimer, Mary H.
  See Coury, Louise Andree
Morton, Lee Jack, Jr. 1928- *32*
Morton, Miriam 1918(?)-1985 ..... *9*
  Obituary *46*
Moscow, Alvin 1925- *3*
Mosel, Arlene 1921- *7*
Moser, Don
  See Moser, Donald Bruce
Moser, Donald Bruce 1932- *31*
Mosesson, Gloria R(ubin) *24*
Moskin, Marietta D(unston)
  1928- *23*

Moskof, Martin Stephen
  1930- *27*
Moss, Don(ald) 1920- *11*
Moss, Elaine Dora 1924-
  Brief Entry *31*
Most, Bernard 1937-
  Brief Entry *40*
Motz, Lloyd *20*
Mountain, Robert
  See Montgomery, R(aymond) A.,
  (Jr.)
Mountfield, David
  See Grant, Neil
Moussard, Jacqueline 1924- *24*
Mowat, Farley 1921- *3*
Moyler, Alan (Frank Powell)
  1926- *36*
Mozley, Charles 1915- *43*
  Brief Entry *32*
Mrs. Fairstar
  See Horne, Richard Henry
Mueller, Virginia 1924- *28*
Muir, Frank 1920- *30*
Mukerji, Dhan Gopal
  1890-1936 .... *40*
  See also CLR 10
Mulcahy, Lucille Burnett *12*
Mulford, Philippa Greene
  1948- *43*
Mulgan, Catherine
  See Gough, Catherine
Muller, Billex
  See Ellis, Edward S(ylvester)
Mullins, Edward S(wift)
  1922- *10*
Mulock, Dinah Maria
  See Craik, Dinah Maria (Mulock)
Mulvihill, William Patrick
  1923- *8*
Mun
  See Leaf, (Wilbur) Munro
Munari, Bruno 1907- *15*
  See also CLR 9
Munce, Ruth Hill 1898- *12*
Munowitz, Ken 1935-1977 .... *14*
Muñoz, William 1949- *42*
Munro, Alice 1931- *29*
Munro, Eleanor 1928- *37*
Munsinger, Lynn 1951- *33*
Munson(-Benson), Tunie
  1946- *15*
Munves, James (Albert) 1922- *30*
Munzer, Martha E. 1899- *4*
Murch, Mel and Starr, Ward [Joint
  double pseudonym]
  See Manes, Stephen
Murphy, Barbara Beasley
  1933- *5*
Murphy, E(mmett) Jefferson
  1926- *4*
Murphy, Jill 1949- *37*
Murphy, Jim 1947- *37*
  Brief Entry *32*
Murphy, Pat
  See Murphy, E(mmett) Jefferson
Murphy, Robert (William)
  1902-1971 .... *10*
Murphy, Shirley Rousseau
  1928- *36*

Murray, John 1923- *39*
Murray, Marian *5*
Murray, Michele 1933-1974 .... *7*
Murray, Ossie 1938- *43*
Musgrave, Florence 1902- *3*
Musgrove, Margaret W(ynkoop)
  1943- *26*
Mussey, Virginia T. H.
  See Ellison, Virginia Howell
Mutz
  See Kunstler, Morton
Myers, Arthur 1917- *35*
Myers, Bernice *9*
Myers, Caroline Elizabeth (Clark)
  1887-1980 .... *28*
Myers, Elisabeth P(erkins)
  1918- *36*
Myers, Hortense (Powner)
  1913- *10*
Myers, Walter Dean 1937- *41*
  Brief Entry *27*
  See also CLR 4
  See also SAAS 2
Myller, Rolf 1926- *27*
Myra, Harold L(awrence)
  1939- *46*
  Brief Entry *42*
Myrus, Donald (Richard)
  1927- *23*

N

Nakatani, Chiyoko 1930-
  Brief Entry *40*
Namioka, Lensey 1929- *27*
Napier, Mark
  See Laffin, John (Alfred Charles)
Nash, Bruce M(itchell) 1947- *34*
Nash, Linell
  See Smith, Linell Nash
Nash, Mary (Hughes) 1925- *41*
Nash, (Frederic) Ogden
  1902-1971 .... *46*
  Earlier sketch in SATA 2
Nast, Elsa Ruth
  See Watson, Jane Werner
Nast, Thomas 1840-1902
  Brief Entry *33*
Nastick, Sharon 1954- *41*
Nathan, Dorothy (Goldeen)
  (?)-1966 .... *15*
Nathan, Robert (Gruntal)
  1894-1985 .... *6*
  Obituary *43*
Natti, Susanna 1948- *32*
Navarra, John Gabriel 1927- *8*
Naylor, Penelope 1941- *10*
Naylor, Phyllis Reynolds
  1933- *12*
Nazaroff, Alexander I. 1898- *4*
Neal, Harry Edward 1906- *5*
Nearing, Penny 1916-
  Brief Entry *42*
Nebel, Gustave E. *45*
  Brief Entry *33*
Nebel, Mimouca
  See Nebel, Gustave E.
Nee, Kay Bonner *10*
Needle, Jan 1943- *30*

Needleman, Jacob 1934- 6
Negri, Rocco 1932- 12
Neigoff, Anne 13
Neigoff, Mike 1920- 13
Neilson, Frances Fullerton (Jones)
  1910- 14
Neimark, Anne E. 1935- 4
Neimark, Paul G. 1934-
  Brief Entry 37
Nelson, Cordner (Bruce) 1918-
  Brief Entry 29
Nelson, Esther L. 1928- 13
Nelson, Lawrence E(rnest) 1928-1977
  Obituary 28
Nelson, Mary Carroll 1929- 23
Nesbit, E(dith)
  1858-1924 ....YABC 1
  See also CLR 3
Nesbit, Troy
  See Folsom, Franklin
Nespojohn, Katherine V.
  1912- 7
Ness, Evaline (Michelow)
  1911- 26
  Earlier sketch in SATA 1
  See also CLR 6
  See also SAAS 1
Neufeld, John 1938- 6
  See also SAAS 3
Neumeyer, Peter F(lorian)
  1929- 13
Neurath, Marie (Reidemeister)
  1898- 1
Neusner, Jacob 1932- 38
Neville, Emily Cheney 1919- 1
  See also SAAS 2
Neville, Mary
  See Woodrich, Mary Neville
Nevins, Albert J. 1915- 20
Newberry, Clare Turlay
  1903-1970 1
  Obituary 26
Newbery, John 1713-1767 20
Newcomb, Ellsworth
  See Kenny, Ellsworth Newcomb
Newcombe, Jack 45
  Brief Entry 33
Newell, Crosby
  See Bonsall, Crosby (Barbara
  Newell)
Newell, Edythe W. 1910- 11
Newell, Hope (Hockenberry)
  1896-1965 24
Newfeld, Frank 1928- 26
Newlon, (Frank) Clarke
  1905(?)-1982 6
  Obituary 33
Newman, Daisy 1904- 27
Newman, Gerald 1939- 46
  Brief Entry 42
Newman, Robert (Howard)
  1909- 4
Newman, Shirlee Petkin
  1924- 10
Newsom, Carol 1948- 40
Newton, James R(obert)
  1935- 23
Newton, Suzanne 1936- 5

Ney, John 1923- 43
  Brief Entry 33
Nic Leodhas, Sorche
  See Alger, Leclaire (Gowans)
Nichols, Cecilia Fawn 1906- 12
Nichols, Peter
  See Youd, (Christopher) Samuel
Nichols, (Joanna) Ruth 1948- 15
Nicholson, Joyce Thorpe
  1919- 35
Nickelsburg, Janet 1893- 11
Nickerson, Betty
  See Nickerson, Elizabeth
Nickerson, Elizabeth 1922- 14
Nicklaus, Carol
  Brief Entry 33
Nicol, Ann
  See Turnbull, Ann (Christine)
Nicolas
  See Mordvinoff, Nicolas
Nicolay, Helen
  1866-1954 ....YABC 1
Nicole, Christopher Robin
  1930- 5
Nielsen, Kay (Rasmus)
  1886-1957 16
Nielsen, Virginia
  See McCall, Virginia Nielsen
Niland, Deborah 1951- 27
Nixon, Hershell Howard
  1923- 42
Nixon, Joan Lowery 1927- 44
  Earlier sketch in SATA 8
Nixon, K.
  See Nixon, Kathleen Irene (Blundell)
Nixon, Kathleen Irene
  (Blundell) 14
Noble, Iris 1922- 5
Noble, Trinka Hakes
  Brief Entry 37
Nodset, Joan L.
  See Lexau, Joan M.
Noguere, Suzanne 1947- 34
Nolan, Dennis 1945- 42
  Brief Entry 34
Nolan, Jeannette Covert
  1897-1974 2
  Obituary 27
Nolan, William F(rancis) 1928-
  Brief Entry 28
Noonan, Julia 1946- 4
Norcross, John
  See Conroy, Jack (Wesley)
Nordhoff, Charles (Bernard)
  1887-1947 23
Nordlicht, Lillian 29
Nordstrom, Ursula 3
Norman, Charles 1904- 38
Norman, James
  See Schmidt, James Norman
Norman, Mary 1931- 36
Norman, Steve
  See Pashko, Stanley
Norris, Gunilla B(rodde)
  1939- 20
North, Andrew
  See Norton, Alice Mary
North, Captain George
  See Stevenson, Robert Louis

North, Joan 1920- 16
North, Robert
  See Withers, Carl A.
North, Sterling 1906-1974 45
  Obituary 26
  Earlier sketch in SATA 1
Norton, Alice Mary 1912- 43
  Earlier sketch in SATA 1
Norton, André
  See Norton, Alice Mary
Norton, Browning
  See Norton, Frank R(owland)
  B(rowning)
Norton, Frank R(owland) B(rowning)
  1909- 10
Norton, Mary 1903- 18
  See also CLR 6
Nöstlinger, Christine 1936-
  Brief Entry 37
Nowell, Elizabeth Cameron 12
Numeroff, Laura Joffe 1953- 28
Nurenberg, Thelma
  See Greenhaus, Thelma Nurenberg
Nurnberg, Maxwell
  1897-1984 27
  Obituary 41
Nussbaumer, Paul (Edmond)
  1934- 16
Nyce, (Nellie) Helene von Strecker
  1885-1969 19
Nyce, Vera 1862-1925 19
Nye, Harold G.
  See Harding, Lee
Nye, Robert 1939- 6

O

Oakes, Vanya 1909-1983 6
  Obituary 37
Oakley, Don(ald G.) 1927- 8
Oakley, Graham 1929- 30
  See also CLR 7
Oakley, Helen 1906- 10
Oana, Katherine D. 1929-
  Brief Entry 37
Oana, Kay D.
  See Oana, Katherine D.
Obligado, Lilian (Isabel) 1931-
  Brief Entry 45
Obrant, Susan 1946- 11
O'Brien, Esse Forrester 1895(?)-1975
  Obituary 30
O'Brien, Robert C.
  See Conly, Robert Leslie
  See also CLR 2
O'Brien, Thomas C(lement)
  1938- 29
O'Carroll, Ryan
  See Markun, Patricia M(aloney)
O'Connell, Margaret F(orster)
  1935-1977
  Obituary 30
O'Connell, Peg
  See Ahern, Margaret McCrohan
O'Connor, Karen 1938- 34
O'Connor, Patrick
  See Wibberley, Leonard (Patrick
  O'Connor)

O'Connor, Richard 1915-1975
Obituary 21
O'Daniel, Janet 1921- 24
O'Dell, Scott 1903- 12
See also CLR 1
Odenwald, Robert P(aul)
1899-1965 11
Odor, Ruth Shannon 1926-
Brief Entry 44
Oechsli, Kelly 1918- 5
Ofek, Uriel 1926- 36
Offit, Sidney 1928- 10
Ofosu-Appiah, L(awrence) H(enry)
1920- 13
Ogan, George F. 1912- 13
Ogan, M. G. [Joint pseudonym]
See Ogan, George F. and Ogan,
Margaret E. (Nettles)
Ogan, Margaret E. (Nettles)
1923- 13
Ogburn, Charlton, Jr. 1911- 3
Ogilvie, Elisabeth May 1917- 40
Brief Entry 29
O'Hagan, Caroline 1946- 38
O'Hanlon, Jacklyn
See Meek, Jacklyn O'Hanlon
O'Hara, Mary
See Alsop, Mary O'Hara
Ohlsson, Ib 1935- 7
Ohtomo, Yasuo 1946- 37
O'Kelley, Mattie Lou 1908- 36
Okimoto, Jean Davies 1942- 34
Olcott, Frances Jenkins
1872(?)-1963 19
Old Boy
See Hughes, Thomas
Old Fag
See Bell, Robert S(tanley) W(arren)
Oldenburg, E(gbert) William
1936-1974 35
Olds, Elizabeth 1896- 3
Olds, Helen Diehl 1895-1981 9
Obituary 25
Oldstyle, Jonathan
See Irving, Washington
O'Leary, Brian 1940- 6
Oleksy, Walter 1930- 33
Olesky, Walter
See Oleksy, Walter
Oliver, John Edward 1933- 21
Olmstead, Lorena Ann 1890- 13
Olney, Ross R. 1929- 13
Olschewski, Alfred 1920- 7
Olsen, Ib Spang 1921- 6
Olson, Gene 1922- 32
Olugebefola, Ademole 1941- 15
Oman, Carola (Mary Anima)
1897-1978 35
Ommanney, F(rancis) D(ownes)
1903-1980 23
O Mude
See Gorey, Edward St. John
Oneal, Elizabeth 1934- 30
Oneal, Zibby
See Oneal, Elizabeth
O'Neill, Judith (Beatrice)
1930- 34
O'Neill, Mary L(e Duc) 1908- 2
Opie, Iona 1923- 3

Opie, Peter (Mason)
1918-1982 3
Obituary 28
Oppenheim, Joanne 1934- 5
Oppenheimer, Joan L(etson)
1925- 28
Optic, Oliver
See Adams, William Taylor
Orbach, Ruth Gary 1941- 21
Orczy, Emmuska, Baroness
1865-1947 40
Orgel, Doris 1929- 7
Oriolo, Joe
See Oriolo, Joseph
Oriolo, Joseph 1913-1985
Obituary 46
Orleans, Ilo 1897-1962 10
Ormerod, Jan(ette Louise) 1946-
Brief Entry 44
Ormondroyd, Edward 1925- 14
Ormsby, Virginia H(aire) 11
Orris
See Ingelow, Jean
Orth, Richard
See Gardner, Richard
Orwell, George
See Blair, Eric Arthur
Osborne, Chester G. 1915- 11
Osborne, David
See Silverberg, Robert
Osborne, Leone Neal 1914- 2
Osborne, Mary Pope 1949-
Brief Entry 41
Osceola
See Blixen, Karen (Christentze
Dinesen)
Osgood, William E(dward)
1926- 37
Osmond, Edward 1900- 10
Ossoli, Sarah Margaret (Fuller)
marchesa d' 1810-1850 25
Otis, James
See Kaler, James Otis
O'Trigger, Sir Lucius
See Horne, Richard Henry
Ottley, Reginald (Leslie) 26
Otto, Margaret Glover 1909-1976
Obituary 30
Ouida
See De La Ramée, (Marie) Louise
Ousley, Odille 1896- 10
Overton, Jenny (Margaret Mary) 1942-
Brief Entry 36
Owen, Caroline Dale
See Snedecker, Caroline Dale
(Parke)
Owen, Clifford
See Hamilton, Charles H. St. John
Owen, Dilys
See Gater, Dilys
Owen, (Benjamin) Evan
1918-1984 38
Oxenbury, Helen 1938- 3

P

Pace, Mildred Mastin 1907- 46
Brief Entry 29

Packer, Vin
See Meaker, Marijane
Page, Eileen
See Heal, Edith
Page, Eleanor
See Coerr, Eleanor
Page, Lou Williams 1912- 38
Paget-Fredericks, Joseph E. P. Rous-
Marten 1903-1963
Brief Entry 30
Pahz, (Anne) Cheryl Suzanne
1949- 11
Pahz, James Alon 1943- 11
Paice, Margaret 1920- 10
Paige, Harry W. 1922- 41
Brief Entry 35
Paine, Roberta M. 1925- 13
Paisley, Tom
See Bethancourt, T. Ernesto
Palazzo, Anthony D.
1905-1970 3
Palazzo, Tony
See Palazzo, Anthony D.
Palder, Edward L. 1922- 5
Palladini, David (Mario)
1946- 40
Brief Entry 32
Pallas, Norvin 1918- 23
Pallister, John C(lare) 1891-1980
Obituary 26
Palmer, Bernard 1914- 26
Palmer, C(yril) Everard 1930- 14
Palmer, (Ruth) Candida 1926- 11
Palmer, Heidi 1948- 15
Palmer, Helen Marion
See Geisel, Helen
Palmer, Juliette 1930- 15
Palmer, Robin 1911- 43
Panetta, George 1915-1969 15
Pansy
See Alden, Isabella (Macdonald)
Pantell, Dora (Fuchs) 1915- 39
Panter, Carol 1936- 9
Papashvily, George
1898-1978 17
Papashvily, Helen (Waite)
1906- 17
Pape, D(onna) L(ugg) 1930- 2
Paperny, Myra (Green) 1932-
Brief Entry 33
Paradis, Adrian A(lexis)
1912- 1
Paradis, Marjorie (Bartholomew)
1886(?)-1970 17
Parenteau, Shirley (Laurolyn) 1935-
Brief Entry 40
Parish, Peggy 1927- 17
Park, Barbara 1947- 40
Brief Entry 35
Park, Bill
See Park, W(illiam) B(ryan)
Park, Ruth 25
Park, W(illiam) B(ryan) 1936- 22
Parker, Elinor 1906- 3
Parker, Lois M(ay) 1912- 30
Parker, Nancy Winslow 1930- 10
Parker, Richard 1915- 14
Parker, Robert
See Boyd, Waldo T.

Parkinson, Ethelyn M(inerva)
1906- *11*
Parks, Edd Winfield
1906-1968 .... *10*
Parks, Gordon (Alexander Buchanan)
1912- *8*
Parley, Peter
See Goodrich, Samuel Griswold
Parlin, John
See Graves, Charles Parlin
Parnall, Peter 1936- *16*
Parr, Letitia (Evelyn) 1906- *37*
Parr, Lucy 1924- *10*
Parrish, Anne 1888-1957 .... *27*
Parrish, Mary
See Cousins, Margaret
Parrish, (Frederick) Maxfield
1870-1966 .... *14*
Parry, Marian 1924- *13*
Parsons, Tom
See MacPherson, Thomas George
Partch, Virgil Franklin II
1916-1984 .... *45*
Obituary *39*
Partridge, Benjamin W(aring), Jr.
1915- *28*
Partridge, Jenny (Lilian) 1947-
Brief Entry *37*
Pascal, David 1918- *14*
Pascal, Francine 1938-
Brief Entry *37*
Paschal, Nancy
See Trotter, Grace V(iolet)
Pashko, Stanley 1913- *29*
Patent, Dorothy Hinshaw
1940- *22*
Paterson, Diane (R. Cole) 1946-
Brief Entry *33*
Paterson, Katherine (Womeldorf)
1932- *13*
See also CLR 7
Paton, Alan (Stewart) 1903- *11*
Paton, Jane (Elizabeth) 1934- *35*
Paton Walsh, Gillian 1939- *4*
See also SAAS 3
Patten, Brian 1946- *29*
Patterson, Geoffrey 1943-
Brief Entry *44*
Patterson, Lillie G. *14*
Paul, Aileen 1917- *12*
Paul, Elizabeth
See Crow, Donna Fletcher
Paul, James 1936- *23*
Paul, Robert
See Roberts, John G(aither)
Pauli, Hertha (Ernestine)
1909-1973 .... *3*
Obituary *26*
Paull, Grace A. 1898- *24*
Paulsen, Gary 1939- *22*
Paulson, Jack
See Jackson, C. Paul
Pavel, Frances 1907- *10*
Payne, Donald Gordon 1924- *37*
Payne, Emmy
See West, Emily G(ovan)
Payson, Dale 1943- *9*
Payzant, Charles *18*

Payzant, Jessie Mercer Knechtel
See Shannon, Terry
Paz, A.
See Pahz, James Alon
Paz, Zan
See Pahz, Cheryl Suzanne
Peake, Mervyn 1911-1968 .... *23*
Peale, Norman Vincent 1898- *20*
Pearce, (Ann) Philippa 1920- *1*
See also CLR 9
Peare, Catherine Owens 1911- *9*
Pears, Charles 1873-1958
Brief Entry *30*
Pearson, Susan 1946- *39*
Brief Entry *27*
Pease, Howard 1894-1974 .... *2*
Obituary *25*
Peck, Anne Merriman 1884- *18*
Peck, Richard 1934- *18*
See also SAAS 2
Peck, Robert Newton III
1928- *21*
See also SAAS 1
Peek, Merle 1938- *39*
Peel, Norman Lemon
See Hirsch, Phil
Peeples, Edwin A. 1915- *6*
Peet, Bill
See Peet, William Bartlett
Peet, Creighton B. 1899-1977 ..... *30*
Peet, William Bartlett 1915- *41*
Earlier sketch in SATA 2
Peirce, Waldo 1884-1970
Brief Entry *28*
Pelaez, Jill 1924- *12*
Pellowski, Anne 1933- *20*
Pelta, Kathy 1928- *18*
Peltier, Leslie C(opus) 1900- *13*
Pembury, Bill
See Gronon, Arthur William
Pemsteen, Hans
See Manes, Stephen
Pendennis, Arthur, Esquire
See Thackeray, William Makepeace
Pender, Lydia 1907- *3*
Pendery, Rosemary *7*
Pendle, Alexy 1943- *29*
Pendle, George 1906-1977
Obituary *28*
Penn, Ruth Bonn
See Rosenberg, Ethel
Pennage, E. M.
See Finkel, George (Irvine)
Penney, Grace Jackson 1904- *35*
Pennington, Eunice 1923- *27*
Pennington, Lillian Boyer
1904- *45*
Penrose, Margaret
See Stratemeyer, Edward L.
Penzler, Otto 1942- *38*
Pepe, Phil(ip) 1935- *20*
Peppe, Rodney 1934- *4*
Percy, Charles Henry
See Smith, Dodie
Perera, Thomas Biddle 1938- *13*
Perkins, Al(bert Rogers)
1904-1975 .... *30*
Perkins, Marlin 1905- *21*
Perl, Lila *6*

Perl, Susan 1922-1983 .... *22*
Obituary *34*
Perlmutter, O(scar) William
1920-1975 .... *8*
Perrault, Charles 1628-1703 ...... *25*
Perreard, Suzanne Louise Butler 1919-
Brief Entry *29*
Perrine, Mary 1913- *2*
Perry, Barbara Fisher
See Fisher, Barbara
Perry, Patricia 1949- *30*
Perry, Roger 1933- *27*
Pershing, Marie
See Schultz, Pearle Henriksen
Peters, Caroline
See Betz, Eva Kelly
Peters, S. H.
See Porter, William Sydney
Petersen, P(eter) J(ames) 1941-
Brief Entry *43*
Petersham, Maud (Fuller)
1890-1971 .... *17*
Petersham, Miska 1888-1960 ..... *17*
Peterson, Esther (Allen) 1934- *35*
Peterson, Hans 1922- *8*
Peterson, Harold L(eslie)
1922- *8*
Peterson, Helen Stone 1910- *8*
Peterson, Jeanne Whitehouse
See Whitehouse, Jeanne
Peterson, Lorraine 1940-
Brief Entry *44*
Petie, Haris 1915- *10*
Petrides, Heidrun 1944- *19*
Petrie, Catherine 1947-
Brief Entry *41*
Petrovich, Michael B(oro)
1922- *40*
Petrovskaya, Kyra
See Wayne, Kyra Petrovskaya
Petry, Ann (Lane) *5*
Pevsner, Stella *8*
Peyo
See Culliford, Pierre
Peyton, K. M.
See Peyton, Kathleen (Wendy)
See also CLR 3
Peyton, Kathleen (Wendy)
1929- *15*
Pfeffer, Susan Beth 1948- *4*
Phelan, Josephine 1905-
Brief Entry *30*
Phelan, Mary Kay 1914- *3*
Phelps, Ethel Johnston 1914- *35*
Philbrook, Clem(ent E.) 1917- *24*
Phillips, Irv
See Phillips, Irving W.
Phillips, Irving W. 1908- *11*
Phillips, Jack
See Sandburg, Carl (August)
Phillips, Leon
See Gerson, Noel B(ertram)
Phillips, Loretta (Hosey)
1893- *10*
Phillips, Louis 1942- *8*
Phillips, Mary Geisler
1881-1964 .... *10*
Phillips, Prentice 1894- *10*
Phillpotts, Eden 1862-1960 .... *24*

Phipson, Joan
  See Fitzhardinge, Joan M.
  See also CLR 5
  See also SAAS 3
Phiz
  See Browne, Hablot Knight
Phleger, Fred B. 1909- 34
Phleger, Marjorie Temple 1
Phypps, Hyacinthe
  See Gorey, Edward St. John
Piaget, Jean 1896-1980
  Obituary 23
Piatti, Celestino 1922- 16
Picard, Barbara Leonie 1917- 2
Pickard, Charles 1932- 36
Pickering, James Sayre
  1897-1969 36
  Obituary 28
Pienkowski, Jan 1936- 6
  See also CLR 6
Pierce, Edith Gray 1893-1977 45
Pierce, Katherine
  See St. John, Wylly Folk
Pierce, Ruth (Ireland) 1936- 5
Pierik, Robert 1921- 13
Pig, Edward
  See Gorey, Edward St. John
Pike, E(dgar) Royston 1896- 22
Pilarski, Laura 1926- 13
Pilgrim, Anne
  See Allan, Mabel Esther
Pilkington, Francis Meredyth
  1907- 4
Pilkington, Roger (Windle)
  1915- 10
Pinchot, David 1914(?)-1983
  Obituary 34
Pincus, Harriet 1938- 27
Pine, Tillie S(chloss) 1897- 13
Pinkerton, Kathrene Sutherland
  (Gedney) 1887-1967
  Obituary 26
Pinkney, Jerry 1939- 41
  Brief Entry 32
Pinkwater, Daniel Manus
  1941- 46
  Earlier sketch in SATA 8
  See also CLR 4
  See also SAAS 3
Pinner, Joma
  See Werner, Herma
Pioneer
  See Yates, Raymond F(rancis)
Piper, Roger
  See Fisher, John (Oswald Hamilton)
Piper, Watty
  See Bragg, Mabel Caroline
Piro, Richard 1934- 7
Pirsig, Robert M(aynard)
  1928- 39
Pitman, (Isaac) James 1901-1985
  Obituary 46
Pitrone, Jean Maddern 1920- 4
Pitz, Henry C(larence)
  1895-1976 4
  Obituary 24
Pizer, Vernon 1918- 21
Place, Marian T. 1910- 3

Plaidy, Jean
  See Hibbert, Eleanor
Plaine, Alfred R. 1898(?)-1981
  Obituary 29
Platt, Kin 1911- 21
Plimpton, George (Ames)
  1927- 10
Plomer, William (Charles Franklin)
  1903-1973 24
Plotz, Helen (Ratnoff) 1913- 38
Plowhead, Ruth Gipson
  1877-1967 43
Plowman, Stephanie 1922- 6
Pluckrose, Henry (Arthur)
  1931- 13
Plum, J.
  See Wodehouse, P(elham)
  G(renville)
Plumb, Charles P. 1900(?)-1982
  Obituary 29
Plume, Ilse
  Brief Entry 43
Plummer, Margaret 1911- 2
Podendorf, Illa E.
  1903(?)-1983 18
  Obituary 35
Poe, Edgar Allan 1809-1849 23
Pogány, William Andrew
  1882-1955 44
Pogány, Willy
  Brief Entry 30
  See Pogány, William Andrew
Pohl, Frederik 1919- 24
Pohlmann, Lillian (Grenfell)
  1902- 11
Pointon, Robert
  See Rooke, Daphne (Marie)
Pola
  See Watson, Pauline
Polatnick, Florence T. 1923- 5
Polder, Markus
  See Krüss, James
Polette, Nancy (Jane) 1930- 42
Polhamus, Jean Burt 1928- 21
Politi, Leo 1908- 1
Polking, Kirk 1925- 5
Polland, Barbara K(ay) 1939- 44
Polland, Madeleine A. 1918- 6
Pollock, Bruce 1945- 46
Pollock, Mary
  See Blyton, Enid (Mary)
Pollock, Penny 1935- 44
  Brief Entry 42
Pollowitz, Melinda (Kilborn)
  1944- 26
Polonsky, Arthur 1925- 34
Polseno, Jo 17
Pomerantz, Charlotte 20
Pomeroy, Pete
  See Roth, Arthur J(oseph)
Pond, Alonzo W(illiam) 1894- 5
Pontiflet, Ted 1932- 32
Poole, Gray Johnson 1906- 1
Poole, Josephine 1933- 5
  See also SAAS 2
Poole, Lynn 1910-1969 1
Poole, Peggy 1925- 39
Poortvliet, Marien
  See Poortvliet, Rien

Poortvliet, Rien 1933(?)-
  Brief Entry 37
Pope, Elizabeth Marie 1917- 38
  Brief Entry 36
Portal, Colette 1936- 6
Porte, Barbara Ann
  Brief Entry 45
Porter, Katherine Anne
  1890-1980 39
  Obituary 23
Porter, Sheena 1935- 24
Porter, William Sydney
  1862-1910 .... YABC 2
Portteus, Eleanora Marie Manthei
  (?)-1983
  Obituary 36
Posell, Elsa Z. 3
Posten, Margaret L(ois) 1915- 10
Potok, Chaim 1929- 33
Potter, (Helen) Beatrix
  1866-1943 .... YABC 1
  See also CLR 1
Potter, Margaret (Newman)
  1926- 21
Potter, Marian 1915- 9
Potter, Miriam Clark
  1886-1965 3
Pournelle, Jerry (Eugene)
  1933- 26
Powell, A. M.
  See Morgan, Alfred P(owell)
Powell, Richard Stillman
  See Barbour, Ralph Henry
Powers, Anne
  See Schwartz, Anne Powers
Powers, Bill 1931-
  Brief Entry 31
Powers, Margaret
  See Heal, Edith
Powledge, Fred 1935- 37
Poynter, Margaret 1927- 27
Prager, Arthur 44
Preiss, Byron (Cary)
  Brief Entry 42
Prelutsky, Jack 22
Presberg, Miriam Goldstein 1919-1978
  Brief Entry 38
Preston, Edna Mitchell 40
Preussler, Otfried 1923- 24
Prevert, Jacques (Henri Marie)
  1900-1977
  Obituary 30
Price, Christine 1928-1980 3
  Obituary 23
Price, Garrett 1896-1979
  Obituary 22
Price, Jennifer
  See Hoover, Helen (Drusilla
  Blackburn)
Price, Jonathan (Reeve) 1941- 46
Price, Lucie Locke
  See Locke, Lucie
Price, Margaret (Evans) 1888-1973
  Brief Entry 28
Price, Olive 1903- 8
Price, Susan 1955- 25
Price, Willard 1887-
  Brief Entry 38
Prideaux, Tom 1908- 37

Priestley, Lee (Shore) 1904- 27
Prieto, Mariana B(eeching)
    1912- 8
Prime, Derek (James) 1931- 34
Prince, Alison 1931- 28
Prince, J(ack) H(arvey) 1908- 17
Pringle, Laurence 1935- 4
    See also CLR 4
Pritchett, Elaine H(illyer)
    1920- 36
Proctor, Everitt
    See Montgomery, Rutherford
Professor Zingara
    See Leeming, Joseph
Provensen, Alice 1918- 9
Provensen, Martin 1916- 9
Pryor, Helen Brenton
    1897-1972 4
Pucci, Albert John 1920- 44
Pudney, John (Sleigh)
    1909-1977 24
Pugh, Ellen T. 1920- 7
Pullein-Thompson, Christine
    1930- 3
Pullein-Thompson, Diana 3
Pullein-Thompson, Josephine 3
Puner, Helen W(alker) 1915- 37
Purdy, Susan Gold 1939- 8
Purscell, Phyllis 1934- 7
Putnam, Arthur Lee
    See Alger, Horatio, Jr.
Putnam, Peter B(rock) 1920- 30
Pyle, Howard 1853-1911 16
Pyne, Mable Mandeville
    1903-1969 9

Q

Quackenbush, Robert M.
    1929- 7
Quammen, David 1948- 7
Quarles, Benjamin 1904- 12
Queen, Ellery, Jr.
    See Holding, James
Quennell, Marjorie (Courtney)
    1884-1972 29
Quick, Annabelle 1922- 2
Quin-Harkin, Janet 1941- 18
Quinn, Elisabeth 1881-1962 22
Quinn, Susan
    See Jacobs, Susan
Quinn, Vernon
    See Quinn, Elisabeth

R

Rabe, Berniece 1928- 7
Rabe, Olive H(anson)
    1887-1968 13
Rabinowich, Ellen 1946- 29
Rabinowitz, Sandy 1954-
    Brief Entry 39
Raboff, Ernest Lloyd
    Brief Entry 37
Rackham, Arthur 1867-1939 15
Radford, Ruby L(orraine)
    1891-1971 6

Radlauer, David 1952- 28
Radlauer, Edward 1921- 15
Radlauer, Ruth (Shaw) 1926- ... 15
Radley, Gail 1951- 25
Rae, Gwynedd 1892-1977 37
Raebeck, Lois 1921- 5
Raftery, Gerald (Bransfield)
    1905- 11
Rahn, Joan Elma 1929- 27
Raible, Alton (Robert) 1918- 35
Raiff, Stan 1930- 11
Rainey, W. B.
    See Blassingame, Wyatt Rainey
Ralston, Jan
    See Dunlop, Agnes M. R.
Ramal, Walter
    See de la Mare, Walter
Ranadive, Gail 1944- 10
Rand, Ann (Binkley) 30
Rand, Paul 1914- 6
Randall, Florence Engel 1917- ... 5
Randall, Janet [Joint pseudonym]
    See Young, Janet Randall and
    Young, Robert W.
Randall, Robert
    See Silverberg, Robert
Randall, Ruth Painter
    1892-1971 3
Randolph, Lieutenant J. H.
    See Ellis, Edward S(ylvester)
Rands, William Brighty
    1823-1882 17
Ranney, Agnes V. 1916- 6
Ransome, Arthur (Michell)
    1884-1967 22
    See also CLR 8
Rapaport, Stella F(read) 10
Raphael, Elaine (Chionchio)
    1933- 23
Rappaport, Eva 1924- 6
Rarick, Carrie 1911- 41
Raskin, Edith (Lefkowitz)
    1908- 9
Raskin, Ellen 1928-1984 38
    Earlier sketch in SATA 2
    See also CLR 1
Raskin, Joseph 1897-1982 12
    Obituary 29
Rasmussen, Knud Johan Victor
    1879-1933
    Brief Entry 34
Rathjen, Carl H(enry) 1909- 11
Rattray, Simon
    See Trevor, Elleston
Rau, Margaret 1913- 9
    See also CLR 8
Rauch, Mabel Thompson 1888-1972
    Obituary 26
Raucher, Herman 1928- 8
Ravielli, Anthony 1916- 3
Rawlings, Marjorie Kinnan
    1896-1953 .... YABC 1
Rawls, (Woodrow) Wilson
    1913- 22
Ray, Deborah 1940- 8
Ray, Irene
    See Sutton, Margaret Beebe
Ray, JoAnne 1935- 9

Ray, Mary (Eva Pedder)
    1932- 2
Raymond, James Crossley 1917-1981
    Obituary 29
Raymond, Robert
    See Alter, Robert Edmond
Rayner, Mary 1933- 22
Rayner, William 1929-
    Brief Entry 36
Raynor, Dorka 28
Rayson, Steven 1932- 30
Razzell, Arthur (George)
    1925- 11
Razzi, James 1931- 10
Read, Elfreida 1920- 2
Read, Piers Paul 1941- 21
Ready, Kirk L. 1943- 39
Reaney, James 1926- 43
Reck, Franklin Mering 1896-1965
    Brief Entry 30
Redding, Robert Hull 1919- 2
Redway, Ralph
    See Hamilton, Charles H. St. John
Redway, Ridley
    See Hamilton, Charles H. St. John
Reed, Betty Jane 1921- 4
Reed, Gwendolyn E(lizabeth)
    1932- 21
Reed, Kit 1932- 34
Reed, Philip G. 1908-
    Brief Entry 29
Reed, Thomas (James) 1947- 34
Reed, William Maxwell
    1871-1962 15
Reeder, Colonel Red
    See Reeder, Russell P., Jr.
Reeder, Russell P., Jr. 1902- 4
Reeman, Douglas Edward 1924-
    Brief Entry 28
Rees, David Bartlett 1936- 36
Rees, Ennis 1925- 3
Reeve, Joel
    See Cox, William R(obert)
Reeves, James 1909- 15
Reeves, Joyce 1911- 17
Reeves, Lawrence F. 1926- 29
Reeves, Ruth Ellen
    See Ranney, Agnes V.
Regehr, Lydia 1903- 37
Reggiani, Renée 18
Reid, Alastair 1926- 46
Reid, Barbara 1922- 21
Reid, Dorothy M(arion) (?)-1974
    Brief Entry 29
Reid, Eugenie Chazal 1924- 12
Reid, John Calvin 21
Reid, (Thomas) Mayne
    1818-1883 24
Reid, Meta Mayne 1905-
    Brief Entry 36
Reid Banks, Lynne 1929- 22
Reiff, Stephanie Ann 1948-
    Brief Entry 28
Reig, June 1933- 30
Reigot, Betty Polisar 1924-
    Brief Entry 41
Reinach, Jacquelyn (Krasne)
    1930- 28

Reiner, William B(uck)
  1910-1976 46
  Obituary 30
Reinfeld, Fred 1910-1964 3
Reiniger, Lotte 1899-1981 40
  Obituary 33
Reiss, Johanna de Leeuw
  1932- 18
Reiss, John J. 23
Reit, Seymour 21
Reit, Sy
  See Reit, Seymour
Rémi, Georges 1907-1983 13
  Obituary 32
Remington, Frederic (Sackrider)
  1861-1909 41
Renault, Mary
  See Challans, Mary
Rendell, Joan 28
Rendina, Laura Cooper 1902- 10
Renick, Marion (Lewis) 1905- 1
Renken, Aleda 1907- 27
Renlie, Frank H. 1936- 11
Rensie, Willis
  See Eisner, Will(iam Erwin)
Renvoize, Jean 1930- 5
Resnick, Michael D(iamond)
  1942- 38
Resnick, Mike
  See Resnick, Michael D(iamond)
Resnick, Seymour 1920- 23
Retla, Robert
  See Alter, Robert Edmond
Reuter, Carol (Joan) 1931- 2
Rey, H(ans) A(ugusto)
  1898-1977 26
  Earlier sketch in SATA 1
  See also CLR 5
Rey, Margret (Elizabeth)
  1906- 26
  See also CLR 5
Reyher, Becky
  See Reyher, Rebecca Hourwich
Reyher, Rebecca Hourwich
  1897- 18
Reynolds, Dickson
  See Reynolds, Helen Mary
  Greenwood Campbell
Reynolds, Helen Mary Greenwood
  Campbell 1884-1969
  Obituary 26
Reynolds, John
  See Whitlock, Ralph
Reynolds, Madge
  See Whitlock, Ralph
Reynolds, Malvina 1900-1978 44
  Obituary 24
Reynolds, Pamela 1923- 34
Rhodes, Bennie (Loran) 1927- 35
Rhodes, Frank H(arold Trevor)
  1926- 37
Rhue, Morton
  See Strasser, Todd
Rhys, Megan
  See Williams, Jeanne
Ribbons, Ian 1924- 37
  Brief Entry 30
  See also SAAS 3

Ricciuti, Edward R(aphael)
  1938- 10
Rice, Charles D(uane) 1910-1971
  Obituary 27
Rice, Dale R(ichard) 1948- 42
Rice, Edward E. 1918-
  Brief Entry 42
Rice, Elizabeth 1913- 2
Rice, Eve (Hart) 1951- 34
Rice, Inez 1907- 13
Rice, James 1934- 22
Rich, Elaine Sommers 1926- 6
Rich, Josephine 1912- 10
Richard, Adrienne 1921- 5
Richards, Curtis
  See Curtis, Richard (Alan)
Richards, Frank
  See Hamilton, Charles H. St. John
Richards, Hilda
  See Hamilton, Charles H. St. John
Richards, Kay
  See Baker, Susan (Catherine)
Richards, Laura E(lizabeth Howe)
  1850-1943 ....YABC 1
Richards, R(onald) C(harles) W(illiam)
  1923-
  Brief Entry 43
Richardson, Frank Howard 1882-1970
  Obituary 27
Richardson, Grace Lee
  See Dickson, Naida
Richardson, Robert S(hirley)
  1902- 8
Richelson, Geraldine 1922- 29
Richler, Mordecai 1931- 44
  Brief Entry 27
Richoux, Pat 1927- 7
Richter, Alice 1941- 30
Richter, Conrad 1890-1968 3
Richter, Hans Peter 1925- 6
Rico, Don(ato) 1917-1985
  Obituary 43
Ridge, Antonia (Florence)
  (?)-1981 7
  Obituary 27
Ridge, Martin 1923- 43
Ridley, Nat, Jr.
  See Stratemeyer, Edward L.
Ridlon, Marci 1942- 22
Riedman, Sarah R(egal) 1902- 1
Riesenberg, Felix, Jr.
  1913-1962 23
Rieu, E(mile) V(ictor)
  1887-1972 46
  Obituary 26
Riggs, Sidney Noyes 1892-1975
  Obituary 28
Rikhoff, Jean 1928- 9
Riley, James Whitcomb
  1849-1916 17
Rinard, Judith E(llen) 1947- 44
Ringi, Kjell Arne Sörensen
  1939- 12
Rinkoff, Barbara (Jean)
  1923-1975 4
  Obituary 27
Riordan, James 1936- 28
Rios, Tere
  See Versace, Marie Teresa

Ripley, Elizabeth Blake
  1906-1969 5
Ripper, Charles L. 1929- 3
Ritchie, Barbara (Gibbons) 14
Ritts, Paul 1920(?)-1980
  Obituary 25
Rivera, Geraldo 1943-
  Brief Entry 28
Riverside, John
  See Heinlein, Robert A(nson)
Rivkin, Ann 1920- 41
Rivoli, Mario 1943- 10
Roach, Marilynne K(athleen)
  1946- 9
Roach, Portia
  See Takakjian, Portia
Robbins, Frank 1917- 42
  Brief Entry 32
Robbins, Raleigh
  See Hamilton, Charles H. St. John
Robbins, Ruth 1917(?)- 14
Robbins, Tony
  See Pashko, Stanley
Roberts, Bruce (Stuart) 1930-
  Brief Entry 39
Roberts, Charles G(eorge) D(ouglas)
  1860-1943
  Brief Entry 29
Roberts, David
  See Cox, John Roberts
Roberts, Elizabeth Madox
  1886-1941 33
  Brief Entry 27
Roberts, Jim
  See Bates, Barbara S(nedeker)
Roberts, John G(aither) 1913- ... 27
Roberts, Nancy Correll 1924-
  Brief Entry 28
Roberts, Terence
  See Sanderson, Ivan T.
Roberts, Willo Davis 1928- 21
Robertson, Barbara (Anne)
  1931- 12
Robertson, Don 1929- 8
Robertson, Dorothy Lewis
  1912- 12
Robertson, Jennifer (Sinclair)
  1942- 12
Robertson, Keith 1914- 1
Robinet, Harriette Gillem
  1931- 27
Robins, Seelin
  See Ellis, Edward S(ylvester)
Robinson, Adjai 1932- 8
Robinson, Barbara (Webb)
  1927- 8
Robinson, C(harles) A(lexander), Jr.
  1900-1965 36
Robinson, Charles 1870-1937 17
Robinson, Charles 1931- 6
Robinson, Jan M. 1933- 6
Robinson, Jean O. 1934- 7
Robinson, Jerry 1922-
  Brief Entry 34
Robinson, Joan (Mary) G(ale Thomas)
  1910- 7
Robinson, Marileta 1942- 32
Robinson, Maudie (Millian Oller)
  1914- 11

Robinson, Maurice R. 1895-1982
    Obituary 29
Robinson, Nancy K(onheim)
    1942- 32
    Brief Entry 31
Robinson, Ray(mond Kenneth)
    1920- 23
Robinson, Shari
    See McGuire, Leslie (Sarah)
Robinson, T(homas) H(eath)
    1869-1950 17
Robinson, (Wanda) Veronica
    1926- 30
Robinson, W(illiam) Heath
    1872-1944 17
Robison, Bonnie 1924- 12
Robison, Nancy L(ouise)
    1934- 32
Robottom, John 1934- 7
Roche, A. K. [Joint pseudonym]
    See Abisch, Roslyn Kroop and
    Kaplan, Boche
Roche, P(atricia) K.
    Brief Entry 34
Roche, Terry
    See Poole, Peggy
Rock, Gail
    Brief Entry 32
Rocker, Fermin 1907- 40
Rockwell, Anne F. 1934- 33
Rockwell, Gail
    Brief Entry 36
Rockwell, Harlow 33
Rockwell, Norman (Percevel)
    1894-1978 23
Rockwell, Thomas 1933- 7
    See also CLR 6
Rockwood, Joyce 1947- 39
Rockwood, Roy [Collective
    pseudonym] 1
    See also McFarlane, Leslie;
    Stratemeyer, Edward L.
Roddenberry, Eugene Wesley
    1921- 45
Roddenberry, Gene
    See Roddenberry, Eugene Wesley
Rodgers, Mary 1931- 8
Rodman, Emerson
    See Ellis, Edward S(ylvester)
Rodman, Maia
    See Wojciechowska, Maia
Rodman, Selden 1909- 9
Rodowsky, Colby 1932- 21
Roe, Harry Mason
    See Stratemeyer, Edward L.
Roever, J(oan) M(arilyn)
    1935- 26
Roffey, Maureen 1936- 33
Rogers, (Thomas) Alan (Stinchcombe)
    1937- 2
Rogers, Frances 1888-1974 10
Rogers, Fred (McFeely) 1928- ... 33
Rogers, Matilda 1894-1976 5
    Obituary 34
Rogers, Pamela 1927- 9
Rogers, Robert
    See Hamilton, Charles H. St. John
Rogers, W(illiam) G(arland)
    1896-1978 23

Rojan
    See Rojankovsky, Feodor
    (Stepanovich)
Rojankovsky, Feodor (Stepanovich)
    1891-1970 21
Rokeby-Thomas, Anna E(lma)
    1911- 15
Roland, Albert 1925- 11
Rolerson, Darrell A(llen)
    1946- 8
Roll, Winifred 1909- 6
Rollins, Charlemae Hill
    1897-1979 3
    Obituary 26
Romano, Louis 1921- 35
Rongen, Björn 1906- 10
Rood, Ronald (N.) 1920- 12
Rooke, Daphne (Marie) 1914- 12
Roos, Stephen (Kelley) 1945-
    Brief Entry 41
Roper, Laura Wood 1911- 34
Roscoe, D(onald) T(homas)
    1934- 42
Rose, Anna Perrot
    See Wright, Anna (Maria Louisa
    Perrot) Rose
Rose, Anne 8
Rose, Carl 1903-1971
    Brief Entry 31
Rose, Elizabeth Jane (Pretty) 1933-
    Brief Entry 28
Rose, Florella
    See Carlson, Vada F.
Rose, Gerald (Hembdon Seymour)
    1935-
    Brief Entry 30
Rose, Wendy 1948- 12
Rosen, Michael (Wayne) 1946-
    Brief Entry 40
Rosen, Sidney 1916- 1
Rosen, Winifred 1943- 8
Rosenbaum, Maurice 1907- 6
Rosenberg, Dorothy 1906- 40
Rosenberg, Ethel 3
Rosenberg, Nancy Sherman
    1931- 4
Rosenberg, Sharon 1942- 8
Rosenblatt, Arthur S. 1938-
    Brief Entry 45
Rosenbloom, Joseph 1928- 21
Rosenblum, Richard 1928- 11
Rosenburg, John M. 1918- 6
Rosenthal, Harold 1914- 35
Ross, Alan
    See Warwick, Alan R(oss)
Ross, Alex(ander) 1909-
    Brief Entry 29
Ross, Dave 1949- 32
Ross, David 1896-1975
    Obituary 20
Ross, Diana
    See Denney, Diana
Ross, Frank (Xavier), Jr.
    1914- 28
Ross, John 1921- 45
Ross, Tony 1938- 17
Ross, Wilda (S.) 1915-
    Brief Entry 39
Rossel, Seymour 1945- 28

Rössel-Waugh, C. C. [Joint
    pseudonym]
    See Waugh, Carol-Lynn Rössel
Rossetti, Christiana (Georgina)
    1830-1894 20
Roth, Arnold 1929- 21
Roth, Arthur J(oseph) 1925- 43
    Brief Entry 28
Roth, David 1940- 36
Rothkopf, Carol Z. 1929- 4
Rothman, Joel 1938- 7
Roueché, Berton 1911- 28
Roughsey, Dick 1921(?)- 35
Rounds, Glen (Harold) 1906- 8
Rourke, Constance (Mayfield)
    1885-1941 .... YABC 1
Rowe, Viola Carson 1903-1969
    Obituary 26
Rowland, Florence Wightman
    1900- 8
Rowland-Entwistle, (Arthur) Theodore
    (Henry) 1925- 31
Rowsome, Frank (Howard), Jr.
    1914-1983 36
Roy, Liam
    See Scarry, Patricia
Roy, Ron(ald) 1940- 40
    Brief Entry 35
Rubel, Nicole 1953- 18
Rubin, Eva Johanna 1925- 38
Ruby, Lois 1942- 35
    Brief Entry 34
Ruchlis, Hy 1913- 3
Ruckman, Ivy 1931- 37
Ruck-Pauquèt, Gina 1931- 40
    Brief Entry 37
Rudeen, Kenneth
    Brief Entry 36
Rudley, Stephen 1946- 30
Rudolph, Marguerita 1908- 21
Rudomin, Esther
    See Hautzig, Esther
Rue, Leonard Lee III 1926- 37
Ruedi, Norma Paul
    See Ainsworth, Norma
Ruffell, Ann 1941- 30
Ruffins, Reynold 1930- 41
Rugoff, Milton 1913- 30
Ruhen, Olaf 1911- 17
Rukeyser, Muriel 1913-1980
    Obituary 22
Rumsey, Marian (Barritt)
    1928- 16
Runyan, John
    See Palmer, Bernard
Rush, Alison 1951- 41
Rush, Peter 1937- 32
Rushmore, Helen 1898- 3
Rushmore, Robert (William)
    1926- 8
Ruskin, Ariane
    See Batterberry, Ariane Ruskin
Ruskin, John 1819-1900 24
Russell, Charlotte
    See Rathjen, Carl H(enry)
Russell, Franklin 1926- 11
Russell, Helen Ross 1915- 8
Russell, Patrick
    See Sammis, John

Russell, Solveig Paulson
1904- 3
Russo, Susan 1947- 30
Ruth, Rod 1912- 9
Rutherford, Douglas
See McConnell, James Douglas
(Rutherford)
Rutherford, Meg 1932- 34
Ruthin, Margaret 4
Rutgers van der Loeff, An(na) Basenau
1910- 22
Rutz, Viola Larkin 1932- 12
Ruzicka, Rudolph 1883-1978
Obituary 24
Ryan, Betsy
See Ryan, Elizabeth (Anne)
Ryan, Cheli Durán 20
Ryan, Elizabeth (Anne) 1943- 30
Ryan, John (Gerald Christopher)
1921- 22
Ryan, Peter (Charles) 1939- 15
Rydberg, Ernest E(mil) 1901- 21
Rydberg, Lou(isa Hampton)
1908- 27
Rydell, Wendell
See Rydell, Wendy
Rydell, Wendy 4
Ryden, Hope 8
Ryder, Joanne
Brief Entry 34
Rye, Anthony
See Youd, (Christopher) Samuel
Rylant, Cynthia 1954-
Brief Entry 44
Rymer, Alta May 1925- 34

S

Saberhagen, Fred (Thomas)
1930- 37
Sabin, Edwin Legrand
1870-1952 .... *YABC 2*
Sabin, Francene 27
Sabin, Louis 1930- 27
Sabre, Dirk
See Laffin, John (Alfred Charles)
Sabuso
See Phillips, Irving W.
Sachs, Marilyn 1927- 3
See also CLR 2
See also SAAS 2
Sackett, S(amuel) J(ohn)
1928- 12
Sackson, Sid 1920- 16
Saddler, Allen
See Richards, R(onald) C(harles)
W(illiam)
Saddler, K. Allen
See Richards, R(onald) C(harles)
W(illiam)
Sadie, Stanley (John) 1930- 14
Sadler, Catherine Edwards
Brief Entry 45
Sadler, Mark
See Lynds, Dennis
Sage, Juniper [Joint pseudonym]
See Brown, Margaret Wise and
Hurd, Edith
Sagsoorian, Paul 1923- 12

Saida
See LeMair, H(enriette) Willebeek
Saint, Dora Jessie 1913- 10
St. Briavels, James
See Wood, James Playsted
St. Clair, Byrd Hooper 1905-1976
Obituary 28
Saint Exupéry, Antoine de
1900-1944 20
See also CLR 10
St. George, Judith 1931- 13
St. John, Nicole
See Johnston, Norma
St. John, Philip
See Del Rey, Lester
St. John, Wylly Folk
1908-1985 10
Obituary 45
St. Meyer, Ned
See Stratemeyer, Edward L.
St. Tamara
See Kolba, Tamara
Saito, Michiko
See Fujiwara, Michiko
Salassi, Otto R(ussell) 1939- 38
Saldutti, Denise 1953- 39
Salkey, (Felix) Andrew (Alexander)
1928- 35
Salmon, Annie Elizabeth
1899- 13
Salten, Felix
See Salzmann, Siegmund
Salter, Cedric
See Knight, Francis Edgar
Salvadori, Mario (George)
1907- 40
Salzer, L. E.
See Wilson, Lionel
Salzman, Yuri
Brief Entry 42
Salzmann, Siegmund
1869-1945 25
Samachson, Dorothy 1914- 3
Samachson, Joseph 1906- 3
Sammis, John 1942- 4
Sampson, Fay (Elizabeth)
1935- 42
Brief Entry 40
Samson, Anne S(tringer)
1933- 2
Samson, Joan 1937-1976 13
Samuels, Charles 1902- 12
Samuels, Gertrude 17
Sanborn, Duane 1914- 38
Sancha, Sheila 1924- 38
Sanchez, Sonia 1934- 22
Sanchez-Silva, Jose Maria
1911- 16
Sand, George X. 45
Sandak, Cass R(obert) 1950-
Brief Entry 37
Sandberg, (Karin) Inger 1930- 15
Sandberg, Karl C. 1931- 35
Sandberg, Lasse (E. M.)
1924- 15
Sandburg, Carl (August)
1878-1967 8
Sandburg, Charles A.
See Sandburg, Carl (August)

Sandburg, Helga 1918- 3
Sanderlin, George 1915- 4
Sanderlin, Owenita (Harrah)
1916- 11
Sanders, Winston P.
See Anderson, Poul (William)
Sanderson, Ivan T. 1911-1973 6
Sanderson, Ruth (L.) 1951- 41
Sandin, Joan 1942- 12
Sandison, Janet
See Cameron, Elizabeth Jane
Sandoz, Mari (Susette)
1901-1966 5
Sanger, Marjory Bartlett
1920- 8
Sankey, Alice (Ann-Susan)
1910- 27
San Souci, Robert D. 1946- 40
Santesson, Hans Stefan 1914(?)-1975
Obituary 30
Sapieyevski, Anne Lindbergh
1940- 35
Sarac, Roger
See Caras, Roger A(ndrew)
Sarg, Anthony Fredrick
See Sarg, Tony
Sarg, Tony 1880-1942 .... *YABC 1*
Sargent, Pamela 29
Sargent, Robert 1933- 2
Sargent, Sarah 1937- 44
Brief Entry 41
Sargent, Shirley 1927- 11
Sari
See Fleur, Anne
Sarnoff, Jane 1937- 10
Saroyan, William 1908-1981 23
Obituary 24
Sarton, Eleanore Marie
See Sarton, (Eleanor) May
Sarton, (Eleanor) May 1912- 36
Sasek, Miroslav 1916-1980 16
Obituary 23
See also CLR 4
Sattler, Helen Roney 1921- 4
Sauer, Julia (Lina) 1891-1983 32
Obituary 36
Saul, (E.) Wendy 1946- 42
Saunders, Caleb
See Heinlein, Robert A(nson)
Saunders, Keith 1910- 12
Saunders, Rubie (Agnes)
1929- 21
Saunders, Susan 1945- 46
Brief Entry 41
Savage, Blake
See Goodwin, Harold Leland
Savery, Constance (Winifred)
1897- 1
Saville, (Leonard) Malcolm
1901-1982 23
Obituary 31
Saviozzi, Adriana
See Mazza, Adriana
Savitt, Sam 8
Savitz, Harriet May 1933- 5
Sawyer, Ruth 1880-1970 17
Say, Allen 1937- 28
Sayers, Frances Clarke 1897- 3
Sazer, Nina 1949- 13

Scabrini, Janet 1953- *13*
Scagnetti, Jack 1924- *7*
Scanlon, Marion Stephany *11*
Scarf, Maggi
   See Scarf, Maggie
Scarf, Maggie 1932- *5*
Scarry, Huck
   See Scarry, Richard, Jr.
Scarry, Patricia (Murphy)
   1924- *2*
Scarry, Patsy
   See Scarry, Patricia
Scarry, Richard (McClure)
   1919- *35*
   Earlier sketch in SATA 2
   See also CLR 3
Scarry, Richard, Jr. 1953- *35*
Schachtel, Roger (Bernard)
   1949- *38*
Schaefer, Jack 1907- *3*
Schaeffer, Mead 1898- *21*
Schaller, George B(eals)
   1933- *30*
Schatzki, Walter 1899-
   Brief Entry *31*
Schechter, Betty (Goodstein)
   1921- *5*
Scheer, Julian (Weisel) 1926- *8*
Scheffer, Victor B. 1906- *6*
Scheier, Michael 1943- *40*
   Brief Entry *36*
Schell, Mildred 1922- *41*
Schell, Orville H. 1940- *10*
Schellie, Don 1932- *29*
Schemm, Mildred Walker
   1905- *21*
Scherf, Margaret 1908- *10*
Schermer, Judith (Denise)
   1941- *30*
Schertle, Alice 1941- *36*
Schick, Alice 1946- *27*
Schick, Eleanor 1942- *9*
Schick, Joel 1945- *31*
   Brief Entry *30*
Schiff, Ken 1942- *7*
Schiller, Andrew 1919- *21*
Schiller, Barbara (Heyman)
   1928- *21*
Schiller, Justin G. 1943-
   Brief Entry *31*
Schindelman, Joseph 1923-
   Brief Entry *32*
Schisgall, Oscar 1901-1984 ....*12*
   Obituary *38*
Schlee, Ann 1934- *44*
   Brief Entry *36*
Schlein, Miriam 1926- *2*
Schloat, G. Warren, Jr. 1914- *4*
Schmid, Eleonore 1939- *12*
Schmiderer, Dorothy 1940- *19*
Schmidt, Elizabeth 1915- *15*
Schmidt, James Norman
   1912- *21*
Schneider, Herman 1905- *7*
Schneider, Laurie
   See Adams, Laurie
Schneider, Nina 1913- *2*
Schneider, Rex 1937- *44*

Schnirel, James R(einhold)
   1931- *14*
Schock, Pauline 1928- *45*
Schoen, Barbara 1924- *13*
Schoenherr, John (Carl) 1935- *37*
Scholastica, Sister Mary
   See Jenkins, Marie M.
Scholefield, Edmund O.
   See Butterworth, W. E.
Scholey, Arthur 1932- *28*
Schone, Virginia *22*
Schongut, Emanuel
   Brief Entry *36*
Schoonover, Frank (Earle)
   1877-1972 ....*24*
Schoor, Gene 1921- *3*
Schraff, Anne E(laine) 1939- *27*
Schrank, Joseph 1900-1984
   Obituary *38*
Schreiber, Elizabeth Anne (Ferguson)
   1947- *13*
Schreiber, Georges 1904-1977
   Brief Entry *29*
Schreiber, Ralph W(alter)
   1942- *13*
Schroeder, Ted 1931(?)-1973
   Obituary *20*
Schulman, Janet 1933- *22*
Schulman, L(ester) M(artin)
   1934- *13*
Schulte, Elaine L(ouise) 1934- *36*
Schultz, Gwendolyn *21*
Schultz, James Willard
   1859-1947 ....*YABC 1*
Schultz, Pearle Henriksen
   1918- *21*
Schulz, Charles M(onroe)
   1922- *10*
Schurfranz, Vivian 1925- *13*
Schutzer, A. I. 1922- *13*
Schuyler, Pamela R(icka)
   1948- *30*
Schwartz, Alvin 1927- *4*
   See also CLR 3
Schwartz, Amy 1954-
   Brief Entry *41*
Schwartz, Ann Powers 1913- *10*
Schwartz, Charles W(alsh)
   1914- *8*
Schwartz, Daniel (Bennet) 1929-
   Brief Entry *29*
Schwartz, Elizabeth Reeder
   1912- *8*
Schwartz, Julius 1907- *45*
Schwartz, Sheila (Ruth) 1929- *27*
Schwartz, Stephen (Lawrence)
   1948- *19*
Schweitzer, Iris
   Brief Entry *36*
Schweninger, Ann 1951- *29*
Scoggin, Margaret C. 1905-1968
   Brief Entry *28*
Scoppettone, Sandra 1936- *9*
Scott, Ann Herbert 1926-
   Brief Entry *29*
Scott, Bill 1902(?)-1985
   Obituary *46*
Scott, Cora Annett (Pipitone)
   1931- *11*

Scott, Dan [House pseudonym]
   See Barker, S. Omar; Stratemeyer,
   Edward L.
Scott, Elaine 1940- *36*
Scott, Jack Denton 1915- *31*
Scott, John 1912-1976 ....*14*
Scott, John Anthony 1916- *23*
Scott, John M(artin) 1913- *12*
Scott, Sally (Elisabeth) 1948- *44*
Scott, Sally Fisher 1909-1978 .....*43*
Scott, Tony
   See Scott, John Anthony
Scott, Sir Walter
   1771-1832 ....*YABC 2*
Scott, Warwick
   See Trevor, Elleston
Scribner, Charles, Jr. 1921- *13*
Scribner, Joanne L. 1949- *33*
Scrimsher, Lila Gravatt 1897-1974
   Obituary *28*
Scuro, Vincent 1951- *21*
Seabrooke, Brenda 1941- *30*
Seaman, Augusta Huiell
   1879-1950 ....*31*
Seamands, Ruth (Childers)
   1916- *9*
Searcy, Margaret Zehmer 1926-
   Brief Entry *39*
Searight, Mary W(illiams)
   1918- *17*
Searle, Kathryn Adrienne
   1942- *10*
Searle, Ronald (William Fordham)
   1920- *42*
Sears, Stephen W. 1932- *4*
Sebastian, Lee
   See Silverberg, Robert
Sebestyen, Igen
   See Sebestyen, Ouida
Sebestyen, Ouida 1924- *39*
Sechrist, Elizabeth Hough
   1903- *2*
Sedges, John
   See Buck, Pearl S.
Seed, Jenny 1930- *8*
Seed, Sheila Turner 1937(?)-1979
   Obituary *23*
Seeger, Elizabeth 1889-1973
   Obituary *20*
Seeger, Pete(r) 1919- *13*
Seever, R.
   See Reeves, Lawrence F.
Sefton, Catherine
   See Waddell, Martin
Segal, Joyce 1940- *35*
Segal, Lore 1928- *4*
Seidelman, James Edward
   1926- *6*
Seiden, Art(hur)
   Brief Entry *42*
Seidler, Tor 1952-
   Brief Entry *46*
Seidman, Laurence (Ivan)
   1925- *15*
Seigel, Kalman 1917- *12*
Seignobosc, Francoise
   1897-1961 ....*21*
Seixas, Judith S. 1922- *17*
Sejima, Yoshimasa 1913- *8*

Selden, George
  See Thompson, George Selden
  See also CLR 8
Self, Margaret Cabell 1902- 24
Selig, Sylvie 1942- 13
Selkirk, Jane [Joint pseudonym]
  See Chapman, John Stanton
  Higham
Sellers, Naomi John
  See Flack, Naomi John (White)
Selsam, Millicent E(llis)
  1912- 29
  Earlier sketch in SATA 1
  See also CLR 1
Seltzer, Meyer 1932- 17
Seltzer, Richard (Warren, Jr.)
  1946- 41
Sendak, Jack 28
Sendak, Maurice (Bernard)
  1928- 27
  Earlier sketch in SATA 1
  See also CLR 1
Sengler, Johanna 1924- 18
Serage, Nancy 1924- 10
Seredy, Kate 1899-1975 1
  Obituary 24
  See also CLR 10
Seroff, Victor I(lyitch)
  1902-1979 12
  Obituary 26
Serraillier, Ian (Lucien) 1912- 1
  See also CLR 2
  See also SAAS 3
Servello, Joe 1932- 10
Service, Robert W(illiam)
  1874(?)-1958 20
Serwadda, William Moses
  1931- 27
Serwer, Blanche L. 1910- 10
Seth, Marie
  See Lexau, Joan M.
Seton, Anya 3
Seton, Ernest Thompson
  1860-1946 18
Seuling, Barbara 1937- 10
Seuss, Dr.
  See Geisel, Theodor Seuss
  See also CLR 9
Severn, Bill
  See Severn, William Irving
Severn, David
  See Unwin, David S(torr)
Severn, William Irving 1914- 1
Sewall, Marcia 1935- 37
Seward, Prudence 1926- 16
Sewell, Anna 1820-1878 24
Sewell, Helen (Moore)
  1896-1957 38
Sexton, Anne (Harvey)
  1928-1974 10
Seymour, Alta Halverson 10
Shackleton, C. C.
  See Aldiss, Brian W(ilson)
Shafer, Robert E(ugene)
  1925- 9
Shahn, Ben(jamin) 1898-1969
  Obituary 21
Shahn, Bernarda Bryson
  See Bryson, Bernarda

Shane, Harold Gray 1914- 36
Shanks, Ann Zane (Kushner) 10
Shannon, George (William Bones)
  1952- 35
Shannon, Monica (?)-1965 28
Shannon, Terry 21
Shapiro, Irwin 1911-1981 32
Shapiro, Milton J. 1926- 32
Shapp, Martha 1910- 3
Sharfman, Amalie 14
Sharma, Partap 1939- 15
Sharmat, Marjorie Weinman
  1928- 33
  Earlier sketch in SATA 4
Sharmat, Mitchell 1927- 33
Sharp, Margery 1905- 29
  Earlier sketch in SATA 1
Sharp, Zerna A. 1889-1981
  Obituary 27
Sharpe, Mitchell R(aymond)
  1924- 12
Shaw, Arnold 1909- 4
Shaw, Charles (Green)
  1892-1974 13
Shaw, Evelyn 1927- 28
Shaw, Flora Louisa
  See Lugard, Flora Louisa Shaw
Shaw, Ray 7
Shaw, Richard 1923- 12
Shay, Arthur 1922- 4
Shay, Lacey
  See Shebar, Sharon Sigmond
Shea, George 1940-
  Brief Entry 42
Shearer, John 1947- 43
  Brief Entry 27
Shearer, Ted 1919- 43
Shebar, Sharon Sigmond
  1945- 36
Shecter, Ben 1935- 16
Sheedy, Alexandra (Elizabeth)
  1962- 39
  Earlier sketch in SATA 19
Sheedy, Ally
  See Sheedy, Alexandra (Elizabeth)
Sheehan, Ethna 1908- 9
Sheffield, Janet N. 1926- 26
Shekerjian, Regina Tor 16
Sheldon, Ann [Collective
  pseudonym] 1
Sheldon, Aure 1917-1976 12
Sheldon, Muriel 1926- 45
  Brief Entry 39
Shelley, Mary Wollstonecraft
  (Godwin) 1797-1851 29
Shelton, William Roy 1919- 5
Shemin, Margaretha 1928- 4
Shenton, Edward 1895-1977 45
Shepard, Ernest Howard
  1879-1976 33
  Obituary 24
  Earlier sketch in SATA 3
Shepard, Mary
  See Knox, (Mary) Eleanor Jessie
Shephard, Esther 1891-1975 5
  Obituary 26
Shepherd, Elizabeth 4
Sherburne, Zoa 1912- 3

Sherman, D(enis) R(onald) 1934-
  Brief Entry 29
Sherman, Diane (Finn) 1928- 12
Sherman, Elizabeth
  See Friskey, Margaret Richards
Sherman, Harold (Morrow)
  1898- 37
Sherman, Nancy
  See Rosenberg, Nancy Sherman
Sherrod, Jane
  See Singer, Jane Sherrod
Sherry, (Dulcie) Sylvia 1932- 8
Sherwan, Earl 1917- 3
Shiefman, Vicky 22
Shields, Brenda Desmond (Armstrong)
  1914- 37
Shields, Charles 1944- 10
Shimin, Symeon 1902- 13
Shinn, Everett 1876-1953 21
Shippen, Katherine B(inney)
  1892-1980 1
  Obituary 23
Shipton, Eric 1907- 10
Shirer, William L(awrence)
  1904- 45
Shirreffs, Gordon D(onald)
  1914- 11
Sholokhov, Mikhail A. 1905-1984
  Obituary 36
Shore, June Lewis 30
Shore, Robert 1924- 39
Shortall, Leonard W. 19
Shotwell, Louisa R. 1902- 3
Showalter, Jean B(reckinridge) 12
Showell, Ellen Harvey 1934- 33
Showers, Paul C. 1910- 21
  See also CLR 6
Shreve, Susan Richards 1939- 46
  Brief Entry 41
Shtainmets, Leon 32
Shub, Elizabeth 5
Shulevitz, Uri 1935- 3
  See also CLR 5
Shulman, Alix Kates 1932- 7
Shulman, Irving 1913- 13
Shumsky, Zena
  See Collier, Zena
Shura, Mary Francis
  See Craig, Mary Francis
Shuttlesworth, Dorothy 3
Shyer, Marlene Fanta 13
Siberell, Anne 29
Sibley, Don 1922- 12
Siculan, Daniel 1922- 12
Sidjakov, Nicolas 1924- 18
Sidney, Frank [Joint pseudonym]
  See Warwick, Alan R(oss)
Sidney, Margaret
  See Lothrop, Harriet Mulford Stone
Siebel, Fritz (Frederick) 1913-
  Brief Entry 44
Siegal, Aranka 1930-
  Brief Entry 37
Siegel, Beatrice 36
Siegel, Helen
  See Siegl, Helen
Siegel, Robert (Harold) 1939- 39
Siegl, Helen 1924- 34

Silas
   See McCay, Winsor
Silcock, Sara Lesley 1947- 12
Silver, Ruth
   See Chew, Ruth
Silverberg, Robert 13
Silverman, Mel(vin Frank)
   1931-1966 9
Silverstein, Alvin 1933- 8
Silverstein, Shel(by) 1932- 33
   Brief Entry 27
   See also CLR 5
Silverstein, Virginia B(arbara
   Opshelor) 1937- 8
Silverthorne, Elizabeth 1930- 35
Simon, Charlie May
   See Fletcher, Charlie May
Simon, Hilda (Rita) 1921- 28
Simon, Howard 1903-1979 32
   Obituary 21
Simon, Joe
   See Simon, Joseph H.
Simon, Joseph H. 1913- 7
Simon, Martin P(aul William)
   1903-1969 12
Simon, Mina Lewiton
   See Lewiton, Mina
Simon, Norma 1927- 3
Simon, Seymour 1931- 4
   See also CLR 9
Simon, Shirley (Schwartz)
   1921- 11
Simon, Solomon 1895-1970 40
Simonetta, Linda 1948- 14
Simonetta, Sam 1936- 14
Simons, Barbara B(rooks)
   1934- 41
Simont, Marc 1915- 9
Simpson, Colin 1908- 14
Simpson, Myrtle L(illias)
   1931- 14
Sinclair, Clover
   See Gater, Dilys
Sinclair, Upton (Beall)
   1878-1968 9
Singer, Isaac Bashevis 1904- 27
   Earlier sketch in SATA 3
   See also CLR 1
Singer, Jane Sherrod
   1917-1985 4
   Obituary 42
Singer, Julia 1917- 28
Singer, Kurt D(eutsch) 1911- 38
Singer, Marilyn 1948-
   Brief Entry 38
Singer, Susan (Mahler) 1941- 9
Sirof, Harriet 1930- 37
Sisson, Rosemary Anne 1923- 11
Sitomer, Harry 1903- 31
Sitomer, Mindel 1903- 31
Sive, Helen R. 1951- 30
Sivulich, Sandra (Jeanne) Stroner
   1941- 9
Skelly, James R(ichard) 1927- 17
Skinner, Constance Lindsay
   1882-1939 ....YABC 1
Skinner, Cornelia Otis 1901- 2
Skipper, G. C. 1939- 46
   Brief Entry 38

Skofield, James
   Brief Entry 44
Skold, Betty Westrom 1923- 41
Skorpen, Liesel Moak 1935- 3
Skurzynski, Gloria (Joan)
   1930- 8
Slackman, Charles B. 1934- 12
Slade, Richard 1910-1971 9
Slate, Joseph (Frank) 1928- 38
Slater, Jim 1929-
   Brief Entry 34
Slaughter, Jean
   See Doty, Jean Slaughter
Sleator, William 1945- 3
Sleigh, Barbara 1906-1982 3
   Obituary 30
Slepian, Jan(ice B.) 1921-
   Brief Entry 45
Slicer, Margaret O. 1920- 4
Sloane, Eric 1910(?)-1985
   Obituary 42
Slobodkin, Florence (Gersh)
   1905- 5
Slobodkin, Louis 1903-1975 26
   Earlier sketch in SATA 1
Slobodkina, Esphyr 1909- 1
Sloggett, Nellie 1851-1923 44
Slote, Alfred 1926- 8
   See also CLR 4
Small, David 1945-
   Brief Entry 46
Small, Ernest
   See Lent, Blair
Smallwood, Norah (Evelyn)
   1910(?)-1984
   Obituary 41
Smaridge, Norah 1903- 6
Smiley, Virginia Kester 1923- 2
Smith, Anne Warren 1938- 41
   Brief Entry 34
Smith, Beatrice S(chillinger) 12
Smith, Betsy Covington 1937-
   Brief Entry 43
Smith, Betty 1896-1972 6
Smith, Bradford 1909-1964 5
Smith, Caesar
   See Trevor, Elleston
Smith, Datus C(lifford), Jr.
   1907- 13
Smith, Dodie 4
Smith, Doris Buchanan 1934- 28
Smith, Dorothy Stafford
   1905- 6
Smith, E(lmer) Boyd
   1860-1943 ....YABC 1
Smith, E(dric) Brooks 1917- 40
Smith, Elva S(ophronia) 1871-1965
   Brief Entry 31
Smith, Emma 1923-
   Brief Entry 36
Smith, Eunice Young 1902- 5
Smith, Frances C. 1904- 3
Smith, Fredrika Shumway 1877-1968
   Brief Entry 30
Smith, Gary R(ichard) 1932- 14
Smith, George Harmon 1920- 5
Smith, H(arry) Allen 1907-1976
   Obituary 20

Smith, Howard Everett, Jr.
   1927- 12
Smith, Hugh L(etcher)
   1921-1968 5
Smith, Imogene Henderson
   1922- 12
Smith, Jacqueline B. 1937- 39
Smith, Jean
   See Smith, Frances C.
Smith, Jean Pajot 1945- 10
Smith, Jessie Willcox
   1863-1935 21
Smith, Jim 1920-
   Brief Entry 36
Smith, Joan 1933-
   Brief Entry 46
Smith, Johnston
   See Crane, Stephen (Townley)
Smith, Lafayette
   See Higdon, Hal
Smith, Lee
   See Albion, Lee Smith
Smith, Lillian H(elena) 1887-1983
   Obituary 32
Smith, Linell Nash 1932- 2
Smith, Lucia B. 1943- 30
Smith, Marion Hagens 1913- 12
Smith, Marion Jaques 1899- 13
Smith, Mary Ellen 10
Smith, Mike
   See Smith, Mary Ellen
Smith, Nancy Covert 1935- 12
Smith, Norman F. 1920- 5
Smith, Pauline C(oggeshall)
   1908- 27
Smith, Philip Warren 1936- 46
Smith, Robert Kimmel 1930- 12
Smith, Robert Paul 1915-1977
   Obituary 30
Smith, Ruth Leslie 1902- 2
Smith, Samantha 1972-1985
   Obituary 45
Smith, Sarah Stafford
   See Smith, Dorothy Stafford
Smith, Susan Carlton 1923- 12
Smith, Susan Mathias 1950- 43
   Brief Entry 35
Smith, Vian (Crocker)
   1919-1969 11
Smith, Ward
   See Goldsmith, Howard
Smith, William A. 10
Smith, William Jay 1918- 2
Smith, Winsome 1935- 45
Smith, Z. Z.
   See Westheimer, David
Smits, Teo
   See Smits, Theodore R(ichard)
Smits, Theodore R(ichard)
   1905- 45
   Brief Entry 28
Smucker, Barbara (Claassen)
   1915- 29
   See also CLR 10
Snedeker, Caroline Dale (Parke)
   1871-1956 ....YABC 2
Snell, Nigel (Edward Creagh) 1936-
   Brief Entry 40

Sneve, Virginia Driving Hawk
1933- 8
See also CLR 2
Sniff, Mr.
See Abisch, Roslyn Kroop
Snodgrass, Thomas Jefferson
See Clemens, Samuel Langhorne
Snook, Barbara (Lillian)
1913-1976 34
Snow, Donald Clifford 1917- 16
Snow, Dorothea J(ohnston)
1909- 9
Snow, Richard F(olger) 1947-
Brief Entry 37
Snyder, Anne 1922- 4
Snyder, Carol 1941- 35
Snyder, Gerald S(eymour) 1933-
Brief Entry 34
Snyder, Jerome 1916-1976
Obituary 20
Snyder, Zilpha Keatley 1927- 28
Earlier sketch in SATA 1
See also SAAS 2
Snyderman, Reuven K. 1922- 5
Soble, Jennie
See Cavin, Ruth (Brodie)
Sobol, Donald J. 1924- 31
Earlier sketch in SATA 1
See also CLR 4
Sobol, Harriet Langsam 1936-
Brief Entry 34
Soderlind, Arthur E(dwin)
1920- 14
Softly, Barbara (Frewin)
1924- 12
Soglow, Otto 1900-1975
Obituary 30
Sohl, Frederic J(ohn) 1916- 10
Sokol, Bill
See Sokol, William
Sokol, William 1923- 37
Sokolov, Kirill 1930- 34
Solbert, Romaine G. 1925- 2
Solbert, Ronni
See Solbert, Romaine G.
Solomon, Joan 1930(?)-
Brief Entry 40
Solomons, Ikey, Esquire, Jr.
See Thackeray, William Makepeace
Solonevich, George 1915- 15
Solot, Mary Lynn 1939- 12
Sommer, Elyse 1929- 7
Sommer, Robert 1929- 12
Sommerfelt, Aimee 1892- 5
Sonneborn, Ruth (Cantor) A.
1899-1974 4
Obituary 27
Sorche, Nic Leodhas
See Alger, Leclaire (Gowans)
Sorel, Edward 1929-
Brief Entry 37
Sorensen, Virginia 1912- 2
Sorley Walker, Kathrine 41
Sorrentino, Joseph N. 6
Sortor, June Elizabeth 1939- 12
Sortor, Toni
See Sortor, June Elizabeth
Soskin, V. H.
See Ellison, Virginia Howell

Sotomayor, Antonio 1902- 11
Soudley, Henry
See Wood, James Playsted
Soule, Gardner (Bosworth)
1913- 14
Soule, Jean Conder 1919- 10
Southall, Ivan 1921- 3
See also CLR 2
See also SAAS 3
Spanfeller, James J(ohn)
1930- 19
Spangenberg, Judith Dunn
1942- 5
Spar, Jerome 1918- 10
Sparks, Beatrice Mathews
1918- 44
Brief Entry 28
Sparks, Mary W. 1920- 15
Spaulding, Leonard
See Bradbury, Ray
Speare, Elizabeth George
1908- 5
See also CLR 8
Spearing, Judith (Mary Harlow)
1922- 9
Specking, Inez 1890-196(?) 11
Speicher, Helen Ross (Smith)
1915- 8
Spellman, John W(illard)
1934- 14
Spelman, Mary 1934- 28
Spence, Eleanor (Rachel)
1927- 21
Spencer, Ann 1918- 10
Spencer, Cornelia
See Yaukey, Grace S.
Spencer, Donald D(ean) 1931- 41
Spencer, Elizabeth 1921- 14
Spencer, William 1922- 9
Spencer, Zane A(nn) 1935- 35
Sperry, Armstrong W.
1897-1976 1
Obituary 27
Sperry, Raymond, Jr. [Collective
pseudonym] 1
Spicer, Dorothy (Gladys)
(?)-1975 32
Spiegelman, Judith M. 5
Spielberg, Steven 1947- 32
Spier, Peter (Edward) 1927- 4
See also CLR 5
Spilhaus, Athelstan 1911- 13
Spilka, Arnold 1917- 6
Spinelli, Eileen 1942- 38
Spinelli, Jerry 1941- 39
Spink, Reginald (William)
1905- 11
Spinner, Stephanie 1943- 38
Spinossimus
See White, William
Splaver, Sarah 1921-
Brief Entry 28
Spollen, Christopher 1952- 12
Sprague, Gretchen (Burnham)
1926- 27
Sprigge, Elizabeth 1900-1974 10
Spring, (Robert) Howard
1889-1965 28

Springstubb, Tricia 1950- 46
Brief Entry 40
Spykman, E(lizabeth) C.
19(?)-1965 10
Spyri, Johanna (Heusser)
1827-1901 19
Squire, Miriam
See Sprigge, Elizabeth
Squires, Phil
See Barker, S. Omar
S-Ringi, Kjell
See Ringi, Kjell
Srivastava, Jane Jonas
Brief Entry 37
Stadtler, Bea 1921- 17
Stafford, Jean 1915-1979
Obituary 22
Stahl, Ben(jamin) 1910- 5
Stair, Gobin (John) 1912- 35
Stalder, Valerie 27
Stamaty, Mark Alan 1947- 12
Stambler, Irwin 1924- 5
Stanek, Muriel (Novella) 1915-
Brief Entry 34
Stang, Judit 1921-1977 29
Stang, Judy
See Stang, Judit
Stanhope, Eric
See Hamilton, Charles H. St. John
Stankevich, Boris 1928- 2
Stanley, Diana 1909-
Brief Entry 30
Stanley, Diane 1943- 37
Brief Entry 32
Stanley, Robert
See Hamilton, Charles H. St. John
Stanli, Sue
See Meilach, Dona Z(weigoron)
Stanstead, John
See Groom, Arthur William
Stapleton, Marjorie (Winifred)
1932- 28
Stapp, Arthur D(onald)
1906-1972 4
Starbird, Kaye 1916- 6
Stark, James
See Goldston, Robert
Starkey, Marion L. 1901- 13
Starr, Ward and Murch, Mel [Joint
double pseudonym]
See Manes, Stephen
Starret, William
See McClintock, Marshall
Stauffer, Don
See Berkebile, Fred D(onovan)
Staunton, Schuyler
See Baum, L(yman) Frank
Steadman, Ralph (Idris) 1936- 32
Stearns, Monroe (Mather)
1913- 5
Steele, Chester K.
See Stratemeyer, Edward L.
Steele, Mary Q. 3
Steele, (Henry) Max(well)
1922- 10
Steele, William O(wen)
1917-1979 1
Obituary 27

Steig, William 1907- *18*
  See also CLR 2
Stein, Harvé 1904-
  Brief Entry *30*
Stein, M(eyer) L(ewis) *6*
Stein, Mini *2*
Stein, R(ichard) Conrad 1937- *31*
Stein, Sara Bonnett
  Brief Entry *34*
Steinbeck, John (Ernst)
  1902-1968 .... *9*
Steinberg, Alfred 1917- *9*
Steinberg, Fannie 1899- *43*
Steinberg, Fred J. 1933- *4*
Steinberg, Phillip Orso 1921- *34*
Steinberg, Rafael (Mark)
  1927- *45*
Steiner, Barbara A(nnette)
  1934- *13*
Steiner, Charlotte 1900-1981 ...... *45*
Steiner, Jörg 1930- *35*
Steiner, Stan(ley) 1925- *14*
Steiner-Prag, Hugo 1880-1945
  Brief Entry *32*
Stephens, Mary Jo 1935- *8*
Stephens, William M(cLain)
  1925- *21*
Stephensen, A. M.
  See Manes, Stephen
Stepp, Ann 1935- *29*
Steptoe, John (Lewis) 1950- *8*
  See also CLR 2
Sterling, Dorothy 1913- *1*
  See also CLR 1
  See also SAAS 2
Sterling, Helen
  See Hoke, Helen (L.)
Sterling, Philip 1907- *8*
Stern, Ellen N(orman) 1927- *26*
Stern, Madeleine B(ettina)
  1912- *14*
Stern, Philip Van Doren
  1900-1984 .... *13*
  Obituary *39*
Stern, Simon 1943- *15*
Sterne, Emma Gelders
  1894-1971 .... *6*
Steurt, Marjorie Rankin 1888- *10*
Stevens, Carla M(cBride)
  1928- *13*
Stevens, Franklin 1933- *6*
Stevens, Gwendolyn 1944- *33*
Stevens, Patricia Bunning
  1931- *27*
Stevens, Peter
  See Geis, Darlene
Stevenson, Anna (M.) 1905- *12*
Stevenson, Augusta
  1869(?)-1976 .... *2*
  Obituary *26*
Stevenson, Burton E(gbert)
  1872-1962 .... *25*
Stevenson, James 1929- *42*
  Brief Entry *34*
Stevenson, Janet 1913- *8*
Stevenson, Robert Louis
  1850-1894 ....*YABC 2*
  See also CLR 10
Stewart, A(gnes) C(harlotte) *15*

Stewart, Charles
  See Zurhorst, Charles (Stewart, Jr.)
Stewart, Elizabeth Laing
  1907- *6*
Stewart, George Rippey
  1895-1980 .... *3*
  Obituary *23*
Stewart, John (William) 1920- *14*
Stewart, Mary (Florence Elinor)
  1916- *12*
Stewart, Robert Neil
  1891-1972 .... *7*
Stewart, Scott
  See Zaffo, George J.
Stewig, John Warren 1937- *26*
Stiles, Martha Bennett *6*
Stiles, Norman B. 1942-
  Brief Entry *36*
Still, James 1906- *29*
Stillerman, Robbie 1947- *12*
Stilley, Frank 1918- *29*
Stine, G(eorge) Harry 1928- *10*
Stine, Jovial Bob
  See Stine, Robert Lawrence
Stine, Robert Lawrence 1943- *31*
Stinetorf, Louise 1900- *10*
Stirling, Arthur
  See Sinclair, Upton (Beall)
Stirling, Nora B. *3*
Stirnweis, Shannon 1931- *10*
Stobbs, William 1914- *17*
Stockton, Francis Richard
  1834-1902 .... *44*
Stockton, Frank R(ichard)
  Brief Entry *32*
  See Stockton, Francis Richard
Stoddard, Edward G. 1923- *10*
Stoddard, Hope 1900- *6*
Stoddard, Sandol
  See Warburg, Sandol Stoddard
Stoiko, Michael 1919- *14*
Stoker, Abraham 1847-1912 ...... *29*
Stoker, Bram
  See Stoker, Abraham
Stokes, Cedric
  See Beardmore, George
Stokes, Jack (Tilden) 1923- *13*
Stokes, Olivia Pearl 1916- *32*
Stolz, Mary (Slattery) 1920- *10*
  See also SAAS 3
Stone, Alan [Collective
  pseudonym] *1*
  See also Svenson, Andrew E.
Stone, D(avid) K(arl) 1922- *9*
Stone, Eugenia 1879-1971 .... *7*
Stone, Gene
  See Stone, Eugenia
Stone, Helen V. *6*
Stone, Irving 1903- *3*
Stone, Jon 1931- *39*
Stone, Josephine Rector
  See Dixon, Jeanne
Stone, Raymond [Collective
  pseudonym] *1*
Stone, Richard A.
  See Stratemeyer, Edward L.
Stonehouse, Bernard 1926- *13*
Stong, Phil(ip Duffield)
  1899-1957 .... *32*

Storch, Anne B. von
  See von Storch, Anne B.
Storey, (Elizabeth) Margaret (Carlton)
  1926- *9*
Storey, Victoria Carolyn
  1945- *16*
Storme, Peter
  See Stern, Philip Van Doren
Storr, Catherine (Cole) 1913- *9*
Stoutenburg, Adrien 1916- *3*
Stover, Allan C(arl) 1938- *14*
Stover, Marjorie Filley 1914- *9*
Stowe, Harriet (Elizabeth) Beecher
  1811-1896 ....*YABC 1*
Strachan, Margaret Pitcairn
  1908- *14*
Strait, Treva Adams 1909- *35*
Strand, Mark 1934- *41*
Strange, Philippa
  See Coury, Louise Andree
Stranger, Joyce
  See Wilson, Joyce M(uriel Judson)
Strasser, Todd 1950- *45*
  Brief Entry *41*
Stratemeyer, Edward L.
  1862-1930 .... *1*
Stratton, Thomas [Joint pseudonym]
  See DeWeese, Thomas Eugene
Stratton-Porter, Gene
  1863-1924 .... *15*
Strayer, E. Ward
  See Stratemeyer, Edward L.
Streano, Vince(nt Catello)
  1945- *20*
Streatfeild, Noel 1897- *20*
Street, Julia Montgomery
  1898- *11*
Stren, Patti 1949-
  Brief Entry *41*
  See also CLR 5
Strete, Craig Kee 1950- *44*
Stretton, Barbara (Humphrey)
  1936- *43*
  Brief Entry *35*
Strong, Charles [Joint pseudonym]
  See Epstein, Beryl and Epstein,
  Samuel
Strong, David
  See McGuire, Leslie (Sarah)
Strong, J. J.
  See Strong, Jeremy
Strong, Jeremy 1949- *36*
Ströyer, Poul 1923- *13*
Stuart, David
  See Hoyt, Edwin P(almer), Jr.
Stuart, Forbes 1924- *13*
Stuart, Ian
  See MacLean, Alistair (Stuart)
Stuart, (Hilton) Jesse
  1907-1984 .... *2*
  Obituary *36*
Stuart, Sheila
  See Baker, Mary Gladys Steel
Stuart-Clark, Christopher
  1940- *32*
Stubis, Talivaldis 1926- *5*
Stubley, Trevor (Hugh) 1932- *22*
Stultifer, Morton
  See Curtis, Richard (Alan)

Sture-Vasa, Mary
  See Alsop, Mary O'Hara
Sturton, Hugh
  See Johnston, H(ugh) A(nthony)
  S(tephen)
Sturtzel, Howard A(llison)
  1894- *1*
Sturtzel, Jane Levington
  1903- *1*
Styles, Frank Showell 1908- *10*
Suba, Susanne *4*
Subond, Valerie
  See Grayland, Valerie
Sudbery, Rodie 1943- *42*
Sugarman, Tracy 1921- *37*
Sugita, Yutaka 1930- *36*
Suhl, Yuri 1908- *8*
  See also CLR 2
  See also SAAS 1
Suid, Murray 1942- *27*
Sullivan, George E(dward)
  1927- *4*
Sullivan, Mary W(ilson)
  1907- *13*
Sullivan, Thomas Joseph, Jr.
  1947- *16*
Sullivan, Tom
  See Sullivan, Thomas Joseph, Jr.
Sumichrast, Józef 1948- *29*
Sumiko
  See Davies, Sumiko
Summers, James L(evingston) 1910-
  Brief Entry *28*
Sunderlin, Sylvia 1911- *28*
Sung, Betty Lee *26*
Supraner, Robyn 1930- *20*
Surge, Frank 1931- *13*
Susac, Andrew 1929- *5*
Sutcliff, Rosemary 1920- *44*
  Earlier sketch in SATA 6
  See also CLR 1
Sutherland, Efua (Theodora Morgue)
  1924- *25*
Sutherland, Margaret 1941- *15*
Sutherland, Zena B(ailey)
  1915- *37*
Suttles, Shirley (Smith) 1922- ... *21*
Sutton, Ann (Livesay) 1923- *31*
Sutton, Eve(lyn Mary) 1906- *26*
Sutton, Felix 1910(?)- *31*
Sutton, Jane 1950-
  Brief Entry *43*
Sutton, Larry M(atthew)
  1931- *29*
Sutton, Margaret (Beebe)
  1903- *1*
Sutton, Myron Daniel 1925- *31*
Svenson, Andrew E.
  1910-1975 .... *2*
  Obituary *26*
Swain, Su Zan (Noguchi)
  1916- *21*
Swan, Susan 1944- *22*
Swarthout, Glendon (Fred)
  1918- *26*
Swarthout, Kathryn 1919- *7*
Sweeney, James B(artholomew)
  1910- *21*

Sweeney, Karen O'Connor
  See O'Connor, Karen
Swenson, Allan A(rmstrong)
  1933- *21*
Swenson, May 1919- *15*
Swift, David
  See Kaufmann, John
Swift, Hildegarde Hoyt 1890(?)-1977
  Obituary *20*
Swift, Jonathan 1667-1745 .... *19*
Swift, Merlin
  See Leeming, Joseph
Swiger, Elinor Porter 1927- *8*
Swinburne, Laurence 1924- *9*
Swindells, Robert E(dward) 1939-
  Brief Entry *34*
Sydney, Frank [Joint pseudonym]
  See Warwick, Alan R(oss)
Sylvester, Natalie G(abry)
  1922- *22*
Syme, (Neville) Ronald 1913- *2*
Symons, (Dorothy) Geraldine
  1909- *33*
Synge, (Phyllis) Ursula 1930- *9*
Sypher, Lucy Johnston 1907- *7*
Szasz, Suzanne Shorr 1919- *13*
Szekeres, Cyndy 1933- *5*
Szulc, Tad 1926- *26*

T

Taback, Simms 1932- *40*
  Brief Entry *36*
Taber, Gladys (Bagg) 1899-1980
  Obituary *22*
Tabrah, Ruth Milander 1921- *14*
Tafuri, Nancy 1946- *39*
Tait, Douglas 1944- *12*
Takakjian, Portia 1930- *15*
Takashima, Shizuye 1928- *13*
Talbot, Charlene Joy 1928- *10*
Talbot, Toby 1928- *14*
Talker, T.
  See Rands, William Brighty
Tallcott, Emogene *10*
Tallon, Robert 1939- *43*
  Brief Entry *28*
Talmadge, Marian *14*
Tamarin, Alfred *13*
Tamburine, Jean 1930- *12*
Tannen, Mary 1943- *37*
Tannenbaum, Beulah 1916- *3*
Tannenbaum, D(onald) Leb
  1948- *42*
Tanner, Louise S(tickney)
  1922- *9*
Tanobe, Miyuki 1937- *23*
Tapio, Pat Decker
  See Kines, Pat Decker
Tarkington, (Newton) Booth
  1869-1946 .... *17*
Tarry, Ellen 1906- *16*
Tarshis, Jerome 1936- *9*
Tarsky, Sue 1946- *41*
Tashjian, Virginia A. 1921- *3*
Tasker, James *9*
Tate, Eleanora E(laine) 1948- *38*
Tate, Ellalice
  See Hibbert, Eleanor

Tate, Joan 1922- *9*
Tatham, Campbell
  See Elting, Mary
Taves, Isabella 1915- *27*
Taylor, Ann 1782-1866 .... *41*
  Brief Entry *35*
Taylor, Barbara J. 1927- *10*
Taylor, Carl 1937- *14*
Taylor, David 1900-1965 .... *10*
Taylor, Elizabeth 1912-1975 ...... *13*
Taylor, Florence Walton *9*
Taylor, Florence M(arion Tompkins)
  1892- *9*
Taylor, Herb(ert Norman, Jr.)
  1942- *22*
Taylor, Jane 1783-1824 .... *41*
  Brief Entry *35*
Taylor, Kenneth N(athaniel)
  1917- *26*
Taylor, L(ester) B(arbour), Jr.
  1932- *27*
Taylor, Mark 1927- *32*
  Brief Entry *28*
Taylor, Mildred D. *15*
  See also CLR 9
Taylor, Paula (Wright) 1942-
  Brief Entry *33*
Taylor, Robert Lewis 1912- *10*
Taylor, Sydney (Brenner)
  1904(?)-1978 .... *28*
  Obituary *26*
  Earlier sketch in SATA 1
Taylor, Theodore 1924- *5*
Teague, Bob
  See Teague, Robert
Teague, Robert 1929- *32*
  Brief Entry *31*
Teal, Val 1903- *10*
Teale, Edwin Way 1899-1980 .... *7*
  Obituary *25*
Teasdale, Sara 1884-1933 .... *32*
Tebbel, John (William) 1912- *26*
Tee-Van, Helen Damrosch
  1893-1976 .... *10*
  Obituary *27*
Teleki, Geza 1943- *45*
Telemaque, Eleanor Wong
  1934- *43*
Telescope, Tom
  See Newbery, John
Temkin, Sara Anne (Schlossberg)
  1913- *26*
Temko, Florence *13*
Tempest, Margaret Mary 1892-1982
  Obituary *33*
Templar, Maurice
  See Groom, Arthur William
Temple, Herbert 1919- *45*
Temple, Paul [Joint pseudonym]
  See McConnell, James Douglas
  (Rutherford)
Tenggren, Gustaf 1896-1970 .... *18*
  Obituary *26*
Tennant, Kylie 1912- *6*
Tennant, Veronica 1946- *36*
Tenniel, Sir John 1820-1914
  Brief Entry *27*
Terban, Marvin
  Brief Entry *45*

ter Haar, Jaap 1922- 6
Terhune, Albert Payson
   1872-1942 15
Terlouw, Jan (Cornelis) 1931- 30
Terris, Susan 1937- 3
Terry, Luther L(eonidas)
   1911-1985 11
   Obituary 42
Terry, Walter 1913- 14
Terzian, James P. 1915- 14
Tester, Sylvia Root 1939-
   Brief Entry 37
Tether, (Cynthia) Graham
   1950- 46
   Brief Entry 36
Thacher, Mary McGrath
   1933- 9
Thackeray, William Makepeace
   1811-1863 23
Thamer, Katie 1955- 42
Thane, Elswyth 1900- 32
Tharp, Louise Hall 1898- 3
Thayer, Jane
   See Woolley, Catherine
Thayer, Marjorie
   Brief Entry 37
Thayer, Peter
   See Wyler, Rose
Thelwell, Norman 1923- 14
Theroux, Paul 1941- 44
Thieda, Shirley Ann 1943- 13
Thiele, Colin (Milton) 1920- 14
   See also SAAS 2
Thiry, Joan (Marie) 1926- 45
Thistlethwaite, Miles 1945- 12
Thollander, Earl 1922- 22
Thomas, Andrea
   See Hill, Margaret (Ohler)
Thomas, Art(hur Lawrence) 1952-
   Brief Entry 38
Thomas, Estelle Webb 1899- 26
Thomas, H. C.
   See Keating, Lawrence A.
Thomas, Ianthe 1951-
   Brief Entry 42
   See also CLR 8
Thomas, J. F.
   See Fleming, Thomas J(ames)
Thomas, Jane Resh 1936- 38
Thomas, Joan Gale
   See Robinson, Joan G.
Thomas, Joyce Carol 1938- 40
Thomas, Lowell (Jackson), Jr.
   1923- 15
Thomas, Victoria [Joint pseudonym]
   See DeWeese, Thomas Eugene
Thompson, Brenda 1935- 34
Thompson, Christine Pullein
   See Pullein-Thompson, Christine
Thompson, David H(ugh)
   1941- 17
Thompson, Diana Pullein
   See Pullein-Thompson, Diana
Thompson, George Selden
   1929- 4
Thompson, Harlan H. 1894- 10
Thompson, Josephine
   See Pullein-Thompson, Josephine

Thompson, Julian F(rancis) 1927-
   Brief Entry 40
Thompson, Kay 1912- 16
Thompson, Stith 1885-1976
   Obituary 20
Thompson, Vivian L. 1911- 3
Thomson, David (Robert Alexander)
   1914- 40
Thomson, Peggy 1922- 31
Thorndyke, Helen Louise
   [Collective pseudonym] 1
Thorne, Ian
   See May, Julian
Thornton, W. B.
   See Burgess, Thornton Waldo
Thorpe, E(ustace) G(eorge)
   1916- 21
Thorvall, Kerstin 1925- 13
Thrasher, Crystal (Faye)
   1921- 27
Thum, Gladys 1920- 26
Thum, Marcella 28
   Earlier sketch in SATA 3
Thundercloud, Katherine
   See Witt, Shirley Hill
Thurber, James (Grover)
   1894-1961 13
Thurman, Judith 1946- 33
Thwaite, Ann (Barbara Harrop)
   1932- 14
Ticheburn, Cheviot
   See Ainsworth, William Harrison
Tichenor, Tom 1923- 14
Tichy, William 1924- 31
Tiegreen, Alan F. 1935-
   Brief Entry 36
Tilton, Madonna Elaine 1929- 41
Tilton, Rafael
   See Tilton, Madonna Elaine
Timmins, William F. 10
Tiner, John Hudson 1944- 32
Tinkelman, Murray 1933- 12
Tinkle, (Julien) Lon
   1906-1980 36
Titler, Dale M(ilton) 1926- 35
   Brief Entry 28
Titmarsh, Michael Angelo
   See Thackeray, William Makepeace
Titus, Eve 1922- 2
Tobias, Tobi 1938- 5
   See also CLR 4
Todd, Anne Ophelia
   See Dowden, Anne Ophelia
Todd, Barbara K. 1917- 10
Todd, H(erbert) E(atton)
   1908- 11
Todd, Loreto 1942- 30
Tolan, Stephanie S. 1942- 38
Toland, John (Willard) 1912- 38
Tolkien, J(ohn) R(onald) R(euel)
   1892-1973 32
   Obituary 24
   Earlier sketch in SATA 2
Tolles, Martha 1921- 8
Tolliver, Ruby C(hangos) 1922-
   Brief Entry 41
Tolmie, Ken(neth Donald)
   1941- 15

Tolstoi, Leo (Nikolaevich)
   1828-1910 26
Tomalin, Ruth 29
Tomes, Margot (Ladd) 1917- 36
   Brief Entry 27
Tomfool
   See Farjeon, Eleanor
Tomkins, Jasper
   See Batey, Tom
Tomline, F. Latour
   See Gilbert, W(illiam) S(chwenk)
Tomlinson, Jill 1931-1976 3
   Obituary 24
Tomlinson, Reginald R(obert)
   1885-1979(?)
   Obituary 27
Tompert, Ann 1918- 14
Toner, Raymond John 1908- 10
Took, Belladonna
   See Chapman, Vera
Tooke, Louise Mathews 1950- 38
Toonder, Martin
   See Groom, Arthur William
Toothaker, Roy Eugene 1928- 18
Tooze, Ruth 1892-1972 4
Topping, Audrey R(onning)
   1928- 14
Tor, Regina
   See Shekerjian, Regina Tor
Torbert, Floyd James 1922- 22
Torgersen, Don Arthur 1934-
   Brief Entry 41
Torrie, Malcolm
   See Mitchell, Gladys (Maude
   Winifred)
Totham, Mary
   See Breinburg, Petronella
Tournier, Michel 1924- 23
Towne, Mary
   See Spelman, Mary
Townsend, John Rowe 1922- 4
   See also CLR 2
   See also SAAS 2
Toye, Clive 1933(?)-
   Brief Entry 30
Toye, William E(ldred) 1926- 8
Traherne, Michael
   See Watkins-Pitchford, D. J.
Trahey, Jane 1923- 36
Trapp, Maria (Augusta) von
   1905- 16
Travers, P(amela) L(yndon)
   1906- 4
   See also CLR 2
   See also SAAS 2
Trease, (Robert) Geoffrey
   1909- 2
Tredez, Alain 1926- 17
Treece, Henry 1911-1966 2
   See also CLR 2
Tregarthen, Enys
   See Sloggett, Nellie
Tregaskis, Richard 1916-1973 3
   Obituary 26
Trell, Max 1900- 14
Tremain, Ruthven 1922- 17
Trent, Robbie 1894- 26
Trent, Timothy
   See Malmberg, Carl

Tresilian, (Cecil) Stuart
  1891-19(?) 40
Tresselt, Alvin 1916- 7
Treviño, Elizabeth B(orton) de
  1904- 29
  Earlier sketch in SATA 1
Trevor, Elleston 1920- 28
Trevor, Glen
  See Hilton, James
Trevor, (Lucy) Meriol 1919- 10
Trez, Alain
  See Tredez, Alain
Trimby, Elisa 1948-
  Brief Entry 40
Tripp, Eleanor B. 1936- 4
Tripp, Paul 8
Tripp, Wallace (Whitney)
  1940- 31
Trivelpiece, Laurel 1926-
  Brief Entry 46
Trivett, Daphne (Harwood)
  1940- 22
Trnka, Jiri 1912-1969 43
  Brief Entry 32
Trollope, Anthony 1815-1882 22
Trost, Lucille Wood 1938- 12
Trotter, Grace V(iolet) 1900- 10
Troughton, Joanna (Margaret)
  1947- 37
Troyer, Johannes 1902-1969
  Brief Entry 40
Trudeau, G(arretson) B(eekman)
  1948- 35
Trudeau, Garry B.
  See Trudeau, G(arretson) B(eekman)
Truesdell, Sue
  See Truesdell, Susan G.
Truesdell, Susan G.
  Brief Entry 45
Truss, Jan 1925- 35
Tucker, Caroline
  See Nolan, Jeannette
Tudor, Tasha 20
Tully, John (Kimberley)
  1923- 14
Tunis, Edwin (Burdett)
  1897-1973 28
  Obituary 24
  Earlier sketch in SATA 1
  See also CLR 2
Tunis, John R(oberts)
  1889-1975 37
  Brief Entry 30
Turkle, Brinton 1915- 2
Turlington, Bayly 1919- 5
Turnbull, Agnes Sligh 14
Turnbull, Ann (Christine)
  1943- 18
Turner, Alice K. 1940- 10
Turner, Ann W(arren) 1945- 14
Turner, Elizabeth
  1774-1846 .... YABC 2
Turner, Josie
  See Crawford, Phyllis
Turner, Philip 1925- 11
Turner, Sheila R.
  See Seed, Sheila Turner
Turngren, Annette 1902(?)-1980
  Obituary 23

Turngren, Ellen (?)-1964 3
Turska, Krystyna Zofia 1933- 31
  Brief Entry 27
Tusan, Stan 1936- 22
Tusiani, Joseph 1924- 45
Twain, Mark
  See Clemens, Samuel Langhorne
Tweedsmuir, Baron
  See Buchan, John
Tworkov, Jack 1900-1982
  Obituary 31
Tyler, Anne 1941- 7

U

Ubell, Earl 1926- 4
Uchida, Yoshiko 1921- 1
  See also CLR 6
  See also SAAS 1
Udall, Jan Beaney 1938- 10
Uden, (Bernard Gilbert) Grant
  1910- 26
Udry, Janice May 1928- 4
Ullman, James Ramsey
  1907-1971 7
Ulm, Robert 1934-1977 17
Ulyatt, Kenneth 1920- 14
Unada
  See Gliewe, Unada
Uncle Gus
  See Rey, H. A.
Uncle Mac
  See McCulloch, Derek (Ivor
  Breashur)
Uncle Ray
  See Coffman, Ramon Peyton
Uncle Shelby
  See Silverstein, Shel(by)
Underhill, Alice Mertie 1900-1971
Ungerer, (Jean) Thomas 1931- 33
  Earlier sketch in SATA 5
Ungerer, Tomi
  See Ungerer, (Jean) Thomas
  See also CLR 3
Unkelbach, Kurt 1913- 4
Unnerstad, Edith 1900- 3
Unrau, Ruth 1922- 9
Unstead, R(obert) J(ohn)
  1915- 12
Unsworth, Walt 1928- 4
Untermeyer, Louis 1885-1977 37
  Obituary 26
  Earlier sketch in SATA 2
Unwin, David S(torr) 1918- 14
Unwin, Nora S. 1907- 3
Usher, Margo Scegge
  See McHargue, Georgess
Uttley, Alice Jane (Taylor)
  1884-1976 3
  Obituary 26
Uttley, Alison
  See Uttley, Alice Jane (Taylor)
Utz, Lois 1932- 5
Uzair, Salem ben
  See Horne, Richard Henry

V

Vaeth, J(oseph) Gordon 1921- 17

Valen, Nanine 1950- 21
Valencak, Hannelore 1929- 42
Valens, Evans G., Jr. 1920- 1
Van Abbé, Salaman
  1883-1955 18
Van Allsburg, Chris 1949- 37
  See also CLR 5
Van Anrooy, Francine 1924- 2
Van Anrooy, Frans
  See Van Anrooy, Francine
Vance, Eleanor Graham 1908- 11
Vance, Marguerite 1889-1965 29
Vandenburg, Mary Lou 1943- 17
Vander Boom, Mae M. 14
Van der Veer, Judy
  1912-1982 4
  Obituary 33
Vandivert, Rita (Andre) 1905- 21
Van Duyn, Janet 1910- 18
Van Dyne, Edith
  See Baum, L(yman) Frank
Van Horn, William 1939- 43
Van Iterson, S(iny) R(ose) 26
Van Leeuwen, Jean 1937- 6
Van Lhin, Erik
  See Del Rey, Lester
Van Loon, Hendrik Willem
  1882-1944 18
Van Orden, M(erton) D(ick)
  1921- 4
Van Rensselaer, Alexander (Taylor
  Mason) 1892-1962 14
Van Riper, Guernsey, Jr.
  1909- 3
Van Steenwyk, Elizabeth Ann
  1928- 34
Van Stockum, Hilda 1908- 5
Van Tuyl, Barbara 1940- 11
Van Vogt, A(lfred) E(lton)
  1912- 14
Van Woerkom, Dorothy (O'Brien)
  1924- 21
Van Wormer, Joe
  See Van Wormer, Joseph Edward
Van Wormer, Joseph Edward
  1913- 35
Van-Wyck Mason, F.
  See Mason, F. van Wyck
Van Zwienen, Ilse (Charlotte Koehn)
  1929- 34
  Brief Entry 28
Varga, Judy
  See Stang, Judit
Varley, Dimitry V. 1906- 10
Vasiliu, Mircea 1920- 2
Vass, George 1927-
  Brief Entry 31
Vaughan, Carter A.
  See Gerson, Noel B(ertram)
Vaughan, Harold Cecil 1923- 14
Vaughan, Sam(uel) S. 1928- 14
Vaughn, Ruth 1935- 14
Vavra, Robert James 1944- 8
Vecsey, George 1939- 9
Veglahn, Nancy (Crary) 1937- 5
Venable, Alan (Hudson)
  1944- 8
Venn, Mary Eleanor
  See Jorgensen, Mary Venn

Ventura, Piero (Luigi) 1937-
  Brief Entry 43
Vequin, Capini
  See Quinn, Elisabeth
Verne, Jules 1828-1905 21
Verner, Gerald 1897(?)-1980
  Obituary 25
Verney, John 1913- 14
Vernon, (Elda) Louise A(nderson)
  1914- 14
Vernor, D.
  See Casewit, Curtis
Verral, Charles Spain 1904- 11
Verrone, Robert J. 1935(?)-1984
  Obituary 39
Versace, Marie Teresa Rios
  1917- 2
Vesey, Paul
  See Allen, Samuel (Washington)
Vestly, Anne-Cath(arina)
  1920- 14
Vevers, (Henry) Gwynne
  1916- 45
Viator, Vacuus
  See Hughes, Thomas
Vicarion, Count Palmiro
  See Logue, Christopher
Vicker, Angus
  See Felsen, Henry Gregor
Vickery, Kate
  See Kennedy, T(eresa) A.
Victor, Edward 1914- 3
Victor, Joan Berg 1937- 30
Viereck, Ellen K. 1928- 14
Viereck, Phillip 1925- 3
Viertel, Janet 1915- 10
Vigna, Judith 1936- 15
Viguers, Ruth Hill 1903-1971 6
Villiard, Paul 1910-1974
  Obituary 20
Villiers, Alan (John) 1903- 10
Vincent, Eric Douglas 1953- 40
Vincent, Félix 1946- 41
Vincent, Mary Keith
  See St. John, Wylly Folk
Vinge, Joan D(ennison) 1948- 36
Vining, Elizabeth Gray
  See Gray, Elizabeth Janet
Vinson, Kathryn 1911- 21
Vinton, Iris 24
Viorst, Judith 7
  See also CLR 3
Vip
  See Partch, Virgil Franklin II
Visser, W(illiam) F(rederick)
  H(endrik) 1900-1968 10
Vlahos, Olivia 1924- 31
Vlasic, Bob
  See Hirsch, Phil
Vo-Dinh, Mai 1933- 16
Vogel, Ilse-Margret 1914- 14
Vogel, John H(ollister), Jr.
  1950- 18
Vogt, Esther Loewen 1915- 14
Vogt, Gregory
  Brief Entry 45
Vogt, Marie Bollinger 1921- 45
Voight, Virginia Frances
  1909- 8

Voigt, Cynthia 1942-
  Brief Entry 33
Voigt, Erna 1925- 35
Voigt-Rother, Erna
  See Voigt, Erna
Vojtech, Anna 1946- 42
von Almedingen, Martha Edith
  See Almedingen, E. M.
Von Hagen, Victor Wolfgang
  1908- 29
von Klopp, Vahrah
  See Malvern, Gladys
Von Schmidt, Eric 1931-
  Brief Entry 36
von Storch, Anne B. 1910- 1
Vosburgh, Leonard (W.)
  1912- 15
Voyle, Mary
  See Manning, Rosemary

W

Waber, Bernard 1924-
  Brief Entry 40
Waddell, Evelyn Margaret
  1918- 10
Waddell, Martin 1941- 43
Wade, Theodore E., Jr. 1936- ... 37
Wagenheim, Kal 1935- 21
Wagner, Jane 33
Wagner, Sharon B. 1936- 4
Wagoner, David (Russell)
  1926- 14
Wahl, Jan 1933- 34
  Earlier sketch in SATA 2
  See also SAAS 3
Waide, Jan 1952- 29
Waitley, Douglas 1927- 30
Wakefield, Jean L.
  See Laird, Jean E(louise)
Wakin, Edward 1927- 37
Walck, Henry Z(eigler) 1908-1984
  Obituary 40
Walden, Amelia Elizabeth 3
Waldman, Bruce 1949- 15
Waldron, Ann Wood 1924- 16
Walker, Alice 1944- 31
Walker, Barbara K. 1921- 4
Walker, (James) Braz(elton)
  1934-1983 45
Walker, David Harry 1911- 8
Walker, Diana 1925- 9
Walker, Frank 1930- 36
Walker, Holly Beth
  See Bond, Gladys Baker
Walker, Louise Jean 1891-1976
  Obituary 35
Walker, Mildred
  See Schemm, Mildred Walker
Walker, (Addison) Mort
  1923- 8
Walker, Pamela 1948- 24
Walker, Stephen J. 1951- 12
Wallace, Barbara Brooks 4
Wallace, Beverly Dobrin
  1921- 19
Wallace, Daisy
  See Cuyler, Margery Stuyvesant
Wallace, John A. 1915- 3

Wallace, Nigel
  See Hamilton, Charles H. St. John
Wallace, Robert A. 1932-
  Brief Entry 37
Wallace-Brodeur, Ruth 1941-
  Brief Entry 41
Waller, Leslie 1923- 20
Wallis, G. McDonald
  See Campbell, Hope
Wallner, Alexandra 1946-
  Brief Entry 41
Wallner, John C. 1945- 10
Wallower, Lucille 11
Walsh, Jill Paton
  See Paton Walsh, Gillian
  See also CLR 2
Walter, Mildred Pitts
  Brief Entry 45
Walter, Villiam Christian
  See Andersen, Hans Christian
Walters, Audrey 1929- 18
Walters, Hugh
  See Hughes, Walter (Llewellyn)
Walther, Thomas A. 1950- 31
Walther, Tom
  See Walther, Thomas A.
Waltner, Elma 1912- 40
Waltner, Willard H. 1909- 40
Walton, Richard J. 1928- 4
Waltrip, Lela (Kingston)
  1904- 9
Waltrip, Mildred 1911- 37
Waltrip, Rufus (Charles)
  1898- 9
Walworth, Nancy Zinsser
  1917- 14
Wangerin, Walter, Jr. 1944- 45
  Brief Entry 37
Wannamaker, Bruce
  See Moncure, Jane Belk
Warbler, J. M.
  See Cocagnac, A. M.
Warburg, Sandol Stoddard
  1927- 14
Ward, John (Stanton) 1917- 42
Ward, Lynd (Kendall)
  1905-1985 36
  Obituary 42
  Earlier sketch in SATA 2
Ward, Martha (Eads) 1921- 5
Ward, Melanie
  See Curtis, Richard (Alan)
Wardell, Dean
  See Prince, J(ack) H(arvey)
Ware, Leon (Vernon) 1909- 4
Warner, Frank A. [Collective
  pseudonym] 1
Warner, Gertrude Chandler
  1890- 9
Warner, Lucille Schulberg 30
Warner, Oliver 1903-1976 29
Warren, Betsy
  See Warren, Elizabeth Avery
Warren, Billy
  See Warren, William Stephen
Warren, Cathy
  Brief Entry 46
Warren, Elizabeth
  See Supraner, Robyn

Warren, Elizabeth Avery
1916- 46
Brief Entry 38
Warren, Joyce W(illiams)
1935- 18
Warren, Mary Phraner 1929- 10
Warren, Robert Penn 1905- 46
Warren, William Stephen
1882-1968 9
Warrick, Patricia Scott 1925- 35
Warsh
See Warshaw, Jerry
Warshaw, Jerry 1929- 30
Warshofsky, Fred 1931- 24
Warshofsky, Isaac
See Singer, Isaac Bashevis
Wartski, Maureen (Ann Crane) 1940-
Brief Entry 37
Warwick, Alan R(oss)
1900-1973 42
Wa-sha-quon-asin
See Belaney, Archibald Stansfeld
Washburn, (Henry) Bradford (Jr.)
1910- 38
Washburne, Heluiz Chandler
1892-1970 10
Obituary 26
Washington, Booker T(aliaferro)
1858(?)-1915 28
Watanabe, Shigeo 1928- 39
Brief Entry 32
See also CLR 8
Waters, John F(rederick)
1930- 4
Waterton, Betty (Marie) 1923- 37
Brief Entry 34
Watkins-Pitchford, D. J.
1905- 6
Watson, Aldren A(uld) 1917- 42
Brief Entry 36
Watson, Clyde 1947- 5
See also CLR 3
Watson, Helen Orr 1892-1978
Obituary 24
Watson, James 1936- 10
Watson, Jane Werner 1915- 3
Watson, Nancy Dingman 32
Watson, Pauline 1925- 14
Watson, Sally 1924- 3
Watson, Wendy (McLeod)
1942- 5
Watson Taylor, Elizabeth
1915- 41
Watt, Thomas 1935- 4
Watts, Bernadette 1942- 4
Watts, Ephraim
See Horne, Richard Henry
Watts, Franklin (Mowry)
1904-1978 46
Obituary 21
Watts, Mabel Pizzey 1906- 11
Waugh, Carol-Lynn Rössel
1947- 41
Waugh, Dorothy 11
Wayland, Patrick
See O'Connor, Richard
Wayne, (Anne) Jenifer
1917-1982 32

Wayne, Kyra Petrovskaya
1918- 8
Wayne, Richard
See Decker, Duane
Waystaff, Simon
See Swift, Jonathan
Weales, Gerald (Clifford)
1925- 11
Weary, Ogdred
See Gorey, Edward St. John
Weaver, John L. 1949- 42
Weaver, Ward
See Mason, F. van Wyck
Webb, Christopher
See Wibberley, Leonard (Patrick
O'Connor)
Webb, Jean Francis (III)
1910- 35
Webb, Sharon 1936- 41
Webber, Irma E(leanor Schmidt)
1904- 14
Weber, Alfons 1921- 8
Weber, Lenora Mattingly
1895-1971 2
Obituary 26
Weber, William John 1927- 14
Webster, Alice (Jane Chandler)
1876-1916 17
Webster, David 1930- 11
Webster, Frank V. [Collective
pseudonym] 1
Webster, Gary
See Garrison, Webb B(lack)
Webster, James 1925-1981 17
Obituary 27
Webster, Jean
See Webster, Alice (Jane Chandler)
Wechsler, Herman 1904-1976
Obituary 20
Weddle, Ethel H(arshbarger)
1897- 11
Wegen, Ron(ald)
Brief Entry 44
Wegner, Fritz 1924- 20
Weihs, Erika 1917- 15
Weik, Mary Hays
1898(?)-1979 3
Obituary 23
Weil, Ann Yezner 1908-1969 9
Weil, Lisl 7
Weilerstein, Sadie Rose 1894- 3
Weiner, Sandra 1922- 14
Weingarten, Violet (Brown)
1915-1976 3
Obituary 27
Weingartner, Charles 1922- 5
Weir, LaVada 2
Weir, Rosemary (Green)
1905- 21
Weis, Margaret (Edith) 1948- 38
Weisberger, Bernard A(llen)
1922- 21
Weiser, Marjorie P(hillis) K(atz)
1934- 33
Weisgard, Leonard (Joseph)
1916- 30
Earlier sketch in SATA 2
Weiss, Adelle 1920- 18
Weiss, Ann E(dwards) 1943- 30

Weiss, Ellen 1953- 44
Weiss, Harvey 1922- 27
Earlier sketch in SATA 1
See also CLR 4
Weiss, Malcolm E. 1928- 3
Weiss, Miriam
See Schlein, Miriam
Weiss, Nicki 1954- 33
Weiss, Renee Karol 1923- 5
Weissenborn, Hellmuth 1898-1982
Obituary 31
Welber, Robert 26
Welch, D'Alte Aldridge 1907-1970
Obituary 27
Welch, Jean-Louise
See Kempton, Jean Welch
Welch, Martha McKeen 1914-
Brief Entry 45
Welch, Pauline
See Bodenham, Hilda Esther
Welch, Ronald
See Felton, Ronald Oliver
Weller, George (Anthony)
1907- 31
Welles, Winifred 1893-1939
Brief Entry 27
Wellman, Alice 1900-
Brief Entry 36
Wellman, Manly Wade 1903- 6
Wellman, Paul I. 1898-1966 3
Wells, H(erbert) G(eorge)
1866-1946 20
Wells, Helen 1910- 2
Wells, J. Wellington
See DeCamp, L(yon) Sprague
Wells, Rosemary 18
See also SAAS 1
Wels, Byron G(erald) 1924- 9
Welsh, Mary Flynn 1910(?)-1984
Obituary 38
Weltner, Linda R(iverly)
1938- 38
Welty, S. F.
See Welty, Susan F.
Welty, Susan F. 1905- 9
Wendelin, Rudolph 1910- 23
Werner, Herma 1926-
Brief Entry 41
Werner, Jane
See Watson, Jane Werner
Werner, K.
See Casewit, Curtis
Wersba, Barbara 1932- 1
See also CLR 3
See also SAAS 2
Werstein, Irving 1914-1971 14
Werth, Kurt 1896- 20
West, Anna 1938- 40
West, Barbara
See Price, Olive
West, Betty 1921- 11
West, C. P.
See Wodehouse, P(elham)
G(renville)
West, Emily G(ovan) 1919- 38
West, Emmy
See West, Emily G(ovan)
West, James
See Withers, Carl A.

West, Jerry
    See Stratemeyer, Edward L.
West, Jerry
    See Svenson, Andrew E.
West, (Mary) Jessamyn 1902(?)-1984
    Obituary 37
West, Ward
    See Borland, Hal
Westall, Robert (Atkinson)
    1929- 23
    See also SAAS 2
Westerberg, Christine 1950- 29
Westervelt, Virginia (Veeder)
    1914- 10
Westheimer, David 1917- 14
Westmacott, Mary
    See Christie, Agatha (Mary Clarissa)
Westman, Paul (Wendell)
    1956- 39
Weston, Allen [Joint pseudonym]
    See Norton, Alice Mary
Weston, John (Harrison)
    1932- 21
Westwood, Jennifer 1940- 10
Wexler, Jerome (LeRoy)
    1923- 14
Wharf, Michael
    See Weller, George (Anthony)
Wheatley, Arabelle 1921- 16
Wheeler, Captain
    See Ellis, Edward S(ylvester)
Wheeler, Cindy 1955-
    Brief Entry 40
Wheeler, Janet D. [Collective
    pseudonym] 1
Wheeler, Opal 1898- 23
Whelan, Elizabeth M(urphy)
    1943- 14
Whistler, Reginald John
    1905-1944 30
Whistler, Rex
    See Whistler, Reginald John
Whitcomb, Jon 1906- 10
White, Anne Hitchcock 1902-1970
    Brief Entry 33
White, Anne Terry 1896- 2
White, Dale
    See Place, Marian T.
White, Dori 1919- 10
White, E(lwyn) B(rooks)
    1899-1985 29
    Obituary 44
    Earlier sketch in SATA 2
    See also CLR 1
White, Eliza Orne
    1856-1947 .... YABC 2
White, Florence M(eiman)
    1910- 14
White, Laurence B., Jr. 1935- 10
White, Ramy Allison [Collective
    pseudonym] 1
White, Robb 1909- 1
    See also CLR 3
    See also SAAS 1
White, Ruth C. 1942- 39
White, T(erence) H(anbury)
    1906-1964 12
White, William, Jr. 1934- 16
Whitehead, Don(ald) F. 1908- 4

Whitehouse, Arch
    See Whitehouse, Arthur George
Whitehouse, Arthur George
    1895-1979 14
    Obituary 23
Whitehouse, Elizabeth S(cott)
    1893-1968 35
Whitehouse, Jeanne 1939- 29
Whitinger, R. D.
    See Place, Marian T.
Whitlock, Pamela 1921(?)-1982
    Obituary 31
Whitlock, Ralph 1914- 35
Whitman, Walt(er) 1819-1892 20
Whitney, Alex(andra) 1922- 14
Whitney, David C(harles) 1921-
    Brief Entry 29
Whitney, Phyllis A(yame)
    1903- 30
    Earlier sketch in SATA 1
Whitney, Thomas P(orter)
    1917- 25
Wibberley, Leonard (Patrick
    O'Connor) 1915-1983 45
    Obituary 36
    Earlier sketch in SATA 2
    See also CLR 3
Wiberg, Harald (Albin) 1908-
    Brief Entry 40
Widdemer, Mabel Cleland
    1902-1964 5
Widenberg, Siv 1931- 10
Wier, Ester 1910- 3
Wiese, Kurt 1887-1974 36
    Obituary 24
    Earlier sketch in SATA 3
Wiesner, Portia
    See Takakjian, Portia
Wiesner, William 1899- 5
Wiggin, Kate Douglas (Smith)
    1856-1923 .... YABC 1
Wight, James Alfred 1916-
    Brief Entry 44
Wikland, Ilon 1930-
    Brief Entry 32
Wilber, Donald N(ewton)
    1907- 35
Wilbur, C. Keith 1923- 27
Wilbur, Richard (Purdy)
    1921- 9
Wilcox, R(uth) Turner
    1888-1970 36
Wild, Jocelyn 1941- 46
Wild, Robin (Evans) 1936- 46
Wilde, Gunther
    See Hurwood, Bernhardt J.
Wilde, Oscar (Fingal O'Flahertie
    Wills) 1854-1900 24
Wilder, Cherry
    See Grimm, Cherry Barbara Lockett
Wilder, Laura Ingalls
    1867-1957 29
    See also CLR 2
Wildsmith, Brian 1930- 16
    See also CLR 2
Wilkie, Katharine E(lliott)
    1904-1980 31
Wilkins, Frances 1923- 14

Wilkins, Marilyn (Ruth)
    1926- 30
Wilkins, Marne
    See Wilkins, Marilyn (Ruth)
Wilkinson, (Thomas) Barry 1923-
    Brief Entry 32
Wilkinson, Brenda 1946- 14
Wilkinson, Burke 1913- 4
Wilkinson, Sylvia (J.) 1940-
    Brief Entry 39
Wilkoń, Józef 1930- 31
Wilks, Michael Thomas 1947- 44
Wilks, Mike
    See Wilks, Michael Thomas
Will
    See Lipkind, William
Willard, Barbara (Mary)
    1909- 17
    See also CLR 2
Willard, Mildred Wilds 1911- 14
Willard, Nancy 1936- 37
    Brief Entry 30
    See also CLR 5
Willcox, Isobel 1907- 42
Willey, Robert
    See Ley, Willy
Williams, Barbara 1925- 11
Williams, Beryl
    See Epstein, Beryl
Williams, Charles
    See Collier, James Lincoln
Williams, Clyde C.
    1881-1974 8
    Obituary 27
Williams, Coe
    See Harrison, C. William
Williams, Eric (Ernest)
    1911-1983 14
    Obituary 38
Williams, Ferelith Eccles
    1920- 22
Williams, Frances B.
    See Browin, Frances Williams
Williams, Garth (Montgomery)
    1912- 18
Williams, Guy R. 1920- 11
Williams, Hawley
    See Heyliger, William
Williams, J. R.
    See Williams, Jeanne
Williams, J. Walker
    See Wodehouse, P(elham)
    G(renville)
Williams, Jay 1914-1978 41
    Obituary 24
    Earlier sketch in SATA 3
    See also CLR 8
Williams, Jeanne 1930- 5
Williams, Kit 1946(?)- 44
    See also CLR 4
Williams, Leslie 1941- 42
Williams, Louise Bonino 1904(?)-1984
    Obituary 39
Williams, Maureen 1951- 12
Williams, Michael
    See St. John, Wylly Folk
Williams, Patrick J.
    See Butterworth, W. E.
Williams, Selma R(uth) 1925- 14

Williams, Slim
  See Williams, Clyde C.
Williams, Ursula Moray
  1911- 3
Williams, Vera B. 1927-
  Brief Entry 33
  See also CLR 9
Williams-Ellis, (Mary) Amabel
  (Nassau) 1894-1984 29
  Obituary 41
Williamson, Henry 1895-1977 37
  Obituary 30
Williamson, Joanne Small
  1926- 3
Willson, Robina Beckles (Ballard)
  1930- 27
Wilma, Dana
  See Faralla, Dana
Wilson, Beth P(ierre) 8
Wilson, Carter 1941- 6
Wilson, Charles Morrow
  1905-1977 30
  Obituary 46
Wilson, Christopher B. 1910(?)-1985
  Obituary 46
Wilson, Dagmar 1916-
  Brief Entry 31
Wilson, Dorothy Clarke 1904- 16
Wilson, Edward A(rthur)
  1886-1970 38
Wilson, Ellen (Janet Cameron)
  (?)-1976 9
  Obituary 26
Wilson, Eric H. 1940- 34
  Brief Entry 32
Wilson, Forrest 1918- 27
Wilson, Gahan 1930- 35
  Brief Entry 27
Wilson, Gina 1943- 36
  Brief Entry 34
Wilson, (Leslie) Granville
  1912- 14
Wilson, Hazel 1898- 3
Wilson, John 1922- 22
Wilson, Joyce M(uriel Judson) ... 21
Wilson, Lionel 1924- 33
  Brief Entry 31
Wilson, Maurice (Charles John)
  1914- 46
Wilson, Ron(ald William) 38
Wilson, Tom 1931- 33
  Brief Entry 30
Wilson, Walt(er N.) 1939- 14
Wilton, Elizabeth 1937- 14
Wilwerding, Walter Joseph
  1891-1966 9
Winchester, James H(ugh)
  1917-1985 30
  Obituary 45
Winders, Gertrude Hecker 3
Windham, Basil
  See Wodehouse, P(elham)
  G(renville)
Windham, Kathryn T(ucker)
  1918- 14
Windsor, Claire
  See Hamerstrom, Frances
Windsor, Patricia 1938- 30
Winfield, Arthur M.
  See Stratemeyer, Edward L.

Winfield, Edna
  See Stratemeyer, Edward L.
Winn, Chris 1952- 42
Winn, Janet Bruce 1928- 43
Winn, Marie 1936- 38
Winston, Clara 1921-1983
  Obituary 39
Winter, Milo (Kendall)
  1888-1956 21
Winter, R. R.
  See Winterbotham, R(ussell)
  R(obert)
Winterbotham, R(ussell) R(obert)
  1904-1971 10
Winterton, Gayle
  See Adams, William Taylor
Winthrop, Elizabeth
  See Mahony, Elizabeth Winthrop
Wirtenberg, Patricia Z. 1932- ... 10
Wise, William 1923- 4
Wise, Winifred E. 2
Wiseman, Ann (Sayre) 1926- 31
Wiseman, B(ernard) 1922- 4
Wiseman, David 1916- 43
  Brief Entry 40
Wisler, G(ary) Clifton 1950-
  Brief Entry 46
Wisner, Bill
  See Wisner, William L.
Wisner, William L.
  1914(?)-1983 42
Witham, (Phillip) Ross 1917- 37
Withers, Carl A. 1900-1970 14
Witt, Shirley Hill 1934- 17
Wittels, Harriet Joan 1938- 31
Wittman, Sally (Anne Christensen)
  1941- 30
Witty, Paul A(ndrew) 1898-1976
  Obituary 30
Wizard, Mr.
  See Herbert, Don
Wodehouse, P(elham) G(renville)
  1881-1975 22
Wodge, Dreary
  See Gorey, Edward St. John
Wohlberg, Meg 1905- 41
Wohlrabe, Raymond A. 1900- 4
Wojciechowska, Maia 1927- 28
  Earlier sketch in SATA 1
  See also CLR 1
  See also SAAS 1
Wolcott, Patty 1929- 14
Wold, Jo Anne 1938- 30
Woldin, Beth Weiner 1955- 34
Wolf, Bernard 1930-
  Brief Entry 37
Wolfe, Burton H. 1932- 5
Wolfe, Louis 1905- 8
Wolfe, Rinna (Evelyn) 1925- 38
Wolfenden, George
  See Beardmore, George
Wolff, Diane 1945- 27
Wolff, Robert Jay 1905- 10
Wolitzer, Hilma 1930- 31
Wolkoff, Judie (Edwards)
  Brief Entry 37
Wolkstein, Diane 1942- 7
Wolters, Richard A. 1920- 35
Wondriska, William 1931- 6

Wood, Audrey
  Brief Entry 44
Wood, Catherine
  See Etchison, Birdie L(ee)
Wood, Don 1945-
  Brief Entry 44
Wood, Edgar A(llardyce)
  1907- 14
Wood, Esther
  See Brady, Esther Wood
Wood, Frances Elizabeth 34
Wood, James Playsted 1905- 1
Wood, Kerry
  See Wood, Edgar A(llardyce)
Wood, Laura N.
  See Roper, Laura Wood
Wood, Nancy 1936- 6
Wood, Phyllis Anderson
  1923- 33
  Brief Entry 30
Wood, Wallace 1927-1981
  Obituary 33
Woodard, Carol 1929- 14
Woodburn, John Henry 1914- 11
Woodford, Peggy 1937- 25
Woodrich, Mary Neville
  1915- 2
Woods, George A(llan) 1926- 30
Woods, Geraldine 1948-
  Brief Entry 42
Woods, Harold 1945-
  Brief Entry 42
Woods, Margaret 1921- 2
Woods, Nat
  See Stratemeyer, Edward L.
Woodson, Jack
  See Woodson, John Waddie, Jr.
Woodson, John Waddie, Jr. 10
Woodward, Cleveland 1900- 10
Woody, Regina Jones 1894- 3
Wooldridge, Rhoda 1906- 22
Woolley, Catherine 1904- 3
Woolsey, Janette 1904- 3
Worcester, Donald Emmet
  1915- 18
Work, Virginia 1946-
  Brief Entry 45
Worline, Bonnie Bess 1914- 14
Wormser, Sophie 1896- 22
Worth, Richard
  Brief Entry 46
Worth, Valerie 1933- 8
Wortis, Avi 1937- 14
Wosmek, Frances 1917- 29
Wriggins, Sally Hovey 1922- 17
Wright, Anna (Maria Louisa Perrot)
  Rose 1890-1968
  Brief Entry 35
Wright, Dare 1926(?)- 21
Wright, Enid Meadowcroft
  1898-1966 3
Wright, Esmond 1915- 10
Wright, Frances Fitzpatrick
  1897- 10
Wright, Judith 1915- 14
Wright, Katrina
  See Gater, Dilys
Wright, Kenneth
  See Del Rey, Lester

Wright, Nancy Means *38*
Wright, R(obert) H. 1906- *6*
Wrightson, Patricia 1921- *8*
  See also CLR 4
Wronker, Lili Cassel 1924- *10*
Wulffson, Don L. 1943- *32*
Wuorio, Eva-Lis 1918- *34*
  Brief Entry *28*
Wyeth, Betsy James 1921- *41*
Wyeth, N(ewell) C(onvers)
  1882-1945 .... *17*
Wyler, Rose 1909- *18*
Wylie, Laura
  See Matthews, Patricia
Wymer, Norman George
  1911- *25*
Wynants, Miche 1934-
  Brief Entry *31*
Wyndham, Lee
  See Hyndman, Jane Andrews
Wyndham, Robert
  See Hyndman, Robert Utley
Wynter, Edward (John) 1914- *14*
Wynyard, Talbot
  See Hamilton, Charles H. St. John
Wyss, Johann David Von
  1743-1818 .... *29*
  Brief Entry *27*
Wyss, Thelma Hatch 1934- *10*

Y

Yaffe, Alan
  See Yorinks, Arthur
Yamaguchi, Marianne 1936- *7*
Yang, Jay 1941- *12*
Yarbrough, Ira 1910(?)-1983
  Obituary *35*
Yaroslava
  See Mills, Yaroslava Surmach
Yashima, Taro
  See Iwamatsu, Jun Atsushi
  See also CLR 4
Yates, Elizabeth 1905- *4*
Yates, Raymond F(rancis)
  1895-1966 .... *31*
Yaukey, Grace S(ydenstricker)
  1899- *5*
Yeakley, Marjory Hall 1908- *21*
Yeatman, Linda 1938- *42*
Yensid, Retlaw
  See Disney, Walt(er Elias)
Yeo, Wilma (Lethem) 1918- *24*
Yeoman, John (Brian) 1934- *28*
Yep, Laurence M. 1948- *7*
  See also CLR 3

Yerian, Cameron John *21*
Yerian, Margaret A. *21*
Yolen, Jane H. 1939- *40*
  Earlier sketch in SATA 4
  See also CLR 4
  See also SAAS 1
Yonge, Charlotte Mary
  1823-1901 .... *17*
Yorinks, Arthur 1953- *33*
York, Andrew
  See Nicole, Christopher Robin
York, Carol Beach 1928- *6*
Yost, Edna 1889-1971
  Obituary *26*
Youd, (Christopher) Samuel 1922-
  Brief Entry *30*
Young, Bob
  See Young, Robert W.
Young, Clarence [Collective
  pseudonym] *1*
Young, Dorothea Bennett
  1924- *31*
Young, Ed 1931- *10*
Young, Edward
  See Reinfeld, Fred
Young, Elaine L.
  See Schulte, Elaine L(ouise)
Young, Jan
  See Young, Janet Randall
Young, Janet Randall 1919- *3*
Young, Lois Horton
  1911-1981 .... *26*
Young, Margaret B(uckner)
  1922- *2*
Young, Miriam 1913-1934 .... *7*
Young, (Rodney Lee) Patrick (Jr.)
  1937- *22*
Young, Percy M(arshall)
  1912- *31*
Young, Robert W. 1916-1969 ..... *3*
Young, Scott A(lexander)
  1918- *5*
Young, Vivien
  See Gater, Dilys
Youngs, Betty 1934-1985
  Obituary *42*

Z

Zaffo, George J. (?)-1984 .... *42*
Zaidenberg, Arthur 1908(?)- *34*
Zalben, Jane Breskin 1950- *7*
Zallinger, Jean (Day) 1918- *14*
Zappler, Lisbeth 1930- *10*
Zarchy, Harry 1912- *34*
Zarif, Margaret Min'imah
  (?)-1983 .... *33*

Zaring, Jane (Thomas) 1936-
  Brief Entry *40*
Zaslavsky, Claudia 1917- *36*
Zeck, Gerald Anthony 1939- *40*
Zeck, Gerry
  See Zeck, Gerald Anthony
Zei, Alki *24*
  See also CLR 6
Zelazny, Roger (Joseph Christopher)
  1937-
  Brief Entry *39*
Zelinsky, Paul O.
  Brief Entry *33*
Zellan, Audrey Penn 1950- *22*
Zemach, Harve 1933- *3*
Zemach, Kaethe 1958-
  Brief Entry *39*
Zemach, Margot 1931- *21*
Zerman, Melvyn Bernard
  1930- *46*
Ziemienski, Dennis 1947- *10*
Zillah
  See Macdonald, Zillah K.
Zim, Herbert S(pencer) 1909- *30*
  Earlier sketch in SATA 1
  See also CLR 2
  See also SAAS 2
Zim, Sonia Bleeker
  See Bleeker, Sonia
Zimelman, Nathan
  Brief Entry *37*
Zimmerman, Naoma 1914- *10*
Zimnik, Reiner 1930- *36*
  See also CLR 3
Zindel, Bonnie 1943- *34*
Zindel, Paul 1936- *16*
  See also CLR 3
Ziner, (Florence) Feenie
  1921- *5*
Zion, (Eu)Gene 1913-1975 .... *18*
Zollinger, Gulielma 1856-1917
  Brief Entry *27*
Zolotow, Charlotte S. 1915- *35*
  Earlier sketch in SATA 1
  See also CLR 2
Zonia, Dhimitri 1921- *20*
Zubrowski, Bernard 1939- *35*
Zupa, G. Anthony
  See Zeck, Gerald Anthony
Zurhorst, Charles (Stewart, Jr.)
  1913- *12*
Zuromskis, Diane
  See Stanley, Diane
Zweifel, Frances 1931- *14*
Zwinger, Ann 1925- *46*